FUTURE PASTS

FUTURE PASTS

The Analytic Tradition in Twentieth-Century Philosophy

Edited by
JULIET FLOYD
SANFORD SHIEH

OXFORD
UNIVERSITY PRESS

2001

OXFORD
UNIVERSITY PRESS

Oxford   New York
Athens   Auckland   Bangkok   Bogotá   Buenos Aires   Cape Town
Chennai   Dar es Salaam   Delhi   Florence   Hong Kong   Istanbul   Karachi
Kolkata   Kuala Lumpur   Madrid   Melbourne   Mexico City   Mumbai   Nairobi
Paris   São Paulo   Shanghai   Singapore   Taipei   Tokyo   Toronto   Warsaw

and associated companies in
Berlin   Ibadan

Copyright © 2001 by Oxford University Press, Inc.

Published by Oxford University Press, Inc.
198 Madison Avenue, New York, New York 10016

Oxford is a registered trademark of Oxford University Press

Library of Congress Cataloging-in-Publication Data
Future pasts : the analytic tradition in twentieth-century
philosophy / edited by Juliet Floyd and Sanford Shieh.
p.   cm.
Includes bibliographical references and index.
ISBN 0-19-513916-X
1. Analysis (Philosophy)   I. Floyd, Juliet, 1960–   II. Shieh, Sanford, 1962–
B808.5 .F88   2000
146'.4—dc21   00-035622

9 8 7 6 5 4 3 2 1

Printed in the United States of America
on acid-free paper

Nonsense is nonsense,
but the history of nonsense is scholarship.

Dedication

The authors wish jointly to dedicate this volume to Burton Dreben (1927–1999), Edgar Pierce Professor of Philosophy, Emeritus, Harvard University, and Professor of Philosophy, Boston University. Dreben exercised a profound influence on American analytic philosophy over the last thirty-five years, especially through his teachings on the significance and nature of the history of the analytic tradition. Every contributor to this volume has been either a colleague or a doctoral student of Dreben and each has written at least partly in reaction to Dreben's views, especially his insistence that the evolution of the analytic tradition represents a failed but noble effort to achieve scientific clarity about the nature of philosophy, and that precisely because of its failures, it is the most profound of twentieth-century philosophical traditions. Dreben took the analytic tradition to have begun with Frege and Russell, and to have been ended by Quine and Wittgenstein (from thoroughly different perspectives), hoist on the petard of its own aspirations to achieve the rigor and clarity of science. His pessimism about the rationality and progress of philosophy, and his simultaneous insistence on the importance of its history, stimulated students and colleagues from many different walks of philosophy over several generations. Some of Dreben's views are discussed in detail in John Rawls's afterword. Rawls speaks for all of us in expressing our gratitude for Dreben's teaching and scholarship. Here we wish to record our collective debt to his colleagueship and constructive criticisms of our work over many years.

Acknowledgments

We are greatly indebted to our contributors for their patience, support, and intellectual stimulation in helping us bring out this volume. Without them the project would have been impossible.

Bernard Prusak's copyediting has improved nearly every page of the manuscript, and we thank him for his help. Several of the contributions—including our own—benefited from his comments. Mihaela Fistioc and Akihiro Kanamori provided us with most helpful feedback on our introduction draft, while Anat Biletzki encouraged and aided our efforts to organize the volume as a whole. We also gladly acknowledge the assistance of Nicolas de Warren in translating several difficult passages from Husserl.

Most of all we thank Burton Dreben, whose thought and teaching inspired so many.

Boston, Massachusetts   J. F.
New Haven, Connecticut   S. S.
June 2000

Contents

Part II Between the Wars: Logical Positivism and Critiques of Metaphysics

Part III After the Wars: Rethinking the Future

Contributors

Stanley Cavell is Walter M. Cabot Professor of Aesthetics and the General Theory of Value, Emeritus, Harvard University.

Juliet Floyd is Associate Professor of Philosophy, Boston University.

Dagfinn Føllesdal is Clarence Irving Lewis Professor of Philosophy, Stanford University, and Professor of Philosophy, University of Oslo.

Michael Friedman is Ruth N. Halls Professor in the Arts and Humanities, Professor of History and Philosophy of Science, and Professor of Philosophy, Indiana University.

Warren Goldfarb is Walter Beverley Pearson Professor of Modern Mathematics and Mathematical Logic, Harvard University.

W. D. Hart is Professor of Philosophy, University of Illinois, Chicago.

Gary Hatfield is Adam Seybert Professor in Moral and Intellectual Philosophy, University of Pennsylvannia.

Jaakko Hintikka is Professor of Philosophy, Boston University.

Peter Hylton is Professor of Philosophy, University of Illinois, Chicago.

Edward H. Minar is Associate Professor of Philosophy, University of Arkansas.

Susan Neiman is Director, Einstein Forum, Berlin.

Rohit Parikh is Professor of Mathematics and Computer Science, Brooklyn College and the Graduate Center, City University of New York.

Charles Parsons is Edgar Pierce Professor of Philosophy, Harvard University.

Hilary Putnam is Cogan University Professor, Harvard University.

W. V. Quine is Edgar Pierce Professor of Philosophy, Emeritus, Harvard University

John Rawls is Conant University Professor, Emeritus, Harvard University.

Thomas Ricketts is Professor of Philosophy, University of Pennsylvania.

Gerald E. Sacks is Professor of Mathematical Logic, Harvard University and M.I.T.

Naomi Scheman is Professor of Philosophy, University of Minnesota.

Sanford Shieh is Associate Professor of Philosophy, Wesleyan University.

Joan Weiner is Professor of Philosophy, University of Wisconsin, Milwaukee.

FUTURE PASTS

Introduction

JULIET FLOYD AND SANFORD SHIEH

Among contemporary philosophers there is a growing interest in recounting the history of philosophy in the twentieth century. The essays in this volume are meant to be contributions, from a variety of perspectives, to this growing histori-cal consciousness. But they are intended to be more than that. Our decision to group together these particular contributions has been determined by our own conception of present difficulties facing a historical perspective on philosophy of the last hundred years. We intend the present volume to provoke discussion of the underlying outlooks and sensibilities that may—and do—inform current work on the history of recent philosophy. Controversies about how history ought to find its way into philosophical practice are, we believe, particularly acute when it comes to discussion of the recent past. It is, after all, especially hard to gain historical distance from a past one has partly lived through. Even more, attempts to write the history of philosophy tend to import with them current philosophi-cal commitments and theories, a whole range of historically conditioned assump-tions, some of them tacit, about what is and is not philosophically central—assumptions that are themselves products of this century.

In particular, it is difficult for contemporary scholars to assess the recent history of philosophy without running up against the tendency to impose ideology upon that history, invoking supposed distinctions between the so-called analytic and the so-called continental traditions, or between philosophy and science, or between metaphysics and antimetaphysics.[1] Thus, for example, there is a widespread ten-dency to identify analytic philosophy with logical positivism, or, more precisely, with a scientistic interpretation of logical positivism. This identification leads to the view that analytic philosophy was founded on the assumption that mathematics and physics are the highest forms of knowledge, that metaphysics should and may be avoided altogether, that the nature of scientific method is the primary issue with which philosophers should be concerned, and that the historical, ethical, sociologi-cal, and psychological contexts in which science has been practiced are irrelevant to an understanding of its nature. Analytic philosophy is thus held responsible for having excluded central topics of traditional philosophy from the domain of philo-sophical discourse, replacing them with adherence to an ahistorical conception of philosophy as problem-oriented. For analytic philosophy, it is held, the history of philosophy is dispensable, or at best of value only insofar as its texts can be mined for arguments that contribute to the present work of philosophical theorizing.

Ironically, however, this picture of the analytic tradition is itself ahistorical in nature, presupposing as it does that detailed attention to this tradition's historical development is not necessary in order to assess its successes, failures, and philosophical significance. Its counterpart is an equally oversimplified and ahistorical picture of so-called continental philosophy as antiscientific in character, uncritically metaphysical, and the lone champion of philosophy conceived of as a discipline designed to contribute to ethical and spiritual life.

Against such ideological caricatures—which dismiss the possibility of learning anything new from a retrospective examination of philosophy of the last hundred years—we wish to set a more complex view. Twentieth-century philosophy, in both the analytic and the continental traditions, presents us with richer and more challenging historical interpretive problems than these caricatures allow: if they did not, they would not be important contributions to the history of philosophy. In particular, following the lead of Burton Dreben, a founder of the historical study of twentieth-century philosophy in America, and a magisterial authority on its texts, we urge that it requires no less hermeneutical and philosophical sensitivity to read a text in the canon of analytic philosophy—say, Frege's *Foundations of Arithmetic* or Carnap's *Logical Syntax of Language*—than it does to read, say, Aristotle's *Prior* and *Posterior Analytics*, or Hegel's *Science of Logic*, or Heidegger's *The Metaphysical Foundations of Logic*. Indeed, what is of lasting philosophical significance in twentieth-century philosophy will be just that work which is amenable to such reading. At its most fruitful, interpretation cuts across received ideological boundaries. If we do not presume to take for granted that we understand what Aristotle or Hegel or Heidegger means by "science," "logic," "proposition," "presupposition," or "argument," we should no more take for granted that we understand what Frege or Carnap means by "science," "logic," "proposition," "presupposition," or "argument." To read truly philosophically, with historical sensitivity, is to read without such preconceptions. For it is only when one attends to what is done with a philosophical notion—to the way in which terms of argumentation and of criticism are applied in a particular context by a particular philosopher—that one is in a position to appreciate that notion's significance. To understand a philosopher's questions philosophically, we need to see the criteria for what she or he counts as satisfactory answers; we cannot rest with "isms" and ideological labels.

The essays of this volume scrutinize recent history in this careful way. We hope they will provoke needed discussion among philosophers, historians of science, and intellectual historians about the complexity, richness, and significance of twentieth-century philosophy.

Before the Wars: Origins of Traditions

Most would agree that analytic philosophy began with Frege's, Russell's, and Moore's rejections of three major currents in mid- and late-nineteenth-century

European thought: psychologism, Hegelian Idealism, and historicism. Although the origins of phenomenology and existentialism are also bound up in a rejection of these nineteenth-century trends, Frege's, Russell's, and Moore's work was distinctive in drawing a sharp distinction between the process of judging—historical, mental, or social—and the judgment which results. For each of them, a judgment is true or false and is what it is, independently of any mental, psychological, or historical facts about the subject who makes that judgment. This conception of judgment goes hand in hand with a nonpsychological, nonhistoricist conception of the justification of judgments. The objectivity of truth and judgment, they argued, must be accounted for in such a way that it is not reduced to facts about mental life, whether metaphysical, transcendental, psychological, or historical.

What lent weight to this call for a break with prior tradition, at least in Frege's and Russell's case, was an account of objectivity bound up with the nature of formal logic. From Kant through Hegel and Marx, formal logic had been viewed as having no special philosophical interest. Kant, for example, held that it was at best a negative touchstone of truth; the law of noncontradiction, for example, helps us to see what cannot be true, but cannot on its own advance knowledge. Moreover, according to Kant, formal logic was a closed and completed body of doctrine which had not been able to make any significant step forward since Aristotle.[2] For philosophy to proceed to genuine knowledge, he insisted, a new, "transcendental logic" must be developed. This logic issued into genuine knowledge, which Kant characterized as a kind of synthetic a priori truth. The post-Kantian Idealists and Marx continued Kant's expansion of the domain of logic. Hegel, in particular, argued (as Kant had not) that formal laws of thought, taken by themselves, are either contradictory or merely empty tautologies lacking in genuine content or truth. His "dialectical" logic, by contrast, was intended to offer a contentful science of reality, history, and mind.[3]

But as Frege's 1879 *Begriffsschrift* showed, formal logic had not yet been completed in its essentials. The greatest single advance in logic since Aristotle was gained through Frege's laying out, for the first time, a formalized language, a language with fully explicit rules of grammar and inference, couched in a notation powerful and flexible enough to exhaustively codify deductive reasoning. The scope of deductive inferences codified by Frege's mathematical logic far exceeds that of any previous logical system, and his language appeared to him to be powerful enough to represent formally all judgments. Indeed, Frege held that this language—which he called "*Begriffsschrift*" ("concept-script")—yields a systematic characterization of correct inference in general, no matter what the subject matter reasoned about. His logic, Frege insisted, is the sine qua non of all rational justification and argument, a universal framework within which all reasoning, insofar as it is reasoning, may be represented. In particular, Frege took himself to have successfully formalized all mathematical reasoning, and he showed in detail how his notation could be used to prove, on the basis of logical (and purely formal) definitions alone, those truths of arithmetic which Kant had insisted were synthetic a priori. This showed, Frege held, that the truths of elementary arithmetic rested upon truths of pure logic and not upon intuition or any sort of empirically conditioned, contingent forms of knowledge. A fortiori, any attempt to ground the truths of mathematics in accounts of the human mind, whether psychological, sociological, or transcendental, is otiose.

Frege's conception of the universal applicability of modern mathematical logic and its singular role in displaying the structure of genuinely objective judgment were the primary concerns of much twentieth-century philosophy. Perhaps this is unsurprising: the effort to delineate the nature of objective judgment has always played a central role in philosophy. Yet questions about the nature and scope of the new logic were from the outset simultaneously taken to be questions about the nature and scope of philosophy. Frege's *Begriffsschrift* opened philosophers up to the question of whether philosophical arguments about the nature and structure of objectivity and truth were to be held to the standards of rigor set by Frege's own formalization of logic. Could all philosophical arguments be formally represented in this new language? Self-reflexive difficulties about the standpoint from which this question might be resolved presented philosophers with continual difficulties in accounting for the nature of their own enterprise. There were many differing accounts within the analytic tradition of the nature and scope of logic and the relation of logic to philosophy. Frege's *Begriffsschrift* did not interpret itself. And few were prepared to agree with Frege's own interpretation of his logic, which shifted after 1891, when he began to propound a distinction between the sense and the reference of linguistic expressions—most famously in his 1892 essay "Über Sinn und Bedeutung" ("On Sense and Reference"). Before the First World War, Russell and Wittgenstein both rejected Frege's sense/reference distinction. Between the wars, it was sometimes interpreted in light of Husserl's phenomenology. After the Second World War—when Frege's writings began to receive widespread attention—the distinction became central to what came to be called the philosophy of language.

It is therefore not surprising that today among historically minded analytic philosophers we find an ongoing attempt to discern a unity in the philosophical legacy of Frege. According to Michael Dummett, Frege's primary achievement was to provide philosophers with the materials for a positive theory of meaning, a new philosophy of language. Dummett argues that the key insight of the analytic tradition as a whole—an insight due to Frege—was to see that an account of thought and of metaphysics must itself proceed through an account of language.[4]

In their contributions to this volume, Warren Goldfarb and Joan Weiner reject the notion that Frege took himself to have provided a theory of meaning. In so doing, they question the extent to which contemporary analytic philosophy may legitimately trace its ancestry to Frege's views. The idea that our notions of logical validity and of justification rest upon a prior notion of meaning is a nearly unquestioned axiom in much contemporary philosophy. And the contemporary so-called semantical account of logical validity in terms of multiple interpretations of a formalized language is now standard. Goldfarb, however, argues that Frege had principled grounds for maintaining that what makes a standard of reasoning a law of logic is not explicable by appeal to *any* facts, much less semantical ones. He thus suggests that the explanatory value of contemporary semantical accounts of logic and language is open to question in light of a proper reading of Frege.

The fact that Frege had no explanation of what makes his formal laws genuinely logical does not, of course, imply that he naively assumed that he had correctly identified universal canons of objectivity and of rationality. As Joan Weiner argues in her essay, Frege explicitly acknowledged the necessity for what he called "elucidations" of his primitive notions. Such elucidations, he admitted, consist of hints, metaphors, and allusions—precisely that which resists being translated into the language of his logic, precisely what cannot be characterized as theoretical or objective by its lights. Weiner argues that Frege not only recognized the limits of theories of meaning, he even held that there is something about the understanding and communication of logic which cannot be argued for, or perhaps even stated. On Weiner's view, far from relying on an unfounded rationalist confidence in the correctness of his logic, Frege is consistently self-conscious and self-critical about the standpoint from which essential requirements for rationality are to be articulated. In this, she holds, he was followed by Wittgenstein.

The year 1900 saw the publication of Volume 1 of Husserl's first phenomenological work, *Logical Investigations*. While Goldfarb and Weiner emphasize a series of distances which seem to separate much contemporary analytic theory from its origins, Dagfinn Føllesdal, Jaakko Hintikka, Thomas Ricketts, and Charles Parsons each stress continuities of concern among philosophers situated at the origins of both the analytic and the continental traditions. Føllesdal, Hintikka, and Parsons argue that Husserl's phenomenology addressed issues central to much contemporary so-called analytic philosophy of language and mind. Like Goldfarb, Føllesdal believes that it was the nineteenth-century philosopher Bolzano who first framed a conception of logic close to the contemporary semantical one.[5] Unlike Goldfarb, Føllesdal is concerned to argue for Bolzano's importance by way of his influence on Husserl. Føllesdal shows how, under Bolzano's influence, Husserl tried to account for the semantics of indexical and demonstrative terms. Such accounts have been central to much philosophy, for these terms seem to express immediate, minimally categorized, and allegedly indubitably certain contact between mind and world. To preempt the charge that Husserl's philosophy forwards a naïve, overly mentalistic model of the mind and its expressive capacities, Føllesdal shows how Husserl developed a thought experiment nearly identical to the well-known Twin Earth scenario later framed by Hilary Putnam to criticize mentalist theories of meaning.[6] As Føllesdal sees it, Husserl was ahead of his time: it would be another sixty years after he wrote before the questions raised in his discussion of indexicals and identity were seriously addressed by philosophers of language.

The principled division between the analytic and the continental traditions is also questioned by Jaakko Hintikka, who argues that Mach should be considered the century's most influential philosopher, a giant on whose shoulders thinkers like Wittgenstein, Husserl, and Heidegger subsequently stood. Hintikka notes—as does Føllesdal—that Frege's direct influence on philosophy proper outside of logic and the foundations of mathematics was for a long time quite minimal. Mach's wider impact is seen in the great importance to much twentieth-century philosophy of the question whether knowledge may be given to us apart from what is conceptualized in thought, in, for example, pure sense perception or nonconceptualized intu-

ition. It was Mach's phenomenalism (or phenomenology), Hintikka claims, which
set the agenda for future discussion of this question. Hintikka notes that this question was central, not only to much twentieth-century epistemology, but also, at
least at the turn of the century, to work within the natural sciences. Mach's disputes with Bolzmann about the reducibility of knowledge to sensation eventually
influenced Einstein and, hence, the development of physics itself. Later on, as
Hintikka sees it, some of the key philosophical ideas of the Vienna Circle—about
verifiability, for example—foundered on the very same difficulties which had earlier beset Mach. Hintikka takes both Husserl and the early Wittgenstein to have
embraced phenomenological conceptions indebted to Mach's ideas. This calls into
question Heidegger's later insistence that phenomenology and phenomenalism are
distinct philosophical traditions.

Thomas Ricketts's chapter shows that in early analytic philosophy—as in other
philosophical traditions—metaphysical doctrines evolved through direct engagement with past traditions. Ricketts treats shifts in Russell's views about truth and
judgment between 1905 and 1910, a period during which Russell attempted to
articulate an atomistic, pluralist, and realist metaphysical alternative to the Idealistic Monism he had embraced in his undergraduate years and his earliest philosophical work. Russell did not dismiss Idealism out of hand; he took it as a metaphysics to be argued against. In the course of formulating his alternative, he
worked his way through several different metaphysical accounts of his own. He
came, for example, to abandon his metaphysics of propositions in favor of a metaphysics of facts. Ricketts shows how internal tensions within Russell's early views
about propositional complexity and truth, as well as efforts to respond to the Idealism of Bradley, shaped the evolution of his views.

In his recent *Origins of Analytical Philosophy*, Michael Dummett has denied that
Husserl was an analytic philosopher on the grounds that Husserl failed to subscribe
to two theses Dummett deems axiomatic for the analytic tradition, namely, "that
a philosophical account of thought can be attained through a philosophical account
of language, and . . . only . . . so attained."[7] Dummett locates the beginning of the
conceptual break between the analytic and the continental traditions in Husserl's
transcendental turn of 1905–1907. According to Dummett, Husserl came to subscribe to a general conception of intentionality which was essentially nonlinguistic.
Charles Parsons agrees with Dummett that Husserl did not view the philosophy of
language as basic to the philosophy of thought, but disagrees with Dummett's account of Husserl. Parsons argues that Husserl was quite aware of the need for an
account of the linguistic expression of thought, but he was focused on grappling
with the problem of whether particular perceptual experiences must have a propositional or language-like structure in order to be said to have genuine content. This
issue lies at the heart of much contemporary debate about thought and consciousness, especially the question of whether the notion of nonconceptual mental content makes sense.[8] In differing with Dummett's interpretation of Husserl, Parsons
is also differing with Dummett's account of the origin and nature of the analytic
tradition. The upshot is once again to question whether the distinction between
the analytic and continental traditions is as philosophically principled a distinction
as many have supposed.

Between the Wars: Logical Positivism and the Critique of Metaphysics

In Kant's terms, Frege, Russell, and Whitehead had come to conceive of formal logic in the same way that Kant had viewed transcendental logic: as an organon of philosophical knowledge, something more than a merely formal canon of rules. In the hands of the young Wittgenstein, this conception of logic underwent a transformation, closing what might be called the classical period of analytic philosophy and ushering in the dominance of what came to be known as logical positivism. Wittgenstein held that "the great work of the modern mathematical logicians . . . has brought about an advance in Logic comparable only to that which made Astronomy out of Astrology, and Chemistry out of Alchemy."[9] But in contrast both to the Idealists and to Frege and Russell, Wittgenstein denied that logic consists of substantive truths or laws. Instead, he insisted, the new logic shows us that the so-called propositions of logic are not true or false in the same sense as are genuine propositions, but are true or false as are tautologies and contradictions: they are redundant; they say nothing about what is or is not the case. Thus did Wittgenstein resuscitate and radicalize both Hegel's complaint that formal logic is empty of content and the early Moore's and Russell's view that tautologies, being empty redundancies, are neither true nor false.[10] Unlike the Idealists, however, Wittgenstein did not recognize anything beyond formal logic that could furnish a basis for metaphysics. Indeed, his aim in the *Tractatus* was to reject *all* metaphysics, whether Realist or Idealist, as nonsensical, as a hopeless attempt to step beyond the limits of sense. From the Fregean idea that there is no standpoint outside logic, he drew the very unFregean conclusion that neither philosophy nor logic could be stated in propositions. Logical form could be "shown" but not "said." Philosophy's proper task, he held, should be the activity of perspicuously displaying the nonsensical character of purported philosophical claims, whether these are claims about knowledge, thought, or value. This, he remarked, was primarily an ethical task.[11]

Frege disliked the *Tractatus*, which Wittgenstein sent him in manuscript form sometime between October 1918 and June 1919.[12] In fact, Frege urged Wittgenstein not to publish it without drastic revision, for he disliked the book's lack of argument and its philosophical spirit, which he took to be unscientific. In contrast, both Russell and Ramsey immediately perceived the *Tractatus* as an important work, and each attempted, though in differing ways, to develop Wittgenstein's conception of logic in a positive direction. But the *Tractatus* was to exercise its widest influence on twentieth-century philosophy through its appropriation by the logical positivists, especially Schlick and Carnap. For the positivists read the *Tractatus* as a doctrinal tract and attempted to apply what they took to be its doctrines across the board, to all metaphysics, past, present, and future. In particular, the positivists took the *Tractatus'* account of the nature of logic to constitute a crucial turning point in the history of philosophy, the means by which empiricism could be made into a scientifically rigorous theory of knowledge. They agreed, first, that Wittgenstein had rigorously demonstrated that purely logical truth reduces to tautologousness, to something wholly formal or "analytic" in character, something void of factual or empirical content. This in turn showed, they believed, that mathematics is equally empty of metaphysical, intuitive, or empirical content. Traditional metaphysics—which had purported to issue into substantive, a priori truths about (logically) necessary features of reality and thought—appeared to the positivists to have been thereby demonstrated to be unnecessary and confused. Logic and mathematics were understood to be stipulative in character, merely conventional formal frameworks to be adopted or rejected independently of the course of experience. Beyond these purely formal domains, the only genuine knowledge, they held, is empirical in character. This view was enshrined in what came to be called the "verificationist theory of meaning," according to which the meaning of a sentence is characterized in terms of its empirical consequences, ultimately the range of (possible) observation statements capable of either confirming or refuting it. The success of Einstein's theory of relativity, in which the (traditional metaphysical) notions of space and time are operationalized in terms of the frames of reference of different observers, was seen as an important application of the verificationist idea. But the positivists also held that ethical utterances are not verifiable, and so do not express genuine propositions, are neither true nor false. Instead, ethical claims are to be construed as expressions of feeling or emotion which are not subject to norms of rational argument. For the positivists philosophy must at last come to be seen for what it is and should be, a purely formal or "analytic" activity of conceptual analysis, scientific in spirit, but limited in its aims and scope. The negative task of this new philosophy was to unmask the emptiness and arbitrariness of purported metaphysics. The positive task was to investigate the logical structure of knowledge. In his 1934 *Logical Syntax of Language*, Carnap explicitly argued that philosophy should reduce to the study of the logic of science—the logic of the only genuine sort of knowledge—and that the logic of science is in turn nothing other than the logical syntax of the language of science, the study of various possible linguistic frameworks which might be used to organize the empirical data of science. With his famous "Principle of Tolerance," Carnap declared that "in logic there are no morals," by which he meant that each philosopher is free to adopt whatever language he or she wishes to adopt (physicalist, phenomenalist, and so on). The only demand Carnap made was that every philosopher must be willing to make explicit the logico-syntactic framework within which he or she is operating, by means of a formalized language. (On this score Carnap argued that Heidegger's metaphysics is wholly unacceptable, because its grammar cannot be set out in a formalized way.)[13]

Wittgenstein rejected the positivists' scientism and disavowed their appropriation of the *Tractatus*. Yet in the 1920s and 1930s, his most enthusiastic and influential readers were the members of the Vienna Circle, and his own attempts at distancing his early work from positivism went largely unheeded. Since Wittgenstein's death in 1951, however, readers of the *Tractatus* have been increasingly inclined to emphasize the sharp differences that separated Wittgenstein's early philosophy from that of the positivists. Some readers now interpret the early Wittgenstein as a metaphysical (or even modal) realist, while others see him as antimetaphysical, but not in a positivist vein. Yet despite such widely various interpretations of the

Tractatus, most contemoprary scholars would agree with what Wittgenstein himself wrote in the Preface to the book: that it was the works of Frege and Russell which stimulated him most in writing it. This is not to say that Wittgenstein agreed with everything—or even anything—contained in these philosophers' works. Juliet Floyd's essay argues that a central aim of the *Tractatus* is to reject Frege's and Russell's most basic logico-philosophical notions, recasting both their conceptions of logical analysis and their conceptions of formal logic itself. Floyd stresses the importance of the fact that in the *Tractatus* Wittgenstein explicitly attacks what Frege, Russell, and the positivists all took Frege to have rigorously demonstrated, namely, that mathematics is a branch of logic. Floyd sees Wittgenstein's rejection of this "logicism" as an index of the great distance separating his philosophy from all these other philosophers. She holds that Wittgenstein's treatment of the grammar of number words in the *Tractatus* is intended to limit or criticize the use of the new logic as a philosophical organon. On this reading, however useful Wittgenstein took the new logic to be for dispelling certain grammatical illusions, he never conceived of it—as did Frege, Russell, and Carnap—as an intrinsically clarificatory tool, as a way to present the logical syntax of a language in a wholly explicit, transparent way. On Floyd's reading, the early Wittgenstein was neither an ideal language philosopher nor a logical positivist, but instead, he began, as he remained, a critic of analytic philosophy's tendency to conceive of logical analysis as a matter of designing or applying formalized languages of the Frege-Russell sort.

If we take seriously Wittgenstein's claim that his aims in writing the *Tractatus* were primarily ethical, though not in the emotivist's sense, then we are in a position to see that Wittgenstein's critique of metaphysics is in some ways closer to Heidegger's effort to criticize traditional metaphysics in *Being and Time* than it is to logical positivism. The aspiration to overcome traditional metaphysics was after all not unique to the analytic tradition, and, like Frege, Russell, and Wittgenstein, Husserl and Heidegger took themselves to be going beyond the presuppositions of nineteenth-century forms of historicism, Idealism, and psychologism. As Edward Minar's essay argues, Heidegger's treatment of skepticism has significant ethical and existential aspects, and evinces concern with issues common to analytic and continental thought. Minar does not take Heidegger to be dismissing modern epistemology as conceptually bankrupt, as Richard Rorty, for example, has maintained. Instead, Minar holds, Heidegger attempts to engage with and account for the power of metaphysics. As Minar reads him, Heidegger does not take received philosophical distinctions between the world of theoretical entities given to us in space and time and the world of sense data or phenomena to be wholly specious or easily dispensable philosophical distinctions. Instead, Heidegger reinterprets these distinctions, seeing them as rooted in the world with which we are practically, morally, and emotionally engaged before we begin philosophizing. On this reading, Heidegger's treatment of the quarrel between common sense and skepticism has significant points of contact with work of Moore, Austin, and Wittgenstein.

We have been heretofore speaking of logical positivism as a philosophical movement, but historically and philosophically speaking, connections among members of this group were multifarious, and there was in fact much disagreement among them as to how best to develop a philosophy for the future. In his essay on Reichenbach's 1938 *Experience and Prediction*, Hilary Putnam argues against the notion that logical positivism represented a unified ideological viewpoint. It is a vast oversimplification, Putnam shows, to suppose that every logical positivist held that all meaningful statements are either empirically verifiable statements about sense data or else purely formal stipulations. Reichenbach, in particular, defended a form of commonsense realism, while at the same time criticizing foundational or metaphysical Realism. For Putnam the most crucial philosophical questions about logical positivism concern, not a unique theory of meaning, but the particular assumptions about rationality, meaning, and objectivity which each positivist brought to bear in arguing against metaphysical doctrines.

These assumptions are the foci of Michael Friedman's essay on Carnap's 1934 *Logical Syntax of Language*. Friedman takes up the question of how best to interpret Carnap's antimetaphysical stance in Carnap's own terms. Focusing on Carnap's attitude toward the foundations of mathematics, Friedman argues that Carnap's deepest philosophical motivation was to offer scientifically minded philosophers an intellectually responsible, undogmatic way out of their philosophical perplexities. These perplexities, Carnap held, were best viewed as questions about choice of language, and his dream was to replace dogmatic metaphysical dispute with the building of formalized languages. Carnap revised what he took to be Wittgenstein's absolutist conception of logical syntax and replaced it with the most general possible pluralism, relativizing the notions of justification and correctness to particular linguistic frameworks. He thereby hoped to provide a precise, purely formal characterization of the intuitive distinction between questions which concern the real natures of objects and those which merely concern alternative ways of speaking. Nevertheless, Friedman argues, Carnap's project foundered on the attempt to formulate his "Principle of Tolerance" in wholly syntactical terms, by way of a language-relative distinction between analytic and synthetic truth. Carnap tried to exploit Gödel's arithmetization of syntax, in which claims made in a metalanguage about the syntax of an object language are represented within the object language itself. But Gödel had used this technique to prove his incompleteness theorem, which states that no syntactically complete, recursively enumerable set of axioms for arithmetic can be devised. This implies, Friedman argues, that there is in principle no wholly formal (no philosophically neutral) way to survey the formal consequences of each and every alternative theory of mathematics. Gödel's logical work thus defeated Carnap's *Syntax* program, despite Carnap's attempt to further his program by applying Gödel's technique. As Friedman sees it, Carnap's work "could not have produced a more disappointing result," for its failure may be seen to stem from its own internal inconsistency.

W. V. Quine's 1952 essay "Two Dogmas of Empiricism" is frequently taken to be a landmark in twentieth-century philosophy. Here Quine rejected both the analytic/synthetic distinction and the view that each sentence of a language carries with it its own fund of empirical meaning—the twin "dogmas," as he held, of logical empiricism. Like the positivists, Quine takes philosophy to be scientific in spirit. Unlike them, he saw no way to draw a scientifically respect-able general distinction between (scientific) questions of fact and (philosophi-cal) questions of meaning. For Quine, philosophy is not a specialized theory of meaning, but is continuous with science. The impact of Quine's vision on phi-losophy after the Second World War has been immense, though the fundamen-tals of Quine's views were already in place by the 1930s. Peter Hylton's essay examines Quine's 1934 Harvard lectures on Carnap, his first attempt to explain Carnap's logical syntax program to an American audience. By pointing out tensions within the exposition Quine offered of Carnap's views, Hylton shows how these lectures already point toward Quine's subsequent disagreements with Carnap over the analytic/synthetic distinction. Hylton finds that in these lectures Quine avoids the Carnapian "fiction" that our actual language contains at the outset a set of implicitly given definitions or rules from which the cat-egory of the a priori arises. Moreover, Quine fastidiously refrains from assum-ing that our language contains at the outset a distinction between the a priori and the empirical. But in the context of an exposition of Carnap's program, this invites a question Quine was soon to ask: What sort of explanation of a given sentence's validity could Carnap's notion of "analytic" provide? Hylton argues that Quine's later well-known holism about meaning, his famed denial of logi-cal empiricism's second reductionist dogma, was not the sole or primary philo-sophical factor shaping Quine's differences with Carnap. According to Hylton, more is at issue between the two, namely, their differing conceptions of what counts as a philosophical explanation.

In his contribution to this volume, Quine confirms that the roots of his view go as far back as the 1930s. Quine reflects on his philosophical development, treating the steadfastness of his faith in extensionalism over the last seventy years as a unifying principle of his whole philosophy. Quine calls two sentences coextensive if they are both true or both false, two general terms or predicates coextensive if they are true of just the same objects, and two singular terms co-extensive if they designate the same object. Extensionalism is, he says, "a pre-dilection for extensional theories." Intensionalism, by contrast, takes difference of meaning or intension as fundamental, prior to sameness or difference of ex-tension. Quine defends his extensionalism by showing how it may be put to work in several different philosophical arenas. For "clarity" and "convenience" in logic, Quine finds the extensionalist viewpoint indispensable; his early admiration of *Principia Mathematica* was, he recalls, nearly "unbounded," but from the start he recoiled from its intensional standpoint. His Ph.D. dissertation of 1932 began the process of reinterpreting the *Principia* extensionally,[14] but the philo-sophical consequences of that reinterpretation continue to be drawn by Quine to this day. Quine conjectures that the intensionalism of Russell and Whitehead lay in their having placed "undue weight on the adjectives that express . . . prop-erties." This led them to take "the giant step" of "reifying meanings." Quine argues that his extensionalism can rise to the challenges posed to it by those seeking scientifically respectable theories of our uses of coextensive yet inten-sionally distinct predicates, our propositional attitude talk, and our talk of logi-cal implication.

After the Wars: Rethinking the Future

A historical approach to the development of twentieth-century philosophy can-not avoid facing the question of whether there has been progress in philosophy over the last hundred years. Some hold that analytic philosophy has come into "a state of crisis."[15] Richard Rorty, for example, has argued that twentieth-century efforts to erect philosophical accounts of scientific method were the final cultural expression of a tradition beginning with Descartes, in which philosophy attempted to defend its own legitimacy as an autonomous discipline by casting itself in the role of an arbiter of scientific knowledge, proposing theories of mind which purported to serve as an a priori foundation for human knowledge in gen-eral, and scientific knowledge in particular.[16] According to Rorty, the illusory nature of this self-conception only came to light in the twentieth century, with the work of philosophers like Heidegger, Wittgenstein, and the American pragma-tists, including Quine: as Rorty sees it, these were the first modern philosophers to successfully question the metaphysical pretensions of modern philosophy. On Rorty's view, the distinctive contribution of twentieth-century philosophy has been its willingness to surrender illusory conceptions of what philosophy can accomplish. Success has consisted in recognizing failures for what they are. The current challenge, Rorty argues, is to follow the path of pragmatism, and to con-struct a philosophical conversation without such pretensions. Rorty's call for a postanalytic pragmatism has been echoed by Cornel West and John Rajchman.[17]

Susan Neiman's chapter argues that there are clear signs of progress in recent philosophy. Arguing that the history of philosophy is best seen as internal to phi-losophy, she explores differences and similarities among appropriations of Kant by such philosophers as Russell, Moore, Schlick, Ayer, Strawson, and Rorty. Neiman argues that each of these philosophers read (or misread) Kant in accor-dance with his own philosophical agenda. Neiman rejects Rorty's reading of modern philosophy as primarily obsessed with grounding philosophy on a cer-tain foundation. Instead, she stresses, the twentieth-century tendency was not so much to project a Cartesian, foundationalist aim onto Kant's writings as to simplify and truncate them, bleeding them of their moral and ethical content. Recent writing on Kant, Neiman argues, has begun to progress precisely in at-tempting to recover the moral dimensions of Kant's theoretical aims, while simul-taneously respecting the subtlety of his own conception of philosophical progress. As Neiman sees it, the theoretical and the practical sides of philosophy form an inseparable unity. Hence, she argues, within the current sense of crisis and con-fusion, we may perhaps discern signs that analytic philosophy is in fact progress-ing, certainly in its attentiveness to great philosophical works of the past.

Naomi Scheman's chapter considers some of the political and cultural ramifi-cations of post–Second World War philosophy. Scheman sees a crucial, positive, and potentially liberating role for philosophy to play in critical reflection on the culture, for she takes philosophical dispute to foster the sort of reflection we re-quire in order to satisfy our deepest needs, the sort of reflection that, she argues, "serious politics" is all about. She agrees with Cornel West that post–Second World War analytic philosophy evaded this truth and was itself a symptom of wider "dis-eases" in the culture. Yet she proposes that Wittgenstein's critique of metaphysics, as interpreted through writings of Cora Diamond and Nancy Fraser, may be useful in actually changing the ways we live—for example, in offering the culturally and politically marginalized something better than the choice between a relativism which leaves the status quo intact and a withdrawal into empty pleas for the realization of ideals. Through the critique of metaphysics, Scheman holds, we may find a route toward reflective and critical engagement with existing political and cultural institutions. Scheman's mode of philosophizing seems to provide what West, Rorty, and others have called for: an epistemically self-critical, morally engaged philosophical conversation.

Rorty's account of modern philosophy assumes a sharp distinction between the practice of philosophy and the practice of science. Yet throughout the modern period philosophy has frequently been in productive interplay with science. In the twentieth century, the development of modern mathematical logic has had both significant scientific and significant philosophical impact, not least on theoretical computer science. Frege's *Begriffsschrift* was arguably the first formalized language capable of producing truths according to wholly explicit, machine-readable rules. Of course, Frege denied that his *Begriffsschrift* was a merely formal device for calculating; he took it to be a meaningful language reflecting thoughts. Yet ironically, by setting out a formalized language, Frege made a crucial contribution toward the development of a precise mathematical account of the notion of an algorithm or computation. Beginning in the 1930s, with work of Jacques Herbrand and Gödel, the modern theory of computability began to develop. In particular, Gödel, Alonzo Church, and Alan Turing gave independent yet extensionally equivalent characterizations of the notion of a computable function.[18] Turing came to advocate a mechanist theory of the human mind, defended in his 1950 paper "Computing Machinery and Intelligence,"[19] where he outlined the famous Turing test for ascribing thought to machines. According to Turing, human thought is essentially reducible to computational algorithms, which can in principle be carried out by computers. Turing's metaphysical use of his mathematical contributions has exercised an enormous influence on subsequent philosophy of mind.

At stake in arguments over mechanism about the mind is the publicity of language and of thought. Traditional philosophy tended to conceive of thinking in terms of ideas, representations, and meanings lodged within an individual human mind. To what extent does contemporary philosophy surrender such conceptions? Rohit Parikh's essay explores three arguments concerned with the social character of language: Quine's thesis of the indeterminacy of translation,[20] Saul Kripke's skeptical paradox concerning the notion of following a rule (attributed by Kripke to Wittgenstein),[21] and John Searle's Chinese room puzzle.[22] Searle argues that computers, as mere manipulators of uninterpreted syntactic systems, cannot express thoughts or meanings as human language users do. Quine and Kripke take a different tack, criticizing philosophically tendentious conceptions of meaning and thought. Quine conjectures the indeterminacy of translation on the basis of a thought experiment he takes to undercut the appeal of philosophical theories—such as Frege's—which postulate a realm of thoughts, meanings,

or propositions expressed by language independent of observable uses of particular
linguistic units on particular occasions. Kripke finds in Wittgenstein's later writings an even more skeptical critique of the notion of meaning, according to which
we can give no content to the notion of a speaker's meaning on a given occasion
of linguistic use. Comparing these philosophical arguments to problems about the
relations between high-level programming languages and the machine languages
into which they must be translated in order to be implemented, Parikh argues
that while these philosophical arguments may appear implausible if couched in
the abstract, they in fact correspond to very real difficulties faced by theoretical
computer scientists. This does not refute mechanism about the mind. But it does
suggest that theoretical computer science and philosophy continue to share certain fundamental conceptual concerns.

The later Wittgenstein's influence began to make itself widely felt after his death
in 1951, with the posthumous publication of his *Philosophical Investigations*.
Though there remains controversy about just what this work contributed to
philosophy, it has already achieved the status of a classic. Stanley Cavell's essay
explores the question of what Wittgenstein's conception of philosophy holds out
as a legacy for future philosophizing. Reflecting on the history of his own interpretation of Wittgenstein, set out in greatest detail in his work *The Claim of
Reason*,[23] Cavell recounts thoughts he has had about the translation of his work
into French. He hopes that Wittgenstein's thought may open up the prospect of
a new, uncharted future for philosophy, in which the split between analytic and
continental approaches is not final or irreparable, but perhaps even fruitful, acknowledged as a philosophical split within each thinker. For Cavell, the academization of philosophy, as the academization of an art, lacks the capacity to impose
any lasting recipe for creative work upon its practitioners. Philosophy is at its
heart autobiographical, not reducible to one or more methods. This implies that
there can be no rules established, either for the production of significant work or
for the protection of philosophy from error. On the other hand, Cavell takes
Wittgenstein to have shown that what is illusory in the philosophical tradition
may be left to fail on its own terms, so that philosophy need not attempt to weed
out error once and for all. After Wittgenstein, we have the prospect of a novel and
open-ended future for philosophy.

Cavell's reading of Wittgenstein is not, however, the one prevalent among those
who have discussed the recent philosophical past. In the face of Quine's claim that
philosophy ought to be conceived as part of ongoing science, many readers have
seen Wittgenstein as providing a defense of the status of philosophy as an autonomous, theoretical, yet a priori discipline. According to the conception of philosophy
prevalent at Oxford beginning in the late 1930s—stemming in part from Oxford's
reading of Wittgenstein's *Tractatus*—philosophy's primary task is to provide a
priori analyses and clarifications of conceptual structure, an activity utterly
different from any empirical inquiry. Philosophy has a special status, it is argued,
because it addresses a special domain: it is prior to natural science, because it
makes possible the identification and dissolution of conceptual confusions. According to this conception, philosophy's most grievous intellectual temptation is
the uncritical worship of science, the illusion that philosophy can mimic scientific

procedures and terminology and uncritically appropriate its results. Peter Hacker, for example, has recently claimed that at its best, analytic philosophy should be conceived of as essentially "*sui generis*, as a critical discipline *toto caelo* distinct from science, as an *a priori* investigation, as a tribunal of sense as opposed to a plaintiff confronting nature," "before which science should be arraigned when it slides into myth-making and sinks into conceptual confusion."[24]

The final four contributions to this volume question such an account of the relationship between philosophy and science, suggesting a rather different course for future philosophical investigation.

Wilbur Hart's chapter uses the logical resources of nonstandard analysis, developed by Abraham Robinson in the early 1960s, to give a rational reconstruction of the philosophically puzzling notion of the infinitesimal. In the seventeenth century, Leibniz had postulated infinitesimals as the subject matter of the calculus, but the notion of an infinitely small quantity was deemed philosophically incoherent by many, including the philosopher Berkeley. In 1961, Robinson claimed, in the first public presentation of his work on nonstandard models of arithmetic, that this work may be seen as making sense of Leibniz' notion.[25] While Hart does not enter into this particular historical debate, he shows how Robinson's ideas may help to shed light on general metaphysical questions which naturally emerge from theoretical physics. Hart does not conceive of his role as a philosopher to be that of adjudicating the epistemological or conceptual warrant of mathematics and physics. Instead, he uses current mathematical work to explore what is conceptually basic or central to the scientific worldview.

Although Quine was largely successful in weaning the majority of post-Second World War empiricists away from reliance on the analytic/synthetic distinction, his dismantling of Carnap's attempt to build a firewall between metaphysics and science opened the way for the practice of metaphysics and with it, ironically, the resurgence of intensionalist doctrines.[26] Contemporary analytic philosophers frequently express agreement with Quine's insistence that no boundary separates the practice of philosophy from the practice of science. Yet challenges to Quine's extensionalist viewpoint inform the vast majority of writings in recent philosophy. Pathbreaking work in the mathematical clarification of quantified modal logic, in particular, appears to many to have made rigorous scientific sense of the modal (and intensional) notions of "possibility" and "necessity"[27]—though not, of course, to Quine.[28] The question thus naturally arose of whether Quine's extensionalism is or is not supported by scientific practice itself. Saul Kripke has challenged Quine by arguing that a scientifically respectable metaphysics and philosophy of language may be constructed upon the basis of modal notions. Kripke's philosophical account of modality, articulated in his 1970 Princeton lectures on the themes of naming and necessity, and later published in his influential *Naming and Necessity* (1980), rejected Quine's arguments—reiterated in his essay in this volume—that modal logic is both unnecessary from an extensionalist perspective and in its quantified version scientifically disreputable.[29] Sanford Shieh's essay attempts to uncover some of the presuppositions about meaning underlying Kripke's arguments in *Naming and Necessity*. Kripke argues against Quine that an essentialist, intensional metaphysics is reflected by ways in which we actually use our language. By examining Kripke's arguments in detail, Shieh argues that this metaphysical conception is not supported by Kripke's inchoate conception of meaning, and that adequate support may require independent metaphysical theses.

Gary Hatfield's essay takes issue with Rorty's characterization of the relationship between philosophy and science in Rorty's *Philosophy and the Mirror of Nature* (1979). Hatfield argues that a closer examination of early modern philosophy yields a far more complex view of the relation between philosophy and science than Rorty suggests. Descartes's epistemological concerns, according to Hatfield, were not a mere pretext for gaining professional authority; rather, Descartes was a practicing scientist whose metaphysics was instrumental in his arriving at the conception of a general physics. Rorty's picture of Locke fares no better, Hatfield claims, for Locke's account of ideas is far more subtle than Rorty's veil-of-ideas picture supposes. Furthermore, Locke's account of probable belief is intended to undermine the notion that science requires or provides us with certainty. Locke's real aim in offering this account of belief, Hatfield believes, was to accommodate the practice of Boylean natural science. This is the reverse of Rorty's idea that modern philosophers' primary aim was to provide an absolutely certain foundation for science's authority in terms of a representationalist theory of knowledge. As Hatfield sees it, the relation between philosophy and the sciences in the early modern European period already lived up to Rorty's ideal of a mutual intellectual conversation; precisely in virtue of its interplay with science, philosophy remained in critical dialogue with its surrounding culture.

The logician Gerald Sacks's chapter issues a self-reflexive, ironical defense of metaphysical speculation outside the bounds of what can be formalized or expressed in a rigorously presented logical system. In the tradition of Lewis Carroll's Red Queen, who argued that "Even a joke should have some meaning," and Philip E. B. Jourdain, who raised the question whether a joke is a joke under all circumstances,[30] Sacks parodies both attempts to dismiss metaphysical doctrines through jokes[31] and attempts to establish them by means of pure logic.

As John Rawls explains in his Afterword to this volume, the issue at stake is neither the mathematical legitimacy of any particular branch of mathematical logic—such as model theory—nor any particular philosophical debate about what is to count as logic—such as whether first-order logic exhausts what we mean by "logic." Rather, Sacks is concerned to reflect on a thesis long defended by Burton Dreben, namely that no mathematical theorem—such as the completeness theorem for first-order logic—can compel us to accept any particular philosophical interpretation of a basic intuitive notion (e.g., the notion of logical validity). Naturally, this position itself cannot be argued for in precise terms; to use Wittgenstein's jargon, such a position can only be shown and not said. Sacks admits that he cannot wholly formalize his own metaphysical views or adduce proofs of their truth. His only hope is to try to display the fun, the seriousness, and the ungroundedness of positions in philosophy, both those that are metaphysical and those that are antimetaphysical. In contrast to the preceding studies of the history of analytic philosophy, Rawls's Afterword is a personal reflection on some aspects of his practice of philosophy, and so a view of that history from within. It seems to us fitting to conclude this volume with this chapter, since it complements historical scholarship with a reminder of the lived dimension of history, and since its subject is Rawls's philosophical relationship with a colleague who, in one way or the other, has influenced the varying approaches to the history of recent philosophy displayed in the preceding essays.

NOTES

1. See, for example, Kevin Mulligan, Review of *The Story of Analytic Philosophy*, ed. Biletzki et al., *Times Literary Supplement*, July 10, 1998.

2. Immanuel Kant, *Critique of Pure Reason*, trans. Norman Kemp Smith (New York: St. Martin's Press, 1929), Preface to the 2d ed., B viii.

3. For a review of the importance of this historical background to early analytic philosophy, see Burton Dreben and Juliet Floyd, "Tautology: How Not to Use A Word," *Synthese* 87, no. 1 (1991): 23–50.

4. Michael Dummett's *Frege: Philosophy of Language*, 2d ed. (London: Duckworth, 1981), *The Interpretation of Frege's Philosophy* (London and Cambridge: Duckworth and Harvard University Press,1981), *The Logical Basis of Metaphysics* (Cambridge, Mass.: Harvard University Press, 1991), and *Origins of Analytical Philosophy* (Cambridge, Mass.: Harvard University Press, 1993).

5. This point was first made by Yehoshua Bar-Hillel, in "Bolzano's Definition of Analytic Propositions," *Theoria* 16 (1950): 91–117. More recently it was rediscovered by John Etchemendy, *The Concept of Logical Consequence* (Cambridge, Mass.: Harvard University Press, 1990), and Michael Dummett, *Origins of Analytical Philosophy*.

6. See Hilary Putnam, 'The Meaning of 'Meaning',' in his *Mind, Language and Reality: Philosophical Papers* (Cambridge: Cambridge University Press, 1975), vol. 2.

7. Michael Dummett, *Origins of Analytical Philosophy*, p. 4.

8. See, for example, Thomas Nagel, "What Is It Like to Be a Bat?" in his *Mortal Questions* (Cambridge: Cambridge University Press, 1979); Gareth Evans, *The Varieties of Reference*, ed. John McDowell (New York: Oxford University Press, 1982); Christopher Peacocke, *A Study of Concepts* (Cambridge, Mass.: MIT Press, 1992).

9. Ludwig Wittgenstein, "On Logic and How Not to Do It," *Cambridge Review* 34 (March 1913): 351.

10. Compare Burton Dreben and Juliet Floyd, "Tautology: How Not to Use A Word."

11. See Wittgenstein's letter to Ficker from Sept. or Oct. 1919, in Paul Engelmann, *Letters from Ludwig Wittgenstein with a Memoir*, trans. L. Furtmüller (New York: Horizon Press, 1967), pp. 143–144.

12. See "Gottlob Frege: Briefe an Ludwig Wittgenstein," in *Wittgenstein in Focus-Im Brennpunkt Wittgenstein*, ed. Brian McGuinness and Rudolf Haller (Amsterdam: Rodopi, 1989), pp. 4–33; an English translation of the letters by Burton Dreben and Juliet Floyd is forthcoming in a special issue of *Synthese*.

13. Rudolf Carnap, "The Elimination of Metaphysics through Logical Analysis of Language," *Erkenntnis* 2; reprinted in A. J. Ayer, ed., *Logical Positivism* (New York: Free Press, 1959).

14. W. V. Quine, *The Logic of Sequences* (reprinted, New York: Garland Publishing, 1990). The significance of the dissertation is explained in Burton Dreben, "Quine," *Perspectives on Quine*, in ed. Robert B. Barrett and Roger F. Gibson (Cambridge, Mass.: Basil Blackwell, 1990), pp. 81–95.

15. Biletzki and Matar, Preface to *The Story of Analytic Philosophy: Plots and Heroes* (New York: Routledge, 1998), p. xi.

16. Rorty, *Philosophy and the Mirror of Nature* (Princeton: Princeton University Press, 1979), *Consequences of Pragmatism: Essays 1972–1980* (Minneapolis, Minn.: University of Minnesota Press, 1982), and *Essays on Heidegger and Others: Philosophical Papers* vol. 2 (Cambridge: Cambridge University Press, 1991).

17. John Rajchman and Cornel West, eds., *Post-Analytic Philosophy* (New York: Columbia University Press, 1985).

18. Kurt Gödel, "On Undecidable Propositions of Formal Mathematical Systems" (*Gödel 1934*) in *Kurt Gödel Collected Works I*, ed. Solomon Feferman et al. (New York: Oxford University Press, 1986); Alonzo Church, "A Note on the Entscheidungsproblem," *Journal of Symbolic Logic* 1 (1936), pp. 101–102; A. M. Turing, "On Computable Numbers, with an Application to the Entscheidungsproblem," *Proceedings of the London Mathematical Society* 2, no. 42 (1936–1937), pp. 230–265 (Church and Turing's papers are both reprinted in Martin Davis, ed., *The Undecidable* (New York: Raven Press, 1965).

19. *Mind* 59 (1950), pp. 433–460.

20. See Quine, *Word and Object* (Cambridge, Mass.: MIT Press, 1960).

21. Saul Kripke, *Wittgenstein on Rules and Private Language* (Cambridge, Mass.: Harvard University Press, 1982).

22. John Searle, "Minds, Brains and Programs," *Behavioral and Brain Sciences* 3 (1980): 417–457, and *Minds, Brains, and Science* (Cambridge, Mass.: Harvard University Press, 1984).

23. Stanley Cavell, *The Claim of Reason* (Oxford: Clarendon Press, 1979).

24. P. M. S. Hacker, "Analytic Philosophy: What, Whence, and Whither?" in *The Story of Analytic Philosophy: Plots and Heroes* ed. A. Biletzki and A. Matar, (London: Routledge, 1998), see especially pp. 25 and 29. Compare Hacker's *Wittgenstein's Place in Twentieth-Century Analytic Philosophy* (Oxford: Blackwell, 1996).

25. See Joseph Warren Dauben, *Abraham Robinson: The Creation of Nonstandard Analysis, a Personal and Mathematical Journey* (Princeton, N.J.: Princeton University Press, 1995), p. 282. An excellent introduction to nonstandard analysis is given by Martin Davis and Ruben Hersh in *Scientific American*, July 1972.

26. See Burton Dreben, "Quine," p. 88, and compare Putnam, "A Half Century of Philosophy," *Daedelus* (Winter 1997): 175–208.

27. Ruth Barcan (Marcus), "A Functional Calculus of First Order Based on Strict Implication," *Journal of Symbolic Logic* 11 (1946): 1–16, "The Deduction Theorem in a Functional Calculus of First Order Based on Strict Implication," *Journal of Symbolic Logic* 11 (1946): 115–118, and "The Identity of Individuals in a Strict Functional Calculus of First Order," *Journal of Symbolic Logic* 12 (1947): 12–15; Jaakko Hintikka, *Knowledge and Belief* (Ithaca: Cornell University Press, 1962), chap. 6 extends to modal logic Hintikka's earlier ideas about model sets published in "A New Approach to Sentential Logic," *Societas Scientiarum Fennica, Commentationes Physico-Mathematicae* 85 no. 2 (1953), "Form and Content in Quantification Theory," *Acta Philosophica Fennica* 8 (1955): 7–55, and "Notes on the Quantification Theory," *Societas Scientiarum Fennica, Commentationes Physico-Mathematicae* 8, no. 12 (1955); Saul Kripke, "A Completeness Theorem in Modal Logic," *Journal of Symbolic Logic* 24, no. 1 (1959): 1–14, "Semantical Considerations on Modal Logic," *Acta Philosophica Fennica* Fax. XVI (1963): 83–94, "Semantical Analysis of Modal Logic I: Normal Modal Propositional Calculi," *Zeitschrift für mathematische Logik und Grundlagen der Mathematik* 9 (1963): 63–96. Dreben was the reader of Saul Kripke's summa cum laude undergraduate honors thesis at Harvard in 1962, which contained major developments in modal logic Kripke had begun while still in high school. Helpful clarification of some of Kripke's and Hintikka's work may be found in Dagfinn Føllesdal's *Referential Opacity and Modal Logic* (Ph.D. Dissertation, Harvard University, 1961) and his "Interpretation of Quantifiers," in B. van Rootselaar and J. F. Staal, eds., *Logic, Methodology and Philosopy of Science*, Proceedings of the Third International Congress for Logic, Methodology and the Philosophy of Science, Amsterdam, 1967 (Amsterdam: North-Holland, 1968), pp. 271–281.

28. Quine's published criticisms of modality began in his "Notes on Existence and Necessity," *Journal of Philosophy* 40 (1943): 113–127, and his "The Problem of Interpreting Modal Logic," *Journal of Symbolic Logic* 12 (1947): 43–48, later fused in

his "Reference and Modality," in his *From a Logical Point of View*, 2d rev. ed. (Cambridge, Mass.: Harvard University Press, 1980), pp. 139–159. See also Quine's "Three Grades of Modal Involvement" (1953) and "Reply to Professor Marcus" (1962), both reprinted in his *The Ways of Paradox and Other Essays* (Cambridge, Mass.: Harvard University Press, 1976), pp. 158–176 and 177–184, respectively.

29. Saul Kripke, *Naming and Necessity*, (Cambridge, Mass.: Harvard University Press, 1980).

30. Lewis Carroll, *Through the Looking Glass, and What Alice Found There* (London: Macmillan 1911), p. 105, and Philip E. B. Jourdain, *The Philosopy of Mr. B*rtr*nd R*ss*l* (London: George Allen & Unwin, 1918), p. 17.

31. See, for example, Burton Dreben, "Quine and Wittgenstein: The Odd Couple" in *Quine and Wittgenstein*, ed. Robert Arrington and Hans-Johan Glock (New York: Routledge, 1996).

1

Frege's Conception of Logic

WARREN GOLDFARB

Frege is of course an important progenitor of modern logic. The technical advances he made were comprehensive. He clearly depicted polyadic predication, negation, the conditional, and the quantifier as the bases of logic; and he gave an analysis of and a notation for the quantifier that enabled him to deal fully and perspicuously with multiple generality. Moreover, he argued that mathematical demonstrations, to be fully rigorous, must be carried out using only explicitly formulated rules, that is, syntactically specified axioms and rules of inference.

Less clear, however, is the philosophical and interpretive question of how Frege understands his formalism and its purposes. Upon examination, it appears that Frege had a rather different view of the subject he was creating than we do nowadays. In lectures and seminars as far back as the early 1960s, Burton Dreben called attention to differences between how Frege viewed the subject matter of logic and how we do. The point has been taken up by several commentators, beginning with Jean van Heijenoort.[1] The technical development historically required to get from a Fregean conception to our own was discussed in my "Logic in the Twenties: The Nature of the Quantifier."[2] Yet there is currently little appreciation of the philosophical import of these differences, that is, the role in Frege's philosophy that his conception of logic, as opposed to ours, plays. Indeed, some downplay the differences and assign them no influence on or role in the philosophy. Thus Dummett says only that Frege was "impeded" from having the modern view by a particular way of looking at the formulas of his *Begriffsschrift*.[3] I want to urge on the contrary that Frege's conception of logic is integral to his philosophical system; it cannot be replaced with a more modern conception without serious disruptions in that system. The reasons for this will, I hope, be instructive about the roots of Frege's philosophizing.

I

The first task is that of delineating the differences between Frege's conception of logic and the contemporary one. I shall start with the latter. Explicit elaborations of it are surprisingly uncommon. (In most writing on issues in philosophical logic, it is implicitly assumed; yet many textbooks gloss over it, for one pedagogical reason or another.) There are various versions; I will lay out the one formulated by Quine in his textbooks[4] as it seems to me the clearest.

On this conception, the subject matter of logic consists of logical properties of sentences and logical relations among sentences. Sentences have such properties and bear such relations to each other by dint of their having the logical forms they do. Hence, logical properties and relations are defined by way of the logical forms; logic deals with what is common to and can be abstracted from different sentences. Logical forms are not mysterious quasi-entities, à la Russell. Rather, they are simply schemata: representations of the composition of the sentences, constructed from the logical signs (quantifiers and truth-functional connectives, in the standard case) using schematic letters of various sorts (predicate, sentence, and function letters). Schemata do not state anything and so are neither true nor false, but they can be interpreted: a universe of discourse is assigned to the quantifiers, predicate letters are replaced by predicates or assigned extensions (of the appropriate r-ities) over the universe, sentence letters can be replaced by sentences or assigned truth-values. Under interpretation, a schema will receive a truth-value. We may then define: a schema is *valid* if and only if it is true under every interpretation; one schema *implies* another, that is, the second schema is a *logical consequence* of the first, if and only if every interpretation that makes the first true also makes the second true. A more general notion of logical consequence, between sets of schemata and a schema, may be defined similarly. Finally, we may arrive at the logical properties or relations between sentences thus: a sentence is logically true if and only if it can be schematized by a schema that is valid; one sentence implies another if they can be schematized by schemata the first of which implies the second.

The notion of schematization is just the converse of interpretation: to say that a sentence can be schematized by a schema is just to say that there is an interpretation under which the schema becomes the sentence. Thus, a claim that a sentence R implies a sentence S, that is, that S is a logical consequence of R, has two parts, each of which uses the notion of interpretation: it is the assertion that there are schemata R* and S* such that

(1)   R* and S*, under some interpretation, yield R and S; and

(2)   under no interpretation is R* true and S* false.

This is often called the Tarski-Quine definition, or (in the Tarskian formulation) the model-theoretic definition, of logical consequence.[5] It is precise enough to allow the mathematical investigation of the notion. For example, using this notion of logical consequence, we can frame the question of whether a proposed formal system is sound and complete, and this question may then be treated with mathematical tools. Better put, though, we should say that the definition is capable of being made precise. For the definition quantifies over all interpretations. This is a set-theoretic quantification; hence, complete precision would require a specification of the set theory in which the definition is to be understood. (However, it turns out that for implications between first-order schemata, the definition is rather insensitive to the choice of set theory. The same implications are obtained as long as the set theory is at least as strong as a weak second-order arithmetic that admits the arithmetically definable sets of natural numbers.)[6]

(As an aside, let me note that this explication of logical consequence has recently come under attack in John Etchemendy's *The Concept of Logical Consequence*.[7] Etchemendy argues that, if S is a logical consequence of R, then there is a necessary connection between the truth of R and the truth of S, and the Tarski-Quine definition does not adequately capture this necessity. Of course, neither Tarski nor Quine would feel the force of such an attack, since they both reject the cogency of the philosophical modalities. Moreover, it is only the Tarski-Quine characterization of logical consequence in terms of various interpretations of a schematism that makes the notion of logical consequence amenable to definitive mathematical treatment.)

On this *schematic conception* of logic, the formal language of central concern is that of logical schemata. Pure logic aims at ascertaining logical properties and logical relations of these formulas, and also at demonstrating general laws about the properties and relations. Applied logic, we might say, then looks at sentences—of one or another formal language for mathematics or science or of (regimented versions of) everyday language—to see whether they may be schematized by schemata having this or that logical property or relation. Thus, there is a sharp distinction between logical *laws*, which are at the metalevel and are about schemata, and logical *truths*, which are particular sentences that can be schematized by valid schemata. The pivotal role in this conception of schemata, that is, of uninterpreted formulas that represent logical forms, gives a specific cast to the generality of logic. Logic deals with logical forms, which schematize away the particular subject matter of sentences. Thus logic is tied to no particular subject matter because it deals with these "empty" forms rather than with particular contents.

Such a schematic conception is foreign to Frege (as well as to Russell). This comes out early in his work, in the contrast he makes between his *begriffsschrift* and the formulas of Boole: "My intention was not to represent an abstract logic in formulas, but to express a content through written signs in a more precise and clear way than it is possible to do through words."[8] And it comes out later in his career in his reaction to Hilbert's *Foundations of Geometry*: "The word 'interpretation' is objectionable, for when properly expressed, a thought leaves no room for different interpretations. We have seen that ambiguity [*Vieldeutigkeit*] simply has to be rejected."[9] There are no parts of his logical formulas that await interpretation. There is no question of providing a universe of discourse. Quantifiers in Frege's system have fixed meaning: they range over all items of the appropriate logical type (objects, one place functions of objects, two place functions of objects, etc.) The letters that may figure in logical formulas, for example, in "(p&q → p)" are not schematic: they are not sentence letters.[10] Rather, Frege understands them as *variables*. Here they are free variables, and hence in accordance with Frege's general rule the formula is to be understood as a universal closure, that is, as the universally quantified statement "$(\forall p)(\forall q)(p\&q \rightarrow p)$." Similarly, logical formulas containing one-place function signs are to be understood not schematically, but as generalizing over all functions.

On Frege's conception the business of logic is to articulate and demonstrate certain true general statements, the logical laws. "$(\forall p)(\forall q)(p\&q \rightarrow p)$" is one; it states a law, we might say, about all objects. Similarly, "$(\forall F)(\forall G)(\forall H)(\forall x)((Fx \rightarrow Gx)\&(\forall x)$ $(Gx \rightarrow Hx) \rightarrow (\forall x)(Fx \rightarrow Hx))$" is a law about all functions.[11] The business of pure logic is to arrive at such laws, just as the business of physics is to arrive at physical laws. Logical laws are as descriptive as physical laws,[12] but they are more general. Indeed, they are supremely general; for, aside from variables, all that figure in them are the all-sign, the conditional, and other signs which are not specific to any discipline, but which figure in discourse on any topic whatsoever. Notions of the special sciences first appear when we apply logic. In applied logic, we infer claims that contain more specialized vocabulary on the basis of the laws of pure logic. For example, in applied logic we might demonstrate, "If Cassius is lean and Cassius is hungry, then Cassius is lean"; or, "If all whales are mammals and all mammals are vertebrates, then all whales are vertebrates." These statements may be inferred from the logical laws given at the beginning of this paragraph. Here we also see a typical situation, that these specialized statements are inferred from the logical law by instantiation of universal quantifiers.

On Frege's *universalist conception*, then, the concern of logic is the articulation and proof of logical laws, which are universal truths. Since they are universal, they are applicable to any subject matter, as application is carried out by instantiation. For Frege, the laws of logic are general, not in being about nothing in particular (about forms), but in using topic-universal vocabulary to state truths about everything.

The question arises immediately of how different these conceptions actually are. They can look very close. Both take pure logic to be centrally concerned with generality. Generality is captured in the schematic conception by definitions that invoke all interpretations of the given schemata, and in the universalist conception by universal quantifiers with unrestricted ranges. In the schematic conception, logic is applied by passing from schemata to sentences that are particular interpretations of them; in the universalist conception, applications are made by instantiating the quantified variables of a general law. Given these close parallels, it is no wonder that many logicians and philosophers would be inclined to minimize the distinction between the two conceptions.

Parallels are not identities, however, and there are philosophically important ways that the conceptions differ. First and most obviously, the schematic conception is metalinguistic. The claims of logic are claims about schemata or about sentences, and thus logic concerns features of discourse. In contrast, on the universalist conception logic sits squarely at the object level, issuing laws that are simply statements about the world. What logical laws describe are not phenomena of language or of representation. As Russell put it, "Logic is concerned with the real world just as truly as zoology, though with its more abstract and general features."[13] This difference will have consequences for the philosophical characterization of logic. For example, the universalist conception leaves no room for the notion that logic is without content; the laws of logic, although very general, have to be seen as substantive. Indeed, in the *Tractatus*, Wittgenstein breaks with the universalist conception in order to arrive at a view in which the propositions of logic are empty. Even if Wittgenstein's characterization of logic is rejected, the metalinguistic conception will inevitably make the nature of discourse, or of our representations, the focus of any account of logic. A sharp sense of this can be obtained by contrasting the remark of Russell's just cited with this one of Dummett's, made unself-consciously and with no argument at all, at the start of laying out his own metaphysics: "Reality cannot be said to obey a law of logic; it is our thinking about reality that obeys such a law or flouts it."[14] On Frege's view, as on Russell's, it is precisely reality that obeys the laws of logic.

Indeed, the universalistic conception is an essential background to many of Frege's ontological views. Frege took not just proper names but also sentences and predicates to be referring expressions, that is, to have *Bedeutung*; in the latter case, the referents were of a different logical sort from those of proper names and sentences. From many contemporary viewpoints, it is odd to think of sentences as names at all; and if predicates are thought to refer, it would be to properties or sets or some other entities that need not be sharply distinguished in logical character from the referents of singular terms.

It should be clear that the universalistic conception *demands* that sentences and predicates refer. As we have seen, for Frege the truth-functional laws look like "$(\forall p)(\forall q)(p\&q \rightarrow p)$" and will be applied by instantiating the quantifiers with sentences. For "If Cassius is lean and Cassius is hungry then Cassius is lean" to count as a genuine instance of the law, the expressions which instantiate the quantified variables have to refer, to things that are values of the variables, just as to count as a genuine instance of "$(\forall x)(x$ is a prime number greater than 2 $\rightarrow$ x is odd)" the name replacing "x" has to refer, and what it refers to must be among the values of "x." (To be is to be the value of a variable as much for Frege as for Quine.) Similarly, since the laws of logic include many that generalize in predicate places, and their application requires instantiating those quantified variables with predicates, here too we are driven to take predicates as referring expressions.

In the case of sentences, it requires a further argument, based on intersubstitutivity phenomena, to conclude that what sentences refer to are their truth-values, and it requires yet other considerations to support taking the truth-values to be of the same logical type as ordinary objects. The former is pretty compelling; the latter has elicited heated objections.[15]

For predicates, however, support for the sharp distinction in logical type of the referent can come from the structure of applications of logic, on the universalist conception. If the position occupied by a predicate in a statement is taken to be generalized on directly, the distinction in logical type is apparent, since the predicate position has argument places; and if an expression has an argument place and so can be used in an instantiation of a quantified predicate variable, then it cannot be used to instantiate a singular term, without yielding expressions that violate the most basic rules of logical (and grammatical) syntax. Thus we see that the universalist conception demands second-order logic.[16] Indeed, it was one of Quine's avowed motivations, in developing the schematic conception, to show that logic did not require us to take there to be anything designated by the predicates in our statements.

Logic, as construed on the universalist conception, is also in back of a doctrine of Frege's that many have found puzzling, namely, that all functions be defined everywhere; for the special case of concepts, this is the requirement that concepts "have sharp boundaries."[17] For Frege, all quantified variables have unrestricted domain. Given this, and given that "$(\forall F)(\forall x)(Fx \lor -Fx)$" is a logical law, Frege's requirement follows at once. If something is a concept, then an expression for it can instantiate the quantifier in this law; thus we can logically derive that, for every object, either the concept holds of it or the concept does not. This is just what Frege means by "sharp boundaries."

II

A second important difference between the two conceptions concerns the role of a truth predicate. Clearly, the schematic conception employs a truth predicate: the definitions of validity and logical consequence talk of the truth under all interpretations of schemata.[18] Since the predicate is applied to an infinite range of sentences, it cannot be eliminated by disquotation. On the universalist conception, in contrast, no truth predicate is needed either to frame the laws of logic or to apply them. Moreover, although Frege sometimes calls logical laws the "laws of truth," he does not envisage using a truth predicate to characterize the nature of those laws.

On the schematic conception, logic starts with the definitions of validity and consequence and goes on to pronounce that a given schema is valid or is a consequence of other schemata. Formal systems may be introduced as a means to establish such facts, but this then requires a demonstration of soundness to show that what the system produces are, in fact, validities and consequences. The introduction of a formal system also raises the (less urgent) question of completeness, of whether all validities and all implications can be obtained by means of the system. Thus it is the overarching notions of validity and consequence that set the logical agenda and provide sense to the question of how well a system for inference captures logic. On this conception, the notion of logical inference rule is posterior to that of consequence: a logical inference rule is one whose premises imply its conclusion or, in the context of a system for establishing validities only, is one that always leads from valid premises to a valid conclusion.

In Frege's universalist conception, there is no analogous characterization of what is a logical law or what follows logically from what. Frege's conception of logic is retail, not wholesale. He simply presents various laws of logic and logical inference rules, and then demonstrates other logical laws on the basis of these. He frames no overarching characteristic that demarcates the logical laws from others.[19] Consequently, the only sense that the question has of whether the laws and rules Frege presents are complete is an "experimental" one—whether they suffice to derive all the particular results that we have set ourselves to derive. For example, at one point, Frege entertains the possibility that a failure to obtain established results while developing an area of mathematics axiomatically could lead us to recognize a new logical inferential principle.[20] The closest Frege comes to providing a notion of logical consequence occurs in "On the Foundations of Geometry," where he defines one truth's being logically dependent on another. The definition is: when the one can be obtained by logical laws and inferences from the other (Frege 1906, p. 423). No further characterization of logical laws and inferences is made. Thus, in direct contrast to the situation in the schematic conception, Frege's notion here rests on the provision of the logical laws and inference rules.

Now Frege does say, "Logic is the science of the most general laws of truth."[21] But he does not intend this as a demarcation of logic, only as a "rough indication of the goal of logic." As we have seen, generality and absence of vocabulary from any specialized science are, on the universalist conception, features of the logical. Frege does not attempt to give any specification of the vocabulary allowable in logic; moreover, there is no reason to think that he would take truth and absence of specialized vocabulary as sufficient for logical status.[22] Yet there is a deeper reason that his phrase gives only a "rough indication," and that has to do with the anomalous status of "true" when used as a predicate.

Frege repeatedly calls attention to that anomalous status. In "Der Gedanke," he presents a regress argument to show that any attempt to define truth must fail, and concludes that "the content of the word 'true' is *sui generis* and indefinable."[23] Both the argument and his subsequent considerations show that he does not mean simply that the notion of truth is a primitive notion, not to be defined in terms of anything more basic. After reflecting that "I smell the scent of violets" and "It is true that I smell the scent of violets" have the same content, so that the ascription of truth adds nothing, he concludes: "The meaning of the word 'true' seems to be altogether *sui generis*. May we not be dealing here with something which cannot be called a property in the ordinary sense at all?" (Frege 1918, p. 61). In " Introduction to Logic,"[24] Frege goes farthest in suggesting that truth is not a property at all: "If we say 'the thought is true' we seem to be ascribing truth to the thought as a property. If that were so, we should have a case of subsumption. The thought as an object would be subsumed under the concept of the true. But here we are misled by language. We don't have the relation of an object to a property" (*PW*, p. 194). In "My Basic Logical Insights,"[25] he connects the use of "true" in characterizing logic with the idea that the ascription of truth to a thought adds nothing:

> So the sense of the word "true" is such that it does not make any essential contribution to the thought. If I assert "it is true that sea-water is salty," I assert the same thing as if I assert "sea-water is salty." This enables us to recognize that the assertion is not to be found in the word "true" but in the assertoric force with which the sentence is uttered. . . . "[T]rue" makes only an abortive attempt to indicate the essence of logic, since what logic is really concerned with is not contained in the word "true" at all but in the assertoric force with which a sentence is uttered. (Frege *1915, pp. 251–252)

Thus, rubrics like "general laws of truth" cannot serve to give a real characterization of logic or a demarcation of the realm of the logical. The notion of truth is unavailable for the role of setting the agenda for logic. Moreover, if we take Frege's scruples seriously, it follows that the schematic conception of logic is simply unavailable to him. To formulate it, as we have seen, use has to be made of a truth predicate. That predicate figures not as a suggestive way of talking, nor as a term whose usefulness arises only from the "imperfection of language," as Frege puts it in (Frege *1915), but as a scientific term in the definitions of the most basic concepts of the discipline. Clearly, Frege would not think that legitimate.

The question then arises of whether Frege's scruples are well-placed, or whether they can be dismissed as merely peripheral phenomena, with no deep systematic connections. Addressing this question requires a careful examination of the arguments Frege adduces. I shall not attempt this here; for a detailed treatment, see Thomas Ricketts' "Logic and Truth in Frege."[26] I limit myself to mentioning the philosophical outlook which I take to be expressed in Frege's scruples about a truth predicate. It is that objective truth is not to be explained or secured by an ontological account. Such an account would take us to have a conception of things "out there" and of their behaviors or configurations that exist independent of our knowledge, and it would depict those behaviors or configurations as being that which renders our thoughts true or false. Such an account is often ascribed to Frege, for it is just what is involved in ascribing a truth-conditional semantics to him. But this ascription is incompatible with Frege's remarks on truth. To take Frege's scruples seriously is to appreciate that there is no general notion of something's making a truth true—that is, that there is no theory of how the thoughts expressed by sentences are determined to be true or false by the items referred to in them. It is thus to put us in a position to appreciate the extraordinarily subtle view Frege can be read as unfolding. On this reading, Frege is not a realist, on the usual philosophical characterizations of that position. He is committed to the objectivity of truth and its independence of anyone's recognition of that truth, but the conception of truth here is immanent within our making of judgments and inferences, our recognitions of truth.

III

Earlier I noted that the most obvious difference between the universalist and the schematic conceptions is that in the former logic operates at the object level, whereas in the latter it operates at the meta-level. Even this by itself has consequences, and it can be used to get at an important role the universalist conception has in Frege's system.

Of course, it is important to avoid anachronism here. At the time Frege was writing, a distinction between object level and meta-level could hardly have been drawn; in fact, it was not to become clear until the 1920s. Nonetheless, we can see a precursor of the distinction as being at issue. Many traditional logicians spoke of logic as being about the forms of judgment, which were to be obtained by abstraction from judgments. Although this conception was far from precise and traditional logic lacked the machinery to work it out, it seems clear that forms of judgment were invoked as a way of capturing the generality of logic and lack of tie to the content of individual judgments. Thus we can see here a proto-schematic conception. (This is particularly visible in Bolzano.) Frege rarely speaks of forms of judgment. It is not hard to surmise some reasons.

First, talk of forms of judgment and of abstracting from individual judgments has a dangerously psychological ring to it. The very locution "forms of judgment" suggests that the forms are of mental acts and so are prime material for psychologistic treatment. Moreover, Frege argued vigorously against any notion of abstraction as needed to get from particulars to general notions.[27] Indeed, elimination of any role for abstraction is central not just to Frege's antipsychologism, but also to his anti-Kantianism. To eliminate abstraction is to eliminate the question, How do we attain the general? Frege replaces it with the question of the relation between the (already given) general and the particular, a question to be answered by logic.

This leads us to the second reason Frege has for discarding talk of the forms of judgment. He has no need of such talk, precisely because his devising of the quantifier gives him a rigorous tool to capture the generality that "forms of judgment" gestures toward. The generality is directly expressed by the quantifier. The relation of general to particular is given by the logical rule of instantiation from former to latter, not by some imprecise, psychological notion of abstraction from the latter to the former.

These two reasons are not relevant to the modern schematic conception, which has found precise nonpsychologistic notions to replace "forms of judgment" and "abstraction" and which uses quantification (in the metalanguage) to capture the desired generality. There is, however, another consideration at work in Frege that is not simply obsolete.

Frege's conception of logic is intertwined with his notion of justification. A cornerstone of Frege's thinking is the sharp distinction between the rational basis of a claim—the truths that it presupposes or depends upon—and what we might call concomitants of thinking or making the claim: the psychological phenomena that occur when a person thinks of the claim, or believes it, or comes to accept it, the empirical conditions someone must satisfy in order to know the claim, the history of the discovery of the claim, and so on. The distinction is emphasized throughout Frege's writings, and particularly vividly in the Introduction to the *Foundations of Arithmetic*. Remarks like these abound: "Never let us take a description of the origin of an idea for a definition, or an account of the mental and physical conditions on which we become conscious of a proposition for a proof of it."[28] The point is more general than antipsychologism, or a distinction between objective and subjective, as the following shows:

A delightful example of the way in which even mathematicians can confuse the grounds of proof with the mental or physical conditions to be satisfied if the proof is to be given is to be found in E. Schröder. Under the heading "Special Axiom" he produces the following: "The principle I have in mind might well be called the Axiom of Symbolic Stability. It guarantees us that throughout all our arguments and deductions the symbols remain constant in our memory—or preferably on paper," and so on. (Frege 1884, p. viii)

Clearly, we would not be able to arrive at correct mathematical arguments if our inkblots were constantly to change. Yet that does not imply that mathematics presupposes the physical laws of inkblots, that those laws would figure in the justifications of mathematical laws.

It is important to note that something must give content to the distinction between rational basis and mere concomitant; something must provide a means for saying what counts as showing that one proposition is the rational basis for another, and showing when one proposition presupposes another. It is Frege's logic that plays this role. Logic tells us when one claim is a ground for another, namely, when the latter can be inferred, using logical laws, from the former. Explanation and justification are matters of giving grounds. For Frege, then, the explanation of a truth is a logical proof of that truth from more basic truths; the justification of a truth is a logical proof of that claim from whatever first principles are its ultimate basis. Thus the laws of logic are explicatory of explanation and justification; on this rests their claim to the honorific title "logic."

Given this role for logic, it should occasion no surprise that Frege's conception of logic and the demands he puts on the notion of justification are closely linked. Now the notion of justification plays a philosophically very important role for Frege, as it is key to his argument for the logicist project. Although we might start off thinking that arithmetical discourse is completely understood, transparent, and poses no problem, Frege urges that we lack knowledge of the ultimate justification of the truths of arithmetic. In order to "afford us insight into the dependence of truths upon one another," we must analyze the seemingly simple concept of number and find the "primitive truths to which we reduce everything" (Frege 1884, p. 2). Frege also brings up "philosophical motives" for the logicist project, asking what looks to be the traditional philosophical question of whether arithmetic is analytic or synthetic. But actually he redefines these notions (as well as those of a priori and a posteriori) so that they concern "not the content of the judgment but the justification for making the judgment" (Frege 1884, p. 3). Here too it is the notion of justification that is doing the work.

Essential to the role of this notion of justification in supporting the logicist project, and to the plausibility of Frege's redefinitions of traditional philosophical terminology, is the applicability to all knowledge of the standards of justification. The canons of justification must be universal in their purview: "Thought is in essentials the same everywhere: it is not true that there are different kinds of laws of thought to suit the different kinds of objects thought about" (Frege 1884, p. iii). Another important feature of justification is explicitness: a justification must display everything on which the truth of the claim being justified depends. To insure that "some other type of premise is not involved at some point without our noticing it," a justification must provide "a chain of inferences with no link missing, such that no step in it is taken which does not conform to some one of a small number of principles of inference recognized as purely logical" (Frege 1884, p. 102).

Obviously, these demands are met when logic, as invoked in Frege's notion of justification, is taken on the universalist conception. That the canons of justification must extend to all areas of knowledge requires utmost generality and universal applicability of the logical principles. Explicitness is vouchsafed by the direct applicability of logic: there are no presuppositions, no implicit steps, in the application of logical laws. To illustrate this, let us examine how, on Frege's picture, logic would be used to justify the conclusion that all whales are vertebrates on the basis of the claims that all whales are mammals and that all mammals are vertebrates. We start with the assertions:

(1)   All whales are mammals.

(2)   All mammals are vertebrates.

We then provide a logical demonstration from first principles that ends with:

(3) $(\forall F)(\forall G)(\forall H)[(\forall x)(Fx \rightarrow Gx) \rightarrow ((\forall x)(Gx \rightarrow Hx) \rightarrow (\forall x)(Fx \rightarrow Hx))].$[29]

Three instantiation steps then license us in the assertion of:

$(\forall x)(x$ is a whale $\rightarrow x$ is a mammal$) \rightarrow ((\forall x)(x$ is a mammal $\rightarrow x$ is a vertebrate$) \rightarrow (\forall x)(x$ is a whale $\rightarrow x$ is a vertebrate$)).$

Or, in ordinary English:

(4)   If all whales are mammals, then if all mammals are vertebrates then all whales are vertebrates.

By *modus ponens* from (4) and (1) we obtain:

(5)   If all mammals are vertebrates then all whales are vertebrates.

Finally, by *modus ponens* from (5) and (2), we arrive at:

(6)   All whales are vertebrates.

Taken together, all these assertions, including those in the logical proof of (3), constitute the justification of the assertion of "All whales are vertebrates" on the basis of the assertions of "All whales are mammals" and "All mammals are vertebrates."

The requirement of explicitness and the need for the logical laws to be directly applicable can be highlighted by consideration of an argument against logicism devised by Henri Poincaré.[30] The version I summarize here is formulated by Charles Parsons.[31] In order to show that arithmetic is logic, one must devise a formal system of logic and show how the theorems of arithmetic can be obtained in that formal system. Now, to give a formal system is to specify, first, the class of formulas and, second, the class of derivable formulas. The usual form of specification is this: certain basic expressions are stipulated to be formulas; other formulas are specified as those and only those expressions obtained from the basic expressions by finitely many applications of certain syntactic operations. Similarly, certain formulas are stipulated to be axioms; the derivable formulas are specified as those and only those formulas obtained from the axioms by finitely many applications of certain inference rules. Thus these specifications are inductive in nature: the notion of a finite number of applications of given operations is essential to them. Therefore, number is presupposed in the logicist foundation for arithmetic. This is a *petitio principii*. Thus there is a logical circle in the logicist reduction.

I believe Poincaré's objection fails, and it is important to see why. The objection would succeed if Frege construed the justification of arithmetic to involve, for one or another arithmetical claim, the following assertion: "This claim is provable in such-and-such formal system." That assertion is a metatheoretic one. It is about the formal system; since Poincaré is quite right that inductive definitions are used to specify the formal system, it follows that the assertion relies on number theory. That is not, however, how Frege conceives of justification. To give a justification of an arithmetical claim is to give the claim with its grounds. It is not to assert that the claim is provable; it is to give the proof. Now, of course, one might want to verify that what has been given is, in fact, a proof by the lights of the formal system. Such a verification would proceed by syntactic means, and does presuppose the specification of the system. The verification is not *constitutive* of the argument's being a justification; it is just a means for us to ascertain that it is. In order for us to be psychologically sure that what we are giving are justifications, we have to use our knowledge of the formal system, that is, our metatheoretic knowledge which is of an inductive nature. But that is different from what the justification of the claim actually is.

Here Frege is relying precisely on the distinction between what we might have to do, in fact, by our natures, in order to be in a position to do mathematics, and what the justification of mathematics is. That we need to set out a formal system to be sure of our justifications is no more relevant to the rational grounds of mathematics than our need to write down proofs because otherwise we will not remember them.

The Fregean rebuttal to Poincaré requires that in what Frege would call a justification, say of an arithmetical truth, everything that is presupposed by the truth does play a role. This lies in back of his demand for "gap-free" deductions.

To gain an appreciation of the role of the universalist conception of logic in this, it is instructive to contrast how a justification abiding by the Fregean requirement of explicitness would have to proceed if logic were taken on the schematic conception. Let us once again undertake a justification of "All whales are vertebrates" on the basis of "All whales are mammals" and "All mammals are vertebrates." We can't simply pass from the latter to the former, with a note ("off to the side," so to speak) that the latter two jointly imply the former, since this does not make explicit what is involved in the inference. Rather, matters have to be laid out as follows. As before, we start by asserting:

(1)   All whales are mammals.

(2)   All mammals are vertebrates.

We then assert, along with whatever grounds needed to show it from first principles:

(3)   There is an interpretation of "$(\forall x)(Fx \rightarrow Gx)$," "$(\forall x)(Gx \rightarrow Hx)$," and
       "$(\forall x)(Fx \rightarrow Hx)$" under which these schemata become (regimented
       versions of) the sentences "All whales are mammals," "All mammals
       are vertebrates," and "All whales are vertebrates," respectively.

We now adduce a mathematical proof culminating in:

(4)   Any interpretation that makes "$(\forall x)(Fx \rightarrow Gx)$" and "$(\forall x)(Gx \rightarrow Hx)$"
       true also makes "$(\forall x)(Fx \rightarrow Hx)$" true.

Using some logical laws and intermediate steps for makings the transition, we can
assert on the basis of (3) and (4):

(5)   If "All whales are mammals" and "All mammals are vertebrates" are
       true, then "All whales are vertebrates" is true.

To apply (5), we must adduce the Tarski paradigms:

(6)   "All whales are mammals" is true if and only if all whales are
       mammals.

(7)   "All mammals are vertebrates" is true if and only if all mammals are
       vertebrates.

(1), (2), (5), (6), (7), and truth-functional laws will allow us to obtain:

(8)   "All whales are vertebrates" is true.

Finally, adducing

(9)   "All whales are vertebrates" is true if and only if all whales are
       vertebrates,

we obtain:

(10) All whales are vertebrates.

   Needless to say, from Frege's point of view this outline already looks terribly cir-
cuitous, and the amount that has to be filled in to provide justifications for (3) and
(4) will make matters worse. Even ignoring Frege's scruples about a truth predicate, the status of the disquotational biconditionals is also troublesome, for, in what
is outlined, those biconditionals figure among the grounds of "All whales are mammals" as much as do assertions (1) and (2). If, for example, they are meant to be
consequences of a substantial semantic theory, then we are in the position of re-

quiring that theory in the justification of "All whales are vertebrates" on the basis of "All whales are mammals" and "All mammals are vertebrates." Matters look less peculiar if the truth predicate is meant to come merely from a Tarski-style definition; but even here an oddly large body of mathematics must figure in order to justify what is, after all, a rather simple logical inference. All this is to say that the schematic conception of logic fits poorly with the Fregean picture of justification.[32]

This lack of fit comes out in another difficulty as well. In the justification as just outlined, various transitions, like that from (3) and (4) to (5), will be made by applying logical rules. On the schematic conception, logical rules are justified only on the basis of their soundness, that is, their yielding logical consequences. But then it looks like the justification we have presented is not fully explicit; there is something left unsaid that it presupposes.

It might be objected, however, that there is a similar problem in the justification given on the universalist conception. In it, inferences are made in accord with certain inference rules. Shouldn't the demand of explicitness be invoked further, to require that whatever principles lie behind the correctness of the inference rules be made explicit and considered part of the justification? In general, the only way of stating these principles are as the soundness or truth-preservingness of the rules and involve semantic ascent and a truth predicate. Thus the "directness" alleged for the universalist conception papers over an elision.[33]

Now I believe Frege would reject the idea that inference rules rest on or presuppose the principles expressing their soundness. Rather, our appreciation of the validity of the rules is not the recognition of the truth of any judgment at all; it is manifested in our use of the rule, in our making one assertion on the basis of another in accordance with the inference rule.[34] There is nothing more to be made explicit, although of course individual instances of the inference rule can always be conditionalized and asserted as logical truths.

To some this may appear to be an evasion. But let us investigate the question we left hanging with respect to the schematic conception. There, the justification looked inexplicit because it omitted a demonstration of the soundness of the logical rules it employed, and, on the schematic conception, logical rules are justified only on the basis of their soundness. Of course, one could adjoin a demonstration of soundness. Naturally, that demonstration will use logical rules. Usually the soundness of those rules will not be vouchsafed by the adjoined demonstration, because the quantified variables in the demonstration will have to range over a larger class than any of the universes of discourses of the interpretations covered by the soundness proof. For example, an everyday soundness proof shows that the usual logical rules are sound with respect to all interpretations whose universes of discourse are sets. The reasoning in that proof involves variables ranging over all sets; hence, the universe of discourse of that reasoning is a proper class. A soundness proof for the logical rules used in the everyday proof would therefore have to show something stronger than everyday soundness, namely, that the rules were sound with respect to interpretations whose universes of discourse were proper classes. This would require a stronger set-theoretic language yet, in which collections of proper classes existed, and the reasoning in the stronger soundness proof would involve variables ranging over such collections. This process continues with no end. To avoid a vicious regress, we have to be able to take the logical rules used in the justification for granted. Yet, on this conception, it has to be admitted that a fuller justification, one amplified by a further soundness proof, is always possible. In passing to that fuller justification, we also pass to a larger universe of discourse. The upshot is that at no level can one think of the quantifier as ranging over everything; there is no absolutely unrestricted quantifier. All the while, though, in enunciating the claims at any level, one is not (yet) in a position to specify how the quantifiers are restricted: they range over everything that at that point one can have. This is a curious position, one which goes far more against Frege's demand for explicitness than our acceptance of a rule of inference without an explicit semantic principle to back it up.[35]

This last argument has brought us rather far afield. My central aims in this paper have been to delineate Frege's universalist conception of logic and contrast it with a more familiar one, to show that this conception connects with many other points in Frege's philosophy, and to suggest that the conception is a well-motivated one, given the nature of Frege's project. Of course, today most of us would find the schematic conception (or some variant of it) far more natural, if not unavoidable. But I hope to have caused us to reflect on how much else has to shift in order to make it so.[36]

NOTES

1. In "Logic as Calculus and Logic as Language," *Synthese* 17 (1967): 324–330. Other discussions of this difference in viewpoint are contained in Burton Dreben and Jean van Heijenoort, "Introductory Note to Gödel's Completeness Papers," in *Kurt Gödel, Collected Works*, vol. I, ed. S. Feferman et al. (New York: Oxford University Press, 1986), pp. 44–59; Jaakko Hintikka, "On the Development of the Model-Theoretic Viewpoint in Logical Theory," *Synthese* 77 (1988): 1–36; and Thomas Ricketts, "Objectivity and Objecthood: Frege's Metaphysics of Judgment," in *Frege Synthesized*, ed. L. Haaparanta and J. Hintikka (Dordrecht: D. Reidel, 1986), pp. 65–95. Hintikka gives a variant version of what I call below the schematic conception of logic.

2. *Journal of Symbolic Logic* 44 (1979): 351–368.

3. *The Interpretation of Frege's Philosophy* (London: Duckworth and Harvard University Press, 1981), p. 151.

4. *Elementary Logic* (Boston: Ginn, 1941) and *Methods of Logic* (New York: Holt, 1950).

5. Tarski's formulation in "On the Concept of Logical Consequence" (in A. Tarski, *Logic, Semantics, Metamathematics* [Oxford: Oxford University Press, 1956, originally published 1935], pp. 409–420) does not introduce schemata, but obtains the same effect for the formalized languages he treats by disinterpreting the nonlogical vocabulary so as to allow for arbitrary reinterpretations.

6. That the arithmetical sets are enough for implications between schemata was shown in David Hilbert and Paul Bernays, *Grundlagen der Mathematik*, vol. 2 (Berlin: Springer, 1939), p. 252. The same proof shows that, for an infinite set of schemata, we need no more than the sets arithmetically definable from that set, but that we may need more than just the arithmetical sets themselves, however, was noted in George Boolos, "On Second-Order Logic," *Journal of Philosophy* 72 (1975): 509–527.

7. (Cambridge, Mass.: Harvard University Press, 1990).

8. "Über den Zweck der Begriffsschrift," *Jenaische Zeitschrift für Naturwissenschaft* 16, supplement (1882): 1–10, p. 1.

9. "Über die Grundlagen der Geometrie," *Jahresbericht der Deutschen Mathematiker-Vereinigung* 15 (1906): 293–309, 377–403, 423–430, p. 384 (hereafter cited as Frege 1906).

10. Throughout this paper I use modern logical notation rather than Frege's.

11. Here, in using modern notation, I am eliding a nicety required by Frege's quantifying over all functions, not just all concepts, namely, his use of the horizontal.

12. *Grundgesetze der Arithmetik, Begriffsschriftlich abgeleitet,* vol. 1 (Jena: H. Pohle, 1893), p. xv.

13. *Introduction to Mathematical Philosophy* (London: Allen & Unwin, 1919), p. 169.

14. *The Logical Basis of Metaphysics* (Cambridge, Mass.: Harvard University Press, 1991), p. 2.

15. For example, see Dummett, *Frege: Philosophy of Language* (London: Duckworth 1973), p. 180 and following. Dummett calls Frege's view on the matter a "gratuitous blunder."

16. Charles Parsons canvasses an objection to Frege's conclusion in his "Frege's Theory of Number" (in C. Parsons, *Mathematics in Philosophy* [Ithaca: Cornell University Press, 1982, original date of publication 1965], pp. 150–172, [hereafter cited as Parsons 1965]), on pp. 499–501. Suppose we take it that predicates are generalized not directly but only via "nominalization," that is, only once they are transformed into names of qualities, properties, sets, or the like: for example, only once "x is malleable" is transformed into "x has (the property of) malleability." Since "malleability" lacks argument places, it may be taken as generalizable using a variable of the same logical type as those over objects. Parsons notes a problem with this: since the assertions with which one starts and ends will contain the unnominalized predicate, one needs a principle to underwrite the transformation, that is, a general principle a particular instance of which will be "$(\forall x)(x$ is malleable $\leftrightarrow$ x has the property of malleability)." But any such principle, it seems clear, will have to contain a generalization directly in the predicate place occupied in this instance by "is malleable." Hence the Fregean conclusion stands. As Parsons notes (1965 p. 503), there is one way around this conclusion. That is to use the method of semantic ascent and understand the principle underwriting the nominalization not as a direct generalization over what predicates refer to, but as an assertion that any assertion of a certain form may be transformed into another form *salva veritate*. To adopt this strategy is simply to give up the universalist conception, as it requires a metalinguistic principle that makes ineliminable use of a truth predicate.

17. *Funktion und Begriff* (Jena: H. Pohle, 1891), p. 20.

18. The truth predicate needed is a predicate of sentences. For Frege, it was not sentences but rather thoughts (senses of sentences) that were true or false. Consequently, those who take Frege to have a form of the schematic conception treat implication as a relation among thoughts. In this version, the definition would require a truth predicate of thoughts.

19. In this Frege differs from Russell, who from the first tries to formulate necessary and sufficient conditions for a truth to be a logical truth. Russell tries to use generality as the key element of the characterization. Wittgenstein takes up the problem, but criticizes Russell's invocation of generality. He takes himself to have solved the problem with the notion of tautology; that notion gives him a general conception of the logical.

20. "Über die Begriffsschrift des Herrn Peano und meine eigene," *Berichte über die Verhandlungen der Königlich Sächsischen Gesellschaften der Wissenschaften zu Leipzig* (Mathematisch-physische Classe) 48 (1897): 362–378, p. 363.

21. "Logic," in G. Frege, *Posthumous Writings* (Oxford and Chicago: Blackwell and University of Chicago Press, 1979), pp. 126–151, p. 128 (hereafter cited as Frege 1979).

22. Richard Heck suggests that Frege may have formulated the principle of countable choice to himself and found himself unable to derive it. "The Finite and the Infinite in Frege's *Grundgesetze der Arithmetik*," in *Philosophy of Mathematics Today*, ed. M. Schirn (Oxford: Oxford University Press, 1998). If so, Frege may have wondered whether that principle is an example of a truth statable without using nonlogical vocabulary, but not itself a truth of logic.

23. *Beiträge zur Philosophie des deutschen Idealismus* 1 (1918): 58–77, p. 60 (hereafter cited as Frege 1918).

24. In Frege (1979), pp. 185–196.

25. In Frege (1979), pp. 251–252 (hereafter cited as Frege *1915).

26. *Proceedings of the Aristotelian Society*, supplementary volume 70 (1996): 121–140.

27. See, for example, "Review of E. G. Husserl's *Philosophie der Arithmetik*," *Zeitschrift für Philosophie und philosophische Kritik* 103 (1894): 313–332.

28. *Die Grundlagen der Arithmetik* (Breslau: W. Koebner, 1884), p. vi (hereafter cited as Frege 1884).

29. See Frege, *Begriffsschrift, eine der arithmetischen nachgebildete Formelsprache des reinen Denkens* (Halle: L Nebert, 1879), §23.

30. In "La logique de l'infini," *Revue de Métaphysique et de Morale* 17 (1909): 461–482. Poincaré was responding to Bertrand Russell's "Mathematical Logic as Based on the Theory of Types," *American Journal of Mathematics* 30 (1908): 222–262.

31. In (Parsons 1965). See also Mark Steiner, *Mathematical Knowledge* (Ithaca: Cornell University Press, 1975), p. 28 and following.

32. Not that it was meant to: Tarski's and Quine's views of justification are different from Frege's.

33. This line of objection is suggested by a remark by Charles Parsons in "Objects and Logic," *Monist* 65 (1982): 491–516, on p. 503.

34. Here I draw on Thomas Ricketts, "Frege, the *Tractatus*, and the Logocentric Predicament," *Noûs* 19 (1985): 3–14, p. 7. See also Ricketts, "Logic and Truth," section 2.

35. The position that there can be no such thing as a truly unrestricted quantifier is due to Parsons in "The Liar Paradox" (in C. Parsons, *Mathematics in Philosophy* [Ithaca: Cornell University Press, 1982, originally published 1974], pp. 221–250. Parsons's argument is based on phenomena associated with the Liar Paradox. The use of the idea in the current context is due to Ricketts.

36. I am greatly indebted to Thomas Ricketts for countless conversations and comments, as well as for access to his unpublished works. Needless to say, he does not agree with all the formulations given in this paper.

2

Theory and Elucidation

The End of the Age of Innocence

JOAN WEINER

One of the mysterious and puzzling claims in Wittgenstein's *Tractatus* appears in the penultimate entry, where he writes, "My propositions serve as elucidations in the following way: anyone who understands me eventually recognizes them as nonsensical, when he has used them—as steps—to climb up beyond them."[1] It is, at least, eccentric to characterize one's propositions as nonsensical, and some readers of the *Tractatus* have been inclined not to take this statement seriously. My aim here will be to examine one strategy for taking it seriously—a strategy derived from a particular reading of Frege's writings.

What burdens are imposed upon an attempt to take this statement seriously? The obvious worry is that, if we take this claim seriously, it is difficult to see what value the *Tractatus* can have. We do not, after all, transcribe and publish the babblings of infants. It is tempting to address this worry by providing an account of how Wittgenstein's propositions really do (imperfectly) communicate truths. This is the strategy Cora Diamond has labeled "chickening out,"[2] and I think her objections to chickening out are convincing. But if the nonsense of the *Tractatus* is not an attempt to show us an inexpressible truth, how can it have value?

It is important to begin by noting that nonsense need not be valueless. One might entertain a young child with a series of nonsense rhymes. And there are many songs, both amusing and serious, with nonsense lyrics. Nor is the use of nonsense syllables limited to entertainment. Singers typically warm up by use of vocalises—repeated patterns of notes sung on various nonsense syllables. Someone who can read, but not speak, a foreign language may find it helpful to learn the sounds of the language by learning to recite a series of nonsense syllables before trying meaningful sentences. It is obvious that nonsense can have value. Hence, Wittgenstein's claim that his propositions are nonsensical does not, by itself, undermine the value of the work. But it is not obvious that this helps us see the value of the sort of nonsense that allegedly appears in the *Tractatus*. The problem is that it is not clear what role, other than stating truths, the sentences of the *Tractatus* are meant to play. The *Tractatus* appears to be a nonfiction book of prose. Were it not for Wittgenstein's odd claims about nonsense, one would, without

43

hesitation, try to read and understand the sentences of the *Tractatus* as if they were meant as statements of truths. But, while Wittgenstein tells us that they are nonsense, he does not appear to tell us how this nonsense is supposed to be of use to us. My burden will be to give an account of what use such nonsense might have.

Although the most striking feature of 6.54 is that Wittgenstein tells us that, when we understand him, we will recognize his propositions as nonsensical, in fact he does not merely tell us that his propositions should be recognized as nonsensical. The sentence begins, "My propositions serve as elucidations in the following way." His claim that anyone who understands him will recognize his propositions as nonsensical is part of his explanation of the way in which they serve as elucidations. On its own, this may not seem to be a particularly helpful observation. What, after all, is elucidation? And how can nonsense be elucidatory? One might expect to find the answers to these questions—if they exist—among the other remarks in the *Tractatus*. But the reader who looks for answers in the *Tractatus* will be disappointed. Unlike Frege, in whose work the notion of elucidation also plays a role,[3] Wittgenstein says very little about elucidation. Nonetheless, I think that the notion of elucidation can be used to shed light on Wittgenstein's comments about nonsense. My strategy will be to use Frege's discussions of elucidation as commentary on Wittgenstein's remarks.

This may seem to be a peculiar interpretive strategy, and it deserves some comment. I do not mean to suggest that the appearance of the term elucidation (*Erläuterung*) in both the writings of Frege and Wittgenstein is sufficient to show that the term has the same significance for both writers. While there is no question that Frege had an influence on Wittgenstein's writings, Wittgenstein's remarks about elucidation and nonsense are not typically viewed as exhibiting that influence. Still, it is interesting that each of the remarks about elucidation in the *Tractatus* appears almost verbatim in Frege's writings. Wittgenstein wrote that he could establish the influence of Frege on the style of his sentences "where at first sight no one would see it."[4] My interpretive strategy is motivated by the suspicion that Wittgenstein's talk about his propositions being nonsensical occurs in one of those places.

Let us begin by looking at the other remarks about elucidation that appear in the *Tractatus*. They are:

> The meanings of primitive signs can be explained by means of elucidations [*Erläuterungen*]. Elucidations are propositions that contain the primitive signs. So they can only be understood if the meanings of those signs are already known. (3.263)

and

> Philosophy aims at the logical clarification of thoughts.
>
> Philosophy is not a body of doctrine but an activity.
>
> A philosophical work consists essentially of elucidations [*Erläuterungen*].

Philosophy does not result in "philosophical propositions" but rather in the clarification of propositions.

Without philosophy thoughts are, as it were, cloudy and indistinct: its task is to make them clear and to give them sharp boundaries. (4.112)

It is not immediately obvious that the mention of elucidation has the same significance in these two entries. After all, the clarification of thoughts and the explanation of the meaning of a primitive sign do not exactly seem to be the same sort of activity. But it is not difficult to imagine cases in which these activities coincide. If our standards of clarity are at all restrictive, then many of the expressions in everyday use will have unclear meaning. Thus, it will be common for someone to attempt to express a thought by using a sentence containing a sign whose meaning is unclear. And in such a situation the clarification of the thought requires an explanation of the meaning of that sign. If the sign is not primitive, one might expect a definition. But if the sign is primitive, elucidation is required. Furthermore, if each proposition has a unique analysis (3.25), one might expect that clarity demands both complete analysis and elucidation of the primitive signs that appear in the completely analyzed proposition.

What are the primitive signs whose meanings are explained in the *Tractatus?* Most of the remarks about primitive signs in the *Tractatus* concern logical notation. Wittgenstein introduces one primitive sign for logic (6), a sign for the general form of a proposition. And he explicitly contrasts this sign with the signs Frege and Russell introduce as primitive signs in their logical notations. The interdefinability of their logical signs, he says, shows that they are not primitive signs (5.42). One aim of the *Tractatus* is the explanation of the most general propositional form. Although Wittgenstein does not introduce a new logical notation, such an introduction might be seen as an important part of the logical clarification of thoughts. And even if it is not, a completely analyzed proposition, one that is expressed in such a way that elements of the propositional sign correspond to the objects of the thought (3.2), cannot be expressed using Frege's or Russell's logical notation. Thus, even if Wittgenstein does not mean to be introducing a logical notation, he certainly means to be issuing a critique of Frege-Russell logical notation.

We can now see a connection between Wittgenstein's avowed elucidations and the stated aims of the *Tractatus.* Wittgenstein says in the preface that his book shows that the reason why the problems of philosophy are posed is that the logic of our language is misunderstood.[5] At one point (3.323–3.325), he says that philosophy is full of confusions that are produced by the use, in everyday language, of one word with different meanings. He goes on to say that, in order to avoid these errors, "we must make use of a sign-language that excludes them . . . that is to say, a sign-language that is governed by logical grammar—by logical syntax." This sort of language will be a logical notation. Wittgenstein's general objection to Frege's and Russell's logical notations is that they do not exclude all mistakes.[6] Particular defects of these notations are described in several other entries of the *Tractatus.*[7] The sign language that is governed by logical grammar will not be a cleaned up version of everyday language. It will be a correct version of the sort of logical notation introduced by Frege.

In the sense described earlier, the introduction of a correct logical notation will require elucidations. For, though Wittgenstein says that "all the propositions of our everyday language, just as they stand, are in perfect logical order" (5.5563), he also says that language disguises thought (4.002) and that Russell "performed the service of showing that the apparent logical form of a proposition need not be its real one" (4.0031). Indeed, since it seems that Wittgenstein's sign for the general form of a proposition will appear in each completely analyzed proposition, the explanation of this sign is, in some sense, a part of the clarification of all thought. The introduction of this sign draws a limit to the expression of thoughts.

There is, however, something odd about this focus on logical notation. Although Wittgenstein does introduce some details of a logical notation in the *Tractatus*, explanations of symbolic expressions occupy only a small part of the book. And although he says a great deal about the propositions of everyday language, he does not proceed to clarify such propositions by translating them into a new notation. His comments about the ways in which Frege's and Russell's notations are defective also occupy only a small part of the book. It does not appear that the introduction of a correct logical notation is really a part of the project of the *Tractatus*. It is not difficult, however, to see that the critique of Frege-Russell logical notation, if compelling, will have serious repercussions for Frege's project.

One of Frege's central tasks is to provide explicit definitions, in his logical notation, of the number one and the concept of number. The formulation of these definitions, on Frege's view, will address a philosophical problem.[8] Among the claims that would be expressible in his notation, should the project be carried out successfully, is the claim that one is a number. But Wittgenstein claims that the expression "1 is a number" is nonsensical (4.1272). His comments indicate that a correct notation will be designed to preclude the expression of such claims. Supposing Wittgenstein can convince us that such a logical notation correctly represents the logic of our language, then his prefatory remark about the problems of philosophy will have been at least partly substantiated. At least one philosophical problem, Frege's problem about the concept of number, results from a misunderstanding of the logic of our language. Here, then, is a pragmatic role for Wittgenstein's (elucidatory) discussion of logical notation: it can prevent us from squandering intellectual time and effort on what will amount to nonsense. But it is difficult to see how this can help with our initial problem—to explain the value of Wittgenstein's avowed nonsense. The discussion of logical notation may fit the description of elucidation, but it does not appear to be nonsensical. It is difficult to imagine that, were it recognizably nonsensical, there would be an identifiable (let alone convincing) critique of Frege. Moreover, if the objection to Frege's project is that it will result in Frege's writing nonsense, why is Wittgenstein's own work not open to this objection?

It is important to begin by noticing that, whatever Wittgenstein's critique might be, it can not be (just) that Frege is writing nonsense. Nothing in the *Tractatus* indicates that one should avoid writing nonsense song lyrics. Moreover, the fact that Wittgenstein is self-consciously writing nonsense in the *Tractatus* suggests that the objection is not based on the assumption that one should not write nonsense in philosophy books. I will argue that the injunction is not to avoid writing nonsense but, rather, to avoid taking nonsense for theory. And I will argue that this injunction can be found in Frege's writings. But, in order for this position to make any sense, it will be necessary to see how there can be a legitimate role for nonsense to play in philosophy. To see this, it will help to look more closely at the nature of Wittgenstein's objection to Frege's use of the term "number."

Wittgenstein says that the word "number" signifies a formal concept (4.1272). We recognize that something falls under a formal concept by the sort of expression we use to make claims about it. He says, "When something falls under a formal concept as one of its objects, this cannot be expressed by means of a proposition. Instead it is shown by the very sign for this object. (A name shows that it signifies an object, a sign for a number that it signifies a number, etc.)" (4.126). At first glance, there may look to be little common ground between this statement and Frege's writings.[9] The expression "formal concept" is not one of the expressions that Wittgenstein borrowed from Frege's writings. And no expression in Frege's writings is used in this way. Yet there is reason to believe that the notion of formal concept, as described in the *Tractatus*, plays an important role in Frege's thought. Although it is obvious that Frege did not take the expression 'number' to be a formal concept in the sense of the *Tractatus*, Frege's treatment of some of the other expressions that Wittgenstein identifies as signifying formal concepts is almost exactly the same as Wittgenstein's. One of these is the word 'object.'

Wittgenstein would surely say that the expression "1 is an object" is nonsensical. And Frege surely would not go that far. But it is easy to see Wittgenstein's talk about nonsense as a more dramatic way of stating something Frege does admit. Frege's actual comments about the expression "is an object" are both more ambiguous and more complex. Frege wants to say that the number one is an object. His introduction of the definition of the numbers begins with the heading "Every individual number is a self-subsistent object."[10] And he concludes his response to Russell's paradox, in an appendix to *Basic Laws*, by identifying "the prime problem of arithmetic" as the attempt to answer the question "By what means are we justified in recognizing numbers as objects?"[11] However, there are important differences, on Frege's view, between the claim that one is a number and the claim that one is an object. The most obvious difference is that, on Frege's view, "number" is definable and "object" is not. But there is a more significant difference than that.

In *The Foundations of Arithmetic*, the work in which Frege first writes that the numbers are self-subsistent objects, he does not support this claim with any demonstrations in his logical notation. Its support is supposed to appear later, in his *Basic Laws*, a work that does consist of proofs in his notation. But *Basic Laws* contains no theorem that numbers are objects. Indeed, there is not even a symbol for predicating objecthood in Frege's logical notation. Nor does Frege attempt to say in words, in the body of *Basic Laws*, that numbers are objects. How, then, does he take himself to have provided the means for justifying our recognizing numbers as objects? By his definitions. What makes the numbers objects, according to *Basic Laws*, is the sort of definitions the numerals must be given. Definitions for object-expressions are different from definitions for concept-expressions. And object-expressions play different roles in the expression of inferences from the roles played by concept-expressions. For example, suppose one has proved a first-order universal generalization from Frege's logical laws, something of the form: $(\forall x)\phi x$. Given that the numeral "1" has been introduced into his notation by an appropriate definition, one can prove $\phi(1)$. In contrast, given that a concept expression, say θ, has been introduced into his notation by an appropriate definition, one cannot prove $\phi(\theta)$. Indeed, given the rules of formation for Frege's notation, the expression that results from putting θ in the argument place will be ill-formed. There is no way to predicate ϕ of a concept named by "θ". Although Frege does not say it quite this way, it is not inappropriate to read the first-order universal generalization as saying, "ϕ holds of every object."

This is very similar to an explicit claim of the *Tractatus*. Wittgenstein says, "Wherever the word 'object' . . . is correctly used, it is expressed in conceptual notation by a variable name" (4.1272). A few lines later he gives an example. He says, "in the proposition 'There are 2 objects which . . . ,' it is expressed by '$(\exists x, y)$ . . .'" (4.1272). In Frege's notation too, the everyday word "objects" in the expression "There are two objects which . . . " will be replaced by two variable signs.[12]

In these respects the word "object," as Frege understands it, seems to signify a formal concept in Wittgenstein's sense. But Wittgenstein also claims that, when the word "object" is used as a proper concept-word, the result is nonsensical. By this criterion, the sentence "1 is an object" is nonsensical. Is there a sense in which Frege recognizes the expression "1 is an object" as nonsensical? Frege uses the predicate "object" throughout his writings. He also, notoriously, refuses to define it. A typical example is,

> When we have thus admitted objects without restriction as arguments and values of functions, the question arises what it is that we are here calling an object. I regard a regular definition as impossible, since we have here something too simple to admit of logical analysis. It is only possible to indicate what it meant. Here I can only say briefly: An object is anything that is not a function, so that an expression for it does not contain any empty place.[13]

One might suppose that, when Frege says we have here something too simple to admit of logical analysis, he is talking about something for which he is going to introduce a primitive term. This notion of primitiveness is mentioned in most of his discussions of systematizing science. In a systematic science, every definable term must be defined, and all inferences must be expressed as gapless proofs in his conceptual notation. Frege says that science only comes to fruition in a system. But he also acknowledges that not all terms are definable. He says,

> My opinion is this: We must admit logically primitive elements that are indefinable. Even here there seems to be a need to make sure that we designate the same thing by the same sign (word). Once the investigators have come to an understanding about the primitive elements and their designations, agreement about what is logically composite is easily reached by means of definition. Since definitions are not possible for primitive elements, something

else must enter in. I call it elucidation. It is this, therefore, that serves the purpose of mutual understanding among investigators, as well as of the communication of the science to others.[14]

Frege's point is that defining needs to stop somewhere. Elucidations are needed for the primitive undefinable terms that will be used in the definitions of the more complex terms of the science.

These general comments about primitive (or undefinable) terms do not quite apply to the term "object." Frege says that the notion of objecthood is a logical notion. If there is to be a primitive term for objecthood in the language of systematic science, this language should be Frege's logical notation. But by the very nature of Frege's logical notation, there can be no term for objecthood. If a term that is to be defined is an object-name, this shows itself in the sort of definition that is given. The purpose of Frege's notation is to express all content that has significance for inference and to leave out all other content.[15] A predicate for objecthood could have no use in simple predications. In order to predicate objecthood of something, one must have an object-name for it. Thus such a predication can express nothing of significance for inference or, indeed, for anything else. As Frege says, "It is not easy to imagine how language could have come to invent a word for a property which could not be of the slightest use for adding to the description of any object whatsoever" (Frege 1884/1980, section 29). Nor would a predicate for objecthood have any other use. Frege would agree that, as Wittgenstein says in 4.126, the content of the everyday expression "object" in such everyday sentences as those beginning "there are two objects which . . ." is exhausted in the logical notation by the use of appropriate variables.

On Frege's view there is no role for a term for objecthood to play in the expression of statements in a systematic science. I have suggested that the reason is that for Frege, as for Wittgenstein in the *Tractatus*, the everyday term "object"—like the terms "concept" and "function"—signifies a formal concept. Although these terms do not appear in any statement of a systematic science, Frege does make use of all these terms in his writings. They appear in the preliminary remarks for setting up his logical notation—his language for systematic science—where they are used to introduce and describe the rules governing the use of different sorts of letters and signs. There are different rules for object signs, first-level function signs, second-level function signs, etc. Of course, the rules for the use of different sorts of letters and signs can be stated without any use of such terms as "object," "function," and "concept." It is certainly possible to think of Frege's notation and rules of inference as an empty game. But Frege's aim is to show that his notation has expressive power. It is supposed to be a tool for expressing what is of significance to inference in the statements of everyday natural language. Without Frege's remarks about the notions of function and object, there is no way to understand how his notation achieves this aim. Without, for example, recognizing Frege's conditional stroke as a function-expression, one could not understand what this sign expresses.[16] The role these everyday terms play in the introduction of Frege's logical notation—the role of explaining the meaning of primitive terms—is just the role that is to be played by elucidation, both in Frege's writings and in 3.263 of the *Tractatus*.

So the advantage of considering Frege's discussions of elucidation is not just that he says more than Wittgenstein says in the *Tractatus*. Because Frege not only needs elucidation to introduce his notation, but also intends to use this notation as a tool, it is easy to see the importance of his elucidation. It is also easy to see how this elucidation is supposed to work. Furthermore, on Frege's view, there is no requirement that elucidations be translatable into his logically perfect language. Indeed, some elucidations cannot be translated into his logically perfect language.[17] This lends plausibility to the claim that the importance of elucidation does not depend on its expressing objective truths.

It is, however, a long way from these conclusions to finding a value for elucidatory nonsense. I have argued above that Frege's views about the expressions "object," "concept," and "function" accord with some of Wittgenstein's remarks about expressions that signify formal concepts. But I have not yet discussed the salient feature of these remarks, namely, that sentences containing such expressions are nonsensical. Thus far, I have argued only that sentences containing such expressions cannot appear in Frege's notation. It does not immediately follow that the sentences in which they appear are nonsensical.

Nevertheless, there is a connection between some of Frege's elucidations and a notion of nonsense very like that of *Unsinn* in the *Tractatus*. Frege says, "what is simple cannot be analysed and hence not defined. If, nevertheless, someone attempts a definition, the result is nonsense [*kommt Unsinn heraus*]. All definitions of function belong to this category."[18] This passage may seem to suggest the contrary of what I have claimed. One might infer that, if attempts at defining the notion of function result in nonsense, then to avoid nonsense the notion should be explained by elucidation. The problem with this inference is that any attempt at elucidation that is designed to explain what it is to be a function will result in nonsense for exactly the same reason that any attempt at a definition results in nonsense. For even an elucidation will be expressed by a sentence in which the term "function" appears and the term "function," along with the related terms "concept" and "object," is defective. Frege's explanation of the defect involved in the word "concept" applies equally to "function." He says, "the word 'concept' itself is, taken strictly, already defective, since the phrase 'is a concept' requires a proper name as grammatical subject; and so, strictly speaking, it requires something contradictory, since no proper name can designate a concept; or perhaps better still, something nonsensical [*einen Unsinn*]" (Frege 1983, p. 192 [pp. 177–178]).

Although Frege is careful to issue such disclaimers, they do not prevent him from using these terms in a way that requires something nonsensical. For the primitive terms of his notation cannot be introduced without the use of these defective terms. Some of Frege's elucidations involve ineliminable nonsense.[19]

Thus for Frege, nonsensical elucidation must have at least some value because it is an ineliminable part of the introduction of a correct conceptual notation. Moreover, by considering Frege's introduction of his logical notation we can see how our attempts to understand apparently meaningful but in fact nonsensical sentences can be of pragmatic value.[20] Although this understanding of how nonsense might function can be applied to the *Tractatus* as well, our problem is still not solved. For the purpose of Frege's nonsense, as described so far, is to introduce his logical notation. Thus we seem to have unambiguous criteria for the success of this nonsense. Further, given the usefulness of Frege's logical notation, there is no difficulty in regarding his elucidatory nonsense as valuable. But this explanation of the value of nonsense is less easy to apply to the *Tractatus*. If elucidatory nonsense can have only pragmatic value, then one might well regard the nonsense of the *Tractatus* as a failure. Wittgenstein's nonsense does not play the role of introducing a logical notation, for Wittgenstein introduces no logical notation. Nor has Wittgenstein's nonsense succeeded in convincing people that there is a difficulty with Frege's and Russell's logical notations. The sort of logical notation Wittgenstein seems to be advocating has not found the acceptance or uses that Russell's has. And while some people may have been convinced by the *Tractatus* to refrain, for example, from the attempt to define the concept of number, this can hardly count as an unambiguous indication of the value of Wittgenstein's nonsense.

But is the value of Frege's nonsense exhausted by its use in introducing his logical notation? If it is, then the subsequent success of his work in logic may seem to rob his philosophical writings of import for us. Today, virtually all philosophy undergraduates are taught a version of the first-order part of Frege's logical notation. This is at least evidence that we think we understand Frege's primitive terms today and, if we are right, there looks to be no role left for his actual elucidations. After all, it is not very difficult to introduce a logical notation to undergraduates. It certainly does not require an understanding of the complex arguments involved in Frege's discussions of the notions of function, concept, and object. Has philosophical (or logical) progress made Frege's elucidations obsolete?

Let us suppose, for the moment, that Frege's elucidations are obsolete. What does this tell us about the value of nonsense in general? First, we have found a case—Frege's elucidations—of an indisputably valuable use of nonsense. Second, the value of this use of nonsense is pragmatic. And there is no reason to believe that it can have no other uses. Indeed, I have just provided an example of a different use for Frege's nonsensical elucidations. In this chapter, I have discussed Frege's use of the terms "function," "concept," and "object," not in order to introduce his notation, but to discuss the interpretation of the *Tractatus* and the nature of elucidation. Thus it is not at all clear that Frege's elucidations should be abandoned.

It is important not to ignore the consequences of this view. If the only value of Fregean nonsense is its successful employment in the communication of the meaning of his primitive logical terms, then it should be no better than any other successful method for communicating this. Should it turn out, for instance, that we could reach the same understanding by taking a pill or undergoing a minor surgical procedure, then the only advantage of Frege's elucidations over the pill or the surgery would be its lack of physical side effects. Or would it?

I have suggested that we suppose for the moment that Frege's elucidations are obsolete. But this assumption of obsolescence makes sense only if the typical introduction of logical notation to undergraduates suffices to communicate what Frege's elucidations communicate. This is not very plausible. The only reason it may seem plausible at this point is that I've emphasized the pragmatic character of Frege's elucidations. Given this emphasis, it is difficult to see what—beyond the ability to translate everyday sentences into logical notation and produce proofs—can be expected of the logic student to whom the notation has been successfully introduced.

Can there be more, then, to the successful introduction of a notation than conveying the ability to use it? Most of my discussion of elucidation so far has concerned the use of Frege's writings to explicate remark 3.263 of the *Tractatus*, the remark in which elucidation is characterized as explanation of primitive signs. But this seems a far cry from Wittgenstein's suggestion, in 6.54, that the use of his propositions as elucidations is supposed to get us to see the world aright. Something is surely missing from my description so far. The objection in the *Tractatus* to Frege's logical notation is not, after all, that Wittgenstein cannot understand how to use its symbols. This attention to the uses to which philosophical nonsense can be put should not be allowed to obscure the significance of something more intimately connected with the idea of seeing the world aright.

Frege says that "when properly expressed, a thought leaves no room for different interpretations" (Frege 1906, p. 384 [p. 315]). He takes this to be true of the proper expression of the primitive laws of logic—their expression in his conceptual notation. But it may well be possible to teach someone to conduct proofs in Frege's notation while regarding it as an uninterpreted calculus. (It is certainly possible to teach undergraduates a similar notation in this way.) On Frege's view, there is a difference between someone who, operating mechanically in accord with Frege's laws and rules, writes down something that is a proof in his notation and someone who proves a theorem using Frege's notation. And this difference is located in their respective understandings of the basic laws and rules.

All this attention to undergraduate logic students, however, is misleading. It is not only one's ability to write out proofs in Frege's notation that may be unaffected by lack of this sort of understanding. Frege's repeated criticisms of mathematicians who, he says, do not understand what the numbers are suggest that this sort of lack of understanding is no impediment to carrying out mathematical research. The inclusion of Weierstrass, a truly great mathematician, among those who do not understand what the numbers are suggests that lack of understanding is not even an impediment to carrying out important mathematical research. Thus an important part of Frege's achievement is meant to be, not an alteration in mathematical practice, but an alteration in our view of arithmetic, our way of regarding its subject matter. This is not to say that Frege does not intend to make any contribution to mathematics. Obviously, he does. My point is, rather, that the aim of Frege's discursive writings, *The Foundations of Arithmetic* in particular, is not exhausted by its role in Frege's mathematical contribution.

To see why there must be something beyond that contribution to mathematics, let us tell a fictional story about Weierstrass, who, according to Frege, did not understand what the numbers are. Suppose Frege's project is carried out successfully; the results (including Frege's discursive writings) are shown to Weierstrass, who reads them and claims he understands and agrees with them. At this point, presumably, Frege would say that Weierstrass does understand what the numbers are. But what, exactly, does this mean? This would surely involve, on Frege's view, Weierstrass's realizing that numbers are logical objects. But the claim that numbers are logical objects is no theorem. Nor is it statable in Frege's notation.

Would this understanding change Weierstrass's technical arsenal or Weierstrass's beliefs about which elementary claims of arithmetic are true? It might. But, except for his views about mathematical definitions, Frege does not insist on any changes in mathematical practice. Nor does he argue that any statements that, prior to his work, had been regarded as truths (falsehoods) of arithmetic are actually false (true). Thus, there is no reason to attribute to Frege the view that such an alteration *must* affect Weierstrass's work. This use of elucidations to change the way we regard arithmetic is not unlike the use suggested by Wittgenstein's claim that the propositions of the *Tractatus*, if they serve as elucidations, will get us to see the world aright.

It should not be surprising that Frege's discursive writings seem designed to do more than introduce a notation, logical laws, and proofs. After all, these writings are lengthy and complicated. The generally accepted view is that they are meant to set out a philosophical theory. It is only Frege's assessment of some of the central statements in these writings as nonsense that requires us to look for another explanation of how Frege means us to understand these writings. And it is not really very plausible that such extensive heuristics should be necessary for the introduction of Frege's mathematical results. Thus, it seems that the value of much of Frege's corpus can only consist in its ability to effect some sort of inexpressible difference of understanding that may have no discernible practical effect. The upshot, unfortunately, is that we have lost one of the advantages of looking at Frege's nonsense rather than the nonsense of the *Tractatus*. It seemed that the problem presented by Frege's nonsense would be easier to confront than that presented by Wittgenstein's nonsense. The reason was that Frege's nonsense seemed designed to accomplish a practical and easily discernible goal. But the practical goal cannot be the point of all of Frege's discursive writings.

I want to argue that the difference in our way of seeing arithmetic and language after reading Frege's writings or the *Tractatus* is of import on its own. I say that I want to argue this, but I cannot really argue this. Or, at least, I cannot provide an argument with this conclusion that proceeds from generally accepted premises and general principles. Yet I have some resources. I do not—not yet—feel driven to stamp my foot.

Before I attempt to make use of these resources, however, it may be worthwhile to stop and answer a question. Why bother? As the above discussion seems to show, both Frege and Wittgenstein have made statements that conflict with some of their other statements. This is not especially surprising, since it is easy enough to take missteps in the attempt to work out a grand project. Moreover, surely it is sound interpretive strategy to discard the obvious missteps. It may seem that the claim that some of one's statements are nonsensical is such an evident misstep that it is a prime candidate for the discard pile.

But if it is so obvious to us that these statements are missteps, why was this not obvious to Frege and Wittgenstein? One might be tempted to say that, at least for Frege, this issue was peripheral and that he simply did not devote a great deal of thought to the difficulties with these statements. But the evidence suggests otherwise. The defective nature of the expression "concept" is a central subject of his paper "On Concept and Object." And the large number of such statements in his *Nachlass*[21] suggests that he devoted a considerable amount of thought to this issue. Insofar as we respect Frege's philosophical acumen, it seems only appropriate to devote some effort to providing an interpretation on which he can be taken at his word.[22] With Wittgenstein, the situation is even clearer. For claims about nonsense occupy a central role in the *Tractatus*. Wittgenstein not only says that his propositions are nonsensical, he also says that most of the propositions and questions in philosophical works are nonsensical and even that such everyday claims as "1 is a number" are nonsensical (4.003, 4.1272, and 6.54). Thus far, most attempts to make sense of Frege's and Wittgenstein's claims about the nonsensical nature of some of their propositions involve the strategy that Diamond calls "chickening out."[23] It is surely worthwhile to attempt to provide an interpretation on which Frege and Wittgenstein are right, both about the nonsensical nature of their propositions and about the value of their enterprises. Let us return, then, to the question of what importance elucidation can have.

The conclusion that there can be importance to a shift in our way of thinking about something—even if that shift is not used for any practical end—is one that I intend to defend by elucidation. But even if I have not yet been reduced to stamping my foot, it is important to emphasize that I will, like Frege, have to ask for goodwill, cooperative understanding, and a grain of salt. Many of us have been confronted by students hell bent for medical school who deny the value of philosophy. Of course, these denials typically appear in the context of an easily countered argument. For example, "You should give me a better grade because my difficulties in the study of this valueless subject should not keep me out of medical school, since, if I am kept out of medical school, I will be prevented from performing great services to humanity." But if this particular challenge is easily countered, that is partly because of the typical lack of strategic sophistication of its formulators. If the student gives up all grandiose ideas of the expected uniqueness and importance of her/his post medical school accomplishments, if the student does not read (except to study), does not listen to music (except as background), does not go to the theater (except for distraction), in short, if the student truly does not value anything but what has recognizable practical value, then there is nothing left to be said. In such a circumstance, one might as well stamp one's foot.

My confidence that I am not now in that circumstance is what leads me to believe that I have more resources. But I do not mean to arouse worries that I am about to provide embarrassing autobiographical details or attempt to discuss the psychological proclivities of philosophers. The elucidation I will discuss is already in print and does not concern the psychology of philosophers. It is not private to me, nor is it even my own. Nor will this be an attempt to use graceful and elegant prose for the purpose of dazzling the reader into accepting something she really thinks is wrong.

Such a discussion, of course, may seem a departure from the elucidatory procedure described in Frege's writings. His comments about investigators reaching a mutual understanding on the meaning of primitive terms may be taken to suggest that elucidation is an improvised activity whose details are dictated by the idiosyncrasies of the investigators. But it is important to remember that Frege says that elucidation serves mutual understanding, not just of the investigators who introduce primitive terms initially, but also for "the communication of science to others" (Frege 1906, p. 301 [p. 300]). Frege himself gives elucidations in order to communicate the meanings of the primitive terms of his logical notation.[24] These elucidations, of course, are not improvised examples in a private conversation. They appear in Frege's written work. Elucidation, like explicit argument and proof, can be available in literature.

The elucidation I will discuss comes from Edith Wharton's novel, *The Age of Innocence*.[25] It will help to begin with a few comments about the plot. Newland Archer, the central character of *The Age of Innocence* is, when the action of the novel commences, a rather silly, unreflective person. The novel opens with a description of the events that take place among a group of people at a performance at the Metropolitan Opera of Gounod's *Faust*. Archer arrives late because it is "not the thing" to arrive on time for the opera and "what was or was not 'the thing' played a part as important in Newland Archer's New York as the inscrutable totem terrors that had ruled the destinies of his forefathers thousands of years ago" (Wharton 1962, p. 14). Nor is Newland Archer an unwilling participant in this New York. We are also told that "Few things seemed to Newland Archer more awful than an offence against 'taste,' that far-off divinity of whom 'form' was the mere visible representative and viceregent" (Wharton 1962, p. 22). Edith Wharton introduces another character, Lawrence Lefferts, as the foremost authority on "form." She continues,

> He had probably devoted more time than anyone else to the study of this intricate and fascinating question; but study alone could not account for his complete and easy competence. One had only to look at him, from the slant of his bald forehead and the curve of his beautiful fair moustache to the long patent-leather feet at the other end of his lean and elegant person, to feel that the knowledge of "form" must be congenital in anyone who knew how to wear such good clothes so carelessly and carry such height with so much lounging grace. As a young admirer had once said of him, "If anybody can tell a fellow just when to wear a black tie with evening clothes and when not to, it's Larry Lefferts." And on the question of pumps versus patent-leather "oxfords" his authority had never been disputed. (Wharton 1962, p. 17)

Edith Wharton tells us that Newland Archer felt himself superior to Lawrence Lefferts and his companions: "he had probably read more, thought more, and even seen a good deal more of the world than any other man of the number. Singly they betrayed their inferiority" (Wharton 1962, p. 17). But, she also tells us, together they represented "New York," and he accepted their doctrine on all the issues called moral (Wharton 1962, p. 17).

On the afternoon before this particular night at the opera, Newland has just become engaged to be married. That night at the opera, these men who represent New York are all talking about a woman sitting in the box belonging to the family of his future wife, May. Ellen Olenska is May's cousin. She has spent most of her life in Europe, married a count, and is now returning to New York under somewhat scandalous circumstances. The announcement of his engagement is moved forward, at his urging, so that he can express support of May's family. This support is complicated by Ellen's odd views and behavior. She regards New York society as quaint and, at least initially, cannot see any reason for following its rules. In the course of the novel, Newland marries May but falls in love with Ellen.

As he begins to see New York society through Ellen's eyes, she begins to see it through his eyes. Even as he begins to see the hypocrisy and triviality of his world and, more significant, to recognize the strict limitations that membership in this society will place on his life, Ellen begins to see its virtues. Ellen's recognition of these virtues convinces her to give Newland up, and Newland's recognition of these virtues, not in his original unthinking way, but as a result of what he learns from Ellen, allow him ultimately to give her up.

Although the novel is almost entirely taken up with the story of this relationship, it does not end with the final separation of Ellen and Newland. At the end of the novel, Edith Wharton returns us to Newland Archer twenty-six years later, as he is contemplating the impending marriage of his now-grown son and, in the process, looking back on the course of his own life. We are informed that the life he has led in the intervening years is very much the sort of life he expected to lead before meeting Ellen Olenska. He has lived his life without the "exquisite pleasures" to which Ellen alludes in one of their discussions. There has been one unorthodox feature of his life and that is that he once was elected to public office. This was the extent of his political career, however, for he was not reelected. His reverie is interrupted by a long-distance telephone call from his son, who convinces Newland to accompany him on a trip to Paris. The final pages of the novel take place in Paris, where Newland comes to terms with the fact that his choice to live a life bounded by the constraints of old New York has made him into a certain sort of person. He is "old-fashioned" and although, since his wife is dead, he is now in a position to experience the exquisite pleasures he once desired without paying for them by anything "hard and shabby and base," he no longer desires them. The Newland Archer who appears in these last pages is, unlike the Newland Archer of the opening pages, an immensely sympathetic character.

Why should this story tell us anything about elucidation? The answer has to do with our reasons for liking Newland at the end of the novel. For the difference has nothing to do with the actions he performs or the rules by which he lives. The life he has lived and the life, as is evident in the ending, he will continue to live, is not so different from Lawrence Lefferts's. But the esteem in which we hold Newland, but not Lawrence Lefferts, is not based on the fact that Newland's idleness is interrupted by his serving a term as an elected official or, in fact, on any of his actions. The most important difference has to do with the way Newland thinks about his actions and his decision to abide by the apparently arbitrary rules of the society in which he lives.

This is not to suggest that the novel shows that actions are unimportant—or that any act is permissible or admirable provided one has reached reflective equilibrium about it. There is no reason to infer that this sort of reflection is the only valuable activity or even that it is the most important sort. But Newland Archer becomes a sympathetic character in the course of the novel to the reader who intrinsically values a certain sort of reflection. And the story about this change in the reader's attitude is an example of how elucidatory justification works. But this may not show that *The Age of Innocence* provides justification. After all, not everyone will respond in the same way to the novel. And as for the sophisticated premedical student, she will surely be unimpressed. It may seem, then, that the novel can provide justification only to someone who already agrees with the moral. But notice that this does not vitiate the use of the novel for Fregean elucidation. Frege says,

> When a straight line intersects one of two parallel lines, does it always intersect the other? This question, strictly speaking, is one that each person can only answer for himself. I can only say: so long as I understand the words "straight line," "parallel" and "intersect" as I do, I cannot but accept the parallels axiom. If someone else does not accept it, I can only assume that he understands these words differently. Their sense is indissolubly bound up with the axioms of parallels. (Frege 1983, p. 266 [p. 247])

Frege believes that no one who understands the axioms of Euclidean geometry can doubt their truth, but it does not follow that we can understand them or see that they are true without elucidation. It is also interesting to note that Frege's confidence that we can reach an understanding and agreement about the axioms of geometry does not prevent him from believing that the question of the truth of the axiom is something that each person must answer privately. Frege says that if someone else does not accept the axiom he can only assume that this person understands the words differently. There is no guarantee of the success of elucidation.

There may seem to be something deceptive about this discussion of elucidatory justification. My aim was to say that there was value in the nonsense of Frege and Wittgenstein. But the text I used for purposes of elucidation was a novel. Its sentences are not nonsensical, or at least they are not nonsensical in the way Frege's claims about concepthood are. The point of the discussion of Edith Wharton's novel, however, was to recognize the value, not of her novel, but of the changes in Newland Archer's way of thinking about the world.

Of course, at this point two shifts in view are under discussion. One of these is the fictional shift of Newland Archer. The other, presumably nonfictional, shift is that undergone by the reader of *The Age of Innocence*. Neither exactly fits Frege's description of the aim of elucidation, that is, serving "the purpose of mutual understanding among investigators, as well as of the communication of the science to others" (Frege 1906, p. 301 [p. 300]). Newland Archer's shift, in particular, is private. And neither shift has anything to do with scientific investigation. However, as I have argued above, the difficulty with identifying the value of shifts accomplished by Fregean elucidation is that they need not have any practical effect on the methods or results of scientific research. If, as I have argued in the discussion of *The Age of Innocence*, the change in Newland Archer's way of thinking is something we value, there seems no reason to deny that we value similar shifts in our ways of thinking about the primitive concepts of some scientific discipline. Moreover, it is of interest to note that the other shift under discussion, that of the reader of *The Age of Innocence*, is something that serves the purpose of achieving mutual understanding, although not of scientific investigators.

But, even so, there may look to be deceit involved. After all, why can the changes in Newland Archer's way of thinking about the world not be characterized as a difference in his substantive beliefs? Surely there are some beliefs that we can attribute to him at the end, but not the beginning of the novel. It is not easy, however, to find a difference in beliefs that characterizes the change in his thought. It is not, for instance, that he comes to believe there are other ways of life. He recognized that before. Indeed, early on in the novel, he prides himself on his friendship with an impoverished reporter as well as his wide experience of the world. Nor does he come to believe that there are other ways he could have lived. He is not really exposed to any other ways of life. He is only exposed to Ellen Olenska's attitude toward his. When he suggests that they run away together to some place where they will not be stigmatized for their behavior, she replies, "Oh my dear—where is that country? Have you ever been there?" (Wharton 1962, p. 231). Edith Wharton writes about the two of them, near the end of the novel, "More than half a lifetime divided them, and she had spent the long interval among people he did not know, in a society he but faintly guessed at, in conditions he would never wholly understand" (Wharton 1962, p. 284). Insofar as he has a vision of other lives or other options, it is only a fantasy. This is not to say that there are no changes in his beliefs. There surely are. But it does not seem that there are any changes in his beliefs that can be said to characterize the change in attitude that constitutes a central drama of the novel. It is not clear that what he has learned can be expressed in words. If this is right, then any attempt to characterize Newland's reflections in explicit words will, like Frege's characterizations of objecthood, result in nonsense.

One might respond that, since Newland Archer's changes are explained to us in a novel, the real characterization of these changes is not what goes through his mind or what he says but, rather, what is said in the novel. Perhaps what is said in the novel is not what Newland Archer has learned, but one might take it as significant that we can be taught about what he has learned without the use of nonsense sentences. This would mark a difference between the elucidation in Edith Wharton's novel and that in the works of such philosophers as Frege and Wittgenstein. But what is the significance of this difference? It is not that novels, because they do not contain nonsense, cannot provide elucidation. Elucidation is, as Wittgenstein says of philosophy, an activity. And there is no reason to suppose that an activity that sometimes involves nonsense must, therefore, always involve nonsense. While vocalises typically make use of nonsense syllables, there is no requirement that only nonsense syllables be used in vocalises. Some singers practice arpeggios on sentences.

But if novels can accomplish our elucidatory aims without engaging in nonsense, should we banish nonsensical philosophical writings in favor of justification by novel? It seems obvious to me that the answer to this question is, No. It is difficult to imagine how, for instance, Frege's logical notation might be introduced by means of fiction. And even if one could come up with some such introduction-by-fiction, why would this be preferable to Frege's? Surely, laughter would be the appropriate reaction of a singer who is criticized for using nonsense syllables in vocalises on the grounds that she could use perfectly good sentences. If Frege's elucidatory nonsense is successful, why should we object that it is nonsense? The conviction that we should object to Frege but not to the singer is, I want to suggest, a symptom of a prevalent and enduring fantasy. This is a fantasy of the perfect transparency and communicability of thoughts.

This fantasy both antedates and survives Frege's and Wittgenstein's writings. And one can find quotations that support its attribution to both of them. For example, Frege uses the term "thought" for what can be true or false, what can be judged.[26] He also says that what is objective is what is law-governed, conceivable, judgeable, what is expressible in words (Frege 1884/1980, section 26). Throughout his writings, it is suggested that all thoughts can be expressed in language. This is also suggested, although perhaps more ambiguously, in the *Tractatus*, where Wittgenstein says, "A thought is a proposition with sense," (4) and that we have "the ability to construct languages capable of expressing every sense" (4.002). And it is suggested in a journal entry from 1916 where he says "Now it is becoming clear why I thought that thinking and language are the same. For thinking is a kind of language. For a thought too is, of course, a logical picture of the proposition, and therefore it just is a kind of proposition."[27] On this view, it seems, what can be thought can be expressed in language. And not only imperfectly—what can be expressed in language can be expressed with precision. In Wittgenstein's words, "what can be said at all can be said clearly" (*Tractatus*, p. 3). In Frege's words, "when properly expressed, a thought leaves no room for different interpretations" (Frege 1906, p. 384 [p. 315]). If I want to communicate something and fail, this might be due to imperfections in the language I am using or to my imperfect use of that language. Or it might be that, due to unclear thinking, there really is nothing I am trying to communicate. In any case, this failure is the failure of an individual. There are no inexpressible thoughts.

Consider the paragraph I have just written. It is certainly not a work of art or an example of particularly felicitous expression. Its primary purpose is to communicate something. And, on this view, what can be communicated must be objective, it must be composed of thoughts. Thus the purpose of my paragraph must be to express thoughts (although this expression might be imperfect). Furthermore, unless there is something really wrong with the above paragraph—unless it amounts to unarticulated gibberish—the thoughts it attempts to express will be expressible precisely.[28] If there is no way to express precisely what is communicated, then the description cannot be communicating anything. Since only thoughts can be communicated, attempts at communication that demonstrably fail to express thoughts will be valueless. Attempts at communication that imperfectly express thoughts should, if the thoughts are important, be reworked so that the thought are stated precisely.

Given these convictions, along with the belief that the above description of the relation between language and thought certainly expresses something, it does not seem unreasonable to attempt to explain this relation more precisely. The interpreters of Frege's writings have been even more unified than those of the *Tractatus* in their conviction that his writings provide methods for doing this. In particular, Frege is credited with introducing the means for developing semantic theories. And, in this way, he has been viewed as beginning the process that will allow philosophy to mature into a science. Philosophy, in Frege's hands, has begun the transformation from a "soft" discipline into a "hard" one. Given this near unanimity among his interpreters, it seems rather surprising that his treatment of language and thoughts differs so radically from his treatment of logic and arithmetic. His writings are full of explicit discussions of what is required for science and his writings are full of arguments that his science of logic meets these requirements. Not only do Frege's discussions of language universally fail to meet these requirements, he never attempts to apply his standards in these discussions. One might suppose that he meant to leave this further work for his followers. But one can only suppose this by ignoring a significant part of his corpus.[29]

I have argued that, on the view I labeled the fantasy of perfect transparency and communicability of thoughts, any attempt to communicate must be an attempt to communicate thoughts and any thought can be precisely communicated. This creates a serious problem for the construal of some of Frege's and Wittgenstein's apparent expressions of thoughts. For the only purpose of these expressions is to communicate something and, as both writers explicitly state, there is no way to replace them with precise expressions. On this view, then, they seem to be without value. Furthermore, these valueless apparent expressions of thoughts are the sentences that appear to be central to the development of a semantic theory. Why have contemporary philosophers not found this more disturbing?

I suspect that one reason has to do with Frege's standards of rigor. Frege is notorious, and justly so, for championing standards of precision and rigor far in excess, not only of those of other writers of his time, but also of what is practical for everyday scientific or mathematical research. Although it is the adoption of these standards that seems to allow Frege's apparent transformation of philosophy into a science, few contemporary philosophers of language seem to have worried about the significance for that transformation of relaxing these standards. More significant, few contemporary philosophers have paid attention to Frege's views about the consequences of adopting his standards of rigor.

It is striking that this philosopher who required proof whenever proof was possible, and gapless proof at that, recognized that our understanding and justification of the primitive laws underlying all these proofs is, in an important sense, subjective and inexpressible. Rather than simply identifying a point at which we must stop defining and proving, Frege recognized a need to say something about that point—something that, of necessity, would not meet his standards. The upshot of taking all of Frege's writings seriously is that, if one values precision and explicit expression, one must also recognize that there is something left over—that without something more our explicit sentences, in some sense, cannot really express truths. When properly expressed, a thought leaves no room for different interpretations—but only provided we have reached a common understanding of the primitive terms. That is, one must realize that the fantasy of the perfect communicability of thought is just that, a fantasy. It is difficult to determine, from Frege's writings, how clear this was to him. Some of my argument depends on drawing connections that Frege does draw but does not quite take with the seriousness we might expect from someone who sees the collapse of this fantasy. In contrast, Wittgenstein's statement that his propositions are nonsensical is what we would expect. And that, I suggest, is why he makes it.

At this point, it is of interest to consider an aspect of Frege's writings that I have been ignoring. This is his tendency to include a brief mention of poetry in many of his discussions of what is expressed by language. In fact, Frege does suggest that there is something other than thoughts—other than what is subject to laws or can be true or false—that is expressed by language. The difference between the use of the term "nag" or "steed" is one of his examples. What is expressed by poetry—just like elucidation—is imperfectly expressed and cannot be made precise. The upshot, although it is unlikely that Frege was entirely aware of this, is that in this sense his writings have the same status as poetry. But he may not have been entirely unaware of this upshot. He also says,

> What are called the humanities are closer to poetry and are therefore less scientific than the exact sciences, . . . for exact science is directed toward truth and truth alone. . . . Where the main thing is to approach by way of intimation what cannot be conceptually grasped, these constituents are fully justified. . . . What is called mood, atmosphere, illumination in a poem, what is portrayed by intonation and rhythm, does not belong to the thought.[30]

It is easy to assume that, because he means to use his philosophical writings to introduce a systematic science of arithmetic, he did not really take them to be part of the humanities. But it is not obvious that this assumption is warranted. Frege is always aware of the difference between his discursive writing and the proofs in his logical notation.[31] Instead of focusing only on Frege's contribution to mathematics, one might heed the remark, in the introduction to *The Foundations of Arithmetic*, that any thorough investigation of the concept of number is bound to turn out rather philosophical.

A final remark. I have argued that the result of viewing Frege's and Wittgenstein's writings as elucidatory nonsense need not deprive them of value. The value in elucidatory nonsense is that, like music and poetry, it can be used to express something that cannot be expressed explicitly; something that cannot be literally true or false. But, in suggesting that some philosophy can be viewed as a kind of art, I do not mean to be suggesting that there needs to be something artful about the nature of the writing. Indeed, philosophers, as a group, are known for the infelicity of their writing style. Rather, I would suggest that the art in philosophy has to do with the inventiveness and the rightness of alternative ways of viewing things. Just as a particular word or expression in a poem can be peculiarly, thrillingly right, so a particular philosophical argument can seem to illuminate some issue in a way that is also peculiarly, thrillingly right.

I do not mean all this to be taken as a celebration of nonsense over theory. Surely theory and statements of truths are preferable when available. But theory is not always available, and if what I have argued is correct, indeed, if Frege is correct, it is not available in a lot of the places many of us thought it was. Sometimes our actual choice is not between theory and elucidation but, rather, between recognizing elucidation for what it is and deluding ourselves into taking metaphor for theory. Perhaps it is time for the end of our age of innocence.

NOTES

This is a version of a paper originally written for and presented at a 1991 conference titled "Elucidation, Understanding, and Truth" at Illinois State University and Illinois Wesleyan University. It underwent substantial revisions in the early 1990s, which were completed in 1994. In preparation for this publication, I have made some minor revisions to the prose and added footnotes to more recent publications in which I have expanded upon some of the topics. However, I have decided not to update the discussions to reflect the substantial literature on this topic that has appeared since 1994. Thus some of the discussion, particularly from the first part of the paper, may seem somewhat dated to those who are familiar with the literature.

In revising the paper, I benefited from discussions with many of the participants in the original conference, as well as from helpful comments from Gary Ebbs, Jamie Tappenden, and, especially, Mark Kaplan. My revisions were also influenced by discussions of nonsense in Cora Diamond, "Ethics, Imagination, and the Method of Wittgenstein's *Tractatus*," in *Bilder der Philosophie, Wiener Reihe* 5, ed. R. Heinrich and H. Vetter (Vienna: R. Oldenbourg Verlag, 1991), pp. 55–90 (hereafter Diamond 1991), and James Conant, "The Search for Logically Alien Thought: Descartes, Kant, Frege and the *Tractatus*," *Philosophical Topics* 20 (1992): 115–180 (hereafter Conant 1992).

1. Ludwig Wittgenstein, *Tractatus Logico-Philosophicus*, trans. D. F. Pears and B. F. McGuinness (London: Routlege and Kegan Paul, 1961), 6.54. Propositions of the *Tractatus* will be cited by their number.

2. Cora Diamond, "Throwing Away the Ladder," *Philosophy* 63 (1988): 5–27 (hereafter Diamond 1988).

3. For accounts of the role elucidation plays in Frege's project, see chapter six of my *Frege in Perspective* (Ithaca: Cornell University Press, 1990), hereafter Weiner (1990), and my "Understanding Frege's Project," in *The Cambridge Companion to Frege*, ed. Thomas Ricketts (Cambridge: Cambridge University Press, forthcoming) (hereafter Weiner forthcoming).

4. Ludwig Wittgenstein, *Zettel*, ed. G. E. M. Anscombe and G. H. von Wright, trans. G. E. M. Anscombe (Berkeley: University of California Press, 1970), §712.

5. *Tractatus*, p. 3.

6. For an interesting and more substantive discussion of the *Tractatus* criticism of Frege's and Russell's notations, see Michael Kremer, "The Multiplicity of General Propositions," *Noûs* 26 (1992) 4: 409–426.

7. 4.1272, 4.1273, 4.431, 5.533, and 5.534.

8. I have argued this in the first three chapters of Weiner (1990). It should be noted that the fact that Frege viewed the formulations of these definitions as addressing a philosophical problem does not in any way preclude his regarding them as contributions to mathematics as well.

9. This connection between Frege's treatment of the expressions "relation," "concept," and "object" and Wittgenstein's notion of a formal concept has been drawn by Leonard Linsky in "The Unity of the Proposition," *Journal of the History of Philosophy* 30, no. 2 (1992): 243–273. Linsky does not explicitly take the further step of connecting Frege's treatment of these expressions with Wittgenstein's remarks about nonsense.

10. Gottlob Frege, *Die Grundlagen der Arithmetik* (Breslau: Wilhelm Koebner, 1884), English trans. by J. L. Austin, *The Foundations of Arithmetic*, 2d rev. ed. (Evanston, Ill.: Northwestern University Press, 1980) (hereafter Frege 1884/1980), section 55.

11. Frege, *Grundgesetze der Arithmetik* (Hildesheim: Georg Olms, 1962) (hereafter Frege 1962), p. 265; English translation on p. 143 of *The Basic Laws of Arithmetic: Exposition of the System*, ed. and trans. Montgomery Furth (Berkeley: University of California Press, 1964) (hereafter Frege 1964). Frege (1964) contains a translation of *Grundgesetze*, vol. 1, Introduction, §§0–52, Appendix I and Appendix II. Translations of *Grundgesetze*, vol. 2, §§56–67, 86–137, 139–144, 146–147, appear in *Translations from the Philosophical Writings of Gottlob Frege*, 3d ed., ed. and trans. Peter Geach and Max Black (Totowa, New Jersey: Rowman and Littlefield, 1980) (hereafter Frege 1980).

From now on all English translation page numbers will appear in square brackets following German page numbers.

12. Although in Frege's notation, unlike Wittgenstein's, to say that there are two objects also involves explicitly stating that these objects are distinct.

13. *Funktion und Begriff* (Jena: Herman Pohle, 1891) (hereafter Frege 1891a), p. 18; English translation on p. 147 of "On Function and Concept," in Frege, *Collected Papers: On Mathematics, Logic, and Philosophy*, ed. Brian McGuinness, trans. Max Black et al. (Oxford: Blackwell, 1984) (hereafter Frege 1984), pp. 137–156.

14. Frege, "Über die Grundlagen der Geometrie," *Jahresberichte der Deutschen Mathematiker-Vereinigun* 15 (1906): 293–309, 377–403, 423–430 (hereafter Frege 1906), p. 301; English translation, Frege (1984), p. 300.

15. See the Preface to Frege, *Begriffsschrift, a Formula Language, Modeled upon that of Arithmetic, for Pure Thought*, in *Frege and Gödel: Two Fundamental Texts in Mathematical Logic*, ed. Jean van Heijenoort (Cambridge, Mass.: Harvard University Press, 1970) (hereafter Frege 1970), p. 6.

16. I have provided a detailed description of how Frege's elucidation of the meaning of the conditional stroke is supposed to work in Weiner (1990), pp. 232–236.

17. Some, but not all. There is no reason to attribute to Frege either the view that all elucidatory hinting must be untranslatable into *Begriffsschrift* or the view that all elucidatory hinting must be nonsense.

18. Frege, *Nachgelassene Schriften* (Hamburg: Felix Meiner Verlag, 1983) (hereafter Frege 1983), p. 290; English translation in Frege, *Posthumous Writings*, eds. Hans Hermes, Friedrich Kambartel, Friedrich Kaulbach, trans. Peter Long and Roger White (Chicago: University of Chicago Press, 1979) (hereafter Frege 1979), p. 271.

19. It is important to emphasize that this is not to say that all sentences in Frege's discursive writings are nonsensical. The nonsense in these writings can usually be recognized by the use of such defective expressions as "function" and "concept." Other sentences in these writings have sense but cannot be directly translated into *Begriffsschrift* because their sense is not sufficiently precise. But this does not distinguish these sentences from most sentences used in scientific research. As I have argued in (Weiner 1990), even the sentences of pre-Fregean arithmetic do not have sufficiently precise sense. For a discussion of Fregean elucidation that is not nonsensical, see Weiner (forthcoming).

There is, however, a difference between the sentences that are meant to be solely elucidatory in Frege's discursive writings and the sentences of pre-Fregean arithmetic. The sentences of presystematic arithmetic are meant to play a role in a mathematical theory. Thus, they must be replaced by systematic sentences, all of whose terms have precise sense that determines a meaning. For this argument, see Weiner (1990), pp. 111–119, 133–139. On the other hand, sentences of Frege's discursive writing, for the most part, are not meant to play a role in any systematic science. I do not have room to give an adequate defense of this claim here. In brief, the reason is that what appears to be the theory to which these sentences belong has, as its cornerstones, true nonsense. This view is defended in my "Burge's Literal Interpretation," *Mind* 104 (1995): 585–597, (hereafter Weiner 1995), and my "Has Frege a Philosophy of Language?" in *Early Analytic Philosophy: Essays in Honor of Leonard Linsky*, ed. W. W. Tait (LaSalle, Il.: Open Court, 1997), pp. 249–273 (hereafter Weiner 1997). In particular, I argue in part II of Weiner (1995) that some of the sentences which have been taken as expressing metaphysical truths about functions are, in principle, not expressible in *Begriffsschrift*.

20. This is only so, of course, presuming that one agrees with Frege that his use of the expressions "concept" and "function" are nonsense. This view is not widely accepted, and I do not have room to defend it here. For an argument that Frege's understanding of the defects of these expressions is correct, see Weiner (1990), pp. 246–258.

21. Among the remarks, not including those from his early draft of "On Concept and Object" are Frege (1983), pp. 129–133, 192, 210, 212, 257–258, 269, 275 (English translation, Frege 1979, pp. 119–122, 177, 193, 195, 239, 249–250, 255). These span most of his subsequent career. The last are included in his "Notes for Ludwig Darmstaedter," dated 1919.

22. Another reason for taking Frege's claims about the nonsensical nature of his statements seriously is that it will not help simply to discard those claims. In this paper, I have argued that in Frege's logical notation there is no role to be played by a term for "object," and I have argued Frege's view of this term, along with "concept" and "function," is, in effect, that they signify formal concepts. But it is not just that there is no apparent role for these terms to play in Frege's *Begriffsschrift*. Nor is it that Frege's claims about objects, concepts, and functions are vague or ambiguous or share any typical logical defects of statements of everyday language. Frege's claims about the nature of objects, concepts, and functions are, in principle, not expressible in *Begriffsschrift*, as I argue in Weiner (1995), Part II.

23. Diamond, "Throwing Away the Ladder," *Philosophy* 63 (1988), pp. 5–27, Diamond (1991), and Conant (1992) are notable exceptions.

24. See, for instance, his introduction of the conditional-stroke in section 12 of Frege (1964). I have discussed how this elucidation works in Weiner (1990), pp. 232–236.

25. Edith Wharton, *The Age of Innocence* (New York: New American Library, 1962; originally published in 1920) (hereafter Wharton 1962).

26. Frege, "Der Gedanke," *Beiträge zur Philosophie des deutschen Idealismus* 1 (1918): 58–77 (hereafter Frege 1918), p. 62; English translation in Frege (1984), pp. 355–356.

27. Ludwig Wittgenstein, *Notebooks, 1914–1916*, ed. G. H. von Wright and G. E. M. Anscombe (Chicago: University of Chicago Press, 1979) (hereafter Wittgenstein 1979), entry of 12.9.16.

28. This is actually a somewhat misleading characterization of Frege's views, although the difference has no significance for the point at issue here. On Frege's actual view, it may not be possible to identify a precise thought that I am attempting to communicate by means of my imperfect sentences. If my sentences are meant as a contribution to a science, then the systematization of this science will require me to substitute precise expressions for my imperfect expressions. The result will be sentences that express precise thoughts but that, of necessity, do not express exactly the same sense as those with which I started. The new sentences, however, will need to preserve something of the senses of the old sentences. I have discussed this at more length in Chapter 3 of Weiner (1990).

29. For example, on Frege's view, every name of the True is a complex expression containing at least one function expression. Thus, were Frege interested in a theory of reference, part of whose point is to give an account of how the truth value of a sentence is dependent on the referents of its parts, an account of how the referents of function expressions contribute to truth value would be a central part of his theory. But such an account would, on Frege's view, be nonsense. For more on this, see Weiner, "Frege and the Linguistic Turn," *Philosophical Topics* 25 (1997).

30. Frege (1918, p. 63 [pp. 356–367]). Because I do not have room to give the full argument here, it may seem that the argument depends on our contemporary use of the English words "humanities" and "science." This is unfortunate, since these words have rather different meanings from the German words (*Geisteswissenschaft* and *Wissenschaft*) they are used to translate. However, the actual argument depends, not on these translations but, rather, on Frege's extensive discussions of what is required for an expression's admissibility for purposes of science. For this argument, see Weiner (1997) and Weiner (1990), pp. 95–120.

It should also be noted that it does not follow, from the fact that sentences that historians regard as expressing truths do not meet Frege's standards, that those sentences are nonsensical. After all, pre-Fregean arithmetic also fails to meet those standards. Rather, as I have argued, these sentences have imperfect (because insufficiently precise) sense (Weiner 1990, pp. 120–141). As I argued there, Frege's definitions of the numbers are meant to capture the sense that, by virtue of scientific practice, was previously associated with the numerals. This argument can be made, as well, about sentences that are taken to express truths about history. However, it may seem less plausible that the expressions used by historians can be given the sort of definitions Frege requires. Although this issue is too complicated to go into here, it is worth noting that the sentences from Frege's writings that he identifies as nonsense are very different from sentences purporting to express truths about history. It is the value of the former sentences that is at issue in this chapter.

31. For example, Frege writes, in the Preface to *Basic Laws*, "The proofs themselves contain no words but are carried out entirely in my symbols" (1964, pp. 1–2). The exposition of his *Begriffsschrift* must, of necessity, be expressed in German, rather than in his notation. But the sections of Part 2 of *Basic Laws* are divided into those with the heading "Analysis" (*Zerlegung*) and those with the heading "Construction" (*Aufbau*). German words (expressions that are not part of his conceptual notation) appear only in the Analysis sections.

3

Bolzano, Frege, and Husserl
on Reference and Object

DAGFINN FØLLESDAL

In lectures, seminars, and conversations, and lately also in publications, Burton Dreben has provided penetrating insights into the origins and development of what we call "analytic philosophy." He has concentrated on Frege, Russell, Wittgenstein, Carnap, Austin, and Quine. I have learned much about these philosophers from him. When I became his colleague at Harvard in 1961, I took up in my lectures another philosopher, Husserl, whom I think should be studied in conjunction with those Dreben lectured on and also in conjunction with their intellectual predecessor, Bernard Bolzano. Yet many resist the idea that Husserl, who inspired and informed what is often called "continental philosophy," has much in common with these champions of the analytic tradition.

In an earlier paper, I used Frege's notion of sense to shed light on Husserl's notion of noema.[1] In that paper, I concentrated on the noema and did not say much about the object. In this chapter, I will take up Husserl's notion of the intentional object and compare and contrast it with Bolzano's and Frege's views on the reference of linguistic expressions. I will also look briefly at Husserl's treatment of indexicals, which I regard as much more insightful than the treatments of Bolzano and Frege.

Bolzano was a main influence on the development of Husserl's phenomenology. Husserl gives generous credit to Bolzano in several of his works and refers to him frequently. Husserl first came across Bolzano when, barely twenty, he read *Paradoxien des Unendlichen*[2] during his studies with Weierstrass in Berlin. And he renewed this acquaintance with *Paradoxien des Unendlichen* in 1884–1885 when he followed Brentano's lectures in Vienna on "Die elementare Logik und die in ihr nötigen Reformen."

But it was only later, in the mid-1890s, that Husserl started serious study of Bolzano's *Theory of Science*,[3] which he earlier had regarded as "strange" ("*fremdartig*"). Husserl had then decided to give up work on the second volume of the psychologistic *Philosophy of Arithmetic* (1891) and had started working on what was to become his first phenomenological work, the *Logical Investigations* (1900–1901). Husserl states that he came to appreciate Bolzano, and in particular his theory of propositions (*Sätze an sich*) and representations (*Vorstellungen an sich*), through studying Lotze's interpretation of Plato's theory of ideas. Husserl interpreted Bolzano in a platonistic manner, which Husserl claimed—I think unjustly—was foreign to Bolzano (XXII, p. 130)[4]

There are indeed many conspicuous similarities between Husserl's phenomenology and Bolzano's philosophy. In presenting Husserl's ideas to philosophers with an analytic background, it is helpful to compare and contrast his views with those of Frege, since Frege is well known to analytic philosophers and the parallels between him and Husserl are striking and help to understand and to appreciate Husserl. It can also be useful, however, to stress Husserl's similarities with Bolzano, especially when one presents Husserl to a mixed audience, some of whom are thoroughly familiar with Frege, others of whom have only a vague idea of Frege and analytic philosophy. There are two reasons for introducing Bolzano into the discussion. First, Bolzano is a great philosopher who deserves to be much better known—until recently he was not even mentioned in the *Encyclopedia Britannica*. Second, Bolzano was also a great pedagogue; he builds up his philosophy in such a clear and systematic manner that students who come from other fields have no difficulty understanding his points and he also makes them see *why* he makes these points—which is a major challenge in teaching philosophy.

I do not claim that Husserl got his phenomenology from Frege or Bolzano; he knew many of the basic ideas and distinctions that he and they use from other philosophers. He did, however, study both Frege and Bolzano carefully. He owned all of Frege's writings and had marked them painstakingly, spotting even small misprints in Frege's proofs. And as we have noted, he studied Bolzano's *Theory of Science* with great care.

Bolzano and Frege were both far ahead of their times in thinking through subtle philosophical issues that became central in Husserl's *Logical Investigations* and later works. I will not have space here to touch on more than a small fraction of all the philosophical connections among Bolzano, Frege, and Husserl. The first issues I will take up relate to the notion of the intentional object in Husserl and the notion of object in Bolzano and Frege. In and of themselves, these issues are rather trivial, but I will take them up because of a recent Husserl interpretation by the competent Husserl scholar, David Bell. From my perspective, his interpretation is based on a misreading of Husserl.

David Bell's Criticism

In his article "Reference, Experience, and Intentionality,"[5] David Bell takes issue with a Fregean interpretation of Husserl to which I subscribe. This interpretation is also pertinent to the relation between Bolzano and Husserl.

Bell does not direct his criticism against me. Instead, he kindly begins his article by praising me for providing a Fregean perspective on Husserl. However, he criticizes five other philosophers for having gone too far in assimilating Husserl to Frege. I quote Bell: "Unfortunately, in certain circles Føllesdal's . . . insight has become something of an orthodoxy—to the effect that Husserl and Frege are in certain respects so doctrinally similar that only terminological differences set them apart" (Bell 1994, p. 185). He then quotes and criticizes passages from Mohanty, Harney, Smith, McIntyre, and Dreyfus.

I was on the dissertation committees for Smith, McIntyre, and Dreyfus, and Bell should have added me to his list of adversaries, for I fully share the view he criticizes. This is that Husserl's notion of the intentional object is similar to Frege's notion of *Bedeutung* (often translated as "reference," as distinguished from Frege's notion of *Sinn*, usually translated as "sense"). In my publications on Husserl, I have focused more on sense than on reference, and I have emphasized parallels between Husserl's notion of noema and Frege's notion of sense. This is, however, mainly because the notion of noema has been more difficult to grasp and more in need of clarification. I certainly also hold that there are close parallels between Frege's notion of *Bedeutung* and Husserl's notion of intentional object. This second parallel is intimately connected with the parallel between Husserl's noema and Frege's sense. There is a similar parallel between Bolzano's notion of the object of a representation (*Vorstellung*) and Husserl's notion of the object of an act.

Although I find Frege's ideas on sense and reference useful for expounding Husserl's phenomenology and understanding what he was up to, I do not allege that Husserl took over these notions from Frege. Husserl studied Frege's writings carefully and corresponded with Frege concerning the distinction between sense and reference. But Husserl was familiar with similar distinctions long before he read Frege, as was Bolzano, from reading Mill and many others. One idea, however, is certainly new in Frege: no earlier author has a systematic discussion of the notion of indirect reference, where an expression refers to what is normally its *Sinn*. Such a discussion is found in Husserl, but we shall not go into it here.

Although there are other interesting and illuminating similarities relating Husserl, Frege, and Bolzano, there are also important and thought-provoking differences. Even with regard to Husserl's notion of noema and Frege's notion of sense—and we could add Bolzano's notion of representations (*Vorstellungen an sich*)—there are many consequential differences, which I discuss in my 1969 paper on Husserl's notion of noema. What shall now concern us are the points of difference Bell finds between Frege's notion of reference and Husserl's notion of object. These differences, if they exist, would hold also between Husserl and Bolzano. Bell thinks these differences are immense.

According to Bell, there are three fundamental differences between Husserl's notion of object and Frege's notion of reference. As Bell sees it, Husserl held, contrary to Frege:

(1)   the object of an act does not exist extramentally; it is nothing in reality (Bell 1994, p. 199);

(2)   an expression or act cannot be meaningful and yet at the same time lack an object (Bell 1994, p. 194);

(3)   an expression or act can have "directedness toward an object" (*Richtung auf einen Gegenstand*) even if its object (*Gegenstand*) does not in fact exist (Bell 1994, p. 194).

I will not contest the third of these theses. There is no doubt that Husserl held this thesis; I disagree with Bell when he says that Frege did not hold it. Yet this thesis does raise some interesting philosophical issues, so I will return to it later.

Examining how Bell goes wrong gives us an opportunity to highlight some features in the interplay between an act's noema and its object and also to bring out some important aspects of Husserl's version of idealism. Bell gives quotations, largely from Husserl's *Logical Investigations*, to support his three theses. Although my discussion of Husserl's views on noema and object pertains primarily to his *Ideas*, where the notion of noema makes its first appearance, on my reading Husserl's view with regard to the points discussed by Bell did not undergo any radical change during the years separating the *Logical Investigations* (1900–1901)[6] from *Ideas I* (1913).[7]

Let us take Bell's first thesis : the object of an act does not exist extramentally. Bell here quotes two passages from *Logical Investigations*:

> The object is *meant*, i.e., to *mean* it is an experience, but it is then merely entertained in thought and is nothing in reality. (LU, p. 386; LI, p. 558; Bell's emphases)

> The *immanent, mental object* is not therefore part of the descriptive or real makeup of the experience, it is in truth not really immanent or mental. But it does not exist extramentally. It does not exist at all. (LU, p. 387; LI, p. 559; Bell's emphases)

As they stand, these passages certainly go against Frege's and Bolzano's realist views about the objects of reference, and also against my interpretation of Husserl and that of my five accomplices whom Bell mentions. The meaning of these passages changes, however, when we read them in context. Both passages occur in a discussion of the exceptional case of an act directed toward the god Jupiter. It is in such exceptional cases that the act has no object. Thus, far from being a general point about all acts and their objects, the passages quoted by Bell relate to an exception from the general rule, that acts normally have an object. Rather than going contrary to Frege, these passages could have been taken from Frege. For Husserl continues the discussion as follows:

> If, however, the intended object exists, nothing becomes phenomenologically different. For consciousness, that which is given is essentially similar, whether the object that is given to consciousness exists, or is fictitious, or is perhaps completely absurd. I think of Jupiter as I think of Bismarck, of the tower of Babel as I think of Cologne Cathedral, of a regular thousand-sided polygon as of a regular thousand-faced solid. (LU, p. 387; LI, p. 559; translation slightly emended)

Let us now turn to Bell's second thesis: an expression or act cannot be meaningful and yet at the same time lack an object. This certainly goes against the observation by Husserl that we just quoted, namely, that there are cases of meaningful acts that lack an object, such as the act of thinking about Jupiter. Bell quotes five passages from Husserl in support of his point. All these passages occur, however, in places where Husserl is explaining to the reader the difference between an expression or an act's meaning and its object. The last passage quoted by Bell makes just this pedagogical point: "Each expression not merely says something, but says it *of* something: it not only has a meaning, but refers to certain *objects*" (LU, p. 52; LI, p. 287; Husserl's emphases). Husserl here wants to bring out the difference between meaning and object and does not complicate the discussion by immediately mentioning expressions that fail to have an object. This he goes into some pages later, in §15, where he discusses cases where expressions and acts lack an object and cases where they lack meaning (LU, p. 60; LI, p. 293).

Husserl goes into much more detail than Frege does, particularly when he discusses meaninglessness. He clearly sees, however, the parallel to Frege's distinction between *Sinn* and *Bedeutung* and points out that Frege uses "one [*Sinn*] for *Bedeutung* in our sense and the other [*Bedeutung*] for the objects" (LU, p. 58; LI, p. 292). There is no indication in Husserl that he has a view about objects that differs radically from Frege's.

Bell's third and last point is that an expression or act can have "directedness toward an object" (*Richtung auf einen Gegenstand*) even if its object (*Gegenstand*) does not in fact exist (Bell 1994, p. 194). This point stands in apparent conflict with his second point, that all acts have an object. As we just noted in our discussion of Bell's second point, Husserl clearly held that acts may lack an object. Acts without an object are nevertheless acts in that they have directedness. The passages that Bell quotes to support his third point are adequate expressions of Husserl's view and help refute Bell's second point.

We could stop here, having achieved our goal of examining how Bell's interpretation of Husserl goes wrong. But here we touch on a very interesting theme in Husserl's philosophy, a theme worth pursuing in order to get a deeper understanding of his notion of "directedness"—the key idea in his theory of intentionality and also in his later idealism.

Bell comes to Husserl with a broad and strong general background in philosophy, and I always read his work on Husserl with great interest. While his first two objections against the Fregean approach to Husserl seem to me to be based on a careless reading of the texts, his misreading of Husserl in connection with his second objection leads him to a more stimulating misreading in connection with his third objection. Since Bell attributes both the second and third theses to Husserl, he tries to interpret Husserl in such a way that there is no conflict between the two theses. Thus Bell tries to interpret Husserl as saying that, although every act has an object (the second thesis), this object does not in fact exist (the third thesis).

Bell always focuses on the early Husserl—Husserl before the transcendental turn of 1906–1907 that led him to idealism and the *Ideas*. Yet in connection with his third thesis, Bell interprets the passages from the *Logical Investigations* in a rather idealist way. Bell finds that these passages present a view according to which language and thought do not hook on to the external world, the nature and the existence of the external world being irrelevant to this connection. I quote Bell:

> What sort of "reference" could it be, we need to ask, that every intelligible expression possesses necessarily, and moreover, possesses independently of there being something that is referred to? The answer seems obvious: it isn't any kind of reference at all. It is, rather, an intrinsic property of an act's *sense*. Husserl's "*Richtung auf ein Objekt*" is not a genuinely relational phenomenon, but is, in his phrase, "an inner determination" of all significant acts; it is not extensional, but is precisely the defining characteristic of intentional phenomena; it is not the point at which language and thought hook onto the external world—on the contrary, as we will see, it is a notion specifically tailored *ab initio* to be such that the nature and the existence of the external world are irrelevant to it. (Bell 1994, p. 195)

Bell here agrees with Guido Küng, who has argued that, "while Husserl took a strong interest in the Fregean notion of sense, his phenomenological inclination prevented him from truly appreciating the importance of the notion of reference."[8] Küng, like Bell, holds that though Husserl may be close to Frege on sense, he deviates importantly—and disastrously—from Frege in his view of reference.

Let us now separate two questions:

(1) Did Husserl deviate from Frege—and Bolzano—in his view of reference?
(2) Is Husserl's view of reference seriously deficient?

The first question, I think, can be answered, "No." Frege, Bolzano, and Husserl all held that in addition to sense there is normally reference and that this reference is usually quite another kind of object, for example, a physical object. And they all three held that in some cases an expression may lack reference. Husserl's view is succinctly expressed in the following passage: "In meaning, a relation to an object is constituted [*In der Bedeutung konstituiert sich die Beziehung auf den Gegenstand*]" (LU, p. 59, LI, p. 293). Apart from the special Husserlian word "constitute" and Husserl's use of *Bedeutung* for Frege's *Sinn*, this passage could just as well have been taken from Frege.

The second question, however, is a much more interesting and difficult one. While Frege is brief and sketchy in his discussion of how sense determines reference, Husserl discusses the issue at length. For Frege, an expression refers to the one and only object, if any, that satisfies the expression's sense. Husserl's view is much more detailed and penetrating. He examines in more detail the reference of different kinds of expression, such as indexicals and demonstratives, and he looks into the complexities that are involved even in the reference of ordinary singular terms, such as names. Much of what Husserl has to say could probably be subscribed to by Frege and by Bolzano, because it is compatible with what they said elsewhere on other issues. But there are many other views, different from Husserl's, that are also compatible with Frege and Bolzano, so we cannot know whether they would have agreed with Husserl. These issues, however, are as pressing for Frege and Bolzano as they are for Husserl, but only Husserl addressed them.

Directedness

For Husserl, as we noted, the sense of an expression and the noema of an act are the locus (if we can use such a word for what is not spatial and also not temporal) where their relation to an object is constituted. Husserl's word *Beziehung*, which Findlay has translated "relation," is in this context not quite like a relation. It may lack a relatum. Expressions, and acts, "stretch out toward" an object, to use a metaphorical expression, but they do not always succeed in hitting one. One of Husserl's favorite locutions for this feature is that the act is or "directed" (*gerichtet*). Just like an arrow, an act may have a direction without there always being an object that it is directed toward. The crucial question then becomes: in what does the directedness of an act consist if there is no object it is directed toward?

This is just one of the main questions Husserl sets out to answer in his phenomenology. He was dissatisfied with Brentano's statement that all acts are characterized by having an object toward which they are directed. There are two problems with Brentano's characterization. First, there is not always an object; and second, Brentano does not address the basic problem of *how* an act can be directed toward an object. What is involved in being directed toward an object? Brentano had little to say about this, as had Frege and Bolzano.

Husserl has long and detailed discussions of this question. According to him, an act's directedness consists in its having an elaborate structure of anticipations, the noema, a large number of features all regarded as features of one and the same object, which is the object of the act, when there is one. Husserl would here agree with Frege and Bolzano, who both said that any physical object has an inexhaustibility of different features. Husserl writes, "No perception of the thing is finally complete; there always remains room for new perceptions which further determine indeterminacies, come to fulfill that which is unfulfilled [*Unerfülltheiten*]" (III,1, pp. 347.5–7; see also III, 1, pp. 319.20–21 and 331.2–4). An object may be experienced at different times and from multiple points of view so different from one another that we may sometimes go wrong in identifying the object. We may believe that there are two or more objects where there is one, and we may believe that there is one object where there are several.

The Determinable X

But what does it mean to go wrong about the identity of an object? What kinds of anticipations are there that are violated when we get mixed up about identity? This is one of the many issues Husserl addresses in his theory of *Sinn* and noema, under the label of the *determinable X*, or the noematic pole. As Bell rightly points out, these reflections on identity are closely related to Peter Geach's observations on intentional identity in *Logic Matters*.[9] They are also related to Jaakko Hintikka's ideas on *de re* modalities and on various kinds of individuation and, as Christian Beyer has pointed out in (1996), to John Perry's idea of *internal* identity.[10]

In the passage from Küng that Bell quotes in support of his claim that Husserl never appreciated the importance of Frege's notion of reference, Küng continues: "[I]nstead of introducing the Fregean notion of referent, Husserl elaborated the phenomenological notion of the-identical-X-meant, namely, the notion of noematic pole. This noematic pole exists even in the cases where there is no referent, and thus, clearly, it still belongs on the level of the Fregean sense" (Küng 1977, p. 341). I have two comments on this claim. First, Küng is right that the determinable X belongs on the level of the Fregean sense, it is part of the noema. There is ample evidence in Husserl that the determinable X is part of the noema and not the object of the act. (See, for example, §131 of *Ideen I.*) It exists even in cases where there is no referent.

Second, unlike Bell and Küng, I do not regard Husserl's discussion of the determinable X as an indication that Husserl failed to appreciate Frege's notion of reference. On the contrary, I take it as an indication that Husserl saw and took on a most important issue in the theory of sense and reference, an issue Frege never considered, namely, the question of what is involved in an expression's referring to an object and, more generally, in an act's being directed upon an object.

Some interpreters of Husserl who properly distinguish between the determinable X and the object of the act make a more subtle mistake. They take the determinable X to be something that *insures* that our experience is of some particular object and not of another one very similar to it. They point out that all our anticipations relate to various *properties* of the object and that these anticipations could fit any similar object. For these interpreters, it is thanks to the determinable X that the object gets fixed. This interpretation of Husserl is in part inspired by so-called direct reference theories, where the reference of an expression is supposed to be fixed by a direct relation to the object or to some individuating essence. This, however, seems to be a rather strange kind of notion, for it can succeed in fixing an experience on one object rather than another even when these objects seem to be qualitatively indistinguishable.

My own interpretation of Husserl's determinable X, which seems to me to fit better with the texts and also to be philosophically more satisfactory, is that the determinable X has to do with reification, or individuation. We structure the world into objects. We are not just experiencing a heap of features, but features of objects.

Two Features of the Determinable X

The determinable X has two characteristic features, both of which are connected with individuation. First, it constitutes the object pole around which the other components of the noema are grouped, such that our experience is of an object, with all its properties, an object that has more to it than what meets the eye and which may remain the same object although its properties change. The object is experienced as the same through "possible manifolds of perception which, continually passing into one another, consolidate into the unity of a perception in which the continually enduring thing shows, in ever new series of adumbrations [*Abschattungsreihen*], ever new (or returning old) 'sides'" (*Ideen I*, §44, III, 1, p. 91.27–32).

Second, the determinable X also gives sense to our notion of several objects being numerically distinct though they may be very similar. When we encounter an object very similar to one we encountered before, we may still raise the question, "Is this the same object, or a distinct one?" And conversely, an object may change its properties, look very different from what it did before, and still be the same object. The notion of the determinable X makes us distinguish two pairs of opposites: identity versus distinctness and similarity versus difference. Things may be distinct in spite of similarities. And things may be identical in spite of changes.

Husserl's view here is in my opinion very similar to that of Quine, my teacher, and Dreben's. Quine writes, in 1995:

> As Donald Campbell puts it, reification of bodies is innate in man and the other higher animals. I agree, subject to a qualifying adjective: perceptual reification (1983). I reserve "full reification" and "full reference" for the sophisticated stage where the identity of a body from one time to another can be queried and affirmed or conjectured or denied independently of exact resemblance. Distinct bodies may look alike, and an identical object may change its aspect. Such discriminations and identifications depend on our elaborate theory of space and time and unobserved trajectories of bodies between observations.[11]

Quine has permitted me to quote from an earlier, unpublished manuscript:

> I wonder whether a dog ever gets beyond this stage. He recognizes and distinguishes recurrent people, but this is a qualitative matter of scent. Our sophisticated concept of recurrent objects, qualitatively indistinguishable but nevertheless distinct, involves our elaborate schematism of intersecting trajectories in three-dimensional space, out of sight, trajectories traversed with the elapse of time. These concepts of space and time, or the associated linguistic devices, are further requisites on the way to *substantial* cognition.[12]

Note how, according to Quine, there is a connection between individuation of objects and a schematism of time and space. A similar kind of connection is found in Husserl. There is a certain kind of package here of notions that comes together. We cannot have some part of it and not other parts. Space, time, and objects are all involved in the way we structure reality.

The determinable X is hence what makes sense of what goes wrong in cases of mistaken identity. It is, as Husserl says in a manuscript from 1911, "[w]hat cannot enter into the unity of an identifying consciousness, what human being cannot in any case confound [*Was kann nicht alles in die Einheit eines identifizierenden Bewußt-seins treten, was kann der Mensch nicht alles verwechseln*]" (XXVI, p. 231.5–6).

Reality

There will not be space here to go into Husserl's many illuminating observations concerning directedness and the determinable X. However, there is space enough to go into one important point that is completely overlooked by Bell and by Küng, a point connected with Bell's belief that for Husserl an act is never directed toward an external object and that "the nature and existence of the external world is irrelevant to it" (Bell 1994, p. 195). For Husserl, our noematic structures do not form a world of their own, unaffected by the surrounding world. There is an all-important component in the noema which Bell does not take into consideration: the thetic component, which engenders the difference between acts of perception, remembering, imagining, etc. In acts of perception and other acts where we are dealing with the real world, the object of the act is not conceived of as part of our own consciousness. Contrary to what Bell says (1994, pp. 197–198), such acts involve a commitment to the existence of external objects. Part of the externality of these objects consists in their not being fully subjugated by our consciousness. They are recalcitrant. Through their influence on our body, they may compel us to restructure our pattern of anticipations, and thus our acts may get a new and different noema.

Intentionality, for Husserl, does not just involve directedness toward an object, but also a "positing" (*Setzung*) of the object, to use Husserl's term, an experience of the object as real and present, as remembered, or as merely imagined, etc. According to Husserl: "I continually find at hand as something confronting me a spatiotemporal reality [*Wirklichkeit*] to which I belong like all other human beings who are to be found in it and who are related to it as I am" (*Ideen I*, §30, III, 1, p. 61.15–18; *Ideas I*, pp. 56–57, translation slightly modified). Husserl stresses the shared, intersubjective nature of the world particularly in §29 of *Ideas I*, which he entitles "The 'Other' Ego-Subjects and the Intersubjective Natural Surrounding World." Here he says: "I take their surrounding world and mine Objectively as one and the same world of which we are conscious, only in different ways [*Weise*]. . . . For all that, we come to an understanding with our fellow human beings and together with them posit an Objective spatiotemporal reality" (*Ideen I*, §29, III, 1, p. 60.16–26; *Ideas I*, pp. 55–56). The same idea of the reality of the world is repeated with almost the same words when Husserl discusses the lifeworld in *The Crisis of European Sciences and Transcendental Phenomenology*, for example in §37, where he says:

> [T]he lifeworld, for us who wakingly live in it, is always there, existing in advance for us, the "ground" of all praxis, whether theoretical or extra-theoretical. The world is pregiven to us, the waking, always somehow practically interested subjects, not occasionally but always and necessarily as the universal field of all actual and possible praxis, as horizon. To live is always to live-in-certainty-of-the-world. (VI, p. 145.24–32)[13]

Husserl discusses this thetic character of intentionality and, correspondingly, of the noema in many of his books and manuscripts. He was particularly concerned with what gives reality-character to the world. Like William James—whom Husserl had already read when he made the transition to phenomenology in the mid 1890s—he stressed the importance of the body, and the inflictions upon our body, for our sense of reality. As James put it, "Sensible vividness or pungency is then the vital factor in reality."[14] Husserl could also have subscribed to James's observation that "[t]he *fons et origo* of all reality, whether from the absolute or the practical point of view, is thus subjective, is ourselves" (James 1950, pp. 296–297).

We may always go wrong; our further experience may conflict with our anticipations, and we may come to see that an object is different from what we had expected it to be, and even that we may have been mixed up about the identity and distinctness of objects. We may discover that there were several objects where we thought there was one, or that there is one where we thought there were several. Husserl is a thoroughgoing fallibilist. In order to be fallible, in order to go wrong, however, there has to be a way of being wrong, and this is what Husserl wants to clarify through his phenomenological analysis of the noema. Far from being out of touch with the external world and its objects, our acts are directed toward them, and our linguistic expressions refer to them. Husserl's phenomenology aims at making us understand how this can happen.

There is much more to say about this, about perception, intuition (*Anschauung*), and the role that our senses, our body, and our actions play in our relation with the world around us and in our concept of reference and reality. But I have written on these questions in other places,[15] and I want to use the rest of my space to make some remarks about Husserl's view of indexicals and demonstratives.

Indexicals and Demonstratives

Any philosopher who holds that sense determines reference will encounter some standard problems. By now these are classical and well-known, but they have not always been so. I will mention three of them and briefly state Husserl's contribution to each.

The Pronoun "I"

Like Bolzano in 1837[16] and Frege in his unpublished *Logik* of 1897,[17] Husserl discusses the peculiarities of the word "I." In the *Logical Investigations* of 1900–1901, Husserl writes: The word *I* names a different person from case to case, and it does so by means of ever new signification [*Bedeutung*]. What in each case its signification is can only be gathered from living speech and the intuitive [*anschaulichen*] circumstances belonging to it (XIX,1, p. 87.32–36). Husserl also points out what many later writers have missed:

> [W]e know that [*I*] is a word . . . with which he who is speaking refers to himself. But the conceptual representation so awakened is not the significa-

tion [*Bedeutung*] of the word *I*. If this were so, we could have simply substituted for the *I*: *the present speaker who refers to himself*. The substitution would obviously lead to expressions that are not merely unusual, but have different signification. (XIX,1, p. 88.1–7)

And Husserl points out that the word "I" is not equivocal:

We have to admit that the two significations [*Bedeutungen*] are here built upon one another in a peculiar way. The first, which relates to the general function, is connected with the word in such a way that it can perform an indicating function in the representing at hand. This now comes to the assistance of the second, singular representation and marks its object as that which is meant *hic et nunc*. The first signification [*Bedeutung*] we call the indicating [*die anzeigende*], the second the *indicated* [*die angezeigte*] signification. (XIX,1, p. 89.4–13)

I will not discuss Husserl's treatment of the pronoun "I" in detail. He came to see that his general approach to indexicals and demonstratives in the *Logical Investigations* was deficient. In a draft for a revision of the second edition (XIX, 2, pp. 812–816), he explores a revised view, and in the Preface to the second edition of *Ideas I* Husserl rejects his original theory of indexicality as a "*Gewaltstreich*." In the English translation, this is unfortunately rendered as tour de force. The context makes it clear that a more appropriate translation would be "act of violence."[18]

Hybrid Names

The first of the passages discussed in part 1 of this section, where Husserl says that "the signification [*Bedeutung*] of the word '*I*' can be gathered from the intuitive [*anschaulichen*] circumstances," hints at the view that Frege later expressed in 1914 in "Logic in Mathematics"[19] and then in 1918–1919 in "Thoughts,"[20] namely, that the circumstances of the utterance are part of the expression. Wolfgang Künne has in an article on Frege called this the theory of "hybrid names."[21]

Twin Earth

The passage I quoted earlier concerning "what human being cannot confound" occurs in a manuscript where Husserl discusses twin earth problems and other examples showing the inadequacy of his earlier theory of demonstratives (XXVI, p. 213.5–6). Husserl discusses in this manuscript the following problem: But what if two persons on two different celestial bodies in surroundings which appear to be completely similar represent 'the same' ['*dieselben*'] objects and orient accordingly 'the same' ['*dieselben*'] expressions? Doesn't the 'this' ['*dies*'] have a different signification in the two cases?" (XXVI, pp. 211.44–212.2). Husserl made several interesting observations about this and similar examples, without arriving at a satisfactory solution to the problems they raise.[22] Yet he saw the problems sixty years before anybody else, and he saw them clearly.

NOTES

1. "Husserl's Notion of Noema," *Journal of Philosophy* 66 (1969): 680–687. For more on this discussion, see also Ethel M. Kersey, "The Noema, Husserlian, and Beyond: An Annotated Bibliography of English Language Sources," *Philosophy Research Archives* 9 (1983): 62–90.

2. Bernard Bolzano, *Paradoxien des Unendlichen*, ed. F. Prihonsky (Berlin: Mayer and Müller, 1889; originally published 1851).

3. Bernard Bolzano, *Theory of Science*, abridged, ed. and trans. Rolf George (Berkeley: University of California Press, 1972, originally published 1837).

4. Roman numerals followed by page and sometimes also line numbers refer to the volumes in the *Husserliana* edition of Husserl's collected works, *Gesammelte Werke* (The Hague: Nijhoff, 1950–).

5. David Bell, "Reference, Experience, and Intentionality," in *Mind, Meaning and Mathematics: Essays on the Philosophical Views of Husserl and Frege*, ed. Leila Haaparanta (Dordrecht: Kluwer, 1994), pp. 185–209, hereafter Bell (1994).

6. All citations will be to volume two of *Logical Investigations*. Page numbers preceded by LU refer to *Logische Untersuchungen*, Zweiter Band, Erster Teil, *Husserliana*, vol. 19, no. 1 (The Hague: Nijhoff, 1984); page numbers preceded by LI refer to J. N. Findlay's English translation, *Logical Investigations* (London: Routledge and Kegan Paul, 1970).

7. Page numbers preceded by *Ideen I* refer to *Ideen zu einer reinen Phänomenologie und phänomenologischen Philosophie. Erstes Buch: Allgemeine Einführung in die reine Phänomenologie, Husserliana*, vol. III (The Hague: Nijhoff, 1976); page numbers preceded by *Ideas I* refer to F. Kersten's translation, *Ideas Pertaining to a Pure Phenomenology and to a Phenomenological Philosophy, Book 1: General Introduction to a Pure Phenomenology* (The Hague: Nijhoff, 1980).

8. "The Phenomenological Reduction as 'Epoche' and Explanation," in *Husserl: Expositions and Appraisals*, ed. F. A. Elliston and P. McCormick (Notre Dame: University of Notre Dame Press, 1977), pp. 338–349 (hereafter Küng 1977), p. 341.

9. Peter Geach, *Logic Matters* (Oxford: Blackwell, 1972), pp. 146–165.

10. John Perry, *The Problem of the Essential Indexical and Other Essays* (New York: Oxford University Press, 1993), pp. 81–89 and 242–244. See Christian Beyer, *Von Bolzano zu Husserl (Phenomenologica)* (The Hague: Nijhoff, 1996) (hereafter Beyer 1996), p. 180.

11. "Reactions," in *On Quine*, ed. Paolo Leonardi and Marco Santambrogio (Cambridge: Cambridge University Press, 1995), pp. 347–361, p. 350.

12. "From Stimulus to Science" (unpublished lecture delivered at Lehigh University, October 15, 1990), p. 21 of the manuscript; see also *From Stimulus to Science* (Cambridge, Mass.: Harvard University Press, 1995), pp. 35–40.

13. The English translation is *The Crisis of European Sciences and Transcendental Phenomenology*, trans. David Carr (Evanston, Ill.: Northwestern University Press, 1970), p. 142.

14. William James, *The Principles of Psychology*, vol. 2 (New York: Dover, 1950), p. 301.

15. See "Phenomenology," in *Handbook of Perception*, ed. Edward C. Carterette and Morton P. Friedman, vol. 1 (New York: Academic Press, 1974), pp. 377–386; "Brentano and Husserl on Intentional Objects and Perception," *Grazer philosophische Studien* 5 (1978): 83–94; "Husserl and Heidegger on the Role of Actions in the Constitution of the World," in *Essays in Honour of Jaakko Hintikka*, ed. E. Saarinen et al. (Dordrecht: Reidel, 1979), pp. 365–378; "Husserl on Evidence and Justification," in *Edmund Husserl and the Phenomenological Tradition: Essays in Phenomenology*, ed. Robert Sokolowski (Washington, D.C.: Catholic University of America Press, 1988), pp. 107–129.

16. For a discussion of Bolzano's view of indexicals, see Markus Textor, *Bolzanos Propositionalismus* (Berlin: de Gruyter, 1996), especially p. 125.

17. Gottlob Frege, *Logik*, in Frege, *Nachgelassene Schriften* (Hamburg: Felix Meiner Verlag, 1983).

18. I owe this observation to Christian Beyer (in discussion).

19. Gottlob Frege, "Logic in Mathematics," in *Posthumous Writings*, ed. Hans Hermes, Friedrich Kambartel, and Friedrich Kaulbach, trans. Peter Long and Roger White (Chicago: University of Chicago Press, 1979), pp. 203–250.

20. "Thoughts," in *Collected Papers: On Mathematics, Logic, and Philosophy*, ed. Brian McGuinness, trans. Max Black et al. (Oxford: Basil Blackwell, 1984), pp. 351–372

21. Wolfgang Künne, "Hybrid Proper Names," *Mind* 101 (1992): 721–731. See also Künne's "Indexikalität, Sinn und propositionaler Gehalt," *Grazer philosophische Studien* 18 (1983): 41–74.

22. For discussions of Husserl's view on indexicals, see Beyer (1996); David Smith, *The Circle of Acquaintance* (Dordrecht: Reidel, 1989); Wolfgang Künne, "The Nature of Acts—Moore on Husserl," in *The Analytic Tradition—Meaning, Thought and Knowledge*, ed. D. Bell and N. Cooper (Oxford: Blackwell, 1990), pp. 104–116; and K. Schumann, "Husserl's Theory of Indexicals," in *Phenomenology—East and West*, ed. F. M. Kirkland and D. P. Chattopadhyaya (Dordrecht: Kluwer, 1993), pp. 111–127. See also Ronald McIntyre, "Intending and Referring," in *Husserl, Intentionality and Cognitive Science*, ed. Hubert L. Dreyfus (Cambridge, Mass.: MIT Press, 1982), pp. 215–231.

4

Ernst Mach at the Crossroads of Twentieth-Century Philosophy

JAAKKO HINTIKKA

Who, historically speaking, was the central figure in the genesis of twentieth-century philosophy? The most prominent thinkers, such as Wittgenstein and Heidegger, stood on the shoulders of earlier giants (or dwarfs); my question is who these giants were at the bottom of things. Of analytic philosophers, the most popular answer to my question would undoubtedly be: Gottlob Frege. According to Frege's fans, he could claim the credit for helping to launch not only one but two of the main contemporary philosophical traditions: analytic philosophy through his work in logic and his philosophy of language and phenomenology through his influence on Husserl. But in sober historical reality such a claim on Frege's behalf is totally ahistorical. What is true is that Frege more than anyone else forged tools that subsequent philosophers, not only analytic ones, have wielded, and he thereby exerted tremendous influence on posterity. But Frege's direct influence on philosophy proper outside logic and the foundations of mathematics was minimal. His philosophy of language caught the eye of theorists only decades after his death, and its influence has in my estimation been far from healthy. Frege was a loner whose direct philosophical influence was for a long time minimal. The one early exception that proves the rule is his criticism of Husserl, which was instrumental in turning the father of phenomenology against psychologism. Yet even though that influence apparently was real, its general historical significance is seen to be considerably less earthshaking than it is sometimes thought when we realize that just about every professional German academic philosopher of that period professed antipsychologism (as Martin Kusch has demonstrated).[1]

Frege's alienation from some of the main philosophical currents of his day, including Husserl's way of thinking, is illustrated by his attitude toward intuition. Husserl's phenomenological reductions aimed at showing the basis of our entire structure of knowledge in the immediately given, which he called *Anschauung*. In contrast, Frege believed firmly that the human mind has access in pure thought to realities that do not reduce to the intuitively given.

Speaking generally, the question of whether all our knowledge is based on what is directly given to us in sense perception—and perhaps even reducible to it—was the overarching issue in the philosophy of science in the early years of this century. It was not merely an issue concerning philosophy as an academic discipline. At issue was to a large extent the question of how natural sciences like physics should be done. On the one hand, there were entire branches of physics such as statistical thermodynamics whose raison d'être lay in the assumption of unobservable entities, such as atoms and molecules. On the other hand, there were physicists like Ernst Mach who were trying to purge their discipline of all traffic in unobservables. This ambition led Mach to his famous criticisms of absolute space and time, which inspired Einstein's theory of relativity. But it also led Mach to reject atomism and a fortiori statistical thermodynamics, as developed by the likes of Boltzmann.

This confluence of the general philosophical problem of reducibility to the given and the problem of unobservable entities in the philosophy of science was the characteristic feature of the intellectual situation around the turn of the century on the continent. The main protagonists of the two opposing standpoints, Ernst Mach and Ludwig Boltzmann, were both philosophers as well as physicists. But both held academic appointments that specifically involved philosophy. Indeed, Boltzmann was Mach's successor in the chair at the University of Vienna devoted to "philosophy, especially the history and theory of inductive sciences." Both were also highly influential popularizers of their views whose writings were widely read by the general educated public. Their controversy was perceived as a true *gigantomachy* between two of the most prominent thinkers of the day. The controversy continued after Boltzmann's death as a dispute between Mach and Planck.

Einstein entered the fray primarily through his theory of relativity, which was initially perceived as a triumph of Machian ideas. But it is perhaps salutary to recall that Einstein's other two major achievements in the annus mirabilis of 1905—his analysis of Brownian movement and his contribution to turning the notion of quantum into a physical reality—were steps toward vindicating the kinds of physical realities that "phenomenological physicists" like Mach eschewed. And in his early work on thermodynamics Einstein followed Mach's great adversary, Ludwig Boltzmann, for whom he expressed great admiration.[2] One particularly interesting argument deployed by the likes of Boltzmann was that the very symbolism physicists used in effect codified assumptions going beyond the domain of observable facts. Boltzmann argued, for instance, that even the use of differential equations presupposes a large number of particular cases to which we have to apply a transition to the limit.[3] He was thus attuned to the assumptions that the very symbolism we use can smuggle into our thinking.

This confluence of scientific and philosophical issues thrust Ernst Mach into a central role unequaled in the development of twentieth-century philosophy. To my opening question, I therefore answer, Mach. Nobody is likely to claim that he was a great philosopher or a great physicist. He became, however, a highly influential exponent of ways of thinking that influenced not only the intellectual climate in turn-of-the-century Vienna but, more widely, twentieth-century philosophy in general.

As far as Mach's influence on Viennese intellectuals is concerned, one of the best informed observers, Hilde Spiel, testifies: "No account of the influence exercised by thinkers or creators in *fin de siècle* Vienna can fail to begin with Ernst Mach."[4] The force of this statement can be appreciated by noting that the other thinkers considered by Spiel include Freud, Adler, Karl Bühler, Weininger, and Herzl.

It is tempting to see the origins of twentieth-century philosophy in the new developments in logic and in the foundations of mathematics or in the various criticisms of idealism and psychologism. Besides such influences, however, there was, we see, the major issue of the reducibility of the entire edifice of our knowledge to immediate experience. Moreover, there is no doubt that this issue was more prominent in the consciousness of the academic community at large than was, for instance, the *Grundlagenkrisis* of mathematics. Ernst Mach's role in the reductivist discussion makes him a crucial figure in the background of twentieth-century philosophy, whether we like it or not. This paper is an attempt to sketch briefly some of the most salient aspects of Mach's role and influence.

I. On Mach As a Philosopher of Science

I will begin by taking a somewhat closer look at Mach's philosophy of science. Mach's ideas here not only show the small print of his empiricism, that is, his idea of reducing all our knowledge to the given. They illustrate more generally Mach's strengths and weaknesses as a philosopher.

For this purpose, I will examine an apparently minor problem. This example was chosen by Mach himself. It is of interest as a case study displaying the prospects of the kind of general reduction to direct experience that Mach was advocating. As a part of his campaign of eliminating theoretical terms from physics, Mach proposed to define mass in terms of the mutual acceleration of the bodies in question. Details need not detain us here. The basic idea is to think of any two particles A, B as forming a two-body system and to observe the accelerations due to their interaction. If we designate these accelerations $a_{A/B}$ and $a_{B/A}$, then we can define mass ratios as

$$m_{A/B} = \frac{a_{B/A}}{a_{A/B}}$$

Then it is an experiential fact that each such quantity can be represented as the ratio of two constants:

$$m_{A/B} = \frac{m_A}{m_B}$$

where m_A and m_B can be defined as the masses of A and B (or, rather, proportional to the masses of A and B). Thus we can according to Mach *define* mass in terms of the observables of Newtonian mechanics. Mach sums up his view in the famous slogan that mass is nothing but a parameter "that merely satisfies an important equation." Later, H. A. Simon sought to systematize Mach's ideas.[5]

Logically sophisticated philosophers eventually became suspicious, however, of Mach's and Simon's claims. Indeed, taken literally, these claims are simply not valid. In 1953, J. C. C McKinsey, A. C. Sugar, and Patrick Suppes proved the indefinability (in the normal logical sense of the word) of mass in an explicit axiomatization of classical particle mechanics.[6] Their work has prompted some philosophers to dismiss Mach's ideas altogether. For instance, Mario Bunge speaks contemptuously of "Mach's mistakes" which could easily be corrected "with the assistance of a bit of logic."[7]

It is not clear, however, who is in need of a tad of logic here. It is amply clear from statements of both Mach and Simon that neither has in mind anything like the strict logical concept of definability. This concept amounts to the derivability of an explicit definition from an underlying theory—meaning that theory alone. In the case of classical particle mechanics, a strictly logical definition of mass would involve the derivability of an explicit definition of mass (one couched in terms of the other primitives) from the classical theory alone. Over and against the strict logical concept of definability, Mach and Simon explicitly have in mind the possibility of fixing the assignment of masses to particles, not on the basis of the theory alone, but on the basis of theory plus suitable observations. This procedure does not satisfy the logicians' notion of definability, but it can be characterized in perfectly explicit logical terms.[8] In fact, it is a generalization of econometricians' concept of identifiability. A parameter is identifiable on the basis of an economic theory if and only if its value can be determined on the basis of the theory plus possible data. In fact, Simon says that his concept of definability is tantamount to statisticians' notion (with which he was of course familiar from econometrics). Unfortunately, neither Mach nor Simon had the logical wherewithal explicitly to characterize the concept of definability they were presupposing. (Simon attempted to loosen up the usual concept of definability, but his ideas are unworkable.)

Once the nature of the notion Mach had in mind is understood, it is in fact possible to show that mass is identifiable under certain conditions. This was shown by Pendse in 1939.[9]

A little bit of logic, then, is all that is needed to show that Mach's ideas on the role of mass in classical mechanics are not simply mistaken, but viable. That it is needed, however, also betrays a major lack of conceptual sophistication on his part. Furthermore, the identifiability of mass in classical particle mechanics does not have the consequences Mach in effect claimed that it did. For instance, it does not imply that mass is eliminable as a primitive term, as Mach seems to have thought. Mach's insights into the conceptual structure of science, perceptive though they were, were not sharp enough to sustain his overall reductivist theory of science. Even worse, Mach's lack of sufficiently strong logical tools is not just a cosmetic defect, but led him to substantially wrong conclusions.

In this respect, it seems to me, the problem of the definability (and identifiability) of mass serves as a small-scale but representative example of Mach's strengths and weaknesses as a philosopher in general. This case study shows among other things that Mach's somewhat simplistic ideas about the relationship of our scientific knowledge to its experiential basis cannot be attributed only to his general phenomenalistic or phenomenological position in philosophy. They also involved what I consider to be a serious mistake concerning the different ways in which a concept can be determined by observational and other experiential evidence. This point requires a few additional comments.

To a considerable extent, Mach's confusions have burdened later discussions too. The notion of identifiability slowly crystallized in the work of econometricians only in the 1930s and 1940s,[10] and it still does not belong to the standard conceptual equipment of philosophers of science. Its potential uses can be illustrated by a couple of examples. Suppose a theory contains a number of observation concepts $O_1, O_2, \ldots$, and a number of *prima facie* theoretical (not directly observable) concepts $H_1, H_2, \ldots$ It may happen that $H_1, H_2, \ldots$ are not definable in terms of $O_1, O_2, \ldots$, given the underlying theory T; but the question remains open whether they are identifiable in terms of the theory plus suitable observations concerning $O_1, O_2, \ldots$ Indeed, this question of identifiability can be highly important in actual theorizing. For if $H_1, H_2, \ldots$ are not identifiable, the theory and the observable "boundary conditions" cannot completely determine what happens in the world, even theoretically.

Conversely, if $H_1, H_2, \ldots$ are identifiable, it might seem that an empiricist should be completely satisfied. For the applicability of all relevant concepts is empirically determinable. But—and this is characteristic of him—Mach would not be satisfied. For the values of an identifiable concept, he would say, need not be directly observable. They may be fixed only on the assumption that the given theory is true. And that theory may again not be directly verifiable or falsifiable. It may be a free theoretical construction.

The failure of mass to be definable in Newtonian mechanics, though not a simple mistake, is thus a serious blow against Mach's philosophy of science. For as these considerations show, he needs a definable concept of mass, not merely an identifiable one.

These observations also put a sharper light on Mach's relationship to other scientists. Physicists such as Boltzmann and Hertz were not anti-empirical. They, too, required that physicists' theories be connected with experience. But for Boltzmann and Hertz that connection had the form of a theoretical—typically mathematical—structure, with its symbolic system of representation. Mach eschewed all such representational systems; indeed, one of his favorite refrains was a complaint about the excessive use of mathematics in physical science.

Mach's wish to avoid reliance upon heavy mathematics was not only a matter of intellectual taste. If all of the theoretical concepts figuring in a scientific theory could be explicitly defined, no heavy mathematical apparatus would be needed to mediate between such theoretical concepts and experience. But if the mathematical structure of a theory is needed as an indispensable framework of identification, the role of mathematics in science becomes much more important philosophically. This is, then, a substantial philosophical issue.

Mach's attitude toward the use of mathematics in physics also determined his relations to Einstein's theory of relativity. Einstein himself acknowledged Mach's influence on the development of the special theory of relativity. What's more, Einstein's later thought displays themes suggesting, if not Mach's direct influence, at the least a close affinity to Mach's ideas. An example is Einstein's quest for what he called *Eindeutigkeit* (uniqueness) in developing his general theory of relativity. This subject has recently been discussed in an interesting way by Don Howard.[11] Einstein's requirement of *Eindeutigkeit* implies that "the course of events in the gravitational field be completely determined by means of the laws that are to be established."[12]

This principle of uniqueness might seem to be congenial to Mach. It seems to require for events what Mach's concept of definability requires for theoretical concepts. But a second look quickly reveals a disagreement with Mach's ideas. No theory ever specifies a unique course of events in the world *simpliciter*. The determination will have to be relative to suitable initial conditions or to other contingent observable truths about the world. For this reason, the uniqueness requirement cannot be understood, *pace* Howard, as an anticipation of the logicians' concept of categoricity according to which all models satisfying a given theory are isomorphic. Uniqueness is related to categoricity rather in analogy to the relation of identifiability to definability. This analogy illustrates significant differences between Mach and the mature Einstein.

Mach's relation to Einstein's theory of relativity, especially to the general theory, has provoked a great deal of discussion and dispute.[13] Mach explicitly rejected the theory of relativity in the preface to his *Principles of Physical Optics*, dated July 1913. The significance of this rejection has been questioned, and it has even been branded a forgery. But on my account, it should not come as a surprise to anyone. Einstein's keen sense of physical reality led him to realize that the Machian project of interpreting physical concepts through direct measurement was too restrictive. In particular, in developing the general theory of relativity, Einstein was forced to give up any direct interpretation of the coordinates, even of an inertial system, in terms of direct measurement (Holton 1992, p. 271). Hence, it is not at all surprising that Mach should have rejected the ideas that eventually led Einstein to the general theory of relativity.

II. Vienna Circle: Machian Neopositivism, or Logical Empiricism?

The role of Mach as a source of inspiration to the Vienna Circle and to logical neopositivism in general is so obvious and well known that in this instance it is more appropriate to clarify the differences than the similarities. The similarities come to a head in the frequent assimilation of the Vienna Circle to the association entitled "Verein Ernst Mach." As Friedrich Stadler has shown, it is nevertheless important to keep the two apart.[14] Running together Mach and the Vienna Circle misplaces Mach in the history of thought.

One way of approaching their differences is terminological. The philosophy of the Vienna Circle is often referred to as "logical positivism." The underlying idea of this appellation is presumably that the logic of the Vienna Circle was contributed by Frege, Russell, and Hilbert while the positivism of the Circle was Mach's heritage. However, several members of the Vienna Circle and their allies preferred the label "logical empiricism." It is not generally known where and how this term originated; it was, to the best of my knowledge, launched by the Finnish philosopher Eino Kaila well before he had visited Vienna and taken part in the activities of the Vienna Circle. His choice of the term was calculated to mark a contrast to Machian positivism. G. H. von Wright writes in his introduction to Eino Kaila's *Reality and Experience: Four Philosophical Essays*:

> Kaila calls his position logical empiricism. ([Kaila 1926], p. 35.) It should be remembered that the year of publication of [his *Die Prinzipien der Wahrscheinlichkeitslogik*] was 1926. According to Kaila's logical empiricist view in [this book], all knowledge which is not formal (logical, mathematical) is based on experiential data which, in the last resort, are given to us *hic et nunc* in sense-experience. The "tie" between the basis and the higher strata of empirical knowledge is *probabilistic*. The logic of knowledge which is to replace traditional epistemology is a probability logic (*ibid.*, p. 34). In order to possess a probability, however, an empirical proposition must imply something which can be given in sensory experience (*ibid.*, p. 152). Kaila calls this requirement the Principle of Possible Experience (*Prinzip der Erfahrbarkeit*). It is a consequence, he says (*ibid.*), of his view of the probability relation as subsisting between a hypothesis and some given truths.
>
> Kaila does not claim absolute novelty for his empiricistic principle. He sees a forerunner of it in Leibniz's *principe de l'observabilité* and in some thoughts which guided Einstein in the construction of relativity theory. He also refers to what Johan von Kries had called the Principle of Interpretation in his *Logik* (1916)—a nowadays undeservedly neglected work.
>
> Kaila recognizes the affinity of his standpoint to positivism (*ibid.*, p. 159*ff.*). But he also notes an important difference. Positivism, he says (p. 159), confuses the fact that every proposition about reality must *imply* some experiential consequences with the requirement that the proposition should be about objects given in direct experience. Therefore traditional positivism has been hostile to the atomic hypothesis. Kaila is thinking of the Mach-Boltzmann controversy over the "reality" of atoms. To this reductionist version of positivism Kaila was always strongly opposed.[15]

It is also significant that the actual members of the Vienna Circle were not all followers of Mach. A certain caution is in order here, for Mach's phenomenological epistemology did not necessarily imply a phenomenalistic ontology. So one could go along with him in epistemology but reject his ontology. And sometimes the Circlers even rejected his epistemology. What was at issue for instance in the Mach-Boltzmann controversy was not the problem of idealism versus realism, but the dispensability of theoretical concepts in science. Nevertheless, even though logical empiricists realized as much, they sometimes found themselves agreeing with Boltzmann and Planck rather than with Mach. Hans Hahn is a case in point. He in fact praises Boltzmann for insisting that "observationally 'unconstitutable terms' (such as atoms, electrons, protons, quanta) should also have a legitimate role in science" and felt that "one should 'in this controversy take Boltzmann's side.'"[16]

Neurath, in another wing of the so-called logical positivist movement, was a materialist who could not swallow a phenomenological epistemology any more than a phenomenalistic ontology. For Carnap a phenomenological basis language was not much more than one possibility among many. Finally, the Circle's general acceptance of a physicalistic basis language—partly under the influence of Neurath on the one hand and of Wittgenstein on the other—marked a sharp departure from Mach's idea that the basis was always the experientially given.

The true similarities and dissimilarities between Mach and the logical positivists are shown by their constructive philosophical work, especially in their work on the problem of constitution. This is a larger subject than can be adequately dealt with here, but a few general remarks may nevertheless be in order. Mach's problem of defining all our empirical concepts in terms of the given seems to be alive and well in Carnap's *Der logische Aufbau der Welt*. But even there we find a discrepancy, for Carnap allows himself the unlimited use of a logical and mathematical conceptual apparatus. And when the logical positivists retreated from the principle of verifiability, they were in effect abandoning the Machian program. Unfortunately, they were to some extent still victims of Mach's curse, for they never developed fully adequate logical and mathematical tools, for instance an explicit concept of identifiability.

III. Mach and Husserl

The late Dutch philosopher and logician E. W. Beth was not an admirer of Husserl. In his lectures, Beth went so far as to accuse Husserl "of having stolen his most important [phenomenological] ideas from Mach's lecture on the principle of comparison in physics, which was reviewed by Edmund Husserl in 1897."[17] One may raise one's eyebrows at Beth's conspiratorial hypothesis and at his moralizing tone, but one cannot deny his acumen. For, unbeknownst to Beth, another philosopher had before him emphatically pointed out Mach's crucial influence on Husserl. This philosopher is Husserl himself. In his Amsterdam lectures, Husserl remarks:

> Around the turn of the century there grew out of the struggle of philosophy and psychology for a strictly scientific method a new science, hand in hand with a new method of philosophical and psychological research. The new science was called *phenomenology*, the reason being that it and its new method arose through a certain radicalization of the phenomenological method that had earlier been propagated and used by individual natural scientists and psychologists. The gist [*Sinn*] of this method, as it was used by men like Mach and Hering, consisted in a reaction against the bottomless theorizing that threatened the so-called "exact" sciences. It was a reaction against theorizing that used unintuitive conceptualizations and mathematical speculations.[18]

Husserl is talking here about natural sciences like physics and of their philosophy. He adds that, "Parallel to this we find some psychologists, in the first place

Brentano, striving to create systematically a strictly scientific psychology based on pure inner experience and on a strict description of what is given in it" (IX, p. 303). Husserl explicitly recognizes also the terminological continuity between his own thinking and that of his "phenomenological" predecessors: "Hence the radicalization of these methodological developments (which incidentally were often already called phenomenological) was what led to a new methodology of purely psychological [*psychisch*] research" (p. 303). Thus Beth was essentially right about the significance of Mach's influence on Husserl, though he was unaware that Husserl had himself acknowledged this influence.

It is even more telling that Husserl's *Encyclopedia Britannica* article summarizing his philosophy includes a similar account of his phenomenology's genesis:

> The term "phenomenology" designates two things: a new kind of descriptive method which made a breakthrough in philosophy at the turn of the century, and an *a priori* science derived from it, a science which is intended to supply the basic instrument (*Organon*) for a rigorous scientific philosophy and, in its consequent application, to make possible a methodical reform of all the sciences. Together with this philosophical phenomenology, but not yet separated from it, however, there also came into being a new psychological discipline parallel to it in method and content.[19]

The passage from the Amsterdam lectures is merely a lightly expanded restatement of the same explanation of the origin of Husserl's phenomenology.

But there is even more evidence of the strength of Husserl's conviction that his phenomenology was a further development of the ideas of philosophers of science like Mach. This conviction was expressed by Husserl in the first of his four drafts of the *Encyclopedia Britannica* article. "By *phenomenology*," he wrote, "one understands the philosophical movement that grew up around the turn of the century and that aims at a radical reconstruction of scientific philosophy and, through it, of all sciences" (IX, p. 237). Alas, this statement of creed was not in line with the subversive purposes of Heidegger, who was assisting Husserl in his work on the *Britannica* article. In the second version of the article, Heidegger replaced Husserl's terse references to turn-of-the-century philosophy of science with a lengthy discourse on phenomenology as a successor of the preoccupation of ancient Greek thinkers with being as being (see IX, pp. 256–257). Husserl did not want to say anything like that, however, and he quickly restored the original idea in an expanded form.

Mach has not received much attention as a precursor of and an influence on Husserl. The reason is, I think, obvious. Neither the self-entitled phenomenologists nor many positivists have found it politically correct to emphasize the Mach-Husserl link. The extremes of this neglect can be gauged by the recent *Encyclopedia of Phenomenology*.[20] In this literally encyclopedic work, the name of Ernst Mach does not even occur in the index. Seldom, if ever, has a major philosophical movement so completely denied its own parentage.

The main exception to this neglect is the work of Manfred Sommer.[21] Sommer repeatedly emphasizes the closeness of Husserl's ideas to early positivism and notes that, even in Husserl's criticism of Mach, there is an element of self-criticism (Sommer 1988, p. 311). By and large, Sommer is nevertheless primarily interested in the perceptual (experiential) basis of our knowledge, as the title of his 1987 book, *Evidenz im Augenblick*, goes to show. It seems to me, though, that the similarities and differences between Mach and Husserl—as well as between Mach and other philosophers—are more directly revealed by their views of how the rest of our knowledge is constituted from the given.

It is sometimes claimed that Mach did not distinguish between the "natural attitude" and the phenomenological reduction and was not, therefore, a significant precursor of Husserl. But Mach does make a distinction that is in some ways comparable with Husserl's. Blackmore describes its terms as the "common sense approach to reference" and "referential phenomenalism."[22] In view of the similarity between Husserlian intentionality and Fregean reference emphasized especially forcefully by Føllesdal, it does not seem farfetched to see in Mach's distinction a partial precursor of Husserl's contrast. True, Mach pays relatively little attention to the transition from the common-sense approach to the phenomenalist approach to reference. But this is an outgrowth of Mach's shallow view of the knowledge which is constituted from the given.

Much more important than the distinction between the natural and the phenomenological attitudes is the nature of the connection between experience and theory. For Mach, all we need to do is to describe the given. For Husserl, in contrast, there are components that cannot be described in their pure unedited state, especially what Husserl called the hyletic data. We have to impose forms on these before they may be articulated in terms of categorially structured particulars, properties, relations, etc. This constitutive process has no counterpart in Mach.

IV. Mach and Wittgenstein

There is a third way in which Mach's ideas came to be utilized in subsequent philosophy. This way is through Wittgenstein's *Tractatus*.[23]

At first sight, such an influence might seem unlikely. Wittgenstein is known to have had a very low opinion of Mach as a thinker and as a writer. He once said to Russell that Mach's writings made him "sick." By contrast, Wittgenstein held Mach's great opponent Boltzmann in high esteem and explicitly counted Boltzmann among the thinkers who had influenced him most strongly. Accordingly, commentators and historians have paid but scant attention to Mach's influence on Wittgenstein.

We have to appreciate, though, the subtlety of Wittgenstein's famous list of those who most influenced him.[24] In this list, Wittgenstein is not speaking of doctrinal influences. For there are no philosophical ideas, views, or concepts that Wittgenstein owed to Kraus, Loos, Weininger, or Spengler. It is even hard to pinpoint any major influences of this kind that could be traced to Boltzmann, Hertz, Schopenhauer, or Sraffa. Of the two remaining thinkers on the list, Frege and Russell, neither understood Wittgenstein's thinking by Wittgenstein's own lights.

This incomprehension is attested to in Russell's case by Wittgenstein, and in Frege's case by Frege himself, whose letters to Wittgenstein confess his puzzlement.

No, the kind of influence Wittgenstein's list acknowledges is inspiration or encouragement to think his own thoughts. For influences in the sense of shared assumptions, we must look elsewhere. An interesting case in point is G. E. Moore, whose name does not appear on the list and of whom Wittgenstein also had a low opinion. In spite of this lack of esteem of Moore as a thinker and writer, it is impossible to understand Wittgenstein's thought—and not only his early philosophy, I believe—without realizing to what extent Wittgenstein shared Moore's idea, elaborated by Russell in his theory of acquaintance, that the basic building-blocks of one's world are the objects of different experiences. Such a view does not make much sense without Moore's "refutation of idealism" and, more specifically, without his sharp distinction between the object of any one experience and that experience itself. This subterranean influence of Moore emerges even in Wittgenstein's detailed views. I have argued (together with Merrill B. Hintikka) that Wittgenstein's ethics and aesthetics in the *Tractatus* are but variations of Moore's themes.[25]

Wittgenstein's list of "influences" thus does not reflect awareness of the true historical *locus* of his own thought. He himself was unaware of what he was taking for granted and where, to speak with Collingwood, his "ultimate presuppositions" came from. These presuppositions are not easy to recognize. Certainly Wittgenstein does not articulate them, let alone highlight them. They have to be gathered by placing Wittgenstein on the map of philosophical currents of his time.

In my view, Wittgenstein's relation to Mach is not unlike his relation to Moore. There are, I hold, at least three major assumptions Wittgenstein shared with Mach. I will not try to establish in this paper whether Wittgenstein actually took them over from Mach or whether they were a part of the *Zeitgeist* Mach had been instrumental in creating. But I will say this much: if we subtract Boltzmann's and Hertz's influence, what remains of Wittgenstein's philosophy of science in the *Tractatus* is Mach's philosophy.

The three ideas I will briefly discuss are: (1) the idea that a priori truths of logic and mathematics are tautological; (2) Wittgenstein's peculiar notion of solipsism; and (3) the idea that empirical science is merely descriptive.

1. Wittgenstein maintained in the *Tractatus* that all (and only) logical truths are tautological. This view is itself a near tautology, given the rest of Wittgenstein's views in the *Tractatus*. All there is to our *Sprachlogik* in the last analysis is, according to him, truth-functional logic. And in truth-functional logic the only logical truths are those propositions that admit all distributions of truth-values to atomic propositions, in other words, that do not exclude any possibility as to what the world might be like. They cannot help being true. Since they do not exclude any possibilities, however, they do not convey any information either.

What are the antecedents of such a view? There is not anything remotely like it in Frege or early Russell. For both of them, the truths of logic are truths about the actual world. Frege admittedly labeled them analytic, but this does not invalidate my point, though it serve as a strong warning not to confuse the concepts "tautological" and "analytic" with each other. Tautological means for

Wittgenstein "uninformative" or "empty." In contrast, "analytic" contains a reference to the way in which the truth of a proposition can be ascertained. Indeed, Russell later claimed to have been shocked by Wittgenstein's tautologicity thesis, in a way that he never was shocked by Frege's purported reduction of arithmetic to analytic truths.

Yet in Wittgenstein's continental context there was little shock value to his claim that logical truths are uninformative. Indeed, the equivalent thesis that all logical inferences are pleonastic was familiar to every reader of Mach's *Erkenntnis und Irrtum* (1905). In the chapter on "Deduktion und Induktion in psychologischer Beleuchtung," Mach argues at some length for that very conclusion. Reflecting on the reasoning required to prove the geometrical theorem of the external angles of a triangle, Mach writes: "But if we carefully remove from our representations [*Vorstellungen*] everything that has not ended up there as an ingredient of the construction or through specialization rather than through the syllogism itself, we find in them nothing but the mere [premises of the syllogism]."[26] A little later, he concludes: "Syllogism and induction hence do not create any new knowledge" (Mach 1905, p. 307). Such views were widespread in German-language philosophy. Another example is found in Moritz Schlick's *Allgemeine Erkenntnislehre* (1918), where Schlick maintains that "all strict, all deductive inference is of analytic nature."[27] And from the context (§14 is entitled "Die analytische Natur des strengen Schliessens"), it can be inferred that analyticity for Schlick entails the absence of all new knowledge.

I am not saying that Wittgenstein got his idea of tautologicity from Mach in any simple sense. Rather it is a "logical" outgrowth of Wittgenstein's belief in truth-functional logic, more specifically, in its exhaustiveness as the logic of our language. I do want to underscore, though, that in historical perspective it is clear that with regard to the emptiness of logical truths Mach, Schlick, and Wittgenstein were members of a tradition to which Frege and Russell did not belong.

Moreover, the realization that Wittgenstein belonged to the Mach-Schlick tradition in virtue of his general background provides an interesting perspective on his development. For example, How was Wittgenstein led to his idea of tautology? Was it his solution to the decision problem for propositional logic?[28] Or was it his "a-b notation" for propositional logic? In spite of the importance of these innovations, it seems to me that they are secondary in relation to Wittgenstein's idea of tautologies as exhausting all possibilities. Wittgenstein's idea of considering all the different distributions of truth-values to elementary propositions was the main application of his thesis that the propositions of logic are tautological, and a decision method for logic was only a by-product of this work. There are perfectly respectable senses in which the truths of first-order logic may be taken as tautological in the sense of admitting all possibilities, even though there is no decision procedure for first-order logic.[29] The tautology thesis, I contend, is also not a corollary of Wittgenstein's "a-b notation." In my view, this notation is best viewed as a way of implementing the tautology thesis. The import of this thesis is also totally independent of whether Wittgenstein (or anyone else) holds that tautologies are "nonsensical" or "senseless," whether logic is conventional, or whether logical connectives can be thought of merely as means of picture construction.[30] On my reading, Wittgenstein's comments about how logical truth is established are all about the (un)informativeness problem. What he called the "a-b notation" shows the uninformativeness for propositional compounds. For in truth-functional propositional logic, tautologies—that is, propositions that agree with all truth-value distributions of elementary propositions—literally exhaust all possibilities concerning the world and hence do not say anything. But Wittgenstein also had to show that all logical truths were such tautologies (and to develop a notation that would show it). What is crucial here is the role of the tautology thesis in the argumentative structure of the *Tractatus*. Wittgenstein needed the idea that logical truths exhaust all possibilities for his attempted extension of the picture theory from elementary propositions to all others.[31] This meant making sure that elementary propositions were independent of each other. Wittgenstein's comments on identity were calculated to contribute to this project by reducing certain apparently nontautological truths of logic to overt tautologies. But in the end, Wittgenstein could not give any general argument to the effect that all logical (conceptual) truths—for instance, color incompatibilities—can be translated into a jargon making their vacuousness blatant.

Again, what has misled many philosophers, in my view, is an unfortunate and ahistorical confusion between the meanings of the terms "analytic" and "tautological." They mean entirely different things. "Analytic" refers to the way a proposition can be established. "Tautological" refers to the information (or, rather, to the lack thereof) that a proposition conveys. These are entirely different ideas. For example, in early modern science, analytic rather than synthetic methods were the main engines of discovering new truths. Later on, Frege maintained that mathematical truths are analytic, that is, can be established by purely logical means. But at the same time, he maintained that logical truths are the most general truths about the world and hence informative. Thus Frege's thesis of the purely analytic character of logical and mathematical truths is in no way equivalent to or an even partial anticipation of Wittgenstein's idea of the tautological character of logical truths. What is remarkable about Mach's and Schlick's anticipations of Wittgenstein's thesis of the tautological character of logic is that they are, in so many words, dealing with the uninformativeness of logical truths, not their analyticity.

Some commentators have claimed that the Vienna Circle misconstrued Wittgenstein's thesis that all logical truths are tautologies. But this claim misses the true dialectic of events. Wittgenstein was merely a member of a long tradition (which included earlier positivists like Mach) when he insisted that logically (conceptually) necessary truths are vacuous. What is peculiar to the *Tractatus* is Wittgenstein's defense of this view by means of his interpretation of all logic as at bottom truth-functional. This defense does not in any way depend on the idiosyncratic notation Wittgenstein happened to use. Wittgenstein gave up this "logic of tautologies" in 1928–1929, but he continued to maintain the factual uninformativeness of logically necessary propositions. The logical positivists did not and could not restrict their logic to truth-function theory, where the tautology thesis was obvious. Their second line of defense was to argue for the conventionalism of logical truths.

2. To my mind, the most intriguing similarity between Mach and Wittgenstein is in what they say about solipsism and the "I." In describing Mach's influence on *fin de siècle* Viennese intellectuals, Hilde Spiel notes first and foremost Mach's concept of self: "Mach maintains that the ego is not a substantial entity but a complex of sensory perceptions. Since its thoughts, sentiments, moods and memories are structured differently every day the self has merely relative continuity. . . . Also, for that reason, it cannot be held responsible for its actions" (Spiel 1987, p. 134). I will argue that this is neither an exhaustive, nor a fully accurate description of Mach's views. The reason I quote Spiel is that she gives a vivid idea of the views that were in the air in Wittgenstein's Vienna. Against that background, several of the tenets of Wittgenstein's *Tractatus* can be seen as, not the bold novelties they are sometimes taken to be, but little more than restatements of views that were current among his contemporaries. I read Wittgenstein's statements about the self in the *Tractatus* as cases in point. I have suggested earlier in Hintikka and Hintikka (1986) that Wittgenstein's solipsism in the *Tractatus* is best understood as a corollary to his phenomenological standpoint. According to this standpoint, my ontology consists ultimately of the objects (of different logical types) that are given to me in my direct experience. Just like Russell's sense-data, these are real objects, not phenomenal shadows. I have to have these objects and *ergo* these experiences in order to understand my own language—the only language I understand. But though the objects are perfectly real, they are objects of my *own* experience. And in so far as I can identify myself with the totality of my experiences, I am my world (5.63) in the sense that all objects in my world are objects of my experience. Moreover, there is nothing apart from this totality that I can identify myself with, philosophically speaking, for my empirical ego is merely one contingent object among others.

What is especially interesting here is the connection between the idea of solipsism and the problem of identifying the self, the ego. David Pears earlier called attention to this connection, although in a manner different from mine.[32] Now this connection and its relation of a kind of solipsism is explicit in Mach. The basic outlook is likewise essentially the same for both Mach and Wittgenstein. For Wittgenstein, reality is fundamentally the totality of (the objects of) my experiences; for Mach, it is the totality of my "sensations," a term Mach uses in a very wide sense. Furthermore, for Mach as well as for Wittgenstein, the phenomenological or, as Mach called it, phenomenalistic ontology was necessitated by semantical considerations. Thus, according to Blackmore: "Mach was frequently if not normally a referential phenomenalist, that is, unlike Kant and John Stuart Mill . . . , Mach often assumed that it was only possible to refer 'meaningfully' either to what was being consciously experienced or to what could be consciously experienced" (1972, p. 32). This is not to say that Mach was entirely clear about his own reasons for holding phenomenalism or clear about what precisely his view was. However, these confusions do not undermine the parallel I am drawing between Mach's and Wittgenstein's standpoints.

Both Mach and Wittgenstein faced the task of finding a niche, if any, for the ego in an experiential (phenomenological) ontology. Blackmore describes Mach's views by way of two different reference concepts, which Mach used, according to Blackmore, in parallel:

In terms of his common sense theory of reference the "ego" did not exist at all. There was no "I" or "self." There were merely sensations related in different ways. This "definition" served as Mach's justification for denying that he was an "idealist" or a follower of George Berkeley. Mach's second definition, which was in terms of his referential phenomenalism, allowed for two "egos," a "narrow" one and an "inclusive" one. The narrow ego consisted of those sensations which phenomenalists identify with a particular person, while the "large" or "inclusive" ego meant the totality of all sensations. (Blackmore 1972, p. 35)

Wittgenstein's position can be described as denying the philosophically privileged status of the narrow conception of the ego. According again to Blackmore, Mach had some sympathy with such a denial: "he did not think it possible to demarcate with complete clarity between a 'narrow' ego and the physical environment around it" (Blackmore 1972, pp. 35–36).

Mach's "inclusive" ego is strikingly similar to Wittgenstein's solipsistic ego in the *Tractatus*. It should not be surprising, then, that Mach too faced the accusation of solipsism. His defense is reminiscent of the *Tractatus*—or should I say vice versa? Blackmore writes: "Mach now had a defense against the possible charge of solipsism. . . . For if there were no 'ego' (and there was none in terms of his common sense theory of reference), then there was no 'self' to be alone in the universe and hence no solipsism" (Blackmore 1972, p. 36). This defense may be compared with Wittgenstein's, who apparently offers a diametrically opposite explanation of his conception of the ego:

The world and life are one. (5.621)

I am my world. (5.63)

The I in solipsism shrinks to an extensionless point and there remains the reality coordinated with it. How can the entire world shrink to an extensionless point in solipsism? The answer is that Wittgenstein's philosophical (as opposed to empirical) I is like Mach's "inclusive"ego. It is the totality of the objects of my experiences—"the limit" of my experience, as Wittgenstein puts it. But I do not, so to speak, play any role in the life of the objects of my experience. They are mine only in the sense of being coordinated with me. Wittgenstein's philosophical "I" therefore disappears in the same way as Mach's "inclusive" ego.

To repeat, Mach's narrower ego corresponds to Wittgenstein's empirical self, which he dismisses as being philosophically irrelevant: "An experiencing, thinking subject does not exist" (5.631). This similarity between Wittgenstein and Mach is not accidental. For it too is based on the similarity of their respective experiential ontologies.

3. Many of Mach's and the early Wittgenstein's views spring from a common source. Both believed, I hold, that the world consists of the objects of immediate experience and that the task of our language, including the symbolism of mathematics, is to enable us to speak of that world without distorting it or adding

anything to the description. What distinguished the early Wittgenstein from Mach, on my reading, is the former's appreciation of the difficulties faced by Mach's program. These entailed showing that the entire system of mathematical representation used in the sciences does not depend on any factual assumptions for its applicability. That it does not is far from clear. Indeed, Boltzmann challenged the phenomenological physicists like Mach on this very point. Mach and others had spoken of the differential equations of mathematical physics as if they were just another method of description. But Boltzmann argued (see 1974, p. 97) that the assumptions on which the use of differential equations depends include assumptions about the limit behavior of a large number of discrete atomistic phenomena. In the same spirit, with an explicit reference to Boltzmann, Hilbert had challenged mathematicians in his sixth problem to formulate physical theories in an axiomatic form in such a way that all factual presuppositions were codified into explicit axioms.[33] Wittgenstein later characterized his work in the *Tractatus* as that of a "logician." There is precious little logic in the technical sense in the *Tractatus*, but there is a great deal of philosophy of logic in it. Indeed, it might be said that the *Tractatus* is an attempt to show that Hilbert's sixth problem could be solved by logical analysis. On my reading, Wittgenstein believed that all mathematics could be expressed in the notation of Whitehead and Russell's *Principia* or, rather, in a corrected form of their logic. And he tried to show that this logic is, at bottom, the logic of truth-functions. Since he also believed that this exhausts our *Sprachlogik*—that is, that the only logical truths are truth-functional tautologies—he concluded to his own satisfaction that the challenges of Boltzmann, Hilbert, and also Hertz could be surmounted through a logical analysis of language. He also thought that these problems could be solved in favor of Mach, over Boltzmann. Wittgenstein thus was not hostile to Mach's conclusions. Rather, his objection was that Mach did not see the problem, let alone solve it.

The same observations serve to put into perspective Wittgenstein's remarks on the philosophy of science in the *Tractatus*. The overall position they reflect scarcely differs, I contend, from Machian positivism. For Wittgenstein, science is purely descriptive. There are no inviolable causal laws in science in the usual sense. Instead, calling a law causal is merely an indication of its form (6.321). There are no explanations in science (6.371) nor any inductive logic (6.363). Induction has only psychological justification (6.3631). (Compare Mach's "Psychologie der Forschung.") Laws of nature are not necessary (6.362). The only necessity is logical necessity (6.37), but that is factually uninformative, for logical truths are tautological. All this is in keeping with Mach's philosophy. Wittgenstein's recognition of the role of simplicity in science even draws him close to Mach's "economy of thought."

Thus, what distinguishes Wittgenstein's remarks in the *Tractatus* on science from Mach's ideas are not his doctrines, but the direction of his interest. For both thinkers, science is purely descriptive. But Wittgenstein is more intensely interested in the means of description actually used in science. This is only to be expected given the overall plan of the *Tractatus*, which called upon Wittgenstein to show that the linguistic, mathematical, and other symbolic means of representation do not contribute any a priori elements to our knowledge. It is also to be expected of an admirer of Boltzmann and Hertz, for they were keenly interested in the modes of representation used in science. Accordingly, Wittgenstein examines the forms of representation used in and outside of science:

> We do not have an *a priori* belief in a law of conservation, but rather *a priori* knowledge of the possibility of a logical form. (6.33)

> All such propositions, including the principle of sufficient reason, the laws of continuity in nature and of least effort in nature, etc. etc.—all these are *a priori* insights about the forms in which the proposition of science can be cast. (6.34)

It is this deep interest in our modes of representation that sets Wittgenstein apart from Mach as a philosopher of science. Ironically, the ultimate aim Wittgenstein had in the *Tractatus* was to show that those modes of representation do not in the last analysis make any philosophical difference, a view with which Mach would have agreed.

The Mach-Boltzmann contrast helps to put into perspective Wittgenstein's change of mind in October 1929—a change, I have suggested, in which Wittgenstein gave up the possibility of a thoroughgoing "reduction to acquaintance," that is, to the language of the immediately given. Wittgenstein characterized his change of mind in terms of a transition from phenomenological language to a physicalistic language. He might as well have spoken of a transition from Machian to Boltzmannian languages.

Post-1929 Wittgenstein rejected the possibility of primary phenomenological languages. Thus his later philosophy, but not the *Tractatus*, stands in sharp contradiction to Mach. It is instructive to see that it is at the time of his change of mind that Wittgenstein began to criticize Mach (albeit not frequently). The early Wittgenstein's relation to Mach is comparable not only to his relation to Moore, but also to his relation to Carnap. Wittgenstein could not stand Carnap's way of expounding his philosophical views. Yet he recognized the fundamental identity of Carnap's ideas, especially of the idea of the primacy of physicalistic languages, with his own post-1929 ideas.[34] Likewise, Wittgenstein detested Mach as a philosophical writer, but deep down he must have recognized the similarity of his early views with those of Mach's. Again, Wittgenstein began to criticize Mach only after—and immediately after—rejecting the primacy of phenomenological languages. In *Philosophical Remarks*, Wittgenstein writes:

> One of the clearest examples of the confusion between physical and phenomenological language is the picture Mach made [in Mach 1959, p. 19] of his visual field, in which the so-called blurredness of the figures near the edge of the visual field was reproduced by a blurredness (in a quite different sense) in the drawing. No, you can't make a visual picture of our visual image.[35]

Just before this passage, but still in §213, Wittgenstein had written that, similarly,

> The use of the word "equal" with quite different meanings is very confusing. This is the typical case of words and phrases which originally referred to the

"things" of the idioms for talking about physical objects, the "bodies in space," being applied to the elements of our visual field; in the course of this they inevitably change their meanings utterly.

This insight had come to Wittgenstein on October 11, 1929, the day he rejected the idea of the primacy of phenomenological languages—that is, his own earlier one. Indeed, in §213 of *Philosophical Remarks*, Wittgenstein is taking Mach to task for the very same mistake he had once made himself. So this criticism of Mach amounts to a criticism of his own earlier ideas. This is clearly seen if we note that the issue of the blurredness of visual space played a key role in Wittgenstein's coming to reject thinking the possibility of primary phenomenological languages.[36] On October 11, 1929, the very first conclusion Wittgenstein draws is in effect the one expressed in the above quotation from *Philosophical Remarks* §213: physical-istic idioms may not be transferred without loss to phenomenological objects. That same day, however, he had written: "[I]nexactness is represented through inex-actness [*Ungenauigkeit wird durch Ungenauigkeit wiedergegeben*]."[37] If this were correct, then it would be possible to make a Machian visual picture of a visual experience. And yet, this is the very idea Wittgenstein had cause to reject as wholly mistaken on that crucial day.

All this illustrates the closeness of Wittgenstein's earlier (pre-October 1929) phenomenological philosophy, including the philosophy of the *Tractatus*, to Mach's ideas.

NOTES

1. See Martin Kusch, *Psychologism* (London: Routledge, 1995).
2. See John T. Blackmore, ed., *Ludwig Boltzmann: His Later Life and Philosophy, 1900–1900. Book 1: A Documentary History*, vol. 1 (Dordrecht: Kluwer Academic, 1995), p. 87.
3. See Ludwig Boltzmann, *Theoretical Physics and Philosophical Problems*, ed. Brian McGuinness (Dordrecht: Reidel, 1974) (hereafter Boltzmann 1974), p. 97.
4. Hilde Spiel, *Vienna's Golden Autumn from the Watershed Year 1866 to Hitler's Anschluss 1938* (New York: Weidenfeld and Nicholson, 1987) (hereafter Spiel 1987), p. 133.
5. See Herbert A. Simon, *Models of Discovery: Topics in the Methods of Science* (Dordrecht: Reidel, 1977).
6. J. C. C. McKinsey, A. C. Sugar, and Patrick Suppes, "Axiomatic Foundations of Classical Particle Mechanics," *Journal of Rational Mechanics and Analysis* 2 (1953): 253–272.
7. Mario Bunge, "Mach's Critique of Newtonian Mechanics," in *Ernst Mach—A Deeper Look: Documents and New Perspectives*, ed. John T Blackmore (Dordrecht: Kluwer Academic, 1992) (hereafter Blackmore 1992), pp. 243–261.
8. See Jaakko Hintikka, "Towards a General Theory of Identifiability," in *Defini-tions and Definability*, ed. J. Fetzer, D. Shatz, and G. Schlesinger (Dordrecht: Kluwer Academic, 1991), pp. 161–183.
9. See Max Jammer, *Concepts of Mass in Classical and Modern Physics* (Cambridge, Mass.: Harvard University Press, 1961).
10. See Tjalling C. Koopmans, "Identification Problems in Economic Model Con-struction," *Econometrica* 17 (1949): 125–144.

11. Don Howard, "Relativity, *Eindeutigkeit* and Monomorphism," in *Origins of Logical Empiricism*, ed. Ronald N. Giere and Alan W. Richardson (Minneapolis: University of Minnesota Press, 1996), pp. 115–164 (hereafter Howard 1996).

12. Einstein, quoted in Howard (1996), p. 117.

13. See, for example, Gerald Holton, "More on Mach and Einstein," in Blackmore (1992), pp. 263–276 (hereafter Holton 1992).

14. Friedrich Stadler, "The 'Verein Ernst Mach'—What Was It Really?" in Blackmore (1992), pp. 363–377.

15. Eino Kaila, *Reality and Experience: Four Philosophical Essays*, ed. Robert S. Cohen (Dordrecht: Reidel, 1979), pp. xxvii–xxviii.

16. Rudolf Haller, *Neopositivismus* (Darmstadt: Wissenschaftliche Buchgesellschaft, 1993), p. 39; compare pp. 134–135.

17. Henk Visser, "Mach, Utrecht, and Dutch Philosophy," in Blackmore (1992), pp. 703–730.

18. Edmund Husserl, *Gesammelte Werke (Husserliana)* (The Hague: Nijhoff [Kluwer], 1950–), vol. 9, pp. 302–303 (hereafter volumes in the *Husserliana* edition will be cited by roman numerals followed by page numbers).

19. Husserl, *Shorter Works*, ed. P. McCormick and F. Elliston (Notre Dame, Ind.: University of Notre Dame Press, 1981), p. 22.

20. Lester Embree et al., eds., *Encyclopedia of Phenomenology* (Dordrecht: Kluwer Academic, 1997).

21. Manfred Sommer, *Husserl und der frühe Positivismus* (Frankfurt am Main: Vittorio Klostermann, 1985); *Evidenz im Augenblick: Eine Phänomenologie der reinen Empfindung* (Frankfurt am Main: Suhrkamp, 1987); and "Denkökonomie und Empfindungstheorie bei Mach und Husserl: Zum Verhältnis von Positivismus und Phänomenologie," in *Ernst Mach: Werk und Wirkung*, ed. Rudolf Haller and Friedrich Stadler (Vienna: Höder-Pichler-Tempsky, 1988), pp. 309–328 (hereafter Sommer 1988).

22. John T. Blackmore, *Ernst Mach: His Work, Life, and Influence* (Berkeley: University of California Press, 1972) (hereafter Blackmore 1972), p. 32.

23. Ludwig Wittgenstein, *Tractatus Logico-Philosophicus*, trans. D. F. Pears and B. F. McGuinness (London: Routlege and Kegan Paul, 1961), 6.54 (propositions of the *Tractatus* will be cited by their number).

24. Wittgenstein, *Vermischte Bemerkungen* (Frankfurt am Main: Suhrkamp, 1977), p. 43.

25. Merrill B. Hintikka and Jaakko Hintikka, *Investigating Wittgenstein* (Oxford: Basil Blackwell, 1986) (hereafter Hintikka and Hintikka 1986), chapter 3, section 12.

26. E. Mach, *Erkenntnis und Irrtum: Skizzen zur Psychologie der Forschung* (Leipzig: Johann Ambrosius Barth, 1905) (hereafter Mach 1905), p. 300.

27. Moritz Schlick, *Allgemeine Erkenntnislehre* (Berlin: Julius Springer, 1918), p. 96.

28. See Burton Dreben and Juliet Floyd, "Tautology: How Not to Use a Word," *Synthese* 87 (1991): 23–49.

29. See J. Hintikka, "G. H. von Wright on Logical Truth and Distributive Normal Forms," in *The Philosophy of G. H. von Wright*, ed. P. A. Schilpp (La Salle, Ill.: Open Court, 1990), pp. 517–537.

30. Compare P. M. S. Hacker, *Wittgenstein's Place in Twentieth-Century Analytic Philosophy* (Oxford: Basil Blackwell, 1997), p. 47.

31. See J. Hintikka, "An Anatomy of Wittgenstein's Picture Theory," in *Artifacts, Representations and Social Practice*, ed. C. C. Gould and Robert S. Cohen (Dordrecht: Kluwer Academic, 1994), pp. 223–256.

32. David Pears, "The Ego and the Eye: Wittgenstein's Use of an Analogy," *Grazer Philosophische Studien* 44 (1993): 59–68; "Connections between Wittgenstein's Treatment of Solipsism and the Private Language Argument," in *A Wittgenstein Symposium*, ed. Josep-Maria Terricabras (Amsterdam: Rodopi, 1993), pp. 79–91; and "Le

Wittgenstein du Hintikka," in *Jaakko Hintikka, Questions de Logique et de Phénomenologie*, ed. Elisabeth Rigal (Paris: J. Vrin, 1998).

33. See Len Corry, "Hilbert on Kinetic Theory and Radiation Theory (1912–14)," *The Mathematical Intelligencer* 20/3 (1998): 52–58; and P. S. Alexandrov, ed., *Die Hilbertschen Probleme: Vortrag "Mathematische Probleme" von D. Hilbert* (Leipzig: Akademische Verlagsgesellschaft, 1971).

34. See J. Hintikka, "Ludwig's Apple Tree," in *Scientific Philosophy: Origins and Developments*, ed. Friedrich Stadler (Dordrecht: Kluwer Academic, 1993), pp. 27–46.

35. Wittgenstein, *Philosophical Remarks* (Oxford: Basil Blackwell, 1975), XX, §213.

36. See L. Wittgenstein, *The Wittgenstein Papers Microfilm* (Ithaca: Cornell University, 1967), MS 107, pp. 161–174.

37. Ibid., p. 162.

5

Truth and Propositional Unity in Early Russell

THOMAS RICKETTS

Russell adopted a new theory of judgment in 1910. Previously he had taken judging to be a two-place relation that relates a mind to a complex entity. When Cassio judges that Desdemona loves Othello, Cassio is related by the relation of judging to the proposition that Desdemona loves Othello, an entity that contains the woman Desdemona, the relation of loving, and the man Othello as constituents. Cassio's judgment is true, because the proposition he judges is true. In contrast, when jealous Othello comes to believe that Desdemona loves Cassio, his belief is false; for the proposition to which he bears the judging-relation is false.[1] In 1910 Russell maintains that judging is not a binary relation, but a multiple relation. When Cassio judges that Desdemona loves Othello, a four-place relation of judging relates Cassio, Desdemona, the relation of loving, and Othello, respectively. This judgment is true, for there exists a corresponding fact, Desdemona's loving Othello. Othello's judgment is similarly a matter of the judging-relation's joining Othello, Desdemona, the relation of loving, and Cassio; but Othello's judgment is false, as there is no corresponding fact of Desdemona's loving Cassio.

Russell's adoption of the multiple relation theory is a fundamental shift in his metaphysics, a shift from a metaphysics of propositions to a metaphysics of facts. The logical and metaphysical costs of this change are enormous. First, Russell never works out an extension of the multiple relation theory from judgments expressed by atomic sentences to those expressed by molecular sentences and generalizations. Second, although the multiple relation theory is mentioned in *Principia Mathematica*, the theory appears incompatible with the ineliminable quantification over propositions and propositional functions present in the formal development of *Principia*. Third, Russell fails to characterize truth satisfactorily, even for judgments expressed by atomic sentences.[2] Moreover, in 1913 Wittgenstein obscurely but furiously criticizes the multiple relation theory.[3] Unable to overcome Wittgenstein's objections, Russell abandons his project of providing foundations for the logic of *Principia*. Even in the face of the obstacles confronting the multiple relation theory, however, Russell does not look back—he never considers returning to the metaphysics of propositions. This is all the more surprising, as

Russell's arguments against the metaphysics of propositions are not decisive objections, as Russell himself recognizes.

Russell forwards his metaphysics of propositions as a pluralist repudiation of Bradley's Idealist monism. In this essay, I argue that the impetus for the shift from the metaphysics of propositions to a metaphysics of facts is the result of connected difficulties Russell faces with his conception of truth and his conception of propositions as complex unities. It is these difficulties that prompt Russell's confusing, opaque distinction between asserted and unasserted propositions in *The Principles of Mathematics*. Russell's efforts in *Principles* to use this distinction to deal with these difficulties are unsuccessful. I believe that Russell thinks these difficulties call into question the basic coherence of his pluralism. The multiple relation theory is his attempt to refashion a coherent pluralism that avoids them.

I

In the preface to *Principles of Mathematics*, Russell acknowledges that he is indebted to G. E. Moore for his conception of propositions.[4] Propositions are what we judge true or false. The sentences we use to express our judgments signify these propositions. Against Bradley's Idealism, Moore and Russell maintain that our judgments are flatly true or false. They do not, however, understand truth as some kind of correspondence between judgment-constituting ideas (mental representations) and reality. Still accepting Idealist criticisms of empiricist theories of judgment, they both appear to hold that a conception of truth as agreement of a mental representation with something nonmental gives rise to conundra that in turn lead to Idealism. Russell, making this point in a 1905 paper (unpublished in his lifetime), "The Nature of Truth," goes on to urge, "that we ought to start out from a quite different point: truth lies not in the correspondence of our idea with fact, but in the fact itself."[5] To understand Russell's viewpoint, we need to consider his conception of propositions.

Propositions are what individuals judge, objects to which judging minds are related. Propositions are themselves nonmental, nonlinguistic complex entities; they do not in any way depend on judging minds for their existence. Russell describes the distinctive complexity of propositions in *Principles* §54:

> Consider, for example, the proposition "A differs from B." The constituents of the proposition, if we analyze it, appear to be only A, difference, B. Yet these constituents, thus placed side by side, do not reconstitute the proposition. The difference which occurs in the proposition actually relates A and B, whereas the difference after analysis is a notion which has no connection with A and B. . . . A proposition, in fact, is essentially a unity, and when analysis has destroyed the unity, no enumeration of constituents will restore the proposition. The verb, when used as a verb, embodies the unity of the proposition, and is thus distinguishable from the verb considered as a term, though I do not know how to give a clear account of the nature of the distinction.[6]

Part of Russell's point here is that an enumeration of the constituents of a proposition does not fix the identity of propositions formed from them; for Desdemona, Othello, and the relation of loving form a single class but two propositions. This observation exhibits the difference between the complexity of classes and the complexity of propositions.[7] There is no class-constituting relation *among* the members of a class that binds them into that class. Propositions are different. Russell holds that every proposition must contain a relation that binds the constituents of the proposition together to constitute that proposition.

Russell elaborates this conception of propositional complexity earlier in chapter IV of *Principles*. In *Principles*, Russell's all-embracing ontological category, his notion of entity, is the category of *terms*: whatever subsists is a term. In describing how propositions are combinations of terms, Russell distinguishes two ways in which items may occur in propositions. In the proposition that Desdemona loves Othello, the individuals Desdemona and Othello occur nonpredicatively, as logical subjects, and the relation of loving occurs predicatively. Russell holds that every term occurs nonpredicatively in some propositions. For example, every term has being. So, for every term x, there is a proposition in which x occurs nonpredicatively, namely the proposition

x has being.

In particular, the relation of loving occurs nonpredicatively in the proposition

Loving has being.[8]

Some terms—Desdemona and Othello, for instance—occur only nonpredicatively in propositions. Terms like loving occur both nonpredicatively and predicatively. In any proposition, it is the predicative occurrence of a relation that unites the constituents of that proposition into a whole, a whole that is either true or false.[9] As for subject-predicate propositions, Russell thinks that in a sentence like "Socrates is wise," the copula "is" names a relation, albeit an extraordinary one. For, in the proposition that Socrates is wise, the term wisdom, although the relatum of the copula relation, nonetheless occurs predicatively in the proposition.[10]

Russell's description in §54 of the unity of propositions via talk of the occurrence of a "verb as verb," of a "relating relation" that unites the constituents of a proposition, is then misleading. This rhetoric suggests that Russell's propositions must all be true. How could loving be a "relating relation" in the proposition that Desdemona loves Cassio, if Desdemona does not love Cassio? Nevertheless, as I have already mentioned, Russell's propositions embrace both truths and falsehoods. Following Moore, in *Principles* Russell assumes the dichotomy of true and false propositions. In later writings, he says that the most persuasive reason for this view is that false propositions are required for the analysis of true propositions expressed by some molecular sentences.[11] For example, Russell holds that hypothetical sentences, material conditionals like

If 5 is even, then 5 is divisible by 2,

or, as Russell would put it,

5 is even implies 5 is divisible by 2,

assert a relation between propositions, a relation which sometimes holds even
when one or both of the propositions are false. The same point holds for belief
attributions, once judging is analyzed as a two-place relation between minds and
propositions. In belief attributions, the clause of indirect discourse signifies the
proposition judged; and even in true belief attributions, this proposition is sometimes false.[12]

In section III, I will return to this very important rhetorical slippage in §54.[13]
For now, I want to concentrate on Russell's view of truth.

Russell's propositions, singular propositions anyway, do not represent anything.[14] Nothing makes the proposition that Desdemona loves Othello true. Nothing falsifies the proposition that Desdemona loves Cassio. Each proposition is
formed by a predicative occurrence of the relation of loving that joins Desdemona
to a second individual. The first proposition is in itself true; the second is false.
The true proposition that Cassio believes and the false one that Othello comes to
believe subsist on a par as ontological equals. Furthermore, Russell does not recognize any fundamental modal distinctions in the truth and falsity of propositions.
Reacting against Bradley, he takes necessity to be a confused notion.[15]

The notion of truth plays a fundamental role in Moore's and Russell's metaphysics. Moore, in his entry for "Truth and Falsity" in Baldwin's *Dictionary*, notes
that once propositions, the objects of belief, are distinguished from mental states
and from sentences,

> it seems plain that a truth differs in no respect from the reality to which it
> was supposed merely to correspond: e.g. the truth that I exist differs in no
> respect from the corresponding reality—my existence. So far, indeed, from
> truth being defined by reference to reality, reality can only be defined by ref-
> erence to truth: for truth denotes exactly that property of the complex formed
> by two entities and their relation, in virtue of which, if the entity predicated
> be existence, we call the complex real—the property, namely, expressed by
> saying that the relation in question does truly or really hold between the
> entities.[16]

What is real does not determine what is true, as on a representation-theoretic view
of a truth, a correspondence conception of truth. Instead, what is real just is what
is true: for Desdemona really to love Othello is for the proposition that Desdemona
loves Othello to be true. In general, for something to have a property or to be related to something else is for a proposition containing the items to be true. Moore
and Russell thus identify facts with propositions that are true.[17] So I call their
metaphysics a metaphysics of propositions.

Moreover, this view applies also to facts about propositions. For Cassio to stand
in the belief-relation to the proposition that Desdemona loves Othello is for it to
be true that Cassio believes that Desdemona loves Othello. In this proposition, a

predicative occurrence of the relation of belief joins Cassio to the proposition that Desdemona loves Othello, a proposition that then occurs as a logical subject in the larger proposition. Similarly, a true material implication is a proposition formed by a predicative occurrence of the relation of implication joining one proposition to another.[18]

This role of truth in Russell's metaphysics informs an argument he presents in "The Nature of Truth" against the correspondence theory of truth:

> But even supposing some other definition of correspondence with reality could be found, a more general argument against definitions of truth would still hold good. An idea is to be true when it corresponds with reality, i.e. when it is true that it corresponds with reality, i.e. when the idea that it corresponds with reality corresponds with reality, and so on. This will never do. In short, if we don't know the difference between a proposition's being true and not being true, we don't know the difference between a thing's having a property and not having it, and therefore we can't define a thing as true when it has a certain property such as corresponding with reality.[19]

Russell's argument here is obscure. He is not, in contrast to Frege, urging that, on a correspondence view of truth, the judgment that p requires a prior, distinct judgment that p is true.[20] Nor is Russell's argument for the indefinability of truth parallel to Moore's for the indefinability of "good".[21] In particular, Russell's argument does not turn on noting the informativeness of any alleged identification of truth with another property. Finally, Russell is not charging proposed definitions of truth with straightforward analytic circularity. His point is not that the concept of truth must reappear as a constituent of any complex property with which truth is identified.

My suggestion is that Russell thinks that to define truth is to move in an explanatory circle. This circle generates a regress that discredits any proposed definition of truth. Russell's correspondence theorist holds that it is ideas that are properly speaking true or false, and that for an idea to be true is for that idea to correspond with reality. Let "F" abbreviate the specification of this relational property in which the truth of an idea consists. So, according to the correspondence theorist, for it to be true that p means: an idea of p is F. Just here Russell brings his understanding of the role of truth to bear on the correspondence theorist's proposed definition. Russell understands the holding of properties in terms of truth. So, for an idea of p actually to be F is for it to be *true* that an idea of p is F. But now, given his definition of truth, Russell's correspondence theorist must identify the original idea's being F with another idea's being F, that is, with an idea of (an idea of p being F) itself being F. The correspondence theorist thus embarks on a regress, and so fails to identify that fact that constitutes the truth of an idea of p. Russell concludes that being true cannot be identified with the possession of any property, because possession of any property (or standing in any relation) is explained in terms of the truth of propositions. It is this priority of the notion of truth in a metaphysics of propositions that renders truth unanalyzable.[22]

Russell's objection to the correspondence theory, however, raises a problem concerning the status of truth within Russell's own metaphysics. Moore and Russell both think of truth itself as a concept or property of propositions. Moore says: "'True' and 'false' as applied to propositions denote properties attaching to propositions which are related to one another in such a way that every proposition must be either true or false."[23] In "The Nature of Truth," Russell says:

> Truth, in the first place, is not a constituent of a true proposition, except in those cases where the proposition happens to be about truth. . . . Truth and falsehood, in fact, are properties attaching to propositions as wholes and are not themselves, in general, parts of propositions. The proposition "It is true that $2+2 = 4$" contains the notion of truth, but is not identical with "$2+2 = 4$."[24]

According to the metaphysics of propositions, for a term x to be F is for the proposition that x is F to be true. As propositions are terms, their possession of properties, including the property of truth, must be understood along these lines. So, for the proposition that Desdemona loves Othello to be true is for the further proposition,

The proposition that Desdemona loves Othello is true,

itself to be true. Here we have, it appears, a regress parallel to the one Russell presents to discredit a correspondence conception of truth. Like the earlier regress, this regress is generated by an explanatory circle in which a term's having a property is identified with the truth of a certain proposition, but a proposition's being true is an instance of something's having a property.

The role of truth in Russell's metaphysics indicates a special status for this notion. Truth is not simply another term that occurs predicatively in some propositions. Russell's murky distinction between asserted and unasserted propositions in *Principles* is an attempt to carve out a special status for truth. Indeed, we shall see that Russell in *Principles* §478 deploys the preceding argument to this end.

II

Russell's distinction between asserted and unasserted propositions concerns neither language nor psychology. In particular, an asserted proposition is not one that someone believes to be true. In his explanations, Russell insists that there is a nonpsychological, logical notion of assertion. His elucidations of this allegedly logical notion are confusing and confused. He offers two very different accounts of the notion; and he appears, for good reason, to be satisfied with neither. Russell's most extensive and most important explanation of logical assertion comes in *Principles*, chapter IV, especially in §52. He returns to logical assertion in appendix A, the survey of Frege's ideas, in §478.

Early on, in §38, Russell applies the distinction between asserted and unasserted propositions in order to respond to Lewis Carroll's paradox about inference in "What the Tortoise Said to Achilles."[25] Although Russell does not explain the distinction in §38, his discussion perhaps motivates his odd terminology. When we linguistically express an inference, we assert the premises and then, saying "therefore," assert the conclusion. Using the assertion stroke that Russell subsequently adopts from Frege, the schema for the expression of a *modus ponens* inference is:

$$\vdash X \supset Y$$
$$\vdash X$$
$$\text{Therefore, } \vdash Y.$$

When an individual linguistically asserts a material conditional, she asserts neither the proposition signified by the antecedent nor the proposition signified by the consequent. What is asserted is the material implication signified by the entire conditional. Underlying this linguistic distinction in a sound *modus ponens* argument, Russell claims, is an ontological distinction. The antecedent and the consequent of the conditional signify propositions, and the conditional signifies a proposition in which these two are joined by the relation of material implication to form a proposition that itself, in a logical sense, asserts that the antecedent implies the consequent, while asserting neither the antecedent nor the consequent. Russell thus posits an ontological difference between what is signified by the antecedent of the conditional in a sound instance of our schema and what is signified by the second premise. The antecedent of the conditional signifies an unasserted proposition; the second premise signifies an asserted proposition. Russell says:

> It is plain that, if I may be allowed to use the word assertion in a non-psychological sense, the proposition "p implies q" asserts an implication, though it does not assert p or q. The p and the q which enter into this proposition are not strictly the same as the p or the q which are separate propositions, at least if they are true.[26]

Russell appears here to be making problems for himself. The reader of Frege will urge that the linguistic facts compel no distinction between what is signified by a sentence standing alone, used to make a linguistic assertion, and what is signified by that sentence when it occurs as a constituent of a compound sentence. In both cases, we can maintain, the sentence signifies one and the same proposition. The only difference is a linguistic/psychological one. In making a linguistic assertion, a person by uttering a sentence puts forward a proposition as true; and that proposition is the one signified by the entire sentence, surrounded by full stops, that the person utters, not one signified by its proper parts. To understand Russell's motivation for introducing logical assertion, we need to look at his later discussions of it.

At the end of section I, I suggested that the role of truth in Russell's metaphysics of propositions appears to require that this notion of truth should have a special status. As Russell puts it in §52, it is the predicative occurrence of a relation in a proposition that joins the logical subjects of the proposition into a whole that is true or false. He attempts to give truth a special status when he offhandedly comments in §52 that "neither truth nor falsity belongs to a mere logical subject." Rather, the truth of a proposition is somehow intrinsic to it without being a constituent of it. Similarly for falsity. Russell's picture here seems to be that there are two ways in which the relation of loving can join two terms so as to form a proposition, the true way and the false way. In the proposition,

Desdemona loves Othello,

the relation of loving joins Desdemona to Othello in the true way. In the proposition,

Desdemona loves Cassio,

loving joins Desdemona to Cassio in the false way.[27] The difference between our two sample propositions is not a matter of one term's having a property another lacks. It is a sort of "internal" difference.

Russell seeks to accommodate this qualification of his metaphysics of propositions by denying that propositions are logical subjects at all. This maneuver requires further modifications, for Russell's analyses of judgment and implication had committed him to the occurrence of propositions in other propositions as logical subjects. Russell reconciles these analyses with his denial of logical subjecthood to propositions by introducing unasserted propositions, propositional concepts, in addition to (asserted) propositions. He suggests that this distinction is linguistically signaled by the difference between sentences and their nominalizations—the difference between "Caesar died" and "the death of Caesar," to use Russell's example. Both a sentence and its nominalization signify a complex composed of the same items, but the relation whose predicative occurrence forms the proposition signified by a sentence does not occur predicatively in the corresponding propositional complex. So the sentence, "Cassio believes that Desdemona loves Othello," signifies a proposition in which the belief-relation joins Cassio, not to a (asserted) proposition, but to a propositional concept. For Cassio's belief to be true is for the object he believes to be true. Russell, accordingly, now maintains that the concepts of truth and falsity hold of propositional concepts, not of the corresponding asserted propositions. On this view, the proposition signified by "Desdemona's loving Othello is true" is a proposition whose subject is a propositional concept. On this approach, for Desdemona actually to bear the external relation of loving to Othello is for the asserted proposition

Desdemona loves Othello,

to contain its own truth, that is, for loving to join Desdemona to Othello "in the true way." Similarly, for the propositional concept signified by "Desdemona's loving Othello" to be externally related to truth is for the proposition

Desdemona's loving Othello is true,

to contain its own truth.

We are now in a position to appreciate the difficulties Russell faces in presenting a consistent theory here. As logical laws are themselves maximally general propositions whose constituents are variables and logical constants, Russell's formulation of logic is accordingly grounded in a theory of the structure of propositions. Propositions are the bearers of truth. Moreover, in *Principles* the notion of truth is univocal and absolute—there are not degrees or levels of truth, as with the Idealists. Russell's discussion of propositions must then, on pain of incoherence, conform to the strictures it lays down. His metaphysics makes no other status available for it. In particular, his generalizations and their instances must themselves signify Russellian propositions.

I noted how Russell thinks that, though there are two ways in which entities occur in propositions, every entity occurs in some propositions as a logical subject. Russell argues for this thesis by observing that its denial is self-thwarting. Suppose the sentence, "x occurs as a logical subject in no proposition," were true. Then it would signify a true proposition whose subject was the term x, the term signified by "x". But then x would occur as a logical subject in a proposition after all. On this basis, Russell maintains that the same term that occurs as logical subject in the proposition signified by, "Loving is a relation," occurs predicatively in the proposition signified by "Desdemona loves Othello."[28]

Russell realizes that his ontological distinction between propositions and propositional concepts is similarly self-thwarting. In §52, he denies that propositions themselves occur as logical subjects in other propositions, but immediately recognizes the conflict between this thesis and his conception of a term. As he writes,

> [I]f I say "*Caesar died* is a proposition," I do not assert that Caesar did die, and an element which was present in "Caesar died" has disappeared. Thus the contradiction which was to have been avoided, of an entity which cannot be made a logical subject appears to have here become inevitable. This difficulty, which seems to be inherent in the very nature of truth and falsehood, is one with which I do not know how to deal satisfactorily.[29]

In Russell's exposition of the distinction between asserted propositions and propositional concepts, he has used sentences that must, if they are to express truths, signify asserted propositions that have asserted propositions as logical subjects. But, according to the account of asserted propositions Russell is presenting, asserted propositions do not occur as logical subjects in any propositions, including those expressed by his sentences. This is "the contradiction which was to have been avoided."

Faced with this contradiction, Russell considers giving up logical assertion, retaining only a psychological/linguistic notion. He is unwilling to take this step: "But there is another sense of assertion, very difficult to bring clearly before the mind, and yet quite undeniable, in which only true propositions are asserted."[30] Russell then tentatively rejects the ontological distinction between propositions and propositional concepts, while retaining assertion. He ends §52 with the remark:

True and false propositions alike are in some sense entities, and are in some sense capable of being logical subjects; but when a proposition happens to be true, it has a further quality, over and above that which it shares with false propositions, and it is this further quality which is what I mean by assertion in a logical as opposed to a psychological sense. The nature of truth, however, belongs no more to the principles of mathematics than to the principles of everything else. I therefore leave this question to the logicians with the above brief indication of a difficulty.

I take Russell here tentatively to advance the following modification of his account. Russell retains the idea that in propositions, predicative occurrences of relations join logical subjects together in either the "true way" or the other way. When a relation joins the logical subjects of a proposition together in the "true way," this feature of the proposition is "the further quality over and above that which it shares with false propositions . . . which is what I mean by assertion in a logical . . . sense." Russell thus decides to restrict the notion of assertion to propositions that contain their own truth. Accompanying this terminological shift is a substantive change: Russell gives up the troublesome distinction between propositions that are not logical subjects and propositional concepts that are.[31] Every proposition occurs as a logical subject in other propositions. Finally, Russell holds that a proposition is externally related to the concept of truth just in case the proposition has the internal quality of assertion. On this view then, assertion, not the concept truth, plays the fundamental fact-constituting role in the metaphysics of propositions—a fact is an asserted proposition.

This maneuver does not, however, rescue Russell from a self-thwarting position. Assertion, on the present view, is a quality or feature of certain propositions. But the possession of this quality is "internal" to the proposition—it is not a matter of the proposition's being related (externally) by the copula to a concept. Russell's thesis that a proposition is true just in case it is asserted is then problematic. His account of propositions and proposition-signifying sentences requires that "asserted" signify a concept. But there is no concept available here to suit Russell's purposes apart from the concept of truth itself. And, if "asserted" signifies truth, Russell's thesis becomes a triviality. There are, then, no sentences signifying Russellian propositions that communicate truths about internal qualities, no coherent conception of such qualities within the metaphysics of propositions. The shoe still pinches. No wonder Russell throws up his hands at the end of §52.

Why is Russell so eager to maintain a nonpsychological notion of logical assertion distinct from the concept of truth? I have suggested that the metaphysics of propositions requires the notion of truth to play a role that no Russellian concept, no propositional constituent, can play. Russell attempts with his notion of logical assertion to find something that can play this role. I believe that §478 confirms this interpretation.

Section 478 occurs in the Frege appendix to *Principles* in the context of Russell's discussion of Frege's concept-object distinction. Russell observes that the Kerry paradox confronting Frege's distinction is analogous to the contradiction on which Russell's distinction between asserted propositions and propositional concepts founders. In §38, Russell had asked, "How does a proposition differ by being actually true from what it would be as an entity if it were not true?" His answer there is: "By being asserted." Why is this answer better than the straightforward one: "By being true"? §478, in effect, addresses this question:

> But assertion does not seem to be a constituent of an asserted proposition, although it is, in some sense, contained in an asserted proposition. If p is a proposition, "p's truth" is a concept which has being even if p is false, and thus "p's truth" is not the same as p and therefore assertion is not a constituent of p asserted. Yet assertion is not a term to which p, when asserted, has an external relation; for any such relation would need to be itself asserted in order to yield what we want.[32]

To begin, let us ask, "How does Desdemona differ by actually loving Othello from what she would be as an entity if she did not?" The answer to our question provided by the metaphysics of propositions seems to be that Desdemona is joined by the relation of loving to Othello to form a proposition that is true— Desdemona's actually loving Othello is constituted by the truth of the proposition that Desdemona loves Othello. Now the same question arises again: "How does the proposition that Desdemona loves Othello differ by being actually true from what it would be as an entity if it were not true?" Or, "How does the proposition that Desdemona loves Othello differ by being actually true from the proposition that Desdemona loves Cassio?" This is Russell's question in §38.

Suppose we answer this question as well by reference to truth:
The proposition that Desdemona loves Othello is actually true, unlike the proposition that Desdemona loves Cassio. I.e., the proposition that Desdemona loves Othello is joined by the copula to the concept truth to form a proposition that is itself true.

But this answer just pushes the question back one more step: "How does the proposition that (the proposition that Desdemona loves Othello) is true differ by being actually true from what it would be if it were not?" The proposition

That Desdemona loves Othello is true,

subsists on an ontological par with the proposition

That Desdemona loves Cassio is true.

In both cases, we have a logical subject joined by the copula to the term truth to form a proposition. The subsistence of the second proposition illustrates the basis for Russell's observation that "p's truth is a concept which has being even if p is false."

In §478, Russell, treating the concept of truth as a propositional constituent, raises the same difficulty canvassed in section I of this paper. The attempt to answer Russell's question by mention of the concept of truth produces a regress that is the product of an explanatory circle in which a term's having a property is identified with the truth of a certain proposition, but a proposition's being true is an instance of something's having a property. Russell calls attention to this explanatory circle when he says that his question cannot be answered by mention of any concept to which the proposition is related, "for any such relation would need to be itself asserted in order to yield what we want." Russell thus uses this regress/circle to conclude that assertion is not a concept to which propositions are externally related by the copula relation. Instead, assertion must be an internal feature of some propositions. Russell, however, realizes that this treatment of assertion leaves him in the dilemma raised in §52.[33]

Russell's difficulties here arise from an explanatory burden he places on the notion of truth. In presenting Russell's metaphysics, I have said things like: "A fact is a proposition that is true: for Desdemona actually to love Othello is for the proposition that Desdemona loves Othello to be true," as though the holding of the relation were constituted by the truth of a proposition. Russell feels himself required to give a general explanation of the difference between something's bearing a relation to an item or not. We have seen how Russell is unable within the confines of the metaphysics of propositions to provide any intelligible explanation. Perhaps these difficulties show that the demand for explanation here is misplaced. Perhaps, Russell should content himself with the unexplanatory material equivalence,

(The proposition) Desdemona loves Othello is true iff Desdemona loves Othello,

and with its generalization, the formal equivalence,

p is true iff p.[34]

Why then does Russell attempt to provide an explanation for the holding of a relation in terms of truth? Why does he think that there is something here that demands a general explanation? The answer to this question will, I believe, uncover the motivation for Russell's shift to a metaphysics of facts.

III

After 1903 Russell remains dissatisfied with the metaphysics of propositions and its treatment of truth. His most prominent pre-1910 expression of dissatisfaction with his metaphysics of propositions occurs in his 1904 examination of Meinong's philosophy. Russell is concerned that his metaphysics is powerless to explain why it is preferable to believe truths rather than falsehoods:

It may be said—and this is, I believe, the correct view—that there is no problem at all in truth and falsehood; that some propositions are true and some false just as some roses are red and some white; that belief is a certain attitude towards propositions, which is called knowledge when they are true, error when they are false. But this theory *seems* to leave our preference for truth a mere unaccountable prejudice, and in no way to answer to the feeling of truth and falsehood.[35]

Russell worries that an account of truth should somehow ground our preference for believing true propositions, but he finds no resources within the metaphysics of propositions to explain this preference. He cannot, after all, within this metaphysics invoke any notion of fact, of reality, to explain why it is better to believe true propositions.

Russell's worry here is not very persuasive.[36] Russell, like a number of philosophers, begins with the truism that true belief is the goal of judgment-making. His philosophical reflections lead him to the notion of a proposition, to the analysis of belief as a dual relation between minds and propositions, and to truth and falsity as unanalyzable properties of propositions. In particular, as noted in section I, Russell persuasively argues in "Meinong's Theory" for the recognition of false propositions on an ontological par with true ones. The absence of any explanation of our preference for true belief is a product of the rejection of a representation-theoretic account of truth as correspondence. Having rejected such accounts of truth, Russell should happily brush off any demand to explain our preference for true belief as the product of a misapprehension of what belief and truth are. That is, it seems that Russell should take toward truth an attitude parallel to Moore's attitude in *Principia Ethica* toward the unanalyzable concept *good*. Indeed, Russell ends "Meinong's Theory" with the remark:

> Thus the analogy with red and white roses seems, in the end, to express the matter as nearly as possible. What is truth and what falsehood, we must merely apprehend, for both seem incapable of analysis. And as for the preference which most people . . . feel in favour of true propositions, this must be based, apparently, upon an ultimate ethical proposition: "It is good to believe true propositions, and bad to believe false ones." This proposition, it is to be hoped, is true, but if not, there is no reason to think that we do ill in believing it.[37]

In 1910 Russell rejects his metaphysics of propositions.[38] He no longer holds that when Othello believes that Desdemona loves Cassio, there is a complex in which the relation of loving joins Desdemona to Cassio, a complex to which Othello is related by a dual relation of belief. His weightiest objection to his former view is:

> If we allow that all judgments have objectives, we shall have to allow that there are objectives which are false. Thus there will be in the world entities, not dependent on the existence of judgments, which can be described as objective falsehoods. This is in itself almost incredible; we feel there could be no falsehood if there were no minds to make mistakes. But it has the further drawback that it leaves the difference between truth and falsehood quite inexplicable. . . . Nevertheless it is quite difficult to abandon the view that, in some way, the truth or falsehood of a judgment depends upon the presence or absence of a "corresponding" entity of some sort. And if we do aban-

don this view, and adhere to the opinion that there are true and false objectives, we shall be compelled to regard it as an ultimate and not further explicable fact that objectives are of two sorts, the true and the false. This view, though not logically impossible, is unsatisfactory and we shall do better, if we can, to find some view which leaves the difference between truth and falsehood less of a mystery.[39]

Russell appears here to be simply reversing his rejection of a representation-theoretic understanding of truth. Had no higher life evolved on the earth, the earth would still orbit the sun; but, as there would be no cognizers, there would be no representation made true or false by this fact. And no representation means no falsehood and no truth. Russell then, in effect, buttresses this objection with the observation from 1904 that the metaphysics of propositions is powerless to explain the significance of the distinction between truth and falsity, powerless to explain our preference for true beliefs. Russell does not consider here his earlier arguments for the posit of false propositions.[40] Nevertheless, I do not think Russell in 1910 is frivolously abandoning a deeply motivated position. Something in the metaphysics of propositions, something connected with truth, is bothering him. I find the clue to the motivation for Russell's rejection of the metaphysics of propositions in his excoriation of false propositions.

Russell's aversion to false propositions has its source, I hold, in his rejection of Bradley's monism. Bradley maintains that there is no coherent conception of how genuinely distinct items can be genuinely related, no coherent conception of unity-in-diversity. Following Peter Hylton, I see Russell as combating Bradley's monism by exhibiting a coherent pluralist metaphysics.[41] The luminous clarity and coherence of Russell's pluralism—together with its formally consistent treatment of the infinitesimally small and the infinitely large[42] —is meant to impugn Bradley's charge of incoherence. Bradley finds Russell's arguments against him variously to miss his point or beg the question. From Russell's vantage point, Bradley's arguments are equally unconvincing.[43]

In his 1910 essay "On Appearance, Error, and Contradiction," Bradley criticizes Russell's metaphysics of propositions in the following terms:

> On the one side I am led to think that [Russell] defends a strict pluralism for which nothing is admissible beyond simple terms and external relations. On the other side . . . he throughout insists upon unities which are complex and which cannot be analysed into terms and relations. These two positions to my mind are irreconcilable, since the second, as I understand it, contradicts the first flatly. If there are such unities, and still more, if such unities are fundamental, then pluralism surely is in principle abandoned as false.[44]

The unities of which Bradley speaks are Russell's propositions. Bradley believes that it is incompatible with pluralism to admit complex unities that are anything over and above their constituents. The pluralist's introduction of these complexes reveals the pluralist's failure to conceive, to make do with, a plurality of genuinely distinct ontological atoms.

Russell replied to Bradley's criticism of complex unities:

> I maintain that there are such facts as that x has the relation R to y, and that such facts are not in general reducible to, or inferable from, a fact about x only and a fact about y only: they do not imply that x and y have any complexity, or any intrinsic property distinguishing them from a z and a w which do not have the relation R. This is what I mean when I say that relations are external. But I maintain also—and it is here that Mr. Bradley sees an inconsistency—that whenever we have two terms x and y related by a relation R, we have also a complex which we may call "xRy," consisting of the two terms so related. This is the simplest example of what I call a "complex" or a "unity." What is called analysis consists in the discovery of the constituents of a complex. A complex differs from the mere aggregate of its constituents, since it is one, not many, and the relation which is one of its constituents enters into it as an actually relating relation, and not merely as one member of an aggregate. I confess I am at a loss to see how this is inconsistent with the above account of relations.[45]

Russell finds the notion of a relating relation transparent. There is no obscurity about Desdemona's loving Othello, about what it means for one thing to bear a relation to another. As Desdemona loves Othello, there is a complex in which the relation of loving relates Desdemona to Othello. Assertion of the existence of a complex is equivalent to assertion of the fact. Indeed, we have here a formal equivalence:

xRy iff there is a complex that is x's R-ing y.

There is no question here as to how a relation relates genuinely distinct individuals. The "unity-in-diversity" that exists when Desdemona loves Othello is transparent and unproblematic.

Or is it? Russell's 1910 reply to Bradley parallels Russell's discussion of relating relations in *Principles* §54, quoted above in the second paragraph of my section I. In both the 1910 reply to Bradley and in the discussion of analysis in §54, false propositions, that is, false complexes, drop out of sight. In *Principles*, Russell deploys the notion of the predicative occurrence of a relation that constitutes a complex as a unity that is true or false. We saw that it is this notion of predicative occurrence, not the notion of a relating relation just canvassed, that must figure in the discussion of analysis in §54. Just here, Russell's *Principles* conception of unity-in-diversity becomes opaque. In the proposition

Desdemona loves Cassio,

a predicative occurrence of loving joins Desdemona to Cassio to constitute the proposition as a unity. But although loving joins Desdemona to Cassio to constitute this proposition, Desdemona does not actually love Cassio. A Bradleyan might put the point like this: according to Russell, a relation can relate without actually relating . . .

I have urged that this contradiction is, on its face, verbal. Russell can stave off the charge of inconsistency here by separating out two notions of a relating relation. One notion is that of the proposition-constituting predicative occurrence of a relation; the other is that connected to truth. In the context of Bradley's challenge to pluralism, however, this maneuver foists on Russell the burden of explaining the relationship between these two notions. What is the difference between the relation of loving joining Desdemona to Othello to form the proposition that Desdemona loves Othello and the relation's actually relating Desdemona to Othello? More generally, in virtue of what does a relation R actually relate one term to another? Clearly, equivalences like

(The proposition) Desdemona loves Othello is true iff Desdemona
loves Othello

do not address these questions. For on Russell's understanding of material equivalence, the proposition signified by this sentence is itself a relational proposition, and so whatever question arises about what it is for Desdemona actually to love Othello arises equally as regards the equivalence of one proposition to another. And without an explanation here, Russell will have failed to vindicate the coherence of his pluralism. Or so, I claim, Russell views matters.

Russell's strategy for defending his pluralism against Bradley then generates the explanatory pressures on the notion of truth within the metaphysics of propositions. We have seen that Russell cannot without vicious circularity explain the second notion of a relating relation in terms of the truth of propositions, if truth is conceived as a propositional constituent. Russell attempts with logical assertion to introduce a 'nonconceptual' notion of truth as the particular way in which, for example, the relation of loving joins Desdemona to Othello to form the proposition that Desdemona loves Othello. The attempt to formulate this view in proposition-signifying sentences, however, leads to a self-thwarting theory. In the end, Russell is forced to surrender the prospect of explanation or clarification of this vital point, this Achilles' heel, of his metaphysics of propositions.

On the interpretation I am presenting, Russell is not worried about the ontological glue that sticks the constituents of a proposition together.[46] In isolation from other features of the metaphysics of propositions, there is no problem of the unity of the proposition. The problem Russell faces is rather the subtler one of relating his conception of propositional unity to his view of truth in the face of Bradley's monism. In *Principles* §54, Russell papers over this difficulty by rhetorically conflating his two notions of relating relations. He realizes that he cannot sustain this rhetoric, and so, alluding back to §52, he confesses himself at the end of §54 unable to give a clear account of relating relations.

It is in significant measure Russell's striving after a transparently coherent pluralism that spurs him to ontological simplification from 1903 onward. He is not complacent about the admission of two basic kinds of complexes, classes and propositions, into his ontology; and he struggles in *Principles*, especially in view of his paradox, to elucidate the notion of a class, to explain how a class, while having many members, is still a whole, although not a propositional unity.[47]

Bradley, in his 1910 paper, seizes on Russell's paradox to criticize Russell's use of classes in *Principles*. Bradley argues that if a collection is nothing over and above its genuinely distinct members, then there is no sense in which the collection is one. So, if a collection is one, it must contain its unity—it must contain itself. "And with this," Bradley remarks, "we end in what is meaningless or else plainly is in contradiction with itself."[48] In his reply, Russell pronounces himself "very largely in agreement" with Bradley's remarks on the idea of a class.[49] Russell has by 1910 eliminated classes from his ontology. Using the regimen of contextual definition of incomplete symbols introduced in "On Denoting," Russell has shown how mention of and quantification over classes can be systematically paraphrased away in favor of mention of and quantification over propositional functions. Classes are thus analyzed away; and the only complexity in the ontology that remains is propositional complexity. Russell attempts to apply this same analytic strategy to propositions as well. What appear in sentences to be designations of propositions are really incomplete symbols that, like class abstracts, disappear on analysis.[50]

In rejecting propositions in favor of facts, Russell adopts a metaphysics in which the only complexity is the complexity of facts. In the metaphysics of facts, there are no false complexes. There is no complex in which the relation of loving joins Desdemona to Cassio. There is only the fact of Desdemona's loving Othello, a complex in which the relation of loving joins Desdemona to Othello. Russell's facts, at least his atomic facts, are thus his old asserted propositions, in the sense of logical assertion in which only true propositions are asserted. Moreover, judgments are themselves facts. For Cassio to judge that Desdemona loves Othello is for a four-place relation of judging to relate Cassio, Desdemona, the relation of loving, and Othello, respectively.[51] Propositions disappear; as surrogates for them, Russell uses existentially general judgment facts. Roughly speaking, the proposition that Desdemona loves Othello gets identified with the fact of someone's judging that Desdemona loves Othello.[52]

In the metaphysics of facts, the notion of a relating relation is univocal. There is then no longer any call to explain what it is for a relation actually to relate one thing to another in terms of the truth of a complex unity. Hence, the metaphysics of facts underwrites Russell's rejection of Bradley's charge of obscurity and contradiction in Russell's account of relations. The rhetorical slippage and hesitancy of *Principles* §54 vanishes; in 1910 Russell can now honestly assert, using the words he does, the transparency of his conception of complex-constituting relating relations. If Russell does not here explicitly mention this change of view, perhaps that is because he wishes to focus on the more fundamental issue of the coherence of a pluralism that admits complex unities whose constituents are genuinely distinct ontological atoms.[53]

All is not, however, in order. The shoe still pinches. Russell faces problems in characterizing the correspondence between judgment-facts and other facts that make the former true or false. In particular, Russell knows that he cannot simply say that the fact of Cassio's judging that Desdemona loves Othello, the fact

Judges (Cassio, Desdemona, Loving, Othello),

is true, if there is a complex in which loving joins Desdemona and Othello. After all, there are two such possible complexes. Russell never satisfactorily solves this problem, and so, to that extent, never makes his pluralism transparent. The difficulties he encounters here are a major source for Wittgenstein's criticisms of Russell's metaphysics of facts and multiple relation analysis of judgment in both the *Tractatus* and pre-*Tractatus* writings.[54]

NOTES

My greatest debt in this paper is to Peter Hylton's writings on Russell and to many years of instructive conversations with him about the topics here discussed. I have also discussed these matters extensively with Warren Goldfarb. This chapter has benefited from comments of William Ewald, Michael Kremer, Danielle Macbeth, Ian Proops, and Charles Raff.

1. My readers, like Russell's in "On the Nature of Truth and Falsehood," should take the Othello story to be flatly true. Fictional discourse is not under discussion here. In Bertrand Russell, *Philosophical Essays* (London: George Allen and Unwin, 1966, pp. 147–159; original publication 1910).

2. For discussions of the problems facing the multiple relation theory, see Nicholas Griffin, "Russell's Multiple Relation Theory of Judgment," *Philosophical Studies* 47 (1985): 213–247; Peter Hylton, *Russell, Idealism, and the Emergence of Analytic Philosophy* (Oxford: Oxford University Press, 1990), pp. 349–361; and my "Pictures, Logic, and the Limits of Sense in Wittgenstein's Tractatus," in *The Cambridge Companion to Wittgenstein*, ed. H. Sluga and D. Stern (Cambridge: Cambridge University Press, 1996), pp. 59–99, especially pp. 64–69.

3. See Brian McGuinness, *Wittgenstein: A Life. Young Ludwig 1889–1921* (Berkeley: University of California Press, 1988), pp. 172–175.

4. Bertrand Russell, *The Principles of Mathematics* (Cambridge: Cambridge University Press, 1903), p. xviii, (hereafter cited as *Principles*).

5. Russell, "The Nature of Truth," in *The Collected Papers of Bertrand Russell*, vol. 4, *Foundations of Logic: 1903–05*, ed. Alasdair Urquhart (London: Routledge, 1994), p. 492. See also G. E. Moore, "Truth and Falsity," in *The Dictionary of Philosophy and Psychology*, vol. 2, ed. John Mark Baldwin (New York: Macmillan, 1901), p. 717, quoted below.

6. *Principles*, §54, pp. 49–50. By "verb" here Russell means relation. Earlier in the passage, he speaks of the difference between a relation in itself and a relation's relating. In my section III, I return to this passage and the unclarity Russell confesses in the last sentence.

7. See *Principles*, §§135–138, pp. 138–141. See also "The Nature of Truth," p. 503. Russell never considers identifying propositions with class-theoretic constructs from their constituents. Indeed, he eventually eliminates classes in favor of propositional functions.

8. See *Principles*, §49, p. 46, and §427, p. 449. Subsequently, Russell employs this argument against Frege's concept/object distinction. See *Principles*, §483, p. 510.

9. Russell speaks of what is left of a proposition when a nonpredicatively occurring term is "removed" as an assertion. Russell uses this notion of assertion to talk about the structure of propositions and about quantification into predicate positions. His remarks on this topic are tentative and do not add up to a coherent, considered view of these matters. See *Principles*, §44, pp. 39–40; §§81–85, pp. 83–88; and §482, pp. 508–510. I think that the details of these discussions of assertion in connection with propositional structure are largely independent of the topic of this essay, the relationship between Russell's view of propositional unity and his view of truth.

10. See *Principles*, §53, p. 49, and §48, pp. 44–45. Russell further thinks that sentences whose grammatical predicate is an intransitive verb prove under analysis to express either propositions whose unifying relation is the copula relation, or propositions of the form

a bears R to something.

11. Russell, "Meinong's Theory of Complexes and Assumptions," part 3, *Mind* n.s. 13 (1904): 509–524, especially pp. 521–522; *The Collected Papers of Bertrand Russell*, vol. 7, *Theory of Knowledge: The 1913 Manuscript*, ed. Elizabeth Eames (London: Routledge, 1983), p. 153; and "On the Nature of Truth," *Proceedings of the Aristotelian Society* n.s. 7 (1906–1907): 28–49, especially p. 48. Furthermore, this point is implicit in Russell's discussion of inference and assertion in *Principles*, §38, discussed in my section II.

12. See "The Nature of Truth," p. 503.

13. Richard Cartwright, Leonard Linsky, and Bernhard Weiss have claimed that the notion of a relating relation that Russell deploys in §54 precludes false propositions. See Richard Cartwright, "A Neglected Theory of Truth," *Philosophical Essays* (Cambridge, Mass.: MIT Press, 1987), pp. 83–84; Leonard Linsky, "The Unity of the Proposition," *Journal of the History of Philosophy* 30 (1992): 243–273, especially see 254; and Bernhard Weiss, "On the Demise of Russell's Multiple Relations Theory of Judgment," *Theoria* 61 (1995): 261–282, especially p. 264. §54 follows closely on §52, where Russell is careful in his discussion of propositional unity to accommodate false propositions. Hence, I charge Russell only with the use of confusing rhetoric, while inquiring into the difficulties in his position that this rhetorical slippage reveals.

14. I believe that a circumscribed notion of representation is implicit in Russell's *Principles* theory of denoting concepts. See Hylton, *Russell*, pp. 207–210 and 249–254. Apart from a worry about the variable, this representation-theoretic element drops out with the elimination of denoting, as explained in Russell's 1905 paper "On Denoting," *Mind* n.s. 14 (1905): 479–493. Russell does link the distinction between meaning and denotation to his notion of assertion in writings from the 1903–1905 period published in *Foundations of Logic: 1903–05*. Though I do not think that the tangles of Russell's views about denoting are centrally relevant to the issues I am addressing in this paper, I do think that more research on this point is necessary.

15. See especially Russell's unpublished 1905 paper, "Necessity and Possibility," in *Foundations of Logic: 1903–05*, pp. 507–520. Russell suggests there that "necessary" is best viewed as a predicate properly applied not to propositions but to propositional functions that yield true propositions for all their arguments, a view to which Russell adheres through 1919. See also "Some Explanations in Reply to Mr. Bradley," *Mind* n. s. 19 (1910): 372–378, especially p. 374. Russell also suggests in the 1905 paper that some uses of "necessary" are best replaced by "analytic," where, he says, a proposition is analytic if it is deducible from the laws of logic.

16. Moore, "Truth and Falsity," p. 717.

17. Russell uses this rhetoric in "The Nature of Truth," p. 495, and "Meinong's Theory," p. 523.

18. See *Principles*, §44, p. 40, and §§37–38.

19. "The Nature of Truth," pp. 493–494.

20. Gottlob Frege, "Der Gedanke," *Beiträge zur Philosophie des deutschen Idealismus* 1 (1918): 58–77, especially p. 60. I discuss Frege's argument in my "Logic and Truth in Frege," *Proceedings of the Aristotelian Society*, supplementary vol. 70 (1996): 121–140, especially pp. 128–131.

21. See Moore's *Principia Ethica* (Cambridge: Cambridge University Press, 1903), §13, pp. 15–17.

22. As I have presented it, Russell's argument against the correspondence theorist is limited in its persuasive force, for it relies on features of the metaphysics of

propositions that any correspondence theorist should reject. To my mind, the chief interest of the argument is the example it gives of the role Russell wants truth to play in his metaphysics and the problems it exposes for that role.

23. Moore, "Truth and Falsehood," p. 717. See also Moore, "The Nature of Judgment," *Mind* n.s. 8 (1899): 176–193, especially pp. 181 and 192.

24. "The Nature of Truth," p. 504.

25. Lewis Carroll, "What the Tortoise Said to Achilles," *Mind* n.s. 4 (1895): 278–280. I will not here be concerned with Russell's flailing discussion of Carroll's paradox.

26. *Principles*, §38, p. 35. I think that this application of the distinction between asserted and unasserted propositions motivates Russell's odd use of the word "asserted".

27. This picture is suggested by Moore's rhetoric in introducing propositions in "Nature of Judgment," p. 180: "A proposition is constituted by any number of concepts, together with a specific relation between them; and according to the nature of the relation, the proposition may be either true or false."

28. See *Principles*, §49, p. 46, and §483, p. 510.

29. At several junctures, the general notions of a term and of a proposition that Russell employs in his metaphysical foundations for logic in *Principles* either produce self-thwarting theses or antinomies. For an illuminating survey of Russell's views here and some other difficulties they encounter, see Leonard Linsky, "Terms and Propositions in Russell's Principles of Mathematics," *Journal of the History of Philosophy* 26 (1988): 621–642.

30. *Principles*, §52, p. 49.

31. I should note that Russell again asserts the distinction between propositions and propositional concepts in the summary of chapter IV in the penultimate paragraph of §55.

32. *Principles*, §478, p. 504.

33. Russell returns to logical assertion one final time in §483. He seems there again to put forward the second account of logical assertion from §52.

34. Russell does not in *Principles* formulate either this formal equivalence or its instances. Perhaps this is because his conception of a proposition permits straightforward generalization into sentential positions, obviating the need for a truth-predicate in the statement of logical laws.

35. "Meinong's Theory," p. 523.

36. Here I differ with Hylton's and Linsky's evaluation of this point. See Peter Hylton, "The Nature of the Proposition and the Revolt against Idealism," *Philosophy in History*, ed. R. Rorty, J. B. Schneewind, and Q. Skinner (Cambridge: Cambridge University Press, 1984), pp. 375–397, especially p. 385. See Leonard Linsky, "The Unity of the Proposition," p. 254.

37. "Meinong's Theory," p. 524.

38. Russell presents the multiple relation theory as a possible alternative to the metaphysics of propositions in §3 of "On the Nature of Truth," *Proceedings of the Aristotelian Society* 7 (1906–07). He embraces this alternative in *Principia Mathematica*, vol. 1 (Cambridge: Cambridge University Press, 1910), pp. 43–44, and in "On the Nature of Truth and Falsehood." He modifies the theory in *The Problems of Philosophy* (Oxford: Oxford University Press, 1959; original publication 1912), chapter 12. He makes more extensive revisions in 1913 in *Theory of Knowledge*, part 2, chapters 1 and 5.

39. "On the Nature of Truth and Falsehood," p. 152.

40. In considering the multiple relation theory in 1906 in "On the Nature of Truth," p. 48, Russell presents compound true sentences that contain a false component sentence as very strong grounds for retaining the metaphysics of propositions. In *Theory of Knowledge*, p. 153, Russell recognizes the force of this point, but postpones treatment of it to a projected third part of the manuscript, "Molecular Propositional Thought," which was never written.

41. See Hylton, *Russell*, especially pp. 10–12 and 105–116. See also Hylton's "Logic in Russell's Logicism," in *The Analytic Tradition: Meaning, Thought, and Knowl-*

edge, ed. David Bell and Neil Cooper (Oxford: Basil Blackwell, 1991), pp. 137–172, especially §1.

42. See especially Russell's seminal 1901 paper, "Recent Work on the Principles of Mathematics," reprinted as "Mathematics and the Metaphysicians" in his *Mysticism and Logic* (London: George Allen and Unwin, 1963; original publication 1918).

43. Burton Dreben has long taught that the most profound debates between philosophers may resemble nothing so much as that old Abbott and Costello comedy routine, "Who's on first?"

44. F. H. Bradley, "On Appearance, Error, and Contradiction," *Mind* n.s. 19 (1910): 153–185. I quote here from p. 179.

45. "Some Explanations," p. 374.

46. Here I differ with the view presented by Bernard Linsky, "Why Russell Abandoned Russellian Propositions," in *Russell and Analytic Philosophy*, ed. A. D. Irving and G. A. Wedeking (Toronto: University of Toronto Press, 1993), pp. 193–209, especially p. 199.

47. Russell's views here are tangled and chaotic. In *Principles*, §71, p. 71, he suggests that the class whose members are the terms A and B is constituted as a whole, as a term via the combination of A and B by a unique kind of combination, itself not a relation, called "numerical conjunction."

48. Bradley, "On Appearance, Error and Contradiction," p. 182.

49. "Some Explanations," p. 376.

50. See *Principia Mathematica*, vol. I, p. 44, and "On the Nature of Truth and Falsehood," p. 151. The multiple relation theory only explains how to eliminate apparent designations of propositions in the context of some propositional attitude ascriptions. Furthermore, unlike the case of classes, Russell never explains how to paraphrase away the apparent generalizations over propositions and propositional functions required by the logic of *Principia*. Russell shows himself aware of this difficulty with the multiple relation theory in *Theory of Knowledge*, p. 155.

51. It is, I think, misleading to say, as Leonard Linsky does, that in the multiple relation theory we have a "psychological solution to the problem of the unity of the proposition." See Linsky, "The Unity of the Proposition," pp. 257 and following. With the adoption of the metaphysics of facts, the problem Russell faces about the relationship between unity and truth in *Principles* vanishes. The unity of a judgment is secured by its status as a fact, a fact constituted by the holding of a relation that happens to be a psychological relation.

52. See *Theory of Knowledge*, p. 115. Somewhat more accurately, Russell identifies the proposition that Desdemona loves Cassio with the existentially general fact:

$$(\exists x)(\exists R)R(x, \text{Desdemona, Loving, Cassio}).$$

53. Russell and Bradley corresponded in April 1910 about Bradley's criticism of *Principles*. "Some Explanations" was published in the July 1910 number of *Mind*. The first published endorsement of the multiple relation theory I know is in "La Théorie des Types Logiques," *Revue de Métaphysique et de Morale* 18 (May 1910): 263–301. The English manuscript of this essay, "The Theory of Logical Types," appears in *Logical and Philosophical Papers: 1909–1913*, ed. John G. Slater, *The Collected Papers of Bertrand Russell*, vol. 6 (London: Routledge, 1992): 3–31. The discussion of the multiple relation theory is in sec. 2 on pp. 10–11. Section iii of chapter 2 of the Introduction to *Principia Mathematica*, which contains *Principia*'s brief discussion of the multiple relation theory, reproduces verbatim sec. 2 of this manuscript. "On the Nature of Truth and Falsehood" is the only previously unpublished paper in *Philosophical Essays*, which appeared in November 1910. Volume one of *Principia* was published in December 1910. The chronological information comes from *Logical and Philosophical Papers: 1909–1913*.

54. See my "Pictures, Logic, and the Limits of Sense in Wittgenstein's *Tractatus*," §§2–3.

6

Husserl and the Linguistic Turn

CHARLES PARSONS

The study of the history of analytical philosophy generally begins with Frege. As a consequence, Edmund Husserl stands in some significant relation to that history almost from its beginning. Husserl and Frege exchanged letters in 1891; Husserl's first book, *Philosophie der Arithmetik* (1891), contained critical comments on Frege's *Die Grundlagen der Arithmetik* (1884); Frege reviewed Husserl's book; and they corresponded again in 1906. The relation between Frege's views and Husserl's, particularly in Husserl's *Logische Untersuchungen*[1] (1900–1901), and the possibility of a significant influence of Frege on Husserl's decisive turn away from psychologism in the late 1890s have been extensively explored. Husserl also enters the history at later points, in particular in the early period of the Vienna Circle. Influence of Husserl on Carnap is in evidence at least as late as *Der logische Aufbau der Welt* (1928),[2] but already then Carnap's philosophical direction is in many ways opposed to Husserl's. Schlick wrote a widely read criticism of Husserl's particular version of the synthetic a priori.[3]

My purpose is not to explore these or other historical relations, but rather to discuss some aspects of Husserl's relation to analytical philosophy in a more philosophical way, following the example of Michael Dummett in his recent *Origins of Analytical Philosophy*. Dummett is interested not only in the origins of analytical philosophy, but also in the origins of the "gulf" between analytical and so-called continental philosophy. From this double point of view, Husserl is clearly of particular interest. In his early period, his thinking was close enough to Frege's so that they could at least have exchanges with one another. Yet Husserl was the founder of the phenomenological movement, at one time the paradigm of continental philosophy at least in the eyes of English-speaking philosophers, and certainly a major source of subsequent continental philosophy. Dummett locates the beginning of the gulf in Husserl's transcendental turn of 1905–1907 and its published manifestation in *Ideas I* in 1913.[4]

I

Dummett's *Origins* is guided by a particular conception of what is fundamental to analytical philosophy, a conception which frames his assessment of Husserl's significance for the history of analytical philosophy and his more detailed discussions of Husserl. It also frames Dummett's more extensive and, as one would expect, more sympathetic discussion of Frege. Dummett's starting point is a thesis concerning what he calls the philosophy of thought; he says that what distinguishes analytical philosophy is "the belief, first, that a philosophical account of thought can be attained through a philosophical account of language, and, secondly, that a comprehensive account can only be so attained" (O, p. 4). He doesn't even attempt to propose an explanation of the term "thought" that wouldn't be tendentious among the different analytical philosophers adhering to this view. Instead, he relies heavily on Frege, whose use of "thought" has roughly the meaning of "proposition" in English-language philosophy.

   I shall make only a few remarks about the accuracy of Dummett's characterization of analytical philosophy, with reference to the different periods of its history.[5] And I shall distinguish two ways of objecting to it. First, Dummett holds that what has long been called the linguistic turn is the essence of analytical philosophy. Second, he offers a very specific statement about what the linguistic turn is, a statement dependent on his conception of a "philosophical account of thought," the search for which is a program he himself has followed and has found inspiration for in Frege. Some counterexamples to Dummett's characterization would impugn only the latter, more specific formulation, not the more general idea that the linguistic turn is the fundamental move distinguishing analytical philosophy, however difficult it might be to give an adequate general statement of what the linguistic turn is.[6] In fact, the idea that a certain kind of reflection on language is fundamental to much of philosophy does in my view characterize quite well one important period in the history of analytical philosophy, that of its rise to dominance in the English-speaking world, roughly from the early 1930s to the early 1960s.[7] But the critical discussions of Dummett's book have argued rather convincingly that his characterization does not fit the wider history.[8]

   Dummett contends that Husserl exemplified a philosophical development essential to the prehistory of analytic philosophy, namely "the extrusion of thoughts from the mind." According to Frege, thoughts are not constituents of the stream of consciousness; they exist independently of being grasped by a subject (O, p. 22). A similar view was held earlier by Bernard Bolzano, whose influence Husserl acknowledges. Just this step is taken by Husserl, first in his polemic against psychologism in the first volume (1900) of the *Logische Untersuchungen*. The result is what has been called a platonist theory of meaning. Evidently, Dummett considers this theory a fundamental step on the road to analytical philosophy. The reason is apparently that the "ontological mythology" that such a view involves gives rise to dissatisfaction that leads naturally to the linguistic turn. According to Dummett, "One in this position has therefore to look about him to find something non-mythological but objective and external to the individual mind to embody the thoughts which the individual subject grasps and may assent to or reject. Where better to find it than in the institution of a common language?" (O, p. 25).

   Dummett projects a highly idealized picture of how analytical philosophy originated, first through the extrusion of thoughts from the mind and then by the step just indicated to the linguistic turn. Husserl took the first of these steps but not

the second. Dummett sees in this a respect in which Husserl has positive importance for the history of analytical philosophy. But he sees Husserl's failure to take
the second step as one of the roots of the separation between continental and
analytic philosophy.

Now had Dummett said nothing more of a positive nature about Husserl's relevance to the history of analytical philosophy, then Peter Hylton would be justified in finding Dummett's claim for Husserl's importance seriously overstated.[9]
Dummett, however, implicitly makes another claim, with which I entirely agree.
This is, roughly, that Husserl is of great interest as an object of comparison. The
point is not to issue a call for an exercise in comparative philosophy. Rather, Frege
and Husserl worked at a time when there was no such schism as the later ana-
lytical-continental one, and the problems faced by each were similar (O, p. 4).
Although the actual debates between them were limited, they might have been
much greater.[10]

I would, somewhat speculatively, enlarge Dummett's case in the following way.
There were two late nineteenth-century scientific developments that had very
great importance for the development of philosophy. One was the beginning of
modern logic and (more broadly but a little less directly) the nineteenth-century
transformation of mathematics, both decisive for early analytical philosophy in
ways by now well known. The other was the development of scientific psychology,
originally institutionally united with philosophy, but gradually emancipated from
it. Many of the important founders of experimental psychology were psychologist-
philosophers, the exemplary and most influential case being Wilhelm Wundt. The
development of experimental psychology went hand-in-hand with the development of a more sophisticated philosophical psychology. Brentano's contribution
was mainly here, although he was a strong proponent of the growth of experimental psychology and through the work of pupils exercised a strong indirect
influence on it as well.

Husserl was perhaps the only major figure in philosophy who was formed intellectually by both the mathematical and the psychological currents of the time, as
is illustrated by the fact that his principal mentors were Weierstrass and Brentano.[11]
Unlike Frege, he was able to see the issues surrounding "psychologism" from both
sides. Although, at least in the *Logische Untersuchungen*, he does in a way "extrude
thoughts from the mind," he never at any time separates the issues concerning
the nature of thoughts from the philosophy of mind. What Frege says about such
matters combines rather traditional elements, such as a conception of "ideas"
hardly differing from that of classical empiricism, with elements derived from or
worked out in connection with his logic. Although Frege has the notion of grasping a thought (or, more generally, a sense), he says little about what this is. Husserl,
for better or for worse, always connects what he has to say about meaning with
a much larger story about mind and consciousness.

Although I am not qualified to engage seriously in the enterprise myself, I ap-
plaud the efforts of recent scholars such as Kevin Mulligan and Barry Smith to
give developments in psychology an important place in the history of philosophy
in the late nineteenth and early twentieth centuries. The attempt to develop a
philosophical psychology by a method that could be called scientific was, I think,

another source of the standards of argument and analysis associated with analytical philosophy, although its influence was not especially marked on the figures of early analytical philosophy.[12]

II

I provide these historical remarks as stage-setting for what is our proper concern,
themes in Husserl that relate him in an interesting way to analytical philosophy
as Dummett characterizes it. Our focus will be Dummett's question, Why did
Husserl not take the linguistic turn? And more generally, What separates Husserl
from analytical philosophy, in particular in *Ideas I*? Dummett's answer to the first
question is that Husserl's introduction of the noema, which Dummett sees as
involving the generalization of the notion of meaning to all acts, made the linguistic turn impossible.[13]

This answer poses a difficulty for Dummett's historical picture, since the essentials for the generalization of meaning to all acts are already present in the *Logische
Untersuchungen*. Acts are intentional experiences. And intentional experiences are
distinguished by the peculiarly intentional relation to an object that for Brentano
was distinctive of "mental phenomena." A point Dummett himself emphasizes is
that linguistic expressions, on actual occasions of use, are meaningful by virtue
of accompanying "meaning-conferring acts" on the part of the speaker. The meaning on that occasion of the expressions the speaker uses is a function of these acts,
which themselves have semantic properties. The Fifth Investigation is devoted
to exploring these matters for acts in general. All acts have matter and quality,
which are analogous to sense and force in Frege's scheme. For present purposes,
it is matter that is important, since it is matter that determines the relation to an
object, not only to what object an act is directed, but how it is directed to it. "The
matter, therefore, must be that element in an act that first gives it reference to an
object, and reference so wholly definite that it not merely fixes the object meant
in a general way, but also the precise way in which it is meant" (LU V, §20, II/1
415, F 589; the emphases added in the second edition are here omitted). Shortly
thereafter, Husserl characterizes the matter as the "sense of the objectual interpretation [Auffassung]" (II/1 416).

Now the matter is, according to Husserl, a moment of the act, whereas according to him meanings are ideal. In the *Logische Untersuchungen*, they are "species,"
that is, universals instantiated by something concrete. But what instantiates them
is the matter of meaning-conferring acts.[14] Husserl introduces this species conception of meaning explicitly only for expressions. Matter and quality together
constitute what he calls the intentional essence of an act. In the special case of
acts "that function or can function as meaning-conferring acts for expressions,"
he talks of the semantic essence (bedeutungsmäßiges Wesen) of the act. "Its ide-
ating abstraction gives rise to the meaning in our ideal sense" (LU V §21, II/1
417, F 590).[15] Husserl makes clear, however, that different acts of other kinds,
for example perception, even of different subjects, can share intentional essence
and matter in particular, and he ends a discussion of different types of acts by

saying that something analogous holds for acts of every kind (II/1 420). The motivation for Husserl's introducing ideal meanings only for expressions is probably his concern to give an account of the meaning of linguistic expressions and not to confine talk of meaning to the case of linguistic expressions alone.

What, then, is the difference made by the introduction of the noema? In the terms of *Ideas I*, the earlier concepts of matter and quality describe aspects of noesis; the matter of an act is a genuine moment of it, so that it is what Husserl calls *reell*. I'm not enough of a Husserl scholar to give a full account of why Husserl became dissatisfied with the conception of ideal meanings as species. Clearly, he thought of the correlation of noesis and noema as more intimate than that between the matter of an act and the ideal meaning it instantiates. On Husserl's account, different noeses, that is, different acts, with exactly the same noema differ only "numerically," or only as events in conscious life; intentionally they are the same. However, the equivalence involved is far more refined than what we would ordinarily recognize as sharing a species. Indeed, in §94 of *Ideas I*, Husserl makes it clear that the correlation of the noemata to acts of judgment is more refined than the assignment of meanings that concerns logic, what we might call the assignment of the proposition expressed. Thus, in the case of linguistic expressions, the move from the species conception of ideal meaning to the noema conception introduces a more refined way of distinguishing among meaning-conferring acts. There remains the question of how equivalences among acts that are not meaning-conferring should be determined. The *Logische Untersuchungen* had suggested the possibility of applying the less refined species account here. Husserl's move to the noema yields a more fine-grained account of act equivalences in this case as well.

In §94 of *Ideas I*, Husserl brings the notion of noema to bear on perceptual judgments. He says that, in the case of an object presented in a certain way, that mode of presentation of that object enters into the noema of the act of judgment (p. 194). Suppose I perceive an apple tree before me and judge that it is in bloom. I might express this by saying, "That apple tree is in bloom." On this view, however, the noema of the judgment would incorporate the noema of the perception of the tree, which already on the level of sense would be far richer than what is communicated in the reference to "that apple tree." The hearer may understand the latter with the help of his own perception of the tree, the perspective of which will differ from the speaker's, so that this perception will have a distinguishable noema. Which apple tree is referred to may of course also be determined in some other way, so that the hearer does not need to perceive the tree in order to understand what apple tree is being said to be in bloom.

Husserl's focus in this passage is on the sense of the judgment as an experience (*Urteilserlebnis*). We should perhaps think of the question as being, first of all, What is the full sense of the judgment when it is made privately, in response to the perception?[16] Husserl explicitly refrains from bringing in at this point the complications of expressing the judgment verbally. The contrast Husserl makes between the full noema that is at issue when we "take 'the' judgment exactly as it is conscious in this experience" and the judgment that concerns formal logic implies, for the reasons just given, that we should not expect full identity of sense between them (pp. 195–196). The contrast Husserl explicitly makes, however, is not one of sense but one drawing on other dimensions of the noema.

Before going further, we have to consider the connection of the concept of noema with Husserl's transcendental idealism. That the introduction of the noema coincided with the transcendental turn is, for Dummett, a reason for locating the beginning of the gulf between analytical and continental philosophy in the development leading to *Ideas I*. This could not be because idealism as such is alien to analytical philosophy; it is not. But it can hardly be disputed that Husserl's version of idealism is alien to *early* analytical philosophy. Even those who dispute the interpretation (held by Dummett) of Frege as a thoroughgoing realist will agree that there is no place in Frege's philosophy for a transcendental ego and its "constitution," whatever that elusive Husserlian term means. And of course Russell and Moore explicitly reacted against British idealism. Although there are echoes of transcendental philosophy in Wittgenstein's *Tractatus*, here too the upshot is quite different from that in Husserl, as for example in Wittgenstein's statement that solipsism in the end coincides with pure realism (5.64).

Thus we need to ask, How far is Husserl's conception of the noema bound up with idealism? It is certainly explained in a way that presupposes the phenomenological reduction, at least in §88 of *Ideas I*, where Husserl uses the example of perceiving with pleasure a blooming apple tree. The explanation of the conception includes the equation of the perceptual sense (noematic sense) with "the perceived as such," of judging with "the judged as such," and so on (p. 182), equations that have given rise to much controversy among Husserl's interpreters. Husserl wants to describe the fact that, when the positing of the world and of particular objects in a perception or a thought has been bracketed, it still remains a perception of, or a thought of, its objects. In his example of perceiving with pleasure a blooming apple tree, the "transcendent" tree itself is bracketed. "And yet, so to speak," Husserl writes, "everything remains as of old. Even the phenomenologically reduced perceptual experience is perception of 'this booming apple tree, in this garden, etc.,' and likewise the reduced liking is a liking of this same thing" (*Ideas I*, pp. 195–196). In the natural attitude, when I see the tree, I take it for granted that it is really there; in Husserl's terms from the *Logische Untersuchungen*, "positing" belongs to the quality of my act. In *Ideas I*, Husserl uses the term "thetic character." It belongs to my perceptual consciousness of the tree to take it to be really there. This is to say both more and less than that I believe the tree to be really there: more because it is part of perceptual consciousness; less because, although my perception may posit the tree, I may because of other knowledge distrust it and believe the tree is not really there. Since this positing is a moment of the perception itself, it does not disappear with the reduction; it is just "put out of action."[17] But what Husserl emphasizes at this point is that what he is calling the sense of the perception is not bracketed.[18] It is not in any case posited in the act itself but, rather, in the phenomenologist's reflection, despite his not being entitled to make any positing regarding the outer world. Since it is the sense of a perception, it must be the sense that the perception has independently of whether its positing is bracketed and independently of what judgments are made on the basis of it. (If there are such judgments, they too are potential fodder for phenomenology, although in that case what is put out of action is an essential element of what makes them judgments as opposed to propositional acts of other kinds.)

On my reading, it is clearly not necessary to undertake the phenomenological reduction in order to talk of the meaning of acts, and in the passage that has concerned me, Husserl says explicitly that "obviously the perceptual sense belongs to the phenomenologically unreduced perception (perception in the sense of psychology)" (*Ideas I*, §89, p. 184). For this reason, I think that Husserl's purpose in bringing in the reduction at this point is to emphasize that the sense of our acts survives it, and the reduction makes it possible to engage in reflections having as objects only objects that are either really immanent in consciousness or are meanings of them (in the broad sense including thetic character as well as sense, but not including reference). The conception of the noema is thus at least to a certain degree independent of the reduction and of transcendental idealism.

Husserl in *Ideas I* is, to be sure, more distant from analytical philosophy than he was in the *Logische Untersuchungen*. What is responsible for this is not, I think, the generalization of meaning to all acts, which I have argued is already present in the *Logische Untersuchungen*. Nor is it the further development of this generalization in Husserl's theory of the noema. Instead it is, I propose, the Cartesianism underlying the transcendental reduction. There is a step from the generalization of meaning to the reduction, but it requires a highly contestable assumption about meaning. Roughly, this assumption is that it is possible to express and to explicate the meaning of our acts, even on a quite global level, without making any presuppositions about reference. In §89 of *Ideas I*, Husserl describes statements about external reality as undergoing through the reduction a "radical modification of sense" (I, p. 183). Bringing to bear Frege's theory of indirect reference,[19] we could describe this reduction as consisting in our putting our whole description of the world into one big intensional context, where what is designated is not the ordinary reference of the words but their sense. This description must assume, however, that these senses do not presuppose, for their very existence and identity, reference to external reality. In particular, it must be assumed that there are no "Russellian" or "object-dependent" thoughts about external reality, which by their very nature involve reference to particular objects, often in the immediate environment. The sort of assumption I have in mind, however, is even stronger than the rejection of such thoughts. For meaning might be dependent on external reference in a more global or diffuse way. For example, it might be that we could not entertain the thoughts we do without an existing external world. Or, short of the nonexistence of the external world, it might be that we could not entertain the thoughts we do about the world if they were radically false. Such a more global dependence of meaning on reference does not imply the existence of Russellian thoughts as they are usually understood. But it is incompatible with the contestable assumption about meaning that leads from Husserl's generalization of meaning to his reduction.

The Cartesian tenor of Husserl's justifications of the reduction in *Ideas I* as well as in other texts, such as his *Cartesian Meditations*, clashes with at least the most characteristic views among analytical philosophers. At the time of *Ideas I*, Husserl's transcendental idealism probably also clashed with more widely held views in

British and American philosophy; that was after all a time of reaction against idealism and the revival of realism.[20] I would suggest, however, that it is only later developments that make this clash a step on the way to the gulf between analytic and *continental* philosophy. As regards Husserl's own thought, such a gulf is always limited by his adherence to rather traditional scientific ideals. I would further suggest that we can't very meaningfully speak of "continental" philosophy in anything like the sense current since the Second World War before Heidegger's *Sein und Zeit* (1927) and other work of the 1920s, such as that of Jaspers.[21] Moreover, we must consider that Husserl's transcendental idealism did not find wide acceptance and was not maintained in anything very close to Husserl's form by the most influential later phenomenological philosophers.

III

On Dummett's reading, Frege parallels Kant in distinguishing between sensibility and understanding, between the faculty of sensation and that of thought. Where Frege takes the linguistic turn, he applies it to the study of thoughts. He has quite a bit to say about ideas (*Vorstellungen*), taking as prominent examples ideas which Kant would have called sensible, in particular sense-impressions. But Frege makes no use of a connection between ideas and language to get at the structures of ideas. This is not only, though, because ideas have subjects as bearers, for so do propositional attitudes, but Frege's writings contain serious suggestions as to how to understand the structure of propositional attitudes by way of an analysis of sentences expressing them.

This simple observation is relevant to the question whether Husserl's generalization of meaning precluded the linguistic turn. For the generalization, that is the extension of the notion of meaning beyond its application to language, is most in evidence when it is applied in domains whose relation to a domain of *thought* is not simple or straightforward. Husserl repeatedly brings up examples from either perception or imagination. Dummett evidently believes that attributing something like a sense to perceptions is incompatible with the linguistic turn (O, p. 27). The question is, Why? An inadequate answer would be that a philosopher who believes that perception involves something fundamentally different from thought could not take the linguistic turn. For Frege and a large number of subsequent analytic philosophers, including Dummett himself, who certainly do take the linguistic turn, also accept the Kantian distinction between perception and thought.[22] In any event, the acceptance of this distinction does not obviously go against Dummett's axiomatic characterization of the linguistic turn: that thought can and must be analyzed in terms of language. So we must seek further to see where and how Husserl might have violated Dummett's axioms of analytical philosophy.

Thoughts as Frege understood them are propositional, and Frege's steps toward the linguistic turn are thus bound up with the context principle. Translated into the terms of an inquiry into thought, the principle says that "there is no such thing as thinking of an object save in the course of thinking something specific about it" (O, p. 5). One might say that, at least in the domain of thought, intentionality is fundamentally propositional. As for perception, according to Frege, something "nonsensible" is necessary for perception to represent an outside world. Discussing Frege's view of perception, Dummett argues that this "nonsensible" must be a complete thought and, at least in most cases, a judgment (O, p. 97). That would give a handle to the linguistic turn, though not one developed by Frege. We are, however, still left with the sensible element, in Frege's case the sense-impressions. For Frege himself that remained an obstacle, because in his view ideas are incommunicable. The notion that there is *something* incommunicable in sensory experience dies hard, as is shown by contemporary controversies about qualia. But is it clear that every philosophical view about such incommunicability is incompatible with Dummett's axioms? To show this, we would have to show that sense-impressions or qualia or whatever either belong to the domain of thought, or else do not exist.

However this may be, Dummett's claim that it is Husserl's generalization of meaning that precludes him from taking the linguistic turn raises other issues than those about sense-impressions.[23] Let us pursue the matter of Husserl's view of the perceptual noema. Dummett attributes to Husserl the view that the noematic sense of acts in general is expressible in language, a view developed by Føllesdal's pupils, particularly Smith and McIntyre.[24] It seems that such expression should give us the same kind of handle on the noematic sense of perceptions as we have on the structure of thoughts. That would call in question Dummett's claim that Husserl's attribution of sense to perceptions precludes him from adopting the twin axioms of the analytical tradition.

Husserl describes the noematic sense of a perception as "the perceived as such"; one way of saying what this involves would be to say that it is the sense that would be expressed by the subject in saying *what* he perceives. Clearly, any one statement would express this sense very incompletely. So the sense would have to be taken to be expressible in the sense that the subject is able to express, through more and more detailed description, everything contained in it. Full expression could be an infinite task. Moreover, there is a criterion of the accuracy of an expression: what is reported should be only what is perceived and not more, although it can and should include what is illusory, provided that it is illusory *perception* and a mistaken judgment of some other kind. This may be a difficult distinction to make, but Husserl's conception of horizon is sensitive to the facts involved. The difficulty, related to other difficulties about meaning discussed in the analytic tradition, is how to separate what belongs to the perception itself from what belongs to the background the subject brings to it and the inferences he makes from it.

Dummett admits that noematic senses generally are expressible. But why does he nonetheless think that Husserl's theory of the senses of perceptions—or of acts generally—makes the resources of an analysis of language unavailable to him?

One reason seems to me to point to something important about perception, though it does not get to the heart of the issue. Dummett refers to two additional components of Husserl's noema beyond the noematic sense, components he says are not expressible. The first such aspect of the noema plays a role like that of Frege's force; an example is the positing involved in normal perception. The second aspect is perhaps not really a dimension of meaning at all; it is what makes an act the particular kind of act that it is—a perception, imagination, or judgment. If there is enough correspondence between language and other embodiments of meaning, we can capture noematic sense and the first of these aspects of the noema by using words of the right sense and force. But how could words *express* the second additional aspect? Words can describe it, as when we say that an act is a perception. And perhaps words could express it in a broader sense of "express," as when we talk of expressing emotion, or when Wittgenstein talks of the natural expression of pain. But these questions of expression, interesting though they are, are not an issue between Husserl and analytical philosophy as Dummett characterizes it. For they concern what *distinguishes* perception from thought.

The second, more fundamental reason why Dummett thinks Husserl's conception of the noema of acts like perceptions violates his axioms of analytical philosophy is expressed in the following telling comment:

> We should expect the veridicality of the perception or memory, the realization of the fear or satisfaction of the hope, and so on, to be explicable as the truth of a judgment or proposition contained within the noematic sense; but we do not know how the constituent meanings combine to constitute a state of affairs as intentional object, since they are not, like Frege's senses, by their very essence aimed at truth (O, 116).

Perception, according to Husserl, is an act directed to the object perceived; if we can attribute to it sense and reference, the reference, if it exists, will be just the object perceived. It thus seems that what the sense would have to "aim at" is reference to this object, something quite different from truth.

Husserl has a reply to Dummett's objection, a reply drawing on a dimension of his philosophy that Dummett does not treat in *Origins* or elsewhere, though it has some relevance to his own views. There is something a meaning-intention aims at, what Husserl calls "fulfillment," which is achieved when the object of the act is given. The schema of intention and fulfillment is central to Husserl's account of meaning, in particular in application to nonlinguistic cases like perception. In external perception the object *is* given, *leibhaft gegeben* in Husserl's famous phrase. That case has, however, a special complexity because external perception always contains unfulfilled intentions toward aspects of the object that are not properly speaking perceived, such as the back and the inside of an opaque object. A full description of the meaning of a perception would have to describe both what is "bodily present" and what would fulfill the unfulfilled intentions in the perception.

The intention-fulfillment schema generalizes not the relation of propositions to truth, but their relation to verification. In fact, in Husserl's discussion of truth, much of what he says suggests a verificationist view.[25] This is of interest because there is a line of descent from Husserl to Heyting's explanation of the intuitionistic meaning of the logical connectives, and from there to much of what Dummett himself has written about an antirealist program in the theory of meaning. It seems to me that, to be consistent with his own views, Dummett has to take the difficulty with Husserl's generalization of the notion of meaning to lie in the manner of its generalization to categories other than sentences, propositions, or judgments, rather than in Husserl's replacement of the notion of truth with the more directly epistemic notion of fulfillment. In his reply to my APA paper, Dummett raises another point, namely that Husserl does not give a compositional theory in his discussions of meaning. This can't really be quarreled with: though Husserl did have ideas for the program of giving such a theory, even in application to linguistic meaning his position is far less developed than Frege's. It is also the case that Husserl does not hold a principle like Frege's context principle; for Husserl, terms are at least as basic units as sentences. But this is not a fatal obstacle, as is indicated by the existence of formalized languages based on the λ-calculus and their application to the semantics of natural language. I suspect that what Dummett sees as fatal to Husserl's taking the linguistic turn is his generalization of the notion of meaning to a domain where a compositional theory is not possible. That that might be the case for perception is not wildly unlikely. But since perception is not thought, the implications of such a conclusion for the linguistic turn as Dummett conceives it are not obvious.

IV

Now let us consider the delicate question of whether fulfillment of a perception (or perhaps of any act) can properly be considered to be, in Dummett's terms, the verification of "judgments or propositions contained in the noematic sense" (O, p. 116, quoted above). Husserl's view was that perceptions are "nominal" and not "propositional" acts; an expression in language of their senses would, I have suggested, be given by saying what is perceived. That would be done more faithfully to Husserl's intention by using noun phrases rather than sentences. Furthermore, Husserl distinguishes the positing involved in perception from that in judgment. The former positing might be compared to using a singular noun phrase with the presupposition that it designates something, though we should not rush to the conclusion that some proposition to the effect that the phrase designates something, or of the form "P exists," where P is the phrase in question, is part of the noema of the act. Still Husserl seems to regard perception as attributing properties to the perceived object.

It is instructive to consider a passage in *Ideas I*, §124, the same section Dummett adduces to justify attributing to Husserl the thesis that noematic senses are expressible (O, p. 114). Husserl writes that:

> For example: an object is present to perception with a determined sense, posited monothetically in the [thus] determined fullness. As is our normal custom after first seizing upon something perceptually, we effect an explicating of the given and a relational positing which unifies the parts or moments singled out perhaps according to the schema, "This is white." This process does not require the minimum of "expression," neither of expression in the sense of verbal sound, nor of anything like a verbal signifying. But if we have *"thought"* or *asserted*, "This is white," then a new stratum is co-present, unified with the purely perceptual "meant as meant." (I, pp. 256–257)

In the next paragraph of §124 (quoted by Dummett), Husserl writes, "'Expression' is a remarkable form, which allows itself to be adapted to every 'sense' (to the noematic 'nucleus') and raises it to the realm of 'logos,' of the *conceptual* and thereby of the *universal*."

The "new stratum," evidently conceptual, must be what prompts Dummett's comment that the noematic sense "can be expressed linguistically, but is not, in general, present as so expressed in the mental act which it informs" (O, p. 114). In the passage I have quoted, Husserl does not use noun phrases to express the sense, as I have suggested he might have done; rather, he uses a sentence. That seems to me, however, not the essential point. It seems that neither the sentence, "This is white," nor a noun phrase like "this white thing" gives quite accurately even that part of the meaning of the perception it is meant to render. On Husserl's conception, nominal acts are simpler than propositional acts; nominal acts simply intend an object, whereas a synthesis connecting such references is necessary for judgment. Moreover, it is by *expression* that the "conceptual" and "universal" are brought in. The reference to explicating "parts or moments" also suggests that it may be Husserl's view that what is meant *perceptually* is the object's particular moment of whiteness, not *that it is white*.[26] If that is so, then the expression in language does not quite give the perceptual sense, since that aspect is not explicitly preserved in the linguistic expression. But elsewhere (for example at the end of §130), Husserl does say that the noema contains "predicates." That seems to be his dominant view in *Ideas I*. If there is equivocation, it is in response to a genuine philosophical difficulty, which, though its particular formulation may be an artifact of Husserl's apparatus and commitments, also arises in other philosophical discussions of perception. The difficulty is how perceptual consciousness is related to belief and judgment. One is reminded of the debate of recent years about whether there is a "nonconceptual" content of experience, with Gareth Evans and Christopher Peacocke taking the affirmative side and John McDowell the negative.[27] More simply put, Does the statement that someone sees that this is white report what he sees, or rather report a judgment he makes on the basis of what he sees?

It is not clear to me how Husserl reconciles the view that nominal acts are inherently simpler than propositional acts with the view of perception as attributing properties to the object and therefore as presumably involving the subject in something that, if not exactly judgment, at least has the content *that x is F*. And the source of my unclarity is not only, I think, the limitations of my knowledge of Husserl.

Let me first consider the view that Mulligan finds in Husserl's earlier writings. In fact, it is not directly inconsistent with the interpretation of *Ideas I* I have favored, according to which the noema of an act attributes properties to the object. For the view Mulligan develops is about the *objects* of perceptual acts. According to it, perception of a white object will contain a perception of its color moment. If the subject's attention is directed to the color moment, however, things will be in a way reversed: the perception of the color moment will, as a perception of a moment of a certain object, "contain" a perception of the object, but now relegated a little bit into the background. It is important to realize that these remarks concern the object and not the noematic sense. But the implication seems to be that an act directed to the moment of whiteness will have its own noematic sense. It seems that we could not rule out different acts, or even different perceptions, having the same moment of whiteness as their object but differing in noematic sense. In what could this difference consist? At least one possible (no doubt partial) answer would take us back where we were before: that different acts would attribute to the moment different *properties*. That seems to be the answer implicit in *Ideas I*, and I am not sure what other answers are available. I confess I also have difficulty understanding what the moments corresponding to properties and relations are. Can I understand what an object's moment of whiteness is without understanding what it is for it to be white? Husserl might concede that I cannot but reply that neither is necessary in order to *see* the object's moment of whiteness. But how is seeing a moment of whiteness different from seeing a white object whose color is visible? That there is some consciousness of the color of an object that is more primitive than applying the specific concept *white* to it will probably be accepted by all parties to such disputes. But if the moment is not derivative from the concept or property, why is its specific description helpful in understanding how perception of a white object can ground the judgment that it is white?[28] It seems as difficult to get from a perception of a white color-moment to the judgment that the object is *white* as to see that the object is white to begin with. If the perception of the moment is thus derivative, have we really captured the greater primitiveness of the consciousness of color? It seems to me that an appeal to perception as perception of moments of properties does not resolve our difficulty.

Another point is that it is not at all clear how Husserl conceives the role of such moments where relations are concerned. In introducing the conception of a property-moment, Husserl says, in his Third Investigation, that "every *non-relational* 'real' predicate therefore points to a part of the object which is the predicate's subject" (LU III §2, II/1 228, F 437; emphasis mine). So far as I have determined, though, he does not say here whether something analogous holds for relational predicates of two or more places. In perceptual cases, he might well say that to relations correspond certain unity-moments of what is perceived as a whole; certainly it was part of his view that there are such moments. Outside the perceptual context, however, that line of argument is highly strained. In the account of the genesis of judgments of the form "*S is p*" in §§50–52 of *Erfahrung und Urteil*, Husserl treats perception of the object *S* and of its *p*-moment. And in §53, he discusses the corresponding issue of simple relational judgments. I don't find his treatment very clear, but at least he avoids claiming that, if *A* is greater than *B*, there is something "in" *A* that is the individual manifestation of its being greater than *B*. Instead, the text seems to favor the interpretation according to which, in general, relations do not have corresponding to them moments of the objects they relate in the way that monadic properties do. For example, Husserl summarizes the discussion with the remark:

Accordingly, we must distinguish:
1. *Absolute adjectivity.* To every absolute adjective corresponds a dependent moment of the substrate of determination, arising in internal explication and determination.

2. *Relative adjectivity*, arising on the basis of external contemplation and the positing of relational unity, as well as the act of relational judgment erected on it.[29]

In cases where the noema of a perception attributes a monadic property (say, whiteness) to the object, it is reasonable to suppose that the perception is, among other things, of a moment corresponding to that property. A perceptual noema will, however, also attribute all sorts of relations; Husserl's view on the extent to which these too are based on perception of moments is not clear to me. Husserl's reluctance to extend such a view to even the most basic relational judgments casts doubt on the attribution to him of the suggestion (to me very implausible) that every relation between objects A and B holds by virtue of a moment of some complex consisting of A and B.

Let us attack again the distinction between perception and perceptual judgment. We can certainly distinguish between seeing a white object, say a white sheet of paper, and seeing of the sheet that it is white, or seeing that there is a sheet of white paper present. Now I may see a white sheet of paper without in any way identifying it as such, for example, if the lighting conditions deceive me as to its color and for some other reason I also do not detect its being paper. In that case, only another person, or I myself in the light of later knowledge, can say that I see (or saw) a sheet of white paper. For this reason, we normally take "x sees y" to be a straightforward predicate, with whatever replaces "y" as purely referential. But in the normal case, our perception is of a sheet of white paper in an intentional sense; on the interpretation we have been following, we could use the phrase "a sheet of white paper" to render part of the noematic sense of the perception. In this situation, we see it as a sheet of white paper. For Husserl, that the conception of the noema as attributing properties such as these does not imply that we judge that the paper is white, as perhaps we do when we express our perception by making a remark to that effect, should be clear from the above-quoted passage from §124 of *Ideas I*. Reserving the locution "see that the paper is white" for the case where there is a judgment would preserve Husserl's view of perception as a nominal and not a propositional act.[30]

I offer these observations in order to clarify the distinction between the noematic sense of a perception and the content of a perceptual judgment. But I still have to consider the question of the simplicity of perception. Our inclination would be to think of predicates in a more or less Fregean way, as sentences with empty argument places, so that, if our perception has the content "a white sheet of paper," that perception would presuppose "x is white" and "x is a sheet of paper." But we should not assume that Husserl thought of predicates in this way.

In his account in *Erfahrung und Urteil*, the clearest difference between the "prepredicative" level of perceptual experience and the level at which predicative judgment emerges is that the attribution of properties to the object at the former level is implicit and only becomes explicit upon both singling out certain properties and, by a synthesis giving rise to a judgment, formulating judgments of the form "S is p." This account would allow Husserl to hold, as Evans did, that there is a level of experience that has content that would be expressed by attributing properties to objects but does not require having the concepts that enter into the judgments. Thus, for example, seeing something as white might be reflected in behavior in various ways without the judgment that it is white being formulated and, in particular, without undertaking the commitment that such a judgment involves.[31] On this account, the perceptual judgment that x is white, for example, makes explicit something implicit in the perception. Husserl clearly thinks that even the most primitive judgment applies to the object a general concept,[32] though the point is obscured in his account of the genesis of a monadic judgment by his emphasis on attending to moments. For him, there is always then still implicit in the judgment a reference to the general essence, say whiteness. Husserl does not tell us, though, how the generality arises. Since he makes clear that something of the kind is already present in pre-predicative experience, however, it too could be a making explicit of what was implicit.

Our problem reduces, finally, to an independent difficulty, namely how a propositional act arises by a "synthesis" of subject and predicate and how it is thus founded on prior nominal acts. Husserl's view seems to me bound to leave mysterious how the generality of the predicate arises. We can agree with Husserl that there is a level where predication remains implicit while also agreeing with Frege that what is thus implicit is something of propositional form, what I have expressed as that x is F. On this strategy, propositional acts are indeed founded on nominal acts, but in the following way: acts with definite propositional content are seen to arise from the making explicit of contents of perception that are already propositional, though implicitly so. This making explicit, by singling out one particular predicate, obviously leaves out much else that is part of the content of the perception. But a simple judgment does have the property of being founded on prior nominal acts, since it is clearly founded on the perception of the object involved.[33] Such is what happens when the noema of a perception is expressed.

Whatever we think about the adequacy of Husserl's analyses, it is important to see that his problems with the relation of the noema of a perception to its expression concern, not thought itself, but how perception relates to thought. The idea that perception has a sense does not, then, make the linguistic turn impossible for Husserl. It is true that the separation between "thought itself" and what is centrally related to it will seem too neat. But then we see a problem with the linguistic turn: the expressibility of the sense of a perception leaves, as both Husserl and Dummett point out, an unavoidable distance between the perception and the expression of it. This is, however, not obviously an artifact of the idea of the noema. For perception and perceptual judgment are not the same thing. Rather, the dependence of thought on perception implies that something important for the study of thought has to be approached by other methods. This might indeed be a reason for not giving the linguistic turn quite the central role many analytic philosophers have given it. The result need not be the adoption of a method like Husserl's phenomenological method, but some method is needed, perhaps an appropriation and analysis of the results of empirical psychology.

Husserl's thinking has another feature that separates him from the mainstream of analytical philosophy. However, it was present in Husserl's thought from the beginning and is not a product of the period of his transcendental turn. That is that for him the basic concept is that of intentionality, where intentionality is consciousness of an *object*. In spite of the fact that he attributes something like force to all acts, nothing like Frege's context principle ever occurs to Husserl. To the contrary, he searches in much of his philosophizing for a level of meaning more basic than anything that takes propositional form. I would see this as the fundamental obstacle to Husserl's taking the linguistic turn. It might well be argued that his treatment of questions clearly within the philosophy of thought as Dummett conceives it suffers as a result. But his explorations of perception and time-consciousness are not obviously part of that domain, and it would take a great deal of argument to show that there too the linguistic turn would provide the key. Ironically, although Husserl's philosophy of perception may be the part of his work that has most attracted analytical philosophers,[34] perception is a domain where the linguistic turn as Dummett formulates it seems to encounter limits.

NOTES

The present chapter is descended from a paper written for a symposium on Michael Dummett's *Origins of Analytical Philosophy* (Cambridge, Mass.: Harvard University Press, 1993) (hereafter O) at the meeting of the Central Division of the American Philosophical Association in Pittsburgh on April 26, 1997, with Richard Cartwright as cosymposiast. That paper concentrated on what Dummett had to say about Husserl. The further work leading to the present paper owes much to Dummett's constructive and interesting reply on that occasion and to comments by Jason Stanley. Dagfinn Føllesdal also commented in detail on a presentation of the same paper at the University of Oslo, and he has made other helpful suggestions. I am indebted to Pierre Keller both for written comments on an intermediate version and for a helpful discussion. Much of the writing of the present version was done during a visit to the University of Oslo, to which I am indebted for hospitality and support, in particular again to Dagfinn Føllesdal. I am grateful to the editors for the many improvements they have proposed.

1. Vol. I (Halle: Niemeyer, 1900), vol. II (Halle: Niemeyer, 1901), 2d. ed., vol. I and vol. II, part 1 (Halle: Niemeyer, 1913), and 2d. ed., vol. II, part 2, (Halle: Niemeyer, 1921) (hereafter LU). I will give page references to the second German edition and to J. N. Findlay's translation of that edition, *Logical Investigations* (London: Routledge and Kegan Paul, 1970) (hereafter F), which I will quote with some modifications. The differences from the first edition, though important for many purposes, play no role in my discussion.

2. This was pointed out to me by Abraham Stone.

3. Moritz Schlick, "Gibt es ein materiales Apriori?" in Schlick, *Gesammelte Aufsätze, 1926–36* (Wien: Gerold, 1938), pp. 19–30.

4. *Ideen zu einer reinen Phänomenologie und phänomenologischen Philosophie. Erstes Buch: Allgemeine Einführung in die reine Phänomenologie* (Halle: Niemeyer, 1913). I will give page references and section numbers for the original German edition (hereafter I); they are included in the two *Husserliana* editions and in F. Kersten's translation, *Ideas Pertaining to a Pure Phenomenology and to a Phenomenological Philosophy, First book. General Introduction to a Pure Phenomenology* (The Hague: Nijhoff, 1982). My quotations will largely follow that translation.

5. With respect to early analytical philosophy (by which I mean roughly the period from Frege through the publication of Wittgenstein's *Tractatus*), see Peter Hylton, Review of *Origins of Analytical Philosophy*, *Journal of Philosophy* 92 (1995): 556–563 (hereafter Hylton 1995).

6. Thus Herman Philipse questions whether Wittgenstein, not only a paradigm analytical philosopher but one to whom Dummett appeals, would embrace the idea of a comprehensive philosophical account of thought; see his "Husserl and the Origins of Analytical Philosophy," *European Journal of Philosophy* 2 (1994): 165–184 (hereafter Philipse 1994), p. 167. In commenting on my APA paper, Dagfinn Føllesdal remarked that Quine, surely an exemplar of the linguistic turn, is skeptical about the very idea of thought as Dummett conceives it; cf. his "Analytic Philosophy: What Is It and Why Should One Engage in It?" *Ratio* n.s. 9 (1996): 193–208, p. 195.

7. The *terminus a quo* is chosen in part because the 1930s saw the beginning of the Oxford tradition of analytical philosophy as well as the emigration of leading logical positivists to the United States. Around 1960 the idea that "analysis of language" should displace "metaphysics" began to lose its hold. Another development of that time was the growing influence of Rawls, which ended analytical moral philosophers' almost exclusive concentration on metaethics.

8. On early analytical philosophy, see Hylton (1995) and more generally Philipse (1994).

9. Hylton (1995). Hylton writes as if the issue were whether Husserl is a "precursor of analytic philosophy," a claim he attributes to Dummett. I think that frames the question of Husserl's relevance too narrowly, at least if one works with a conception like Dummett's of what analytical philosophy is, or even with Hylton's contrasting understanding of what is essential in early analytical philosophy.

10. For example, if Frege had been a little younger when LU appeared and had not gone through the period of greatest discouragement in his life in the years just afterward.

11. Husserl himself confirmed as much at a celebration of his seventieth birthday in 1929. See Karl Schuhmann, *Husserl-Chronik* (The Hague: Nijhoff, 1977), p. 345. (Thanks to Dagfinn Føllesdal for pointing this out.)

12. These considerations would also suggest that the antipsychologism of Frege, Husserl, and other figures of the turn of the century should be studied with close attention to the views of those they were criticizing. Much valuable work of this kind has been done by Eva Picardi, herself a former student of Dummett who played a role in the origins of *Origins* (O, p. vii).

13. Dummett's reading of Husserl is clearly much influenced by Dagfinn Føllesdal. That is also true of my own. It would be interesting to see the issues considered here discussed by a commentator who disputes Føllesdal's theses concerning the noema (see Føllesdal, "Husserl's Notion of Noema," *Journal of Philosophy* 66 [1969]: 680–687). Philipse is apparently such a commentator (see O, p. 71), but the discussion of Husserl in Philipse (1994) takes another direction.

14. Compare Peter Simons, "Meaning and Language," in *The Cambridge Companion to Husserl*, ed. Barry Smith and David Woodruff Smith (Cambridge: Cambridge University Press, 1995) (hereafter Smith and Smith 1995), pp. 106–137, p. 114.

15. Husserl says he will have to investigate later whether all acts can serve as meaning-conferring acts.

16. We will consider later the problem of perception as attributing properties to an object. If I see a blooming apple tree, its being in bloom is plausibly already part of the noematic sense of the perception.

17. "As phenomenologists we abstain from all such positings. But on that account, we do not reject them by not 'taking them as our basis,' by not 'joining in' them. They are there; they belong essentially to the phenomenon" (I, §90, p. 187).

18. I ignore the fact that phenomenology also involves an eidetic reduction.

19. In fact, Husserl echoes Frege's theory in this passage, though probably not consciously, in using words such as "plant" and "tree" in quotes to indicate the modification of their meaning (I, p. 184).

20. Husserl gave lectures in London in 1922. There does not seem, though, to have been much understanding between him and the British philosophers he met.

See Herbert Spiegelberg, "Husserl in England: Facts and Lessons," *Journal of the British Society for Phenomenology* 1 (1970): 4–17

21. Consider Husserl's own comment, referring to his preface to the first English translation of *Ideas I*, which appeared in 1931:

> No account is taken, to be sure, of the situation in German philosophy (very different from the English), with its philosophy of life [*Lebensphilosophie*], its new anthropology, its philosophy of "existence," competing for dominance. Thus no account is taken of the reproaches of "intellectualism" or "rationalism" which have been made from these quarters against my phenomenology, and which are closely connected with my version of the concept of philosophy. In it I restore the most original idea of philosophy, which, since its first definite formulation by Plato, underlies our European philosophy and science and designates for it a task that cannot be lost ("Nachwort zu meinen *Ideen zu einer reinen Phänomenologie und phänomenologischen Philosophie*," appendix to *Ideen, Drittes Buch* [*Husserliana* V], ed. Marly Biemel [The Hague: Nijhoff 1952], p. 138; my translation).

22. Dummett explicitly affirmed this view in his reply to my APA paper.

23. In fact, Dummett is almost silent on Husserl's notion of hyletic data and does not rest any of his case on it.

24. See David Woodruff Smith and Ronald McIntyre, *Husserl and Intentionality* (Dordrecht: Reidel, 1982).

25. See LU VI §§36–39. These sections treat complete verification, however, as only an ideal possibility, and even that possibility is later called into question by the thesis of *Ideas I* that the inadequacy of perception of transcendent objects is essential to them. These issues are instructively discussed in Gail Soffer, *Husserl and the Question of Relativism* (Dordrecht: Kluwer, 1991), chapter 3.

26. This is the view taken by Kevin Mulligan in his rich and illuminating article, "Perception," in (Smith and Smith 1995). His interpretation refers, however, to *The Logische Untersuchungen* and Husserl's 1907 lectures, *Ding und Raum* (*Husserliana* XVI), ed. Ulrich Claesges (The Hague: Nijhoff, 1973), so to texts earlier than the *Ideas*. Still, that Husserl continued to hold this view in later years is indicated by his account of the genesis of perceptual judgment in *Erfahrung und Urteil* (Hamburg: Claassen, 1948) (hereafter Husserl 1948); see below.

27. See Gareth Evans, *The Varieties of Reference* (Oxford: Clarendon Press, 1982), chapter 5; Christopher Peacocke, *A Study of Concepts* (Cambridge, Mass.: MIT Press, 1992); and John McDowell, *Mind and World* (Cambridge, Mass.: Harvard University Press, 1994), lecture 3. The discussion in *Origins* of the consciousness of animals seems to be responding to this debate, and Dummett mentions McDowell's view in his reply to my APA paper. I have found it difficult to place Husserl's position on these issues. Mulligan clearly interprets the earlier Husserl as being on Evans's side, and the conception of "pre-predicative experience" in *Erfahrung und Urteil* does look to tend in that direction. But the fact that the noema is very much in the background in that work makes it difficult to draw any definitive conclusion.

28. The view that the perceptual moment is not derivative from the property seems to me more plausible in itself and probably as an interpretation of Husserl. Consider an object that is red in a particular way, say one that is scarlet. If its color moment derives from the property, then it seems it will need to have both a moment of redness and a moment of scarletness, and these would have to be distinguished. But I do not find any phenomenological basis for such a distinction.

29. Husserl (1948), §53, p. 267; the translation is by James S. Churchill and Karl Ameriks, *Experience and Judgement* (Evanston: Northwestern University Press, 1973) (hereafter Husserl 1973), pp. 224–225.

30. The suggestion of using a distinction between seeing as and seeing that in this connection was made to me in conversation by Pierre Keller, to whom I am much indebted here.

31. One difference between Husserl's discussion and the contemporary one is that he does not emphasize what does or does not belong to the "space of reasons," though I think the question is not entirely absent from his work.

32. Husserl (1948), §49, pp. 240–241; translation, Husserl (1973), p. 204.

33. Dagfinn Føllesdal suggested in conversation that the greater simplicity of perception is a matter of its thetic character. I think these remarks express some of what he had in mind; I would have liked, however, to pin the idea down more precisely.

34. That is certainly true of Føllesdal and his pupils and also of Mulligan.

PART II

Between the Wars

Logical Positivism and Critiques of Metaphysics

1921
Publication of Wittgenstein's
Tractatus Logico-Philosophicus

7

Number and Ascriptions of
Number in Wittgenstein's *Tractatus*

JULIET FLOYD

How are we to place the *Tractatus*'s remarks on arithmetic within the development of early analytic philosophy in relation to the work of Frege and Russell? Heretofore, the understandable focus of most readers has been Wittgenstein's characterization of the nature of logic and of the fundamental logical notions. The logical positivists took Wittgenstein's characterization of logic as "tautologous" or "analytic" to be the crux of his philosophical contribution, the key to the turning point in modern philosophy. Since they also held that Frege and Russell had demonstrated that arithmetic is a branch of logic, they happily applied the terms "tautologous" and/or "analytic" to mathematics as well, ignoring the fact that Wittgenstein never characterized logic and mathematics as a unity.

Indeed, in the *Tractatus*, Wittgenstein explicitly rejected the Frege-Russell attempt to prove that such a unified characterization is mandatory, holding that mathematics consists, not of tautologies, but of equations. Wittgenstein questioned the notion that Russell's axioms of Infinity and Reducibility are fundamental principles of logic (5.535, 6.1232, 6.1233), asserted that the Frege-Russell definition of the successor relation "suffers from a vicious circle" (4.1273), and remarked that "the theory of classes is superfluous in mathematics" (6.031). Ramsey felt that Wittgenstein's account of logic should be used to render the logicism of Frege and Russell "free from the serious objections which have caused its rejection by the majority of German authorities," but also held that the *Tractatus* view of mathematics as consisting, not of tautologies, but of equations, "is obviously a ridiculously narrow view of mathematics, and confines it to simple arithmetic."[1] Of the many philosophers who took Wittgenstein's terms "tautology" and "analytic" to appropriately characterize the nature of logic—both positivists and antipositivists— nearly all shared Ramsey's dismissive attitude toward Wittgenstein's treatment of arithmetic.[2]

Thus the problems of analysis that centrally occupied Frege and Russell in their works—the objectivity of arithmetic, the grammatical structure of ascriptions of number, explicit definitions of the natural numbers in logical terms, derivations of fundamental principles of arithmetic from logical axioms—were (until recently)[3] treated as peripheral to Wittgenstein's main philosophical concerns in the *Tractatus*.

This essay will attempt to remedy this tendency to pass over the *Tractatus* remarks on arithmetic in silence by exploring their relation to the philosophies of Frege and Russell. I haven't the space to do full interpretive justice to these remarks here. Nor shall I even attempt an exhaustive characterization of Wittgenstein's responses to Frege and Russell's philosophies of arithmetic. Instead, I shall argue that one cannot appreciate the full philosophical force of Wittgenstein's treatment of logic without taking his remarks on mathematics into account. The structure of this paper is then as follows. I first argue for the centrality of Wittgenstein's *Tractatus* remarks on mathematics to his early philosophy (section I) and probe the origins and significance of the terminology he uses in the *Tractatus* to characterize mathematics (section II). Next, I discuss what I take to be Wittgenstein's recasting of Frege's analogy between the grammatical structures of sentences and the grammatical structures of number words (section III). This sets the stage for an explication of Wittgenstein's unFregean, unRussellian handling of the grammar of ascriptions of number (section IV), and his idiosyncratic treatment of the variable (section V). Finally (in section VI), I characterize Wittgenstein's formal specification of the natural numbers in the *Tractatus* and his conception of the grammar of mathematical sentences.

I. Anti-Logicism in the *Tractatus*

An obvious question about the *Tractatus*'s treatment of number words concerns what Wittgenstein has to say about the logic of ascriptions of number, statements such as "there are three men on the street," and inferences such as "Tom has two peanuts and Larry has four peanuts, so together they have six peanuts." An analysis of the deductive structure of inferences involving such statements was arguably one of the principal glories of Frege and Russell. Max Black held that Wittgenstein failed even to address this issue.[4] Others disagree, arguing that the *Tractatus*'s treatment of arithmetical equations offers at least the beginnings of an account of the deductive structure of ascriptions of number: equations may be seen to express rules licensing the interchange of certain definite descriptions and numerical terms in nonarithmetical propositions.[5] Yet such a response fails to address the question of how Wittgenstein treated the grammar of extramathematical ascriptions of number ("Tom has two peanuts") unless we (wrongly) assume that he took these to be equations as well. Wittgenstein took equations to be neither identities nor genuine propositions. But extramathematical sentences ascribing number would seem to be genuine propositions: that Tom has three peanuts is either true or false. So a failure to account for the grammar of such sentences would appear to be a failure on Wittgenstein's part to account for the nature of the proposition. It should certainly incline us to think that Wittgenstein embraced a kind of formalism about mathematics of just the sort which Frege and Russell so effectively criticized in their works. Frascolla remarks that "[Wittgenstein]'s brief outline [of mathematics], without further elaboration, is not enough to account for numerical specifications in ordinary language asserting the number of the elements of the extension of a material concept and for the formal relations between these statements" (Frascolla 1994, p. 23).[6]

If this is correct, however, we are faced with a puzzle. For Wittgenstein had familiarized himself with Frege's *Grundgesetze*,[7] Russell's *Principles of Mathematics*,[8] and Whitehead and Russell's *Principia Mathematica*[9] well before writing the *Tractatus*. He knew at firsthand Frege's and Russell's emphases on the importance of applications of number and arithmetic. Frege and Russell *begin* by analyzing statements of cardinal number; they emphasize that only their analyses show how to represent the use of elementary arithmetic in ordinary inferences. Indeed, Frege's primary argument against formalism is that it cannot account for the logic of such inferences; hence, it cannot account for the content or "applicability" of arithmetic, that which differentiates arithmetic from a mere game like chess. Frege wrote in the *Grundgesetze*:

> Why can arithmetical equations be applied? Only because they express thoughts. How could we possibly apply an equation which expressed nothing and was nothing more than a group of figures, to be transformed into another group of figures in accordance with certain rules? Now, it is applicability alone which elevates arithmetic from a game to the rank of a science. So applicability necessarily belongs to it.[10]

Wittgenstein explicitly remarks in the *Tractatus* that mathematics consists essentially of equations that, as pseudo-propositions [*Scheinsätze*], "express no thoughts" (6.2–6.21). Since it is wholly unlikely that Wittgenstein simply ignored Frege's and Russell's treatment of the application of arithmetic—this is too central to their writings—it may seem inevitable that we must conclude, as many readers do, that Wittgenstein was quite self-consciously adopting what may be legitimately described as a version of the philosophical doctrine of formalism.

At stake is not merely the question of the adequacy of the *Tractatus*, or the relative impact on Wittgenstein of Frege and Russell. Even more, there is the question of the sense, if any, in which Wittgenstein may be said to have shared Frege's and Russell's aims and ideals, their conception of what philosophical logic can and should set out to accomplish. This question cannot be answered apart from detailed consideration of the extent to which the *Tractatus* takes account of the internal workings of Frege's and Russell's philosophies. As Michael Dummett has written,

> The arguments Frege uses in favour of his answer to the question 'What is a number the number of?' and against answers proposed by others, are arguments for adopting his analysis of ascriptions of number. Since that analysis is both syntactic and semantic in character, they are also suasions in favour of his semantic theory: it is, among other reasons, because that theory is capable of giving a convincing account of ascriptions of number, and rival semantic theories are not, that we now take for granted the correctness of a semantics at least generally along Fregean lines, and *do not so much as stop to consider* one of those implicitly underlying the views Frege . . . so decisively refutes.[11]

We, however, should stop so to consider. As I shall argue, Wittgenstein did treat the logic of ascriptions of number in the *Tractatus*. Yet ironically, his treatment further served to undercut the philosophical purpose and interpretation that Frege and Russell imposed on the (different) logical systems each of them devised. Thus in questioning the adequacy of their purported analyses of the grammar of number words and of arithmetic Wittgenstein is questioning their analyses of logic itself. The *Tractatus'* treatment of arithmetic is thus a crucial index and expression of Wittgenstein's philosophical stance toward Frege and Russell, a small part of the book which (like so many of its parts) exemplifies the whole. It is not the mathematics of Frege and Russell per se to which Wittgenstein objected: nothing he wrote could ever hope to jettison any genuine result about the mathematical structure of, say, quantification theory. Instead, he took Frege's and Russell's purported accounts of logic and arithmetic to mislead in purporting to provide a logical framework which could be used to resolve the philosophical questions, How does arithmetic apply to the world?, What gives our number words definite meaning? and How is it that arithmetic is more than a mere formalistic game with symbols? For Wittgenstein, Frege's way of construing the question "What is a number?" makes no sense. It is not that Wittgenstein proposed an alternative foundationalist or reductive solution to the question. He was neither a formalist nor an antiformalist. Rather, he challenged both the Frege-Russell and the formalist's conceptions of how logic might figure in resolving the philosophical debate.

Not surprisingly, the *Tractatus* has usually been read through the lens of the new logic, through the eyes of Frege and/or Russell. We see Wittgenstein making remarks about variables, functions, names, objects, concepts, truth-functions, numbers, and quantifiers, and we suppose that we know whereof he speaks. On the contrary, what the *Tractatus's* remarks on number and arithmetic show, I believe, is that we misread the *Tractatus* when we impose either a Fregean or Russellian conception of such notions on its terminology. If we focus on Wittgenstein's treatment of number in the *Tractatus*,[12] we can see that he rejects Frege's and Russell's conceptions of what logical analysis can accomplish.

Consider, then, that in the *Tractatus* Wittgenstein never once applies the term "function" to what we would ordinarily call mathematical functions. What could be more striking—or more misleading for his readers? Few are prepared to follow him here. Commentators standardly assume that Wittgenstein's notion of (propositional) function may be explicated by appealing to mathematical examples, just as Frege did in explaining his notion of function.[13] Wittgenstein himself suggests that his use of "function" is reminiscent both of Frege's and of Russell's uses of the term: he writes in the *Tractatus* that "I conceive the proposition—like Frege and Russell—as a function of the expressions contained in it" (3.318). But this is misleading, and not only because Frege's and Russell's conceptions of functions differ from each other. Mathematical functions are not functions in the sense of the *Tractatus*. By insisting that function and operation never be confused with one another (5.25), and then calling mathematics essentially a calculus of operations (6.233–6.234), Wittgenstein is rejecting, not only Frege's and Russell's conceptions of mathematics, but also their (respective) conceptions of the notions of function, proposition, and sentence.

From a mathematical point of view, one main task of building arithmetic up out of "logic"[14] was to show how to define arithmetical functions and numbers

in terms of purely logical concepts or functions (for Frege) or in terms of propositional functions (for Russell). Frege and Russell took themselves to have clarified
our notion of a mathematical function by analyzing it in purely logical terms. But
to so analyze, they generalized the notion of function beyond its customary mathematical use, applying it uniformly to the structure of all sentences, in order to call
it a logical notion. One point I take to be central to the *Tractatus*: Wittgenstein is
resisting this sort of generalization. He is denying that one function/argument
scheme is adequate to an analysis of logic and mathematics. In particular, he
denies that number words and nonmathematical names (or adjectives) must be
given the sort of unified logico-grammatical treatment that Frege and Russell gave
them. He denies both that number words are names (are object expressions) and
that they are adjectives (are function expressions). He refuses to treat those
ascriptions of number which he takes to express genuine propositions as identities. As he sees it, not all complexity in the structure of sentences is function/argu-
ment complexity. To assume so is to fall prey to the ghost of what he calls "the
old logic," the fantasy of a generally applicable subject/predicate distinction.[15]

Attention to the use of language in philosophizing is as basic to the *Tractatus*
as it is to Wittgenstein's later thought. Yet it has been held—for example, by
G. E. M. Anscombe—that there is nevertheless a distinction between the kind of
use on which Wittgenstein focused in the *Tractatus* (Anscombe calls this "logico-
syntactic use") and the kind on which he focused in his later philosophy (Anscombe
1971, pp. 91–92, labels this "role in life" or "practice"). But I think we do better
to say that in the *Tractatus*, just as in his later philosophy, Wittgenstein focuses
on use in order to wean us from misconstruing the character and scope of those
distinctions we are inclined to enshrine as "logical"—especially the distinctions
drawn by Russell and by Frege.[16]

Wittgenstein's categorial (logical) distinctions thus fail to coincide with those of
Frege and Russell, despite the coincidence of their terminology. This is best viewed,
I believe, as the manifestation of his desire to expose the apparent clarity of their
analyses as illusory, to show that their systems of logic, when treated as "great
mirrors" of thought and reality (5.511), distort like the mirrors of a funhouse. It
is not that Wittgenstein purports to correct Frege's and Russell's logic, as if he
sees himself having discerned the true categorial reality lying behind the functioning of language when he draws unFregean and unRussellian categorial distinctions among kinds of expression. There are no arguments in the *Tractatus* as
to the correctness of such distinctions. Instead, in drawing the distinctions he
does, Wittgenstein is attempting to recover ordinary modes of speaking about
language—about mathematics in particular—in the face of what he regards as
Frege's and Russell's mis-systematization. His denial that numerals are names,
that numbers are objects or (second order) properties, is best read as recasting the
whole idea of what the drawing of categorial or logical distinctions can accomplish. He is attempting to shift our attitude toward (pre- and post-Fregean)
categorial talk, toward our use of notions such as *name, subject, predicate, object,
number, concept, function, proposition,* and so on. By fashioning his own categorial
distinctions and notational proposals for a *Begriffsschrift*, he does without the
analyses of Frege and Russell, and thus shows us how misleading is their categorial

talk. He builds his own funhouse of mirrors to show us the way out of theirs. His aim is to unmask metaphysical idolatry of notation.

Wittgenstein is quite clear that his own Tractarian remarks mislead as to their categorial status: though they appear to make sense, to satisfy all ordinary grammatical criteria for propositionhood, they fail to find uses as genuine propositions according to the lights of the *Tractatus* itself (6.54). This was the price Wittgenstein paid for attempting to unmask the purported analyses of Frege, Russell, and others as nonsensical rather than false. But Wittgenstein's deepest philosophical insight in the *Tractatus* was to try to get us to see that not every grammatically well-formed propositional sign, not every sentence, finds a use in thinking and, conversely, that there is thinking by means of sentences which are not propositional signs, which fail to fit purportedly universal logical categories of propositionhood. The best commentators on *Philosophical Investigations* and related works all agree that this is a key insight of the later Wittgenstein. Implicit throughout this chapter is the claim that this insight is already present in the *Tractatus*.[17] For already in the *Tractatus*, Wittgenstein is questioning the idea that any one logical grammar is adequate to guarantee or represent all forms of sense. Proofs within a formalized, pure logic, just as proofs within elementary arithmetic, are mere mechanical expedients, mere calculations (6.126ff, 6.2, 6.2331ff). But in the *Tractatus*, Wittgenstein is trying to show that there are no such mechanical expedients in philosophy, no general logico-syntactic means for showing that an apparently grammatically well-formed sentence does or does not have (a certain kind of) use. Some thinking cannot—except misleadingly—be captured by a logic which represents all inferences as movements from truth to truth (from proposition to proposition) in accordance with generally applicable logical laws. Some insights (including the insight that a particular grammatically well-formed propositional sign finds no use in thinking) take thinking, but no particular thoughts, to see (compare Floyd 1998b).

Thus in the *Tractatus*, Wittgenstein is showing us that no fixed logico-grammatical criteria—even those of the *Tractatus* itself—are sufficiently rich to explicate the meaningfulness or meaninglessness of any particular configuration of signs in a generally applicable way. This is how I interpret Wittgenstein's rejection of Frege's and Russell's view that pure logic and pure mathematics consist of propositions in a paradigmatic sense of "proposition" extendable uniformly across all of language. His treatment of basic logical notions takes place in a context intended to complicate our conception of what it is to express or fail to express a proposition or thought, of what it is to think, in ways Frege and Russell could not accept. Indeed for Wittgenstein—unlike for Frege or Russell—a pure logic, a *Begriffsschrift*, is a mere *Schrift*, a mere script of signs used to keep track of wholly formal operations. In application to genuine propositions—by way of genuine concept words and names—it is a mechanical expedient in certain circumstances (when, for example, the generality sign is not present, as Wittgenstein explicitly remarks at 6.1203) for helping us to recognize that certain propositional signs which meet the rules of ordinary grammar nevertheless fail to express propositions or thoughts (6.1263). But pure logic does not in itself limn the underlying structure of all thoughts. Insofar as it is framed and treated as a maximally general science of the laws of truth or thought, as a universally applicable framework within which generally applicable logical distinctions are enshrined and a single interpretation of the signs is fixed, in which thought as such is characterized, it is *unsinnig*, nonsensical, its structure misleads. Differently put, Wittgenstein believes that Frege and Russell assimilated the logic of our language much too closely to the (mechanical) workings of a systematic notation such as the decimal system, in which every numeral can be generated by a mechanical operation from its predecessor, and in which all properly spelled numerical signs signify—automatically, as it were—numbers. In so doing, Frege and Russell misrepresented both the nature of language and the nature of arithmetic.

II. The Terminology of "Operations"

Here are some of the terms used by Wittgenstein in the *Tractatus* to characterize mathematics:

6.2   Mathematics is a logical method.
          The propositions [*Sätze*] of mathematics are equations, and therefore
          pseudo-propositions [*Scheinsätze*].
6.21   Mathematical propositions express no thoughts.
6.211   In life it is never a mathematical proposition which we need, but we
          use mathematical propositions only in order to infer from proposi-
          tions which do not belong to mathematics to others which equally
          do not belong to mathematics.
6.2323   The equation characterizes only the standpoint from which I consider
          the two expressions, that is to say the standpoint of their equality of
          meaning (*Bedeutung*).
6.233   To the question whether we need intuition for the solution of mathe-
          matical problems it must be answered that language itself here sup-
          plies the necessary intuition.
6.2331   The process of calculation brings about just this intuition.
          Calculation is not an experiment
6.234   Mathematics is a method of logic.
6.2341   The essential of mathematical method is working with equations. On
          this method depends the fact that every proposition of mathematics
          must be self-evident.
6.24   The method by which mathematics arrives at its equations is *the method
          of substitution*.
          For equations express the substitutability of two expressions, and we
          proceed from a number of equations to new equations, replacing ex-
          pressions by others in accordance with the equations (last emphasis
          mine).
6.241   Thus the proof of the proposition $2 \times 2 = 4$ runs:
          $(\Omega^{\nu})^{\mu'}x = \Omega^{\nu \times \mu'}x$ Def.
          $(\Omega^{2 \times 2'})x = (\Omega^2)^{2'}x = (\Omega^2)^{1+1'}x = \Omega^{2'}\Omega^{2'}x = \Omega^{1+1'}\Omega^{1+1'}x$
          $= (\Omega'\Omega')(\Omega'\Omega)'x = \Omega'\Omega'\Omega'\Omega'x = \Omega^{1+1+1+1'}x = \Omega^{4}x.$

As I explain below (in section V) "Ω" is a variable ranging over what Wittgenstein calls "operations."

The terms Wittgenstein uses to characterize mathematics in the *Tractatus*—as a "calculus," an art of manipulating "substitutive signs" in "equations," in abstraction from their "meaning," by the use of "operations" according to "the method of substitution"—were familiar in the late nineteenth and earlier twentieth century, especially in algebra. They appear, for example, in Whitehead's *Universal Algebra* (1898)[18] and *Introduction to Mathematics* (1911),[19] works it is not unlikely that Wittgenstein saw.[20] In these remarks, Wittgenstein is rejecting Frege's and Russell's stretching of the notion of function by exploiting this traditional terminology and adapting it to apply to the new logic.

The term "operation" was primarily used to characterize any algorithmic manipulation of signs in a purely formal manner, in abstraction from any particular interpretation of the symbols. "Operation" thus came to be associated with (what Frege and Russell would later criticize as formalist) conceptions of logical and mathematical symbolism as calculi, as algebras in which logical signs are to be treated as variables, as empty formulae awaiting interpretation and/or reinterpretation. When in his *Universal Algebra* Whitehead defines the term "operation," he applies it, not only to mathematical operations such as addition and multiplication, but also to deductive inference, footnoting Bradley's *Principles of Logic* treatment of inference (Whitehead 1898, pp. 7–9). Not surprisingly, like the other post-Kantian Idealists, Bradley viewed deductive logical inference as empty, merely formal thought. Chapter 1 of Whitehead's *Universal Algebra*, "On the Nature of a Calculus," begins with words that echo those of the *Tractatus* :

1. SIGNS. Words, spoken or written, and the symbols of Mathematics are alike signs. Signs have been analysed [by Stout and Peirce][21] into (α) suggestive signs, (β) expressive signs, (γ) substitutive signs.

A suggestive sign is the most rudimentary possible, and need not be dwelt upon here. An obvious example of one is a knot tied in a handkerchief to remind the owner of some duty to be performed.

In the use of expressive signs the attention is not fixed on the sign itself but on what it expresses; that is to say, it is fixed on the meaning conveyed by the sign. Ordinary language consists of groups of expressive signs, its primary object being to draw attention to the meaning of the words employed. . . .

A substitutive sign is such that in thought it takes the place of that for which it is substituted. A counter in a game may be such a sign: at the end of the game the counters lost or won may be interpreted in the form of a money, but till then it may be convenient for attention to be concentrated on the counters and not on their signification. The signs of a Mathematical Calculus are substitutive signs.

The difference between words and substitutive signs has been stated thus, "a word is an instrument for thinking about the meaning which it expresses; a substitute sign is a means of not thinking about the meaning which it symbolizes [n. Cf. Stout, 'Thought and Language,' *Mind*, April 1891]."

2. DEFINITION OF A CALCULUS. In order that reasoning may be conducted by means of substitutive signs, it is necessary that rules be given for the manipulation of the signs. The rules should be such that the final state of the signs after a series of operations according to rule denotes, when the signs are interpreted in terms of the things for which they are substituted, a proposition true for the things represented by the signs. . . .

3. EQUIVALENCE. In a calculus of the type here considered propositions take the form of assertions of equivalence. (Whitehead 1898, pp. 7–9)

Whitehead explicitly denies that such assertions of equivalence are mere identities. As for the term "operation," Whitehead takes it in its traditional sense, linking it to what he explicitly calls "the method of substitution":

OPERATIONS. Judgments of equivalence can be founded on direct perception, as when it is judged by direct perception that two different pieces of stuff match in colour. But the judgment may be founded on a knowledge of the respective derivations of the things judged to be equivalent from other things respectively either identical or equivalent. It is this process of derivation which is the special province of a calculus. The derivation of a thing p from things $a, b, c, \ldots$, can also be conceived as an operation on the things $a, b, c, \ldots$, which produces the thing p.

. . . Instead of reasoning with respect to the properties of one scheme in order to deduce equivalences, we may substitute the other scheme, or conversely; and then transpose at the end of the argument. This device of reasoning, which is almost universal in mathematics, we will call the method of substitutive schemes, or more briefly, the method of substitution. (Whitehead 1898, pp. 7–9)

When in the *Tractatus* Wittgenstein calls all the sentences of logic "tautologies," he is denying both that every grammatically well-formed sentence expresses a proposition and that there are any genuine logical propositions: even the Idealists and the early Moore and Russell had denied that tautologies are genuine propositions (see Dreben and Floyd 1991, p. 27). When he remarks that the essence of mathematics is work with equations according to "the method of substitution" by way of "calculation" (6.23–6.24), and when he calls the same method in logic a "mechanical expedient" (6.1262), he is resuscitating traditional algebraic terminology in order to undercut, not Frege's and Russell's mathematical logic per se, but their claims for its contentfulness and success in simultaneously analyzing both logic and mathematics. There can be little doubt that he chose his terminology with care. For when in 1923 Ramsey ventured to lower Austria to discuss the *Tractatus* with Wittgenstein, and they went through the book line by line,[22] there were just a few marginal remarks Wittgenstein wrote into Ramsey's copy of the *Tractatus* as suggested revisions, and these surrounded the treatment of number. Wittgenstein suggested adding to the text (at 6.02, see section V below): "The fundamental idea of mathematics is the idea of calculation represented here by the notion of operation," "number is the fundamental idea of calculus and must be introduced as such," and "the beginning of logic presupposes calculation and so number."[23] Something like Poincaré, Wittgenstein is suggesting that in setting out the formal language by means of which logic and arithmetic will be analyzed, Frege, Whitehead, and Russell have already invoked the use of a specifically mathematical procedure, that of operation.[24] Unlike Poincaré, he is denying that this shows that mathematical procedures (e.g., mathematical induction) require special mathematical insight or intuition (cf. 6.233). For on his view, in both mathematics and logic, calculation is fundamental.

In both the *Principles of Mathematics* and in *Principia Mathematica*, aided by whitehead, Russell himself reverts to old-fashioned talk of "operations" (applying it to, e.g., addition and multiplication), but when and only when he is bracketing his logicistic analysis of number and arithmetic, when and only when he is abstracting away from what is symbolized or denoted, and focusing on the symbols alone.[25] Of course, Frege and Russell never apply the notion of operation either to the logical connectives or to logical inference. This is the hallmark of their philosophies: logic, on their view, is a universal science, something more than an artful manipulation of uninterpreted signs, something more than a mere calculus. In logic, they hold, we express thoughts and propositions and our words have meaning. Once the logicist definitions of the natural numbers are in place and the basic theorems about the natural numbers are derived from logical laws via these definitions, there is no excuse other than convenience for supposing that we may continue to hold meaning or interpretation in abeyance when we speak of mathematics. The notions of calculus and operation do not really apply, except misleadingly, either to logic or to mathematics. Since mathematics is a branch of logic, it is part of a universal science, and in it there is genuine truth, genuine content expressed at each step of a deduction. For Frege, the *Begriffsschrift* is not a mere uninterpreted formalism. It is a genuine (formalized) language. Similarly, for Whitehead and Russell (what Wittgenstein calls [e.g., at 3.325]) the *Begriffsschrift* of *Principia Mathematica* is not a mere uninterpreted formalism. These *Begriffsschriften* are taken by their framers to express thoughts and meanings, to involve us in the recognition of truth. Insofar as mathematics enjoys the same status as logic, for Frege and Russell it is no calculus.

It is, however, a remarkable historical irony that in spite—or perhaps even because—of their philosophical commitments, Frege, Russell, and Whitehead provided us with quite formidable tools for forging a mechanistic conception logic and mathematics. Their formalisms—as opposed to what they conceived their formalisms to express—are a means by which thought may apparently be made irrelevant, not of course to the discovery of formal derivations, but to the formal assessment of a logical structure as indeed a derivation in accordance with the rules of the system. For the remarkable thing about the new logic is that transitions from one step to the next in a formal derivation may be checked and even generated by a machine, without regard to the meanings of the various expressions at work in the proof it may be said to represent. Both Frege and Russell attacked the idea that thinking is calculating. Both attacked the idea that mathematics and logic involve a mechanical manipulation of signs. Yet, arguably, what they did was to produce what might be called the first computer program, the first truly mechanical way of handling the patterns of inference characteristic of logic and mathematics. Wittgenstein characterizes mathematics in the ordinary terminology of his day to suggest that Frege and Russell, who aimed to bring arithmetic under the auspices of their logic, give the wherewithal for a philosopher to claim instead that their logic is just another sort of calculus. Wittgenstein was not alone in suggesting a mechanical metaphor for characterizing the logic of *Principia Mathematica*—at about the same time C.I. Lewis,[26] quickly followed by E. L. Post,[27] suggested it too[28]—but Wittgenstein made the move with the philosophies of Frege and Russell as self-consciously constructed targets of his criticisms, the only immediate student of both to do so. In the *Tractatus*, Wittgenstein revitalizes the standard algebraic talk of "operations," hurling the old-fashioned language back at Frege and Russell—its greatest critics—while at the same time transforming it to meet the Frege-Russell demand that the logical form of number words be accounted for.

III. Differing Grammatical Analogies between Arithmetical Terms and Sentences

Wittgenstein writes that "in order to recognize the symbol in the sign we must consider the sign's significant use [*sinnvollen Gebrauch*]" (3.326)—that is, its use in expressing propositions, true or false. A proposition is itself a "symbol" or "expression" as opposed to a mere sign; it expresses a sense, truly or falsely (3.31). We can separate the sign from the symbol—the propositional sign from the proposition or the numeral from the number—but neither a particular sign token (e.g., two, man) nor that token's type (e.g., "two," "man") can be considered expressions apart from considering their contributions to the articulation of propositions on given occasions. Different (types of) signs may be used to express the same symbol: I might express the same proposition either in English or in German. Conversely, the same (type of) signs may be used in different ways to express different symbols or expressions, as in (the ambiguous) configuration of signs "Green is green" (3.321ff). Yet a sign is also a symbol or expression. A propositional sign, for example, is just that which is perceptible in the proposition, in the symbol, that which in use exhibits the symbol (3.32). Wittgenstein's way of speaking could be cleaned up and systematized: propositions might be spoken of as propositional signs appropriately used in thinking, while propositional signs might be spoken of as those which are perceptible in such uses. But he prefers to rest with a constant ambiguity in his remarks, inviting, for dialectical purposes, a metaphysical misreading. This is part of his funhouse, part of his subversive treatment of Frege's and Russell's terminology for their most basic logical notions. By an "expression" or "symbol" he means, not merely a (part of a) sign, but a sign which aids in expressing a sense. This makes it sound as if symbols, expressions, propositions, and senses are entities shown or reflected in our uses of signs (cf. 2.22). But I believe that Wittgenstein himself draws no hard and fast distinction between what is articulated and articulation, between what is exhibited by a sign and the sign doing the exhibiting, between thought and thinking. Symbols and expressions are aspects or patterns of the uses of signs in thinking; propositions, senses, and thoughts are nothing but appropriate uses of particular propositional signs, and propositional signs are perceptible facts on which we operate (3.12, 3.14).

The apparent relation of the signs to what they express is "internal" or "formal" or "operational." For Wittgenstein, thinking goes on, but there are no (imperceptible, abstract) thoughts or propositions which are somehow mirrored or shown in propositional signs. A thought is nothing but an applied (*angewandte*), bethought (*gedachte*) propositional sign (3.5); it expresses itself perceptibly in thinking (3.1). This Frege did not say and would not have said.[29] Wittgenstein thus exploits the ambiguity of the German word *Satz* (sentence/proposition) by inflicting an ambiguity on the words *Ausdruck* (expression) and symbol. Sometimes he speaks of these as linguistic categories, types of sign. Sometimes he speaks of them as what signs in these categories reflect. Inevitably, he makes remarks which appear to reify propositions, symbols, expressions, thoughts, and senses. But this is part of the reason Wittgenstein takes his own remarks to be—if construed as propositional signs—nonsensical (*unsinnig*), potentially misleading. Although one might try to say that thought expresses itself perceptibly in a propositional sign (3.1)—as if there are thoughts or senses which are shown—one must also see that thinking is nothing but a way of using a configuration of sensibly perceptible signs, in the first instance nothing but the appropriate use of a sentence-sense (*Satz-Sinn*) to project a state of affairs (*Sachlage*) by operating with a propositional sign (3.11).

Wittgenstein's refusal to sharply distinguish use from mention, linguistic from extralinguistic, is an index of how deeply he rejects Frege's conception of the kind of articulateness which sentences have. As has often been emphasized, by comparing propositions with pictures, Wittgenstein sharply distinguishes propositions from names, as Frege had not. After 1891 Frege explicitly assimilated the grammatical structure of all sentences to that of his conception of arithmetical terms[30] (e.g. "2^3", "$8+144$"). He thereby came to construe all sentences as (functionally complex) names of truth-values, just as he had always construed arithmetical terms as (functionally complex) names of numbers. In this way Frege came to apply to sentences his post-1891 distinction between the *Sinn* and the *Bedeutung* of a name. Frege's analysis of number in his *Grundlagen der Arithmetik* in no way depended upon his lumping sentences and names together in one logico-grammatical category. But the lumping is a natural outgrowth of his original (*Begriffsschrift*) idea that he could use what he took to be the notion of function (naturally applicable to the grammatical structure of arithmetical terms) to account for the logical structure of all sentences—including of course extramathematical ascriptions of number and sentences of arithmetic—in a uniform way.

In the *Tractatus*, I claim, Wittgenstein does not wholly reject Frege's notion that the grammatical structures of (at least some) sentences are analogous to those of arithmetical terms. He grants Frege's analogy but turns it against Frege, uses it to abandon the assumptions Frege always had made, that numerals and arithmetical terms are names and that arithmetical sentences (arithmetical equations) express (functionally complex) propositions. Wittgenstein's unwillingness to apply a univocal notion of function—his sharp distinction between functions and operations—is thus crucial for understanding how he differs from Frege (and from Russell) on the nature of the proposition.[31] For to try to break the hold of their conceptions of logic, he reconceived the relation between the logic of the sentence and the logic of the arithmetical term.

Wittgenstein's anti-Fregean analogy between propositions and numbers has several different facets.[32] The first concerns notation and the grammar of elementary propositions. The decimal Arabic notation in which arithmetic is ordinarily carried out is, as a symbolism, a systematic notation, a system of picturing or representing numbers. In this system, a fixed alphabet is set out, and spelling rules are set down, so that just ten separate numerals may be used to express any number whatsoever. Configurations of these numerals in immediate juxtaposition represent (or "picture") natural numbers through column positionality—positionality which makes any numeral arithmetically (operationally) articulate, even, for example, the numeral "2". Such configurations (e.g., "372") may be calculated with, expanded by means of arithmetical operation signs in a systematic way ("300 + 70 + 2", "(3 × 102) + (7 × 101) + (2 × 100)") in order to show what they express.

Now in a similar way in the *Tractatus*, Wittgenstein construes that portion of our language used to express propositions as consisting in the first instance of a fixed stock of names, each of which has, in the context of (positioned within the expression of) a genuine proposition, a *Bedeutung*. The logically simple names of the *Tractatus* are analogous to numerical digits, and their modes of possible combination with one another—the function expressions—like alphabetical spelling rules, like the positionality convention of the decimal notation. Vacuous names and redundant names (differing signs with the same *Bedeutung*) are idealized away, as actually happens in the decimal notation. Elementary propositional signs are configurations of names which, in immediate juxtaposition, express functionally articulate propositions (4.22), just as configurations of numerals in the decimal notation are arithmetically articulate. Any such elementary proposition may be expanded by means of (truth) operations to show what it expresses ("p" by "p v p," "¬p⊃p," and so on), just as any numeral may be expanded by means of arithmetical operations into polynomials of powers of ten. Of course, the analogy is not perfect, for the alphabetical rules of the decimal system are fixed once and for all via column positionality, whereas the alphabetical rules of a language capable of being used to express propositions are not so rigidly fixed.

That we are using the decimal system with the numerals "1", "2", "3" . . . (and not some other), and that the use of this notation is adequate to express every natural number, come out in our uses of the notation, in the ways we operate with the numbers, both within and outside of arithmetic. But we cannot use the decimal system in and of itself to say that these things are so. Similarly, in the *Tractatus* Wittgenstein is suggesting that we cannot say within our language (of propositions) that our names have the *Bedeutungen* they do, or that our (grammatically well-formed) sentences are adequate to express all propositions, thoughts, senses; these too are matters shown in our uses of sentences, in the ways in which we operate with them systematically. It might seem that Wittgenstein's distinction between what can be shown and what can be said (4.1212) may be escaped or defeated by bringing in the notion of a metalanguage or a hierarchy of languages. This was what Russell suggested and Carnap thought.[33] But as we shall see, Wittgenstein's Tractarian notion of operation portrays any such move as already surrendering the philosophical quest for an overarching function/argument scheme in terms of which we may represent the logic of all terms and sentences, both mathematical and nonmathematical.

I have just argued that like Frege, Wittgenstein draws an analogy between the way in which numerals may be conceived to signify and the way in which elementary propositional signs may be conceived to signify—though I have also insisted that for Wittgenstein, unlike for Frege, the point of the analogy is to bring us to see that neither numerals (qua pictures of numbers) nor elementary propositions (qua pictures of states of affairs) play the same role as digits or names do. A further, deeper aspect of Wittgenstein's recasting of Frege's analogy concerns the structure of logically complex, molecular sentences. For Wittgenstein, as for Frege, the grammatical structure of arithmetical terms (e.g., "1+4", "52+34+2") is analogous to that of molecular propositional sentences. But for Wittgenstein, unlike for Frege, this is so only insofar as each sort of sign reflects, not functional, but operational complexity—arithmetical operations in the case of arithmetical terms and logical operations in the case of molecular sentences. In other words, Wittgenstein constructs a parallel between the (arithmetical) operation by means of which a number is constructed from another and the (logical) truth-operation by means of which a new proposition is constructed from another.[34]

Operation signs—number words and truth-operation signs—figure in the articulation of propositions. But the occurrence of a sign for a particular operation in a sentence is never essential for characterizing the sense, if any, of the sentence (5.25). The capacity of operations to be iterated and combined with one another, their specific mutual interplay, is what any adequate notation for them must capture; arithmetic and truth-operational logic demand systematic notations for their articulation. This capacity for iteration—for "self-reference," if you like—is what sharply distinguishes operations from functions on Wittgenstein's view. If, for example, we tried to make a particular kind of structural configuration of names express the operation of negation (e.g., writing a propositional sign upside down, or writing it in red), we would not have succeeded in devising a notation capable of expressing every proposition of our language unless we could see how this particular way of expressing negation could be iterated and combined with disjunction, conjunction, and so on. Like operation signs in the language of arithmetic, truth-operation signs form a system, a formally integrated network, as names and (material) function expressions do not. When Wittgenstein remarks that elementary propositions are logically independent of one another, he means to say that names and function expressions do not form such a systematically interconnected network, as a system of operation signs always does.

Wittgenstein attempts to articulate this distinction in several different ways. Operations may be iterated to form significant expressions (as in "p, ¬p, ¬¬p" [propositional signs] or "2", "2×2", "2×2×2" [numerals]), but a name or function expression can never be so iterated (neither "Harry Harry is a man" nor "is a man Harry is a man" are significant expressions). This unbounded capacity for iteration goes hand in hand with the systematic interconnectedness of signs in a notation capable of expressing operations. Neither names nor function expressions can ever cancel out the contributions of other names or function expressions to the articulation of a proposition. But an operation sign can do so. Thus, for example, in the tautology p v ¬p, the logical operators for negation and disjunction cancel out the expressive contributions (the senses) of p and ¬p. It is intrinsic to operations that their effects on the articulation of propositions can be captured by using an alternative configuration of operations belonging to the same system. "2", "+", "2+4", "not", "or" "all" and "some" are all operation signs. Wittgenstein remarks that such signs are nothing but punctuation marks, like commas or semicolons or periods (5.4611, *WA*, vol. 1, p. 41), because any particular configuration of such signs used to express a proposition can always be systematically eliminated from its expression, systematically replaced with another equivalent configuration, and the same thing still said. In the system of arithmetical operations, a single number can be expressed in an unlimited number of different ways, each systematically interconnected with every another ("two" may be expressed by "1+1", by "0+2", "3–1", and so on). This is essential to the number's numberhood, to its operational character. Every proposition ascribing a particular number may be expressed in an unlimited number of ways (the "three" in "three apples" may be expressed by "3", "2+1", "21/7", "4–1", and so on, or even simply shown in the use of three distinct names [see Section IV below]). Such a system of alternative ways of expressing ourselves is not, on Wittgenstein's view, characteristic of our uses of names or function expressions.

Differently put, Wittgenstein deems it essential to the expressive power of our language that differing configurations of truth-operational signs can be used to express the very same proposition and, conversely, that no single configuration of the standard truth-operational signs is ever necessary to the expression of any proposition. It is essential to any proposition p that p may be expressed by "p v p," "p v (q &¬q)," "(q v¬q) v p," and so on (5.515). If we focus just on the possibilities of the truth and falsity of each of these propositions based on the possibilities of truth and falsity of their components p and q, each way of expressing p says exactly the same thing, expresses, on Wittgenstein's view, the same sense (*Sinn*). Indeed, each mode of expressing a sense presupposes all its other modes of expression. What Wittgenstein calls a "logical form" is that which is common to all these different ways of expressing the same proposition, that which is essential to the expression of its sense (cf. 5.42, 5.441). This is something we show in our use of a system of operations, not something we say in a proposition. Logical form in Wittgenstein's sense cannot be expressed through a single configuration of truth-operation signs; it is not a genuine property of sentences to be formalized with reference to any unique (truth-operational or quantificational) structure. Logical form emerges instead through a system of operations used to express propositions. Operation signs are thus construed by Wittgenstein—as they were by the algebraists of his day—as variables of a certain special sort (5.24ff).

IV. Propositional Ascriptions of Number in the *Tractatus*

In Wittgenstein's denial that numbers are objects and that arithmetical terms are names, there is something reminiscent of Russell, who also resisted both Frege's assimilation of sentences to names and Frege's construal of arithmetical terms as names. Neither Frege's *Grundgesetze* or Russell and Whitehead's *Principia Mathematica* postulate any primitive arithmetical terms; that is the point of the program of reducing arithmetic to logic. But unlike Frege, Russell construed arithmetical terms as definite descriptions, hence, as expressions contextually eliminable, via the theory of descriptions, in favor of certain canonically related, functionally complex proposition expressions. For Russell, after 1905, the logistic reduction consists in explicitly defining (nondenoting except in context) "descriptive" terms for mathematical entities and functions in terms of (genuinely denoting) expressions reflecting propositional functions.[35] As he writes in the *Principia*:

> The functions hitherto considered, with the exception of a few particular functions . . . have been propositional, i.e., have had propositions for their values. But the ordinary functions of mathematics, such as x^2, sin x, log x, are not propositional. Functions of this kind always mean "the term having such and such a relation to x." For this reason they may be called descriptive functions, because they describe a certain term by means of its relation to their argument. Thus "sin $\pi/2$" describes the number 1; yet propositions in which sin $\pi/2$ occurs are not the same as they would be if 1 were substituted for sin $\pi/2$. This appears e.g. from the proposition "sin $\pi/2 = 1$", which conveys valuable information, whereas "1=1" is trivial. Descriptive functions, like descriptions in general, have no meaning by themselves, but only as constituents of propositions. (Whitehead and Russell, *30)

Russell thus takes his theory of descriptions to obviate the need for an account of the informativeness of denoting phrases in terms of what they denote. It thereby obviates the need for anything like Frege's (post-1891) attempt to account for the informativeness of non-trivial identity statements (e.g., 2+2=4) through a distinction between the *Sinn* and the *Bedeutung* of names and definite descriptions. It allows Russell to introduce new (arithmetical) terms into his system without extra-logical ontological commitment, e.g., without independent commitment to the existence of classes.

Like Russell, Wittgenstein rejects Frege's (post-1891) distinction between *Sinn* and *Bedeutung*, but not on the basis of the theory of descriptions (6.232ff). Wittgenstein does allude to the theory of descriptions in the *Tractatus* (3.24), but he never proposes applying it as it stands. Russell's analysis relies on using identity, which Wittgenstein will not countenance. As we shall see, Wittgenstein does fashion an alternative treatment of descriptions for what he would consider to be genuine propositions. But unlike Russell, Wittgenstein never suggests applying this treatment to arithmetical expressions. For he rejects both Russell's treatment of arithmetical terms as functionally complex expressions replaceable by propositional signs and Russell's treatment of arithmetical sentences as propositional signs. Wittgenstein does not take there to be any one logico-syntactic category of "description" in the way Russell does. In *Principia Mathematica*, a key constraint on the logistic reduction is the ability of the axioms to support derivations of such (typically ambiguous) propositions as "There is a unique square of three." For Wittgenstein, "there is a unique square of three" is, like "there is only one number one," nonsensical (*unsinnig*) if construed as an ascription of number like "there is only one man in the room" (4.1272). So construed, such expressions vacillate or "dither," to use a phrase of Cora Diamond's, between treating an expression as a variable and treating it as a constant (Diamond 1997, pp. 78ff). This is simultaneously to assimilate numerals both to function expressions and to names. Frege and Russell both tried to use phrases like "the square of three" and "there is only one number one" to articulate constraints on what would count as a proper analysis of arithmetic. Wittgenstein takes the fact that Frege and Russell's logic make these look like genuine (constituents of) propositions, like any (logical part of a) proper ascription of number, to be a mark against their analyses.

As is evident from ordinary first-order quantification theory, number words are not needed to articulate propositions ascribing particular finite natural numbers—if, that is, one is prepared to use identity. For "there are exactly three women" write

$$(\exists x,y,z)(Wx \,\&\, Wy \,\&\, Wz \,\&\, x{\neq}y \,\&\, y{\neq}z \,\&\, x{\neq}z) \,\&$$
$$\neg(\exists x,y,z,w)(Wx \,\&\, Wy \,\&\, Wz \,\&\, Ww \,\&\, x{\neq}y \,\&\, x{\neq}z \,\&\, x{\neq}w \,\&\, y{\neq}z \,\&\, y{\neq}w \,\&\, z{\neq}w);$$

for "b follows a by two in the R-series" write

$$(\exists x,y,z)(xRy \,\&\, yRz \,\&\, x{\neq}y \,\&\, y{\neq}z \,\&\, x{\neq}z \,\&\, x{=}a \text{ and } z{=}b).$$

It was in order to be able to speak more generally about (ascriptions of) any, some or all finite number(s) n that Frege's and Russell's (second-order) analyses were proposed. Their analyses lean essentially on the use of identity. For Frege analyzed ascriptions of cardinal number ("the number of F's is n") in terms of equinumerosity ("there are just as many F's as G's"), which he in turn analyzed by means of the notion of a 1–1 correlation, hence, in terms of identity. Furthermore, he took number words to be substantivals: ascriptions of cardinal number, he argued, should be construed as identities (e.g., "there are two cups on the table" as "the number belonging to the concept *cup on the table* = 2"). The Frege-Russell definitions of the individual natural numbers also rely on identity (Frege defines "1" as "the extension of the concept *is a concept* gleichzahlig *to the number zero*," Russell as "the class of all 1–membered classes").

In 1923 Wittgenstein wrote the marginal remark "identity" in Ramsey's copy of the *Tractatus* beside 6.031 ("the theory of classes is altogether superfluous in mathematics"). Identity is indeed key to his anti-Fregean, anti-Russellian treatment of ascriptions of number in the *Tractatus*.[36]

5.53 Identity of the object I express by identity of the sign and not by means of a sign of identity. Difference of the objects by difference of the signs . . .

5.5303 Roughly speaking: to say of two things that they are identical is nonsense, and to say of one thing that it is identical with itself is to say nothing. . . .

5.531   I write therefore not "f(a,b).a=b," but "f(a,a)" (or "f(b,b)"). And not
         "f(a,b) . ¬a=b", but "f(a,b)."

5.532   And analogously: not "(∃x,y) . f(x,y).x=y", but "(∃x).f(x,x)"; and not
         "(∃x,y).f(x,y).¬x=y", but "(∃x,y) . f(x,y)."
         (Therefore instead of Russell's "(∃x,y).f(x,y)":
         "(∃x,y) . f(x,y) . v . (∃x) . f (x,x)."

5.5321   Instead of "(x): fx ⊃ x=a" we therefore write e.g.
         "(∃x) . fx . ⊃. fa: ¬∃(x,y) . fx . fy."
         And the proposition "only one x satisfies f( )" reads: "(∃x).fx:
         ¬(∃x,y).fx.fy."

5.533   The identity sign is therefore not an essential constituent of logical
         notation (*Begriffsschrift*).

5.534   And we see that apparent propositions (*Scheinsätze*) like: "a=a", "a=b.
         b=c.⊃a=c," "(x).x=x," "(∃x) . x=a," etc. cannot be written in a cor-
         rect logical notation (*einer richtigen Begriffsschrift*) at all.

Here Wittgenstein appears to be proposing certain analyses—laying down conditions on what is to count as a "correct logical notation"—using Russell's notation. But his remarks undercut the possibility of his formulating a formal system
in either Russell's or Frege's sense. For Wittgenstein proposes to formalize the
notions of identity and numerical individuation by means of an anti-Russellian,
anti-Fregean reading of the variable. Wittgenstein is not defining these notions—
as one might define a name or function expression—but treats them as operations by absorbing them into the interpretation of the notation's form.[37]

   For consider Wittgenstein's proposal for writing in logical notation an ascription of number such as "there is exactly one F":

$$(\exists x) . Fx . \& . \neg(\exists x,y) . Fx . Fy$$

This does not succeed in saying what Wittgenstein takes it to say unless we interpret it so that the range of "y" is restricted to names that differ in *Bedeutungen*
from whatever names might be taken to instantiate the second existentially quantified "x". The ranges of significance of these two variables are "exclusive," to use
Hintikka's phrase.[38] Now Hintikka distinguished two sorts of ways in which we
might interpret Wittgenstein's "exclusive" construals of the variable: the "weakly
exclusive" reading would apply only to variables within the scope of a (sequence
of) quantifier(s), whereas the "strongly exclusive" reading would demand that
every distinct bound variable throughout the whole sentence have a range restricted by all the previously occurring quantifiers. The latter reading might take
various forms (Hintikka 1956, p. 230, n. 11). For example, if the same variable
letter is bound by different quantifiers in different parts of one sentence—as "x"
is in the example above and also in 5.5321—one might in effect read it as a different letter in its two differing bound occurrences and, hence, as being instantiable
only by names with differing *Bedeutungen*. Alternatively, one might require that
the same letter, even if bound in different occurrences by distinct quantifiers, be
instantiated by names with the same *Bedeutung* throughout the sentence as a

whole. (On the weakly exclusive and the first of the strongly exclusive readings, the restrictions on instantiation of distinct bound variables begin over again from scratch after the sign for conjunction in the above formula; on the second of the two strongly exclusive readings, these restrictions would apply throughout the whole sentence, and the range of the second bound occurrence of "x" would be restricted to the particular instance picked out for the first occurrence: the existential quantifier would function like a descriptive phrase, or constant.) On all of these readings, bound variables occurring within sequences of more than one quantifier (whether in a subformula or in a sentence) are interpreted as having ranges of significance which are restricted as we move from left to right through the sentence. In the second half of 5.5321, the variable "y" expresses "any y except the previously chosen value for x," however we interpret the phrase "x."

Thus we should ask ourselves how Wittgenstein would interpret a sentence such as "$(\exists x)Fx \ \& \ \neg(\exists y)Fy$" (equivalently, "$(\exists x)Fx \ \& \ (y)\neg Fy$"). This is a contradiction, both in standard logic and on the weakly exclusive interpretation of the variable, but is not a contradiction according to either one of the strongly exclusive readings of the variable. For on the latter reading, "$(\exists y)Fy$" (or "$(y)\neg Fy$") is taken to mean "every y but the previously chosen x." Now Hintikka has argued that Wittgenstein should be read as having advocated a weakly expressible interpretation of the variable in the *Tractatus* (Hintikka 1956, p. 230). But it seems to me that Wittgenstein's remarks in the *Tractatus* are insufficiently precise to decide this interpretive question. This in itself, if true, is significant; it tells us something important about Wittgenstein's philosophical aims. For it indicates that on Wittgenstein's way of construing the variable—however we might try to make it precise—the application of logic to sentences which express genuine propositions takes priority over the formal systematization of pure logic (that is, logic which consists of sentences which do not express propositions, but instead contradictions and tautologies). To take just one example: Wittgenstein sharply distinguishes between the role of the *Satzvariable* "x loves y" and that of the *Satzvariable* "x loves x." "Harry loves Harry" expresses a proposition falling within the range of the latter, but not the former. Although "x loves Harry," "Harry loves x," "y loves Harry," and "Harry loves y" are functional expressions which contribute to articulating the proposition that Harry loves Harry, "x loves y" does not. Thanks to the restrictions on instantiation Wittgenstein imposes on the variable, on his view Harry's loving Harry can have nothing to do, logically speaking, with the proposition expressed by "$(\exists x)(\exists y)(x \text{ loves } y)$," as it does for both Frege and for Russell. For Wittgenstein takes the latter to say that someone loves someone else, someone different from him or herself. For Wittgenstein, "$(x)(y)(fxy \ \& \ fyx) \supset (x) fxx$" does not express a truth of logic, as it does in the logic of Frege and Russell. Instead, it expresses a proposition. If true, it tells us something informative about the relation f.

Thus Wittgenstein's remarks drastically limit the usual ways in which quantification theory is presented.[39] Indeed, this is evidence that a smooth-running system of pure logic holds no interest for Wittgenstein. He wishes to explore patterns in the ways in which differing kinds of sentence contribute to our expressive capacities, but he has no interest in presenting a systematic way of deriving patterns of quantificational structure from other patterns of quantificational structure.

5.5321 (quoted above) only suggests a notational technique for representing ascriptions of finite cardinal number without identity in those cases in which a (genuine) function expression is involved. It thereby provides an alternative to Russell's treatment of definite descriptions, but only in these cases (for "the so-and-so" write "there is exactly one so-and-so"; compare White 1979, pp. 164ff.). The notational proposal presupposes, however, that cardinal individuation is given immediately with the forms of elementary propositions. For what Wittgenstein has done is to build cardinality and ordinality directly into their forms of representation. That is, he takes numerical individuation as a primitive notion. Nothing could be further from Frege and Russell. It requires Wittgenstein to reject the Frege-Russell claim that number words are to be construed as constants or substantivals, either as names or as function expressions.

It should come as no surprise that Wittgenstein's restrictions on (what we would call) instantiations of quantifiers reflect aspects of the representational form of elementary propositions. This is one hallmark of his treatment of logic, that all propositions may be conceived to result from successive application of his operator N to the elementary propositions (6; see Section V below). Since number words figure in genuine propositions—in ascriptions of number—their expressive power must also so result. But how is this possible? Answer: If "a" and "b" are names with distinct *Bedeutungen*, then the number two is part of the form of representation (*Form der Darstellung*) of any proposition in which they figure, and two is itself represented in the form of the proposition. Wittgenstein conceives of numerals and number words as abbreviations of such depicting features of the symbolism, as forms. Such depicting features do not play the grammatical role that names and functional expressions do, but are variables, operation signs, and thus in a certain sense indefinable (*WVC*, p. 224).

Take, for example, the elementary proposition that aRb. The propositional sign "aRb" may be used to say that a bears R to b. The distinctness of these names in and of itself shows (though it does not say that there is) the possibility of there being at least two different R-relata (*CL*, p. 126; *WA*, vol. 1 p. 7). The elementary proposition aRb also shows the possibility of there being at least one R relatum of (the object) a distinct from a, the possibility of b's being the relatum under R of at least one distinct object and the possibility of there being at least two distinct objects whose names are "a" and "b." These "possibilities" are not ineffable, nonfactual possibilities. They are instead reflections of the use of the propositional sign to say what it says, true or false (that aRb).[40] Such possibilities are *shown* by aRb's being in the range of the *Satzvariable* "xRy," the variable Wittgenstein's notational proposal would use to articulate the ascription of number $(\exists x,y)xRy$, which says that there are at least two distinct R-relata.[41] For "xRy" does not range over any proposition of the form "xRx" according to Wittgenstein's restricted use of the variable.

That number is built as a primitive into the "form" of the elementary propositions may be seen a different way by considering Wittgenstein's differences with Frege and Russell over the nature of identity. At *Principia* *13, "x = y" is defined by what Russell takes as a version of Leibniz' law of the identity of indiscernibles: "$(\varphi)(\varphi x \equiv \varphi y)$," where "$\varphi$" is understood to range over all predicative functions. To this Wittgenstein objects that "Russell's definition of '=' won't do; because according to it one cannot say that two objects have all their properties in common. (Even if this proposition is never true, it is nevertheless significant.)" (5.5302.) Suppose that we take a language with the names "a" and "b" and the function expression "f(x)," and suppose too that the *Bedeutungen* of "a" and "b" are distinct. In this language there would be two elementary propositions, f(a) and f(b). Each would say something about a, and the same thing about b, that is, something about two f's. It would make sense to say in this language that two different f's had all their properties in common. But Russell's definition of identity systematically rules out any such language: he claims that from the supposition that a and b cosatisfy the propositional function f(x) we can deduce that a = b. As Russell would later write in objecting to Ramsey's use of the *Tractatus* treatment of identity, Wittgenstein takes numerical diversity to be a "primitive idea."[42] For Wittgenstein, Leibniz' law expresses a proposition: if it happens to be true, it can only be contingently so, and its making sense at all depends on a range of elementary propositions already in use—a range which presupposes numerical diversity and unity from the outset.

Wittgenstein's suggested interpretation of the Russellian notation is adequate for expressing all those propositions which ascribe a finite cardinal number via a genuine material function, so long as sufficiently many names with distinct *Bedeutungen* are available in the language. If there were, for example, only two names in the language with distinct *Bedeutungen*, then the language would still contain the grammatical forms of the number words by way of the arithmetical operations which Wittgenstein distills from general form of operation (see Section VI), and we would still have arithmetical terms and all the sentences of arithmetic. But we would have no means of using arithmetical terms to construct propositions ascribing numbers greater than two via material functions.[43] Furthermore, Wittgenstein's proposal does not suffice to set out in advance a way of saying that there is some number of ϕ's for a (genuine, material) function expression ϕ, much less that there are n objects (without functional qualification). For Wittgenstein, to try to say such things would be to try to construe number words as names or function expressions. He prefers to rest content with a specification of the numbers which allows us to write down a *Satzvariable* for the formal series of propositions "there is one ϕ, there are two ϕ's, there are three ϕ's and so on," up to the point where names with different *Bedeutungen* are exhausted. This is not an explicit definition of the kind Frege and Russell demanded. But, as we shall see, Wittgenstein did not think his definition worse off than theirs on that score.

This will perhaps become clearer if we focus on the basic logical notion of the variable, a notion essential to both Frege's and Russell's articulation of their respective notions of function. We have seen that Wittgenstein insists that any element of a systematic notation—any operation sign—is expressed by a variable, and in so insisting he follows at least verbally the manner of speaking he inherits from the nineteenth-century algebraists. Conversely, he treats variables as themselves operation signs. Thus he extends the algebraical notion of operation back across all the most basic notions of Frege's and Russell's (respective) philosophies of logic. Since it is by means of variables that Frege, Russell, and Wittgenstein articulate categorial (logical) distinctions among kinds of sign (e.g., operation signs versus function expressions versus names), we should expect that fundamental differences among these philosophers about the aims, scope, and character of logical distinctions would be reflected in differing conceptions of the variable. That this is so is the argument of the following section.

V. Variables as *Satzvariablen*: Operations and the Limits of Expression

For Wittgenstein—unlike for Frege, unlike for contemporary logicians—variables are not letters of the alphabet. They are what he calls *Satzvariablen*.

3.311   An expression presupposes the forms of all propositions in which it can occur.
         It is the common characteristic mark of a class of propositions.
3.312   It is therefore presented by the general form of the propositions which it characterizes.
         And in this form the expression is constant and everything else variable.
3.313   An expression is thus presented by a variable whose values are the propositions which contain the expression.
         (In the limiting case the variable becomes constant, the expression a proposition.)
         I call such a variable a "*Satzvariable*."

Satzvariablen are written by taking a particular expression—in the first instance, a propositional sign—and substituting in for its expressional parts a sign such as "x" or "ϕ." To return to our example, we may view "x is a man" and "ϕ(Harry)" as *Satzvariablen*, "variables" which exhibit what Wittgenstein calls "logical prototypes," "symbols," or "expressions" (3.315). ("Harry is a man" is a limiting case of a *Satzvariable*.) For Wittgenstein, a *Satzvariable* like "x is a man" or "ϕ(Harry)" is not a sign capable of differing interpretations; it is not just an open sentence. "Something variable," a "general form" common to a class of propositions,[44] is expressed by what Frege—but not Wittgenstein—would call a "variable," the letter "x" or "ϕ". Now Frege never conceived of "x is a man" as a variable. But for Wittgenstein variable letters such as "x" do not have an independent significance of their own, nor may they be said to range over objects or to stand for argument places in propositions which, when completed with objects or functions, yield propositions. For what variables such as "x is a man" do is to determine classes of propositions through ("presupposing," as Wittgenstein says at 3.311) the totality of elementary propositions. Variables have no content for Wittgenstein apart from this predetermined range. They are nothing but proxies. So it is not that Wittgenstein takes the variable name "x" to range over a fixed domain of all objects in the universe, as does Frege. Indeed, according to the *Tractatus*, all variables—variable names, variable function expressions, operation signs (including truth-operational signs, quantifiers, number words, and arithmetical terms), and variables ranging over operations—range, directly or indirectly, over elementary propositions.

3.314   An expression has meaning [*Bedeutung*] only in a proposition.
Every variable can be conceived as a *Satzvariable*.
(Including the variable name [*der variable Name*]) (my emphasis).

"The variable name"—for example, "x"—appears in, for example, "x is a man." One might suppose that the variable name "x" marks out a form, namely, the class of all names, those elements from which all propositions are composed (3.202). But on its own, "x" doesn't mark out or range over anything. On its own, it is the sign (not a symbol) for "the pseudo-concept *object*" (see 4.1272)—which is to say that in a concept-script, it has no significance on its own. Differently put, "x" makes no contribution (essential or otherwise) to the articulation of any proposition, but only serves to help mark out a class of propositions when it is written beside a function expression (or variable function expression) in the context of a *Satzvariable*. Then it aids in marking out a range (or category) of expressions—that is, names. To Frege it makes sense to ask what sort of entity a variable is: it is a letter of the alphabet used to indicate argument places. To Wittgenstein, it makes no sense to pose or to answer this question.

The *Tractatus*'s remarks about *Satzvariablen* are much more closely linked to Russell's talk about the variable than to Frege's, and specifically to what Russell calls "propositional variables" and "propositional functions" in *Principia Mathematica*. An expression like "x is a man" is, according to Russell, "such that it becomes a proposition when x is given any fixed determined meaning" (Whitehead and Russell, vol. 1, p. 14), and the range or collection of values of a propositional variable consists "of all the propositions (true or false) which can be obtained by giving every possible determination to x" (Whitehead and Russell, vol. 1, p. 15). For Russell, as for Wittgenstein, an expression like "x is a man" is not on its own either a propositional sign or a sign for a propositional function, and each bound or "apparent" variable occurring within the scope of a quantifier has a determinate but restricted "field" or range.

Russell allowed each propositional variable to be used to refer "ambiguously" to "an arbitrary member of the class of propositions it demarcates" (Whitehead and Russell, vol. 1, pp. 14–15). Thus he took as a primitive logical idea the notion of asserting a linguistic form with a "real" variable in it, calling this "ambiguous assertion" but insisting that it "cannot be defined in terms of the assertion of propositions" (Whitehead and Russell, vol. 1, p. 17). Russell held that the notion of ambiguous assertion is required in order to analyze mathematics, and specifically (1) reasoning by means of representative particulars (e.g., reasoning in geometry about a particular, arbitrarily chosen triangle in the course of proving a general theorem about all triangles of this kind); (2) reasoning by means of equations; and (3) expressions of general truths about numbers (Whitehead and Russell, vol. 1, p. 18). The claims are tied, as we shall see, to Russell's difficulties with the theory of types and worries about vicious circles.[45]

As early as 1913, in the "Notes on Logic," Wittgenstein had written that "there are no propositions containing real variables," for

> [t]hose symbols which are called propositions in which "variables occur" are in reality not propositions at all, but only schemes of propositions, which only become propositions when we replace the variables by constants. There is no proposition which is expressed by "x=x", for "x" has no signification; but there is a proposition "(x).x=x" and propositions such as "Socrates=Socrates" etc.
>
> In books on logic, no variables ought to occur, but only the general propositions which justify the use of variables.[46]

At this stage of his thinking, Wittgenstein is anticipating the *Tractatus*'s conception of *Satzvariablen*. He dismisses Russell's notion that formulae with real variables must sometimes be asserted (as if they expressed genuine propositions) in logical deductions (compare Hylton 1997, p. 98 n.). A Tractarian *Satzvariable* simply goes proxy for (*vertritt*) the collection of propositions it determines; it cannot be used to name a class ("the theory of classes is superfluous") nor can it be used to reach through to the *Bedeutungen* of any of the particular expressions over which it ranges (cf. 3.317). We operate with it systematically.

Wittgenstein preserves his fundamental distinctions between names, function expressions, and operation signs in the notation he proposes for *Satzvariablen*. If "O" stands for any operation sign and "O'x" stands for "the result of applying operation O to x," then the variable for the operation takes on a special form:

5.2522   The general term of the formal series "a", "O'a", "O'O'a" write thus: "[a,x,O'x]." This expression in brackets is a variable. The first term of the expression in brackets is the beginning of the formal series, the second the form of an arbitrary term x of the series, and the third the form of that term of the series which immediately follows x.

5.2523   The concept of the successive application of an operation is equivalent to the concept "and so on."

The "and so on," essential to the formal potential of any operation sign, is expressed by Wittgenstein's square bracketed *Satzvariablen*. These variables are proxies for collections of propositions ordered internally by the repeated application of an operation to its own result ad infinitum, beginning from a particular basis. They capture the systematic quality of the notation for any operation.

Wittgenstein specifies three sorts of ways in which a *Satzvariable* may go proxy for its values:

5.501   An expression in brackets [*Klammerausdruck*] whose terms are propositions I indicate—if the order of the terms in the bracket is indifferent—by a sign of the form "($\bar{\xi}$)". "ξ" is a variable whose values are the terms of the expression in brackets, and the line over the variable indicates that it stands for all its values in the bracket.
(Thus if ξ has the 3 values P, Q, R, then ($\bar{\xi}$) = (P,Q,R).)

The values of the variables are determined.

The determination is the description of the propositions which the variable stands for [*vertritt*].

How the description of the terms of the bracket expression takes place is unessential.

We may distinguish 3 kinds of description:

1. Direct enumeration. In this case we can simply set out its constant values instead of the variable.

2. Giving a function *fx*, whose values for all values of *x* are the propositions to be described.

3. Giving a formal law, according to which those propositions are constructed. In this case the terms of the bracket expression are all the terms of a formal series.

"How the description of the terms of the bracket expression takes place is unessential": this means that *Satzvariablen* of the first and second kind may be used within square bracketed *Satzvariablen*. In this way, square bracketed *Satzvariablen* may be used to collect together more than one formal series (or: formal series with multiple series of complexity). For example, if we let ξ = (p, q), for some definite collection of propositions p and q, then "ξ" is a *Satzvariable* of the first kind (an enumeration). And "[$\bar\xi$, x, ¬x]"—or alternatively, "¬'($\bar\xi$)"—collects together two formal series, namely, "p, ¬p, ¬¬p, ..." and "q, ¬q, ¬¬q, ..." As for generality, Wittgenstein's generalized Sheffer stroke of joint denial—operator N—may be used to jointly deny all values of a *Satzvariable* by use of the bar notation, so that (to stick to our example) "[$\bar\xi$, $\bar{x}$, N'$\bar{x}$]" ranges over "N(p,q), N(N(p,q)), N(N(N(p,q))) . . . ," or equivalently "¬p & ¬q, ¬ (¬p & ¬q), ¬¬(¬p & ¬q) . . . ." If we let our basis be the *Satzvariable fx*, then the *Satzvariable* "[$\bar{fx}$,$\bar\xi$, N'$\bar\xi$]—alternatively "N'($\bar{fx}$)"— ranges over the propositions in the formal series "N($\bar{f[x]}$), N(N[($\bar{f(x)}$)])), N(N(N($\bar{f(x)}$))) . . .", or equivalently "¬(∃x)($f(x)$), ¬(¬(∃x)($f(x)$))), ¬(¬(¬(∃x)($f(x)$)))) . . . ."

This process of generalizing the square bracket notation by means of *Satzvariablen* within *Satzvariablen* culminates in what Wittgenstein calls "the general propositional form." Let '*p*' stand for any elementary proposition. Then

6   The general form of truth-function is: [$\bar{p}$, $\bar\xi$, N($\bar\xi$)]
      This is the general form of proposition.

6.001   This says nothing else than that every proposition is the result of successive applications of the operation N'($\bar\xi$) to the elementary propositions.

In the Appendix, I give several examples of how (what we would call) first order quantificational schemata may be formally constructed through a finite number of applications of operator N to a basis (collection) of elementary propositions.[47]

Wittgenstein had earlier remarked that all propositions are truth-functions of elementary propositions (5). Yet he holds that the truth-functions are not really functions, are not "material" functions (5.44). As the *Tractatus* unfolds, he shifts his way of speaking, trading away the phrase "truth-function" in favor of "truth-operation." This divides Frege's and Russell's notions of function up into kinds, into material or genuine functions and merely formal operations, restricting the application of the notion of *function*. All propositions are on this view results of truth-operations on elementary propositions (5.3), the elementary propositions being limiting cases of empty operations on themselves. On Wittgenstein's view, the generality of the general form of proposition is not quantificational, but operational. No proposition talks about the general form of proposition; the square bracketed *Satzvariable* is not a propositional sign. Its values are determined through (operations on) elementary propositions. Indeed, none of the three kinds of *Satzvariablen* Wittgenstein mentions (in 5.501) can be used to express a proposition, except in the limiting case of a lone propositional sign: (1) to enumerate propositions is to list, but to list is not to say that anything is the case, it is not to articulate a genuine proposition, true or false; (2) an expression such as "x is a man" cannot be used to assert a proposition, true or false; (3) no square bracketed expression such as "p, O'p and so on" can be used to assert a proposition, true or false.

Neither Frege nor Russell took the notion of an operation as a basic notion. This is no accident, for the *Satzvariablen* which express them thwart the general applicability of a function/argument scheme. The "and so on" was the very notion Frege and Russell wished to eliminate from the foundations of logic (and mathematics) by means of their ancestral construction. Wittgenstein is insisting against them that ellipsis is essential to our uses of the signs of logic and mathematics, and therefore that operations—not only truth-operations, but also arithmetical operations—figure essentially in the power of our language to articulate propositions (compare N, pp. 89–90).

This has special force against the presentation of the theory of types in *Principia Mathematica*, which depends essentially on the use of such an iterable mode of expression. The so-called logical constants—used, for example, in expresssing what Russell conceives of as general logical laws—"must," Russell explains, either be confined "to disjunctions and negations of elementary propositions, or we must regard them as really each multiple, so that in regard to each type of propositions we shall need a new primitive idea of negation and a new primitive idea of disjunction" (Whitehead and Russell, vol. 1, p. 128). Russell claims that "by merely repeating the process" he sets forth, "propositions of any order can be reached" (Whitehead and Russell, vol. 1, p. 128), but this requires the use of systematic ambiguity, for logical laws such as *modus ponens* must be assumed afresh in Russell's shift from elementary propositions to quantified propositions. In addition, every enunciation of a logical law requires ambiguity of type in its variables. (Wittgenstein explicitly objects to this at 6.123.) Furthermore, like Frege, Russell and Whitehead have no general treatment of relations of arbitrary *n*-adicity: the *Principia* proceeds without the Wiener/Kuratowski reduction of order to class, so that their theorems must be proven afresh for unary, dyadic, triadic relations, and so on (compare WA, vol. 1, pp. 27–28).[48] Furthermore, the definition of the natural numbers within type theory stratifies the universe, so that new numbers must be defined afresh at each step in the progression of the hierarchy of types. That there are a particular number of first-level individuals cannot, as is explicitly said, "be proved logically; . . . it is only ascertainable by a census, not by logic" (Whitehead and Russell, vol. 2, p. x). Even after such a census, however, there is no way to assert the cardinal number of things in the universe. Nor can one say whether or not there is a unique number of classes at each particular type (Whitehead and Russell, vol. 2, p. xiii). At best what Russell and Whitehead can write down are "symbolically identical primitive propositions" (Whitehead and Russell, vol. 2, p. ix), at best they can indicate mere constancy of symbolic form, form which may be shown or seen but not said. Writes Russell,

from symbolic analogy we "*see*" that the process can be repeated indefinitely. This possibility rests upon two things:

(1) A fresh interpretation of our constants—v ~, !, (x)., (∃x)—at each fresh stage;

(2) A fresh assumption, symbolically unchanged, of the primitive propositions which we found sufficient at an earlier stage—the possibility of avoiding symbolic change being due to the fresh interpretation of our constants, primitive propositions.

. . . if, at any stage, we wish to deal with a class defined by a function of the 30,000th type, we shall have to repeat our arguments and assumptions 30,000 times. But there is still no necessity to speak of the hierarchy as a whole, or to suppose that statements can be made about "all types."

. . . we "*see*" that whatever *can be proved* for lower types, whether functional or extensional, can also be proved for higher types. . . . Hence we assume that it is unnecessary to know the types of our variables, though they must always be confined within some one definite type.

. . . when we have proved a proposition for the lowest significant type, we "*see*" that it holds in any other assigned significant type. Hence every proposition which is proved without the mention of any type is to be regarded as proved for the lowest significant type, and extended by analogy to any other significant type.

By exactly similar considerations we "*see*" that a proposition which can be proved for some type other than the lowest significant type must hold for any type in the direct descent from this . . . .

To "assert a symbolic form" is to assert each of the propositional functions arising for the set of possible typical determinations which are somewhere enumerated. We have in fact enumerated a very limited number of types starting from that of individuals, and we "*see*" that this process can be indefinitely continued by analogy. The form is always asserted so far as the enumeration has arrived; and this is sufficient for all purposes, since it is essentially impossible to use a type which has not been arrived at by successive enumeration from the lower types. (Whitehead and Russell, vol. 2, pp. ix–xii; emphases [but not scarequotes] on "see" are mine)

This is the *Principia*'s way of drawing the distinction between showing and saying. In order to present arithmetic without "having to repeat our arguments and assumptions 30,000 times," it fashions a way of speaking about symbolic form and symbolic analogy apart from particular interpretations or "meanings." This involves the authors, as they fully realize, in what can only be seen, and not couched or asserted in propositions. Whitehead classifies "formal numbers" as those which are "constant" (those numbers σ for which there is a symbol α such that whenever α is determined as to type, σ is identical with Nc'α, the cardinal number of all objects at α), and those which are "functional," or functionally complex.[49] Distinctions among formal numbers depend, he says, "on the symbolism and not on the entity denoted, and in considering them it is symbolic analogy and not denotation which is to be taken into account" (Whitehead and Russell, vol. 2, p. xiv). So he adopts the algebraic terminology of "operations" and "symbolic forms": "Addition, multiplication, exponentiation, and subtraction will be called the arithmetical operations; and in $\mu +_c \nu$, $\mu \times_c \nu$, μ^ν, $\mu -_c \nu$, μ and ν will each be said to be subjected to these respective operations" (Whitehead and Russell, vol. 2, p. xv). In the context of the theory of types, ordinary rules of substitution in equalities must be restricted. Whitehead distinguishes between kinds of occurrences of formal numbers in symbolic forms: some are argumental, some are equational, and some are logical. In, for example, in

$$*100.511. \ \vdash: \exists! \ Nc'\beta \ .\supset. \ sm''Nc'\beta = Nc'\beta$$

the formal numbers are Nc'β and sm''Ncβ. The first occurrence of "Nc'β" is logical, the second argumental, the third equational, and the only occurrence of "sm''Ncβ" is equational (cf. Whitehead and Russell, vol. 2, p. xix). Whitehead defines an "arithmetical equation" as an "equation between purely arithmetical formal numbers whose actual types are both determined adequately" (Whitehead and Russell, vol. 2, pp. xxiv–xxv). This allows us to "pass with practical immediateness" from a typically ambiguous equation to the substitution of one symbolic form (one formal number) for another. Whitehead dubs this the "Principle of Arithmetical Substitution" (Whitehead and Russell, vol. 2, p. xxivff). In this way, he allows that "all discrimination of the types of indefinite inductive numbers may be dropped; and the types are entirely indefinite and irrelevant (Whitehead and Russell, vol. 2, p. xxxi).

Whitehead has wiped out the expressive difficulties facing his theory of types by reverting to his older algebraical language of "operations," "symbolic form," and "substitution." Naturally, Whitehead and Russell take this as a mere convenience, rather than a conceptual analysis of the nature of mathematics and logic. But when Wittgenstein takes the notion of operation to be basic in the *Tractatus*, he is construing their appeal to what we can "see" if we proceed to go on "in the same way"—that is, what they do, as opposed to what they (try to) say they do—as fundamental to logic and mathematics:

5.252   Only [by means of an operation] is the progress from term to term in a formal series possible (from type to type in the hierarchy of Russell and Whitehead). (Russell and Whitehead have not admitted the possibility of this progress but have made use of it all the same.)

VI. Wittgenstein's Formal Specification of the Natural Numbers, Mathematical Sentences, and Ascriptions of Number in Mathematics

Space permits only a very brief characterization of Wittgenstein's treatment of mathematical sentences, including ascriptions of number within mathematics.

Wittgenstein's treatment of arithmetical terms turns the *Principia*'s appeal to "symbolic analogy" and "showing" on its head by taking the notions of a formally iterable operation and of a rule of substitution as primitive notions. The difference between Wittgenstein's use of the notions of operation and symbolic rule and the ordinary algebraist's use of these terms is that Wittgenstein ties his notions directly to his characterization of the general form of proposition and, hence, to the forms of the elementary propositions. Wittgenstein constructs a *Satzvariable* for his notion of operation on the basis of his *Satzvariable* for the general form of proposition:

6.002   If we are given the general form of the way in which a proposition (*Satz*) is constructed, then thereby we are also given the general form of the way in which by an operation out of one proposition another can be created.

6.01   The general form of the operation $\Omega'(\eta)$ is therefore:
$[\bar{\xi}, N(\bar{\xi})]' (\bar{\eta}) (= [\bar{\eta}, \bar{\xi}, N(\bar{\xi})])$.
This is the most general form of transition from one proposition to another.

According to Wittgenstein, every operation gives us a way of making systematic ("formal") transitions from one proposition to another. In "$[\bar{\eta}, \bar{\xi}, N(\bar{\xi})]$", "$\bar{\eta}$" ranges over all possible bases for operations, "$\bar{\xi}$" over all propositions (i.e., all possible results of steps in the development of a formal series) and "$N(\bar{\xi})$" over all propositions (i.e., all possible results of applying operator N). Wittgenstein does not mean that operator N is the only operation, but is instead stipulating that nothing he counts as an operation has a basis or a result that cannot be used— whether directly or indirectly—to make a systematic sort of formal transition from one proposition to another.

The *Tractatus* characterizes the natural numbers by extracting from Wittgenstein's notation for the general form of operation a notation to express the notion of a result appearing at a particular stage (after a particular *number* of steps) in the development of a formal series.

6.02   And thus we come to numbers: I define
$x = \Omega^{0}{}'x$ Def. and
$\Omega'\Omega^{\nu}{}'x = \Omega^{\nu+1}{}'x$ Def.
According, then, to these symbolic rules we write the series
$x, \Omega'x, \Omega'\Omega'x, \Omega'\Omega'\Omega'x \ldots$ as:
$\Omega^{0}{}'x, \Omega^{0+1}{}'x, \Omega^{0+1+1}{}'x, \Omega^{0+1+1+1}{}'x \ldots$

Therefore I write in place of "$[x, \xi, \Omega' \, \xi]$"
   "$[\Omega^{0'}x, \Omega^{v'}x, \Omega^{v+1'}x]$."
And I define:
   $0+1 = 1$ Def.
   $0+1+1 = 2$ Def.
   $0+1+1+1 = 3$ Def.
and so on.

6.021 A number is the exponent of an operation.

"Ω" is a variable ranging over operations, "v" is shorthand for finite sequences of this variable. Thus "$\Omega'\Omega'$" stands in for two steps in the development of any formal series, "$\Omega'\Omega'\Omega'$" for three such steps, and so on. "x" ranges over all possible bases of formal series "$\Omega^{0'}x$" over results of first steps in the development of any formal series, "$\Omega^{0+1'}x$" over the results of second such steps, and so on.

As Frascolla (1994) sets out in admirable detail, Wittgenstein construes the natural numbers as abbreviations of sequences of variables, variables that range over all operations. Natural numbers are thus "exponents" or "pictures" (not "indices")[50] common to the development of any formal series, to the iteration of any operation, though of course numerals and arithmetical terms "picture" numbers in a different way than propositions picture states of affairs.[51]

Numerals are operation signs. For Wittgenstein's specification of the numbers uses the "and so on" and is thus itself equivalent to a square bracketed *Satzvariable*. It would not pass muster with Frege as a "definition," it is not explicit. But it shows that the series of natural numbers (0, 1 ,1+1, 1+1+1, and so on) models or pictures (shares the form of) the iterability of any operation, and therefore that each natural number models or pictures (shares the form of) the generation of a formal series up to a certain point. It shows that any notation for the system of numbers must be a systematic notation. Differently put, there could be no notation for the natural numbers which construed them as proper names or function expressions, any more than there could be a notation which construed the truth-operations as proper names or function expressions (compare *WVC*, p. 226). "$[0, \xi, \xi+1]$", a variable ranging over exponents of operations, shows the general form of natural number (6.03). Like the general form of proposition, it is a (very general) *Satzvariable* that is not a propositional sign. Just as no proposition can be framed using the general notion of proposition, no proposition can be framed using the general notion of natural number.

We have already seen that Wittgenstein takes equations to be essential to mathematics. Equations do not in his view express propositions (about, say, all numbers), they are operationally, but not functionally, complex. They set forth rules for the substitution of one numerical (or operational) sign for another, either in other mathematical equations or in genuine propositions (extramathematical ascriptions of number). Mathematical equations contain no signs used in the way function expressions and names are used; they contain only (abbreviations of) variables and signs for equality. "$3+1=4$" might be shown (or operated on) in any one of an unlimited number of ways (e.g., $3=4-1$, $3+1-4=0$, $3+1+1=4$, and so on). Each result of operating on the equation yields a different aspect of the equation, a different representation or standpoint from which to consider the operation signs figuring in it (6.2323; cf. 2.173, 1994, vol. 2, p. 56).

Ascriptions of number within mathematics (e.g., "there is only one solution to x+1=1"), take a special grammatical form: they are not propositions, true or false, but rather grammatical rules of variables:[52] they show us ways we may interchange numerical operations in genuine propositions without affecting the sense expressed. Arithmetical 'proofs' of equalities between particular number words are calculations with operation signs by means of the method of substitution (6.241, quoted above).

In the *Tractatus*, Wittgenstein never excludes the possibility that his remarks might be used to develop a notation which would interweave signs for quantifiers and truth operations with arithmetical operation signs.[53] But not until he returned to England in 1929 did Wittgenstein begin seriously to investigate the question of whether and how such interweaving might be accomplished in an unmisleading way, without glossing over his sharp distinction between function expressions and operation signs. It was only then that he began to try to develop his view of mathematics beyond elementary arithmetic, to the point where he considered quantification over numbers. Even then, however, he still treated the roles of quantifiers and truth-operations in equational contexts as utterly different from their role in nonmathematical propositions, and he never did accept Frege's and Russell's uses of the ancestral construction to account for the logic of ascriptions of number. Not because he was a finitist or constructivist, but because he rejected their conceptions of what the basic logical notions are.

I am not claiming that Wittgenstein's treatment of number owes nothing to Frege and Russell. Like the logicists, he takes cardinal number words to reflect an aspect of the logical form of propositions; he construes our method of representing the numbers in language as part and parcel of our use of sentences to express propositions.[54] Like Frege and Russell, he attends carefully to the grammar of sentences involving number words—including extramathematical ascriptions of number—and eschews the quest for a philosophical account of number which depends upon any sort of psychological or transcendental account of the mind, including mental processes of abstraction, or synthetic a priori intuition. His notational proposal for representing the grammar of number words might even be said to give expression to Frege's idea that we may "characterize as a concept that which has number" (Frege 1984, p. 114): according to the *Tractatus*, it is part of what it is to be a genuine concept word (a genuine function expression) to be configurable in propositional signs which are used to ascribe particular finite numbers and in elementary propositional signs, in which concept words aid in the representation of numbers (as forms). Furthermore, his handling of the grammar of ascriptions of number might be formulated in a Fregean way, as Wittgenstein himself wrote in 1929: in a sense, he construes an ascription of number as an assertion about a concept (*WA* vol. 1, p. 8). Finally, Wittgenstein himself remarks in the *Tractatus* that "mathematics is a method of logic" (6.2, 6.234, quoted above).

For all these reasons, it may still seem appropriate, as Frascolla has maintained, to call Wittgenstein a "logicist" about mathematics (Frascolla 1994, pp. 25–26,

37–39). But I have argued that Wittgenstein's differences with Frege and Russell on the respective natures (the respective grammars) of logic and mathematics evinces a conception of the fundamental notions of logic which is fundamentally at odds with theirs. It is quite misleading to label him a "logicist," as the tradition has so often done.

VI. Conclusion

In closing, I would like to make a few remarks about why I believe it is important for readers of the *Tractatus* to be willing to scrutinize the inner details of the text with the kind of circumspect attention I have paid to them in this essay.

The *Tractatus* counts as one of the most influential works in all of twentieth-century philosophy, certainly within anything one would be willing to count as the "analytic" tradition. We therefore cannot understand recent philosophical history unless we come to see precisely what Wittgenstein's interpreters did (and do) with his writings: how they read him selectively and partially, according to their philosophical needs and demands, and how he in turn so read his own philosophical predecessors, especially Frege and Russell. If we look at the history of interpretations of the *Tractatus*, it may be said (speaking very generally) that since at least Elizabeth Anscombe's *Introduction to Wittgenstein's Tractatus* (1959) there has been a growing consensus that the early Wittgenstein was not a logical positivist, however influential the *Tractatus* was on that philosophical movement. (This trend has paralleled the wider philosophical culture's increased distancing of itself from positivism.) Readers interested in situating the *Tractatus* within the history of twentieth-century philosophy are far more likely nowadays to emphasize Wittgenstein's philosophical debts to Hertz, to Russell, and especially to Frege than they are to emphasize what he had to say about analyticity, verificationism, or phenomenalism. (This trend echoes the fact that Frege is far more carefully and enthusiastically read today than he was before the mid-1940s.) Meanwhile, the resurgence of interest in ontology within the analytic tradition since the 1960s seems to have tempted at least some readers to interpret the *Tractatus* as a metaphysical, rather than antimetaphysical work: as defending, for example, either a form of modal realism, or a cognitive metaphysics of thought, or a critical realism of the Kantian variety (albeit one according to which the transcendental standpoint is not expressible in factual language, but can only be shown). There is some justification within Wittgenstein's text for each of these interpretations, and each has certain merits. Most recently, however, a number of American scholars of early analytic philosophy—most notably Cora Diamond, Burton Dreben, and Warren Goldfarb—have reacted against such metaphysical ways of reading the *Tractatus* and have attempted to defend a more sophisticated antimetaphysical reading of the book, albeit one which still distances Wittgenstein's philosophy from positivism in key respects.[55] Their readings of the *Tractatus* have sparked heated yet philosophically fruitful debate,[56] precisely by stimulating philosophers to re-examine the (frequently highly ambiguous) text of the *Tractatus* itself, exploring the philosophical and interpretative possibilities latent within it.

In this essay, focusing on what may seem rather technical or peripheral parts of Wittgenstein's early philosophy, I have defended a version of this antimetaphysical yet antipositivist reading of the *Tractatus*. I make much of the fact that Wittgenstein accepted neither the Frege-Russell analysis of the grammar of number words, nor their reduction of logic to mathematics, nor even their account of the application of logic within mathematics. This fact separates Wittgenstein's philosophy sharply from the positivists as well. But my primary aim has been to emphasize Wittgenstein's differences with Frege and Russell. This is because most recent antimetaphysical interpreters of the *Tractatus* have, by contrast, tended to stress affinities between Frege and the early Wittgenstein, partly in order to reassess received readings of Frege (see Floyd 1998b).

Here Cora Diamond's reading of the early Wittgenstein—to which I am greatly indebted—stands out (Diamond 1991a, 1991b, 1997). Diamond argues that the early Wittgenstein may be seen to have inherited a distinction between showing and saying from Frege and then used it (like Frege, on Diamond's reading of him) to resist the attractions of both realist and idealist theories of the logical structure of language and/or world. Diamond's interpretation the *Tractatus* places heavy weight on what she has called the "framing" remarks of the *Tractatus*: the Preface and closing lines of the book, where Wittgenstein suggests that the reader should take the remarks of the *Tractatus* to be purely nonsensical. On her "therapeutic" reading, the *Tractatus* is pure nonsense, but at the same time is a work of great imaginative and philosophical force, designed to depict the attractions of various sorts of realism and idealism and, simultaneously, to show us that every such effort to erect a metaphysical theory of logical structure steps beyond the bounds of sense. She argues (rightly I think) that the early Wittgenstein—like the later Wittgenstein—aimed to help his readers overcome the felt need to propound theories of necessity, meaning, and ontology. His Tractarian strategy, she holds, is to indulge such felt needs imaginatively, by constructing an arrangement of remarks (e.g., "objects form the substance of the world" [2.021]) in such a way as to display their nonsensical character—a character which, Diamond insists, is not nonsense-with-a-certain-kind-of-ineffable-or-poetical-significance, but rather nonsense pure and simple, on a par with gibberish (e.g., "Socrates is frabble"). Just here, she claims, Frege provided Wittgenstein with a model. For Frege took sentential forms resembling those of the *Tractatus* to play a key role in his philosophy. He called them "elucidations," conceiving of them as constructions which are strictly speaking nonsensical, but which nevertheless serve as hints, aids to help a reader catch on to the use of genuine language—that is, to his concept-script. According to Diamond, it is by means of such elucidatory forms as "There are functions" or "No concept is an object"—neither of which can be expressed in Frege's notation—that Frege tries to inculcate our understanding of that language. Yet it is on her view only by working within genuine, meaningful language—e.g., the language of Frege's concept-script—that a reader can come to appreciate the status of Frege's primitive, undefinable logical distinctions. Frege's appreciation of the nonsensical character of his elucidations is thus, for Diamond, part and parcel of his appreciation of the nonsensical character of certain forms of realism. And this, she believes, Wittgenstein took from Frege. As she writes,

Philosophical uses of 'object' *dither* between wanting the word to have the kind of logical significance it has functioning as a variable and wanting the word to mean some property, to be a genuine property-word. The idea of a notation in which, instead of the word 'object,' we always did just have a variable is then supposed by Wittgenstein to be possibly helpful: we should come to see that the notation enables us to say everything we wanted to say and so we may be cured of the *irresolute dithering* use of 'object'. The notation itself then helps achieve the therapeutic goals Wittgenstein describes at *Tractatus* 6.53. The ordinary language use of 'object' as a variable goes over into that notation in one way; and the use of 'object' as a genuine property word goes over differently. The translation into the logical notation thus reveals that the use of 'object', as a word logically parallel to 'potato', involves no logical error but does involve using a word which, in that use, has been assigned no meaning. The importance of translation into logical notation is thus that the notation doesn't, as ordinary language does, make it easy to conceal one's dithering from oneself. (Diamond 1997, p. 79)

On Diamond's reading, Wittgenstein's diagnosis of the nonsense that arises in philosophizing is that it comes from unclarity about the "logical significance" of the terms that we use, an unclarity abetted by ordinary language and (possibly) dispelled by the use of a perspicuous logical notation. Diamond insists that her account of the Wittgenstein-Frege notion of the "logical significance" of an expression is not a semantical or meaning-theoretic one. Instead, it is to be made out wholly in terms of the inferential relations that a judgment voiced using that expression bear to other judgments (1997, p. 75–76). For example, from "There's a potato in the window" may be seen to follow "there's an object in the window," but in two quite differing ways, ways which would be differently expressed in Fregean notation. Philosophical confusion arises, on the view Diamond ascribes to Wittgenstein and Frege, from the fact that one and the same term of ordinary language ("object") may be used in expressions of judgments conforming to entirely distinct patterns of inferential relations. And herein lies the therapeutic usefulness of the "notation," the concept script which perspicuously marks—or attempts to perspicuously mark—all (genuine) inferential distinctions syntactically. As she writes,

If a language is capable of expressing thoughts at all, it must (here Frege and Wittgenstein agree) have as the logical component of its grammar what every language has. The point about *the* logical grammar applies not only to any natural language but also to a concept-script designed with the intention that the logical characteristics of the thoughts expressed in its sentences should be shown clearly in the perceptible structure of those sentences. A concept-script is unsatisfactory when it treats in the same way what is logically different (what *the* logical grammar treats as different) or treats in different ways what is logically similar. (Diamond 1997, pp. 126–127; emphases are hers)

This conception of a *Begriffsschrift* involves the idea that there is a single inferential order of judgment and thought which it is the aim of a perspicuous logical notation to capture or make explicit. This suggests that Diamond takes Tractarian therapy designed to dispel the power of metaphysics to involve—at least in part—the devising of a *Begriffsschrift*. But not just any old *Begriffsschrift*. A proper *Begriffsschrift* reflects "*the*" logical order of thought insofar as it prevents us from dithering in the relevant respect when we express thinking in language. A *Begriffsschrift* that failed to reflect this order would be one that encouraged us to "treat in the same way what is logically different," or "in different ways what is logically similar."

Yet, as I have argued in this essay, by examining the details of what Wittgenstein actually *did* with the *Begriffsschriften* of Frege and Russell in the *Tractatus*, we can see that he is rejecting this ideal of clarity of expression. According to this ideal—vividly set out by Diamond—we imagine ourselves to be depicting *the* inferential order among thoughts (or sentences of our language) when we work with a logical notation. But on my reading, one aim of the *Tractatus* is to depict such notions as "*the* inferential order," "*the* logical grammar of language," and "*the* logical form of a proposition" as chimeras. In this sense, the Frege (Russell) ideal stands as a primary philosophical target of the *Tractatus*, and not just an ideal Wittgenstein inherited from them. For Frege and Russell write as if, at least ideally, there is a single context of expression within which we may discern the structure of thought, a systematically presented *Begriffsschrift* within which we can use logical notation to make perspicuous *the* logical order. In contrast, I have emphasized Wittgenstein's insistence in the *Tractatus* that no single imposition of a logico-syntactic order on what we say is or can be the final word, the final way of expressing or depicting a thought. In the *Tractatus*'s view (as I interpret it), there is thinking, but thinking without thoughts, thinking without an inferential order. For Wittgenstein—even in the *Tractatus*—however useful the formalized languages of Frege and Russell may be for warding off certain grammatical and metaphysical confusions, these languages must simultaneously be seen as sources of new forms of philosophical illusion—indeed the deepest kind of illusion of all, the illusion of having found ultimate clarity. Wittgenstein is certainly indebted to Frege's and Russell's work—he himself writes that we need a good logico-syntactic notation in order to avoid certain philosophical confusions (3.325). But I do not think he shared either Frege's or Russell's (or for that matter the logical positivists') conception(s) of what an ideal or formalized language could do for us in philosophy. Unlike these philosophers, he does not think any notation can depict *the* grammar of language, or make clear *the* limits of sense, *the* logical order.

This, it seems to me, is the best answer that can be given to those critics of Diamond (and other antimetaphysical readers of the *Tractatus*) who find incoherent her insistence that the remarks of the *Tractatus* are no more and no less nonsensical than any other gibberish. It is a good question how Wittgenstein's *Tractatus* could have been so philosophically influential and insightful if it consists of nothing but gibberish or ironically intended remarks.[57] The answer, it seems to me, is that Wittgenstein's use of the term "nonsense" ("*unsinnig*")—in the *Tractatus* as

in his later philosophy—has no freestanding use, but is instead a kind of dialectical punctuation mark, used in context to stop the reader from imposing a single
order of grammar (or thought) upon a particular philosophically minded choice
of words. In my view, Wittgenstein's deepest philosophical insight—even in the
Tractatus—was not one that concerns the notion of *nonsense* as a generic grammatical category or a term of philosophical criticism with a systematic use.
Rather, Wittgenstein's insight was that there is no general category of nonsense
to be made out by the philosopher, no way for philosophy to achieve a perspective from which to systematically chart the bounds of sense.[58] We can appreciate this about the *Tractatus* only by penetrating inside the so-called framing remarks and exploring the details of Wittgenstein's own philosophical remarks.
Only in this way may we see that there is no clear distinction to be drawn between
the frame of the *Tractatus* and what is inside the frame.

I have argued in this essay that one way to see that Wittgenstein had no ineffable theory of logic, thought, or mathematics is to see that he had no theory—
no notation for—the effability of logic, thought, or mathematics. I am well
aware that to emphasize, as I have, the distance separating the philosophy of
the *Tractatus* from the philosophies of Frege and Russell is to portray the tradition of early analytic philosophy as a conversation in which parties disagree
with one another on fundamentals, rather than finding themselves bound together by a common conception of method (e.g., the use of a system of modern
mathematical logic to depict the logico-syntactic grammar of language) or
doctrine (e.g., that the structure of thought can [and can only] be gleaned from
an analysis of the structure of language).[59] I am holding that there is a point at
which Wittgenstein's criticisms of Frege and Russell are external criticisms,
criticisms which evince a philosophical perspective and spirit radically different
from theirs—even if at particular points in the *Tractatus* (as Diamond for one
has shown) we may also take him to have been working through insights he
gleaned from both Frege and from Russell, and pointing toward internal tensions in their philosophies which he hoped to resolve (or, better, dissolve). It is
for this reason that I have insisted on grappling with the *Tractatus*'s treatment
of number in such detail in this essay. Until we see what Wittgenstein asked us
to *do* with the *Begriffsschriften* of Frege and Russell, we cannot see what his aims
really were in the *Tractatus*.[60]

Appendix

Wittgenstein holds that a proposition may be conceived as the result of a finite
number of successive applications of operator N to elementary propositions
(*Tractatus* 5,6). It has been alleged that this is false, since pure quantification
theory does not reduce to purely truth-functional logic, but I do not think this
reduction is at issue in the *Tractatus*, and therefore I do not take this objection to
refute his claim (see footnote 39). In response, I give below an indication of how
it is that Wittgenstein understands his claim, using the notation he proposes in

the *Tractatus* to express quantificationally complex propositions as results of the application of operator N to elementary propositions. I have departed from the *Tractatus* notation in adding indices to the use of operator N whenever it is used to express generality; in such cases, operator N is applied to a (potentially infinite) number of elementary propositions all at once, by means of a *Satzvariable*; and the index in my variant of Wittgenstein's notation indicates the *Satzvariable* to which this particular use of operator N is tied. Some such system of indexing—some such notational differentiation among uses of operator N to express generality—is needed in order to unambiguously express multiple generality, for we need to be able to notationally tie each such use of operator N to a unique *Satzvariable*. Any such system of indexing goes beyond what Wittgenstein actually proposes in the *Tractatus*, but not in a way that undercuts his insistence that quantification is an operation on elementary propositions. The fact that Wittgenstein never bothered to propose any such indexing system indicates, it seems to me, just how uninterested he was in developing a formalized quantificational language of the Frege-Russell sort.

In the tables below, rows represent steps in the finite sequence of applications of operator N to elementary propositions. To express generality, operator N applies, not to a (single) set of elementary propositions, but directly to the elementary propositions themselves. I have rendered such applications as two-part steps (e.g., 3a., 3b., in the table below), because I conceive of these as really one application of operator N.

To Express One Universal Quantifier with Operator N:
e.g., "Everything is an apple"

English	Russellian Notation	Wittgenstein's Operator N Notation	Comments
1. *a* is an apple	Aa	Aa	Elementary Proposition, hence no variables and we assume "A", "a" are all simple names
2. *a* is not an apple	$\neg Aa$	$N(Aa)$	Quantifier-free Proposition
3a. *x* is not an apple	$\neg Ax$	$N(Ax)$	*Satzvariable* from 2, $x \rightarrow a$
⇓	⇓	⇓	⇓
3b. It's not the case that there is a non-apple.	$\neg(\exists x).\neg Ax$	$N_x(\overline{N(Ax)})$	Quantified Proposition
4. Everything is an apple.	$(\forall x).Ax$	$N_x(\overline{N(Ax)})$	Russellian abbreviation of 3b; Quantified Proposition

To Express Multiple Dependent Quantifiers with Operator N: e.g., "Someone fathers everyone except himself"

English	Russellian Notation	Wittgenstein's Operator N Notation	Comments
1. Adam fathers Cain	aFc	aFc	Elementary Proposition, hence no variables and we assume "a", "c", "F" are all simple names
2. Adam is not the father of Cain	$\neg aFc$	$N(aFc)$	Quantifier-free Proposition
3a. Adam is not the father of y	$\neg aFy$	$N(aFy)$	*Satzvariable*, 2, $y \rightarrow c$
$\Downarrow$	$\Downarrow$	$\Downarrow$	$\Downarrow$
3b. It's not the case that there is someone whom Adam does not father	$\neg(\exists y).\neg(aFy)$	$N_y(\overline{N(aFy)})$	Quantified Proposition
4. Adam is the father of all	$(\forall y).aFy$	$N_y(\overline{N(aFy)})$	Russellian abbreviation of 3b Quantified Proposition
5a. x is the father of all	$(\forall y):x \neq y. \supset .xFy$	$N_y(\overline{N(xFy)})$	*Satzvariable*, 4, $x \rightarrow a$
$\Downarrow$	$\Downarrow$	$\Downarrow$	$\Downarrow$
5b. It's not the case that there is someone fathers everyone but himself	$\neg(\exists x)(\forall y):x \neq y. \supset .xFy$	$N_x(\overline{N_y(\overline{N(xFy)})})$	Quantified Proposition
6. Someone fathers everyone except himself	$(\exists x)(\forall y):x \neq y. \supset .xFy$	$N(N_x(\overline{N_y(\overline{N(xFy)})}))$	Quantified Proposition

The General Term for the Successor Series for an Arbitrary Relation R Using Operator N:

English	Russellian Notation	Wittgenstein's Operator N Notation	Comments
1. b immediately succeeds a in the R-series	aRb	aRb	Elementary Proposition
2. b succeeds a by one in the R-series	$(\exists x){:}aRx.xRb$	$N(N_x(N(N(aRx), N(xRb))))$	Quantified Prop.
2.1	$aRc.cRb$	aRc,cRb	Elem. Props.
2.2	$\neg aRc, \neg cRb$	$N(aRc),N(cRb)$	Quant.-free Props
2.3	$aRc.cRb$	$N(N(aRc),N(cRb))$	Quant.-free Prop.
2.4a	$aRx.xRb$	$N(N(aRx),N(xRb))$	Satzvar, 2.3, $x{\to}c$
$\Rightarrow$	$\Rightarrow$	$\Rightarrow$	$\Rightarrow$
2.4b	$\neg(\exists x){:}aRx.xRb$	$\overline{N_x(N(N(N(aRx), N(xRb)))}$	Quantified Prop.
	$(\exists x){:}aRx.xRb$	$N(N_x(N(N(N(aRx), N(xRb)))))$	Quantified Prop.
2.5 = 2.		$N(N_x(N(N_y((N(N(aRx), N(xRy), N(yRb)))))))$	Quantified Prop.
3. b succeeds a by two in the R-series	$aRc.cRd.dRb$	$aRc.cRd.dRb$	Elem. Props.
3.1	$aRc.cRd.dRb$	$N(aRc),N(cRd),N(dRb)$	Quant.-free Prop
3.2	$\neg aRc, \neg cRd, \neg dRb$	$N(N(aRc),N(cRd),N(dRb))$	Quant.-free Prop
3.3	$aRc.cRd.dRb$	$N(N(aRc),N(cRy),N(yRb))$	Satzvar, 3.3, $y{\to}d$
3.4a	$aRc.cRy.yRb$	$\Rightarrow$	$\Rightarrow$
$\Rightarrow$	$\Rightarrow$	$\overline{N_y(N(N(N(aRc), N(cRy), N(yRb)))}$	Quantified Prop.
3.4b	$\neg(\exists y){:}aRc.cRy.yRb$	$N(N_y(N(N(N(aRc), N(cRy), N(yRb)))))$	Quantified Prop.
3.5	$(\exists y){:}aRc.cRy.yRb$	$N(N_y(N(N(aRx),N(xRy),N(yRb))))$	Satzvar, 3.5, $x{\to}c$
3.6a	$(\exists y){:}aRx.xRy.yRb$	$\Rightarrow$	$\Rightarrow$
$\Rightarrow$	$\Rightarrow$	$\overline{N_x(N(N_y((N(N(aRx), N(xRy), N(yRb))))))}$	Quantified Prop.
3.6b	$\neg(\exists x)(\exists y){:}x{\neq}y.aRx.xRy.yRb$	$N(N_x(N(N_y((N(N(aRx), N(xRy), N(yRb)))))))$	Quantified Prop.
3.7 = 3.	$(\exists x)(\exists y){:}x{\neq}y.aRx.xRy.yRb$		

And so on . . . .

Formal Series for Ascriptions of Number: e.g., "There are (at least) n apples"

English	Russellian Notation	Wittgenstein's Operator N Notation	Comments
1. There are no apples	$\neg(\exists z).Az$	$N_z(Az)$	Quantified Prop.
1.1	Aa	Aa	Elementary Prop.
1.2a	Az	Az	Satvar., 1.1,$z{\rightarrow}a$
⇓	⇓	⇓	⇓
1.2b = 1	$\neg(\exists z).Az$	$N_z(\overline{Az})$	Quantified Prop.
2. There is 1 apple	$(\exists z).Az$	$N(N_z(\overline{Az}))$	Quantified Prop.
2.1	Aa	Aa	Elementary Prop.
2.2a	Az	Az	Satzvar,2.1, $z{\rightarrow}a$
⇓	⇓	⇓	⇓
2.2b	$\neg(\exists z).Az$	$N_z(Az)$	Quantified Prop.
2.3 = 2.	$(\exists z).Az$	$N(N_z(Az))$	Quantified Prop.
3. There are 2 apples	$(\exists y)(\exists z):Ay.Az$	$N(N_y(N(N_z(\overline{N(N(Ay,)N(Az))}))))$	Quantified Prop.
3.1	Aa,Ab	Aa, Ab	Elementary Props.
3.2	$\neg Aa,\neg Ab$	$N(Aa),N(Ab)$	Quant.-free Props
3.3	$Aa.Ab$	$N(N(Aa),N(Ab))$	Quant.-free Prop
3.4a	$Aa.Az$	$N(N(Aa),N(Az))$	Satzvar,3.3, $z{\rightarrow}b$
⇓	⇓	⇓	⇓
3.4b	$\neg(\exists z):Aa.Az$	$N_z(\overline{N(N(Aa), N(Az))})$	Quantified Prop.
3.5	$(\exists z):Aa.Az$	$N(\overline{N_z(N(N(Aa), N(Az)))})$	Quantified Prop.
3.6	$(\exists z):Ay.Az$	$N(N_z(\overline{N(N(Ay), N(Az))}))$	Satzvar, 3.6, $y{\rightarrow}a$
⇓	⇓	⇓	⇓
3.6b	$\neg(\exists y)(\exists z):y{\neq}z.Ay.Az$	$N_y(\overline{N(N_z((N(N(Ay), N(Az))))})$	Quantified Prop.
3.7=3	$(\exists y)(\exists z):y{\neq}z.Ay.Az$	$N(N_y(\overline{N(N_z(N(N(Ay), N(Az))))})$	Quantified Prop.
4. There are 3 apples	$(\exists x)(\exists y)(\exists z):y{\neq}z.$ $x{\neq}y.x{\neq}zAx.Ay.Az$	$N(N_x((N(N_y((N(N_z((\overline{Ax.Ay.Az})))))))))$[61]	Quantified Prop

And so on . . .

NOTES

This chapter is reprinted from E. Reck, ed., *Perspectives on Early Analytic Philosophy: Frege, Russell, Wittgenstein* (New York: Oxford University Press, forthcoming). The only distinction between the two printings are due to differences in the systems of citation.

All references to the *Tractatus* are made in the standard way using Wittgenstein's paragraph numbers. Citations are to *Tractatus Logico-Philosophicus*, trans. C. K. Ogden (London: Routledge and Kegan Paul, 1922; English translation reprinted with corrections 1933).

Abbreviations of citations of Wittgenstein's other works are as follows:

CL   *Ludwig Wittgenstein: Cambridge Letters: Conversations with Russell, Keynes, Moore, Ramsey, and Sraffa*, ed. B. McGuinness and G. H. von Wright (Malden, Mass.: Blackwell, 1997).

N   *Notebooks 1914–1916* (Chicago: University of Chicago Press, 1979).

RFM   *Remarks on the Foundations of Mathematics*, ed. G. H. von Wright, R. Rhees, G. E. M. Anscombe, trans. G. E. M. Anscombe, rev. ed. (Cambridge, Mass.: MIT Press, 1978).

RLF   "Some Remarks on Logical Form," *Proceedings of the Aristotelian Society*, supplementary, vol. 9 (1929): 162–171, reprinted in *Ludwig Wittgenstein: Philosophical Occasions 1912–1951* (Indianapolis: Hackett Publishing, 1993).

WA   *Wiener Ausgabe*, 5 vols., ed. Michael Nedo (New York: Springer Verlag, 1994).

WVC   *Ludwig Wittgenstein and the Vienna Circle*, shorthand notes recorded by F. Waismann, ed. B. McGuinness, trans. J. Schulte and B. McGuinness (Oxford: Blackwell, 1973).

1. F. P. Ramsey, "The Foundations of Mathematics," in Ramsey, *The Foundations of Mathematics*, ed. R. B. Braithwaite (Paterson, N.J.: Littlefield, Adams, 1960) (hereafter Ramsey 1960), pp. 1, 17.

2. An interesting exception was Friedrich Waismann; see his *Introduction to Mathematical Thinking: The Formulation of Concepts in Modern Mathematics* (New York: Harper Torchbooks, 1951) and *Lectures on the Philosophy of Mathematics* (Amsterdam: Rodopi, 1982). On Wittgenstein and Waismann, see S. G. Shanker, *Wittgenstein and the Turning Point in the Philosophy of Mathematics* (Albany, N.Y.: SUNY Press, 1987). For a discussion of the history and reception of Wittgenstein's term "tautology," see Burton Dreben and Juliet Floyd, "Tautology: How Not to Use a Word," *Synthese* 87 (1991): 23–49 (hereafter Dreben and Floyd 1991).

3. Important exceptions here are Michael Wrigley, *Wittgenstein's Early Philosophy of Mathematics* (Ph.D. Dissertation: University of California, Berkeley, 1987), and "Wittgenstein's Philosophy of Mathematics," in S. G. Shanker, ed., *Ludwig Wittgenstein: Critical Assessments*, vol. 3 (London: Croom Helm, 1986); P. Frascolla, *Wittgenstein's Philosophy of Mathematics* (New York: Routledge, 1994) (hereafter Frascolla 1994); and Mathieu Marion, *Wittgenstein, Finitism, and the Philosophy of Mathematics* (New York: Oxford University Press, 1998) (hereafter Marion 1998).

4. Max Black, *A Companion to Wittgenstein's Tractatus* (Ithaca, N.Y.: Cornell University Press 1964), p. 313 (hereafter cited as Black 1964).

5. See P. M. S. Hacker, *Insight and Illusion: Themes in the Philosophy of Wittgenstein*, revised 2d ed. (Oxford: Oxford University Press, 1989), p. 124, and Frascolla (1994); pp. 20–23.

6. J. L. Bell and William Demopoulos, in "Elementary Propositions and Independence," *Notre Dame Journal of Formal Logic* 37 (1996): 112–124 (hereafter Bell and Demopoulos 1996), also take Wittgenstein to have failed to account for the application of arithmetic, finding this failure "ironic" in light of Frege's work.

7. Gottlob Frege, *Grundgesetze der Arithmetik*, vol. 1 (Jena: H. Pohle, 1893), vol. 2 (Jena: H. Pohle, 1903).

8. Bertrand Russell, *The Principles of Mathematics* (New York: W. W. Norton, 1938) (hereafter Russell 1938).

9. A. N. Whitehead and B. Russell, *Principia Mathematica*, vol. 1 (Cambridge: Cambridge University Press, 1910), vol. 2 (Cambridge: Cambridge University Press, 1912) (hereafter Whitehead and Russell).

10. Gottlob Frege, *Translations from the Philosophical Writings of Gottlob Frege*, 3d ed., ed. Peter Geach and Max Black (Totowa, N.J.: Rowman and Littlefield, 1980), p. 167.

11. Michael Dummett, *Frege: Philosophy of Mathematics* (Cambridge, Mass.: Harvard University Press, 1991), p. 74, last emphasis mine. Dummett is writing here about Frege's *Grundlagen* (Breslau: W. Koebner, 1884), which we cannot be sure Wittgenstein had read before the First World War. But what Dummett says applies equally to Frege's treatment of ascriptions of cardinal number in the *Grundgesetze*, with which Wittgenstein was acquainted before writing the *Tractatus*.

12. A proper treatment of the *Tractatus*'s treatment of number words would explore the extent to which Wittgenstein altered, and the extent to which he retained, his early philosophy of arithmetic in the period 1922–1934. Such a treatment lies

beyond the scope of this chapter (though see Steve Gerrard, "Wittgenstein's Philosophies of Mathematics," *Synthese* 87 (1991): 125–142). Many interesting remarks
are, however, to be found in Wittgenstein's manuscripts from the 1929–1934 *WA*
that shed much light, I believe, on the *Tractatus* itself. Below I shall occasionally quote
from these manuscripts (and the related *N*) in order to flesh out my reading, fully
realizing that these texts must be used with great care, as they may reflect ideas which
are not fully Tractarian in character.

13. See Black (1964), pp. 129–130, and G. E. M. Anscombe, *An Introduction to
Wittgenstein's Tractatus* (Philadelphia: University of Pennsylvania Press, 1971
[1959]) (hereafter Anscombe 1971), pp. 102ff.

14. I am not going to enter here into the vexed question whether second-order logic
is or is not "logic," is or is not "set theory in sheep's clothing," to use Quine's phrase.

15. "The old logic" thus applies even to Frege and to Russell, despite the fact that
each of them criticized traditional logic (and metaphysics) for naively assuming the
general applicability of a subject/predicate distinction. See 6.125, *N*, p. 109, and
RFM, V §§13, 48.

16. As Cora Diamond writes in "Realism and Resolution," *Journal of Philosophical Research* 22 (1997): 75–86, p. 77 (hereafter Diamond 1997),

> while there are some *Tractatus* remarks which are apparently intended to give
> some general guidance [about logical analysis], the bulk does . . . take the guid-
> ance necessary for logical analysis to be largely negative. Clarity about logic (of
> the sort the *Tractatus* aims at) is meant to head us off wrong paths in analysis.

17. This is the heart of what I propose as a development of the insight, most vividly pressed in Cora Diamond's "Ethics, Imagination and the Method of Wittgenstein's
Tractatus," in *Bilder der Philosophie: Reflexionen über das Bildliche und die Phantasie*
ed. R. Heinrich and H. Vetter (Vienna/Munich: Oldenbourg, 1991), pp. 55–90 (hereafter Diamond 1991a) and *The Realistic Spirit* (Cambridge, Mass.: MIT Press, 1991)
(hereafter Diamond 1991b), that there is no ineffable (nonfactual, nonliteral) *content* which is shown in the *Tractatus*. Compare my "The Uncaptive Eye: Solipsism in
Wittgenstein's *Tractatus*," in L. S. Rouner, ed., *Loneliness* (South Bend, Ind.: University of Notre Dame Press, 1998), pp. 79–108 (hereafter Floyd 1998b). Both Peter
Hacker, in "When the Whistling Had to Stop" (forthcoming), and David Pears have
questioned the arguments—textual and philosophical—that Diamond and others
have offered for such readings, but neither has addressed the question of how
Wittgenstein's treatment of mathematics bears on the issue.

18. A. N. Whitehead, *A Treatise on Universal Algebra with Applications* (Cambridge:
Cambridge University Press, 1898) (hereafter Whitehead 1898).

19. A. N. Whitehead, *An Introduction to Mathematics* (London: Williams and
Norgate, 1911) (hereafter Whitehead 1911).

20. Burton Dreben suggested to me that Whitehead (1898) might have been what
Wittgenstein was alluding to in his entry of June 22, 1915, in *N*, p. 70 (see especially
Whitehead 1898, pp. 9–10). Whitehead (1911) also contains some remarks about
mathematics which may be profitably compared with the *Tractatus*. In what follows, I
quote from these books in order to show how Wittgenstein is reinterpreting their terminology. Whether or not it was these particular works that stimulated Wittgenstein,
I shall take them to be sufficiently representative to illustrate the force of his remarks.

21. Whitehead has a footnote here:

> Cf. Stout, "Thought and Language," *Mind*, April 1891, repeated in the same
> author's *Analytic Psychology*, (1896), ch. x. §1: cf. also a more obscure analysis
> to the same effect by C. S. Peirce, *Proceedings of the American Academy of Arts and
> Sciences*, 1867, vol. vii. p. 294.

22. See Ray Monk, *Wittgenstein: The Duty of Genius* (New York: Free Press, 1990),
pp. 216–217.

23. Ramsey had written his review of the *Tractatus* (reprinted in [Ramsey 1960]) before meeting with Wittgenstein in Austria. A photograph of the annotated page from Ramsey's copy of the *Tractatus* is reproduced in M. Nedo and M. Ranchetti, eds., *Wittgenstein: Sein Leben in Bildern und Texten* (Frankfurt am Main: Suhrkamp Verlag, 1983), pp. 192–193, and the provenance of the annotations discussed in Casimir Lewy, "A Note on the Text of the *Tractatus*," *Mind* 76 (1967): 416–423, where it is noted that Wittgenstein seems to have questioned the translation of "Anschauung" as "intuition" at 6.233–6.2331.

24. See also Jacques Bouveresse, *Le pays des possibles: Wittgenstein, les mathématiques, et le monde réel* (Paris: Les Éditions de Minuit, 1988) and Marion (1998), though they take this to indicate that Wittenstein is a constructivist or even a finitist, both labels I would resist pinning on the *Tractatus*. Warren Goldfarb, in "Poincaré Against the Logicists," in *Minnesota Studies in the Philosophy of Science xi: History and Philosophy of Modern Mathematics*, ed. W. Aspray and P. Kitcher (Minneapolis: University of Minnesota Press, 1988), pp. 61–81, argues that Poincaré's objection has no force against the positions of either Frege or Russell, as it imports a psychologistic conception of reasoning into the argument. That would be one reason for hesitating before we ascribe Poincaré's objection to Wittgenstein.

25. Russell (1938), pp. 117, 377, the latter reference containing an explicit reference to Whitehead (1898); Whitehead and Russell, vol. 1, pp. 297, 345, vol. 2, p. xv. Compare Section IV below. Russell attributes the remarks in volume II of *Principia* to Whitehead. See Russell, "Whitehead and *Principia Mathematica*," *Mind* 57 (1948): 137–138.

26. C. I. Lewis, *Survey of Symbolic Logic* (Berkeley: University of California Press, 1918), pp. 354ff.

27. Emil L. Post, "Introduction to a General Theory of Elementary Propositions," *American Journal of Mathematics* 43 (1921): 163–185.

28. See the discussion of Post and Lewis in Burton Dreben and Jean van Heijenoort, "Introductory note to 1929, 1930 and 1930a," in S. Feferman et al., eds., *Kurt Gödel: Collected Works*, vol. 1 (New York: Oxford University Press, 1986), pp. 44–48.

29. Cf. Gottlob Frege, *Posthumous Writings*, ed. H. Hermes, F. Kambartel, F. Kaulbach, trans. P. Long, R. White (Chicago: University of Chicago Press, 1979), p. 206, and *Collected Papers on Mathematics, Logic, and Philosophy*, ed. B. McGuinness, trans. M. Black et al. (Oxford: Blackwell, 1984) (hereafter Frege 1984), pp. 159–160, 354.

30. As opposed to simple numerals (e.g., "2") or arithmetical sentences (e.g., "2+2=4").

31. Peter Hylton's "Functions, Operations and Sense in Wittgenstein's Tractatus," in W. W. Tait, ed., *Early Analytic Philosophy* (Chicago/Lasalle: Open Court, 1997), pp. 91–106 (hereafter Hylton 1997), sheds much helpful light on Wittgenstein's distinction between functions and operations in connection with the truth-operations. I do think, however, that Hylton overspeaks in claiming that the truth-operations are the primary examples of operations on which we should focus in order to gain an understanding of how Wittgenstein's views compare to those of Frege and Russell (Hylton 1997, p. 92, n. 3).

32. While the explanation of this analogy is mine, and is somewhat conjectural about the *Tractatus*, the analogy itself is made explicit in *WVC*, pp. 225–226. I am arguing that the analogy is implicit already in the *Tractatus*.

33. See Rudolf Carnap, *The Logical Syntax of Language* (London: Routledge and Kegan Paul, 1937), pp. 53, 101, 282–284. For a different reading of Wittgenstein's show/say distinction in connection with metalanguages (and Gödel's arithmetization of syntax, which Carnap took to have refuted that distinction), see Juliet Floyd, "On Saying What You Really Want to Say: Wittgenstein, Gödel and the Trisection of the Angle," in J. Hintikka, ed., *From Dedekind to Gödel: The Foundations of Mathematics in the Early Twentieth Century* (Dordrecht: Kluwer, 1995), pp. 373–426, and "Prose versus Proof: Wittgenstein on Gödel, Tarski and Truth," forthcoming in *Philosophia Mathematica*.

34. At *WVC*, pp. 218–219, the parallel is drawn explicitly.

35. For a discussion, see Peter Hylton, "Functions and Propositional Functions in *Principia Mathematica*," in A. Irvine and G. Wedeking, eds., *Russell and Early Analytic Philosophy* (Toronto: University of Toronto Press, 1994), pp. 342–360.

36. Roger White, "Wittgenstein on Identity," *Proceedings of the Aristotelian Society*, n.s. 78 (1979): 157–174 (hereafter White 1979), R. J. Fogelin, "Wittgenstein on Identity," *Synthese* 56 (1983): 141–154 (herafter Fogelin 1983), and *Wittgenstein* (New York: Routledge and Kegan Paul, 1987) (hereafter Fogelin 1987) deem Wittgenstein's treatment adequate to express ascriptions of finite cardinal number, though they do not explore the deductive power of Wittgenstein's notational proposal (discussed below). Marion (1998) and Peter Sullivan, "Ramsey's Definition of Identity: A Tractarian Criticism," in J. Hintikka and K. Puhl, eds., *The British Tradition in 20th Century Philosophy* (Vienna: Austrian Ludwig Wittgenstein Society, 1994), pp. 501–507, and "Wittgenstein on the 'Foundations of Mathematics', June 1927" (forthcoming) scrutinize Wittgenstein's (post-Tractarian) exchanges with Ramsey about identity.

37. It might seem as if Wittgenstein is adopting a view of identity such as Frege had embraced in his 1879 *Begriffsschrift, eine der arithmetischen nachgebildete Formelsprache des reinen Denkens* (Halle: L. Nebert, 1879), §8. There Frege held that identity "necessarily produces a bifurcation in the *Bedeutung* of all signs," for in identity contexts names "suddenly display their own selves"—that is, suddenly name themselves. This apparent confusion of use and mention was remedied, in Frege's mind, by his later distinction between the *Sinn* and the *Bedeutung* of a name. On Frege's (vacillating) attitude toward the project of logically defining identity see Dummett (1991), pp. 141ff., and my "Frege, Semantics and the Double Definition Stroke," in Anat Biletzki and Anat Matar, eds., *The Story of Analytic Philosophy* (New York: Routledge: 1998), pp. 141–166 (hereafter Floyd 1998a). I am, however, reading Wittgenstein as altogether denying that names flank mathematical uses of the equality sign. Wittgenstein is explicit in the *Tractatus* that use of the identity sign between names is a mere matter of convenience in genuine propositions, but cannot assert anything about the *Bedeutung* of distinct signs (4.241ff.). Unlike Frege, Wittgenstein sharply distinguished between signs which represent forms and signs which are names or function expressions.

38. Jaakko Hintikka, "Identity, Variables and Impredicative Definitions," *Journal of Symbolic Logic* 21 (1956): 225–245 (hereafter Hintikka 1956).

39. Were someone to actually try to construct a deductive system of logic on the basis of Wittgenstein's notational proposals—which he never tried to do—it might be that only a decidable fragment of first-order logic would result, since on at least one reading, no coinstantiation of distinct variables is allowed. Such an applied "logic" really would be tautologous. Yet even in this case, the question of a *general* decision procedure for logic as a whole could not be formulated in Wittgenstein's terms, for his notational remarks about identity at 5.53ff. apply only to genuine propositions, and not the sentences of pure logic and mathematics. Dreben and Floyd (1991) argues (against, e.g., Fogelin [1987]) that even at the time of writing the *Tractatus* Wittgenstein did not hinge his characterization of logic as "tautologous" on the existence of a general decision procedure for "all of logic" as such.

40. For a perspicuous criticism of readings of the *Tractatus* which reify possibilities, see Warren Goldfarb, "Metaphysics and Nonsense: On Cora Diamond's *The Realistic Spirit*," *Journal of Philosophical Research* 22 (1997): 57–73 (hereafter Goldfarb 1997), especially pp. 65–66.

41. The falsity of an ascription of number lies in there being no way to instantiate the *Satzvariablen* at work in the propositional sign expressing the ascription and get a truth. If we wrongly suppose that two names, say, "Morning Star" and "Evening Star," have distinct *Bedeutungen*, then we shall be wrong in our counting of astronomical bodies and wrong in other propositions as well. But for Wittgenstein this would be as much a matter of our being mistaken about the significance of names

and *Satzvariablen*—that is, being mistaken about which symbols these signs may be used to express—as it would be an error about heavenly bodies. That there are two distinct astronomical bodies called "the Morning Star" and "the Evening Star" is not necessarily false: in a language in which these names did not share a *Bedeutung*, it would make sense (and be true) to say that there are two stars which appear in such and such a way in the sky, the morning star and the evening star, while it would be nonsense to try to say that these two stars are one (5.5303). But in a language such as ours, these names share the same *Bedeutung*, and then according to Wittgenstein's notational proposal the *Satzvariable* "x is a star appearing in such and such a way in the sky and y is a star appearing in such and such a way in the sky" does not range over "the Morning Star is a star appearing in such and such a way in the sky and the Evening Star is a star appearing in such and such a way in the sky." Every proposition over which this *Satzvariable* ranges is false.

42. Bertrand Russell, "Review of Ramsey's *Foundations of Mathematics,*" in *The Collected Papers of Bertrand Russell, Vol. 10, A Fresh Look at Empiricism 1927–1942,* ed. J. G. Slater and P. Köllner (New York: Routledge, 1996), p. 108.

43. As Anscombe (1971), pp. 147–149, reports, Ramsey objected to Wittgenstein's interpretation of the variable, pointing out that apparent ascriptions of number such as $(\exists x,y)(\phi x$ and $\phi y)$ and $\neg(\exists x,y,z)(\phi x$ and ϕy and $\phi z)$ would turn out to be problematic if the number of objects in the universe were exceeded by the number of distinct variables in the language. To Wittgenstein the above quantificational form would be a structure with symbolic redundancy, in the case of a language in which there were only two distinct names, for there would be no way to find distinct instances of the variables x, y, z in the second half of the conjunction. Ramsey suggested that in this case the statement would imply a contradiction at the point at which two distinct variables were instantiated with the same name. But in the *Tractatus* we are dealing with a picture of language in which we may not so instantiate, because all redundancy in names has been eliminated, and the values a variable may take on are determined by the range of available distinct names. In the kind of case Ramsey imagines, what appears to be a grammatically well formed sentence, what appears to meet all logical criteria for counting as a propositional sign, is not a propositional sign after all. (Fogelin [1987], pp. 70–71, also holds that the extra variable ["z" in the above example] would be, because useless, meaningless.) I should add that Wittgenstein does not rule out the possibility of an infinite number of names in the language (5.535), but it is difficult to see how he would set out such a stock of names without a general formal rule. Any such rule would of course treat names as part of a system, hence, as operation signs, undermining the *Tractatus*'s distinction between operation signs and names and his claim for the logical independence of elementary propositions. This is what appears to happen in *RLF*.

44. Which class? There is a question, originally raised by Ramsey, whether second-order *Satzvariablen* such as "ϕ(Harry)" may be read widely—so as to include in the range of propositions they demarcate all molecular propositions which include the constant expressions contained in them—or narrowly, so that these *Satzvariablen* would be conceived of as ranging only over the elementary propositions sharing the forms they exhibit. For example, does "ϕHarry)" range over "Harry is not a horse" and "Harry is not a man or Pete is not a man"? Molecular propositional signs are built up, not only out of object and function expressions, but out of operation expressions as well. Yet operations do not contribute essentially to the senses of propositions in which they figure: whatever they reflect is parasitic on the interplay between senses of elementary propositions.

My view is that Wittgenstein would have no in principle objection to the usual treatment in second-order logic, which would read the variables widely. But he is not attempting to provide smooth-running axiomatization of logic. The advantage of reading these second-order *Satzvariablen* narrowly, as ranging in the first instance over elementary propositions, is that we are less likely to be misled by the grammar of the variable into assimilating very different sorts of expressions to one another. We see logico-syntactical structure more clearly if we distinguish truth-operations from function expressions in our use of *Satzvariablen*.

45. A proper treatment of Russell's use of systematic ambiguity to present the theory of types lies outside the scope of this paper. But see Peter Hylton, *Russell, Idealism and the Emergence of Analytic Philosophy* (Oxford: Oxford University Press, 1990), for an excellent treatment.

46. N, pp. 98, 100. The example of "x=x" is treated in Whitehead and Russell; see vol. 1, pp. 18, 39, vol. 2, pp. vii–viii.

47. I agree with Peter Geach, "Wittgenstein's Operator N," *Analysis* 41 (1983): 573–589; Scott Soames, "Generality, Truth Functions and Expressive Capacity," *Philosophical Review* 92(1983): 573–589; and Göran Sundholm, "The General Form of the Operation in Wittgenstein's *Tractatus*," *Grazer Philosophische Studien* 42 (1992): 57–76, that Fogelin (1983) and Fogelin (1987) err in holding that Wittgenstein failed to specify the totality of propositions by means of a finite number of applications of operator N to the elementary propositions. The key to Wittgenstein's construction is to allow arbitrary collections of elementary propositions to begin formal series generated by means of operator N, and then to index applications of N by way of a *Satzvariable*. My proposed construction is closest to the one proposed by Sundholm, which I take to be closest to Wittgenstein's intent; for unlike Sundholm, Geach and Soames build reference to classes into their respective constructions. Bell and Demopoulos (1996) go so far as to credit Wittgenstein with having invented the algebraic notion of a free generator of a logical calculus. Fogelin (1987, p. 82) argues, against all such interpretations, that Wittgenstein failed to specify any such construction on the ground that Wittgenstein is "plainly . . . committed to a decision procedure for the propositions of logic." Dreben and Floyd (1991) argue that Wittgenstein is not so committed.

48. A treatment of relations of arbitrary *n*-adicity could be obtained for the *Principia* by adding different primitives to the object language, as in W. V. Quine, *The Logic of Sequences* (Ph.D. Dissertation, Harvard University; New York: Garland Publishing, 1990). Cf. Burton Dreben, "Quine," in R. B. Barrett and R. F. Gibson, eds., *Perspectives on Quine* (Oxford: Blackwell, 1990), pp. 81–95, for a discussion. Russell's and Whitehead's appeal to "symbolic analogy" in connection with the theory of types is, by contrast, intrinsic to its presentation and could not be eliminated by building stronger primitive notions into the object system.

49. This distinction between "constant" and "functional" formal numbers is not exclusive, for $1+_c2$, the cardinal sum of 1 and 2, is both constant and functional (Whitehead and Russell, vol. 2, p. xiv).

50. Like operation expressions, indices are contrasted by Wittgenstein with arguments, with names and function expressions (5.02). But unlike operation expressions, indices are not formally interconnected with other indices in a systematic network; they do not, for example, generate formal series, and do not have to belong to a systematic notation. In calling the numbers "exponents of operations" rather than "indices," Wittgenstein takes number to reflect the process of iterating or applying an operation; he is not thinking of the uses of number words as tags, as in codes, passwords, or bank account numbers.

51. Wittgenstein never explicitly says in the *Tractatus* that numerals and arithmetical terms are used as "pictures." His aim in this work is to stress grammatical differences, to show that our language involves more than one sort of sentence, and he uses the notion of *picture* in part to distinguish genuine propositions—which he explicitly construes as pictures (*Bilder*)—from the sentences (*Sätze*) of pure mathematics, which, to repeat, he views as merely apparent propositions (*Scheinsätze*), not as propositional signs. In the late 1920s, however, he explicitly remarks that a natural number is a form of representing (*eine Art der Darstellung*), and in contexts which I believe are essentially Tractarian in character. For numbers as modes of represent-

ing, see *WA*, vol. 1, p. 7. On construing natural numbers as pictures, see *WVC*, pp. 220–226, especially p. 223. An analogy between mathematical proofs and pictures remains a governing motif of Wittgenstein's later philosophy, and it too, I suggest, has its roots in the *Tractatus*'s treatment of arithmetic. Compare Frascolla (1994), pp. 29, 33, 49; Mathieu Marion, "Operations and Numbers in the Tractatus," in *From the Tractatus to the Tractatus: Wittgenstein Studies*, ed. G. Oliveri (Dordrecht: Reidel, forthcoming), and Juliet Floyd, "Wittgenstein, Mathematics, Philosophy," in *The New Wittgenstein*, ed. A. Crary and R. Read (New York: Routledge, 2000).

52. *WA*, vol. 4 p. 239:

$x^2 = 1$ has two roots versus on the table are 2 apples. The former is a grammatical rule of the variable. . . . Can I determine a variable by saying that its values should be all objects which satisfy a certain function? Not if I don't know this some other way—if I don't, the grammar of the variable is simply not determined (expressed).

53. A full answer to Frege and Russell would require this, not least because of the need to account for (apparent) inferences like "four apples and three pears make seven fruits."

54. In *WVC*, p. 225, Wittgenstein is recorded having said that "*the method of representing numbers is the method of picturing*" (*die Methode der Darstellung der Zahlen ist die Methode der Abbildung*).

55. See, for example, Diamond (1991a, 1991b, 1997); Dreben and Floyd (1991); Goldfarb (1997); and Warren Goldfarb, "Objects, Names and Realism in the *Tractatus*" (unpublished manuscript [1979]).

56. V. Hofman gives an engaging account of a recent meeting of the Boston Colloquium for Philosophy of Science attended by Diamond, Dreben, Floyd, Goldfarb, Hacker, Hintikka, Hylton, Pears, and Ricketts at which the *Tractatus* was heatedly discussed ("Ein Bostoner Streitgespräch über Wittgensteins *Tractatus*," *Frankfurter Allgemeine Zeitung*, June 10, 1998). Marie McGinn gives an overview of the contrast between what she calls "therapeutic" and "metaphysical" readings of the *Tractatus*, defending an intermediate position between the two ("Between Metaphysics and Nonsense: Elucidation in Wittgenstein's *Tractatus*," *Philosophical Quarterly* 49 [1999]: 491–513 [hereafter McGinn 1999]).

57. See, for example McGinn (1999); Hacker (forthcoming).

58. For further discussion of this point, see Floyd (1998b) and M. Ostrow, *Wittgenstein, Plato, and the Liberating Word* (Ph.D. Dissertation: Boston University, 1999).

59. Compare Michael Dummett, *Origins of Analytical Philosophy* (Cambridge, Mass.: Harvard University Press, 1993).

60. Earlier versions of this paper were presented at the May 1996 Brazilian Logic Association meeting in Salvador, Bahia—where I profited greatly from discussions with Professors Itala D'Ottaviano, Pasquale Frascolla, Mathieu Marion, Carlo Penco, Richard Valée, and Michael Wrigley—at the Philosophy Departments at the University of Stockholm and the University of Oslo—where I received equally helpful criticism from Professors Peter Martin Löf, Peter Pagin, Dag Prawitz, Göran Sundholm and Dagfinn Follesdal—and in Burton Dreben's fall 1996 seminar at Boston University. Thanks are also due to Rosalind Carey, Arthur Collins, Alex George, Warren Goldfarb, Montgomery Link, Andrew Lugg, Matthew Ostrow, Rohit Parikh, and especially Thomas Ricketts for much good discussion of the *Tractatus* and comments on earlier drafts which led to substantial improvement of the paper, as well as to the American Council of Learned Societies and the Dibner Institute for the History of Science and Technology for generous financial and intellectual support. My debt to Burton Dreben is greatest, for he aided in all these ways and more.

61. For reasons of space, I here abbreviate the conjunction of *Ax, Ay, Az* with the Russellian notation: *Ax.Ay.Az*.

8

Heidegger's Response to Skepticism in *Being and Time*

EDWARD H. MINAR

In this essay, I consider Heidegger's assertion that human being is what he calls Being-in-the-world[1] as a key element in his response to the traditional epistemological problem of skepticism about the external world. The claim that human being is Being-in-the-world, I try to show, is not a mere insistence that to look at the knowing subject as potentially detached from its world is to leave something vital out of one's understanding of what it means to be human. It is better read as part of an elaborate dialectical strategy that obligates the epistemologist to reexamine the description of the human being's place in the world with which the traditional problem begins and which accounts for its intellectual grip. My way of reading Heidegger is deeply indebted to Burton Dreben's (almost phenomenological) instruction in the need to return to our starting points in philosophy, to his understanding of the later Wittgenstein, and to his lessons in reading texts. I am extremely grateful as well for Burt's generosity, his openness, and his uncanny ability to transmit his boundless intellectual energy to his students.

A satisfying challenge to the meaningfulness of the traditional epistemological project of explaining our knowledge of the external world would identify flaws in the picture of our relation to the world that informs the traditional enterprise while accounting for the force that that picture retains even in the face of its possible entanglements with skepticism.[2] Martin Heidegger's analysis of Being-in-the-world in Division I of *Being and Time* can be read as attempting—in my view, with some success—to provide such a challenge. Heidegger seeks, that is, a response to skepticism having the diagnostic depth sufficient to enable us to recognize, and thereby to resist, the considerable attractions of the traditional picture.

According to Heidegger, epistemological questions about the relation of human beings to the world in which they dwell presuppose the independence of the knowing subject and its experiences from the world in which it exists. This conceptual "isolation" gives rise to questions about how the subject can transcend its "inner 'sphere'" to apprehend a world of objects (60/87/56). For Heidegger, this setup and the skeptically oriented concerns that arise from it are virtually constitutive of epistemology. He thinks that, given epistemology's uncritical conceptions of reality and our place in it, knowledge of the external world will inevitably appear

problematic (61/87/57); efforts to secure our relation to the world will lead to
"inextricable impasses" (206/250/191). Wanting to offer a competing conception of our relation to the world, Heidegger redescribes *Dasein* or human being
as, in essence, Being-in-the-world.[3] Human beings, that is, take on their identities through dealing with things in "worldly" settings in which they find themselves already ensconced. *Dasein*, unlike the traditional subject, cannot be identified in terms shorn of reference to its worldly involvements. As a result, Heidegger
admits no general question of whether a subject so conceived could transcend its
own immanent realm to gain access to what he generally calls "*Welt*," "world"
(with scare quotes), defined as "the totality of entities which can be present-at-
hand within the world [*das innerhalb der Welt vorhanden sein kann*]" (64/93/60).[4]
As we come to recognize *Dasein* as Being-in-the-world, we bear witness to the
dissolution of the "pseudo-problem of the reality of the external world" (Heidegger
1984, p. 151).

Heidegger stakes out his position by differentiating it, in no uncertain terms,
from Kant's. Kant had found that "it still remains a scandal to philosophy and to
human reason in general that the existence of things outside us . . . must be accepted on faith,"[5] and he attempted to address the situation in the Refutation of
Idealism. Heidegger, by contrast, challenges the very need for the kind of proof
the Refutation proposes. "The 'scandal of philosophy' is not that this proof has
yet to be given," he writes, "but that *such proofs are expected and attempted again
and again*" (205/249/190; Heidegger's emphasis). Kant's goal of finding a "cogent proof for the '[existence] of things outside of us' which will do away with
any scepticism" (203/247/189) is misguided; to counter skeptical doubts about
the existence of the external world directly, by way of proof, is not merely futile,
but confused, empty, even absurd. "The question of whether there is a world at
all and whether its Being can be proved makes no sense if it is raised by *Dasein* as
Being-in-the-world; and who else would raise it?" (202/247/188) Or: "If *Dasein*
is understood correctly, it defies such proofs, because, in its Being, it already *is*
what subsequent proofs deem necessary to demonstrate for it" (205/249/190).

We are bound to wonder whether these pronouncements offer more than a
rather dogmatic declaration that the act of raising a general question about the
grounds of our beliefs about the external world somehow defeats itself. I think
that Heidegger does offer more, and I try to defend that claim here. I begin (in
part I) by sketching Heidegger's antiskeptical strategy as laid out in §43 of *Being
and Time*—where he confronts Kant's allegedly misguided approach to the problem of "Reality"—and by highlighting its apparent vulnerabilities. If the contention that skeptical questioning undermines itself depends on the bare claim that
human beings are constituted by Being-in-the-world and, as such, are "always
already" involved in everyday dealings with external objects, a skeptically minded
philosopher will demand that this assertion be justified. To view Heidegger as
avoiding this demand, as side-stepping the skeptical problematic in the interest
of offering an alternative model of our position in the world, would be to leave
the skeptic unmoved and us without a viable—that is, philosophically useful—
understanding of Heidegger's basic claim that *Dasein* is Being-in-the-world.
Accordingly, in part II, I turn to the task of developing a reconstruction of the

Heideggerian strategy that eschews mere side-stepping and confronts the skeptic in the right place. The intent is to strip skepticism of its world-threatening significance through depriving its starting point—its picture of the objective world as something to which we may or may not stand in a particular, uniform epistemic relation—of the apparent obviousness on which its appeal rests.[6]

I

"We, the *Dasein*, in apprehending beings, are always already in a world. Being-in-the-world itself belongs to the determination of our own being."[7] In what respects, and by what lights, will Heidegger's designation of human being as Being-in-the-world be superior to the subject/object picture he rejects? Insistence on the primacy of engaged activity over theoretical detachment will seem to thinkers operating within the traditional framework to pose no threat to their projects. More important, *we* shall not be persuaded to view raising skeptical doubts as anything less than intellectual scrupulousness. Insofar as the suggestion that there is no position from which a skeptical inquiry can be launched rests on an ostensible pragmatic contradiction in the skeptic's attempt to voice a general question about our relation to the world, its whole weight seems to be derived from the contention that the inquirer, as *Dasein* or human being, is "always already" Being-in-the-world. To assess Heidegger's antiskeptical strategy, we must examine the credentials of this claim.

Does Heidegger want to circumvent skepticism by simply refusing to acknowledge a standpoint from which philosophical questions about the content and justification of our sense-based beliefs would appear to be perfectly in order and to demand answers?[8] Professing ontological rather than epistemological aims, he writes, in *The Basic Problems of Phenomenology*, that "it is nowhere prescribed that there must be a problem of knowledge" (1982, p. 162). Epistemology is not, however, deemed merely irrelevant to Heidegger's aims; to pursue ontology is "to deprive [epistemological difficulties] of their sham existence, to reduce the number of problems and to promote investigation which opens the way to the matters themselves" (1982, p. 162). Circumvention, it seems, is not Heidegger's intention, in that even grasping what it *is* to pursue ontology in his sense will require a critique of epistemology and its picture of subject and object. "The ontological problem," he writes, "has nothing at all to do with the acclaimed pseudo-problem of the reality of the external world and the independence of beings-in-themselves from the knowing subject. The ontological problem *consists* [*besteht*], rather, in *seeing* that this so-called epistemological problem cannot be posed at all if the being-in-itself of existing things is not clarified in its meaning. But this cannot even be posed as a problem, much less solved, if it is not yet clear how the question about the meaning of being as such must be posed" (Heidegger 1984, p. 151; my emphases). Ontology will yield a better understanding of the sphere with which so-called epistemology had concerned itself; presumably, once our relation to world and the beings in it has been elucidated, a skeptical problem will no longer seem germane to our relation to world *überhaupt*. One of the goals of ontology is learning to see human being, Being-in-the-world, in a "phenomeno-logically adequate" way, and Heidegger conceives of this process as removing the disguises in which this existential structure (Being-in-the-world) has been con-cealed by the traditional conception of the subject/object distinction and its epis-temological ramifications.

It seems, then, that Heidegger conceives of his ontological task as undoing epistemological resistance to his phenomenological descriptions of human beings, and that he acknowledges the obligation to confront the epistemologist's qualms about his claim that *Dasein* is Being-in-the-world. Further reflection on the na-ture of ontology will, however, elicit a deeper skeptical worry about Heidegger's approach. The ontological question of "Reality," posed in §43 of *Being and Time*, asks what it is for "Real" beings or entities to exist "in themselves" and "indepen-dent of us" (see 202/246/188). Heidegger thinks we can only make sense of this question about the Being of real entities in terms of how *we* understand entities of the appropriate kind, those particular beings we take to have the characteris-tic independence. Accordingly, he locates a kind of truth in idealism: "Only be-cause Being is 'in the consciousness'—that is to say, only because it is understand-able in *Dasein*—can *Dasein* also understand and conceptualize such characteristics of Being as independence, the 'in-itself,' and Reality in general" (207/251/192; see also 230/272/211). In this context, the notion that *Dasein* is Being-in-the-world—to be distinguished from the assertion that human beings exist among real, independent, spatiotemporal entities—acquires particular significance. *World* is the background or practical context within which beings are picked out, iden-tified, dealt with, that is, understood.[9] "Before the experience of beings as extant [*vorhanden*, present-at-hand], world is already understood" (Heidegger 1982, p. 166). "Even the Real can be discovered only on the basis of a world which has already been disclosed" (203/247/188). Any encountering of objects (includ-ing perceiving or for that matter dreaming them) requires an understanding, not necessarily explicit or theoretical, of what it is to be such an object. Cru-cially, however, "the 'world' as entities within-the-world (that in which one is concernfully absorbed)" is necessary to render this understanding concrete and definite: "*With the disclosedness of the world, the 'world' has in each case been discov-ered too* [*je auch schon entdeckt*; in Stambaugh, 'is always already discovered too']" (203/247/188). Understanding of world opens up to human beings only insofar as they find themselves involved with particular things in "contexts of signifi-cance,"[10] amidst a background in which things already make the sense they do. Having first gone from beings to world by way of the need for some context in which the Being of beings can be understood, we then pass from world back to particular beings as we come to see that world just *is* a general context involving some of these beings in their significance, that is, in their relatedness to each other and to us. Reversing our path in this way therefore seems to have an antiskeptical upshot. On Heidegger's account, a world populated with particular entities is always available to any *Dasein*, to any being that understands itself as dealing understandingly with a "context of significance."[11]

We are meant to see that knowledge of world *itself* can never come to be at issue, because legitimate questions of knowledge or certainty only arise given a background understanding of world. Hence, "the 'problem of Reality' in the sense of the question whether an external . . . world can be proved turns out to be an impossible one, not because the consequences lead to inextricable impasses, but because the very entity [*Dasein* as Being-in-the-world] which serves as its theme is one which . . . repudiates any such formulation of the question" (206/250/191). The question appears to make sense only "after the primordial phenomenon of Being-in-the-world has been shattered" (206/250/191). A philosophical imposition creates the illusion of the need to reassemble the shards of the "phenomenon" (subject and object or "world") through a process by which the subject somehow manages to "assure itself of a world" (206/250/191).

How should we expect the skeptic to respond to the allegation that his question fails to make the sense he wants it to? Perhaps he would suggest that Heidegger has at most established that acting *as if* one occupies a world of involvements with real entities is unavoidable. This, he would hold, hardly establishes the unintelligibility of asking whether we actually *do* encounter such a world or whether the world is, generally speaking, the way we believe it to be. To reply on Heidegger's behalf that Being-in-the-world just *is* comporting oneself as if one is dealing with real entities would represent an unappealing retreat.[12] In its face, the skeptic would observe that his question of whether the external world is really accessible via *knowledge* remains both intact and unanswered. He might take himself to have wrested an admission that no "assurances" of the sort he has sought will ever be forthcoming; he would not be surprised that this groundlessness is a matter of practical indifference. The Heideggerian conception of ontology would, in the skeptic's estimation, have added no plausibility to the bald assertion that the skeptic's question is meaningless because this question ventures outside a restricted, practical realm. In the absence of independent argument for this point, the skeptic's lurking sense that the legitimacy of his inquiry has been impugned solely on the (unsatisfying) ground that it "will lead to inextricable impasses" would seem well-founded. We want more than the retreat. If Heidegger's conclusions about the meaninglessness of the skeptic's stance are to be compelling, it must be shown that the skeptic has misunderstood the nature, substance, and force of the claim that *Dasein* is Being-in-the-world. For at this point, the skeptic's failure to understand hardly seems obtuse. Further explanation of Heidegger's meaning is thus required.[13]

We may begin to look for Heidegger's response to skeptical suspicion in his reaction to the charge that his notion of world harbors a "most extreme subjective idealism" or "the heresy of subjectivism" (Heidegger 1982, p. 167). His opponent, anticipating a major concession, might say, "If the world belongs to the being that I myself in each instance am, to the *Dasein*, then it is something subjective" (Heidegger 1982, p. 167). Heidegger does express willingness to acquiesce in the conclusion that world is subjective, but with two major qualifications. First, as he repeatedly notes, there is no further implication that present-at-hand beings, in particular the things of nature that populate the "world," are themselves in any sense subjective. True, their Being as real entities is embodied in our understanding, in the ways we comport ourselves toward them and in the questions we find it intelligible to put to them. These factors comprise what it is for real entities to be objective, the sense it makes to call them so. Whether some particular present-at-hand entity actually exists is what Heidegger calls an ontical affair, a matter of beings, something to be discovered about the way things actually are—and paradigmatically objective matters of this sort are not settled by our understanding of Being alone. Second, and more important, Heidegger's confession of "subjectivism" is somewhat disingenuous. For as he writes in *The Metaphysical Foundations of Logic*, "There is world only insofar as *Dasein* exists. But then is world not something 'subjective'? In fact it is! Only one may not at this point reintroduce a common, subjectivistic concept of 'subject.' Instead, the task is to see that being-in-the-world, which as existent supplies extant things [*dem Vorhandenen*, present-at-hand entities] with entry to world, fundamentally transforms the concept of subjectivity and of the subjective" (Heidegger 1984, p. 195; see Heidegger 1982, pp. 167–168). Heidegger thus turns the allegation of subjectivism into an opportunity to register his incessant complaint that his adversaries presuppose an indeterminate, ill-defined conception of the subject. They simply posit subjectivity as an "inner realm" that must be transcended for experience to penetrate world. On rejecting this picture of subjectivity, Heidegger can say with impunity that world is "subjective in some sense." The teeth of this particular skeptical worry have been pulled.[14]

An effective Heideggerian counter to skepticism must, it would seem, vindicate the claim that *Dasein* is Being-in-the-world in a way that precludes a retreat into a subjectivism granting too much to the traditional notion of the subject. One could argue, however, that to insist on addressing skeptical scruples about the Heideggerian strategy is to risk taking traditional epistemology too seriously, too much on its own ground. After all, it might be said, Heidegger's intention is to break free of epistemology, to refuse to encounter it, self-consciously to sidestep its concerns.[15] The force of Heidegger's criticism, on this view, would depend on the effects of his polemical efforts to wean us from outworn intellectual habits. Heidegger's descriptions of human being would provide an alternative to the epistemologist's picture of the isolated subject which (as the alternative is supposed to reveal) underestimates the importance of practical activity. Insisting that a concern with addressing the skeptic is fruitless, adherents of a side-stepping interpretation of Heidegger's critique may grant that Heidegger's claim that *Dasein* is Being-in-the-world amounts to a particular (pragmatically oriented) theory of our encounters with beings that the skeptic will regard as groundless. They will protest, however, that the theory is perfectly acceptable by any ordinary standard and that the skeptic's demand for justification of our basic commitments is obsessive. Here, clearly, the skeptic will feel that he has been ignored, and it is hardly clear what will settle the issue between him and an opponent who finds his labors pointless.

Reaching this standoff, can we do better than to acknowledge the futility of getting clear of it (and getting clear about the force of Heidegger's description of *Dasein*)? The difficulty here is apparent in Charles Guignon's treatment, in which, "given Heidegger's alternative model of Being-in-the-world," the skeptic will be unable to "make sense of a clear division between our ways of talking about the world and the way the world is in itself" (Guignon 1983, p. 175). This raises two questions in the skeptic's mind. First, by what standard is Heidegger's "model" better? Second and more important, why should the skeptic be forced to *make* sense of a distinction that seems already to be perfectly intelligible? Guignon himself questions whether the very quest for "a new and better model of our situation in the world" won't tend "to perpetuate a traditional set of puzzles" that Heidegger had hoped to overcome (Guignon 1983, p. 241). The skeptic, once again, would have to be shown that his "model" is not rejected simply because of the "inextricable impasses" (206/250/191) to which it may well lead; and he is owed an account of where, in appealing to an appearance/reality distinction, he has illicitly generalized his question or changed the subject.

Any reading of Heidegger's efforts must circle back to and acknowledge his claim that *Dasein* is Being-in-the-world. I have suggested that *understanding* the substance and relevance of this claim as well as its point *has* to involve an attempt to address the skeptic's concerns without falling into a conciliatory subjectivist stance or into mere circumvention. If this is so, then providing a "better model" of our situation that will somehow independently reveal its superiority is not exactly Heidegger's strategy. Looking more closely at where the traditional epistemologist will balk in the face of Heidegger's descriptions puts this point in sharper focus.

The epistemologist can afford to admit that descriptions of human being as involved activity are wholly accurate in their own "pragmatic" domain. In this realm, certain basic "assumptions" will at any given point be held unavailable to questioning and justification, and the overall reliability of our methods of inquiry will be taken for granted. In itself, limitation to a practical realm is unobjectionable, although the epistemologist will later determine that it prevents us from attaining a proper perspective on the status of our "assumptions." At the outset, he need only point out that the restricted perspective reflects an interest in the practical aspects of human being and a complementary suspension of equally legitimate philosophical concerns with an ideal of objectivity. From the point of view of capturing these concerns, Heidegger's more pragmatic or involved descriptions have no priority. More important, *given* a concern with objectivity, the epistemologist's depiction of our position as that of the detached subject appears to be a product not of metaphysical conjecture, but of a constructive conception of what objectivity *is* that involves the idea of factoring out "our contribution" to our views of things.[16] All that inquiry into our general cognitive situation starts with, the epistemologist will think, is a set of possibilities (dreaming, evil geniuses, brains in vats) that reveal gaps between how things seem and how they are. If skeptical quandaries emerge from these starting points, so be it. In response to these quandaries, we want a Heidegger who looks less like a G. E. Moore. Granting that the existence of the external world is made manifest in everydayness, the burden remains of explaining the significance of this phenomenological point by revealing the distortions implicit in the epistemologist's starting point.

Is there a reading on which Heidegger achieves this goal? I shall argue that in §43 of *Being and Time* Heidegger does provide material for locating specific confusions in the skeptic's starting points and thereby breaking the impasse. In refusing to take skepticism on its own terms, Heidegger is not offering a defense of common sense, proposing a legitimation of the so-called natural attitude, or issuing a license to ignore the skeptic. He is proposing that we cannot forgo our existing as Being-in-the-world even to raise a question about whether the "assumptions" manifest in everyday existence are justifiable. In order to inhabit the supposedly presuppositionless perspective from which the natural attitude—conceptualized in part as our "belief" in the external world—first appears questionable, we would have to rely on presuppositions that cannot be imported without simultaneously introducing skepticism itself, begging the question. For skepticism to appear as a potential discovery—a possibility that *strikes* us as counter to our common commitments and ordinary beliefs—the very act of occupying the perspective from which it appears as such must have predetermined the outcome of the investigation in the skeptic's favor. Appearances to the contrary—the apparent naturalness of the skeptic's detachment—arise through a reliance on common commitments (and not just on an allegedly superior model of these commitments which Heidegger purports to offer) which the skeptic must disavow. In this case, however, the sense of discovery dissolves. If Heidegger can make it dissolve, his criticism of skepticism is formidable.

II

On Heidegger's account, and contrary to what he takes to be Cartesian ontological preconceptions, the world does not first emerge as meaningless, with meaning a later achievement. Instead, the world is always already disclosed as meaningful: "Being-in-the-world as concerned understanding lets us encounter something self-signifying in self-meaning. This self-signifying meaning [*sich deutendes Bedeuten*] constitutes meaningfulness and is the presence of the world, insofar as it is discovered in understanding concern. *Presence of the world is the worldhood of the world as meaningfulness*. The correlations of meaning which we now take as references are not a subjective view of the world" (Heidegger 1992, p. 213).[17] Heidegger must convince us not that world *is* disclosed as significant—that world emerges as meaningful is in some sense undeniable—but that the meaningfulness inherent in world cannot be explained in terms commensurate with the "epistemological directions" (207/250/192) epitomized by realism, idealism, and skepticism. To do so, he will stand "wholly outside of an orientation to [idealism and realism] and their ways of formulating questions" (Heidegger 1992, p. 167). Thus, in turning to the question of reality, he announces that "it is necessary, by means of a summary consideration, to extricate the question of world understood as meaningfulness from a perverse horizon oriented to some theory or other of the reality of the external world" (1992, p. 214). In §43 of *Being and Time*, Heidegger emphasizes his desire to distance himself from idealism while holding fast to the truth toward which, he believes, it gropes: "If idealism emphasizes that Being and Reality are only 'in the consciousness,' this expresses an understanding of the fact that Being cannot be explained through entities" (207/251/192). In order to avoid the falsity and "emptiness" to which idealism is prone (207/251/192), Heidegger turns away from an idealist analysis of the consciousness of the subject to an analysis of the Being of *Dasein* in terms of what he calls "care" (*Sorge*). "Being (not beings)," he writes, "is dependent upon the understanding of Being; that is to say, Reality (not the Real) is dependent upon care" (212/255/196).

Heidegger opens §43(a) by proposing that the question of "what 'Reality' signifies in general" has been confused with the putative "problem of the external world" (202/246/188). Because the meaning of "Reality" must be understood in terms of the ways we encounter and grasp real entities, reflection on this meaning tends to focus on how we have access to world. Heidegger has earlier (in §13) claimed to find a characteristic philosophical error in interpreting this access as "primordially" a matter of knowledge of present-at-hand reality. This knowledge, he now suggests, must be grounded in "beholding" or "intuitive knowing [*das anschauende Erkennen*]" (202/246/188). "Such knowing," he goes on to comment, "'is' as a [particular] way in which the soul—or consciousness—behaves." Heidegger wants to pose a problem for the picture that represents the real as independent of consciousness and makes access appear to be problematic. If, however, the real is directly available to consciousness, its independence seems to be attenuated.

Heidegger's response to this problem will not be to suggest some other possible resolution for a view that takes knowing as our primary means of access to world. Rather, he will try to subvert the primacy of knowing by asserting that "the question of whether there is a world at all and whether its Being can be proved makes no sense if it is raised by *Dasein* as Being-in-the-world" (202/246–247/188). He urges that the issue of Reality stems from a lack of clarity concerning the Being of that which, on the traditional picture, is to be transcended. On Heidegger's account, human being, as Being-in-the-world, just *is* "transcendent," "overstepping," "familiar in a world."[18] *Dasein* is always already alongside entities, open to them. At this juncture, at the beginning of his attempt to undo the problem of Reality, Heidegger abruptly raises the worry about question-begging. The traditional way of posing the problem is beset by "a double signification [*Doppeldeutigkeit*; Stambaugh translates 'ambiguity']" (202/247/188)—in particular, a potential for confusion between the world and the "world" and the kinds of access we have to them. Whereas "the world is disclosed [*erschlossen*] essentially *along with* the Being of *Dasein*," Heidegger writes, the totality of entities present-at-hand ("world") is "discovered [*entdeckt*]" (203/247/188). Heidegger represents this distinction as crucial; what, really, is its force?

For Heidegger, world-disclosure is a precondition of our comporting ourselves toward or dealing with entities in any meaningful way. Disclosure provides the background on which inquiry into the things of the "world" proceeds. Heidegger writes, "The Real can be discovered only on the basis of a world which has already been disclosed. And only on this basis can anything Real remain *hidden*" (203/247/188). World-disclosure constitutes our working understanding of what it is for real entities to exist; Heidegger explicitly links it to our grasp of our ways of assessing claims about particular present-at-hand beings. "A being can be uncovered [*entdeckt*]," he writes, "whether by way of perception or some other modes of access, only if the being of this being is already disclosed—only if I already understand it. Only then can I ask whether it is actual or not and embark on some procedure [*Weg*] to establish the actuality of the being" (Heidegger 1982, p. 72). Recall that Heidegger holds that the worldly basis of our understanding of beings already involves us with particular things (see 203/247/188). If this is correct, our "procedures" for ascertaining the existence and character of particular real entities are not innocent of commitments to the real "world."

How does confusion about the distinction between the discovered "world" (as present-at-hand beings) and the disclosed world (as background to any understanding of beings) "encumber" the "question of whether there is a world at all and whether its Being can be proved" (202/246–247/188)? Prior to his discussions of Kant's Refutation of Idealism, of realism and idealism, and of the meaning of the "independence" that characterizes real objects, Heidegger remained unforthcoming about this question, assuring us that traditional quests for proof have failed sufficiently to clarify the "*phenomenon of world* as such" (203/247/188). What he has in mind can, I think, be captured in the following way: the harmful "ambiguity" between "world" as the totality of entities and world as that *in* which we have our Being feeds confusion about what proofs of the external world seek to ascertain. If the question is one of the "world," then our concern turns to particular entities, and there is no immediate reason why our given procedures for or ways of determining existence should not be taken as relevant, legitimate, and potentially successful. If, however, what is at issue is the *world* as the basis for our ways of dealing with things, including our ways of inquiring into them, then there is no telling what establishing its existence, and therefore asking about it, would be. Particular doubts cannot be understood in isolation from the ways we go about trying to resolve them. Heidegger is combating the idea that a completely general "question of Reality" has even been posed. Failing, on the one hand, to see how a significant doubt about the "world" has arisen in this philosophical context, he remains, on the other hand, mystified about what would *count* as genuine doubt concerning the *world* as a whole. His treatment of Kant's Refutation of Idealism renders this schema for resisting the pull into epistemology more concrete.

Heidegger holds that a bankrupt picture of the knower and the known as present-at-hand informs Kant's task in the Refutation of Idealism and his conception of how this refutation is to be accomplished.[19] Heidegger's criticism involves "ontical" (in Stambaugh, "ontic") and "ontological" facets.[20] His ontical complaint is that in adopting "the Cartesian approach of positing a subject one can come across in isolation," Kant assumes "the ontical priority of the isolated subject and inner experience" (204/248/189). This "subject—the 'in me'"— remains the "starting point" from which we must "leap off" to the "outside of me" (204/248/189). How can these descriptions of the subject's original situation be supported? According to Kant, the determination of a subject's experience in time demands an enduring, independently existing framework, a "permanent in perception" that "cannot . . . be something in me" (B275). Heidegger contends that this Kantian requirement is based on a prior conceptualization of the self's experience as a series of self-contained, "transitory and variable" moments (Bxli). As Heidegger sees it, to claim with Kant that no permanent is to be found in me, and that, as it were, my experiences themselves do not come complete with some objective reference points, is not to report innocently on the results of introspection. Heidegger's sense is that actual phenomenal findings—accurate descriptions of experience—would belie the "ontical priority of the isolated subject and inner experience" (204/248/189); they would, in fact, present experience as open to the external world. This suggestion loosens the grip of the Kantian setup by suggesting that its conception of experience can only be produced by the distorting lenses of prior *ontological* conviction.

Even were Heidegger to present the "phenomenal evidence" in sufficient detail to sustain this criticism, failure to find support in it for Kant's picture of the empirical subject would hardly be sufficient to sustain the charge of distorting our epistemic situation. Heidegger's deeper, ontological challenge probes the Cartesian-Kantian reconceptualization of the subject and its experiences by scrutinizing what it *means* to view our standing in the world in terms of a relation between inner and outer spheres. Heidegger asks what Kant's proof has to do with *Dasein* as Being-in-the-world. How, that is, do Kant's results apply to us? "It has not been demonstrated," Heidegger writes, "that the sort of thing which gets established about the Being-present-at-hand-together of the changing and the permanent when one takes time as one's clue will also apply to the connection between the 'in me' and the 'outside of me'" (204–205/248–249/190). Kant, it is alleged, draws conclusions about the special case of "subject and object . . . present-at-hand together" from general considerations about change and permanence. To assume that *Dasein* instantiates such an abstract, present-at-hand notion of subject is to misapprehend what would be involved in a satisfactory account of how the Kantian picture applies to our situation. This is the substance of Heidegger's contention that "it is not that the proofs are inadequate, but that the kind of Being of the entity which does the proving and makes requests for proofs *has not been made definite enough*" (205/249/190; Heidegger's emphasis). This dark point bears further examination.

The key, I think, lies in taking seriously the idea that the Being of the inquirer has been left indeterminate on the picture under attack. The being that asks for proof of the external world is individual *Dasein* making an issue of itself. *I* raise the question of how *I* have access to world. This first-personal aspect of the problem constitutes its distinctive character. *If* it were given that the justifiability of *all* of my beliefs about the external world is at stake, I would not be satisfied by an approach that takes my accepted "ways of knowing" about particular objects for granted. What I *can* ask before even considering the challenge to legitimate those "ways of knowing," however, is whether I genuinely have reason to accept the given idea that the justifiability of all of my beliefs is at stake. In broaching this question, I turn on my own dissatisfaction with approaches to understanding my Being-in-the-world that *have* accepted the legitimacy of some of my procedures. Is that (skeptically oriented) dissatisfaction based on more than prejudice? After all, upon "looking into myself," I will find that the testimony of experience suggests that I dwell amidst a world of independent entities—unless, that is, I have eliminated this possibility on a priori grounds. Am I obliged to regard myself, from a first-person point of view, as closeted in a "cabinet of consciousness" (62/89/58)? *Can* I? Faced with this question, I may find myself wondering what reason I have *not* to pre-empt further pursuit of the philosophical problem of the external world.

As inquirer, I cannot point to anything in the subject-object setup that makes it applicable to *me* in particular. This is how it should be; the epistemologist will point out that this feature of the issue is a product of its generality and involves no imposition of a particular "theory" of the subject. Surely, distinctive features of individual knowers are irrelevant to the problem he wants to raise. Nevertheless, the subject position "outside the world" is *not* my place; or, to repeat, I need a reason to take it as such, I need to be apprised of its relevance to my situation. Can the epistemologist adequately explain the relevance of his model?

I think it is plausible to read Heidegger as intending to accuse the epistemologist of abstracting not only from the idiosyncrasies of individual knowers, but also from what we can call "the conditions of inquiry." From out of our worldly understanding of things, we grasp how to go about raising questions, gathering information, and drawing conclusions. We have definite means of putting our "ontical" questions to entities and of ascertaining their characteristics. Heidegger has maintained that these conditions find their place only where the "world . . . has already been disclosed" and where, in addition, some present-at-hand entities have "in each case been discovered" (203/247/188). The "worldly" nature of our routes of inquiry is manifested in the ontologically committed nature of the evidence we adduce for the existence of particular objects and in the equally rich methods and rules of thumb we have for distinguishing seeing and other forms of veridical experience from hallucinating and the like.

Heidegger's point is that *given* the conditions of inquiry—the ways we understand ourselves as questioning the world and determining the facts—we cannot without further explanation see what sense it makes to call the *disworlded* subject of the traditional picture an inquirer. Initially, our Being as inquirers must be described in terms that grant our situatedness, our involvements with things in the world. The skeptic then demands justification of the claim that we actually *are* involved with things, a proof of the external world. Here he moves beyond our initial conception of our cognitive situation. In particular, because the conditions of inquiry that comprise our understanding of how to investigate particular claims implicate our involvements with world, they must be relinquished for purposes of pursuing the skeptic's desired proof. At this point we can counter the skeptic's movement by asking, How is the examination of our capacity as knowers to proceed once the conditions of inquiry have been suspended? What would *count*, under those conditions, as establishing that remarkable thing, that the world exists—or that we don't know that it does? What means do we have of pursuing the question, if indeed it is a question? The ontical question of the reality of the world is a merely general question about beings. (Do any exist?) It would be settled by our ordinary means of evaluating claims about the world; but clearly, with its forgone conclusion, it does not capture what interests the skeptic. Do we really have another question, one to which we so far have no approach? All is well with the skeptic's query if we are willing to assume that we as inquirers are represented by the worldless subject; but Heidegger has asked the epistemologist to *show* that this notion reflects our condition, and it is not even clear how the task can be embraced, let alone what would comprise success.

The epistemologist may refuse to try to explain the relevance of his picture. He may say, "We know what inquiry is, we know how to ask, so we can investigate how the worldless subject gets to the world, whether or not our particular 'procedures' have been suspended. A question is a question." The Heideggerian strategy has not yielded an argument that the skeptic's question is unintelligible, in that there has been no conclusive demonstration that we cannot see the inquirer in the worldless subject. How, after all, could it be proved that there could be no satisfactory way of making sense of the relevance of the epistemologist's picture? Still, by distancing the traditional scheme from the concrete makeup of our situation, Heidegger makes a strong case that we cannot simply take for granted that we can ask what we seem to want to ask about our situation. The epistemologist's refusal to explain begins to seem willful.

In the face of the problem of external reality, our "real need" has not been for proof, but instead for a *reminder* that we are Being-in-the-world.[21] Demands for proof come too late. Heidegger's ontical criticism shows that we are not forced into this late stage; we arrive there through a philosophical interpretation of "the subject," not a consideration of any intrinsic or phenomenal aspects of our subjectivity. His ontological criticism exhibits what is *wrong* with reaching this stage: when we bracket the manifest albeit apparently presuppositious commitments of our epistemic procedures, we shift the problem so that it no longer makes contact with what we had thought we wanted to know about ourselves as knowers. We deal only with an indeterminate subject.

Have Heidegger's efforts to challenge the applicability of the traditional picture of the subject to our position in the world really led to a better understanding of why inquiring *Dasein* "repudiates" (206/250/191) the problem of the external world? Until we have a better grasp of where the skeptic's investigation fails and why, if it does fail, it appears to make sense, we remain circumspect. Substantial clarification results if we interpret the "ambiguity" or "double signification" (202/247/188) in the question of the world (between "world" and world, discovery and disclosure) in terms of an inability or unwillingness to achieve a stable understanding of the nature of the question. For Heidegger, the appearance of coherence in the skeptic's questioning depends on his ability to slide between matters ontical (concerned with beings) and ontological (concerned with the Being of beings). This is suggested by the brief discussion of the relative merits of realism and idealism that concludes §43(a). "The thesis of *realism* that the external world is Really present-at-hand," Heidegger admits, represents a misleadingly expressed apprehension of his claim that, "along with *Dasein* as Being-in-the-world, entities within-the-world have in each case already been disclosed" (207/251/192). Realism, further, "is right to the extent that it attempts to retain *Dasein*'s natural consciousness of the extantness [or presence at hand] of the world." (Heidegger 1992, p. 223). (Heidegger's mock-conciliatory attitude toward realism is his way of registering his sense that his analyses of the world afford as robust a sense of objectivity as could coherently be desired.) Nevertheless, realism commits the cardinal sin of maintaining "that the Reality of the 'world' not only

needs to be proved but also is capable of proof" (207/251/192). It betrays "a lack
of ontological understanding" in trying to "explain Reality ontically by Real connections of interaction between things that are Real" (207/251/192). Though
this charge is best understood as implying that realism, as Heidegger understands
it, is bound to a causal theory of perception that renders its "proofs" ineffectual
in vanquishing the skeptic, the details are less important than a general point:
skepticism and realism share a commitment to the subject-object construction
that severs *Dasein*'s internal relations to the world as its "wherein" (see 202/247/
188), thereby fueling the illegitimate demand for proof. Particular idealist views
also tend to remain in thrall to an empty, indefinite notion of the disworlded subject, but idealism in a broad sense contains a decisive insight in embryo: it can be
said to "amount to the understanding that Being can never be explained by entities [Stambaugh translates, 'being is never explicable by beings']" (208/251/
193). It points, in other words, toward ontological difference.

The significance of this crucial Heideggerian notion to the problem of reality
becomes clearer in §43(c), "Reality and Care." Reality, as a "kind of Being," is
"referred back to the phenomenon of care" (211/255/196). The meaning of a
kind of Being (for example, presence-at-hand, readiness-to-hand, or existence,
Dasein's mode of Being) is correlative to our way of understanding the entities
subsumed under that kind. Ontological categories, that is, are just as they are
reflected as being in our ways of treating or comporting ourselves toward beings
in the appropriate mode.[22] We understand present-at-hand entities as those
beings which make up the "world" of real objects, independent and potentially
accessible via sensible intuition; what this signifies is embodied in our practices
with regard to these entities, centrally our making assertions about the objective "world" and justifying them on the basis of experiential evidence.[23] Ontological determinations do not *reduce* to facts about our practices, if for no other
reason than that our practices need not and cannot be characterized in terms that
are themselves free of ontological commitments. Still, for Heidegger, accurate
descriptions of the relevant practices in ontologically rich terms would *fully* capture the thinghood and independence of the present-at-hand entities that populate the external "world." There is no getting behind the ontological distinctions
and categories expressed in our ways of dealing with beings to prior facts that
would justify these categories or our understanding of them—there is nowhere
else to look for their "natures." (To think otherwise is a paradigmatic example of
looking to beings to explain Being—of neglecting ontological difference.)

In the light of his understanding of ontology, Heidegger thinks he can embrace
some superficially paradoxical claims: "Of course only as long as *Dasein is* (that
is, only as long as an understanding of Being is ontically possible) 'is there' ['*gibt
es*'] Being. When *Dasein* does not exist, 'independence' 'is' not either, nor 'is' the
'in-itself' . . . *In such a case* it cannot be said that entities are, nor can it be said
that they are not. But *now*, as long as there is an understanding of Being and
therefore an understanding of presence-at-hand, it can indeed be said that *in this
case* entities will still continue to be" (212/255/196). Given the prior determination of the Being of present-at-hand entities by our ways of understanding, their
independence is undeniable. If such an entity actually exists in the "world," it will

be independent of our ways of treating and representing it; here, naturally, nothing debars the recognition that such independent beings could have existed before there was *Dasein* around to discover them.[24] We should rest assured, however, that we have no reason—really, no room—to ponder whether the *Being* of beings existed before any human beings, with their ways of understanding and coping with beings. To raise this question would be to regard Being as *a* being which has been determined in *its* Being in a manner that allows us sensibly to assert that it (Being) either existed before *Dasein* or not. To take *this* as a possibility is, once again, to ignore ontological difference by asking of Being a question appropriate only to beings. We ought not think of this confusion as resulting from an attempt to inquire about Being in a way that is precluded by Being's mysterious nature; in doing so, we would remain under the misapprehension that ontology, the study of Being, advances theses about an independently grasped, although ineffable, entity. Misapprehensions here are failures to appreciate the inextricable relation between ontology and *Dasein*'s understanding.[25]

How would neglecting ontological difference give rise to the skeptic's problem? In suggesting that the demand for clarity about the Being of the inquirer creates a need to explain how a disworlded subject could represent *Dasein*, I distinguished between an ontical question of the existence of the real world and a question the skeptic seemed to want to ask. What was the nature of that as yet unformulated question? On the ontical level, determining whether a given object exists is a practice that follows accepted paths within a worldly context. We have no reason *not* to accept that, within world-disclosure, some entities are discovered; thus on the ontical plane, with our ways of dealing with beings held in place, no interesting dispute arises about whether the world exists. The skeptic's question was supposed to emerge from the suspension of the appropriate ontical procedures. According to Heidegger, however, such procedures are internal to our grasp of the notions of reality and independence that have figured into the formulation of the problem of the external world. Skeptically, to seek a justification of our methods for uncovering the facts about beings appears intended to raise an issue about our very grasp of the Being of real or present-at-hand entities.

That is to say: the skeptic asks an ontological question, in Heidegger's sense. Or does he? Here Heidegger's proposal is that skepticism trades on an equivocation between ontical and ontological issues. The skeptic's concern with the existence of the external world must begin with objects; first, because he is trying to raise a demand for a proof of the existence of a something (in effect, a present-at-hand entity, to which we are related by perceptual knowledge) and, second, because the demand is based on a specific ground for doubting whether external objects really are as I now experience them to be (for example, the possibility that I might now be dreaming). In order for the skeptic's question to have the general significance he wants, however, the legitimacy of our day-to-day ways of deciding such ontical matters must be held in abeyance. The ontical starting point allows the skeptic to pose his problem; the apparent shift to the ontological level creates the global, all-encompassing character of his doubt by forcing the suspension of *all* our ways of dealing with matters ontical. Heidegger's problem with the shift is that we have transferred the question of the existence of the world to a new context without retaining any means for approaching it. If one is going to treat the world as an object, must not doing so involve everything that goes into our understanding of objects? Doesn't one have to allow the procedures appropriate to determining whether objects exist to take their course? If the skeptic denies that he is treating the world as an object—and world in Heidegger's technical sense is *not* to be so treated—then his purpose becomes murky and the substance of his doubt questionable. The skeptic is likely to insist that the generalization of his doubt, his suspension of our ways of pursuing questions about objects, is not produced by any suspicious shift to an "ontological" level. His doubts, he will say, rest on nothing more than an appraisal of his current situation: he is just asking whether this, now, might not be a dream. Heidegger's dialectical response will be to continue to press on the question of why taking possibilities of this kind to have world-threatening significance is not *simply* to adopt the question-begging hypothesis that we *Daseins* are disworlded, detached subjects. To the extent that Heidegger succeeds in keeping this question alive, he can conclude that there is as yet no single, well-defined question concerning the existence of the external world and our access to it. Whether the issue is ontical or ontological, no skeptical quandary has rendered our relation to the world the focus of inquiry, let alone threatened it with dissolution.

We have sought an approach to the Heideggerian response to skepticism that renders it immune to two charges: first, that Heidegger simply asserts that *Dasein* is Being-in-the-world without explaining why that claim lies beyond skeptical doubt; and, second, that his accusation of senselessness in the skeptic's demand for a proof or justification of the existence of the external world rests on a subjectivism that renounces a pretheoretical conviction that we have access to things themselves. At this point, the skeptic might want to phrase the latter concern as a worry about verificationism: has the imputation of the meaninglessness of his inquiry been made on the basis of our incapacity to settle claims of a particular kind or about a particular realm? (My talk of "procedures" and "ways of telling," and particularly the suggestion that the skeptic's question may not be recognizable as real if detached from ontically relevant approaches to it, may reinforce such anti-verificationist suspicions.) Heidegger's contention that in seeking a proof of the external world *Dasein* stands in contradiction to its own Being appears susceptible to both these problems: first, that *Dasein* is Being-in-the-world does appear to have been built in from the beginning; second, the unavoidability of *Dasein*'s acting *as if* it has a world seems to have been taken to exhibit the unintelligibility of raising the skeptic's question. Does the contention we have been examining—that the skeptic's problem arises from a conflation of ontical and ontological questions—avoid these difficulties?

The interpretation I have proposed attempts to disarm these charges by turning on the skeptic's questions. Heidegger's "verificationism" would consist in his refusal to take for granted the coherence of the idea of a bare reality in which ontological categories could be grounded, along with his "phenomenological" insistence that philosophical constructions and theories be rendered understandable—in particular, that epistemological restrictions on the "presuppositiousness" of average everyday Being-in-the-world be motivated. The skeptic's intentions begin as conservative. He wants to use standards we acknowledge to criticize actual beliefs and cognitive practices. He seeks to eliminate "assumptions" of worldly involvement in order to explore how we know anything at all about the existence and character of the world. He takes his question to be a factual one, but not one that can be approached via the ontologically rich and committed means we use to decide particular factual claims. Heidegger's point here is that, once normal means of access to the "realm" of factual knowledge are waived, we must ask, Why presume that *knowledge* is at issue here? His conclusion is not that the skeptic is *wrong* for having moved outside everyday standards and procedures, but that we lack a ready-made conception of what factual knowledge consists in that could operate on a level on which all commitments to the world have been suspended. "World" as the collection of spatio-temporal objects is, for all we have seen, established through the discovery of beings; *world* as the background on which beings are discovered and understood has not been made a target of epistemological inquiry. But then it is not clear what the skeptic is asking in demanding a justification of our belief in the external world. At this point, it is fair to say that his innocence is compromised and that he must try to *make* sense out of the question he wants to raise by *excluding* the meaningfulness of the world as context for *Dasein*'s dealings. The price is the credibility of his conviction that his question is self-evident and his way of pursuing it fully natural.

When we allow Heidegger's phenomenological descriptions to remind us that our inquiries begin *in mediis rebus* and, more generally, that the everyday world is manifestly meaningful, we need feel no sense of dissatisfaction, of restriction, or of limitation in our everyday perspectives—unless we have decided to be skeptics from the outset. Heidegger's case can never be final, demonstrative. Nothing guarantees that the need for Heideggerian reminders will not recur at any point in our attempts to understand our position in the world. Still, the traditional epistemologist must face up to the possibility that in ignoring these reminders he sacrifices the veneer of easy intelligibility that lent his questions their force.[26]

NOTES

1. I follow the Macquarrie-Robinson translation of *Being and Time* (New York: Harper & Row, 1962) in rendering Heidegger's "*Sein*" in the capitalized form "Being" and in rendering "*in-der-Welt-sein*" as "Being-in-the-world." I shall cite *Being and Time* in my text by the German page of *Sein und Zeit*, 7th ed. (Tübingen: Max Niemeyer, 1993, first ed. 1927) followed by the page of the Macquarrie-Robinson translation and, next and last, the page in the recent translation by Joan Stambaugh, *Being and Time* (Albany: State University of New York Press, 1996). I shall quote, with slight modification, the Macquarrie-Robinson translation because of its familiarity. Variant translations of significant or possibly confusing Heideggerian terminology will be noted in brackets.

2. On the traditional epistemological project, its ends and prospects, and its relation to global skeptical challenges, see Barry Stroud, *The Significance of Philosophical Scepticism* (Oxford: Clarendon Press, 1984) (hereafter Stroud 1984), and "Understanding Human Knowledge in General," in *Knowledge and Skepticism*, ed. M. Clay and K. Lehrer (Boulder, Colo.: Westview Press, 1989), pp. 31–50. Throughout, I use "[traditional] epistemologist" and "skeptic" in much the same way, because the focus is on the skeptic's initial querying of our epistemic relation to the external world, and

not on his (negative) conclusions, which provide the occasions for his disagreements with other traditional epistemologists.

3. On *Dasein* as "human being," see Hubert Dreyfus, *Being-in-the-World* (Cambridge, Mass.: MIT Press, 1991) (hereafter Dreyfus 1991), chapter 1, especially p. 13: "'*Dasein*' in colloquial German can mean 'everyday human existence,' and so Heidegger uses the term to refer to human being." *Dasein*, that is, is the kind of Being of beings or entities that have the characteristics definitive of humans in, we might say, their humanity—where for Heidegger this is not a matter of, say, species membership, but of the capacity to make one's Being an issue for oneself. "*Dasein*" can also refer to those beings or particular entities that have the relevant kind of Being; for the most part, this is how I use the term here.

4. Heidegger relates his notion of "world" to the Kantian notion of nature as a "dynamic totality of appearances" in *The Metaphysical Foundations of Logic*, trans. Michael Heims (Bloomington: Indiana University Press, 1984) (hereafter Heidegger 1984), on p. 176; see also p. 180. In *Being and Time*, to conceive of beings as present-at-hand within the "world" is to conceive of them as external, law-governed, spatiotemporal objects. Stambaugh translates "*Vorhandenheit*" not as "presence-at-hand" but as "objective presence."

5. Immanuel Kant, *Critique of Pure Reason*, trans. Norman Kemp Smith (New York: St. Martin's Press, 1965), Bxxxixn. Hereafter cited by the standard A/B number system.

6. I hope to bring out that Heidegger's claim that *Dasein* is Being-in-the-world can only be understood when we come to be in a position to resist those false pictures or philosophical constructions that he is concerned to combat in making the claim. In other words, the claim can only be grasped in terms of the philosophical work it does, and not *simply* as an alternative description of our position in the world. I hope to show as much by tracing how the claim is employed in Heidegger's response to skepticism. In the course of doing so, I trust that we shall gain insight into the point as well as the meaning of some of Heidegger's technical terminology and, in particular, his notion of Being-in-the-world.

Dorothea Frede, "Heidegger and the Scandal of Philosophy," in *Human Nature and Natural Knowledge*, ed. A. Donagan, A. N. Perovich Jr., and M. V. Wedin (Dordrecht: Reidel, 1986), pp. 129–151, and Charles Guignon, *Heidegger and the Problem of Knowledge* (Indianapolis: Hackett 1983) (hereafter Guignon 1983), are important studies with significant points of contact (and agreement) with what follows. Frede (see p. 144) emphasizes the importance of the ontic/ontological distinction; my concern is to show how the distinction is put to work by bringing out how Heidegger's suggestion that the problem of the external world arises due to neglect of ontological difference constitutes an attempt to block the skeptic's demand for a proof of the external world from getting off the ground (see below). Guignon's important account emphasizes that the skeptic's inquiry undermines the conditions of its own intelligibility (see, for example, pp. 173–176); my concern is to go into detail about why the skeptic ought to feel obligated to take this kind of point seriously.

7. Martin Heidegger, *The Basic Problems of Phenomenology*, trans. Albert Hofstadter (Bloomington: Indiana University Press, 1982) (hereafter Heidegger 1982), p. 167.

8. Heidegger's insistence that *Dasein* as Being-in-the-world cannot raise the question of the reality of the external world might strike one as similar to G. E. Moore's strategy in "A Defense of Common Sense," in Moore, *Philosophical Papers* (London: George Allen and Unwin, 1959), pp. 32–59; one might, moreover, be tempted to find an affinity to the Moore of "Proof of an External World," in *Philosophical Papers*, pp.127–150. Arguing that in "Proof" Moore "gives the impression of having no idea what the sceptical philosopher really wants to say or do," Barry Stroud interprets Moore as either failing or refusing to discern even an apparent sense in which a philosophical question about knowledge would not be addressed by gesturing at his hands (Stroud 1984, p. 124; see pp. 124–126). The appearance of similarity between

Moore and Heidegger is, in the end, misleading, but saying how it misleads would be one way of trying to articulate the chances Heidegger's strategy has for successfully responding to skepticism.

9. See chapter III of Division I of *Being and Time*; Dreyfus (1991), ch. 5; and Mark Okrent, *Heidegger's Pragmatism* (Ithaca, N.Y.: Cornell University Press, 1988), pp. 39–44.

10. See Heidegger (1982), p. 165.

11. Here we see why Heidegger tries to invert Descartes's *cogito*: "The '*sum*' is . . . asserted first, and indeed in the sense that 'I am in a world.' As such an entity, 'I am' in the possibility of Being towards various ways of comporting myself—namely, *cogitationes*—as ways of Being alongside entities within-the-world" (211/254/195). See also 24/46/21: The *cogito* reasoning cannot provide a "determinate" notion of the subject.

12. A sophisticated version of what the skeptic will regard as a retreat is presented by Frederick Olafson: "In ordinary situations we do not behave as though we were standing in any such extramundane place from which the existence of the world would have to be worked out in terms of argument and inference" (*Heidegger and the Philosophy of Mind* [New Haven: Yale University Press, 1987], p. 12). If the contention is that "we are already operating on the very 'presuppositions' about the world and our being in it that realism seeks to justify" (p. 12), the skeptic will point out that this vocabulary invites us to ask what justifies the presuppositions involved.

13. This paragraph represents an attempt to express, in terms arising naturally from the Heideggerian context, skeptical hesitations about the scope and legitimacy of transcendental arguments, about reliance on verificationist premises, and, more generally, about attempts to restrict meaningful knowledge claims to the "inside" of a predefined realm of sense. On transcendental arguments and verificationism, see Barry Stroud, "Transcendental Arguments," *Journal of Philosophy* 65 (1968): 241–256; more generally, see Stroud (1984).

14. Or rather the substance of the charge is no longer clear. In *The History of the Concept of Time*, trans. Theodore Kisiel (Bloomington: Indiana University Press, 1992) (hereafter Heidegger 1992), Heidegger writes that "[t]he peculiar thing is just that the world is 'there' [*da*] *before* all belief. . . . Inherent in the being of the world is that its existence *needs no guarantee in regard to a subject*. What is needed, if this question comes up at all, is that the *Dasein* should experience itself in its most elementary constitution of being, as being-in-the-world itself. This experience of itself—unspoiled by any sort of epistemology—eliminates the ground for any question of the reality of the world" (p. 216).

15. The idea that Heidegger's contribution lies in advising us to ignore the traditional epistemological problematic is associated with Richard Rorty; see "Heidegger, Contingency, and Pragmatism," in Rorty, *Essays on Heidegger and Others* (Cambridge: Cambridge University Press, 1991), pp. 27–49. But Heidegger is less prone than Rorty to maintain that we should *just* forget about the problems bequeathed by bad epistemological pictures and get on with matters of greater interest. For side-stepping, see P. F. Strawson, *Skepticism and Naturalism: Some Varieties* (New York: Columbia University Press, 1985), p. 24, where Heidegger is enlisted for the "naturalist" cause of pursuing a "response to skepticism which does not so much attempt to meet the challenge as to pass it by" (p. 3). Strawson's naturalist realizes that "professional skeptical doubt . . . is idle, unreal, a pretense" (p. 19), as is the attempt to rebut such doubt with argument. Heidegger could hardly be said to disagree wholly with this point (see 229/271–272/210); still, he does not want to "pass by" the skeptic.

John Richardson holds that "Heidegger's claim that . . . concernful understanding is inescapable"—which is essential to his dissolution of the need to prove the external world—"implies that we can never really know, and hence a skeptical answer in epistemology" (*Existential Epistemology* [Oxford: Clarendon Press, 1986], p. 118). Heidegger, Richardson suggests, deemphasizes this skeptical upshot because he takes the *goal* of gaining access to things as they are in themselves to be "one we adopt misguidedly—because we suppose it a means to an end that it does not contribute to, or else that itself ought not be pursued" (p. 120). Richardson's interpretation is, I contend, misleading in that it locates the problem in having a certain goal, rather than in the way we (try to) conceive of what the goal might be. I read Heidegger as suggesting not that we do not know things in themselves, but that we have not yet arrived at an adequate understanding of what it is for something to be "in itself" (see 75–76/106/71).

16. On the role notions of objectivity play in the epistemologist's task, see Bernard Williams, *Descartes* (New York: Penguin 1978), ch. 2, and Stroud (1984), ch. 2.

17. See *Being and Time*, §21, and (Heidegger 1992), p. 219: "If I take perception to be the simple perception of a thing, the world is no longer accessible in its full worldhood, in its full meaningfulness as it encounters concern. In the pure perception of a thing, the world shows itself instead in a *deficient meaningfulness*."

18. See Heidegger (1982), p. 301.

19. See the discussion of Kant's views on perception and their connection to actuality in Heidegger (1982), §9. From Heidegger's perspective, the placement of the Refutation after the Second Postulate of Empirical Thought—"that which is bound up with the material conditions of experience, that is, with sensation, is *actual*" (A218/B266)—would tend to corroborate the claim that Kant treats what is at issue in the Refutation as a matter of the subject's relations to present-at-hand entities. Kant associates problematic idealism with doubts about whether the existence of unobserved objects or properties can be inferred; the upshot of the Second Postulate is that such inferences are legitimate (justifiable) as long as the inferred objects are properly connected (by empirical laws) to actual perceptions (A225/B272) and are themselves objects of *possible* perceptions. The Refutation is supposed to remove the prospect that there might be no such objects.

20. On the distinction between "ontical" and "ontological," see (11/31/9), especially Macquarrie and Robinson's n. 3: "Ontological inquiry is concerned primarily with Being; ontical inquiry is concerned primarily with entities [that is, beings] and the facts about them." See also (Dreyfus 1991), p. 20; like Stambaugh, Dreyfus translates "*ontisch*" as "ontic."

21. On our "real need" in philosophy, see Ludwig Wittgenstein, *Philosophical Investigations*, 3d ed., eds. G. E. M. Anscombe and R. Rhees, trans. G. E. M. Anscombe (Oxford: Blackwell, 1953), §108; on reminders, see §§89–90 and §127. If my understanding of Heideggerian ontology is correct, there is a strong affinity between it and the sense of his own method Wittgenstein expresses in §§89–90. For present purposes, though, it is more important to note that Heidegger, like Wittgenstein, is attempting to head off a philosophical questioning that imposes a demand for a kind of grounding for our everyday practices without fully justifying or motivating that demand in a way that satisfies its own standards.

22. There is, of course, no implication that our reflections on how ontological categories are expressed in our comportments will be unerring.

23. See Robert Brandom, "Heidegger's Categories in *Being and Time*," in *Heidegger: A Critical Reader*, ed. H. Dreyfus and H. Hall (Cambridge, Mass.: Blackwell, 1992), pp. 45–64, pp. 55–62.

24. See, for example, 212/255/196: "Being (not entities) is dependent upon the understanding of Being; that is to say, Reality (not the Real) is dependent upon care"; and Heidegger's striking discussion of "world-entry" in *The Metaphysical Foundations of Logic* (Heidegger 1984), pp. 194–195.

25. This discussion of the ontological meaning of the independence of beings is supported by Heidegger's treatment of truth in §44, where he writes, "'[t]*here is*' truth only in so far as Dasein is and so long as Dasein is" (226/269/S208) and "[b]*ecause the kind of Being that is essential to truth is of the character of Dasein, all truth is relative to Dasein's Being*" (227/270/208; Heidegger's emphases). Saying that truth depends

on *Dasein* is intended to jar, but it is Heidegger's way of expressing a predominantly negative idea. Truth in what Heidegger takes to be its essence—as the disclosedness of entities without which we could not make sense of correspondence—*is* simply *Dasein*'s openness to world, which is to say that according to Heidegger there is no perspective from which we need a "theory of truth."

26. Earlier versions of this chapter were presented to the Columbia University Philosophy Department and the University of Arkansas Philosophy Department; I thank the members of those audiences for their generous and useful questions. Wolfgang Mann has been of great help. Several critical insights of Daniel Brudney have led to significant improvement. I am most grateful to Randall Havas both for his careful reading of this chapter throughout the process of writing and for years of thoughtful discussion of Heidegger. And I thank also Burton Dreben for remarks about my approach to the issues discussed here that served as impetus in the early stages of writing this essay.

1932
W. V. Quine submits his Harvard Ph.D.
Dissertation, *The Logic of Sequences*

9

Confessions of a Confirmed Extensionalist

W. V. QUINE

I am neither an essentialist nor, so far as I know, an existentialist. But I am a confirmed extensionalist. Extensionalism is a policy I have clung to through thick, thin, and nearly seven decades of logicizing and philosophizing. I shall now define it, though I was heeding it before knowing the word or having the concept clearly in mind.

I shall call two closed sentences *coextensive* if they are both true or both false. Two predicates or general terms or open sentences are coextensive, of course, if they are true of just the same objects or sequences of objects. Two singular terms are coextensive if they designate the same object. And finally to the point: an expression is *extensional* if replacement of its component expressions by coextensive expressions always yields a coextensive whole. *Extensionalism* is a predilection for extensional theories.

In defining coextensiveness, I lumped predicates, general terms, and open sentences together. They are what can be predicated of objects or sequences of objects, and in that capacity they all three come to the same thing. They are what the schematic predicate letters in quantification theory stand for. Open sentences are the most graphic of the three renderings. Two open sentences are coextensive if they have the same free variables and agree with each other in truth-value for all values of those variables.

The clarity and convenience conferred by extensionality are evident: free interchangeability of coextensive components *salva veritate*. When in particular those components are singular terms, indeed, their interchangeability would seem mandatory from any point of view; for this is simply the substitutivity of identity. Still, "Tom believes that Cicero denounced Catiline" and "Tom believes that Tully denounced Catiline" might be respectively true and false despite the identity of Cicero and Tully. We must come to terms with such cases either by compromising extensionalism or in some happier way, whereof more anon.

Meanwhile, extensionalism faces a challenge from another quarter. Karel Lambert has argued[1] that an irreferential singular term such as "Pegasus" can disrupt extensionality. The predicates "flies if existent" and "flies and exists" are coextensive, since everything exists. But the sentence, "Pegasus flies if existent" is vacuously true, since Pegasus is not existent, whereas "Pegasus flies and exists" is false. So these two sentences are not extensional; their truth values are switched by switching coextensive predicates.

Happily this threat is thwarted by my practice, for lo these many decades, of treating all singular terms as singular descriptions—thus "Pegasus" as "$(\iota x)(x$ pegasizes)." We may think of the descriptions as defined contextually, following Russell. Under his definition, where "F" stands for any predicate, "$F(\iota x)(x$ pegasizes)" becomes

$$\exists x(x \text{ and only } x \text{ pegasizes } . Fx),$$

and this is false regardless of "F." So both of Lambert's predicates, both "flies if existent" and "flies and exists," must issue in falsehood when the subject is "Pegasus." Then there is no breach of extensionality.

To reckon "Pegasus flies if existent" true, as Lambert does, we would have to analyze "Pegasus flies if existent" into "If Pegasus exists then Pegasus flies," using two predicates. Then, treating "Pegasus flies and exists" correspondingly, we do find the sentences respectively true and false, as he claims. But our predicates are no longer the coextensive pair "flies if existent" and "flies and exists" that raised the problem. When singular description is evaporated into primitive notation, all is in order.

Lambert already recognized this, writing that my way with singular terms bypasses his challenge to extensionalism. This would indeed have been a good reason for that early move on my part, but actually my motive for it back then was just simplicity of foundations.

The elimination of singular terms bears also, it might seem, on our question regarding the singular terms "Tully" and "Cicero." But that is another story, and I shall continue to postpone it.

I have discussed extensionality thus far without mentioning classes. I hasten to do so, for classes are deemed the very paradigms of extensionality. Thus far I only defined extensionality of an *expression*: "Replacement of its parts by coextensives always yields a coextensive whole." But classes are not expressions. They are objects, abstract objects. To bring them into the act I turn rather to the familiar expression for specifying a class: the class abstract "$\{x: Fx\}$." Being a singular term, "$\{x: Fx\}$" may be thought of as defined as a singular description in the obvious way, namely as "$(\iota y)((\forall x)(x \in y. \equiv .Fx))$," and then dissolved into Russell's contextual definition of descriptions.

The expression "$\{x: Fx\}$ " is indeed extensional by my definition. For, if "Fx" and "Gx" stand for coextensive open sentences, then the singular terms "$\{x: Fx\}$" and "$\{x: Gx\}$ " designate the same class, the same abstract thing, and such was my definition of coextensiveness of singular terms. If now we transfer the epithet "extensional" from the class abstract to the class itself, saying that classes are extensional just means that they are determined by their members.

The one difference between classes and properties, apart from metaphor and free association, is extensionality: a class is determined by its members. A property is not in general determined by its instances. I am told that among normal animals the property of having a heart and the property of having kidneys are coextensive, but we would never call them the same property. Classes are extensional, properties not.

We have no clear basis in general for saying what coextensive properties qualify as identical and what ones do not. In a word, properties lack a clear principle of *individuation*. Groping for such a basis, one settles for obscure talk of essence and necessity. Anything that can be described in terms of properties and not equally directly in terms of classes is unclear to my mind. I doubt that I have ever fully understood anything that I could not explain in extensional language.

Now that I have slipped back into the first person, I shall continue in that mode for a while; for the pertinent definitions are now explicitly before us. Afterward, I shall resume the selfless business of making the world safe for extensionalism.

My first inarticulate hint of extensionalism may date from boyhood, when my liking for some Jewish schoolmates collided with someone's occasional derogatory remark about Jews. I reasoned in effect that a class is to be evaluated, if at all, by evaluating its members individually.

By my senior year in Oberlin College, 1929–1930, my extensionalism was full blown. I was majoring in mathematics with honors reading in mathematical logic. There was little mathematical logic in America, and none at Oberlin. But my professor, W. D. Cairns, had got me a reading list, culminating in Whitehead and Russell's *Principia Mathematica*.

My admiration for the three volumes, mostly in logical symbols, was almost unbounded. There was the spectacular analysis, the reduction of classical mathematics to a few basic notions of so-called logic, really logic and set theory. Further, there was the rigor, explicitness, and clarity of the definitions, theorems, and proofs.

My admiration was not quite unbounded. It was bounded by the explanations in prose that were preposed and interposed as explanatory chapters and in briefer bits among the expanses of symbols.

Doubtful of the reality of classes, our authors undertook to accommodate them as fictions, eliminable by contextual definition in terms of purportedly more substantial things called propositional functions. These were functions which, when applied to objects, yielded propositions, which were the meanings of sentences. Thus the propositional functions of one variable were evidently identifiable with properties, and those of two or more variables were identifiable with relations "in intension."

Extensionality was seen by our authors as having to be worked for by devious contextual definition. The *intentional*, for all its failure of individuation, was the given. I suppose the reasoning was that, since the propositions and propositional functions are the *meanings* of sentences, adjective phrases, and verb phrases, surely they are clear to us insofar as we understand the expressions whose meanings they are.

If so, the authors' fallacy lay in tacitly taking in stride the giant step of reifying those meanings. Reification incurs the responsibility to individuate the reified entities, for there is no entity without identity. I suspect that our authors thus put undue weight on the adjective phrases that express the properties; for the phrases could differ conspicuously even if the properties did not.

Along with this regrettably intentional orientation, but independent of it, there was a detail that calls for notice only because of its disproportionate consequences in subsequent literature. The truth-functional conditional "$p \supset q$" or "not p or q" was called material implication in *Principia* and read indifferently as "if p then q" and "p implies q." On the face of it this was a grammatical aberration, independently of logical considerations. The grammar of "if p then q" requires "p" and "q" to stand for sentences, whereas that of "p implies q" requires them to stand for nouns, in this case names of sentences.

C. I. Lewis lashed out against material implication,[2] but his objection was not to the grammar. He was protesting, and rightly, that the truth function "not-or" was a hollow mockery of implication, demanding as it does no semantic relevance of the one component sentence to the other. He supplanted the weak "$\supset$" by a stronger connective "$\dashv$" for what he called strict implication. He explained "$p \dashv q$" as meaning "necessarily if p then q," and offered no further reduction. It was an emphatic departure from extensionalism, and it pioneered modal logic. Succeeding modal logicians have not all persisted in the grammatical confusion between "if-then" and "implies," but they still sacrifice extensionality to their "necessarily if-then."

I find the truth-functional conditional "$p \supset q$" a satisfactory rendering of "if-then" in the indicative mood. Implication is quite another thing, in strength as well as in grammar. It is a relation between sentences, expressed by putting the verb "implies" between names of the sentences, and it is established by steps of deduction.

Whitehead and Russell's regrettable use of "implies" virtually spoiled the word, prompting subsequent logicians to cast about for synonyms such as "entails" for the real thing. But I have been stubborn on that point.

Unlike the enduring intentionality of modal logic, the intentionality of propositional functions in *Principia* was mercifully just a flash in the pan. The propositional functions carry over only briefly into the formulas as values of quantified variables: only long enough to introduce classes as fictions by contextual definition. From there on the constructions proceed on greased wheels, greased by extensionality.

I was quite aware of these matters when I graduated from Oberlin in 1930, but my admiration for *Principia* was still almost unbounded. I proceeded to Harvard for graduate work in philosophy because Whitehead was in philosophy there. My doctoral dissertation was in mathematical logic still, under Whitehead's sponsorship, and was devoted to improving *Principia*. He seemed tickled by my little shortcuts and clarifications, except that I cannot have swayed him in my extensionalism. Anyway, I imposed it in my dissertation. Individuals, classes, and sequences of them were all there was.

Mathematical logic, scarce in America, was sketchy even at Harvard. *Principia* was still the last word, and little was done even with it. I did not know that in Poland, Germany, and Austria the subject had been proceeding apace and that classes were the unquestioned staple from scratch. In 1931, while I wrote my dissertation, logicians in Europe were freely pursuing logic and set theory on the frugal conceptual basis of just truth-functions, quantification, and membership.

This startling economy came of Kazimierz Kuratowski's discovery in 1921 that the ordered pair of x and y can be construed as the class whose two members are the class of x alone and the class of x and y. Kuratowski's definition had been anticipated by a slightly less elegant one in 1914 by a young American, Norbert Wiener, but his three-page paper in the Proceedings of the Cambridge [England] Philosophical Society escaped notice everywhere.[3] Both contributions, Wiener's and Kuratowski's, escaped notice in America.

The economies over *Principia* that I achieved in my dissertation had thus been long surpassed, as I learned only after getting to Europe the following year, 1932, complete with doctorate. But in 1937 I published a more extreme reduction, assuming just class inclusion and class abstraction.[4]

The reduction of classical mathematics to one or another so meager a conceptual basis was amazing and illuminating, but calling it a reduction of mathematics to logic—*logicism*, in a word—gave the wrong message. Logic was proverbially slight and trivial. Mathematics proverbially ranged from the profound to the impenetrable, and reduction of mathematics to logic challenged belief, as indeed it well might. The reduction was to the unbridled theory of classes, or set theory, which, far from being slight and trivial, is so strong as to tangle itself in paradox until bridled in one way or another. This is no fault of extensionalism, be it noted; properties are enmeshed in those paradoxes too. But what it shows is that the startling reduction of mathematics is to something far richer than traditional logic. I prefer to limit the term "logic" to the logic of truth functions, quantification, and identity, drawing the line at the reification of classes. Above that line we have set theory, the mathematics of classes.

I think of logic in this narrow sense as the grammar of strictly scientific theory. When a bit of science is thus regimented, the one place where extralogical vocabulary enters the picture is as interpretation of the schematic predicate letters. Within this grammar, extensionality prevails.

But extensionality had no evident charm for the Harvard philosophers during my two years of graduate study. Whitehead, Lewis, and Sheffer all swore by properties and propositions. It was with Carnap in Prague and Tarski, Lesniewski, and Łukasiewicz in Warsaw the following year that my extensionalism went without saying as a matter of course.

So much for reminiscence. But I have more to say of extensionalism, for properties and necessity are not its only hurdles. The domain of meanings of expressions is hopelessly intensional and in trouble over individuation. Propositions, seen as meanings of sentences, are conspicuous here. Properties themselves might be seen correspondingly as meanings of adjective phrases.

Properties, meanings, and necessity were violations of extensionality that I repudiated without regret. But the breach of extensionality that I cited early in this essay is of another sort: "Tom believes that Cicero denounced Catiline." Those idioms of propositional attitude—belief, hope, regret, and the rest—are not to be lightly dismissed. It is not clear how to do without them. But there is a strategy by which, in the majority of cases, they can be rendered extensional.

I call it *semantic ascent*. It is the strategy of talking about expressions instead of using those expressions to talk about something more dubious. It already did us routine service in correcting Whitehead and Russell's confused treatment of "implies" as a connective to be written between sentences. We lifted it to its rightful place as a transitive verb between names of sentences. Now the strategy can be used also on ascriptions of belief, artificially this time, by reconstruing belief as a relation between believers and sentences: thus

Tom believes "Cicero denounced Catiline"

or perhaps, for usage sticklers,

Tom believes true "Cicero denounced Catiline."

This reinterpretation of the propositional attitudes, as relating the person to the sentence, does not require him to know the language. The quoted sentence is the ascriber's expression of what he would be prompted to assert if he were in the state of mind in which he takes the subject to be. The effect of semantic ascent here is to seal the belief off from the context in which it is ascribed, so that Tom's disbelief of "Tully denounced Catiline" will not violate extensionality of the combined ascriptions of belief and disbelief.

Some ascriptions of propositional attitudes resist semantic ascent. For example,

There was an orator whom Tom believes to have denounced Catiline.

This example switches us from what are called propositional attitudes *de dicto* to attitudes *de re*. In ascribing a belief *de re* the ascriber ventures to assign a role within the ascribed belief to a denizen of the ascriber's real world. Such identifications can depend in varying degrees upon collateral information or conjecture about the subject's past behavior.[5] Semantically these idioms *de re* of belief and other attitudes are comparable to the contrary-to-fact conditional, which depends so utterly for its truth upon tacit factual knowledge or assumptions that the interlocutors are assumed to share. The particles "you," "I," "here," "there," "now," and "then" are simpler examples of such dependence on circumstances of utterance. So the propositional attitudes *de re* belong with these extraneous idioms, ancillary to the self-contained language of scientific record.

Finally, I turn to some further thoughts about our extensionalizing strategy of semantic ascent from use to mention. To the extensionalist eye, the ascent could seem paradoxically to be rather a descent from bad to worse, from frying pan to fire. We mention expressions by quoting them, and nothing could be less extensional on the face of it than quotation. Within a quotation, you cannot supplant a word by even the strictest synonym without changing the designatum of the quotation, namely the quoted expression itself. Nothing could be farther from extensionality than quotation.

This quandary is dispelled by recognizing the quotation as merely a graphic abbreviation, analyzable into spelling. We possess or coin a name for each of the simple signs of our language, and one for the space, and one for the operation of juxtaposition. Then we spell out the quoted expression. The spelling leaves no word of the quoted expression intact for replacement by a synonym. It thus blocks this latest little debacle before it begins.

Spelling is similar to polynomials and multidigit numerals. It reduces similarly to truth-functions, quantification, and predicates, with the help of contextual definition of singular description.

We have been seeing semantic ascent at work in achieving extensionality, but it has other uses. Someone's revolutionary scientific idea may prove difficult to promote because it undercuts one of the principles on which his colleagues' very thought and judgment depend. Holding that principle at bay for impartial assessment leaves the judge himself at a loss for a basis for judging. Semantic accent, then, to the rescue. The innovator ascends from his subject matter to the formulas and laws themselves, dwells on their simplicity, and shows that they logically imply his strange new hypothesis together with essentials of the antecedent theory. The change of subject matter, from waves or quarks or fields to the formulas themselves, has bridged the gaps in his colleagues' intuition. Something like this perhaps went on at crucial points in the advance of science, though with no awareness of an ascent from use to mention.

NOTES

1. Karel Lambert, "Predication and Extensionality," *Journal of Philosophical Logic* 3 (1974): 255–264.

2. C. I. Lewis, *A Survey of Symbolic Logic* (Berkeley: University of California Press, 1918), pp. 222–339.

3. Norbert Wiener, "A Simplification of the Logic of Relations," *Proceedings of the Cambridge Philosophical Society* 17 (1914): 387–390.

4. "Logic Based on Inclusion and Abstraction," *Journal of Symbolic Logic* 2 (1937): 145–152. Reprinted in Quine, *Selected Logic Papers*, enlarged ed. (Cambridge, Mass.: Harvard University Press, 1995).

5. See Robert Sleigh, "On a Proposed System of Epistemic Logic," *Noûs* 2 (1968): 391–398.

10

Tolerance and Analyticity in Carnap's Philosophy of Mathematics

MICHAEL FRIEDMAN

In *The Logical Syntax of Language*[1] Carnap attempts to come to terms philosophically with the debate in the foundations of logic and mathematics that raged throughout the twenties—the debate, that is, between the three foundational "schools" of logicism, formalism, and intuitionism. Carnap himself, as a student of Frege, Russell, and Wittgenstein, is of course most sympathetic to the logicist school. Nevertheless, he recognizes that traditional logicism cannot succeed: we cannot reduce mathematics to logic in some antecedently understood sense, whether in the sense of Frege's *Begriffsschrift* or Whitehead and Russell's *Principia Mathematica*. And, at the same time, Carnap is sensitive to the contributions, both technical and philosophical, of the other two competing schools. In particular, he is sensitive to the notion of constructibility emphasized by the intuitionist school and, especially, to Hilbert's conception of metamathematics emphasized by the formalist school. Indeed, Carnap begins *Logical Syntax* by explaining that the metalanguage, in which we speak about the formulas and rules of a logical system, represents "what is essential in logic" (Foreword). The point of Carnap's book is then to develop a precise and exact method, logical syntax, wherein these "sentences about sentences" can be formulated.

Nevertheless, Carnap by no means shares Hilbert's foundational program. Carnap is fully cognizant, in particular, of Gödel's recently discovered incompleteness theorems and accordingly states explicitly that "whether . . . Hilbert's aim can be achieved at all, must be regarded as at best very doubtful in view of Gödel's researches on the subject" (§34i). Carnap thus shows no interest whatever in the foundational project of proving the consistency of classical mathematics within an essentially weaker, finitary, metalanguage. Moreover, it is also clear that Carnap does not share the foundational concerns of traditional intuitionism or constructivism. To be sure, Carnap devotes a considerable portion of *Logical Syntax* (Parts I and II) to the articulation and investigation of a logical system, Language I, in which "[s]ome of the tendencies which are commonly designated as 'finitist' or 'constructivist' find, in a certain sense, their realization" (§16). Indeed, Carnap had originally felt substantial sympathy with the constructivism of

Brouwer, Heyting, and Weyl.[2] Nevertheless, although in harmony with these sympathies Carnap had at first intended to develop Language I alone, he soon adopted the standpoint of "tolerance" according to which a language containing all of classical arithmetic, analysis, and set-theory, Language II, is equally possible and legitimate.[3] In this sense, Carnap abandons all constructivist philosophy in *Logical Syntax* and instead views his particular constructivist system, Language I, as simply one possible formal-logical system among an infinity of equally possible such systems.

Carnap in fact intends to represent the most general possible logico-mathematical pluralism in *Logical Syntax*. We are entirely free to set up any system of formal rules we like, whether or not these rules represent the point of view of logicism, formalism, intuitionism, or any foundational school at all. And we are entirely free here because there can be no question of "justification" or "correctness" *antecedent* to the choice of one or another formal-logical system. From the point of view of the metalanguage—that is, from the point of view of logical syntax—our task is neither to justify nor to criticize any particular choice of rules, but rather to investigate and to compare the consequences of any and all such choices:

> From this point of view the dispute between the different tendencies in the foundations of mathematics also disappears. One can set up the language in its mathematical part as one of the tendencies prefers or as the other prefers. There is no question of "justification" here, but only the question of the syntactic consequences to which one or another choice leads—including also the question of consistency. (Foreword)

As Carnap here intimates, once we have made the choice of a particular formal-logical system, there is then a specific notion of logical "correctness" fixed by the rules in question, a notion of logical "correctness" *relative to* the formal rules (and their syntactic consequences) to which we have committed ourselves. For the choice of one such formal system over another, however, there is and can be no notion of "correctness." Here we are faced with a purely pragmatic or conventional question of suitability and/or convenience relative to one or another given purpose. If one is especially concerned to avoid the threat of inconsistency, for example, the choice of a relatively weak constructivist or intuitionist language such as Carnap's Language I is prudent. If, however, one wants the full power of classical mathematics (perhaps in view of ease of physical application), then one has no choice but to adopt a much richer language such as Carnap's Language II.[4] As Carnap expresses the resulting *principle of tolerance*: "*we do not wish to set up prohibitions, but rather to stipulate conventions*" (§17).

I

We have seen that Gödel's incompleteness results form an essential part of the background to *Logical Syntax*. Indeed, Carnap himself ascribes a central role in the genesis of *Logical Syntax* to his own interactions with Gödel in connection with these fundamental discoveries:

[T]he members of the Circle, in contrast to Wittgenstein, came to the conclusion that it is possible to speak about language and, in particular, about the structures of linguistic expressions. On the basis of this conception, I developed the idea of the logical syntax of a language as the purely analytic theory of the structure of its expressions. My way of thinking was influenced chiefly by the investigations of Hilbert and Tarski in metamathematics. . . . I often talked with Gödel about these problems. In August 1930 he explained to me his new method of correlating numbers with signs and expressions. Thus a theory of the forms of expressions could be formulated with the help of the concepts of arithmetic. He told me that, with the help of this method of arithmetization, he had proved that any formal system of arithmetic is incomplete and incompletable. When he published this result in 1931, it marked a turning point in the development of the foundations of mathematics.

After thinking about these problems for several years, the whole theory of language structure and its possible applications in philosophy came to me like a vision during a sleepless night in January 1931, when I was ill. On the following day, still in bed with a fever, I wrote down my ideas on forty-four pages under the title, "Attempt at a metalogic." These shorthand notes were the first version of my book *Logical Syntax of Language*. In the spring of 1931 I changed the form of language usage dealt with in this essay to that of a coordinate language of about the same form as that later called "language I" in my book. Thus arithmetic could be formulated in this language, and by use of Gödel's method, even the metalogic of the language could be arithmetized and formulated in the language itself.[5]

Given the central importance, for Carnap, of Wittgenstein's more general conception of logic and logical syntax, it is crucial for him to reject Wittgenstein's doctrine of the inexpressibility of logical syntax in favor of his own project of developing an explicit formal theory of logical syntax.[6] And it is no wonder, then, that Carnap took Gödel's discoveries to be so important.

Yet Gödel himself, in a contribution written for inclusion in *The Philosophy of Rudolf Carnap* but never published, argues that the incompleteness results are incompatible with Carnap's position in *Logical Syntax*.[7] Gödel argues that, if the choice of logico-mathematical rules is really to be viewed as conventional, then we must have independent assurance that these rules do not have unintended empirical or factual consequences. We must know, that is, that the rules in question are conservative over the purely conventional realm. We therefore need to show that the rules are consistent, and this, by Gödel's second theorem, cannot be done without using a metalanguage whose logico-mathematical rules are themselves even stronger than those whose conservativeness is in question. Hence, we can have no justification for considering mathematics to be purely conventional, for an unintended incursion into the empirical or factual realm cannot be excluded without vicious circularity. Gödel takes this state of affairs to support his own view, in opposition to Carnap's logicism, that there is no in principle distinction between the mathematical and the empirical or factual sciences: both deal with realms of objects given to us by intuition (rational and sensible respectively).

Thomas Ricketts and Warren Goldfarb have recently contributed subtle and perceptive discussions of *Logical Syntax* which seek, among other things, to defend Carnap against Gödel's challenge.[8] They point out, in particular, that Gödel's argument proceeds from the assumption that we are given antecedently a clear notion of the factual or empirical realm. Carnap is then depicted, accordingly, as starting with an unproblematic realm of empirical facts to which the logico-mathematical sentences are to be conventionally or stipulatively added.[9] Ricketts and Goldfarb rightly emphasize that such a language-independent notion of the factual or empirical realm is foreign to Carnap himself. Instead, Carnap holds that the very distinction between the conventional and the factual itself only makes sense relative to, or within, a given formal language: the conventional statements relative to a given formal-logical system are just the sentences that are *analytic* relative to this system; the empirical statements relative to a given formal-logical system are just those sentences that are *synthetic* relative to this system.[10] To be given a formal language is thus to be given at the same time a distinction between analytic and synthetic (conventional and factual) sentences, and there can therefore be no further question of showing that the logico-mathematical or analytic sentences of the language do not turn out, inadvertently as it were, to include factual sentences.[11]

Carnap presents a formal explication of the distinction between analytic and synthetic sentences in §§50–52 of *Logical Syntax*. This explication is carried out within what Carnap calls "general syntax," and it is thus meant to apply to arbitrary formal languages. It is meant to apply, in particular, to languages (such as the language of mathematical physics) which contain both *logical* rules, such as the principles of arithmetic and analysis, and *physical* rules, such as Maxwell's field equations. For such languages the problem is then precisely to distinguish the two types of rules. Carnap proceeds in two steps. First, he defines a distinction between *logical* and *descriptive* expressions. The logical expressions, such as the connectives, quantifiers, and primitive signs of arithmetic, are those expressions such that all sentences built up from these expressions alone are determinate relative to the rules of the language.[12] In contrast, for descriptive expressions such as the electromagnetic field functor, whereas some sentences containing them are determined by the rules of the framework alone (for example, Maxwell's equations themselves), this is not true for all such sentences (for sentences ascribing particular values of the electromagnetic field to particular space-time points, for example). Intuitively, then, to determine the truth-values of the latter sentences we need extralinguistic information—such as, for example, observational information (§50). Given this distinction between logical and descriptive expressions, the distinction between logical and physical rules (and thus analytic and synthetic sentences) follows easily (§51): the logical or analytic sentences are just those consequences of the rules of the formal language that contain only logical expressions essentially and thus remain consequences of the rules for all substitutions of nonlogical or descriptive vocabulary.[13]

In an earlier paper, I attempted to show that a problem closely related to the one raised by Gödel is fatal to this Carnapian explication of the concept of analyticity.[14] My point was that, if Carnap's explication is to have the desired result that classical arithmetic is analytic (relative to a suitable formal language) then the logical rules of the language in question have to include a nonrecursively enumerable (and indeed nonarithmetical) consequence relation; otherwise, all arithmetical sentences are not determinate. But then, just as in Gödel's argument, we must have a metalanguage that is essentially stronger than the object language in question, and Carnap's project again appears threatened by vicious circularity. One might view this argument as an internal version of Gödel's argument. It attempts to show that Carnap's view of mathematics as conventional still founders on the incompleteness results, even when we work throughout with Carnap's explicitly language-relative version of the conventional/factual distinction.

Goldfarb and Ricketts also provide an extensive discussion of the issues raised by this latter argument. They question whether any vicious or otherwise objectionable circularity is involved in Carnap's use of a strong metalanguage here. After all, Carnap himself is perfectly aware of the technical situation, and he explicitly states that the principle of tolerance is to be applied both at the level of the object-language and at the level of the metalanguage (§45), where we are entirely free to use an "indefinite" (nonrecursive) notion of analyticity (compare §34a).[15] Goldfarb and Ricketts further object that my own attempt to explain why the Gödelian situation nonetheless presents a problem for Carnap proceeds by attributing to him a conception of logic that too closely assimilates his view to the foundational conception of Hilbert. In particular, I suggested that Carnap's logicism requires that the metalanguage, the language of logical syntax, should itself embody a purely combinatorial (and thus recursive) notion of analyticity or logical truth, so that Carnap in effect has two distinct notions of analyticity: a relativized, conventional notion for the various object-languages and a privileged, combinatorial (and thus foundational in the sense of Hilbert) notion for logical syntax. Goldfarb and Ricketts argue, first, that there is no evidence at all for such a foundational conception in Carnap's text and, second, that the point of the principle of tolerance is precisely to wean us away from all such foundational concerns. According to Goldfarb and Ricketts, neither Gödel's original objection nor my internal variant takes adequate account of the absolutely central position of this principle in Carnap's philosophy of mathematics.[16]

II

Carnap first explicitly formulates the principle of tolerance in *Logical Syntax*. Yet, as he explains in his intellectual autobiography, it actually represents a characteristic attitude toward philosophical problems that remained constant throughout his career:

Since my student years, I have liked to talk with friends about general problems in science and practical life, and these discussions often led to philosophical questions. . . . Only much later, when I was working on the *Logischer Aufbau*, did I become aware that in talks with my various friends I had used different philosophical languages, adapting myself to their ways of thinking and speaking. With one friend I might talk in a language that could be characterized as realistic or even materialistic; here we looked at the world as consisting of bodies, bodies as consisting of atoms. . . . In a talk with another friend, I might adapt myself to his idealistic kind of language. We would consider the question of how things are to be constituted on the basis of the given. With some I talked a language which might be labeled nominalistic, with others again Frege's language of abstract entities of various types, like properties, relations, propositions, etc., a language which some contemporary authors call Platonic.

I was surprised to find that this variety in my ways of speaking appeared to some to be objectionable and even inconsistent. I had acquired insights valuable for my own thinking from philosophers and scientists of a great variety of philosophical creeds. When asked which philosophical position I myself held, I was unable to answer. I could only say that my general way of thinking was closer to that of physicists and of those philosophers who are in contact with scientific work. Only gradually, in the course of the years, did I recognize clearly that my way of thinking was neutral with respect to the traditional controversies, e.g., realism vs. idealism, nominalism vs. Platonism (realism of universals), materialism vs. spiritualism, and so on.

This neutral attitude toward the various philosophical forms of language, based on the principle that everyone is free to use the language most suited to his purpose, has remained the same throughout my life. It was formulated as [the] "principle of tolerance" in *Logical Syntax* and I still hold it today, e.g., with respect to the contemporary controversy about a nominalist or Platonic language.[17]

Nevertheless, the particular ways in which Carnap attempted to implement this neutral or tolerant attitude varied with the problem situation in which he found himself.

In his very first publication, his doctoral dissertation of 1921–1922, Carnap attempts to resolve the contemporary conflicts in the foundations of geometry involving mathematicians, philosophers, and physicists by carefully distinguishing among three distinct types or "meanings" of space: *formal, intuitive*, and *physical* space. Carnap argues that the different parties involved in the various mathematical, philosophical, and physical disputes are in fact referring to different types of space, and, in this way, there is really no contradiction after all: "All parties were correct and could have easily been reconciled if clarity had prevailed concerning the three different meanings of space" (Carnap 1922, p. 64). Thus, mathematicians who maintain that geometry is purely logical or analytic are correct about formal space; philosophers who maintain that geometry is a synthetic a priori deliverance of pure intuition are correct about intuitive space; and physicists who maintain that geometry is an empirical science are correct about physical space.[18] In this way, in a tour de force of logical, mathematical, physical, and philosophical analysis, Carnap hopes to resolve the contemporary disputes about the foundations of geometry by showing how each of the conflicting parties—when they are limited to their proper domains—has a significant *part* of the truth.

As Carnap suggests above, however, it is in his next major publication, the *Aufbau* of 1928, that his neutral attitude toward alternative "philosophical languages" comes fully into its own. And there are in fact two importantly different aspects to this neutrality. In the first place, although Carnap develops one particular "constitutional system" in the *Aufbau*, the "system form with autopsychological basis," he also indicates the possibility of alternative systems, notably, the "system form with physical basis." Whereas the first logically reconstructs scientific knowledge from an epistemological point of view, by sketching a reduction of all scientific concepts to the given, the second logically reconstructs scientific knowledge from a materialistic or realistic point of view, by defining all scientific concepts (even those of introspective psychology) in terms of the fundamental concepts of physics. Both of these systems, according to Carnap, are equally possible and legitimate. In the second place, however, even within the domain of epistemology proper, Carnap also maintains an attitude of tolerance and neutrality toward the diverging, and apparently incompatible, philosophical epistemological schools:

> [T]he so-called epistemological tendencies of realism, idealism, and phenomenalism agree within the domain of epistemology. Constitutional theory represents the neutral basis [neutrale Fundament] common to all. They first diverge in the domain of metaphysics and thus (if they are to be epistemological tendencies) only as the result of a transgression of their boundaries. [19]

Thus, since all epistemological schools agree that knowledge begins with the experiential given and then proceeds to build up all further objects and structures via a "logical progress," Carnap's autopsychological system (which does just this in a logically precise fashion) represents what is clear and correct in all of them. The schools in question only disagree, therefore, when they indulge in metaphysical questions about which constituted structures are ultimately "real."

The vehicle of Carnap's philosophical neutrality, in the *Aufbau*, is the logic of *Principia Mathematica*. It is this system, understood in accordance with the logicist viewpoint Carnap had first imbibed from Frege, that constitutes the fixed set of logical rules within which the various "philosophical languages" he considers are then formulated. When he became involved in the disputes on the foundations of logic and mathematics in the late 1920s, however, Carnap could no longer persist in this state of happy logical innocence. [20] For he was now faced with a situation in which the background rules of logic were precisely what was at issue. Even worse, logic and mathematics were now embroiled with philosophical questions about mathematical intuition, the "reality" of mathematical objects, and the relation of such objects to the thinking subject—just the kind of questions that logicism had hoped to be done with once and for all. Fruitless and interminable philosophical disputes, which Carnap himself had hoped to avoid through the tolerance and neutrality of the *Aufbau* project, were now threatening the very basis of that project. But how can disputes about the foundations of logic themselves be logically resolved?

Carnap's first idea was to incorporate the apparently conflicting demands of intuitionism and formalism within logicism. Carnap sketches this idea in contributions to two symposia on the foundations of mathematics in 1930.[21] With respect to intuitionism, we drop the purely philosophical doctrine that "arithmetic rests on an original intuition [*Ur-Intuition*]" while retaining only the "*finitist-constructivist* requirement [of] renouncing pure existence proofs without constructive procedures"—we thereby obtain an accommodation with formalism, which also recognizes this constraint in the realm of metamathematics (Carnap 1930a, pp. 308–309.). Logicism, by contrast, has run into problems concerning the need for special existence assumptions expressed in the axioms of infinity, choice, and reducibility. Carnap is happy to adopt Russell's expedient of considering infinity and choice as nonlogical premises or conditions in theorems for which they are needed, and he here focuses his efforts at reconciliation on the axiom of reducibility. Although Ramsey has made an excellent case for rejecting the ramified theory of types in favor of the simple theory, his justification for impredicative definitions embodies an "absolutistic" and "theological" assumption of the existence, prior to any definition or construction, of the totality of all properties—which assumption, however, is clearly incompatible with the "finitist-constructivist requirement."[22] Carnap's own not fully developed countersuggestion is to restrict ourselves to finitely definable properties while still retaining at least the most important impredicative definitions.[23] Finally, the chief remaining difference between logicism and formalism is that logicism develops definitions of the natural numbers via properties or classes, whereas formalism considers them as primitive signs. If, however, we reflect on the need to account also for the application of arithmetic, and thus to construct a formal system in which empirical statements involving numbers are also derivable, then, Carnap suggests, a formal system meeting this desideratum might very well lead us back to the logicist definitions.[24] In this way, Carnap hopes, we may attain "a problem-solution that will appear as satisfactory from [all three] different points of view."[25]

Yet Carnap's idea of articulating a single formal-logical system that would simultaneously fulfill the demands of all three foundational schools was never successfully carried out.[26] Instead, he adopts the fundamentally new standpoint encapsulated in the principle of tolerance in *Logical Syntax*. The way to dissolve the fruitless foundational disputes is not to develop a single logical system simultaneously embracing the demands of all parties. Rather, we should view the choice of underlying logic, too, as simply the choice of one form of language among an infinity of equally possible alternatives. Intuitionism is correct that we can, if we wish, develop a language, Language I, embodying finitist-constructivist restrictions on existential quantification. But logicism is equally correct that we can also, if we wish, develop a much stronger language, Language II, in which the full unrestricted existence claims of classical analysis and set-theory are analytic. Indeed, by employing the device of "coordinate languages" in which numerical expressions appear as the basic individual constants, we can, since such numerical expressions are logical in the sense of §50, even count the axiom of infinity as logical (§38a). Nor is there any need to scruple over the admissibility of impredicative definitions, for there is again only the question of what form of language we *wish* to adopt.[27] Further, and for kindred reasons, the axiom of choice is also a perfectly admissible, though optional, logical principle (§§34h, 38a). Finally, we can easily reconcile the demands of logicism and formalism—not, however, by an argument that a single formal system embracing the application of arithmetic must eventually lead us back to the logicist definitions of the arithmetical terms, but simply by the mere possibility of a single "*total language* that unites the logico-mathematical and the synthetic sentences" (§84).[28]

III

As we noted at the beginning (see note 3 above), Carnap credits Karl Menger's 1930 paper, "Der Intuitionismus," for first representing the standpoint of tolerance within the foundations of mathematics:

> One may assume that the tolerant attitude intended here, applied to special mathematical calculi, comes naturally to most mathematicians without customarily explicitly articulating it. In the conflict over the logical foundations of mathematics it has been represented with particular force (and apparently for the first time) by *Menger* [*Intuitionismus*], pp. 324f. *Menger* points out that the concept of constructivity, which intuitionism absolutizes, can be taken narrowly or widely.—How important it is for the clarification of philosophical pseudo-problems also to apply the attitude of tolerance to the form of the total language will become clear later (cf. §78). (§17)

On reflection, however, this passage helps us rather to articulate what is entirely unique in Carnap's own understanding of the principle of tolerance.

Menger's representation of "tolerance" appears in §10 of his paper, entitled "General Epistemological Remarks" (1930, pp. 323–325 [Menger 1979, pp. 56–58]). Referring to his own earlier work on the set-theoretical meaning of various ideas of Brouwer's, Menger suggests that one might develop constructivity requirements corresponding to the admissibility of stronger and stronger sets—finite sets, denumerable sets, analytic sets, and finally arbitrary sets of real numbers. In this way, one can envision a variety of systems meeting a variety of constructivity requirements (the weakest being mere consistency). There is then no need, as intuitionists customarily do, to attach oneself dogmatically to one particular notion of constructivity: "For in mathematics and logic it does not matter which axioms and principles of inference one *assumes*, but rather what one can *derive* from them or with their help respectively" (Menger 1930, p. 324 [1979, p. 57]). According to this "implicationist" standpoint, we are concerned only with the purely mathematical problem of which consequences follow from which given assumptions. We are interested in the "mathematics" of constructivity, not in the purely "biographical" question of which principles appeal to which actual mathematicians.

Menger's attitude toward the philosophical debate over the foundations of logic and mathematics is therefore one of stark dismissal: let us put all such merely "dogmatic" and "biographical" questions aside once and for all and simply get on with the real mathematical work. In this sense, Menger perfectly represents the attitude of the "ordinary working mathematician" to which Carnap refers. Yet Carnap's own attitude is very different, for he, unlike Menger, is intensely interested in the philosophical foundational debate. Like Menger, to be sure, he wants to do away once and for all with "the dogmatic attitude through which the discussion often becomes unfruitful" (§16). But the whole point of Carnap's principle of tolerance is to articulate a systematic method for resolving or dissolving such philosophical disputes. Carnap's principle, we might say, is crafted for and directed at philosophers: it aims to offer (scientifically minded) philosophers a way out of their impasses and perplexities. From a purely mathematical point of view, of course, Carnap's constructions are of very limited interest. In this sense, Carnap's principle is not a call, like Menger's, for mathematicians to leave behind philosophy.[29]

Carnap's reference to §78 signals precisely this difference between his own attitude and Menger's, for in this section of *Logical Syntax* Carnap puts forward nothing less than a general characterization of the peculiar type of confusion arising in philosophy: "That in philosophical debates, even in those that are free of metaphysics, unclarities occur so frequently, and that in philosophical discussions there is so much talk at cross purposes, is due for the most part to the use of the material mode of speech instead of the formal [mode]" (§78).[30] We are misled, in the first place, to think we are debating about "extra-linguistic objects, such as numbers, things, properties, experiences, states of affairs, space, time, etc." instead of about "language structures and their interconnections . . . such as numerical expressions, thing-designations, spatial coordinates, etc." We are thereby misled, in the second place, to ignore the *relativity to language* that is a central feature of the formal or syntactic concepts. We thus ignore the all-important point that properly formal or syntactic claims must first specify the language in question: they can apply to all languages, some languages, one given language, or (perhaps most interestingly) they can serve as *proposals* to formulate the total language of science (or some part thereof) in one or another particular fashion.

Carnap immediately applies these ideas to a debate in the foundations of mathematics, namely, the debate between logicism and formalism. If the logicist asserts, in the material mode, that "numbers are classes of classes of things," and the formalist asserts, also in the material mode, that "numbers belong to a peculiar, original type of objects," we are hopelessly stuck: "Then between the two an endless and fruitless discussion can be carried out over who is correct and what the numbers really are. The unclarity vanishes if the formal mode of speech is applied." Accordingly, we translate the above two sentences into "the numerical expressions are class expressions of the second level" and "the numerical expressions are expressions of the zeroth level," respectively. It now becomes clear that we are talking about two different languages, and, since both languages are perfectly possible, "the dispute vanishes." The only remaining possibility is that "the discussants understand one another as intending their theses as suggestions [for the language of science]. In this case one cannot debate about the truth and false-hood of the theses, but only whether this or that form of speech is simpler or more suitable for such and such purposes." In this way, we offer our (scientifically minded, nonmetaphysical) philosophical friends a way of transforming their fruit-less dispute into a fruitful one. They are not really debating about the "true na-ture" of mathematical objects but merely proposing different language forms, each having various advantages and disadvantages, for the total language of science.

It cannot be stressed too much, I think, that this diagnosis and transformation of philosophical problems constitutes the main point of both the principle of tol-erance and the method of logical syntax more generally. Thus, in his intellectual autobiography Carnap states that "the investigation of philosophical problems was originally the main reason for the development of syntax," and he expands on this statement as follows:

> [I]t seemed to me important to show that many philosophical controversies actually concern the question whether a particular language form should be used, say, for the language of mathematics or of science. For example, in the controversy about the foundations of mathematics, the conception of intuitionism may be construed as a proposal to restrict the means of expres-sion and the means of deduction of the language of mathematics in a cer-tain way, while the classical conception leaves the language unrestricted. I intended to make available in syntax the conceptual means for an exact for-mulation of controversies of this kind. Furthermore, I wished to show that everyone is free to choose the rules of his language and thereby his logic in any way he wishes. This I called the "principle of tolerance"; it might per-haps be called more exactly the "principle of the conventionality of language forms." As a consequence, the discussion of controversies of the kind men-tioned need only concern, first, the syntactical properties of the various forms of language and, second, practical reasons for preferring one or the other form for given purposes. In this way, assertions that a particular language is the correct language or represents the correct logic such as often occurred in earlier discussions, are eliminated, and traditional ontological problems, in contradistinction to the logical or syntactical ones, for example, problems about "the essence of number," are entirely abolished. (Carnap 1963a, pp. 54–55)

Carnap is perfectly serious about this: traditional philosophy should be replaced by the new and logically exact enterprise of "language planning."[31] Only so can we achieve an exact diagnosis of the true character of traditional philosophical problems and, at the same time, find a new (albeit still characteristic) task for the philosophy of the future.[32]

Carnap thus adopts a deflationary stance toward traditional philosophy, but it is nonetheless a characteristically philosophical form of deflationism. Carnap does not simply leave philosophy behind in favor of the standpoint of the "working scientist." Rather, he systematically articulates a radically new vision of the philosophical enterprise, in which, in particular, philosophy is to retain its special, nonempirical status:

> Metaphysical philosophy claims to go beyond the empirical-scientific questions of a scientific domain and pose questions about the essence of the objects of the domain. The non-metaphysical logic of science also takes up a different standpoint than that of empirical science—not, however, by means of a metaphysical transcendence, but rather by the circumstance that it makes the linguistic forms themselves the objects of a new investigation. (§86)

In this way, we obtain a radically new conception of philosophical problems and, in particular, of the true character of the philosophical debate in the foundations of logic and mathematics. It is this transformation and reformulation of the philosophical debate with which Carnap (in sharp contrast to a "working scientist" like Menger) is most concerned.[33]

IV

This transformation and reformulation of traditional philosophy involves Carnap himself in a philosophical task. How do we precisely characterize the distinction between questions that do concern the "true natures" of objects (questions investigated in natural science and mathematics) and those that merely concern forms of language (questions for philosophy)? How do we show our (scientifically minded, nonmetaphysical) philosophical friends that their problems are actually of the second kind? In §§76–77 of *Logical Syntax* the distinction is drawn with the help of the concept of *universal words* (*Allwörter*). Formally or syntactically considered, a universal word is a predicate of a language such that every predication thereof is logically or analytically true in that language. Thus "number" is a universal word in the language of arithmetic whereas "prime number" is not, and "being a space-time point" is a universal word in the language of mathematical physics (§40) whereas "being a space-time point characterized by such-and-such value of mass-density" (or charge-density, or electromagnetic field, and so on) is not. From a formal or syntactic point of view, universal words are entirely dispensable, for they can always be replaced by distinctive types of variables. In philosophical discussions, however, we characteristically find universal words used in the material mode of speech: "The investigation of universal words is especially important for the analysis of philosophical sentences. They occur very frequently in such sentences, both in metaphysics and in the logic of science, and mostly in the material mode of speech" (§76). It is this that misleads us into asking questions about the "reality" or "true nature" of numbers or the "reality" or "true nature" of space-time points. The syntactic transformation in the formal mode, by contrast, makes it clear that we are really posing questions about the form of language and, in particular, about what types of variables are to occur at various levels.[34]

Here we have the germ of Carnap's celebrated later distinction between *internal questions*, which are rationally answerable on the basis of the rules of a given language or linguistic framework, and *external questions*, which rather concern the prior choice of one or another such framework as the language for the investigation in question.[35] External questions are therefore noncognitive or nontheoretical, and concern only the purely practical problem of which framework is adapted or expedient for one or another given purpose. Questions of "reality" or existence thus make theoretical sense within a given framework as internal questions—"Is there a prime number greater than a hundred?" "Are there space-time points having such-and-such values of mass-density?" But they have no such sense taken as external questions—"Are there really numbers?" "Are there really space-time points?"[36] In "Empiricism, Semantics, and Ontology" (1950a), Carnap applies these notions, once again, to the philosophical problem of the foundations of mathematics:

> [P]hilosophers who treat the question of the existence of numbers as a serious philosophical problem . . . might try to explain what they mean by saying that it is a question of the ontological status of numbers; the question whether or not numbers have a certain metaphysical characteristic called reality (but a kind of ideal reality, different from the material reality of the thing world) or subsistence or status of "independent entities." Unfortunately, these philosophers have so far not given a formulation in terms of the common scientific language. Therefore our judgement must be that they have not succeeded in giving to the external question and to the possible answers any cognitive content. Unless and until they supply a clear cognitive interpretation, we are justified in our suspicion that their question is a pseudo-question, that is, one disguised in the form of a theoretical question while in fact it is non-theoretical; in the present case it is the practical problem whether or not to incorporate into the language the new linguistic forms which constitute the framework of numbers. (Carnap 1950a, §2, p. 209)

The kinship with the program of *Logical Syntax* should be evident.[37]

In the philosophical debate in the foundations of mathematics, questions about the existence of numbers (and higher set-theoretical objects) arose in connection with the need for strong existential axioms (such as infinity, choice, and reducibility) in the wake of the discovery of the paradoxes. Carnap's remarks on "Existence Assumptions in Logic" in §38a of *Logical Syntax* are therefore of particular interest. In the case of the axiom of infinity, for example, which is demonstrable in both Language I and Language II, Carnap holds that we are here concerned only with the choice of a so-called coordinate language, in which numerical expressions are of zeroth type. In such languages, numerical expressions are logical rather than descriptive in the sense of §50, and the axiom of infinity therefore counts as an analytic truth. For precisely this reason, there can be no genuine ontological issue here:

> The [sentences containing only logical expressions] (and with them all sentences of mathematics) are, from the point of view of material interpretation, expedients for the purpose of operating with the [sentences containing

descriptive expressions]. Thus, in laying down [a sentence containing only logical expressions] as a primitive sentence, only usefulness for this purpose is to be taken into consideration. (§38a)[38]

There can be no genuine theoretical question whether a primitive mathematical existence assertion is acceptable or not *precisely because* such sentences contain only logical expressions. If we add such a sentence to our language we obtain merely a new analytic truth, and whether a language with this or that primitive analytic truth is acceptable or not can only be a purely pragmatic question.[39] In this sense, "existence assumptions in logic" must, in Carnap's later terminology, count as external questions.

The situation is quite otherwise in the empirical sciences. In the language of mathematical physics (§82), for example, we postulate both logical rules (L-rules) and physical rules (P-rules), where the latter consist customarily of "certain most general laws" called *"fundamental laws [Grundgesetze]"* and their logical consequences (p. 316 [244]). Maxwell's equations for the electromagnetic field are paradigmatic of such "P-fundamental sentences" (p. 319 [247]). Just as in the case of "existence assumptions in logic," then, there is a question whether or not to add such primitive sentences to the rules of our language. Here, however, we are *not* faced with a purely pragmatic, external question. For such a P-fundamental sentence, like any other sentence containing descriptive expressions essentially, can and must be empirically tested:

> A sentence of physics, whether it is a P-fundamental sentence or an otherwise valid sentence or an indeterminate assumption (i.e., a premise whose consequences are investigated), is *tested*, in that consequences are deduced from it on the basis of the transformation rules of the language until one finally arrives at propositions of the form of protocol-sentences. These are compared with the protocol-sentences actually accepted and either confirmed or disconfirmed by them. If a sentence that is an L-consequence of certain P-fundamental sentences contradicts a proposition accepted as a protocol-sentence, then some alteration must be undertaken in the system. (P. 317 [245])

To be sure, what precise change we then make is not itself determined by rules, and faced with such a situation, we might even make a change in the L-rules. Nevertheless, there remains an essential distinction:

> If we assume that a newly appearing protocol-sentence within the language is always synthetic, then there is nonetheless the following difference between an L-valid and thus analytic sentence S_1 and a P-valid sentence S_2, namely, that such a new protocol-sentence—whether or not it is acknowledged as valid—can be at most L-incompatible with S_2 but never with S_1. (Pp. 318–319 [246])[40]

In this sense, "[t]he laws have the character of *hypotheses* relative to the protocol-sentences" (p. 318 [245]), and such hypotheses, despite their postulational character as primitive rules of the language of mathematical physics, "are to be tested by empirical material, i.e., by the actually present and ever newly added protocol-sentences" (p. 320 [248]). Therefore, the conventional element in the adoption of P-fundamental sentences is strictly limited. It does not derive, as in the case of L-rules, from the utter logical irrelevance of empirical material, but rather from the circumstance of empirical underdetermination.[41]

It follows that the question of adopting a given P-fundamental sentence—despite the fact that such a sentence, like the fundamental logico-mathematical sentences, is definitive of the rules of the language—is not, in Carnap's later terminology, a purely external question. The answers to internal questions, Carnap says, "may be found either by purely logical methods or by empirical methods," and, in the later case, "[r]esults of observation are evaluated according to certain rules as confirming or disconfirming evidence for possible answers" (Carnap 1950a, §[0–9], pp. 206–207). Such "rules of evaluation" may, as in *Logical Syntax*, consist merely in the hypothetico-deductive method. In this case, the relevant rules are clearly analytic. Or, as in *Logical Foundations of Probability*, we might incorporate a confirmation function into our language. Here, again, however, our "rules of evaluation" are still analytic.[42] In all cases, then, the rules definitive of internal questions are logical or analytic rules: it is precisely the possibility of coming to a decision on the basis of such rules that makes a question more than purely pragmatic.[43] Hence, what is crucial, for Carnap, is not the bare idea of a formal language or linguistic framework as such. After all, any scientific decision whatsoever, even whether or not to accept a given empirical theory, can be represented as the choice of a particular formal language. What is crucial is the distinction, *within* any formal language or linguistic framework, between analytic and synthetic sentences. It is because analytic sentences (and therefore L-rules) are true solely in virtue of meaning whereas synthetic sentences (and therefore P-rules) must also respect the empirical facts that changes in the former, but not the latter, are purely pragmatic.[44]

V

Following out the implications of Carnap's own understanding of the principle of tolerance has led us back to the absolutely central position of the analytic/synthetic distinction in his philosophy. Carnap's tolerance is not simply that of the "working scientist," who urges us to leave philosophical problems behind once and for all in order to return to the real scientific work. It is rather directed precisely at those caught in serious philosophical perplexities, and it aims to offer such people (provided, of course, that they are inclined toward scientific rather than metaphysical philosophizing) a way of transforming their hitherto fruitless disputes into fruitful ones. We are invited, in particular, to recognize the true character of philosophical problems as questions about the logico-linguistic form in which the total language of science is to be cast. They are not genuine theoretical questions, such as are treated in the mathematical and natural sciences themselves, but purely pragmatic external questions governed by canons of expedi-

ence rather than truth. And, as we have seen, what shows us that such external
questions really are purely pragmatic is precisely the circumstance that they
concern, in the end, only the question of which primitive *analytic* sentences to
adopt. It is for *this* reason that such questions involve us with no "matters of fact."

Thus, in the case of philosophical problems in the foundations of mathematics, their true character is revealed when we recognize mathematical sentences
as mere formal auxiliaries within the total language of science:

> The application of synthetic and analytic sentences in science is as follows.
> Factual science lays down synthetic sentences, e.g., singular sentences for
> the description of observed facts or general sentences that are laid down as
> hypotheses and are applied experimentally. From the sentences thus laid
> down the scientist now tries to derive other synthetic sentences, e.g., to make
> predictions about the future. The analytic sentences serve as auxiliaries for
> these inferential operations. Considered from the point of view of the total
> language, the whole of logic, including mathematics, is nothing else but an
> auxiliary calculus for handling synthetic sentences. *Formal science* has no
> independent meaning. It is rather introduced into the language as an auxil-
> iary component on technical grounds, so as to make the linguistic transfor-
> mations required for *factual science* technically easier. The great importance
> pertaining to formal science, and thus to logic and mathematics, in the total
> system of science is thereby in no way denied but rather precisely empha-
> sized, through a characterization of the particular function [of this science].
> (1935a, p. 35 [1953, p. 127])[45]

And it is precisely in virtue of this "particular function" of logic and mathematics as mere deductive auxiliaries that we can apply the principle of tolerance here:

> [I]f we regard interpreted mathematics as an instrument of deduction within
> the field of empirical knowledge rather than as a system of information, then
> many of the controversial problems are recognized as being questions not of
> truth but of technical expedience. The question is: which form of the mathe-
> matical system is technically most suitable for the purpose mentioned? Which
> one provides the greatest safety? If we compare, e.g., the systems of classical
> mathematics and of intuitionistic mathematics, we find that the first is much
> simpler and technically more efficient, while the second is more safe from
> surprising occurrences, e.g., contradictions. (Carnap 1939, §20)

Without clear and precise distinctions, within the total language of science, between logical and descriptive expressions, logical and physical rules, analytic and
synthetic sentences, we could not use the principle of tolerance to dissolve the
philosophical disputes in question.[46] So it is no wonder, then, that Carnap continually reiterates the importance of these distinctions.[47]

With this account of the connection between the principle of tolerance and the
analytic/synthetic distinction in mind, let us go to Carnap's logicism and, in particular, to his conception of his debt to Frege:

[T]he following conception, which derives essentially from Frege, seemed to me of paramount importance: it is the task of logic and mathematics within the total system of knowledge to supply the forms of concepts, statements, and inferences, forms which are then applicable everywhere, hence also to non-logical knowledge. It follows from these considerations that the nature of logic and mathematics can be clearly understood only if close attention is given to their application in non-logical fields, especially in empirical science. Although the greater part of my work belongs to the fields of pure logic and the logical foundations of mathematics, nevertheless great weight is given in my thinking to the application of logic to non-logical knowledge. This point of view is an important factor in the motivation of some of my philosophical positions, for example, for the choice of forms of languages, for my emphasis on the fundamental distinction between logical and non-logical knowledge. (1963a, pp. 12–13)

As Carnap explains, this Fregean view that "knowledge in mathematics is analytic in the general sense that it has essentially the same nature as knowledge in logic" later "became more radical and precise, chiefly through the influence of Wittgenstein" (1963a, p. 12). For it was Wittgenstein, according to Carnap, who first taught him that logic (and therefore mathematics) is entirely independent of all "matters of fact":

The most important insight I gained from [Wittgenstein's] work was the conception that the truth of logical statements is based only on their logical structure and on the meaning of the terms. Logical statements are true under all conceivable circumstances; thus their truth is independent of the contingent facts of the world. On the other hand, it follows that these statements do not say anything about the world and thus have no factual content. (1963a, p. 25)

Wittgenstein's doctrine of tautology is thus the fulfillment, for Carnap, of Frege's logicism.[48] And logicism so understood is an integral part of Carnap's own understanding of the principle of tolerance.[49]

Wittgenstein's doctrine of tautology rests on a sharp distinction between the logical constants and all other meaningful signs. Tautologies remain true for all combinations of existence and nonexistence of states of affairs. That the logical signs themselves are held constant in this process of evaluation does not, however, limit the resulting independence of logic from the totality of facts constituting the world. For the logical constants, unlike all other primitive signs, are not representative of objects according to Wittgenstein:

The possibility of the proposition rests on the principle of the representation of objects by means of signs.

My fundamental thought is that the "logical constants" are not representative. That the *logic* of the facts can not be represented. (Wittgenstein 1922, 4.0312)

The logical constants obtain this uniquely privileged status in virtue of the circumstance that all meaningful propositions, for Wittgenstein, are the results of truth-operations on elementary propositions. All meaningful propositions arise by iteratively applying the operations of truth functional composition and quantification to a given initial collection of propositions that are themselves logically simple and thus contain no logical constants. In this sense, the logical constants "vanish," since they merely afford us a means for expressing the combinatorial compositional structure necessary for any system of linguistic representation as such.[50]

Thus for Wittgenstein, there is a single privileged set of logical constants common to all possible systems of linguistic representation: the classical truth functional connectives and quantifiers. Classical truth functional and quantificational logic is the only conceivable possibility for expressing the "*logic* of the facts." By contrast, "[Wittgenstein's] absolutistic conception of language, in which the conventional element in the construction of a language is overlooked," is precisely what Carnap's own explanation of the logical constants and the resulting notion of logical or analytic truth aims to avoid (§52). In particular, in accordance with his principle of tolerance, Carnap wants to allow both underlying logics differing from classical logic and, in the case of classical mathematics itself, an expansion of the logical constants to include the identity sign, the numerals taken as primitive signs, and the full higher-order apparatus of classical analysis and set-theory. For both of these reasons, Wittgenstein's minimalist, purely combinatorial conception of the logical constants is clearly inadequate. How, then, can Carnap continue to profess allegiance to the Wittgensteinian doctrine of tautology? How can he continue to maintain that the meanings of the logical constants—now explicitly *relativized* to the choice of one or another formal language or linguistic framework—are entirely independent of all "matters of fact"?

Section 50 of *Logical Syntax* contains Carnap's answer to these questions. For Carnap here presents, in general syntax, a characterization of the distinction between logical and descriptive expressions that is to hold for any possible formal language or linguistic framework and is intended to represent formally the idea that the logical expressions, relative to any given framework, are entirely independent of all extralinguistic factors:

> If a material interpretation is given for the language L, then one can divide the signs, expressions, and sentences of L into logical and descriptive, namely, into those with purely logico-mathematical meaning and those that signify something extra-logical, e.g., empirical objects or properties or the like. This classification is not only unsharp, but it is also non-formal, and thus not usable in syntax. If, however, we reflect that all interconnections of logico-mathematical concepts are independent of extra-linguistic determinations, e.g., empirical observations, and must be already completely fixed solely by the transformation rules of the language, we then find that the formally comprehensible distinguishing peculiarity of the logical signs and expressions is the circumstance that every sentence constructed from them alone is determinate.

The transformation rules of a language include, in general, both logical and physical rules, so not every sentence determined by the transformation rules is an analytic sentence. But the logico-mathematical expressions (in contradistinction to descriptive expressions like the electromagnetic field functor, for example) are such that *everything* about their use is already predetermined by the transformation rules (whereas some particular sentences containing the electromagnetic field functor, for example, are not determined by the transformation rules even in the presence of Maxwell's equations). And it is in this precise and formal sense that the logical expressions are independent of all extralinguistic factors or "matters of fact."

Carnap's formal characterization of the logical signs thereby transforms and replaces both the vague and intuitive conception of expressions that fail to "signify something extra-logical" and Wittgenstein's minimalist and "absolutistic" purely combinatorial conception. It allows us, in a precise and formal way, to harmonize the relativity to language encapsulated in Carnap's principle of tolerance with Wittgenstein's insight into the utter independence of logic from all "contingent facts of the world."[51] And, at the same time, it gives precise and formal expression to the fundamental idea that the truths of logic and mathematics are true solely in virtue of the meanings of the terms they contain. Analytic sentences, in contrast to synthetic sentences, contain only logical expressions essentially (§51), so their truth can be due only to the latter. But, in the case of logical expressions, everything about their use is already predetermined by the transformation rules and is in this sense purely linguistic. So here we have the best possible case of truth in virtue of meaning alone.[52] Finally, by transforming and replacing the intuitive, pretheoretical distinction between those expressions that signify empirical objects and properties and those that do not, Carnap's formal characterization makes it clear that he is not caught in the predicament depicted by Gödel discussed in section I above. Carnap does not take for granted a realm of empirical facts somehow intuitively given, but rather formally characterizes— relative to one or another formal language or linguistic framework—the very distinction between the formal and the factual itself.[53]

VI

From this point of view, Carnap's formal characterization of the distinction between logical and descriptive expressions in §50 of *Logical Syntax* bears considerable philosophical weight. Although Carnap has indeed given up the traditional logicist project of reducing classical mathematics to logic in some antecedently understood sense, he nonetheless maintains that classical mathematics consists only of analytic truths and is thus entirely independent of the facts of the actual world. Moreover, it is logicism in precisely this sense that then allows him to apply the principle of tolerance to the choice of logico-mathematical rules (whether classical or otherwise), which choice is now seen as concerning only the "linguistic form" of our total scientific system rather than its content. And, in particular, the choice of logico-mathematical rules (including the strong existential assumptions of classical arithmetic, analysis, and set-theory) is now seen to have no ontological implications whatsoever.[54] Nor need Carnap accept Gödel's demand for a (nontrivial) consistency proof for the logico-mathematical rules in order to show that they do not lead to unintended empirical consequences. Since Carnap's own version of empiricism is simply the requirement that synthetic sentences essentially containing descriptive expressions should be testable via the deduction of further synthetic sentences (protocol-sentences), logico-mathematical rules themselves—which, by definition, contain no descriptive expressions—cannot possibly have empirical consequences (see note 10 above). And security against inconsistency, according to the principle of tolerance, is simply one more pragmatic virtue among others.[55]

Yet Carnap's formal characterization of the distinction between logical and descriptive expressions also poses serious problems for his principle of tolerance. That principle bids us to view the dispute in the foundations of logic and mathematics between logicism, formalism, and intuitionism as a purely pragmatic question of which logico-mathematical rules we wish to adopt as the "linguistic form" of our total system of science. It appears, then, that in order properly to address this reformulation of the dispute we should first step back from the decision itself so as impartially to investigate the formal consequences of each and every option:

> It is important to be aware of the conventional components in the construction of a language system. This view leads to an unprejudiced investigation of the various forms of new logical systems which differ more or less from the customary form (e.g., the intuitionistic logic constructed by Brouwer and Heyting, the systems of logic of modalities constructed by Lewis and others, the systems of plurivalued logic as constructed by Lukasiewicz and Tarski, etc.), and it encourages the construction of further new forms. The task is not to decide which of the different systems is "the right logic" but to examine their formal properties and the possibilities for their interpretation and application in science. It might be that a system deviating from the ordinary form will turn out to be useful as a basis for the language of science. (Carnap 1939, §12)

Hence, on a very natural understanding of the principle of tolerance, before we make any substantial decision about the logico-mathematical form of the language of science, we are to engage in a prior investigation, from a neutral and impartial vantage point, of the syntactic consequences of each and every "linguistic form" under consideration.[56]

As we pointed out in section I above, however, a variant of Gödel's objection shows that Carnap's own metatheoretical standpoint cannot be neutral and impartial in this sense. Carnap's characterization of the distinction between logical and descriptive expressions requires, in the case of classical mathematics, that the consequence relation expressed in the transformation rules for the language of mathematical physics be nonrecursively enumerable (and indeed nonarithmetical). In giving a metatheoretical description of this language, we therefore need a metalanguage even stronger than the language of classical mathematics itself (containing, in effect, classical mathematics plus a truth-definition for classical mathematics). And we need this strong metalanguage, not to prove the consistency of the classical linguistic framework in question, but simply to describe and define this framework in the first place so that questions about the consequences of adopting it (including the question of consistency) can then be systematically investigated. In order even to begin to investigate this framework in logical syntax, we can in no way step back from the decision whether or not to adopt such a strong set of logico-mathematical rules. On the contrary, the only way in which we can describe this framework, in Carnap's terms, is to step up into an even stronger set of logico-mathematical rules where the decision under consideration has itself already been made.

We also pointed out above that Carnap is perfectly clear about the technical situation, and he shows no qualms whatsoever about the use of such a strong metalanguage (compare note 14 above). Indeed, it might now seem, as Carnap explicitly states in §45, that the principle of tolerance should apply, in turn, to the choice of metalanguage as well, so that no conflict with this principle could possibly arise here.[57] But, from our present point of view, the situation is not so simple. Consider, for example, the choice between classical logico-mathematical rules for the total language of science and the much weaker logico-mathematical rules endorsed by the intuitionist. In order to apply the principle of tolerance, we must view this choice as a purely pragmatic decision about "linguistic forms" having no ontological implications about "facts" or "objects" in the world. It is a matter of simply weighing one purely pragmatic virtue, ease of application, against a conflicting purely pragmatic value, safety against contradiction. Accordingly, we must view the logico-mathematical rules in question, in both linguistic frameworks, as sets of purely analytic sentences. Given Carnap's own explication of the distinctions between logical and descriptive terms, analytic and synthetic sentences, however, we must have already adopted the classical logico-mathematical rules in the metalanguage. Thus, to understand the choice between classical and intuitionistic logico-mathematical rules in accordance with the principle of tolerance, we must have already built the former logico-mathematical rules into our background syntactic metaframework. We must have already biased the choice against the intuitionist in the very way in which we have set up the problem. The principle of tolerance, on Carnap's own understanding of it, appears to undermine itself.[58]

In particular, the principle of tolerance by no means yields an initial situation of equal opportunity, where we are then free to adopt any of the positions in question in light of how they fare with respect to one or another set of purely pragmatic virtues. On the contrary, in the case of the philosophical debate in the foundations of mathematics that the principle was originally intended to dissolve, the very decision at issue has itself been already prejudged.[59] By contrast, the logicist side of Carnap's position appears to be completely self-consistent—and even, in a way, self-supporting. According to Carnap's logicism, we are urged, despite the possibility of contradiction, to adopt the full strength of the classical logico-mathematical rules. And we are told, in addition, that these rules are purely

analytic truths which thus function as mere "formal auxiliaries" having no ontological import for the "objects" and "facts" in the world. Then, by adopting the
classical logico-mathematical rules in the metalanguage as well, we can employ
Carnap's formal characterization of the distinctions between logical and descriptive expressions, analytic and synthetic sentences, to cash out—and indeed to
prove—these philosophical claims via translations into the formal mode in logical syntax. If we are willing to adopt classical mathematics as the background
logic of our metaframework, we can prove, at least to ourselves, that this particular choice of logic is indeed analytic.[60]

Yet a Carnapian proponent of classical mathematics can also prove to himself—
by precisely the argument sketched above—that his logicism stands in conflict
with his tolerance. He can show that the mere idea that classical mathematics is
analytic itself rules the intuitionist out of court. By contrast, the choice of a restricted metalanguage equally acceptable to all parties to the dispute is much
better suited to Carnap's profession of tolerance. In such a metalanguage, we can
still show that classical logico-mathematical rules (now described by a recursive
proof relation rather than a non-recursively enumerable consequence relation)
are much stronger than the intuitionistic rules, so that, for example, the mean
value theorem is easily provable in the former framework but not the latter. We
can see, even in this restricted metaframework, that the classical rules are much
more expedient for physical applications, while the intuitionistic rules provide far
more safety against contradiction. Hence, in accordance with the spirit of the
principle of tolerance, we can view the choice between the two frameworks as a
fundamentally pragmatic one. The only step we cannot take is to adopt Carnap's
characteristic philosophical concept of analyticity so as to find translations in the
formal mode of the philosophical claims constituting Carnap's logicism. We cannot set up a sharp contrast between *merely* pragmatic questions of "linguistic
form" having no ontological import, on the one side, and genuine theoretical
claims, on the other.[61] It is in this precise sense that the spirit of the principle of
tolerance stands in conflict with Carnap's logicism—and therefore, as we have
seen, with the letter of that principle.[62]

VII

How damaging is this situation to Carnap's philosophical position? My own view
is that it reveals a fundamental tension between his logicism and his tolerance
which, in particular, renders his attempted dissolution of the philosophical debate in the foundations of logic and mathematics otiose. Yet Carnap himself never
explicitly considers this problem. After accepting Tarski's theory of truth and
adding the methods of formal semantics to logical syntax, Carnap officially repudiates the characterization of the distinctions between logical and descriptive
expressions, analytic and synthetic sentences, offered in §§50–52 of *Logical Syntax*.[63] On this basis, he also frankly acknowledges that, although he can still make
the relevant distinctions for particular individual formal languages in "special
semantics," he no longer has an overarching characterization in "general seman-

tics." Accordingly, "[t]he problem of the nature of logical deduction and logical truth . . . can still not be regarded as completely solved."[64] Nevertheless, Carnap sees no *fundamental* problem here, and he remains hopeful, throughout his career, that the desired explication can and will be found.[65] Certainly, Carnap never sees any tension at all between the principle of tolerance and the analytic/synthetic distinction.[66]

As we have seen, Carnap aims to offer scientifically minded philosophers a systematic escape from their philosophical perplexities. We can systematically transform obscure and fruitless ontological disputes about the "reality" or "true nature" of some contested class of entities (such as numbers and other mathematical objects) into precise and fruitful disputes about the logico-linguistic form in which the total language of science is to be cast. We are invited to recognize, in particular, that there is, after all, no genuine ontological import—no implications as to the "objects" and "facts" in the world—in the philosophical questions with which we have hitherto been struggling in vain. For, when we attain Carnapian philosophical self-consciousness, we see that we have actually been concerned with the much more fruitful—albeit purely pragmatic—question of language planning. In this way, Carnap's attempt to transform traditional philosophy into the new enterprise of language planning is intended to bring peace and progress to the discipline, much as his work on "the construction of an auxiliary language for international communication" was intended to contribute toward peace and progress for humankind in general.[67] It cannot be stressed too much, I believe, that Carnap himself was extraordinarily, and equally, serious about both of these ambitions.

In the end, what is perhaps most discouraging to Carnap's philosophical ambitions is that his invitation to scientifically minded philosophers to transform their understanding of the discipline in this way has been almost universally ignored. A large number of philosophers, to be sure, have enthusiastically embraced the use of formal-logical methods, many of which were first pioneered by Carnap himself. Yet such philosophers, on the whole, have not simultaneously embraced Carnap's particular conception of the wider philosophical significance of these formal-logical methods. They have not come to conceive their enterprise as a purely pragmatic exercise in language planning having no theoretical or ontological implications whatsoever. Indeed, the three scientifically minded philosophers who worked most closely with Carnap during the formulation and elaboration of his *Logical Syntax* project—Gödel, Tarski, and Quine—all came explicitly to oppose Carnap's philosophical position. All three appeared to take considerations very close to those on which we have been focussing to constitute formidable, if not fatal, obstacles to Carnap's philosophical project. Gödel, as we have seen in section I above, took problems associated with the need for a strong metalanguage in the light of his incompleteness results to pose a conclusive refutation of Carnap's philosophy of mathematics. Tarski opposed a sharp distinction between logical and descriptive expressions, and, on this basis, he publicly joined with Quine in rejecting the analytic/synthetic distinction.[68] And Quine, by far the most important philosopher among Carnap's students, appealed to the technical problems surrounding §§ 50–52 of *Logical Syntax* that we have explored here in carrying out a full-scale attack on all of the most fundamental notions of Carnap's philosophical framework, an attack which led to the widespread promulgation of a naturalistic form of pragmatism wherein Carnap's most cherished Fregean distinction—that between logical and psychological investigations—eventually fell by the wayside as well.[69] Carnap's invitation to transform radically the philosophical enterprise, an invitation deeply based, as we have seen, on a radically new conception of the debate in the philosophical foundations of logic and mathematics, could not have produced a more disappointing result.

NOTES

An earlier version of this paper was presented at a workshop on Carnap's philosophy in Flagstaff, Arizona, in October 1996. I am indebted to the other participants, Richard Creath, Warren Goldfarb, Alan Richardson, and Thomas Ricketts, for very valuable comments and criticisms. And I am particularly indebted to Goldfarb and Ricketts for discussions of these issues throughout the years. Finally, I would like to acknowledge a substantial debt to Burton Dreben for stimulating and encouraging my interest in the philosophical history of logical positivism.

1. Rudolf Carnap, *Logische Syntax der Sprache* (Vienna: Springer, 1934) (hereafter Carnap 1934a)—trans. A. Smeaton *The Logical Syntax of Language* (London: Kegan Paul, 1937) (hereafter Carnap 1937). I cite this work in the text parenthetically via section numbers (and, in some cases, by page numbers of the English translation, followed in square brackets by those of the German original). As Carnap explains in his Preface, the 1937 English version contains some important sections that were written for the original but not included because of lack of space; these sections appear in the translation with lowercase letters appended to the original numbering. Translations from Carnap's German are my own.

2. See Carnap's "Intellectual Autobiography," in P. A. Schilpp, ed., *The Philosophy of Rudolf Carnap* (La Salle, Ill.: Open Court, 1963), hereafter Schilpp (1963), pp. 3–86, "Intellectual Autobiography" is hereafter (Carnap 1963a), p. 49: "[T]he constructivist and finitist tendencies of Brouwer's thinking appealed to us [viz. the Vienna Circle] greatly. . . . I had a strong inclination toward a constructivist conception." Here Carnap is referring to the period surrounding Brouwer's famous lecture to the Circle on intuitionism (which apparently also greatly influenced Wittgenstein) in March 1928. For discussion, see L. Golland, B. McGuinness, and A. Sklar, eds., *Reminiscences of the Vienna Circle and the Mathematical Colloquium* (Dordrecht: Kluwer, 1994) (hereafter Menger 1994), pp. 130–139. Menger, as Carnap notes in the same passage, had in turn studied with Brouwer in Amsterdam in 1925–1926.

3. See Carnap (1963a), pp. 55–56: "Originally, in agreement with the finitist ideas with which we sympathized in the Circle, I had the intention of constructing only language I. But later, guided by my own principle of tolerance, it seemed desirable to me to develop also the language form II as a model of classical mathematics. It appeared more fruitful to develop both languages than to declare the first language to be the only correct one or to enter into a controversy about which of the two languages is preferable." As Carnap notes in *Logical Syntax* (§17), he was here influenced especially by Karl Menger, "Der Intuitionismus," *Blätter für deutsche Philosophie* 4 (1930): 311–325 (hereafter Menger 1930)—translated as "On Intuitionism," in Menger's *Selected Papers in Logic and Foundations, Didactics, and Economics* (Dordrecht: Reidel, 1979) (hereafter Menger 1979). See my section III below.

4. See Carnap (1963a), p. 49: "It is true that certain procedures, e.g., those admitted by constructivism or intuitionism, are safer than others. Therefore, it is advisable to apply these procedures as far as possible. However, there are other forms and

methods which, though less safe because we do not have a proof of their consistency, appear to be practically indispensable for physics. In such a case there seems to be no good reason for prohibiting these procedures as long as no contradiction has been found." Compare "Foundations of Logic and Mathematics," *International Encyclopedia of Unified Science* I/3 (1939) (hereafter Carnap 1939), §20.

5. Carnap (1963a), pp. 53–54. See §18 of *Logical Syntax*, entitled "The syntax of [language] I can be formulated in [language] I," where Carnap explains how Gödel's arithmetization of syntax (§19) allows us to overcome Wittgensteinian scruples.

6. I discuss both Carnap's debt to Wittgenstein and their divergence over the expressibility of logical syntax in my "Carnap and Wittgenstein's *Tractatus*," in *Early Analytic Philosophy: Frege, Russell, Wittgenstein*, ed. W. Tait (La Salle: Open Court, 1997), pp. 19–36 (hereafter Friedman 1997).

7. Gödel preserved six drafts of this contribution, entitled "Is Mathematics Syntax of Language?" two of which have been published in *Kurt Gödel: Collected Works*, ed. S. Feferman et al.,Volume 3 (New York: Oxford University Press, 1995) (hereafter Gödel 1995), pp. 334–365 (hereafter Gödel *1953/9).

8. See Thomas Ricketts, "Carnap's Principle of Tolerance, Empiricism, and Conventionalism," in *Reading Putnam*, ed. P. Clark and B. Hale (Oxford: Blackwell, 1994) (hereafter Ricketts 1994); Warren Goldfarb and Thomas Ricketts, "Carnap and the Philosophy of Mathematics," in *Science and Subjectivity*, ed. D. Bell and W. Vossenkuhl (Berlin: Akademie, 1992) (hereafter Goldfarb and Ricketts 1992); and Warren Goldfarb, "Introductory Note to Gödel *1953/9" in Gödel (1995), pp. 324–333.

9. Thus Gödel begins the third draft of "Is Mathematics Syntax of Language?" by citing the following passage from the conclusion of Carnap's "Formalwissenschaft und Realwissenschaft," *Erkenntnis* 5/1 (1935): 30–36, hereafter (Carnap 1935a), p. 36: "When formal science is added to factual science [*Realwissenschaft*] *no new objects* are thereby introduced, as many philosophers who oppose the 'formal' or 'spiritual [*geistig*]' or 'ideal' objects to the 'real [*real*]' objects of factual science believe. *Formal science has no objects at all*; it is a system of auxiliary sentences, free of objects and empty of content" (Gödel *1953/9, p. 335, footnote 9). Carnap (1935a) is translated as "Formal and Factual Science," in *Readings in the Philosophy of Science*, ed. H. Feigl and M. Brodbeck (New York: Appleton-Century-Crofts, 1953), pp. 123–128 (hereafter Carnap 1953).

10. Carnap explains the dependence of the distinction between formal and factual science on his analytic/synthetic distinction in "Formalwissenschaft and Realwissenschaft" itself—which here simply follows *Logical Syntax*. From this point of view, as Goldfarb and Ricketts rightly emphasize, statements like that cited by Gödel in note above are simply colorful formulations, in the material mode, of the idea that logico-mathematical sentences are analytic.

11. According to Carnap's own explication of the analytic-synthetic distinction, if a language is inconsistent then there turn out to be no synthetic sentences (for all sentences are then determinate and all expressions logical). From Carnap's point of view, this is just one more respect in which an inconsistent language is an extremely inexpedient choice for the language of science, but it creates no fundamental difficulties for his underlying conception of analyticity. Compare Ricketts (1994), pp. 192–193.

12. A formal language is defined by formation rules and transformation rules. The transformation rules yield a consequence relation between sentences of the language. Sentences that are consequences of every sentence of the language are valid in that language. A sentence is determinate if it or its negation is valid.

13. It is this, for Carnap, that captures Wittgenstein's insight into the tautologousness of logical truth: the idea that logical truths hold in all conceivable circumstances and thus say nothing about the world. See Friedman (1997) and see also section V below. In Carnap's *Introduction to Semantics* (Cambridge, Mass.: Harvard University Press, 1942) (hereafter Carnap 1942), §16, 2a, this same idea is given a

semantical reading: the logical or analytic truths remain true for all *interpretations* of the descriptive predicates. As Carnap explains, this change accommodates Tarski's work and, in particular, the existence of indefinable properties.

14. Michael Friedman, "Logical Truth and Analyticity in Carnap's 'Logical Syntax of Language'," in W. Aspray and P. Kitcher, eds., *History and Philosophy of Modern Mathematics* (Minneapolis: University of Minnesota Press, 1988), pp. 82–94 (hereafter Friedman 1988). I was not at the time acquainted with Gödel's drafts. I did, however, make essential use of the insightful paper by Evert Beth, "Carnap's Views on the Advantages of Constructed Systems over Natural Languages," in Schilpp (1963), pp. 469–502 (hereafter Beth 1963), which makes a point very similar to Gödel's.

15. Accordingly, Carnap explicitly points out (1935, p. 36 [1953, p. 128]), that "certain concepts referring to S_1 (e.g., 'analytic in S_1' . . .) cannot be defined with the means of S_1 itself but only with those of a richer language S_2,"—which assertion is proved in §60c of *Logical Syntax*. (In 1935 Carnap cites Gödel's incompleteness paper and an earlier paper of his own which reported the results of §60c before the appearance of the English translation.) Indeed, already in §18 of *Logical Syntax*, Carnap qualifies his claim to have captured logical syntax within the object-language: "[W]e shall *formulate the syntax of I*—so far as it is definite [recursive]—*in I itself.*" In this sense, Carnap's anti-Wittgensteinian use of Gödel's method of arithmetization is also qualified (see notes 4 and 5 above).

16. This is not to say, however, that Goldfarb and Ricketts see no serious problems arising for Carnap's philosophy of mathematics in the wake of Gödel's incompleteness results. On the contrary, they hold that Carnap's use of a strong metalanguage to define analyticity has the damaging consequence of "not allow[ing] the conventional or non-factual nature of mathematics to be fully and explicitly displayed" (Goldfarb and Ricketts 1992, p. 70), and they give qualified endorsement to the related criticism developed by Beth (see note 13 above).

17. Carnap (1963a), pp. 17–18. Compare pp. 44–45.

18. As Carnap explains in detail in "Der Raum. Ein Beitrag zur Wissenschaftslehre," *Kant-Studien Ergänzungshefte im Auftrag der Kant-Gesellschaft* 56 (1922) (hereafter Carnap 1922), chapter 3, there is also a very substantial *conventional* element in our knowledge of physical space. For discussion, see my "Carnap and Weyl on the Foundations of Geometry and Relativity Theory," *Erkenntnis* 42 (1995): 247–260 (hereafter Friedman 1995).

19. Carnap, *Der logische Aufbau der Welt* (Berlin: Weltkreis, 1928) (hereafter Carnap 1928), trans. R. George, *The Logical Structure of the World* (Berkeley: University of California Press, 1967) (hereafter Carnap 1967), §178. For further discussion of both aspects of Carnap's neutrality in the *Aufbau* see my "Carnap's *Aufbau* Reconsidered," *Noûs* (1987) 21: 521–545 (hereafter Friedman 1987) and my "Epistemology in the *Aufbau*," *Synthese* 93 (1992): 15–57 (hereafter Friedman 1992).

20. Although the *Aufbau* was first published in 1928, most of the work on it was completed in the years 1922–1925, before Carnap moved to Vienna to join Schlick's Circle in 1926. It was only after moving to Vienna that Carnap became involved in the disputes on the foundations of mathematics. See Carnap (1963a), pp. 16–20, 46–50.

21. The first contribution, "Die Mathematik als Zweig der Logik," *Blätter für deutsche Philosophie* 4 (1930): 298–310 (hereafter Carnap 1930a), was prepared for a symposium on the philosophical foundations of mathematics in the *Blätter für deutsche Philosophie*, wherein intuitionism was treated by Menger (see note 2 above) and formalism by Paul Bernays. The second is the better known paper, "Die logizistische Grundlegung der Mathematik," *Erkenntnis* 2: 91–105 (hereafter Carnap 1930b), presented to the Second Conference on the Epistemology of the Exact Sciences in Königsberg in September 1930. This paper appeared in *Erkenntnis* along with papers by Arend Heyting representing intuitionism and John von Neumann representing

formalism. All three of the latter papers are translated in *Philosophy of Mathematics: Selected Readings*, ed. Paul Benacerraf and Hilary Putnam, 2 ed. (Cambridge: Cambridge University Press, 1983) (hereafter Benacerraf and Putnam 1983).

22. (1930a). See also Carnap (1930b), p. 102; Benaceraff and Putnam (1983), p. 50.

23. See Carnap (1930b), pp. 103–105; Benaceraff and Putnam (1983), pp. 50–52.

24. Carnap (1930a) pp. 309–310. See also Rudolf Carnap, Arend Heyting, and Johan von Neumann, "Diskussion zur Grundlegung der Mathematik," *Erkenntnis* 2 (1931): 91–121 (hereafter (Carnap, Heyting and von Neumann 1931), pp. 141–144, for Carnap's more detailed presentation of this idea.

25. Carnap (1930a), p. 310. See also Carnap's remarks introducing his discussion in (Carnap, Heyting, and von Neumann 1930), p. 141: "Many listeners have received the depressing impression from the three lectures that the problem-situation is tangled, confused, and hopeless: here are three tendencies, none of which understand any of the others and each of which wants to construct mathematics in a different way. But in reality the situation is not as bad as this, as we will see." He concludes (p. 144): "I believe that this execution [of the ideas of all three schools] will finally lead to a common result."

26. Carnap does not explain why he gave up on this idea, but we may plausibly conjecture that interaction with Tarski and Gödel convinced him that the definability restrictions on arithmetical properties he had envisioned would not lead to a satisfactory version of classical analysis. He may have been influenced, in this regard, by Tarski's work on definable sets of real numbers (1930–1931), which he cites in the bibliography to the English version of *Logical Syntax*. It is not clear what the relation is between the finitist-constructivist ideas of Carnap's 1930 contributions and the early versions of *Logical Syntax* restricted to Language I alone (see note 3 above). Carnap (1963a, p. 33) notes that he had planned to develop a version of the "Zermelo-Fraenkel axiom system of set theory, but restricted in the sense of a constructivist method" already in 1927.

27. See §44: "One can permit such definitions or exclude them, without giving a justification. But if one wants to justify the one or the other procedure, then one must first exhibit the formal consequences of this procedure." Goldfarb and Ricketts (1992, p. 68) note the contrast between this attitude and that of Carnap (1930b) (and compare Goldfarb and Ricketts's pp. 62–63).

28. Indeed, as noted at the very beginning, Carnap does not pursue the traditional logicist project of defining the arithmetical terms via logical terms in the earlier sense (connectives, quantifiers, identity) at all in *Logical Syntax*. He instead treats the arithmetical terms as primitive in both Language I and Language II. They nonetheless count as logical in the new sense of §50. Carnap observes in §84 that the question of logicism in the traditional sense is not even well defined: "[W]e have given a formal distinction between logical and descriptive signs in general syntax; but a sharp division of the logical signs in our sense into logical signs in the narrower [traditional] sense and mathematical signs has not yet been given by anyone." Goldfarb and Ricketts note the resulting attenuation of traditional logicism (1992, p. 68).

29. In the introduction to the corresponding section (Menger 1979, pp. 13–14), Menger makes several revealing remarks in his anxiety to establish exclusive priority for the idea of tolerance. Thus, he first addresses Carnap's attribution, in the above passage from §17 of *Logical Syntax*, of an attitude of tolerance to "most mathematicians." To this Menger remarks that the "prominent mathematicians . . . who have dealt with the foundations of mathematics," such as Poincaré, Hilbert, Weyl, and Brouwer, have been quite opposed to this attitude—thereby missing Carnap's point, namely, that the "ordinary working mathematician" tacitly embraces tolerance. Menger then considers the passage from Carnap's intellectual autobiography, cited at the beginning of section II above, in which Carnap says that the attitude of tolerance "has remained the same throughout my life." Here Menger simply remarks that

Carnap's memory must have been faulty. In this way, Menger not only misses the point that it is only specifically *logico-mathematical* tolerance that is new in *Logical Syntax*, also misses the deep roots of Carnap's principle in a much more general attitude toward philosophical problems as such.

30. Compare §75: "[By means of the diagnosis of the material mode of speech] the character of philosophical problems in general will become clear. The unclarity about this character is traceable mainly to the deception and self-deception brought about via the application of the material mode of speech."

31. See Carnap (1963a), §11, especially pp. 67–69.

32. Ricketts, in his paper cited in note 8 above and, especially, in his "Rationality, Translation, and Epistemology Naturalized," *Journal of Philosophy* 79 (1982): 117–136 (hereafter Ricketts 1982), correctly emphasizes Carnap's concern with the difference between genuine rational disputes and traditional philosophical talk at cross purposes. But he then characterizes Carnap's main problem as that of applying this distinction to actually occurring intellectual debates so as to determine which type of case we are faced with in fact: there is a genuine dispute if and only if the investigators in question share a common language or linguistic framework. From this point of view, Carnap immediately runs up against a difficult problem in *descriptive* syntax, namely, how to tell whether or not actual investigators share a common language, and Quine's challenge—that, in Ricketts's terms, of supplying a "criterion of analyticity"—then proves to be fatal to the entire enterprise. I do not think Ricketts's presentation fits Carnap's own conception of his project. Carnap is not worried about determining, in actual cases, which disputes are genuine and which are not. He is already perfectly clear about this: *philosophical* disputes are characteristically fruitless, whereas *scientific* questions (in either natural science or mathematics) are patently rationally negotiable. Carnap's problem is not to discriminate the fruitless disputes from the fruitful ones but to offer those enmeshed in the former—philosophers—a way out. This is what the construction and investigation of a variety of formal languages is for. Descriptive syntax can fall where it may: Carnap is concerned with the constructive task—belonging to *pure* syntax—of language planning.

33. Carnap tirelessly reiterates this new conception of the true character of philosophical problems, normally with the debate in the foundations of mathematics as paradigmatic. See, for example, "On the Character of Philosophical Problems," *Philosophy of Science* 1 (1934): 2–19 (hereafter Carnap 1934b), *Die Aufgabe der Wissenschaftslogik* (Wien: Gerold, 1934) (hereafter Carnap 1934c)—translated as "The Task of the Logic of Science," in *Unified Science*, ed. B. McGuinness (Dordrecht: Reidel, 1987) (hereafter Carnap 1987)—especially §7 of the supplementary remarks, and *Philosophy and Logical Syntax* (London: Kegan Paul, 1935) (hereafter Carnap 1935b), especially pp. 75–82.

34. In §76 Carnap traces this idea to Wittgenstein's doctrine of "formal concepts" in *Tractatus Logico-Philosophicus*, trans. C. K. Ogden (London: Kegan Paul, 1922) (hereafter Wittgenstein 1922).

35. See Carnap, "Empiricism, Semantics, and Ontology," *Revue Internationale de Philosophie* 4 (1950): 20–40 (hereafter Carnap 1950a), reprinted as supplement A in Carnap's *Meaning and Necessity*, 2d. ed. (Chicago: University of Chicago Press, 1956) (hereafter Carnap 1956). My page references are to this volume.

36. Carnap points out that "There are numbers" and "There are space-time points" also have entirely trivial internal readings on which they are obviously analytically true, but these are not questions in which anyone—philosopher or scientist—is seriously interested: see Carnap (1950a), §2, pp. 209, 213.

37. Carnap explains (1950a, §3, pp. 213–214), that external questions primarily concern the choice of a distinctive type of variable.

38. As Carnap explicitly points out, this argument also applies to the existential axioms of set theory (§38a). Similarly, in the language of mathematical physics, sentences asserting the existence of (a nondenumerable infinity of) space-time points

are similarly analytic and thus devoid of genuine ontological import. As we noted at the end of section II above, this attitude toward such mathematical existential assumptions marks a sharp break from Carnap's earlier treatment.

39. As Goldfarb has emphasized to me in discussion, the concept of a "primitive sentence" is not well-defined on the basis of a notion of *consequence* (or validity) alone. In this connection, especially, Carnap himself also employs a notion of *derivability* in characterizing formal languages (§§13, 14, pp. 30–33, 47, 48). In any case, the heart of Carnap's point can be formulated without relying on the notion of primitive sentence: whether a language in which this or that analytic sentence is valid is acceptable or not can only be a purely pragmatic question.

40. The Smeaton translation has "incompatible" rather than "L-incompatible" here.

41. See p. 320 [249]: "That there is still always a conventional element in the hypotheses, despite their subjection to empirical control by the protocol-sentences, rests on the circumstance that the system of hypotheses is never uniquely determined by the empirical material, no matter how rich." Ricketts (1994, pp. 193–195) interprets Carnap's empiricism as the requirement that *indeterminate* sentences be testable via protocol-sentences, whereas Carnap himself clearly extends this requirement to all *synthetic* sentences, including, in particular, the P-rules.

42. See R. Carnap, *Logical Foundations of Probability* (Chicago: University of Chicago Press, 1950) (hereafter Carnap, 1950b), Preface: "[A]ll principles and theorems of inductive logic are analytic." As Goldfarb and Ricketts have emphasized to me in discussion, there is another possible reading of the second passage from "Empiricism, Semantics, and Ontology" just cited, according to which the "rules of evaluation" in question include P-rules (such as general laws of nature) as well as L-rules. In view, however, of Carnap's explicit use of the notion of *confirmation* here, together with the circumstance that "Empiricism, Semantics, and Ontology" belongs to the same period as *Logical Foundations of Probability*, I consider this reading to be less plausible (so that, on my reading, the examples of internal questions in the "thing language" Carnap presents here should be conceived of as singular predictions not requiring laws of nature). In any case, what is central to my argument is that Carnap nowhere (to my knowledge) suggests a confirmational asymmetry between P-rules and indeterminate synthetic sentences, whereas he consistently maintains a clear confirmational asymmetry between P-rules and analytic sentences (see next note).

43. I am therefore entirely in agreement with Ricketts's description of the situation (1982, p. 123): "Observation reports can confirm and disconfirm theories within frameworks, but they can never confirm or disconfirm the logical machinery of a framework. This logical machinery is required to constitute a framework-relative notion of evidence. Only against the background of such a notion does talk of confirmation make any sense at all. So, in changes of theory, the application of pragmatic considerations is confined to confirmationally acceptable theories and thus governed by the logical machinery of the framework. In changes of framework, however, pragmatic considerations operate untrammeled: there is nothing else." What I am adding here is simply the observation that P-rules are subject to the same rules of confirmation as are indeterminate synthetic sentences. In more recent work, by contrast, Ricketts uses the point that P-rules are just as definitive of a formal language as are L-rules to urge that we should divorce the distinction between change of theory and change of language (and the related distinction between internal and external questions) from the analytic/synthetic distinction (see, for example, Ricketts 1994, p. 189).

44. See R. Carnap, "W. V. Quine on Logical Truth," in Schilpp (1963, pp. 915–921) (hereafter Carnap 1963b), p. 921. Here Carnap considers Quine's argument that no statement of science is immune from revision. Carnap admits (as §82 of *Logical Syntax* had already stated explicitly) that logico-mathematical rules—just like physical rules—can be revised, and in both cases one has "a transition from a lan-

guage L_n to a new language L_{n+1}." However: "My concept of analyticity as an expli-
candum has nothing to do with such a transition. It refers in each case to just one
language. . . . That a certain sentence S is analytic in L_n means only something about
the status of S within the language L_n; as has often been said, it means that the truth
of S in L_n is based on the meanings in L_n of the terms occurring in S."

45. Compare also (1939), §§1, 7, 23.

46. This explicit link between the principle of tolerance and the analytic/synthetic
distinction marks the central difference between the present interpretation and the
viewpoint of Goldfarb and Ricketts. I believe that this difference is traceable, in the
end, to the circumstance that Goldfarb and Ricketts are operating against the background of Ricketts's general understanding of the principle of tolerance, according
to which Carnap's central concern is that of determining, in the context of *descriptive* syntax, whether or not two different investigators share a common linguistic
framework. From this point of view—the point of view of Quine's demand for a "criterion of analyticity" (compare Goldfarb and Ricketts 1992, p. 75, fn. 21)—the real
problem concerns the general notion of linguistic framework as such, together with
the accompanying notion of "true in virtue of the adoption of a framework." From
this point of view, the distinctions, within a given framework, and in *pure* syntax,
between logical and descriptive expressions, logical and physical rules, are of decidedly secondary importance. See notes 32, 41, and 43 above.

47. Thus, for example, in his "E. W. Beth on Constructed Languages," in the
"Replies and Expositions" section of Schilpp, *Philosophy of Carnap* (1963c), p. 932,
Carnap considers Tarski's view that there is no sharp distinction between logical
and descriptive expressions: "[This disagreement] is to a large extent to be explained
by the fact that Tarski deals chiefly with languages for logic and mathematics, thus
languages without descriptive constants, while I regard it as an essential task for
semantics to develop a method applicable to languages of empirical science. I believe that *a semantics for languages of this kind must give an explication for the distinction between logical and descriptive signs and that between formal and factual truth*,
because it seems to me that without these distinctions a satisfactory methodological analysis of science is not possible." And, more simply, Carnap states in §13 of
(1942), which is concerned precisely with the distinction between logical and
descriptive signs, that "[t]he problem of the nature of logical deduction and logical truth is one of the most important problems in the foundations of logic and
perhaps in the whole of theoretical philosophy."

48. Compare (1963a), p. 46.

49. Goldfarb and Ricketts (1992, p. 68) present a minimalist reading of Carnap's
logicism, as simply the proposal for a "total language, which contains both logico-
mathematical and synthetic sentences" adequate for representing the application
of mathematics (§84). By contrast, it is crucial to my interpretation that the "logico-
mathematical" or analytic sentences have a formally specifiable general character
in virtue of which they are thereby entirely independent of all "matters of fact."

50. See (Wittgenstein 1922), §§5.4, 5.441, 5.47. For further discussion of these
ideas, in connection with Carnap's conception of the logical constants sketched
below, see Friedman (1997).

51. It is important to note here that Carnap articulates a sense in which the truths
of logic and mathematics are "empty of content" without invoking protocol-sentences and thus a notion of *empirical* content. That sentences essentially containing
descriptive expressions should be testable via the deduction of protocol-sentences is
then a separate requirement, which serves to differentiate legitimate (theoretical)
descriptive concepts such as the electro magnetic field functor from illegitimate
descriptive concepts such as "entelechy" (§82, p. 319 [247]). The requirement that
P-rules, in particular, should be testable is thus in no way a trivial one.

52. In this sense, there is a notion of truth in virtue of meaning already in *Logical
Syntax*, and Carnap's later use of this notion in the remarks cited in note 44 above

apply equally here. More generally, Carnap's project in *Logical Syntax* is not to reject all talk about meaning, but rather to translate or reinterpret such talk in purely syntactical terms (as he does in §50 and also, for example, in §62 and §75). Primarily for the purpose of formally developing inductive logic, Carnap will later introduce "meaning postulates" to capture what he takes to be meaning relations involving *descriptive* expressions as well. But this extension of the notion of truth in virtue of meaning does not affect Carnap's philosophy of logic and mathematics (where, as I say in the text, we have the best possible case).

53. I thus find myself in substantial agreement with Ricketts's discussion of §50 of *Logical Syntax* and its implications for Gödel's objection (1994, pp. 189–193). Once again, however, for Ricketts what is of paramount importance is the problem in descriptive syntax of "finding" a given formal language or linguistic framework in the speech dispositions of actual speakers. From this point of view, the notion of what speakers are committed to simply in virtue of the adoption of a framework—which includes both logico-mathematical rules (L-rules) and physical rules (P-rules)—is more important than the distinction, within a given framework, between logico-mathematical and physical rules (see notes 43 and 46 above). Accordingly, Ricketts again takes the point of §50 to be entirely deflationary: it "displaces, more than analyzes, the notion of truth-in-virtue-of" (p. 191). On my reading, by contrast, the point of §50 is precisely to *explicate* the pretheoretical notion of truth in virtue of meaning (compare notes 44 and 52 above). This is one notion Carnap does not at all wish to deflate, on pain of undermining both his commitment to logicism and the principle of tolerance.

54. The last sentence of Carnap (1950a, §5, p. 221), recasts the principle of tolerance so as to emphasize the duality between "linguistic forms" (external questions involving analytic sentences) and genuine "assertions" (internal questions). And in footnote 5 in §3 (p. 215), after referring to Paul Bernays's "Sur le platonisme dans les mathématiques" (a penetrating discussion of the foundations of logic and mathematics from a frankly ontological point of view), Carnap observes that "Quine does not acknowledge the distinction which I emphasize above [between internal and external questions], because according to his general conception there are no sharp boundary lines between logical and factual truth, between questions of meaning and questions of fact, between the acceptance of a language structure and the acceptance of an assertion formulated in the language." This passage strongly suggests, I believe, that Carnap himself sees a close connection between the analytic/synthetic distinction and the distinction between internal and external questions (see note 43 above).

55. Moreover, the distinction between logical and descriptive expressions gives Carnap a sense in which logico-mathematical rules are empty of content that does not rely on his empiricism (note 62). Carnap is thus not vulnerable to a second objection leveled by Gödel: namely, that Carnap's notion of content arbitrarily begs the question in favor of empiricism (see Gödel *1953/9, pp. 354–355, for example). By the same token, however, this point further underscores the importance, for Carnap, of giving a general explication of the distinction that *formally characterizes* the pretheoretical idea of independence from all extralinguistic facts. (I am indebted to Goldfarb for emphasizing the importance of this second Gödelian objection here.)

56. Compare also the passage from §44 of *Logical Syntax* cited in note 27 above, which suggests an enterprise of "investigating consequences" logically prior to (pragmatic) "justification."

57. This idea, as we have seen, is central to Goldfarb and Ricketts (1992, see especially p. 69): "Carnap would surely disavow any pretense that there is one metalanguage that will always be acceptable to all parties in all controversies: there is no more a universal metalanguage than there is a universal object language."

58. Goldfarb and Ricketts (1992, pp. 69–70) explicitly consider this situation and again see no problem for Carnap. What they fail to consider, from the present point

of view, is how the principle of tolerance involves Carnap's (mathematically very strong) concept of analyticity, so that the pragmatically motivated intuitionist will then also be barred from embracing this principle as Carnap understands it. In my opinion, Goldfarb and Ricketts here, once again, fail properly to appreciate the absolutely central role of Carnap's distinctions between logical and descriptive expressions, analytic and synthetic sentences, for the principle of tolerance itself. Note that the pragmatically motivated intuitionist will eschew the use of a strong metalanguage for the very same pragmatic reason that weighs against the choice of a strong object-language, namely, the cautious desire to be as safe as possible against contradiction.

59. In a different context, Goldfarb and Ricketts remark that "the method of logical syntax is meant to provide a level playing field for all contested views" (1992, p. 76). If the present interpretation is correct, however, this is precisely what Carnap's understanding of the principle of tolerance does not do.

60. This situation may be what Goldfarb and Ricketts have in mind when they write (1992, p. 71) that "[Carnap's] position is not circular so much as self-supporting at each level. If the mathematical part of a framework is analytic, then it's analytic; and so invoking mathematical truths at the level of the metalanguage is perfectly acceptable, since they flow from the adoption of the metalanguage."

61. We are now in a position precisely to pinpoint the mistake I made in my earlier treatment (1988) of these issues. I there argued that Carnap's logicism needs to respect Wittgenstein's conception of the logical constants and that Carnap is thereby committed to a minimalist, purely combinatorial conception of logic in the metalanguage. However, whereas Carnap does need to respect Wittgenstein's conception of the logical constants, the whole point of logical syntax, in this matter, is to generalize and relativize Wittgenstein's conception in the manner of §50. And this generalized conception does not lead to a minimalist version of logical syntax in the metalanguage, but rather to an extremely strong classical version. It is then the spirit of the principle of tolerance, not Carnap's logicism, that pushes us toward a minimal version of logical syntax, so that, in the end, Carnap's logicism stands in conflict with his tolerance.

62. Thus, what I am calling the spirit of the principle of tolerance is better represented by the (much less philosophically loaded) pragmatic attitude of the "ordinary working scientist" discussed in III above. It also fits Quine's opposing, naturalistic version of pragmatism. See, in particular, the conclusion of W. V. Quine, "Carnap and Logical Truth," in Schilpp (1963, pp. 385–406, pp. 405–406): "Now I am as impressed as Carnap with the vastness of what language contributes to science and to one's whole view of the world; and in particular I grant that one's hypothesis as to what there is, e.g., as to there being universals, is at bottom just as arbitrary and pragmatic a matter as one's adoption of a new brand of set theory or even a new system of bookkeeping. Carnap in turn recognizes that such decisions, however conventional, 'will nevertheless usually be influenced by theoretical knowledge.' (This footnote is to §2 of Carnap 1950a.) But what impresses me more than it does Carnap is how well this whole attitude is suited also to the theoretical hypotheses of natural science itself, and how little basis there is for a distinction."

63. See Carnap (1942, §39). Carnap's reasons for abandoning §§50–52 have nothing to do with the problems we have been discussing. The main reason appears to be that he now wants to recognize logical systems, such as first-order logic with identity, in which not all sentences containing only logical expressions are determinate. For an interesting discussion of the transition from syntax to semantics containing a rather different suggestion as to what motivates Carnap to abandon §§50–52, see Thomas Ricketts, "Carnap: From Logical Syntax to Semantics," in *The Origins of Logical Empiricism*, ed. R. Giere and A. Richardson (Minneapolis: University of Minnesota Press, 1996) (hereafter Ricketts 1996).

64. Carnap (1942, §13). For the importance of a characterization in what Carnap is now calling "general semantics," see note 55 above.

65. See, for example, the quotation from Carnap (1963c) in note 47 above.

66. Thus the problem referred to in note 63 above can be viewed as a narrowly technical rather than a truly fundamental one. (Moreover, from the point of view of *Logical Syntax*, this problem does not seem particularly important, since no one would seriously suggest logico-mathematical rules for the total language of science consisting solely of first-order logic with identity.) The closest Carnap comes to recognizing the problems with which we have been occupied is in his exchange with Beth (Schilpp 1963). Beth uses ideas very close to our considerations to suggest that the need for a strong metalanguage entails a "limitation regarding the Principle of Tolerance" (Beth 1963, p. 479, and see also pp. 499–502). In his reply, Carnap explains that, in a dispute between two parties touching also the question of the metalanguage: "It may be the case that one of them can express in his own language certain convictions which he cannot translate into the common language; in this case he cannot communicate these convictions to the other man. For example, a classical mathematician is in this situation with respect to an intuitionist" (Carnap 1963c, pp. 929–930). Yet Carnap never takes up Beth's theme of a "limitation regarding the Principle of Tolerance."

67. See again §11 of Carnap (1963a) for his parallel interest in both forms of language planning.

68. For his relations with Tarski in connection with these issues, see Carnap (1963a, pp. 13, 30–31, 35–36, 60–67). See further Beth (1963, pp. 482–488), together with Carnap's reply (1963c, pp. 931–932).

69. For Quine's discussion of §§50–52 of *Logical Syntax*, see Quine (1963, §VII). For Carnap's view of the importance of a sharp distinction between logical and psychological investigations, see, for example (1934b), p. 6; (1934a), §72; (1934c), §I; (1935b), pp. 31–34; "Von der Erkenntnistheorie zur Wissenschaftslogik," in *Actes du Congrès international de philosophie scientifique* (Paris: Hermann, 1936), (1950b), §§11–12.

11

"The Defensible Province of Philosophy": Quine's 1934 Lectures on Carnap

PETER HYLTON

In November 1934 Quine, then twenty-six years old, gave a series of lectures at Harvard on Carnap, in particular on Carnap's *Logische Syntax der Sprache*.[1] Quine had visited Carnap in Prague in the spring of the previous year and been inspired. He returned to Harvard as a Junior Fellow in the Harvard Society of Fellows. His evident enthusiasm for Carnap's philosophy led to a request that he lecture on that topic. The lectures were written out in full and have now been published.[2]

Quine later said of himself at this time, "I was very much his [Carnap's] disciple for six years."[3] In a comment on the lectures, he says simply that they were "uncritical" (Hahn and Schilpp 1986, p. 16); he also speaks of them as "abjectly sequacious."[4] These later claims to uncritical discipleship are largely borne out by the lectures themselves, which are a brilliant exposition of Carnap's views of the *Syntax* period. To read the lectures, indeed, is to be forcefully reminded of the power of Carnap's thought. The third and last lecture, a discussion of Carnap's way of transforming philosophical problems into questions of syntax, is particularly striking. Its final paragraph reveals how completely the young Quine accepts the Carnapian view of these matters:

> Views will differ as to the success of Carnap's total thesis that all philosophy is syntax. Carnap has made a very strong case for this thesis; but it must be admitted that there are difficulties to be ironed out. We cannot be sure that we have found the key to the universe. Still Carnap *has* provided us, at the worst, with a key to an enormous part of the universe. He has in any case shown conclusively that the bulk of what we relegate to philosophy can be handled rigorously and clearly within syntax. Carnap himself recognizes that this accomplishment stands *independently* of the thesis that *no* meaningful metaphysics remains beyond syntax. (Pp. 102–103; emphases in the original)

If there is such a thing as damning with faint praise, this may surely be described as a case of endorsing with very faint qualification.

In spite of their uncritical nature, the lectures afford us insight into the basis of Quine's subsequent disagreement with Carnap. In particular, there is an internal tension in the lectures: they reveal fundamental assumptions that are at odds with the views they espouse—especially about analyticity. Or so at least I shall argue in what follows. I shall not much be directly concerned with the question of how far Quine's (1934) Carnap is our Carnap (or, if sense can be made of the idea at all, Carnap's Carnap); nor with a comparison of the 1934 Quine with the later Quine familiar to us. Questions of these two sorts lead in fascinating directions, but would take us too far aside from our main theme. (I shall, however, touch on them in notes and asides from time to time.)

As is indicated by the passage from the lectures quoted above, Quine clearly sees that the central issue in Carnap's *Syntax* is the nature and status of philosophy itself. Referring to that book, published in German earlier that year, Quine says on the first page of the lectures: "Carnap's central doctrine, which is the main concern of these lectures, is the doctrine that philosophy is syntax" (p. 47). Let us begin by sketching the way in which the issue of the nature of philosophy arises for Carnap.

The context of Carnap's concern with this issue is set by Wittgenstein's *Tractatus Logico-Philosophicus*,[5] which rejects all philosophy (including itself, so to speak) as nonsensical. The basis of this rejection is the idea that all propositions are of one of two kinds. On the one hand, we have empirical propositions—"propositions of natural science," as Wittgenstein says. These propositions, he immediately adds, have "nothing to do with philosophy" (*Tractatus*, 6.53; here, it is worth noting, Wittgenstein is himself following Russell). On the other hand, there are propositions of logic. Wittgenstein calls these "tautologies." On his account, they make no claim about the world—they say nothing and so are called "propositions" only as a matter of courtesy or convenience. Wittgenstein assumes that supposed philosophical propositions cannot be tautologies. So there simply is no status that such (alleged) propositions could have; hence his conclusion that there are no philosophical propositions. Attempts at such propositions result in nonsense. There is a clarificatory *activity* that might be called philosophy, but no propositions, no theory: "Philosophy is not a body of doctrine but an activity. . . . Philosophy does not result in 'philosophical propositions,' but rather in the clarification of propositions" (*Tractatus*, 4.112).

Carnap accepts much of Wittgenstein's view, but makes crucial modifications. Perhaps the most important is the idea that there are languages that differ from one another not merely in superficial ways but fundamentally—in their expressive power, or in the logic they embody. Carnap thus rejects the (apparently) Wittgensteinian or Russellian idea that there is at bottom only one language.[6] This aspect of Carnap's thought is fundamental, because he thinks that much of the task of philosophy consists in formulating different languages for this or that purpose.

Like Wittgenstein, Carnap gives central importance to a category of sentences which lack genuine content, which make no claim on the world. In *Syntax* and after, however, he no longer speaks of such sentences as "tautologous"; instead he calls them *analytic*.[7] There is more than a nominal change here. Wittgenstein's tautologies are truths of logic, what we should now call instances of valid schemata. Wittgenstein's idea of a tautology, however, applies much more clearly to truth-functional logic than to anything beyond. Thus a formidable task faced those philosophers, such as Ramsey, who wanted to argue that mathematics is tautologous in this sense (this was not a conclusion that Wittgenstein himself accepted). They had to use the technical machinery of *Principia Mathematica*, or something akin to it, to show that mathematics reduces to logic. Worse, they had to argue that the logic they employed was to be counted as tautologous in Wittgenstein's sense. This was an uphill task at best.[8]

Carnap's view in *Syntax* presents a sharp contrast. He exploits the idea of implicit definition, often attributed to the mathematician David Hilbert.[9] The assumption here is, roughly, that a language is constituted by rules that imply the truth of certain sentences; the rules may, indeed, simply stipulate that certain classes of sentences are true. This connects with definition via the idea that the meaning of a term is thought to be fixed when we have fixed the truth-values of the sentences that contain it.[10] The stipulations constitute an implicit rather than explicit definition of the term because they do not give its meaning by equating it with some other form of words; they do so, rather, by saying that all of a certain class of sentences containing that term are true. The correctness of certain sentences is thus part of the framework of the language, so to speak; and these are the analytic sentences of the language.[11] (We shall return to the idea of implicit definition shortly, when we examine Quine's exegesis of Carnap.) On this account, the analyticity of mathematics for a language does not require use of anything like the reduction of *Principia Mathematica* (though some languages may exploit that reduction). We—as artificers of the given language—can, rather, build certain axioms and rules into its framework. It remains to be shown, of course, that the axioms or rules that we have built in suffice to yield (all or most of) mathematics, and that they make sense of the applicability of mathematics. But the crucial point is that the rules we need are obtained by building them into the structure of the language, not by showing them to be part of logic, in some antecedently given sense.

Carnap also accepted, and also modified, Wittgenstein's rejection of philosophy. While rejecting almost everything that had previously gone under that head, he still wished to leave room for something that might be called "philosophy"— for the results of his own philosophical activity. Like Wittgenstein, he held (very roughly) that there are only empirical assertions and sentences of logic; nothing else makes sense. This view was sometimes expressed within the Vienna Circle by saying that there is only the empirical and the analytic: there is no synthetic a priori, no a priori knowledge of the world. What then of philosophy? Carnap confined it, at least officially, to the task of establishing artificial languages, deriving theorems about them, and making linguistic recommendations or decisions, recommendations or decisions to accept this or that language for a certain purpose. (One purpose which was to assume particular prominence is that of *explication*: giving a precise definition of a concept which is useful but unclear or in some other way troubling. We can think of this as giving a miniature artificial language.) On this view of philosophy it cannot be put forward as a *doctrine*, exactly, that there are only empirical assertions and sentences of logic. This can itself be no more than a linguistic decision to use a language which permits nothing else.

Let us turn now to Quine's elaboration, in his 1934 lectures, of the Carnapian ideas sketched above. In outline at least, Quine follows Carnap. In contrast to his later view, he sharply distinguishes philosophy from the empirical sciences (see pp. 66, 87, 93–94). Philosophical sentences are to be neither empirical nor about some nonempirical (metaphysical) reality. They are, rather, of two kinds. Some are analytic sentences about the syntax of this or that language. These sentences are not empirical claims about some actually existing language; they are analytic sentences about the syntax of some proposed formal language, which may or may not resemble an actual language.[12] Other philosophical sentences are not assertions or claims at all, not even analytic ones. Their function is, rather, to record syntactic recommendations or decisions—recommendations or decisions to use this or that language, or a language with this or that syntactic feature. Assertions that give rise to metaphysical questions can be thought of as misleading ways of expressing such decisions and recommendations; when we adopt this attitude, we cease to think of them as genuine assertions at all, and we thus avoid metaphysical questions as to their truth. The statement that there are numbers, for example, may look like a nonempirical claim about extralinguistic reality; it is, however, best thought of not as an assertion about numbers but rather as recording the author's decision to use a language containing numerals as primitive expressions, and perhaps also his recommendation that others do likewise. Thought of in this way, no unanswerable questions about the *truth* of the sentence arise, for it makes no claim.

The notion of analyticity is central to this picture. The picture is based on the idea that all truly contentful sentences are empirical. Analyticity is then to account for logic and mathematics, as well as for those philosophical sentences that do not simply record our syntactic decisions or recommendations. The fundamental doctrine here is that there is no synthetic a priori, that the a priori is analytic. But what of this doctrine itself? Is it not a philosophical thesis, of just the kind that it claims to be impossible? According to Quine, we do not have to see it that way. The view that the a priori is analytic, and thus the view that philosophy consists (roughly) of syntactic decisions, is itself a syntactic decision. It is, however, a decision that Quine clearly thinks it would be foolish of us not to make:

> The modern convention has the advantage of a great theoretical economy; the doctrine that the *a priori* is analytic remains only a syntactic decision. It is however no less important for *that* reason: as a syntactic decision it has the importance of enabling us to pursue foundations of mathematics and the logic of science without encountering extra-logical questions as to the source of the validity of our *a priori* judgments. . . . [I]t shows that all metaphysical questions as to an *a priori* synthetic are gratuitous, and let in only by ill-advised syntactic procedures. (Pp. 65–66)

What is the notion of analyticity that is to have this effect of enabling us to avoid the synthetic *a priori* and, more generally, all questions about the validity of our *a priori* judgments? It is the idea we have already touched on, that analytic truths arise from implicit definitions. Here Quine gives a masterly exposition.[13] Very roughly, the idea is this: we start, in the ideal case, with all the "admittedly true sentences" (p. 49), or the "whole range of accepted sentences" (p. 65), or "all those sentences which, in 1934, we find ourselves accepting as true" (p. 87).[14] We may suppose that we have already carried out as many *explicit* definitions as possible, so that these sentences contain a minimum number of terms. Then we decide upon the first term—word or unitary idiom—to be (implicitly) defined; let us follow Quine and call it K (see p. 49). The choice of K is arbitrary, but it will be convenient to take a term of very wide use, such as a connective of truth-functional logic. (Some choices of terms may be so inconvenient that the whole method is unworkable. The important point behind the idea of arbitrariness, however, is that no particular order is forced on us.) Some of our accepted sentences will contain the term K; let us call these the accepted K-sentences.

As we briefly saw, the idea of an implicit definition is that it gives us the meaning of a given term not by equating it with other terms but by fixing the truth-values of (some or all of) the sentences in which it occurs. As Quine puts it in "Truth By Convention": "[I]n point of *meaning* . . . a word may be said to be determined to whatever extent the truth or falsehood of its contexts is determined" (Quine 1976, p. 89). Thus if we were to stipulate that all of the accepted K-sentences are true, that stipulation would constitute an implicit definition of K; and, trivially, the truth of all the accepted K-sentences would follow from this definition. Matters are not that simple, in part because of the fact that many sentences contain more than one term essentially.[15] Let us suppose that we give a definition which stipulates as true all the accepted K-sentences that contain only K essentially. Now what of those that essentially contain both K and one or more other terms? Are such sentences to have their truth-values stipulated as part of the implicit definition of K, or as part of the implicit definitions of one of their other terms? Here again decisions are called for. Considerations of the simplicity, even the feasibility, of the whole project may in practice sharply curtail our options; subject to these constraints, however, we are free to make what choices we like.

Having given our implicit definition of K—that is, our stipulation of some of the accepted K-sentences as true—we then move on to another term, say J. Here we repeat the procedure, stipulating as true all the accepted J-sentences that essentially contain only J, or only J and K, and also (perhaps) some other of the accepted J-sentences. And so on with other terms: we proceed in order through various stages. At each stage all accepted sentences essentially containing only the term defined at the given stage plus terms defined at earlier stages will be stipulated as true; sentences also essentially containing terms not defined at that stage may or may not be stipulated at the given stage.

I have spoken of stipulating truths as if we were simply to list a number of sentences and say: each one is true. This is indeed one method of stipulating truths, but it is not an adequate one, for there are too many truths to stipulate in this fashion. So we do something like laying down axioms and rules of inference: each

of *these* sentences is to count as true, we will say, and also all those that can be
obtained from sentences already established as true by one of *these* methods. Quine
uses logic as an example (and surely it is crucial that this example is available).
Suppose we have defined all the truth-functional connectives in terms of one—
joint denial, let's say. Then we can take as an implicit definition of this one term
a set of axioms and rules of inference for truth-functional logic phrased using only
joint denial. All truths of truth-functional logic (phrased using only joint denial)
become true by implicit definition; if we add definitions of other truth-functional
connectives, then we may lift the parenthetical restriction. Having done this for
joint denial, and thus for all truth-functions, we can then go on to extend the logic,
by adding, say, quantification in the same way. We simply take a new term—
the universal quantifier, perhaps—and lay down axioms and rules of inference
which, together with those for truth-functional logic, yield all the truths essentially containing only quantifiers and truth-functions. All of first-order logic thus
becomes true by implicit definition. (This is of course first-order logic without
identity; implicit definition of the identity symbol will extend the idea to first-
order logic with identity.)[16]

Although it is logic which forms Quine's illustration of this procedure, he sees
it as more widely applicable. On his account, indeed, it is applicable—it *could* be
applied—as broadly as we wish: it is in principle possible to carry on the process
of giving implicit definitions, thereby creating analytic truths, until every term
is defined and all truths reckoned as analytic. He is explicit on this point:

> But where should we stop in this process? Obviously we could go on indefi-
> nitely in the same way. . . . Then *every* accepted sentence, no matter in what
> words, would be provided for by the implicit or explicit definitions; every ac-
> cepted sentence would become analytic, that is, directly derivable from our
> conventions as to the use of words. (Pp. 61–62; emphasis in the original)[17]

It is for our purposes of fundamental importance that Quine sees the process of
giving implicit definitions, and creating analytic truths, as one that can be carried on indefinitely. For we are then faced with the question, How are we to decide
where to end the process of giving implicit definitions? And it is this question
which reveals the tension in Quine's thought.

One possible answer to our question is that we should continue the process until
we have made all the a priori truths (and no others) analytic; here it would be
presupposed that we have at the outset a distinction between the a priori truths
and the others. But this is not Quine's answer. The initial stock of true (or accepted) sentences is meant to include all the truths. Although Quine uses the
expressions "a priori" and "empirical," his uses seem to be loose, and more or less
for the sake of argument. He does not seem to endorse the idea that our stock of
initially accepted truths is divided into a priori and a posteriori. Speaking of the starting point, he says explicitly, "The distinction between *a priori* and empirical does
not concern me here" (p. 49). And on page 61 he speaks of "so-called logical words,"
and "so-called mathematical" words, and "so-called empirical" words; he pointedly
refrains from endorsing the existence of such distinctions at the outset.

Quine, then, does not begin by presupposing a distinction between the a priori and the empirical. The process of carrying out implicit definitions, and thus of rendering truths analytic, is not answerable to any antecedent facts about what is a priori and what is not. Quine's use of the notion of the a priori, we might say, is purely negative: it is the illusion or the confusion that is to be eliminated. We do not begin with a class of a priori truths. Nor does the language have a class of analytic truths prior to and independent of the imposition of definitions. The definitions are thus not answerable to such prior facts about the language; the matter is simply one for syntactic decision. We may define this class of truths as analytic, or that class; there is no right or wrong to it.

The fact that there is no right and wrong here, that the definition of the class of analytic truths for a given language is simply a matter for "syntactic decision," highlights the question of the *purpose* of such a definition.[18] If we are not recording an antecedent fact (that such-and-such are the analytic or a priori truths of our language), then we are recording a decision or a recommendation to define "analytic" for that language in the given way. But decisions and recommendations are answerable to purposes: *why* does it seem to be a good idea to define analyticity in this way for this language? Or, indeed, to define it at all?[19] We have already seen Quine's (1934) answer to this point. To repeat: the definition of analyticity "has the importance of enabling us to pursue foundations of mathematics and the logic of science without encountering extra-logical questions as to the source of the validity of our *a priori* judgments. . . . [I]t shows that all metaphysical questions as to an *a priori* synthetic are gratuitous, and let in only by ill-advised syntactic procedures" (pp. 65–66). The implication here is that there are questions as to the validity of some of our judgments, questions that threaten to lead us into metaphysics; and that such questions can be answered by the definition of analyticity.

At the risk of some overstatement, or simplification, we may thus say that the purpose of the definition of analyticity, as Quine sees it, is to give nonmetaphysical answers to questions about "the source of the validity" of some of our judgments. It is to explain how we come to know certain sentences, or at least to accept them as true (there is no reason to take "validity" here as more than truth).

Can a system of implicit definitions achieve this aim? This question is by no means straightforward. Suppose we imagine ourselves speaking the language established by those definitions—speaking that language and no other. Then we may think that in the imagined situation the question of the validity of certain of our sentences would not arise, or would be easily answered by reference to the definitions.[20] If one holds (as Carnap perhaps does) that the question of justification makes sense only when formulated within some such language, then one may hold that, given an appropriate choice of language, the question will have an acceptably nonmetaphysical answer. But Quine's rhetoric, at least, suggests that even in 1934 he does not hold this view. The imagined situation is, of course, merely imagined—and imagined by us, at home in our actual language and our actual system of knowledge. It is from this vantage point that Quine contemplates the creation of a system of implicit definitions and speaks of its (supposed) advantages. And from this point of view—our actual point of view—it may seem that

Quine's (1934) notion of analyticity cannot meet the demands placed on it. In particular, if that notion is seen as *explaining* our acceptance of certain sentences, then it may seem inadequate to its task.

The problem here is not so much the arbitrariness of any particular system; it is, rather, the fact that the definition is erected on the basis of a body of "admittedly true" sentences. This is our starting point. If a sentence comes out of the process of implicit definitions with the label "analytic", then it went into the process wearing the label "true"; it was already accepted, before the system of definitions was constructed. So how can the system of implicit definitions be "the source of [the sentence's] validity"? How can the notion of analyticity, as Quine explains it, account in a nonmetaphysical way for the correctness of (some of) our beliefs?

Let us elaborate and fill in some details. Quine's starting point, as we have seen, is "the expository fiction that we have at hand all those sentences which, in 1934, we find ourselves accepting as true" (p. 87). We have stressed that he does not presuppose, at the outset, that these sentences are separated into the empirical and the a priori; and that it would undermine his purposes if he were to do so. The sentences whose truth or acceptability is presupposed at the outset are of course sentences of a certain language—more or less the ordinary American English of 1934, let's say, supplemented by mathematical and other symbols as needed to express the knowledge of 1934 in perspicuous ways. This point may seem quite trivial, but it is significant that, at least in thinking about where the process begins, Quine sticks with this more or less ordinary language, and does not proceed at once to thinking about artificial or formalized languages. Even in 1934, Quine takes the starting point of philosophy to be our actual language, and our actual system of knowledge, as going concerns.

The starting point, then, is accepted sentences, couched in some more or less natural language. Now what is the role of *definitions* in this language? Here again there are foreshadowings of the later Quine. His fundamental picture of language is as constituted not by rules or definitions, but by patterns of behavior (we shall shortly note a qualification to this, but it does not affect the main point). This becomes clear in a passage that, apart from the first sentence, could have been written by Quine at any time in the subsequent sixty-odd years of his career:

> The analytic depends upon nothing more than definition, or conventions as to the uses of words. But in the ordinary uncriticized language of common sense we have little to do with deliberate definition. We learn our vocabulary through the usual processes of psychological conditioning. We proceed glibly to use our vocabulary, and so long as we move among compatriots we get on without much difficulty: for their conditioning has been substantially the same as ours. At this level we feel no need of defining terms, or introducing deliberate conventions as to the use of language. (P. 49)

This is the view that lies behind the idea that the system of implicit definitions, which Quine envisages the philosopher as imposing on language, is *arbitrary*. The system is not trying to capture definitions or conventions that are already implicit in the language; there are no such definitions. There is only the process of shared "psychological conditioning" that enables us to interact with our compatriots. (The habit of accepting some sentences as true is presumably one aspect or outcome of this conditioning. Later, of course, Quine was to go into far more detail here—but the later detail is an elaboration of the same underlying picture.)

This picture is, as I have indicated, qualified. The natural language that we start with is not spoken by wholly unreflective people; it is spoken by us. And in more or less complex and technical subjects we have already made use of definitions, prior to the philosophical process of imposing implicit definitions. Thus the passage quoted immediately above continues, "This [defining our terms, introducing deliberate conventions as to the use of language] comes only at a more sophisticated stage—for example in mathematics and science." Later Quine, commenting on the unreality of his "expository fiction," observes that our language contains "technical words which we never had, prior to their definitions, but have deliberately coined and introduced through their definitions" (p. 65). Having said this, however, he immediately lessens the impact of the point: "On the other hand it is likewise true that mathematics itself has not, traditionally, developed through the sole process of deliberately presenting implicit and explicit definitions, but has merely systematized and generated firmly accepted sentences of an abstract kind." In other words, even in our most technical subjects, the body of accepted sentences largely precedes definition; attempts to systematize by the imposition of definitions are mostly subsequent to the acceptance of the sentences themselves.

With minor qualification, then, Quine takes it that the language the philosopher sets out to systematize is not already regimented by definitions. The system of definitions is not a clearer or more precise version of what is already there. This makes more pressing our question of the explanatory value of a notion of analyticity based on implicit definitions. The starting point is a body of truths which we accept, independently of any system of definitions. How could this acceptance be explained by the subsequent imposition of a system of definition?

Only at one point does Quine seem to see that his position invites such a question. Having sketched the idea of imposing implicit definitions, thereby giving rise to a class of analytic sentences, Quine raises the issue of the relation of the analytic (thus conceived) to the a priori and to the "inward necessity" that is thought to characterize a priori judgments. Revealingly, he compares the relation between the two to the well-known conundrum of the chicken and the egg: Which comes first?[21] On the issue of the priority of analyticity and the a priori, Quine comments as follows:

> When it is claimed that the *a priori* is analytic, the usual procedure is to suggest that the *a priori* has the character of an inward necessity only because it is analytic; first we have definitions, and thence we get the *a priori*. During this hour I have adopted the opposite fiction, that we first have our whole range of accepted sentences, without any definitions, and frame our definitions to fit these sentences. (Pp. 64–65)

(Quine then goes on to enter the partial qualification to this "fiction" which we have already discussed.)

In spite of what he says, however, Quine's procedure is not exactly "the oppo-site fiction." Once the issue is posed as a question of which comes first—as a chicken-and-egg conundrum—this point can be seen quite clearly. The one fic-tion is the supposition that language, from the outset, more or less tacitly con-tains definitions and that the a priori arises out of them. This fiction Quine explic-itly avoids. The opposite fiction is that we begin with the a priori, and create definitions to match it or capture it. But this fiction also, as we have emphasized, is not Quine's procedure. He begins with *neither* presupposition: neither that the language already contains a distinction between the a priori and the empirical and that our definitions are established to enshrine that distinction; nor that the language is, to any significant extent, already tacitly regimented by definitions which, when made explicit, give rise to a distinction between the a priori and the empirical. His starting point is, near enough, an undifferentiated body of accepted sentences. The system of definitions that he envisages presupposes the validity of these sentences, and so, one might suppose, it cannot be the source of their validity.

The tension that we have found in Quine's lectures could be phrased like this: does the notion of analyticity have any explanatory value? Does it, in particular, have an explanatory role in epistemology, as an account of the basis of the truth of some of the sentences we are inclined to accept (those generally thought of as a priori)? The way in which Quine articulates the notion of analyticity suggests negative answers to both these questions (and such, I think, would accord with Carnap's view of the matter). His account of the purpose of analyticity, of the reason for wanting to construct such a notion in the first place, however, suggests a posi-tive answer: again, "enabling us to pursue foundations of mathematics and the logic of science without encountering extra-logical questions as to the source of validity of our *a priori* judgments" (pp. 65–66). Perhaps the suggestion of a posi-tive answer is defeasible; or perhaps the tension could be resolved by finding an ambiguity or unclarity in the idea of explanation, as it is deployed here. From the point of view of the mature Quine, however, I think that no such resolution is possible. This gives us a way of crystallizing the debate between Carnap and Quine: the question becomes whether analyticity—and philosophical concepts in general—are to be explanatory; whether philosophy aims to be explanatory in the same sort of way as natural science is. That this tension is to be found in Quine's 1934 lectures suggests that even then, even at the height of his Carnapianism, he was more or less unwittingly drawn to a rather different view, according to which the concepts and questions of philosophy have a role akin to those of natural science.

These ideas are encouraged by hints in the lectures that the tension over ana-lyticity is a sign of a larger and more general issue. At least at moments, Quine's words suggest the (unCarnapian) idea that there really are philosophical prob-lems and that our aim is to *solve* them—not, or at least not in all cases, merely to show that they are illusory. Early in the third lecture Quine says: "In all our gen-eral thinking, whether within metaphysics itself or in the natural sciences or in mathematics, we seem invariably to come up finally against some philosophic, non-empirical problem which cannot be permanently swept aside" (p. 88). He goes on to suggest that, at least to a large extent, these problems are not to be dismissed as meaningless but, rather, resolved by "the methods of syntax." The bulk of the penultimate paragraph of the lectures reads as follows:

> [Carnap's] purpose is not merely to advance a negative doctrine, not to construe philosophy as trivial. His concern is rather to clear away confusion and lay the foundations of a rigorous and fruitful study of the logic of science: for it is the logic of science, in the broadest sense of the phrase, the analysis, criticism and refinement of the *methods* and the *concepts* of science that Carnap regards as the defensible province of philosophy. (Pp. 102–103)

It is tempting to see here an echo of Russell's statement, "Philosophy is not a short cut to the same kind of results as those of the other sciences: *if it is to be a genuine study, it must have a province of its own*, and aim at results which the other sciences can neither prove nor disprove."[22]

The Quine of 1934 is strongly attracted to the Carnapian picture of philosophy; he comes, indeed, almost as close as one could wish to being a true believer. The above quotation, however, suggests that he is trying to square that picture with an inchoate view that is quite different: a robust conception of the subject— philosophy as confronting genuine problems and offering genuine explanations and solutions. The tension over analyticity, I suggest, indicates the difficulty of reconciling the two views.

Our discussion also suggests a somewhat different issue, which concerns not the explanatory power of the notion of analyticity but rather the idea that there is something here in need of explanation. Quine's starting point, we have emphasized, is simply those sentences which we accept as true: he does not begin by making any epistemological distinctions among them. But then what is it that analyticity is to explain? The obvious answer is that it is to explain our acceptance of those of our accepted sentences that cannot be justified by the usual empirical methods. But this answer presupposes that the sentences we accept fall into one or other of two categories: those that can be justified by "the usual empirical methods" and those that cannot. This, however, is just the sort of distinction Quine seems unwilling to presuppose—so what is there to be explained? This issue emerges in and immediately following the passages we have just been discussing.

Quine's claim that he is adopting "the opposite fiction" to the usual one seems, as we have seen, to require an initial distinction between the a priori and the empirical. Having made the claim (and qualified it), however, Quine goes on to make not that distinction, but one that differs from it in crucial ways. In a voice that could be that of the mature Quine, he says:

> But in any case there are more or less firmly accepted sentences prior to any sophisticated system of thoroughgoing definition. The more firmly accepted sentences we choose to modify last, if at all, in the course of evolving and revamping our sciences in the face of new discoveries. And among these sen-

tences which we choose to give up last, if at all, there are those which we are not going to give up at all, so basic are they to our whole conceptual scheme. These, if any, are the sentences to which the epithet "*a priori*" would have to apply. (P. 65)

We wait for the conclusion the mature Quine was to draw: that calling sentences "a priori," or "analytic," adds nothing to calling them "firmly accepted"—adds, that is, nothing by way of explanation to the bare behavioral fact that these are sentences about which we will change our minds only under the most extreme circumstances, if at all.[23]

We wait, of course, in vain: this is, after all, not the mature Quine but a twenty-six-year-old prodigy still ("abjectly"?) following his great teacher. His point is not that the term "analytic" fails to be explanatory—that it adds nothing to the fact that some sentences are more firmly accepted than others—and is thus to be condemned. His point, rather, is that there really is something that needs to be explained—namely the status of those sentences we most firmly accept. This becomes clear immediately:

[I]t is *convenient* so to frame our definitions as to make all these sentences [the most firmly accepted ones] analytic. . . . [W]e are equally free to leave some of our firmly accepted sentences outside the analytic realm, and yet to continue to hold to them by what we may call deliberate dogma, or mystic intuition, or divine revelation: but what's the use, since suitable definition *can* be made to do the trick without any such troublesome assumptions? If we disapprove of the gratuitous creation of metaphysical problems, we will provide for such firmly accepted sentences within our definitions, or else cease to accept them so firmly. (P. 65)

This is a very curious passage. Why should our firmly accepted sentences, if not explained as analytic, threaten "the gratuitous creation of metaphysical problems"?

Let us begin with what may appear to be a relatively minor point. Though the notion of being unrevisable appears to be behavioristic, in Quine's use it is not untainted by philosophical theory. If it were a truly behavioristic notion, it would not discriminate between "2 + 2 = 4" and (to use a later Quinean example) "there have been black dogs." But Quine here has in mind only cases of the former kind, not the latter. This is clear because he has in mind a class of sentences that threaten to raise metaphysical problems; he hopes to pick this class out by means of the behavioral concept of being unrevisable, but the prospect of doing this seems unpromising.[24]

This seemingly minor difficulty serves to point the way to the underlying problem. Never mind how we pick out the relevant class of sentences (or whether we can); the pivotal question is, Why should Quine think that some of our sentences threaten "metaphysical problems" (problems of justification, presumably) unless we give a system of definitions which makes them out to be analytic? The obvious answer here—indeed, so far as I can see, the only remotely satisfactory answer—is that a problem arises if there is a notion of empirical justification which applies to some of the sentences we accept, but not to others (and not, in particular, to the sentences of logic and mathematics). In that case we are, presumably, faced with the need to give some nonempirical—and hence metaphysical—justification for logic and mathematics (at least). Some such idea as this, indeed, seems to be presupposed in the basic picture of which analyticity is a part. According to that picture, sentences divide exhaustively into the contentful, which are empirical, and the contentless, which are analytic: there is no awkward category of the synthetic-but-contentful left over to threaten empiricism.[25] This picture implies that we have a notion of empirical justification, however inchoate, that applies to some sentences but not to others. It is thus very striking that, at least in his lectures, Quine does not seem to accept any such distinction among sentences. As we have emphasized, he takes it that the starting point for philosophy is the set of accepted sentences; the sentences are more or less firmly accepted, but no philosophically loaded distinctions among them are presupposed. And in the passages most recently quoted he seems to go out of his way to avoid a notion of empirical justification which would effect such a distinction.

Quine's view of the role that analyticity is to play—of what it is meant to explain—thus seems to require epistemological assumptions that other points he makes give us reason not to attribute to him. What are we to make of this tension? We might try, on this basis, to attribute to the young Quine a complex epistemological view reconciling the various points we have seen in a satisfactory way. But I doubt that there is such a view. Also, that tactic would seem (in marked contrast, of course, to all that has gone before) to run the risk of over-reading: there is, apart from the points to which we have drawn attention, simply no sign of any epistemological view in the lectures. And this seems to me to indicate the correct way to understand the tension that we have uncovered: the young Quine was first and foremost a logician, and secondarily a philosopher of language; he did not, at this point, hold any definite views about matters epistemological.[26] Indeed, he does not seem to have seen clearly that epistemology is directly relevant to the analytic-synthetic distinction as he articulates it. Saying this, however, may seem simply to exacerbate the problem: if Quine holds no epistemological theory, how can he hold that some sentences—the sentences of logic, for example—require some special explanation? Surely this view arises only as the result of an epistemological theory—and one, moreover, that the young Quine does not seem to hold?

The answer to these questions, I think, is that in philosophy the line between theory and data is always wavering. For us, it may be clear that the idea that logic and mathematics require some special sort of explanation is not a *datum*, but is rather the product of a theory. For Quine in 1934, however, it would have been far from clear: it is entirely understandable that he could have taken for granted the (alleged) *datum* while not endorsing the theory from which (as we now see) it actually arises. And what makes us so much wiser than the young Quine in this regard? It is, I think, the fact that we have access to a theory according to which the special epistemological status of logic and mathematics is not a *datum* at all. (Only with a rival theory are we able to reconceive what counts as data.) In particular, we have access to the epistemological holism that is so characteristic of the later Quine. Of this view, there is no sign at all in the lectures. (We might fondly take Quine's starting with all our accepted sentences, without presupposing distinctions among them, as a sign of nascent holism. As an anticipation of holism, however, this is faint, even by our present generous standards.)

One crucial element in the mature Quine's rejection of analyticity is his insistence that this concept, if it is to be philosophically acceptable, must play a genuinely explanatory role. We have found foreshadowings of this point in the lectures. The other crucial element, however, is epistemological holism; and of this we find no sign. Without it, there will seem to be a need for *something* to explain our knowledge of logic and mathematics; even without adherence to any very substantive view of empirical justification, these subjects are likely to seem problematic. One may then think that there is a genuine question which the notion of analyticity is trying to answer, even if one is dissatisfied with the answer.[27] Only with something like Quine's full-blown holism does it become clear that there simply is no question here to answer, nothing for analyticity to explain.[28]

Let us attempt to summarize the discussion. The young Quine wishes to give a sympathetic treatment of Carnap. Central to this treatment is an exposition of the analytic-synthetic distinction. But we have found a tension in Quine's exposition of this distinction. The role Quine ascribes to the notion of analyticity, indeed the reasons he gives for accepting the distinction in the first place, suggest that the point of analyticity is that it should have explanatory power. Yet it is hard to see how analyticity, as Quine articulates it, could explain anything. This point of tension in the lectures reflects a fundamental strand in the thought of the mature Quine: the idea of philosophy as substantive and explanatory in something of the same way as the natural sciences are taken to be.

A further, though rather less clear-cut point of tension in the lectures concerns the question of whether there is anything in need of the kind of explanation that Quine sees the analytic-synthetic distinction as affording. Although Quine holds that there is such a need, this position seems to rest on epistemological views which he does not endorse, and seems tacitly to reject. Here one might attempt to discern foreshadowings of another central doctrine of the later Quine: his holistic approach to knowledge. But there is no sign of such a view in the lectures— what we see there is something more like a gap which was later to be filled up with that view. It remains a virtue of Quine's 1934 account that it suggests to a later reader (even if its author did not clearly grasp) that epistemological matters are of direct relevance to analyticity. This is a virtue, of course, to a reader sympathetic to the mature Quine;[29] perhaps a Carnapian reader would rather count it a vice, arising from confusion or from perversity on the part of the Quinean reader.

NOTES

I am indebted to Juliet Floyd and W. D. Hart for their comments on an earlier version of this essay.

My greatest debt, however, is to my teacher, the late Burton Dreben, not only for comments on an earlier draft of this essay, but even more for inspiration and instruction over many years, and for his example of intellectual depth and honesty.

1. Carnap, *Logische Syntax der Sprache* (Vienna: Springer,1934), trans. A. Smeaton, *The Logical Syntax of Language* (London: Kegan Paul, 1937) (hereafter *Syntax)*.

2. In R. Creath, ed., *Dear Carnap, Dear Van: The Quine-Carnap Correspondence and Related Work* (Berkeley: University of California Press, 1990) (hereafter Creath 1990), pp. 47–103. I shall call them simply "the lectures"; page numbers standing alone refer to them as published in Creath. The brief history in this paragraph is drawn chiefly from Creath's introduction and from Quine's "Autobiography," in *The Philosophy of W. V. Quine*, ed. Lewis Edwin Hahn and P. A. Schilpp (LaSalle, Ill.: Open Court, 1986) (hereafter Hahn and Schilpp 1986), pp. 3–46.

3. "Homage to Rudolf Carnap," *Boston Studies in the Philosophy of Science* 8 (1971): xxii–xxv (hereafter Quine 1971), was presented in Boston in October 1970, at a memorial meeting under the auspices of the Philosophy of Science Association. Reprinted in *Ways of Paradox* (Cambridge, Mass.: Harvard University Press, 1976) (hereafter Quine 1976) and also in Creath (1990). The passage quoted is from Quine (1976, p. 41), and Creath (1990, p. 464).

4. "Two Dogmas in Retrospect," *Canadian Journal of Philosophy* 21 (1991): 265–274, p. 266. Here it is worth mentioning that, when he first met Carnap, Quine was by no means a convinced Carnapian. An entry in Carnap's professional log for March 31, 1933, reads as follows: "He [Quine] said after reading my MS 'Syntax': 1. Is there a principled distinction between the logical laws and empirical statements[?] He thinks not. Perhaps though it is only [as] an expedient I seek a distinction, but it appears he is right: gradual difference. They are the statements that we want to hold fast." I quote from Neil Tennant, "Carnap and Quine," in *Logic, Language, and the Structure of Scientific Theories*, ed. Wesley Salmon and Gereon Wolters (Pittsburgh: University of Pittsburgh Press,1994), pp. 305–344; I'm indebted to Quine for this reference. Whether these words represent the consideration of a significant change of doctrine is, I think, unclear.

5. First published under the title *Logische-Philosophische Abhandlung* in *Annalen der Naturphilosophie* 44 (1921): 185–262 (*Tractatus Logico-Philosophicus*, trans. C. K. Ogden [London: Kegan Paul, 1922], cited in the text as *Tractatus*, followed by Wittgenstein's system of numbering).

6. My parenthetical "apparently" qualifies the attribution of this idea to Russell and to Wittgenstein in two rather different ways. Russell seems to be committed to this view by his writings, especially his discussions of logical form, at least in the period 1900–1918, but the matter is not entirely clear. Wittgenstein's *Tractatus*, by contrast, does appear to be quite clearly committed to this view—provided that we ignore the last few sections of the book, which might suggest that it is not committed to anything. At any rate, Carnap took it that Wittgenstein accepts this doctrine; see *Syntax*, pp. 53 and 186.

7. See Burton Dreben, "Quine," in *Perspectives on Quine*, ed. Robert Barrett and Roger Gibson (Oxford: Basil Blackwell, 1990) (hereafter Dreben 1990), pp. 81–95, especially p. 86.

8. The so-called ramified type theory of *Principia Mathematica* does not yield mathematics unless we assume the Axiom of Reducibility, which could have struck only the most convinced as tautologous. In his doctoral dissertation *The Logic of Sequences: A Generalization of* Principia Mathematica (Ph.D. dissertation, Harvard University, 1932; New York: Garland Publishing, 1990), Quine, like Ramsey (but independently), reformulated *Principia* in such a way as to avoid the use of this axiom. Unlike Ramsey, however, the young Quine was not concerned to argue that mathematics is tautologous in Wittgenstein's sense; see Dreben (1990, especially p. 81). The resulting system (Quine's or Ramsey's) is stronger than ramified type theory and hence, presumably, harder to show to be tautologous.

Even granted the tautologousness of *Principia*, or of a variant system, there are still difficulties. Many of the results proved in *Principia* are conditional in form, with the antecedent of the conditional being an assertion of the infinitude of objects, or of the

Axiom of Choice, or of their conjunction. For a discussion of the nontechnical aspects of the achievement of *Principia*, see my "Logic in Russell's Logicism," in *The Analytic Tradition*, ed. David Bell and Neil Cooper (Oxford: Basil Blackwell, 1990), pp. 137–172.

9. Quine, however, traces the idea back to the early nineteenth-century thinker Gergonne. See Quine (1976, pp. 88 and 133).

10. For the purposes of this essay, I will refrain from going into any disputes about this idea. It is, however, subject to an important qualification. Fixing the truth-values of all the sentences constructed from certain terms does not in general (uniquely) determine the meanings and referents of those terms (the component parts of the sentences). If we think of ourselves as finding a model for the set of true sentences constructed from those terms, then in general there will be more than one such model available. We do not, however, have to be thinking in explicitly model-theoretic terms to see this point. It emerges also, for example, in Russell's criticism of the idea that we can define the natural numbers as whatever satisfies Peano's Postulates (in *Introduction of Mathematical Philosophy* [London: Allen & Unwin,1919], chapter 1). Russell points out that many different progressions will satisfy those axioms, so no unique set of objects can be determined in such a manner. Implicit definition may determine the truth-values of sentences, but it does not determine the referents of component parts of sentences.

The most important application of this fact, from the point of view of the present essay, is in the mature Quine's doctrine of ontological relativity. In this doctrine, Quine accepts that fixing the truth-values of sentences is the best we can do by way of fixing the meanings of terms. He then exploits the fact that implicit definition does not (uniquely) determine the referents of terms to argue for empirical slack in any account of these referents. See especially "Ontological Relativity," in *Ontological Relativity and Other Essays* (New York: Columbia University Press, 1969) (hereafter Quine 1969), pp. 69–90, and many other sources in Quine's later writings; see also my "Reference, Ontological Relativity, and Realism," *Aristotelian Society Supplementary Volume* LXXIV (2000), pp. 281–299.

11. For the idea of implicit definition as giving rise to analytic truths, see Quine's ironically entitled "Implicit Definition Sustained," *Journal of Philosophy* 61 (1964): 71–74, reprinted in Quine (1976). Quine there draws on Löwenheim's theorem, in a strengthened version due to Hilbert and Bernays, to argue that, given any (axiomatizable) set of truths, we can come up with a definition making these truths arithmetically true. For those who take arithmetic as paradigmatically analytic, this might seem to completely vindicate the idea that implicit definitions give rise to analytic truths. But such is not, of course, Quine's conclusion in 1964. He ends the essay like this: "Now we see that such claims to analyticity [that is, those generated by a system of implicit definitions] are every bit as firm as can be made for sentences whose truth follows by definition from arithmetic. So much the worse, surely, for the notion of analyticity" (Quine 1976, p. 136).

12. Thus Quine writes: "[T]he quasi-syntactic sentences of philosophy itself, when translated into the syntactic form, appear rather as sentences of formal syntax. These sentences are not synthetic, but analytic or contradictory" (p. 102).

13. "Truth by Convention" (in *Philosophical Essays for A. N. Whitehead*, ed. O. H. Lee [New York: Longmans, 1936], pp. 90–124) written about a year after the lectures and overlapping with them, also contains such an exposition, in some ways clearer on philosophical points. This essay is reprinted in Quine (1976, pp. 77–106); subsequent page references will be to this reprinting. In this later essay, Quine shuns the expression "implicit definitions," speaking instead of "the use of postulates"; see, for example, Quine (1976, p. 88). The underlying point is the same; it would be interesting to speculate about the reason for the change in terminology.

14. Clearly Quine here makes nothing of the distinction between the true sentences and the (firmly) accepted sentences. In this respect, the Quine of 1934 is en-

tirely consonant with later Quine, who holds that there is no standpoint outside the body of our firmly accepted beliefs from which we can demarcate them into the true and the false. Any distinctions within the body of beliefs must be made piecemeal and on internal grounds—which is not to say that critical scrutiny of our firmly accepted beliefs will not lead to our doubting, or even rejecting, some of them.

15. The notion of essential occurrence is, very roughly, that a term occurs *essentially* in a sentence if replacing it at all occurrences by another term may alter the truth-value of the sentence. If the truth-value of the sentence is immutable under this operation, then the term occurs *vacuously*. See Quine (1976, pp. 80–28), and footnote 2 of "Carnap and Logical Truth," in Schilpp (1963, pp. 385–406) (hereafter Quine 1963).

In a logically valid sentence, for example, all the nonlogical terms occur vacuously: the truth of "If Socrates is a person and all people are mortal then Socrates is mortal" is unaffected by (consistent and grammatically acceptable) replacements of "Socrates," "person," and "mortal." If we consider the first premise—"Socrates is a person"— by itself, however, then "Socrates" has an essential occurrence: there are replacements for "Socrates" that will alter the truth-value of the resulting sentence.

Even apart from the complication of sentences that essentially contain more than one term, it is not always necessary—and may sometimes not be conveniently possible—to stipulate the truth of *all* the accepted K-sentences. I shall, however, ignore this point and its close analogues in what follows.

16. The claim that *all* of first-order logic (with or without identity) thus becomes true by implicit definition relies on the existence of sound and complete axiom systems for first-order logic.

17. This statement might seem to raise a puzzling point. Gödel's incompleteness theorem shows that there is no recursive first-order axiomatization of all mathematical truths and hence (a fortiori) not of all truths. Will this not preclude a system of definitions, implicit and explicit, from which all truths may be obtained? The answer here depends on exactly how one requires that the truths be *obtained*. In *Syntax*, Carnap adopts a liberal understanding of this idea, which permits the use of Hilbert's ω-rule. This does not, of course, refute the theorem. It does, however, avoid its effects— though at the price of an indefiniteness about the notion of consequence.

Quine later made much of the problems that these issues pose for Carnap; see especially Quine (1963). In the lectures, however, and also in Quine (1936), he seems not to be aware of those problems.

18. Compare the far more skeptical remarks of "Two Dogmas of Empiricism," *The Philosophical Review* 60 (1951): 20–43 (hereafter Quine 1951), given as a talk at the meeting of the Eastern Division of the American Philosophical Association in December 1950 and reprinted in Quine's *From a Logical Point of View* (Cambridge, Mass.: Harvard University Press, 1953) (hereafter Quine 1953). On page 33 of Quine (1953), he is commenting on the Carnapian idea that we can give semantical rules for some formal language, L_0, and thereby specify the analytic statements of that language. One way of understanding this idea is as giving an answer to the antecedently understood question, What are the analytic truths of L_0? But here we need to understand the notion of analyticity in order to understand the question. So this method will not advance our understanding of analyticity. Suppose, then, that we do not understand Carnap's specification as answering an antecedently understood question. Quine writes, "[W]e may, indeed, view the so-called rule as a conventional definition of a new simple symbol 'analytic-for-L_0,' which might be better written untendentiously as 'K' so as not to seem to throw any light on the interesting word 'analytic.' Obviously any number of classes K, M, N, etc. of statements can be specified for various purposes or for none; what does it mean to say that K, as against M, N, etc. is the class of the 'analytic' statements of L_0?"

19. Carnap takes up this question, and in particular the passage quoted in the previous footnote, in his posthumously published reply to "Two Dogmas":

Now Quine distinguishes two cases with respect to the question of how these rules [semantical rules giving rise to a definition of analyticity] are to be understood. (1) They may be meant as assertions or as information that such and such sentences are analytic in L_0. That, however, helps us not at all, Quine says, because we do not understand the word "analytic." (2) The rules are meant merely as a convention, as a definition of a new, presumably not previously understood expression "analytic in L_0." In this case, so he says, it would be better, less misleading, to take not a symbol already in current use, but rather a new symbol, perhaps "K," "so as not so seem to throw light on the interesting word 'analytic.'" Our rules are meant neither in the first sense nor the second sense, neither as an assertion nor as a mere nominal definition, which serves as an abbreviation. Their purpose is, rather, the explication of an inexact concept already in current use. . . . [W]e advance the claim that the defined concept embraces what philosophers have meant, intuitively but not exactly, when they speak of "analytic sentences." (Creath 1990, pp. 429–430; my emphasis)

Note that here Carnap does seem to presuppose—as Quine in the lectures does not—that our starting point is a body of sentences already at least roughly demarcated into the analytic and the synthetic, or the a priori and the a posteriori. Carnap wrote this passage, of course, some twenty years after *Syntax*.

20. We *may* think this. The mature Quine, of course, would not. See especially section VIII of Quine (1963).

21. Quine speaks of hens and eggs, but I adopt the more colloquial form. Note that, in the case of chickens and eggs, it is undeniable that we do in fact have both; in the case of analyticity and the a priori the conundrum can be evaded by denying the corresponding claim.

22. Bertrand Russell, *Our Knowledge of the External World*, 2d ed. (London: George Allen and Unwin, 1926), p. 27; emphasis added.

23. Here it is apparent that the idea that the analytic-synthetic distinction is a vague or gradual one is not the crucial point in the disagreement between Carnap and the mature Quine. The point is rather whether calling a sentence "analytic" has any explanatory value—whether it adds anything at all to saying that it is firmly accepted, or whether the word is simply an idle label. —Hence it is quite unclear whether Carnap was contemplating any real concession in his notes of March 31, 1933; see note 5, above.

24. Note that in taking the unrevisability of certain beliefs to be the *explanandum*, Quine seems to contradict Carnap. For Carnap, no belief is unrevisable; it's just that, for some beliefs, their revision amounts to a change of language. For a very explicit statement of this position, see Carnap's "Reply to Quine" in (Schilpp 1963), p. 921. The difference may arise from the fact that Quine begins with our actual beliefs cast in our actual language; or from the fact that a more Carnapian starting point would make the emptiness of analyticity, from a Quinean point of view, even more apparent.

25. For an articulation of this picture, see Carnap's "Autobiography" in Schilpp (1963, pp. 47 and 64).

26. A footnote in "Truth by Convention" may seem to challenge this view, but in fact, I think, reinforces it. This is footnote 20 (Quine 1976, p. 100), in which Quine speaks of the likely success of the reductionist program of Carnap's *Der logische Aufbau der Welt* (Berlin: Weltkreis, 1928) (hereafter Carnap 1928). Quine's comments might be taken to suggest an interest in epistemology as early as 1933 or 1934. But a better reading, I believe, would be that they show exactly the opposite. Carnap himself had abandoned the program of *Der logische Aufbau* by 1933, and for convincing reasons. Quine's speaking optimistically of that program strongly suggests that epistemology was far from the center of his attention.

27. Thus Quine's statement in his "Autobiography" about his views in the early to mid-1940s: "Because of its negativity, my repudiation of analyticity was noth-

ing I felt impelled to write about" (Hahn and Schilpp 1986), p. 19. The "negativity" here, I think, is that he rejected analyticity as unexplanatory or ill-defined, but had nothing to put in its place—nothing else that could explain the status of logic and mathematics.

28. See Quine's "Reply to Hellman":

The second dogma of empiricism, to the effect that each empirically meaningful sentence has an empirical content of its own, was cited in "Two Dogmas" merely as encouraging false confidence in the notion of analyticity; but now I would say further that *the second dogma creates a need for analyticity as a key notion of epistemology, and that the need lapses when we heed Duhem and set the second dogma aside."* (Hahn and Schilpp 1986, p. 207; emphasis added)

29. Compare Quine's statement from the early or mid-1980s: "I now perceive that the philosophically important question about analyticity and the linguistic doctrine of logical truth is *not* how to explicate them; it is the question rather of their relevance to epistemology." "Reply to Hellman," Hahn and Schilpp (1986, p. 207).

12

Hans Reichenbach:
Realist and Verificationist

HILARY PUTNAM

In *Meaning and the Moral Sciences*, I remarked that "it is *not* clear that [Reichenbach's] form of verificationism (the 'probability theory of meaning') is incompatible with realism."[1] (I added, however, that I thought it was wrong on other grounds.[2]) And after rehearsing the reasons why the identification of meaningfulness with "conclusive verifiability in principle" (accepted by the Vienna Circle at one point[3]) *is* incompatible with realism, I went on to ask,

> Why should it be impossible from a realist point of view that (1) every meaningful sentence have some weight or other in some observable situation; and (2) every difference in meaning be reflected in some difference in weight in some observable situation? (These are . . . the two principles of Reichenbach's "probability theory of meaning.") At least it should be an open question for the realist *qua* realist whether this is so or not, and not something that realism rules out. (Putnam 1978, p. 113)

What I want to argue here (and did not argue at that time) is that this observation is essential to understanding the structure and content of Reichenbach's only work in pure epistemology, *Experience and Prediction*.[4] That is, not only is it the case that one might *suppose* that realism and Reichenbach's form of verificationism are compatible, but that was, so to speak, the *point* of *Experience and Prediction*. What Reichenbach was trying to do in the whole book was *simultaneously* to be a particular sort of realist (a materialist, in particular) *and* to preserve a weak form of the verifiability theory of meaning—weak, but not *too* weak to exclude metaphysics. This is not to say that Reichenbach did not feel some discomfort; after all, his friend, Rudolf Carnap (with whom he co-founded *Erkenntnis*), and the other members of the Vienna Circle as well[5] had characterized the realism/idealism issue as a pseudo-issue, and Reichenbach defers to this view to the extent of claiming that the issue is just a question of a choice of a linguistic framework. But I wish to claim that the arguments Reichenbach gave only make sense if we realize that his realism was much more robust than these disclaimers suggest.

To argue this claim properly would require a much longer paper than this one. What I shall do here is point to places in Reichenbach's argumentation at which his realism is most evident, and also briefly discuss the claim just alluded to, that the issue is one of choosing a "language."

I also want to consider another aspect of Reichenbach's thought, one not, as far as I know, mentioned in his writings. When I was Reichenbach's student, he repeatedly expressed the view that in "Testability and Meaning"[6] and thereafter Carnap had "converged" to a position close to or perhaps identical with (my memory is not clear here) Reichenbach's own position. I want briefly to consider this idea and argue that, though there is a superficial appearance of convergence, Carnap's way of thinking is really very far from what I have described as Reichenbach's realism, even after "Testability and Meaning" and, in fact, to the end of Carnap's life.

Background: The Probability Theory
of Meaning

I have already mentioned the two principles of "the probability theory of meaning." Here they are in Reichenbach's words: "(1) [A] proposition[7] has meaning if it is possible to determine a weight, i.e., a degree of probability, for the proposition;[8] and (2) every difference in meaning is reflected in some difference in weight in some observable situation" (1938, p. 54). It is necessary to add that at this time neither Reichenbach nor Carnap considered any other possible meaning for "probability" than relative frequency and that Carnap questioned whether it was possible to assign numerical degrees of probability (in this sense) to hypotheses.[9] (The "chief difficulty," Carnap wrote—citing Popper as the origin of this criticism—"lies in how we are to determine for a given hypothesis the series of 'related' hypotheses to which the concept of frequency is to apply" [1936, p. 427].)

Reichenbach, as we shall see, viewed scientific hypotheses in a very different way from how they are most often viewed (although his view has some affinity to "bootstrapping" views about scientific confirmation, such as those proposed by Clark Glymour). His belief that we can assign a numerical probability to, say, the existence of electrons was based on the idea that electrons are by no means mere "constructs," added to the language of physics for the sake of predictive efficacy. Electrons are *things*, much as billiard balls are things, and we *infer* their existence. Moreover, the very inferences by which we infer their existence permit us to assign a probability to that existence. It is obvious that this is (intuitively at least) a realistic conception, in stark contrast to that of the Vienna Circle.

There are many other symptoms of Reichenbach's attraction to realism, indeed to an almost naive materialism, in the opening chapter (titled "Meaning") of *Experience and Prediction*. Not only does Reichenbach emphasize that linguistic symbols are "physical things" (although this plays no role whatsoever in the probability theory of meaning), but, oddly, he adopts what sounds like a naive correspondence account of reference, writing: "Let us formulate our first answer [to the question, "What is meaning?"] as follows: *Meaning is a function which symbols acquire by being put into a certain correspondence with facts*" (1938, p. 17; emphasis in original). And again:

[I]f "north" means a certain relation of a line to the North Pole of the earth, the symbol "north" will occur in connection with the symbols "London" and "Edinburgh," as for example in the sentence, "Edinburgh is north of London," because the objects London and Edinburgh are in the relation to the North Pole corresponding to the word "north." So the carbon patch "north" before your eyes has a meaning because it occurs in relation to other carbon patches in such a way that there is a correspondence to physical objects such as towns and the North Pole. Meaning is just this function of the carbon patch acquired by this connection. (1938, p. 17)

This pair of sentences in *Experience and Prediction*, contrary to what one might expect, is not the beginning of a sustained discussion of how one gets from putting symbols in correspondence with "facts" or "objects" to the definition of the concept "truth-value of a sentence." (There is no hint of Tarskian semantics in *Experience and Prediction*.) In fact, although we have just been told that meaning depends on a "correspondence," Reichenbach moves at once to other topics—that meaning is a property of a proposition as a whole, that it is related to the direction of actions—and then to the discussion of the "truth theory of meaning"— that is, the Viennese theory that meaningfulness requires the possibility of "verification"—and to his own "probability theory of meaning." *"Correspondence" is never mentioned again.* So what are these assertions doing here?

I submit that they represent declarations of faith. Reichenbach is telling us that he subscribes to an intuitive realist picture of meaning as correspondence. He has already told us (1938, p. 5) that epistemology deals with "rational reconstruction" (Reichenbach takes the term from Carnap's "*rationale Nachkonstruction*" in the *Aufbau*.) The subsequent discussion, which does not mention correspondence, is, I believe, precisely Reichenbach's *rational reconstruction* of the notion of meaning, but the initial declarations I have quoted show that it is not offered as a repudiation of realism, but intended to make these realist intuitions more precise.

Reichenbach's Cubical World Argument

The most interesting but also the most difficult chapter of *Experience and Prediction* is titled "Impressions and the External World." The difficulties begin with the title. Although Reichenbach adopts the strategy of speaking of "impressions" in this chapter, and makes the traditional assumption that impressions are what we "directly observe," he opens the very next chapter, "An Inquiry Concerning Impressions," by attacking that whole way of thinking. "The foregoing chapter," he writes,

was based on the presupposition that impressions are observable facts. We introduced them because we found that physical observations, even of the most concrete type, can never be maintained with certainty; so we tried to reduce them to more elementary facts. It may be doubtful, we said, that there is a table before me; but I cannot doubt that at least I have the impression of a table. Thus impressions came to be the very archetype of observable facts.

This train of thought is of convincing power, and there are not many philosophers who have been able to resist it. As for myself, I believed it for a long
time until I discovered at last some of its weak points.[10]

Although there is something correct in these reflections, it seems to me
now that there is something in them which is essentially false. (1938, p. 163)

Reichenbach immediately goes on (p. 164) to declare, "I cannot admit that
impressions have the character of observable facts. What I observe are things,
not impressions." To be sure, Reichenbach does not doubt the existence of impressions: "I believe that there are impressions but I have never sensed them.
When I consider this question in an unprejudiced manner, I find that I infer the
existence of my impressions" (p. 164).

What is happening in chapter II of *Experience and Prediction*, then, is not
really an account of how we infer the existence of things from impressions; if
Reichenbach's view (in chapter III) is correct, there is no such problem. Rather,
it is an account of how we infer the existence (and behavior) of unobserved things
from the existence and behavior of observed things. What Reichenbach assumes
for the purposes of chapter II is that if "things" only existed when observed by me
and had only the properties that they appear (to me) to possess, then these "things"
would be, to all intents and purposes, just as "phenomenal" as the empiricist
impressions; this justifies, he thinks, identifying (temporarily) the traditional
problem of justifying "the inference from impressions to the external world" with
the problem of justifying the inference from observed things to unobserved things.

Reichenbach argues vigorously against what he calls the "positivist" view (he
never accepted the label as applied to himself) that talk about unobserved objects
is just highly derived talk about one's own impressions and/or about observed
objects. Instead, he likens it to inferring the existence of birds we cannot see, but
whose shadows are visible to us on the ceiling of the cage. To make the inference
more complicated, he imagines a setup in which the human race is confined to
an enormous cubical room with translucent walls. There are birds outside the
cube, and a mirror which causes the images of the birds to be reflected onto a side
wall of the cube, so that each bird produces two "shadows," one on the ceiling
and one on the side wall. To make sure that it is physically impossible for human
beings directly to verify the existence of the birds, Reichenbach also stipulates that
there is a "system of repulsive forces" which makes any near approach to the walls
"impossible for men" (1938, p. 117). And he asks, "Will these men discover that
there are things outside their cube different from the shadow-figures?" (1938,
p. 116).

The answer he gives is the following:

After some time, however, I think there will come a Copernicus. He will direct telescopes to the walls and discover that the dark spots have the shape
of animals, and, what is more important still, that there are corresponding
pairs of black dots, consisting of one dot on the ceiling and one dot on the
side wall, which show a very similar shape. (1938, pp. 116–117)

Reichenbach goes on to describe how this Copernicus will

> surprise mankind by the exposition of a very suggestive theory. He will main-
> tain that the strange correspondence between the two shades of one pair
> cannot be a matter of chance but that these two shades are nothing but effects
> caused by one individual thing situated outside the cube within free space.
> He calls these things "birds" and he says that there are animals flying out-
> side the cube, different from the shadow figures, having an existence of their
> own, and that the black spots are nothing but shadows. (1938, p. 118)

Reichenbach now imagines a positivist who insists that the "birds" are just
logical constructions and that in fact they can be identified with pairs of black
spots (1938, p. 119). But Reichenbach counters that a physicist would reject this
positivist interpretation:

> The physicist, however, would not accept this . . . theory. . . . It is not because
> he wants to combine with the term "causal connection" some metaphysical
> feelings, such as "influence from one thing to another" or "transubstantia-
> tion of the cause into the effect." . . . Freed from all associated representa-
> tions, his inference has this form: Whenever there were corresponding
> shadow-figures like the spots on the screen [in the case of similar phenom-
> ena observable within the cubical world], there was, in addition, a third body
> with an independent existence; it is therefore highly probable that there is
> also such a third body in the case in question. It is this probability inference
> which furnishes a different weight [probability] for the projective complex
> and the reducible complex. (1938, p. 123)

In this last quotation, two technical terms appear: "projective complex" and "reducible complex." A "projective complex" is an item to whose existence we infer
with probability on the basis of similar cases in the past; a "reducible complex" is
something whose existence is guaranteed by the existence of the evidence because
it is a mere logical construct out of that evidence. Reichenbach is arguing that,
on the (early Vienna Circle) view he is attacking, the existence of the "birds" (unobserved objects) is certain, because they are nothing more than logical constructs
out of the observables (pairs of shadow figures). But on the view he regards as
correct, their existence has a probability less than one and is thus not logically
equivalent to the existence of the logical constructs. On Reichenbach's "probability theory of meaning," the two propositions which the "positivists" regarded as
equivalent in meaning are quite distinct assertions.

"Illata" versus "Abstracta"

Two quite opposed reactions are possible to this argument. First, a traditional
epistemologist might say that the argument simply begs the question. Reichen-

bach's inference presupposes that there are places outside the cubical world at which unobserved objects can be situated. But is this not precisely begging the question of "the existence of unobserved objects" (Reichenbach's "stand-in" for the question of the existence of objects other than our sense impressions)?

Reichenbach's answer to this objection is stated in what he himself acknowledges to be Carnapian language, which leaves him open to the suspicion (which he himself shared) that the difference between Reichenbach and "the positivist" is just the difference between the Carnap of, say, "Testability and Meaning" and the earlier positions of the Vienna Circle. (This is the second possible reaction.) What Reichenbach says in answer to the first reaction is that the decision to postulate places we do not observe, and to allow inductive speculation about the behavior of (possible) objects at such places, is a matter of "the difference of two languages." I shall discuss this claim in a later section, as well as the question of whether, indeed, there is an identity of view between the Reichenbach of *Experience and Prediction* and the Carnap of "Testability and Meaning." But certainly, regarding the status of statements about objects we do not observe but could (physically possibly) have observed, what Carnap writes in "Testabililty and Meaning" is in full agreement with Reichenbach's position. Discussing "the following sentence discussed by [C. I.] Lewis and Schlick: 'If all minds (or: all living beings)[11] should disappear from the universe, the stars would still go on in their courses,'" Carnap writes:

> Both Lewis and Schlick assert that this sentence is not verifiable. This is true if "verifiable" is interpreted as "completely confirmable." But the sentence is confirmable and even testable, though incompletely. . . . The sentence in question is meaningful from the point of view of empiricism, i.e., it has to be admitted in an empiricist language, provided generalized sentences are admitted at all and complete confirmability is not required. (Carnap 1937, pp. 37–38)

The "partial confirmation" Carnap speaks of here is just the confirmation (during our lifetimes) of "the laws C of celestial mechanics" (1937, p. 37).

In his lectures at UCLA, Reichenbach used to employ the following example: suppose I see a tree-shaped shadow in front of me on the ground. Whether I turn around and look at the tree or not, I infer that there is a tree behind me, because I have confirmed—in situations in which I was in a position to see the place in question—that, whenever there is a tree-shaped shadow on the ground, then (almost always, if we allow for a small number of cases where the shadow is cast by something else), in the place at which the base of the tree-shaped shadow is located, there is also a real tree. The statement that there is an unobserved tree behind me is simply a deduction (or an induction, if the generalization is statistical) from a generalization which is itself inductively confirmed. Concerning this view, I wrote in *Meaning and the Moral Sciences*:

> What seems right to me about this is that if we had no inductive logic at all—
> if we had only pattern recognition and deductive logic—there would be no

basis for ascribing to us any concept of an "unobserved object." Our linguistic behavior would fit the account "tree" means "observed tree"—and, more generally, "object" means "observed object." In this sense our inductive logic is part of our concept of an unobserved object, and hence of an object at all. (Putnam 1978, p. 112)

But Reichenbach does not only speak of the inference from observed objects (birds, trees) to unobserved objects. As already remarked, he regards the inference to unobservable[12] objects—for example, "electricity, radio waves, atoms"—as of exactly the same nature. Such theoretical entities, he claims, are *illata* (inferred entities),[13] not *abstracta* (logical constructions). With respect to this claim, I want to make two remarks, one historical and one purely philosophical.

The historical claim is that the agreement between Carnap and Reichenbach regarding the status of sentences about unobserved objects decidedly did not extend to agreement about the status of unobservable objects, such as the "electricity and radio waves" Reichenbach mentions. The predicates we need even to speak about such objects are only "partially interpreted," Carnap insisted to the end of his life; talk about them is highly derived talk about observables (and, strange to say, sets of observables, sets of sets of observables, etc.). Although these "theoretical constructs," as Carnap's followers continued to call them,[14] were no longer claimed to be individually definable in "observational vocabulary," the theory of contemporary science as a whole was held to be expressible in a language with no primitive vocabulary except "observation terms."[15] This is precisely the attitude Reichenbach rejected.

The philosophical remark (a critical one) is that Reichenbach's view is, however, almost certainly incompatible with his own doctrines respecting inductive logic. For Reichenbach, induction is simply the projection of an observed relative frequency, and induction in this sense is the only legitimate method of nondemonstrative inference.[16] Even if we accept (as I think we should) some inferences to the existence and behavior of physical things too small to see or touch as of essentially the same character as the inference to the existence of the birds outside the cubical world, what Reichenbach ignores is the problem of inferences that are not to the existence of little things at all, but to the existence of fields (modifications of space itself) and novel magnitudes of all kinds. (It is striking that, when Reichenbach discusses his doctrine of "*illata*," he writes that "modern physics has shown that electrons, positrons, protons, neutrons, and photons are the basic elements out of which all things are built up in the form of reducible complexes" [1938, p. 215; emphasis added]. Here he entirely ignores the predicates involved, and thinks only of the objects!) In *The Philosophy of Space and Time*, Reichenbach allows himself to pretend that there are arbitrarily small "clocks" and "measuring rod[s]." But however useful and legitimate such a device may be in explaining relativity theory, we cannot seriously suppose that an inference to the existence of such a magnitude as electricity and to the differential equations that it obeys is simply an "inductive" inference (in Reichenbach's limited sense) to the behavior of arbitrarily small measuring instruments!

The problem will appear strange to most philosophers, since we are used to thinking, with Mill, that something called the "hypothetico-deductive method" is an essential part of the apparatus of "induction" and that it is by confirming the predictions of theories about electricity, etc., that we confirm the existence and behavior of electricity. But Reichenbach rejected the hypothetico-deductive method, or, rather, he had a Bayesian attitude toward it: the method is legitimate only when sanctioned by Bayes' Theorem, which requires a knowledge of the prior probabilities of the alternative hypotheses. But the difficulty is in seeing how Reichenbach's inductive method can assign any probability at all to hypotheses about such "*illata.*"

The reason that Reichenbach held such a restrictive view of induction has to do, strangely, with a rationalist strain in his thinking: he believed that he had found a deductive vindication of induction and that this limited sort of induction was the only method for which such a deductive vindication could be given.[17]

Just "the Difference between Two Languages"?

In §16 of *Experience and Prediction*, entitled "An Egocentric Language," Reichenbach formulates the difference between positivism and realism as a matter of choice between an "egocentric language" (in which things exist only when observed to exist by the subject, and have all and only the properties they appear— to that same subject—to have) and "usual language" (which allows inferences to unobserved objects). (A similar distinction occurs in Carnap's "Testability and Meaning," although not under these labels.) At the beginning of §17, "Positivism and Realism As a Problem of Language," Reichenbach writes that "the difference of the positivistic and the realistic conception of the world has taken a different turn; this difference has been formulated as the difference of two languages." And he immediately adds, "This form of consideration, *which has been applied particularly by Carnap*, seems to be a means appropriate to the problem in question, and we shall make use of it for illustration of our results" (1938, p. 145; emphases added).

What a reader of Carnap would expect at this point is some such argument as the following: the more liberal language ("usual language") allows the formulation of statements from which we can deduce or induce many useful predictions which are not permitted by the restrictions of the older positivism (because the statements cannot be formulated in "egocentric language"). In short, the statements science makes about, for example, objects too small to see, or events before there were sentient beings, are part of a system leading to valuable predictions about what we observe here and now, predictions each scientist could in principle test for herself. But Reichenbach offers a remarkably different argument:

> The insufficiency of a positivist language in which talk of events after my death is construed as a device for predicting my experiences while I am alive is revealed as soon as we try to use it for the rational reconstruction of the

thought processes underlying actions concerned with events after our death, such as expressed in the example of [purchasing] life insurance policies." (1938, p. 150)[18]

I contend that this argument makes a deep point, and one quite unlike anything to be found in Carnap's writing. What Reichenbach is telling us is that it if I view my whole language as just a device for predicting what experiences I *myself* will have—if even statements about my family, and about what will happen to them after I die, are no more than gears in a prediction machine, a machine whose whole purpose is to predict what I will experience here and now—then that view will violate the deepest intuitions we have about *what we are doing* when we utter sentences about others and about events after (and before) our own lives. One might add (although Reichenbach unfortunately did not) that, even if I deny that such statements are *translatable* into an "egocentric language," if the only account I have of what it is to *understand* a "realist" language is that it consists in being able to use it to predict *one's own* sensory stimulations, the view remains just as unsatisfactory. As I have myself recently put this further "moral":[19] *"to preserve our commonsense realist convictions it is not enough to preserve some set of "realist" sentences; the interpretation you give those sentences, or, more broadly, your account of what understanding them consists in, is also important!"* I do not claim that Reichenbach drew this further moral. Indeed, I have argued elsewhere that he failed to see that in consistency his argument required him to give a nonpositivist account of *understanding*.[20] But the intuition behind Reichenbach's little argument about "life insurance policies" is, I think, quite clear.

Conclusion

In closing, it is appropriate to ask, when all is said and done, Just what did Reichenbach understand by his contrast of "the positivistic and realistic conceptions of the world"? I think that it is safe to make two points. First, a realistic conception of the world did not, in Reichenbach's eyes, involve anything like a metaphysical realist account of truth.[21] Reichenbach was not defending metaphysical realism (if we prescind from his materialism, anyway), but a common-sense realism. His realism was not a proposal for a metaphysical foundation of some kind, but, in the main, a *rejection* of a picture he saw as inadequate to our scientific lives and, in the remarkable paragraph quoted above, to our humanity as well. Second, Reichenbach did not, however, *think through* the question of whether what he retained from positivism was fully adequate to his "realistic conception of the world."

NOTES

I am sure that many other contributors will have said that (1) Burton Dreben has been an enormous influence on their philosophy, even when they have not been able to wholly agree with him, and (2) that he has done perhaps more than anyone to bring about an immense deepening of our understanding of the history of analytic philosophy through his teaching and his influence as well as his own papers. But both propositions happen to be true, and I have to say them because of the debt of gratitude that I feel.

1. "Reference and Understanding," part III of my *Meaning and the Moral Sciences* (London: Routledge and Kegan Paul, 1978) (hereafter Putnam 1978). The remark I quote occurs on p. 112.

2. See Putnam (1978, p. 114), for a statement of these grounds.

3. In his "Testability and Meaning, Part I" (*Philosophy of Science* 3 [1936]: 420–471; hereafter Carnap 1936) Carnap wrote that this identification was "exhibited in the earliest publications of our Vienna Circle; it is still held by the more conservative wing of this Circle" (p. 422).

4. Hans Reichenbach, *Experience and Prediction* (Chicago: University of Chicago Press, 1938) (hereafter Reichenbach 1938).

5. Reichenbach, it should be noted, was not a Vienna Circler; he led his own group, the Berliner Gesellschaft für empirische Philosophie. Its most famous members, besides Reichenbach, were C. G. Hempel and Olaf Helmer. *Erkenntnis*, founded in 1930, was the official journal of both the Wiener Kreis and the Berliner Gesellschaft. In 1933, a few days after Hitler took power, Reichenbach fled Europe. *Experience and Prediction*, which appeared in 1938, was written in Istanbul, where dozens of refugee professors from Nazi Germany found positions.

6. Carnap (1936) and "Testability and Meaning, Part II," *Philosophy of Science* 4 (1937): 2–38 (hereafter Carnap 1937).

7. "Proposition" is Reichenbach's term for a sentence. "The words 'sentence' and 'statement,'" he writes, "are also in use. But this distinction being of little importance and rather vague, we shall make no distinction between 'propositions' and 'sentences' and 'statements'" (1938, p. 21n.).

8. Reichenbach neglects to say "on the basis of some possible observation," but the formulation of the second principle makes it clear that this is what he means.

9. At least we know that, as late as "Testability and Meaning" (1936–1937), Carnap could write (speaking of Reichenbach's probability theory of meaning) "It presupposes the thesis that the degree of confirmation of a hypothesis can be interpreted as the degree of probability in the strict sense which this concept has in the calculus of probability, i.e. as the limit of relative frequency. Reichenbach holds this thesis" (1936, p. 427). Of course, Carnap was later to develop his theory that "degree of confirmation" is itself a quantitative notion and a possible interpretation of "probability" different from "the limit of the relative frequency." But in "Testability and Meaning," he wrote (1936, p. 427), "It seems to me that at present it is not yet clear whether the concept of degree of confirmation can be defined satisfactorily as a quantitative concept, i.e. a magnitude having numerical values."

10. One of those "weak points," in Reichenbach's view, is the assumption that no proposition could be known with probability unless some basic propositions were known with certainty. In a remarkable paper titled "Are Phenomenal Reports Absolutely Certain?" (*Philosophical Review* [1952] 61: 147–159) and delivered at a symposium with C. I. Lewis and Nelson Goodman, Reichenbach returns to this question late in his life and argues devastatingly against Lewis's defense of this assumption. Compare my "Reichenbach and the Myth of the Given" (hereafter Putnam 1991a); in my *Words and Life* (Cambridge, Mass.: Harvard University Press, 1994) (hereafter Putnam 1994a), pp. 115–130. Of the "exceptional" philosophers cited by Reichenbach, only Richard Avenarius had been able to resist the idea that impressions are observable facts. This is interesting because we know that it was reading Avenarius that first inspired William James to turn to his own version of direct realism. David C. Lamberth, *Metaphysics, Experience and Religion in William James' Thought* (Cambridge: Cambridge University Press, 1997) provides a detailed account of the development of James's metaphysics.

11. The parenthetical remark is Carnap's addition.

12. I use the term "unobservable" here as the logical empiricists themselves did. In my *Dewey Lectures* 1994, "Sense, Nonsense and the Senses; An Inquiry into the Powers of the Human Mind" (*Journal of Philosophy* 91 [1994]: 445–517) lecture III, I criticize the idea that things we observe only with the aid of scientific instruments are "unobservable" in any epistemologically significant sense. But the view I defend there is not compatible with Reichenbach's view that all scientific knowledge comes from (1) unaided human perception and (2) what he was prepared to allow as "inductive logic." On the problems with the latter, see my "Reichenbach and the Limits of Vindication" in Putnam (1994a, pp. 131–148).

13. Reichenbach writes, "We use the participle *illatum* of the Latin *infero* to denote this kind of thing" (1938, p. 212).

14. This term appears repeatedly in the volumes of *Minnesota Studies in the Philosophy of Science* edited by Carnap's ally Herbert Feigl during Carnap's lifetime.

15. For references, and also for a criticism of this view, see "What Theories Are Not," in my *Philosophical Papers. Vol. 1: Mathematics, Matter and Method*, 2d ed. (Cambridge: Cambridge University Press, 1979), pp. 215–227.

16. See part V of (Reichenbach 1938), "Probability and Induction."

17. See again part V of (Reichenbach 1938).

18. In my "Logical Positivism and Intentionality" (in Putnam 1994a, pp. 85–98) pp. 90–93, I argue that Reichenbach fails to realize that this defense of realist language is, in fact, incompatible with the defense he offers of the claim that all that is at stake is a choice of a language. His defense of realist language assumes, in particular, that my understanding of the language doesn't consist merely in my ability to assign weights to sentences on the basis of my own experiences, but this assumption implies that some account of reference is needed.

19. In my "Richard Rorty on Reality and Justification," in *Festschrift for Ben-Ami Scharfstein*, ed. Shlomo Biderman (forthcoming) (hereafter Putnam forthcoming).

20. See Putnam (forthcoming).

21. See Putnam (forthcoming).

PART III

After the Wars

Rethinking the Future

13

Sure Path of a Science: Kant in the Analytic Tradition

SUSAN NEIMAN

There is progress in philosophy.

Anyone who has had the fortune to study with Burton Dreben can imagine his reactions to such a statement, and I confess that I make it to provoke him. In its defense I wish to offer a piece of evidence which seems incontrovertible, namely, the differences between the ways in which Kant is taught and studied today and the ways in which his work was approached some twenty-five years ago. However significant may be the differences among those of us who have devoted some portion of our lives to Kant scholarship, we must all agree that it has gotten remarkably better. Indeed, the very quantity of work can itself be taken as a sign of improvement, for it indicates the acceptance of an activity which was formerly marginalized. The increase in attention to detail, in willingness to learn from Kant, and in scrupulousness about reading our own needs into his texts, all signal a vastly welcome combination of openness and modesty which are themselves philosophical virtues, sorely lacking in discussion of Kant during much of the century.

Yet all these are points which Dreben himself might grant without much ado. Reputedly, after all, garbage is distinct from scholarship. The unexpected proliferation of good Kant scholarship over the past few decades need not have, by itself, philosophical relevance. But the distinction between philosophy and the history of philosophy, so firmly a part of analytic philosophy for most of its history, is itself one which has fallen increasingly into question, not least as a result of Dreben's own influence. His attention to analytic philosophy as an object of historical investigation was in part the result of his rejection of an assumption critical to most of analytic philosophy: that good philosophy must, somehow or other, proceed according to models of the (natural) sciences. Kant himself was used to defend this idea, on those few occasions when it was thought to require defense. Probably none of Kant's sentences is more frequently cited in analytic philosophy than his very problematic claim, to which I will return, to have put metaphysics on the sure path of a science.

Once the belief in the continuity of philosophy and science was cast in doubt, the belief in the distinctness of philosophy and its history could be more easily abandoned. Of course, this development could be given a negative interpretation: unlike science, philosophy continually returns to examine its sources because, unlike science, it makes no progress beyond them. But few, today, would make such a claim. Rather, the increasing recognition that critical engagement with its history is a central part of the process of doing philosophy has led to philosophical growth both for those people who list "history of philosophy" as an area of specialization in professional contexts and those who do not. For the former, historical work has become more subtle, active, discerning. Nor would most philosophers who view themselves to be engaged in pure, contemporary, problem-centered research take the sort of liberties with historical figures which were commonly taken not long ago.

This paper will examine some of those liberties. Two different sorts of questions are here of interest: how was it possible for analytic philosophers to read Kant in a manner so utterly different from Kant's self-understanding, and the understanding of most of his near-contemporaries? The second question is that of the effects which such readings of Kant had on analytic philosophy, itself. If these problems guide the following remarks, however, the reader should not expect an answer to them. For first, if anything casts doubt on the idea that there is one thing called analytic philosophy, it might be a glance at the ways in which leading analytic philosophers read Kant. Yet despite differences of emphasis and problem as well as attitude, there is a set of common features which can, I think, be elicited. A complete examination of them is beyond the scope of this paper. Indeed, one could usefully write a history of twentieth-century philosophy from the perspective of its successive uses of Kant. Rather than attempting such a history, I wish to draw attention to certain material such a project might take into account. If the remarks which follow raise more questions than they answer, I hope it will be in the spirit of the teacher to whom this book is dedicated.

In his 1804 memorial essay for Immanuel Kant, Schelling wrote the following:

> The claim that only the great event of the French Revolution gained him the general public regard that his philosophy alone would never have earned is fictitious. A few of his enthusiastic adherents, not without perceiving some special work of fate, marveled at the coincidence of these two revolutions, which, in their eyes, were equally important. They did not realize that it was one and the same long-developing spirit that, in accordance with the distinctive features of the two nations and circumstances, expressed itself in one case as a real revolution and in the other as an ideal one.[1]

The claim that Schelling feels a need to defend should strike the contemporary reader as astonishing: Kant's philosophical preeminence is not merely a result of the connections between his work and the French Revolution; the work alone has intrinsic value, though it can be seen as one expression of the same spirit which lead to the French Revolution. Should we view Schelling's remarks as an aberration inspired by the emotional impact of recent events (whether the death of the Sage of Königsberg himself or the political developments in France and

Germany), we may advance a few decades in expectation of a more sober view of Kant's achievement. Instead we find, in Heine's *Zur Geschichte der Religion und Philosophie in Deutschland*, a series of passages like the following:

> One really gives Maximilian Robespierre too much honor when one compares him with Immanuel Kant. . . . But although Kant, the great destroyer in the realm of thought, far surpassed Robespierre in terrorism, he had many similarities which invite a comparison between the two men. First, we find in both the same unrelenting, cutting, unpoetic, sober honesty. We also find in each the same talent for mistrust; only the one exercises it against thought and calls it critique, the other uses it against men and calls it republican virtue. In the highest degree, however, we find in both the model of the bourgeois: nature determined them to weigh coffee and sugar, but fate would have them weigh other things, and put on the scales a king for one, and for the other a God.[2]

It seems safe to say that few who studied Kant in an English-speaking philosophy department during the better part of the twentieth century would recognize the figure here described.[3] Let us turn now to that Kant on which most of us were raised. To recall that more familiar figure, I have chosen quotations from three analytic philosophers who, different enough to be representative, dominated their fields during portions of the century. My interest is not primarily in considering English-language Kant scholarship, but in the picture of Kant which was received and transmitted by central analytic philosophers.[4] I am also less concerned with their discussion or criticism of any particular features of Kant's project than with their most general understanding of what that project was.

We may begin with Bertrand Russell, though not the Russell whose dislike of Kant is unabashed and open, nor the Russell who claimed to destroy the Critical Philosophy with the proof that the propositions of mathematics are reducible to logical ones. Rather, let us take Russell where we might expect to find him at his best in matters Kantian, namely in his general discussion in *A History of Western Philosophy*.[5] Russell's history, though more comprehensive, provides interesting comparison with Heine's. A century separates them in time. Both are witty, popular works written for a general rather than a professional audience. Perhaps as a consequence, both are explicitly less concerned with summarizing philosophical arguments than with presenting philosophical views as part of a social and historical context. Russell's 895-page work begins with the following sentences:

> Many histories of philosophy exist, and it has not been my intention merely to add one to their number. My purpose is to exhibit philosophy as an integral part of social and political life: not as the isolated speculations of remarkable individuals, but as both an effect and a cause of the character of the various communities in which different systems flourished. (Russell 1945, p. ix)

Unlike many later analytic philosophers, therefore, Russell is hardly unconcerned with social and political issues in which philosophy may be entwined; his stated purpose here is to raise them. Yet his portrait of Kant begins with the claim that "Kant, the founder of German idealism, is not himself politically important" (Russell 1945, p. 703). That this is intended as a positive claim with content rather than an oversight is underscored by Russell's statement that, like other idealists who followed him, Kant was "not intentionally subversive" (Russell 1945, p. 704). Rather, the reader learns that "Kant's most important book is the *Critique of Pure Reason*. The purpose of this work is to prove that, although none of our knowledge can transcend experience, it is nevertheless in part *a priori* and not inferred inductively from experience" (Russell 1945, p. 706). Russell follows this statement with an exposition of the analytic/synthetic distinction, a very brief summary of the antinomies and Kant's demolition of traditional proofs of God's existence, and an even briefer discussion of the categorical imperative, before embarking on a sustained discussion of what he calls the most important part of the *Critique*: Kant's theory of space and time. Recall that little more than a century earlier, Schelling felt compelled to argue that Kant's work was not *merely* of political significance; Russell confidently asserts that it has none. Rather, Kant's importance lies in his contribution to discussion of the status of certain claims of knowledge, and a false and confused theory of space and time. Perhaps for this reason, Russell, though ready to acknowledge Kant's importance, tells the reader of his disagreement with the general estimate of Kant as the greatest of modern philosophers.

Let us turn to remarks from a more sober and professional text, P. F. Strawson's *Individuals*. This book begins with a distinction between descriptive and revisionary metaphysics. The former "is content to describe the actual structure of our thought about the world," and the latter "is concerned to produce a better structure" (Strawson 1966, p. 9). The formulation allows for the question: Structure of what?—for a metaphysician might hope to revise the structure of thought or the world, but the context suggests that Strawson does not consider the latter possibility at all. Only the assumption that the revisionary metaphysician can have nothing else in mind but revising the structure of thought can make sense of Strawson's claim that "revisionary metaphysics is at the service of descriptive metaphysics"; only because metaphysics needs no justification other than that of the value of pure inquiry can the value of a revision of our description be dependent on the value of the description. A revisionary metaphysics which wanted to affect the world itself would have to make the opposite claim.

Oxford is not perhaps the most likely place to look for adherents of the eleventh thesis on Feuerbach, and it would be foolish to fault Strawson's distinction for failing to leave room for it. Far more puzzling is his definition of metaphysics as concerning the structure of our thought *about* the world—whether in descriptive or revisionary form. For surely metaphysics is equally concerned with the relations *between* thought and world, a question which has dominated philosophy since Plato. Note that, while putting the matter this way can as easily lead to Absolute Idealism as to Marx, it opens the door for a more active, and political, conception of metaphysics than Strawson's own formulation. This is as true for conservative thinkers as it is for radical ones: Hume's argument for a particular set of relations between thought and world was explicitly taken up by Burke, who used claims about the impotence of reason and the mind's subsequent dependence on custom and habit to argue against radical attempts to change the established order.

But though the *Critique* itself denotes the question of the relationship between thought and reality as the first of the major questions on which there has been progress in metaphysics (A853/B882), Strawson does not; and though Strawson does not hold any metaphysician to have been either wholly descriptive or wholly revisionary, he places Kant among the former. Even within Strawson's distinction this placement seems surprising. One need not consider little-known quotes like those of Schelling and Heine; one may choose, for methodological reasons, to discount Kant's remarks, some of them autobiographical, about the worthlessness of pure inquiry undertaken for its own sake. But what of Mendelssohn's familiar, all-destroying Kant? Or Kant's own oft-quoted reference to a Copernican revolution in thought? Strawson's placid ordering of Kant in the category of descriptive metaphysics (along with Aristotle instead of Plato, to whom Kant explicitly claimed allegiance) is of a piece with the reading of Kant's project to which Strawson's later work would much contribute. The mapping of the boundaries of thought, the articulation of our most general concepts and ideas, has for Strawson no need to seek further legitimacy than that inherent in all forms of pure intellectual inquiry. In Kant's hands, however, it does have what Strawson seems to take as a fortunate by-product, namely, of revealing "the link between objectivity and the necessary unity or connectedness of experience" (Strawson 1966, p. 121). Whether or not Strawson takes Kant to be successful in doing so, the "proof of the necessary conformity of nature to law in general" is seen as an outcome so central to Kant's undertaking to survey our conceptual structure that it can be seen as its very heart (Strawson 1966, pp. 116, 121).

Less elegantly and carefully, Jonathan Bennett would describe the empiricist threat of "total chaos" which Kant is concerned to avert. According to Bennett, the empiricist grants

> that if the causal order failed we could apply no concepts to, have no rational grasp of, our experience; but now see how much comfort you have lost and how horridly intractable your experience may, for all you know to the contrary, at any moment become.
> Kant wishes to show that this nightmare is impossible.[6]

The words "nightmare" and "comfort" may be more vivid than those used by most, but they only serve to dramatize an assumption which most of analytic philosophy viewed as uncontroversial. Whether successful or not, Kant's goal was to provide guarantees for the security of our experience. Missing from any such discussion was the recognition that prominent among initial reactions to Kant's work was hardly the sense of security or comfort, but the experience of loss and fear.[7]

The Kant we find in Richard Rorty's *Philosophy and the Mirror of Nature*[8] is particularly worth considering, as Rorty gives Kant the major share of responsibility for the mistakes of modern philosophy. Rorty's book also falls somewhere between the first two considered in point of audience: while it was a book that could hardly be avoided by philosophers, it also reached a wider public outside the profession, and thus provides an especially useful means of gauging which assumptions about Kant were most generally transmitted. Rorty gives Kant the dubious credit of having professionalized the subject, "if only by making it impossible to be taken seriously as a 'philosopher' without having mastered the first *Critique*" (Rorty 1979, p. 149). Kant did so, Rorty claims, by simultaneously determining philosophy's history and fixing its problematic, through building a particular conception of cognitive experience "into our conception of a 'theory of knowledge' (and thus our conception of what distinguished philosophers from scientists)" (Rorty 1979, p. 149). Kant's concern is "the problem of reason," which Rorty describes as "that of how to spell out the Greek claim that the crucial difference between men and beasts is that we can *know*—that we can know not merely singular facts but universal truths, numbers, essences, the eternal" (Rorty 1979, pp. 34–35). Rorty is particularly helpful in restating and emphasizing the assumptions on which his reading of Kant is based; so he tells us elsewhere that the modern problem of reason is "the notion that there is a problem about the possibility or extent of accurate representation which is the concern of a discipline called 'epistemology'" (Rorty 1979, p. 126). For Kant, therefore, philosophy is centered in epistemology; after Kant, the paradigmatic concern of the subject becomes "the study of representing" (Rorty 1979, pp. 133, 164). Marvelously, Rorty is so convinced that Kant's problem of reason is the study of representing that his own historical research does not call it into question. While noting that the term "theory of knowledge" was only invented after Kant's death, and only used widely after Hegel's, Rorty remarks that "the first generation of Kant's admirers used '*Vernunftkritik*' as a handy label for 'what Kant did' (Rorty 1979, pp. 134–135). That Rorty's understanding of "what Kant did" is a more accurate rendering of "*Vernunftkritik*" seems a matter unworthy of argument.

From Rorty's perspective, Kant's philosophical goal, then, was to develop a theory of knowledge which would be foundational, "providing a permanent ahistorical framework for inquiry" (Rorty 1979, p. 257). Presumably, Kant's search for such foundations was a development of the Cartesian-initiated professionalization of philosophy which signaled

> the triumph of the quest for certainty over the quest for wisdom. From [Descartes's] time forward, the way was open for philosophers either to attain the rigor of the mathematician or the mathematical physicist, or else to explain the appearance of rigor in these fields, rather than to help people attain peace of mind. Science, rather than living, became philosophy's subject. (Rorty 1979, p. 61)

The quest for certainty rather than wisdom, science rather than living, is one that, Rorty's later work will tell us, the "strong poet" is brave enough to forego; and whatever the differences between Rorty's Kant and Heine's, both take the judgment that he was unpoetic to be an easy one to make. Rorty's most sustained discussion of the historical problematic that might have led Kant on a quest for foundations suggests a Kant who was not merely weak but positively venal. In this discussion, epistemology was invented in order to find a way of demarcating philosophy from the sciences:

> Without this idea of a "theory of knowledge," it is hard to imagine what "philosophy" could have been in the age of modern science. Metaphysics—considered as a description of how the heavens and earth are put together—had been displaced by physics. The secularization of moral thought, which was the dominating concern of European intellectuals in the seventeenth and eighteenth centuries, was not then viewed as a search for a new metaphysical foundation to take the place of theistic metaphysics. Kant, however, managed to transform the old notion of philosophy—metaphysics as "queen of the sciences"—because of its concern with what was most universal and least material—into a notion of a "most basic" discipline—a *foundational* discipline. Philosophy became "primary" no longer in the sense of "highest" but in the sense of "underlying." Once Kant had written, historians of philosophy were able to make the thinkers of the seventeenth and eighteenth centuries fall into place as attempting to answer the question "How is knowledge possible?" and even to project this question back upon the ancients. (Rorty 1979, p. 132)

Here Kant's recentering of philosophy as epistemology appears to be the result of the worst aspect of professionalization. Not merely a pedant's inability to think of more interesting projects than those laid before him, but a careerist's desire to retain control of a field threatening to disappear in the face of progressive encroachments on it, is the source of Kant's (and the Kantians') invention of the theory of knowledge.

A final, and related though less reprehensible, motivation for Kant's turn to epistemology is given through his relationship to natural science: "since Kant, the physical sciences had been viewed as a paradigm of knowledge, to which the rest of culture had to measure up" (Rorty 1979, p. 322). Kant, according to Rorty, was swept away in a pre-Kuhnian idolization of the natural sciences. Viewing science as the bearer of objectivity and certainty, and the model for any other disciplines that (unreflectively and naturally) sought those properties, Kant's desire to set up epistemology as a foundational science might seem clear. On the one hand, epistemology looked like a better candidate than metaphysics or ethics for a field that might hope to attain the status of a science.[9] On the other hand, Kant could perform a professional *coup* by presenting a science that would ground and adjudicate the very model whose success had threatened to undermine his profession itself. Through a mixture, then, of diffidence, professional vanity, and fetishization of science, Kant turned the course of philosophy from the relatively loose and dynamic (if often misguided) consideration of a large number of interesting questions to the near-exclusive focus on variants of a boring question.[10] Rorty concludes:

> Our post-Kantian sense that epistemology or some successor subject is at the center of philosophy (and that moral philosophy, aesthetics and social phi-

losophy, for example, are somehow derivative) is a reflection of the fact that the professional philosopher's self-image depends on his professional preoccupation with the image of the Mirror of Nature. (Rorty 1979, p. 392)

Here it should be noted that, though Rorty's representation is the least pleasant to contemplate, his is a polemical work. But the distance between the picture of Kant the Jacobin,[11] and the figure whose guiding mission and achievement was to create pure academic philosophy as we know it, had already long been traveled before Rorty reached it. Our samples vary in tone according to the value which their authors place on pure academic philosophy, but the difference in substance is insignificant. The unsubversive Kant portrayed by Russell is hardly other than Strawson's placid practitioner of descriptive metaphysics, whose work may issue in some reassurances about the security of ordinary experience. Rorty's own desire to challenge a professional guild leads him to represent Kant as a particularly brilliant consolidator of that guild; yet his desire to attack the Kant who has been given to us by analytic philosophy may not be wholly mysterious.

My intention in the foregoing has not at all been to attempt a comprehensive discussion of Russell's, Strawson's, or Rorty's views of Kant, but merely to provide selections typical enough to be representative. For my interest is not in examining the faults in any of the Kant interpretations offered or taken for granted in analytic philosophy, but rather to elicit a picture of Kant which was common and transmitted through most of them. Major features of that picture, reflected in the writers just quoted as well as in other material, can be summarized as follows.

1. The *Critique of Pure Reason* aims to put philosophy, after centuries of uncertainty and disagreement, on the sure path of a science. If Kant's efforts are successful, philosophy will henceforth have the sort of certainty that Newton's achievement provided for the natural sciences.
2. To this end, Kant shows that previous failure to resolve definitively most traditional philosophical problems was not accidental. Rather, classical metaphysics is impossible because its objects are in principle unknowable. Kant demonstrates this through use of principles of meaning and legitimacy that can be easily translatable into an empiricist idiom.
3. After doing away with metaphysics, Kant offers us epistemology: if we can no longer claim to know necessary truths about the world as it is in itself, we can know necessary truths about our knowledge of it. Those truths serve to prove objectivity, giving foundations to something in need of them: either ordinary knowledge of experience, or science, or both.

Those things were in need of foundation, or guarantee, because of the challenge of skepticism. In the persons of Descartes and Berkeley, skepticism threatens our ordinary beliefs ultimately by raising the specter of solipsism: we have no proof that anything besides our own representations exists. In the person of Hume, the threat is deepened by the challenge to the objectivity of the causal order, which also impugns the reliability of that scientific law whose discovery was, for the eighteenth century, the crown of human achievement.

While the above three features adequately characterize the first *Critique*, Kant's major work, Kant *also* had an ethics which he expounded in other works. This ethics is sometimes seen to be partly motivated by metaphysical concerns, such as the need to defend freedom of the will against the increasing advances of natural science, but it is separable from, and usually secondary to, metaphysical and epistemological questions. If ethics are secondary, politics are absent; English-speaking Kant readers seemed to share Russell's conviction so thoroughly that they found this fact unnecessary to mention.

This is, I hope, a fair sketch of the Kant who was transmitted to those of us schooled in analytic departments of philosophy. My purpose at present is not to argue against this picture, though I have tried to do so elsewhere.[12] For purposes of contrast, however, it may be helpful to summarize points at which each aspect of this picture may be challenged, and has been challenged in various ways, by Kant interpretations of recent years.

1. Kant's notion of science is far more, his notion of philosophy far less, developed than this view suggests. Far from participating in the idolization of the natural sciences which characterized many later thinkers, Kant's conception of science was the first to include standard elements of the later twentieth-century critique of positivist philosophy of science. His conception of philosophy, however, is the least developed aspect of his entire work. There are several different accounts of the status of his own philosophy, and of whatever is to come after it, to be found in Kant's texts. Though one such account can be summarized by the statement of intention to put metaphysics on the sure path of a science, it is far from clear that this is the most coherent one.

2. If the failure of traditional metaphysics was not accidental, it must have been necessary, and it is just this necessity which Kant emphasizes in the very first sentence of the first *Critique*, as well as in his account of transcendental illusion. Thus Kant's efforts must be directed not to dissolving the problems of metaphysics but to redirecting them. Ideas of metaphysics, properly understood, may have a great deal of significance without being objects of knowledge; thus it follows that an empiricist interpretation of Kant's account of meaning will prove contrary to the deepest purposes of the work.

3. Kant does substitute epistemology for ontology—which is not, except for Heidegger, the equivalent of metaphysics—but its role in even the first *Critique* is far less central than the traditional analytic picture suggests. Though Kant provides an account of objectivity, it is coherentist rather than foundationalist. Though fond of architectural metaphors, where Kant is concerned with foundations of knowledge it is not for its own sake but for the sake of things he considered to be in need of more solid grounding.[13]

4. Kant viewed the idealism and skepticism of Descartes and Berkeley as "cobwebs," intellectual curiosities of interest only to the dogmatic Schools

he contemned (Bxxiv–xxv). Kant does think there are pressing philosophical problems that necessarily and equally concern everyone, from
the most highly educated philosopher to those of the most common
understanding, insofar as we are human (A830/B858). These do not
include the worry that the external world might not exist. Hume's skepticism is a more serious challenge, not because of its possible threat to
Newtonian science, about whose solidity Kant is never in doubt; but
rather because of Hume's ability to raise more general problems from his
views on causality.[14]

5. The interdependence of metaphysics and political philosophy, epistemology and ethics, is not only a feature characteristic of Kant's work, but of
all serious philosophy through the late nineteenth century. This is as true
of empiricist philosophers as of systematic ones: Hume and Mill are no
less holistic on this score than are Spinoza and Hegel; and it would be
hopeless to begin to try to separate Nietzsche's ethics from his metaphysics, much less to understand one without the other. How this separation
came to seem natural within analytic philosophy is a question to be studied independently. But to read this separation into earlier writers is simply to misunderstand them. One who emphasizes this interdependence
will likely be viewed as emphasizing the importance of ethical and political concerns for understanding metaphysical ones, since these have lacked
attention within analytic history of philosophy. But reduction would be
as pointless in one direction as the other. Though Kant himself invented
the phrase "the primacy of the practical," I think he would agree that the
claim that his work is more concerned with ethics than with metaphysics would be as senseless as the claim that Tolstoy's is more concerned
with love than with justice. To suggest that the first *Critique* be read as
metaphysical background to Rousseau's *Emile* is not to deny that it stands
in a similar relation to Newton's *Principia*; rather, it is precisely to demand
attention to a wholeness which analytic philosophy has lost.

The Kant interpretations that were current within analytic philosophy have been
challenged from many directions by the philosophical scholarship of recent decades, but these five points seem fundamental enough to suggest that our basic
assumptions about Kant are in the process of major revision. The Kant taught
today will be, as a rule, closer to the texts, and to a larger number of texts, than
the Kant taught twenty years ago; closer to Kant's own statements of his aims,
with some attention paid to the views of his contemporaries, and some attempt
to place them in context; more philosophically sound and coherent; even quite
simply more interesting than the Kant represented in the past. If our picture of
Kant, therefore, is very different, and frankly better, than the older one, we may
ask: just how did the older picture arise?

One answer close to hand is that analytic philosophers couldn't read. More
exactly: careful attention to historical texts was not viewed as an important part
of philosophical practice. Certainly, there was a strong and stated preference in
analytic philosophy for examining historical figures, if at all, with the intention

of evaluating the philosophical merit of their arguments rather than determining what they actually thought. With the conceit of hindsight, we can ask how the former was thought to be possible without the latter; yet a few hours browsing among certain volumes of classical German scholarship can lend sympathy for the earlier impulse to find less passive approaches to the history of philosophy. Still, the reaction led many analytic philosophers to regard the most basic elements of scholarly practice—say, reading whole books instead of parts of them or checking translations of languages one hasn't mastered—as unnecessary, even pedantic.

Certainly, some of this disregard accounts for major lapses, at least within later analytic philosophy. Few readers today would be quick to accuse Kant of a simple error, or a non sequitur of numbing grossness, in a part of the book which could be explained by looking at another.[15] And whatever the difficulties in the translation of the verb *aufheben*, even fewer would be tempted to *quote* Kant as having "destroyed [*sic*] reason [*sic*] to make room for faith" (Rorty 1979, p. 138). Even more importantly, the analytic picture of Kant was made possible not only by simple failures of reading, but particular habits of it. The structural unity of the first *Critique* was viewed as artificial, part of Kant's peculiarly baroque taste for architectonic, and consequently ignored; the "Transcendental Analytic" was viewed as the "positive" part of the book, the "Transcendental Dialectic" as the "negative," with a sense of certainty about what those designations implied; and a course on the first *Critique* that made it through the "Second Analogy" was considered ambitious. These habits insured that most of the sections presenting the clearest challenge to the traditional picture remained unread.[16] But these practices of reading were furthered, if not positively decided, by the traditional picture itself; it primarily determined which parts of which texts were considered important. Practices of reading and aspects of interpretation were mutually supportive, but one cannot be isolated as the origin of the other.

Perhaps most importantly and surprisingly: early analytic philosophers *could* read. That is: a look at early analytic references to Kant shows far more attentive reading than might be expected. We have already seen Russell's interest in considering the social and political contexts in which philosophy is written; the treatment of such contexts as immaterial must be seen as part of the Americanization of analytic philosophy, not obvious at its inception.[17] Moreover, Russell's concern with historical sources could be genuine and acute. He writes, for example, that "Hume, for Kant, was an adversary to be refuted, but the influence of Rousseau was more profound" (Russell 1945, p. 704). This is, to be sure, only a sentence, but it is one which would have been welcome in the Kant discussion of later analytic philosophy, which wrote as if the only significant influences on Kant were Hume and Leibniz.[18]

If Russell showed some attention to history, Moore showed some attention to texts. His "Proof of an External World"[19] might have proceeded by carelessly mentioning Kant as the source for a particular set of problems Moore wished to address before going straight to his own solution of a fixed problematic which he unreflectively ascribed to the tradition. Such is what some current views of analytic philosophers as illiterate Philistines, at least in matters historical, could lead us to expect. Instead, we find a text which begins with the first *Critique*'s "scandal to philosophy" passage (Bxl) quoted both in English and German, and close exegesis extending over pages. Moore's exegesis begins:

> It seems clear from these words that Kant thought it a matter of some importance to give a proof of "the existence of things outside us" or perhaps rather (for it seems to me that the force of the German words is better rendered in this way) of "the existence of *the* things outside us"; for had he not thought it important that a proof should be given, he would scarcely have called it a "scandal" that no proof had been given. And it seems clear also that he thought that the giving of such a proof was a task which fell properly within the province of philosophy; for if it did not, the fact that no proof had been given could not possibly be a scandal to *philosophy*. (Moore 1959, pp. 127–128)

This is clearly reading. I think it is just as clearly the wrong reading, particularly regarding the word "scandal." Scandals are not scandals without an element of shock or surprise. Generally, the surprise is created by disproportion between expectations of capacities or aspirations and their realization. It makes good sense to say, "It is a scandal that an official entrusted with the highest administration of justice should himself be suspected of a contemptible violation of it," or "It is a scandal that a leader of the world's most powerful country cannot spell the word 'potato'." It may be a failure, but it isn't a scandal, if a judge acting in good faith improperly adjudicates a complex matter of law or if a politician of whom one expects nothing more than a good general education shows ignorance of the latest developments in physics. Philosophy's failure to prove the existence of the external world is a scandal because such a proof should be neither difficult nor momentous but rather something a good philosopher should be able to do, so to speak, with one hand.[20]

Thus even without considering the context of the passage which he took such pains to explicate, reflections on the use of the word "scandal" might have lead Moore to a better understanding of why Kant chose it.[21] I believe it signals his disgust with the gap between the "essential aims of metaphysics" (Bxl) to determine the great questions driving all the interests of reason and its pathetic results, which leave us uncertain of the simplest of truths clear to the most ordinary understanding. Kant does think the scandal should be resolved, but only so that philosophy can overcome the "scorn" and "dishonor" into which it has fallen—not, he suggests, without reason (Aviii). A judge accused of perjury must clear his reputation before returning to the administration of justice. But a judge charged with deciding a nation's laws who spent the rest of his career assembling proofs of his own honesty would be as ludicrous as a discipline expected to reflect on humankind's essential interests which spent the rest of its duration assembling . . . proofs of the existence of the external world.

If any one text is to blame for the analytic picture of Kant as the philosopher directed toward giving final demonstration of the reality of ordinary objects, it is probably Moore's. Yet the problems in Moore's interpretation do not result from

a simple lack of interest in reading. Perhaps because, as a member of the first generation of analytic philosophers, he was conscious of his relation to the tradition
he helped to overthrow, Moore is a far more alert and self-conscious reader than
many who would follow him. It is easy to see that he should have read *more*, but
this is true of all of us.

Similarly, if any group of philosophers is thought to have taken up and popu-
larized Kant's claim that good philosophy should be scientific, it must be the
Vienna Circle. So A. J. Ayer described the Circle's members as having "thought
they succeeded, where Kant had failed, in finding a way to 'set philosophy on the
sure path of a science'."[22] Though by 1959 Ayer's conviction in their failure to
achieve this goal suggests it to have been a faintly naïve one, neither he nor others
seem to doubt either the sense of Kant's remark or the fact that that remark was
indeed their slogan. Yet Schlick, for example, is much more circumspect in his
use of it, describing Kant as having said "that from now on philosophy might
begin to work as securely as only science had worked thus far."[23] Schlick's cir-
cumspection is justified by his very accurate discussion of that one of Kant's passages most likely to undermine the equation of philosophy and science:

> Kant used to say in his lectures that philosophy cannot be taught. However,
> if it were a science such as geology or astronomy, why then should it not be
> taught? It would then, in fact, be quite possible to teach it. Kant therefore
> had some kind of a suspicion that it was not a science when he stated "The
> only thing I can teach is philosophizing." By using the verb and rejecting the
> noun in this connection Kant indicated clearly, though almost involuntarily,
> the peculiar character of philosophy as an activity, thereby to a certain ex-
> tent contradicting his books, in which he tries to build up philosophy after
> the manner of a scientific system. (Schlick 1967, p. 51)

While Schlick is mistaken in seeing the contrast to be between Kant's books and
his lectures—the first *Critique* contains a long, albeit unclear discussion of the
claim that "we cannot learn philosophy" (A838/B866)—this is a minor oversight. Far more important is the fact that Schlick sees and discusses exactly the
central tension in Kant's own views on the nature of philosophy: on the one hand,
philosophy should become a field as certain and unified as science; on the other,
philosophy is so far from being a body of scientific knowledge that it is an activity
which cannot be learned or taught.[24] Schlick uses the latter strain in Kant's views,
very accurately described, to lend support to his own argument that philosophy,
since it cannot be science, must be the activity of finding meaning which is needed
in order to clarify the concepts of the sciences. His ability to read Kant clearly on
this score does not lead him to wonder what is so sure in the path of a science—
that is, to reject the view that "all real problems are scientific questions, there are
no others" (Schlick 1967, p. 51). Nor did it have any impact on the way in which
Kant's own metaphilosophical views were transmitted; though the Vienna Circle
provides a more sophisticated account of the relations between science and philosophy, Kant's views of those relations continue to be broadcast through the
same naïve slogan.[25]

A final example serving to complicate this story is given by Strawson, whose statement of what he calls "Kant's principle of significance" is a perfect statement of that Kant who, as Strawson immediately acknowledges, was made for modern empiricism. This principle, Strawson writes, was

> repeatedly enunciated and applied by Kant throughout the *Critique*. This is the principle that there can be no legitimate, or even meaningful, employment of ideas or concepts which does not relate them to empirical or experiential conditions of their application. If we wish to use a concept [otherwise] we shall not merely be saying what we do not know; we shall not really know what we are saying. (Strawson 1966, p. 16)

Yet Strawson is an acute enough reader to acknowledge that Kant's use of this principle can be restricted: that some ideas which have no significance according to this principle of significance nevertheless have significance. This acknowledgment leaves room for claims like Kant's stinging "in respect of the moral law [experience] is, alas, the mother of illusion!" (A318/B375). But it does not leave much room. The question is really why. Strawson recognizes the nonempirical significance of moral ideas, but confines their discussion to a footnote. He also recognizes that "[c]ertain ideas which had in themselves no empirical application or significance . . . might even have some useful function in stimulating the indefinite extension of empirical knowledge" (Strawson 1966, p. 17). In the hands of Buchdahl and others, this recognition would lead to a dramatic revision of Kant's philosophy of science and thus ultimately of his theory of knowledge itself; for Strawson it amounts to no more than a responsible qualification. Strawson does, however, acknowledge that Kant's intentions are "not only to curb the pretensions of dogmatic metaphysics to give us supersensible knowledge; he is concerned also to curb the pretensions of sensibility to be coextensive with the real" (Strawson 1966, p. 22). Now anyone whose work includes the latter concern is mounting a full-scale attack on the basic tenet of empiricism, not a defense of it. To deny that sensibility is coextensive with the real is a fortiori to deny that significance can be tied to empirical conditions. One might perhaps deny the latter without denying the former, by developing a theory of significance which was not tied to empirical reality; but Kant, as Strawson here signals, is in fact making a much stronger claim. The contradiction between Strawson's principle of significance and his recognition of Kant's interest in restricting sensibility's claim to exhaust reality seems so patent that one would expect Strawson either to accuse Kant of fundamental error (as he is willing to do elsewhere) or reconsider his own readiness to recast Kant in empiricist terms. Yet Strawson does neither. Rather than abandon the centrality of the empiricist idiom in understanding Kant's philosophy, he is willing to explain restrictions on it by reference to an interpretation already ridiculed by Heine, and attacked by Hegel, as unworthy of a philosopher of stature.[26]

The examples above could probably be multiplied; here I only wish to recapitulate my own perplexity. We cannot explain the predominance of an inaccurate picture of Kant by supposing that leading figures in the analytic tradition simply failed to see features of Kant's work which have rightly come under scrutiny in recent years. Russell emphasizes the importance of social and political factors as both effect and cause of philosophical views, recognizes that Rousseau influenced Kant more profoundly than did Hume, yet concludes that Kant is of no political significance. Moore perceives that the phrase "scandal to philosophy" is peculiar enough to warrant close attention—and spends pages misreading it. Strawson's recognition that a crucial part of Kant's intention is to restrict sensibility's claims to be coextensive with reality does not prevent him from emphasizing an empiricist principle diametrically opposed to it. Ayer saw that Kant's philosophy of science was far more progressive than Hume's, and hastens to dissociate logical positivism from the latter (Ayer 1952, p. 137); Schlick points out the irresolvable tension in Kant's metaphilosophy; yet the Vienna Circle would be remembered as following the most naïve version of Kant's determination to make philosophy scientific and would itself contribute to transmitting that version to our store of general assumptions about Kant's project. A wider reader than I will surely find other points at which the challenges raised by current work on Kant were perceived by earlier readers—and not perceived as challenges. Here we have to do with questions of tone and weight and gravity which, in one case, leave an untidy residue around an image and, in the other, transform the image itself.[27]

But misreading is never simple, or simply misreading. All the figures mentioned above were not, I have emphasized, primarily interested in Kant, but in agendas of their own. (One might ask why they bothered to attach that agenda to Kant rather than simply dismissing him as they dismissed Hegel and starting afresh, were it not the case that most revolutionaries want to stand on the shoulders of giants. Both in thought and in action, few will try to overthrow an old tradition without claiming connection to an even older one.) This is easy enough to note. The difficulty lies in isolating elements of an agenda common to those in analytic philosophy who appealed to Kant as an authority to help establish it; elements which could, but need not, be reasonably ascribed to Kant. Particularly interesting are elements that reinforce themselves: that is, those which have enough textual plausibility to find foothold in Kant's work, which is then used as an authority for supporting the assumptions themselves. Again, elaborating these is such an extensive and general project that I can but hope to sketch a piece of it, but two such elements loom particularly large.

The first is a focus on the relationship between philosophy and science which might easily be described as obsessional. Although it was not until Quine that an analytic philosopher went so far as to assert the identity of (usable) philosophy with science, most philosophers of this tradition were insistent that it be closely connected to science, and were unreflective in assuming that the renewed attempt to make one's philosophy scientific was characteristic of all major philosophical thought.[28] That analytic philosophy could not be exactly like science seemed fairly clear from its inception. What is striking is the amount of space analytic philosophers nevertheless devoted to the attempt to specify the nature of the connection between them, indicating the firmness of the belief that, however one ultimately characterized the relationship between philosophy and sci-

ence, it was this relationship that would be crucial. This devotion is traceable to
two factors. First, science seemed naturally to embody a host of values that philosophy wished to share: not only the theoretical merits of certainty, solidity, and
the ability to end disagreement, but the moral ones of cooperation and solidar-
ity, patience and responsibility characteristic of what Carnap called "a certain
scientific atmosphere."[29] The second factor motivating the preoccupation with
defining philosophy's relationship to science did seem to be the thought that if
science is supreme in embodying those values, it must inevitably encompass any
worthwhile field of inquiry within its own territory. While some were untroubled
by the prospect that philosophy itself would thus eventually disappear, others
seemed concerned enough to demarcate an independent space for philosophy in
the face of science to make some of Rorty's charges seem warranted.

Kant's own discussion of the relationship between philosophy and science may
be, as I have argued elsewhere, the most confused and confusing part of his
work.[30] It may thus seem ironic—or perhaps merely inevitable—that, of all he
contributed to philosophy, it was the most equivocal aspect of his theory that
should be transformed into a slogan for this twentieth-century conviction.[31] Let
us try to unravel a bit of the confusion by pointing out that Kant unquestionably
shared the first motivation named above. Indeed, the tendency to associate the
theoretical desiderata of certainty and solidity with moral desiderata like community, responsibility, patience, and humility seemed—for him and most Enlightenment thinkers—as natural as it would prove problematic. But the second factor behind the twentieth-century need to make clear the right kind of connection
between philosophy and science is one which Kant would have found completely
foreign. The eighteenth century had no problem about how philosophy was to
be demarcated from the sciences because it wasn't: the idea of principled distinctions between fields of inquiry had not yet taken hold. *General desire to emulate
Newton was not equivalent to a general desire to emulate or appropriate the methods of
natural science.* Newton was simply a model of human intellectual achievement,
but that achievement had yet to be divided into disciplines of which some were
more steadfast than others. (Imagine, by contrast, a serious contemporary philosopher aspiring to be the Einstein of the mind, or an even more serious one
describing another as having attained that aspiration.)

These considerations should show that, however inchoate Kant's account of
philosophy may be as a whole, even had he succeeded in putting philosophy on
the path of a science, it would not have been sent in the direction of logical empiricism.[32] Still, the shared moral values common to commitment to the Enlightenment, and the shared confusion between moral and theoretical values, made
it unsurprising that analytic philosophy should find its own scientism reflected
in Kant. (Had it not done so, not merely the picture of Kant in the tradition but
the tradition itself might have been different.) This scientistic appropriation of
Kant *could* make sense.[33] Once Kant had been thus appropriated, the picture of
Kant as the philosopher who wanted to introduce scientific method to philosophy could be reinforced not merely by focusing on particular sections in Kant's
texts, but by using the methods of natural science to read, or refuse to read, the
others. Here I have in mind, for example, the fact that Kant's own autobiographi-

cal remarks about the meaning and purpose of his work were virtually ignored in analytic philosophy. This meant that a set of questions which might have challenged traditional interpretation—for example, how a work directed to proving technical claims about the status of knowledge might be viewed as a contribution to restoring the rights of humanity—inevitably remained unasked. But on the sort of assumptions set out so well in the preface to Carnap's *Aufbau* (Carnap 1967), such questions must remain at most part of the preface to a scientific book. In understanding and evaluating the truth of the work, Kant's claims about the rights of humanity can be no more interesting than Newton's claims about the glory of God—as Kant himself, qua scientific philosopher, must surely agree.

Closely related to the scientistic elements of the traditional agenda was a commitment to empiricist criteria of meaning. Like the attempt to specify the demand that philosophy be scientific, the attempt to specify the demand that significant statements be related to experience took so many forms within analytic philosophy that it might seem too general to be informative. Yet the demand was made, insofar as analytic philosophers engaged in constructing theories of meaning at all. If the nature of the connection between meaning and experience remained obscure, the very preoccupation with explaining it despite repeated failures to do so reveals a commitment as deep as any.[34]

Here Kant could seem an eminently usable source of authority. Does not the Introduction to the first *Critique* begin by asserting that "[t]here can be no doubt that all our knowledge begins with experience" (B1)? Does not Kant's attack on metaphysics, as consisting of claims transcending all experience, remarkably prefigure the positivists' own? Kant repeatedly claims that comprehension even of the possibility of things in themselves is in principle impossible. From his assertion that "the entire use, *indeed the meaning* of the categories" stops at the limits of experience (B309, emphasis added), it would seem but the shortest of steps to condemn all nonempirical employment of ideas and concepts as meaningless. If one included the Tractarian insight that the matters of which one can thereby speak are the least significant, the step might just be ventured; but even this qualification would fail to capture the differences between Kant's notion of meaning and an empiricist one.[35]

It is undeniable that Kant spends a great deal of effort in arguing that genuine claims to knowledge (which analytic statements were not) are either knowledge of experience or, in a few instances, of the conditions of its possibility. Yet one of Kant's greatest achievements is to distinguish knowledge from thought, truth from significance; indeed, the first *Critique* as a whole can be read as an explication of this distinction.[36] The empiricist reading might have paused at the fact that those things whose significance Kant was most concerned to explicate were precisely those entities logical empiricism was concerned to deny, or at most relegate to a secondary, noncognitive status. (In denying that ideas of God, or freedom, or justice can be items of knowledge, Kant of course denies their cognitive status; but the distinction between understanding and reason is meant to undermine the assumption that cognitive status is primary.) But a reader already convinced that *some* empiricist criterion of meaning was the only sensible one could easily find confirmation of his conviction in much of the first half of the first *Cri-*

tique. Then the criterion itself could be implicitly used to justify dismissing most of the second half as a vestige of Kant's dogmatic and pre-Critical education! Since Kant there clearly spoke of what the first half seemed to tell us couldn't be expressed, it could seem mere politeness to ignore his time-bound lapses and focus on that part of the book in which he figures as a prescient precursor of modern scientific philosophy. That this manner of reading and the conviction in the truth of some empiricist criterion of meaning would continue to prove mutually reinforcing is clear; the noblesse oblige implicit in this use of the principle of charity may be less so. Perhaps the fact that one thereby begs the very questions about the relations between thought and reality which Kant is most concerned to raise must have remained unnoticed so long as empiricist assumptions about meaning seemed unassailable.

Using methods of one's teachers to reach different conclusions may seem an odd form of tribute and certainly a risky one. Given the material just presented, what could possibly justify the claim with which this essay began? If leading philosophers contributed to a misreading of Kant that itself infected analytic philosophy's own self-understanding, not even in ignorance but in partial awareness of facts which would count against it, what hope might there be for progress in philosophy?

Predictions in such matters are clearly presumptuous; as Kant himself reminds us, progress is not a constitutive idea. Yet he also acknowledges our need to seek an occasional sign. Signs, he emphasizes, are far from certainties, and the events to which they point may issue very differently. I submit that such signs of progress can be found in the very confusion in which philosophy now finds itself. The collapse of clear programs within analytic philosophy is both result and cause of the loss of conviction in the presuppositions about science and meaning just discussed; while they will surely continue to be explored, it will just as surely be without the tenacity which formerly animated them. And this loss accounts for a spirit of openness which is widespread and international. On the one hand, there has developed an enormous increase in encounters between philosophy and its history, coupled with a refusal to draw sharp distinctions between such encounters and philosophy proper, whether "scientific" or "systematic." On the other hand, there has been almost as great an increase in encounters between contemporary philosophical traditions themselves. The sense of confusion in which such encounters occur suggests that, where we do meet traditions other than those in which we were educated, we will be more likely to learn from them than to appropriate them. Nothing can insure that future philosophers will refrain from uncovering a dogma or two in our current stances. But the very difficulty of identifying such a dogma ("empiricism" is clearly inappropriate, but "post-modernism" would be rejected by just as many) is itself encouraging.

I have mentioned collapse, loss, and confusion, all of which might more likely be viewed as an invitation to nihilism than its opposite. Before taking such a view, we should recall Kant's sharp description of the skeptic as merely a counter-dogmatist (A755/B781 ff). Dogmatism, the unquestioned conviction in a set of methods which will provide final truths about the nature of reality, is what Kant calls the first step of reason, marking its infancy. Skepticism is born in reaction to it, a phase which Kant views as the adolescence of reason, necessary but—it is to be hoped—transient. Skepticism remains enduring if it remains purely reactive, tied to its disappointment in the failure of the dogmatist's programs because it cannot conceive of any other. To assume that philosophy is at best an uneasy form of amusement if it cannot provide us with certain and systematic knowledge is to let dogmatism define the terms of debate.

Far preferable is to conclude with Kant that the path to reason's maturity is elsewhere. It may begin in the recognition that "The consciousness of my ignorance, instead of ending my enquiries, ought rather to be itself the reason for entering upon them" (A758/B786). And it must include the acknowledgment that the most difficult of all its tasks is that of self-knowledge (Axi). If the ability to explore and confront one's origins is a signal of adulthood, in philosophy as elsewhere, the current explosion of interest in all aspects of the history of philosophy can be viewed as a sign that we are beginning to come of age.

NOTES

1. Quoted in Dieter Henrich, *Aesthetic Judgement and the Moral Image of the World* (Stanford: Stanford University Press, 1992), p. 87.

2. Heinrich Heine, *Zur Geschichte der Religion und Philosophie in Deutschland*, in *Sämtliche Schriften*, Band 3 (München: Carl Hanser, 1971), p. 594–596.

3. The story of Kant's reception in Germany is itself a long and complicated one which I cannot discuss here. It is interesting to note, however, that certain features of the picture of Kant taken for granted in the analytic tradition are also prominent in German neo-Kantianism, though never to the degree prevailing in the English-speaking world. These include a focus on the *Critique of Pure Reason*, trans. Norman Kemp Smith (New York: Macmillan, St. Martin's Press, 1965) (hereafter cited by the standard A edition/B edition numbering), and indeed on the first portions of that book, to the exclusion of other works; a corresponding tendency to view epistemology as Kant's most central concern; and a desire, clearly inspired by a reaction to Hegelian idealism, to make philosophy more "scientific" in what was taken to be Kant's sense. These trends are all the more interesting in view of the fact that many neo-Kantians were explicit in viewing Kant as a source of political inspiration; so Cohen wrote that "Kant is the true and real originator of German socialism." But Gerhard Lehmann writes:

> Der anthropologische Neukantianismus nimmt Kant in die realistische Bildungsbewegung auf, macht ihn zum Bestandteil der Arbeiterbildungs- bzw. Arbeiterbewegung selbst. Das ist kein geringes Verdienst. Es hat aber mit philosophischer Forschung nichts zu tun." (Gerhard Lehmann, "Kant im Spätidealismus," in *Materialien zur Neukantianismus Diskussion*, ed. Hans-Ludwig Ollig (Darmstadt: Wissenschaftliche Buchgesellschaft, 1987)
> [Anthropological neo-Kantianism enlisted Kant in the realist education movement [Bildungbewegung], made him part and parcel of workers' education [Arbeitersbildung]—that is, the workers' movement itself. That is something of no small merit. But it has nothing to do with philosophical research.]

See also Klaus Christian Köhnke, *Enstehung und Aufstieg des Neukantianismus: die deutsche Universität zwischen Idealismus und Positivismus* (Frankfurt am Main: Suhrkamp, 1986).

4. Of course the two cannot be entirely separated, as the few English works devoted to Kant influenced and supported the view of Kant received by the general philosophical public, but I have focused on the latter. So I am at least as interested in Strawson's

Individuals: An Essay in Descriptive Metaphysics (London: Methuen, 1959) as his *The Bounds of Sense* (London: Methuen, 1966) (hereafter Strawson 1966), the most influential English Kant interpretation of the 1960s and 1970s, as a means of exposing the most general and unconsidered assumptions. Even the latter, of course, was offered by Strawson as a reading rather than a piece of scholarship (Strawson 1966, p. 11).

5. (London: George Allen and Unwin, 1945) (hereafter Russell 1945). Russell's 1912 summary of Kant in *The Problems of Philosophy* (London: William and Norgate, 1912) is very close to that given in the later text.

6. Jonathan Bennett, *Kant's Analytic* (Cambridge: Cambridge University Press, 1966), p. 101.

7. I have in mind, for example, the reactions of such profoundly different and opposed figures as Mendelssohn and Jacobi. While the latter's call for return to a Humean-based leap of faith was expressed with bravado, it can hardly be described as unperturbed. See Frederick Beiser, *The Fate of Reason: German Philosophy from Kant to Fichte* (Cambridge, Mass.: Harvard University Press, 1987) (hereafter Beiser 1987), for historical discussion.

8. (Princeton: Princeton University Press, 1979) (hereafter Rorty 1979).

9. Of course, this is a very twentieth-century perspective. It was Rousseau whom Kant designated as the Newton of the mind and the problem of evil whose solution Kant thought merited this designation. See my "Metaphysics, Philosophy: Rousseau and the Problem of Evil," in *Reclaiming the History of Ethics: Essays in Honor of John Rawls*, ed. B. Herman, C. Korsgaard, and A. Reath (Cambridge: Cambridge University Press, 1997), pp. 140–169.

10. That I share something of this view of what happened to much of analytic philosophy—or even to Kant in the hands of analytic philosophy—is undeniable, though I think the motivations for the shift to put epistemology in the center of philosophy are more problematic than Rorty's narrative suggests. The puzzling question is why this shift should be attributed to Kant. One might bite an antihistorical bullet and ask what, besides piety, turns on the question of who took the wrong turn; one who agrees with Rorty's charge that philosophy went in the wrong direction, and with some of his description of the direction itself, might feel indifferent about just how we got there. I find this an interesting question, for which I have no answer at present but to repeat the dictum about the fate of those who forget the past.

11. On the widespread acceptance of the view of Kant as the "philosophical foreman of the French Revolution," see especially Hannah Arendt, *Lectures on Kant's Political Philosophy* (Chicago: University of Chicago Press, 1982), and Frederick Beiser, *Enlightenment, Revolution, and Romanticism: The Genesis of Modern German Political Thought, 1790–1800* (Cambridge, Mass.: Harvard University Press, 1992).

12. *The Unity of Reason: Rereading Kant* (New York: Oxford University Press, 1994) (hereafter Neiman 1994).

13. The *Prolegomena* underlines:

Our laborious Analytic of the understanding would be superfluous if we had nothing else in view than the mere knowledge of nature as it can be given in experience; for reason does its work, both in mathematics and in the science of nature, quite safely and well without any of this subtle deduction. (*Gesammelte Schriften* [Berlin: G. Reimer, 1910–], vol. IV, p. 331)

14. As the *Critique of Practical Reason* explains:

Hume . . . desired, as is well known, nothing more than a merely subjectively necessary concept of cause, i.e. habit, be assumed in place of all objective meaning of necessity in the causal concept; he did this in order to deny to reason any judgement concerning God, freedom and immortality; and he knew very well how to draw conclusions with complete cogency when once the principles were conceded. (*Gesammelte Schriften* [Berlin: G. Reimer, 1910–], vol. V, p. 13)

15. Bennett's and Strawson's carelessness on this score have been pointed out by many.

16. As they would necessarily remain in the abridged Modern Library edition of the *Critique* published by Random House in 1958. Kemp Smith, who might be expected to know better, provided his editorial services and, not surprisingly, an excellent introduction. But he concludes: "This abridged edition is designed for the use of the general reader, and of students entering upon the study of the Critical Philosophy. It may also, I trust, prove helpful to those who are engaged in the study of the complete text. *I have endeavoured to detach what is essential in Kant's teaching from the mass of minor detail in which it is embedded, and by which it is frequently obscured*" (p. xvi, emphasis added). Kemp Smith's remarks are particularly surprising since the print is sufficiently small so that very few pages are actually cut in this edition; but among the minor details he chooses to omit is the entire "Canon of Pure Reason," which according to Kant gives the sum total of the principles of the correct employment of reason, as the Analytic did for the understanding, and therewith the answer to the problem with which the book began (A796/B825).

17. The best-known and clearest case in which analytic philosophy was viewed to have both a political context and a goal was that of the Vienna Circle. Jean Améry's *Unmeisterliche Wanderjahre* (Stuttgart: E. Klett-Cotta, 1971) provides a particularly vivid recollection of the ways in which Carnap's work was thought to undermine Heidegger's proto-fascism along with his metaphysics. Such considerations show the one-sidedness of the Frankfurt School's critique of positivism as inherently conservative, though it seems as unclear as it is interesting how a group whose self-understanding was politically revolutionary could nevertheless produce a body of work of which Frankfurt School criticisms could be fairly raised. For a beginning of discussion of this issue, see Burton Dreben, "Cohen's Carnap, or Subjectivity is in the Eye of the Beholder," in *Science, Politics and Social Practice*, ed. Kostas Gavroglu, John Stachel, and Marx W. Wartofsky (Dordrecht: Kluwer Academic Publishers, 1995), pp. 27–42.

18. Indexes to standard analytic works on Kant of the 1960s and 1970s contain, variously, references to Rescher, Ross, Russell, and Ryle, but none to Rousseau. Among historical figures, Descartes, Hume, Leibniz, and Locke are well represented.

19. In Moore, *Philosophical Papers* (New York: Humanities Press, 1959), pp. 127–150 (hereafter Moore 1959).

20. An ironic reading of the conclusion of Moore's essay might suggest that he was in fact aware of the implications of Kant's use of the word "scandal"; but the intricacy of the bulk of the essay, as well as Moore's later epistemological writings, indicate the opposite. John Hollander has pointed out to me that the original meaning of "scandal" is "stumbling-block," and argued that Kant must have known this from the New Testament. The thought that a proof of the existence of the external world would prove a stumbling-block to philosophy has been more than amply demonstrated.

21. The passage occurs in a footnote, and it is preceded by the long discussion telling us, among other things, that "[c]riticism alone can sever the roots of *materialism, fatalism, atheism, free-thinking, fanaticism, and superstition*, which can be injurious universally; as well as of *idealism* and *skepticism*, which are dangerous chiefly to the Schools, and hardly allow of being handed on to the general public" (Bxxxv). Moreover, it occurs in the preface added in the B edition. Many of the additions in B, as well as the structure of the *Prolegomena*, were clearly motivated by Kant's barely concealed fury at the Garve-Feder review, which had accused him of presenting nothing other than a new form of Berkeleyan idealism. (See Beiser 1987 for an account of the surrounding controversy.) Kant's concern to reject what seemed to him a perverse misinterpretation could make this set of issues seem more central than was originally intended. Misreading is possible in any era, and its results can be harmful: the fact that this was the very first review of the first *Critique* is a piece of histori-

cal bad luck, never entirely dispelled by the well-known circumstances surrounding the review. (It is known as the Garve-Feder review because neither Garve nor Feder was happy to claim authorship of it; so the piece was originally published anonymously. Garve claimed that Feder, as editor of the *Zugaben zu den Göttinger gelehrte Anzeigen*, the journal where it was originally published, "mutilated" his original review, and the question of who was responsible for the final production has provided occupation for Kant scholars until this day. From its publication in 1782, however, there was widespread agreement that the review was a deep distortion of Kant's views, though there would be much disagreement about the nature of the distortion.) But despite the addition of discussions of idealism clearly motivated by this external circumstance, the *Prolegomena* is full of passages describing the more central goals of the Critical Philosophy. Indeed, the B preface itself, though unsystematic, provides a remarkably clear, thorough, and balanced overview of the first *Critique*.

22. "Editor's Introduction," in *Logical Postivism*, ed. A. J. Ayer (Glencoe, Ill.: Free Press, 1959), pp. 3–28, p. 9.

23. "The Future of Philosophy," in *The Linguistic Turn*, ed. Richard Rorty (Chicago: University of Chicago Press, 1967) pp. 43–53 (hereafter Schlick 1967), p. 44.

24. That first *Critique* passage, to be sure, suggests that, when the final scientific metaphysics is created, it will be teachable, but other passages in Kant's works suggests that the problem is in principle resistant to solution.

25. Examples taken almost at random, since this feature of our picture of Kant seems the least controversial: see Strawson (1966), p. 17.

26. Strawson writes: "The proof of our necessary ignorance of the supersensible safeguards the interests of morality and religion from our skepticism as well as from our knowledge" (Strawson 1966, p. 22). This explanation draws on the so-called tragic view of Kant—as Heine demonstrated, equally characterizable as farcical— as one who had hoped simply to provide better metaphysical proofs of the existence of God and freedom than his rationalist predecessors, but had to content himself with demonstrating their immunity to empiricist refutation. Again, the prevalence of such a reading—particularly of the notorious "I have found it necessary to deny knowledge in order to make room for faith"—in many traditions attests to its naturalness. Perhaps only the unnaturalness of attributing such a weak set of arguments to a philosopher of Kant's powers is enough to call it into question.

27. It should be clear that early analytic philosophers were not uniformly good readers and often made errors which were simply grotesque. Russell's claim ("Logical Positivism," in Russell, *Logic and Knowledge* [New York: Macmillan, 1956] (hereafter Russell 1956), pp. 367–382, on p. 367, that Kant stands in a line of great philosophers who thought mathematics a model for philosophy can only be based on his own interests, since few things in Kant are as clear or as constant as the view that the methods of mathematics cannot be those of philosophy. Ayer's claim that the difference between Kant's view of metaphysics as "production of nonsense" and his own is found in Kant's belief that knowledge of the objects of metaphysics is merely restricted as a matter of fact is similarly glaring, since few things in Kant are repeated as often as the claim that our inability to know noumena is a matter of necessity (*Language, Truth and Logic* [New York: Dover 1952] [hereafter Ayer 1952], p. 34). It would be easy to collect other examples. My interest has been to show that instances of this sort of gross error are fewer than might be expected; that early analytic philosophers sometimes read more accurately than later students, even scholars of Kant; and that they nevertheless set the assumptions for misreadings that would plague Kant students, and analytic philosophy itself, for nearly a century.

28. For a few statements of the claim that this attempt was fundamental to the history of philosophy, see Richard Rorty, "The Editor's Introduction" of *The Linguistic Turn*, ed. Richard Rorty (Chicago: University of Chicago Press, 1967), Russell (1956), and Schlick (1967). Schlick exempts Socrates, whom he describes as having

despised science, but still holds the attempt to make philosophy into a science to be characteristic of all modern philosophy—despite the fact that he also holds this attempt to be responsible for much that is mistaken in the history of philosophy.

29. Rudolf Carnap, *The Logical Structure of the World*, trans. Rolf A. George (Berkeley: University of California Press, 1967) (hereafter Carnap 1967), p. xvi.

30. See Neiman (1994), ch. 5, "The Task of Philosophy."

31. It is, at least, historically ironic if one considers the fate of the metacritics, that group of Kant's contemporaries who argued that Kant's metaphilosophy was so incoherent that it vitiated everything else in his work. (See Beiser 1987.) That we remember Kant today and not the metacritics is a sign, perhaps, that methodological and foundational questions are of less importance in philosophy than others. At the same time, it is striking to note, in view of how little of their methodological criticism was ever refuted, that it was some aspect, or impulse, of Kant's method that would be taken up by analytic philosophy.

32. That "*Wissenschaft*" cannot be translated as "*natural* science" means that Kant's claim could not be understood as some recent writers seem to assume, but this was hardly unknown to the members of the Vienna Circle. Even should the term be taken to include, as is proper, *Geistes- und Sozialwissenschaften*, there is still more "*Wissen*" in "*Wissenschaft*" than some of Kant's metaphilosophical considerations allow.

33. Although there was evidence against such appropriation even within English Kant *scholarship*: in 1923 Kemp Smith wrote that Kant's "real intention is to show that scientific knowledge is not coextensive with human insight, but he employs a misleading terminology" (*A Commentary to Kant's Critique of Pure Reason*, 2d. rev. ed. [London: Macmillan, 1979], p. lv). But Kemp Smith's own insight is rather buried in his vast *Commentary*, and we have seen his editing to exclude as tangential the one place in the *Critique* where Kant most clearly expounds this point.

34. Despite the short life of verificationism proper, its influence is revealed even in the choice of examples used in later theories of meaning. The nonobservable entities which seem to present problems are those of natural science; other sorts seem already to have succumbed to the earlier criterion.

35. The absence of discussion of Wittgenstein's use of Kant is entirely deliberate; the subject is too large to be tackled in even a paper of this generality.

36. I have argued for such a reading in "Understanding the Unconditioned," *Proceedings of the 8th International Kant Congress* (Memphis, Tenn.: Marquette University Press, 1995), pp. 505–519; the centrality of the distinction is pointed out by Hannah Arendt, *The Life of the Mind* (New York: Harcourt Brace Jovanovich, 1971); and much of Hermann Cohen's work can be read in this vein. But the claim is also implicit in the above quoted statements of Kemp Smith and Strawson.

1949
John Dewey's ninetieth birthday
celebration reported in *Time*

14

Non-Negotiable Demands: Metaphysics, Politics, and the Discourse of Needs

NAOMI SCHEMAN

> One might say: the axis of our examination must be rotated, but about the fixed point of our real need.
>
> Wittgenstein, *Philosophical Investigations*, §108

> I do not explicitly learn the propositions that stand fast for me. I can *discover* them subsequently like the axis around which a body rotates. This axis is not fixed in the sense that anything holds it fast, but the movement around it determines its immobility.
>
> Wittgenstein, *On Certainty*, §152

> I am by no means sure that I should prefer a continuation of my work by others to a change in the way people live which would make all these words superfluous.
>
> Wittgenstein, *Culture and Value*, p. 61

Perhaps, one might say, we discover our real need by the movement around it: as we attempt to rotate the axis of our examination—learn to ask different questions, problematize the taken-for-granted, stir up trouble where there seemed to be consensus—we discover something about who "we" are, what our stake is in the forms of life within which we are made intelligible. If we succeed in changing the ways people live, will the philosophical problems that have engaged us become superfluous, no longer articulating anxieties that arise from our attempts to make sense of who and how we are? Might what we now take to be the problems of philosophy cease to be *our* problems?

I want to address these questions by bringing together two lines of thought: Cora Diamond's articulation of a Wittgensteinian critique of philosophical demands (her term is "requirements") and Nancy Fraser's work (drawing critically on Habermas and Foucault) on the politics of needs discourse.[1] What I want to suggest is this: what our "real need" might be in any particular case will frequently be deeply contested; discovering it will mean discovering who we are and who

315

we might best become. Such discovery (merging with invention) is what serious politics, in an Aristotelian sense, is about; such discovery also creates, in an unavoidable circle, the possibility of serious politics. Serious politics is the struggle to create the possibility of engaging in the social activity of self-discovery and self-creation by means of socially discovering and creating ourselves as persons capable of engaging in that struggle. Serious politics must be, then, disorienting, as it involves excavating the ground under your own feet, chipping away at the bedrock that ordinarily turns your spade;[2] and it calls for the deepest of trust in one's fellow citizens—trust that issues only from long political struggle.

The circularity is Aristotelian: it takes the well-ordered polis to create the citizens who can create the well-ordered polis, much as an individual becomes virtuous by cultivating the habit of acting virtuously. In either case, however, the circle needn't be vicious; it can be, and ideally is, precisely virtuous. But if the polis or the person is initially vicious, it can be hard to see how the circle could fail to be so; and actual politics is frequently marked by the various suspicions that variously located political actors have that the conditions for the circle's being virtuous are not—perhaps cannot be—met. In the face of this despairing of serious politics, the two most common twentieth-century replacements for it are aiming for the satisfaction of what are taken to be scientifically determined "real needs" and fighting for the granting of painstakingly detailed rights or "demands." These strategies, though, are especially fraught with tension for the relatively disenfranchised, who are rightly suspicious both of the supposedly objective specification of their real *needs* by those who control the production of knowledge and by the embodiment of *rights* in institutions that have historically explicitly or implicitly excluded them.

The tensions between the two strategies—rights versus needs—have fueled much of recent political philosophy,[3] and it is not my intent to recapitulate those controversies. Rather, I want to develop a way in which we can better understand both the problematic nature of the "demands" that (as Diamond argues Wittgenstein shows) philosophy typically and problematically makes and the sources of those demands: why it is that we (and Wittgenstein, in the recurring voice of his interlocutor) find it so hard to stop,[4] to find peace (PI §133), to accept that, in refusing to meet those demands, Wittgenstein is not "denying something" (PI §305).

The Evasion of History

When Americans say something is history, that means it's irrelevant.
                                                                    Polish journalist

More dangerous than Hitler?
                                        Caption on a photograph of John Dewey,
                                        cover of *Time* magazine, March 17, 1952

In *The American Evasion of Philosophy*, Cornel West examines the role of pragmatism in American philosophical and cultural life and emphasizes its resolute evasion of ("epistemology-centered") philosophy, in favor of an "unashamedly moral emphasis and . . . unequivocally ameliorative impulse."[5] What I want to suggest in the present essay (in line with West's own arguments) is that analytic philosophy, especially as practiced in the United States after World War II, focusing on ahistorically articulated abstract "problems," has identified with and deepened the obverse evasion—of a moral and (politically ameliorative) conception of philosophy in favor of epistemological projects that rest on and reinforce the idea that knowledge, though it will in various ways be in the service of power, is not fundamentally constituted by it. The protection of philosophy from politics similarly rests on and reinforces the idea that philosophy's demands—for example, for theoretically tidy accounts of our moral and epistemic relationships to each other and to the rest of the natural world—can be met by purely intellectual investigation, that there are answers to philosophy's questions that lie in something other than what we do, something out of our hands and not of our making, something that has no significant (extraphilosophical) history.

The abstraction of the problems of philosophy from historical context is something that has, itself, a history, one that can be understood in the context of the specifically American evasion of serious politics, especially after World War II. Serious history (meaning history that makes a difference to how we experience the present)—along with serious politics—was regarded as suspiciously European; to the extent that it was not already dead, it was dangerous. For the generation born after the war, a too-vivid sense of history stood in the way of our all becoming self-made "men," even those of us whose cousins had, shortly before our birth, been murdered on a continent that took (and still takes) history very seriously indeed.[6] For the generation of our teachers, however, history must have been an ever-present ghost, something I dare say they had in mind even as they wove for our delight and empowerment a "problem-oriented" introduction to this marvelous twenty-five-hundred-year conversation. My own philosophical mentors were overwhelmingly women and Jewish men. Their own places in the profession and the academy, and subsequently mine, had needed within their lifetimes to be fought for, a fact that cannot have escaped their notice; and it was, I now recognize, an extraordinary gift that they so arranged things that for a shockingly long time it utterly escaped my notice. I managed to regard myself as an entirely unexceptional heir to the history of philosophy, an enabling ignorance made possible only by the abstraction of philosophy's history from history more generally.

"History," however, was what brought analytic philosophy to North America, via refugees from Hitler's Europe. But the flight from Nazism became in effect a flight from politics, as the post-war mood in the United States was hardly receptive to the often left-wing political convictions of many of the refugees, convictions that in many cases had actually passionately motivated what came to be characterized as the excessively dry and formal abstractions of logical positivism.[7] Cold war attitudes stigmatized ideas associated, rightly or wrongly, with Communism; and a revulsion against the Nazi labeling of "Jewish" science and philosophy reinforced the view of both those fields as ideally independent of any ideological considerations. The attempt to stamp out suspiciously "un-American" political thinking led to the McCarthy era's terrorizing of the politically serious professoriate, both immigrant and native-born. Ironically, distinctively American philosophy was among the casualties, surviving only as a marginalized and neglected specialty, whose recent resurgence owes much to the raising of explicitly historical and political questions in relation to metaphysics and epistemology. Pragmatism was tainted both by its association with progressive politics and by its being insufficiently pragmatic (in the popular sense of that term) because of its attention to why we ask the questions we do and why we care about the answers.

Formalisms of various sorts—the best known example being New Criticism in literature—can be seen in part as responses to the chilling effect of McCarthyism on American universities. "Problems" are formal puzzles whose raison d'être is simply that they are there—and that we have tools that seem suited to answering them. For my peers and those who have followed us, this ahistorical inheritance of the field has made it more readily ours, since we did not, in theory, have to confront what it meant that the likes of us should be among its heirs—including, as we do, not only Jews but many white women and, though far too few, men and women of color. In practice, many of us have come to believe that we do have to confront the terms of this inheritance and to ask, not only if the answers philosophers have given will work in the varying contexts of our lives, but more deeply if—and in what ways—the questions philosophers have asked are ours.[8] The dehistoricizing of the field, seen in connection with the depoliticizing of the academy, has facilitated the inclusion in philosophy of many who are coming to question the terms of that inclusion—much as the liberal inclusion of previously excluded groups in political discourse has led to the questioning of liberalism. In both cases, those who facilitated our inclusion, in part by shielding us from the depth of the historical resistance to it, understandably tend to see such questioning as counterproductive, dangerous, and ungrateful: it troubles our relationship to a field that only too recently allowed us in at all.[9]

The Problems of Philosophy

I have argued in a series of essays[10] that central philosophical problems (among those that West sees pragmatism as evading, arising from worries about whether or not the world is my world, whether I can know it or be known in it, whether my words can refer and my sentences be true or false, whether I inhabit it with intelligible others and whether I am intelligible to them, whether we matter to each other or to anything beyond ourselves) are not best understood as timeless and acontextual, nor is that how they were understood by the earlier philosophers who first articulated them in something like their present form. Rather, they are attempts to meet the specific needs that arose as the irresolvable residue of projects of crafting and enacting privileged subjectivity, projects in which canonical philosophers were explicitly engaged in ways that clearly connect with their epistemological and metaphysical questioning and theorizing. Philosophy could not actually meet those needs (nothing could), but expressing them in the form of

philosophical demands helped to allay the symptoms (for everyone but philosophers) of the "dis-ease" they represented—the disconnection, for example, of the
knowing subject from the objects of his knowledge, starting with his own body.

Thus, philosophy did, indirectly, meet (some of) the needs of those who benefited from the construction of privilege: the placebo effect does work. The situation is more complicated with respect to those who are variously marginalized
or subordinated. The same philosophical problems will be ours to the extent that
we come to have, or to believe we have, a stake in the structures of privileges we
lack (and that we will frequently have such a stake and even more frequently be
justified in believing we do is one of the reasons political organizing against these
structures is so difficult). It may even seem, for reasons I will discuss, that those
who are marginalized or subordinated have a specific, perhaps even greater, interest
in the posing of philosophical demands.

I want to argue, however, with respect to three deeply entrenched metaphysical pictures, that, though each seems to meet the real needs of those who are
marginalized or subordinated, that offer is an illusion. In each case, I will argue,
the metaphysical picture promises what it cannot deliver and diverts attention away
from the commitment to political struggle that might, to paraphrase Wittgenstein's
words, change the way we live and dissolve the philosophical problem to which
the metaphysics was meant to be a solution.[11] I want to suggest that the failure
in each case stems from a similar move (the initial one in the conjuring trick, the
one that escapes notice, PI §308): for understandable reasons, the circularity of
genuine needs discourse is rejected in favor of the posing of demands that are
taken, in a way that precludes examination, to represent the satisfaction of real
needs—what *must* be the case if our needs are to be met.

Mind-Independent Reality

Arguments about the nature of reality—in particular, about what it means to say,
and whether it is true, that the physical world exists independently of our attempts
to know it—are in some form or other as old as philosophy. One recent turn on
these disputes starts with the argument, often from the academic left, that realism is politically suspect, that the requirement of mind-independent reality as the
ground for truth claims about the world is an ideological fiction that serves to
occlude the human activities of world-structuring. A reply to that, from political
allies, is that it is those who would argue against the *status quo* who most need
independence—as the ground for the truth of such claims as that gender is a system of subordination, whether or not anyone thinks so. Furthermore, it is argued,
surely we want to be able to say that those who promulgate sexist, racist, homo-
phobic theories about the nature of women, people of color, gays and lesbians,
are just wrong and that the theories we and our allies come up with are not just
more to our liking, but are actually true (or, at least, truer).[12]

One standard way of explaining what is meant by mind-independent reality is
to say that it entails that no matter how far we may progress in our understanding of the world, no matter how confident we may be in the truth of our theories,

we could turn out to be wrong, even if we might never actually or perhaps even possibly discover that fact. No amount of justification entails truth; metaphysics (what is true) is independent of epistemology (what we are justified in believing).[13]

It does seem right to me that liberatory theorists have good reasons to be realists. Those reasons include a recognition of the problems of arrogance: surely it is salutary to cultivate an attitude of openness to being surprised by reality, a discipline of attentiveness, a readiness to discover that the world eludes one's classificatory and explanatory grasp, rather than conforming to it as a matter of definition.[14] What is seriously at issue is how to characterize realism—in particular, what characterization best captures the insights into the necessarily perspectival nature of knowledge that have been developed by feminist theorists and others.

Such insights (including arguments against an Archimedean point, or God's-eye, objectivity, and for the relevance of social location to how one comes to conceive of the world) have often been interpreted as arguments against realism—replacing reality with views of reality. Such arguments are, I think, fundamentally misguided: perspectivalism (which I take to be basically correct, in some form or other, and there are many) makes sense only as a form of realism. To say that perspectives differ is to say that those who are relevantly differently located will perceive things differently—and this simply makes no sense unless what is being perceived, the perceivers, and their locations are all real. One can, in fact, often differentiate between real and imagined things precisely by asking if those who are differently placed have different perspectives on them—if from where you stand, you can see the pink elephant I see, and if the way it looks to you is different in the ways it ought to be from the way it looks to me. It's not only that, if you fail to see it, we may conclude that it's my hallucination, but, if, standing on the other side of the room, you see just what I see, we may conclude that we're *both* hallucinating: perspectives are supposed to differ, and to do so predictably, or at least in ways we can come to understand.

Metaphysical realism may well be compatible with perspectivalism. But, as Wittgenstein put it, "a wheel that can be turned though nothing else moves with it, is not part of the mechanism" (PI §271). Whether or not something is part of the mechanism has to do with what we are doing: what is the "real need" to which mind-independent reality is the answer?[15] While all persons have an interest in their theories' being true, independently of anyone's thinking that they are, the need for realism specifically on the part of those who are marginalized or subordinated is acute, since the alternative—truth's consisting in some sort of agreement in practice—would leave them not only epistemically but metaphysically in the cold, their beliefs condemned to being not only unjustified but false.

But does metaphysical realism answer this real need? What it does is to put the truth beyond a necessarily receding horizon: anything that could be known to turn with the parts we have our hands on could, on this view, not be reality—the possibility of not being part of the mechanism is its whole point. It is, in this way, suspiciously like a Kingdom of Heaven promised especially to those who are on the losing end of all the kingdoms on earth. The keys to this heavenly kingdom do not unlock any earthly doors; the message of transcendence is necessar-

ily one of deferral. One suspects that the function of the two transcendent gestures is the same—the deflection of attention from what might change the situation of the wretched of the earth here on the earth, by shifting the structures of
power that keep them wretched.

What might this mean in the case of metaphysical realism? What other account
of realism might meet those real needs in reality, not just in fantasy? Rather than
being able to say, without being able to show, that there is a fact of the matter
that makes one's views the truth, or at least nearer the truth than one's opponents, what would actually do some work would be making a space for critical
engagement. An account of realism that starts with the perspectival nature of
knowledge provides such a space by its insistence on the problematic partiality
of any account that has failed to engage relevant critiques. What makes a critique relevant, and what counts as engagement, are matters for argument; but
for a perspectival realist, it remains always an open possibility that, however stable
a current consensus might be, there are potential critics who ought to be heard
and who, if heard, would properly upset that consensus. A perspectival account
of realism places on those who would maintain a particular view the burden of
seeking out critics or, at the very least, of scrutinizing the practices that might be
keeping critics silent or distorting what they might say. It requires that a commitment to objectivity and truth be backed up by vigorous projects of discursive
affirmative action.[16] Rather than resting with the metaphysical possibility that
we might be wrong—a possibility that, since it is necessarily transcendent, remains with equal force no matter what we do—it draws our attention to what
we need to *do* if we care about truth. To say that reality might turn out to be different from what we take it to be doesn't direct our attention; to say that our accounts of reality are incomplete because relevant perspectives have not contributed to them directs us to those who have been marginalized or subordinated by
social structures.

Another way of putting the point is that metaphysical realism is a thesis about
the ontological status of the objects of knowledge; it is mute about the subjects of
that knowledge. By contrast, the recognition that specific forms of bias inhere in
privileged perspectives on the world underwrites the call for what Sandra Harding
calls "strong objectivity," which "puts the subject or agent of knowledge in the
same critical, causal plane as the object of her or his inquiry."[17] What responds
to the real needs of the marginalized or subordinated is realism about knowing
subjects as rigorous as the realism about the objects of their knowledge. Such a
need is especially crucial when the objects of knowledge are the marginalized or
subordinated themselves—scrutinized, pathologized, exoticized, and anatomized
by those whose epistemic privilege consists precisely in their being exempt from
such scrutiny, in their occupying subject positions encoded as generic, and in their
being allowed (often, in fact, required) to present what they claim to know in
anonymous, impersonal, "objective" form, a requirement that idealizes the conditions of their knowledge-construction, effectively masks their social location,
renders them "unreal," and removes them from reciprocal critical examination.[18]

In seeming to offer a ground for truth claims, metaphysical realism may be a
source of comfort for liberatory theorists, but it has—can have—no teeth. At best,

one can hope that reality will eventually bite back against one's opponents. Perspectival realism, by contrast, is programmatic: it allows one to distinguish between those who have a genuine commitment to objectivity and truth and those who do not. Such a view of realism can be argued for independently of any particular perspective, but those whose voices are already heard are less likely to see, from their own perspective, the need for it: it doesn't, in the same direct way, respond to their "real needs." But rotating the axis of our examination around the real needs of the "others"—needs for legitimated entry into the processes of knowledge-creation—shifts the constraints on an adequate account of the nature of realism and moves us away from the metaphysical demand for—and problem of—inaccessible reality and toward the politics of democratic critical engagement.

As with any serious politics, however, such a project is unavoidably circular. In particular, what are the terms of democratic critical engagement, starting with the question of how "we" are to decide who is to participate in it? There is no way prior to such a project to lay down the rules for engaging in it. In the absence of the trust that could ground such boot-strapping, there may be no way effectively to answer the interlocutor who persists in the demand for absolute, metaphysically guaranteed bedrock. What would allow us to give peace to such a demand would be the confidence that the real needs that give it force stood some real chance of being, at least, attended to. For this reason, breaking the hold of the metaphysical picture requires a change in the way we live.

Transcendent Moral Standards

Similar arguments have occupied moral philosophers. A standard question has been, Are there grounds for moral judgment that transcend particular, historically and culturally variable forms of practice? Further, are such grounds required if moral judgments are to be objectively (or even universally intersubjectively) true or false? What might the source of such moral authority be, and how might we be connected to it epistemically and motivationally? How do we know what it commands, and why do its commands speak to us? Arguments for one or another form of moral realism have mirrored those for metaphysical realism, including the point that it is especially those whose interests are not reflected in dominant practices who have the greatest stake in not reducing claims about what we ought to do to claims about what we in fact do or even what we think we ought to do.[19] It would seem that some sort of moral realism is required to make sense of the claim of the radical critic that the form of life she inhabits is an immoral one.

As with metaphysical realism, the apparent need is to have it both ways—to ensure the objectivity of moral judgments by locating their source outside of our practices, but also to connect those judgments to our practices in ways that make them both knowable to us and binding on us. Plausible accounts of moral epistemology or of moral motivation risk losing moral objectivity, while accounts of moral objectivity risk making moral truths inaccessible or alien. Attempts at reconciling these conflicting demands have frequently rested on substantive claims about allegedly universal human needs or interests; the problem comes in specifying those needs or interests in ways that avoid being either too thin to do any real work or too thick to be nontendentious.

Wittgenstein is frequently read as urging us to forego these attempts altogether—to recognize that justification is itself a practice, which, like all practices, rests not on some transcendent ground but on what we do, on our agreement "in form of life" (PI §241). ("The end is not an ungrounded presupposition: it is an ungrounded way of acting.")[20] This "pluralist conservative" reading of Wittgenstein[21] has been contested, notably by Sabina Lovibond, who has argued that Wittgenstein is best read as a moral realist and, as such, provides a way of making the radical critic intelligible by construing objectivity in terms of a project rather than an already existing ground.[22] Properly understood, moral practices are intrinsically critical. Rather than a transcendent ground, we have a rolling horizon, and keeping it rolling is the work of the moral critic: this is what we—at least some of us—do.[23]

Putting the matter this way makes moral objectivity not a given, but a commitment. If "we" *don't* contest the *status quo*, then justification may well come to an end, not because it *couldn't* be carried further, but because no one has taken on the task of disturbing its grounds. Wittgenstein writes, "If I have exhausted the justifications I have reached bedrock, and my spade is turned. Then I am inclined to say: 'this is simply what I do'" (PI §217). "Bedrock" is no more absolute, however, than is the riverbed in *On Certainty*. It may be that the "hard rock" of the bank is "subject to no alteration or only to an imperceptible one" (OC §99), but that doesn't mean that it can't be disturbed: it's simply a matter of fact that it isn't. So if we find its obduracy problematic, we have our work cut out for us. If our demands for justification are met with the reply "this is simply what I do," we need to ask ourselves: "Is this what *I* do? And, if so, do I do it less than wholeheartedly," as Lovibond puts it (*Realism and Imagination*, pp. 159–163)? Do I know others who are similarly (or perhaps differently) estranged from this "we"? Why, precisely, does what is being justified seem to me or to others unjustified?

It is a peculiar feature of commitments to both moral and metaphysical realism that they typically take as definitive a resistance to being thus "cashed out." In the course of such resistance, "where your mouth is" is precisely where your money is not supposed to be. This can seem especially responsive to the needs of those without money: indefinite deferral means that the line of credit will never come due. But, as in the financial realm, getting credit requires more assurance of solvency than simply pointing out that there's a lot of time before one will have to make good. The "real needs" of the moral critic are not met by an inner assurance of ultimate vindication. If one's criticisms are ignored (the privileged insist their spades are turned), such inner assurance will be cold comfort, assuming one is even able to maintain it. To take moral realism seriously would mean to be committed to the belief that, if others did or could live a form of life deeply different from ours, there would still be the possibility of critical engagement with them, that their different ways are possibilities for us and pose a critical challenge to us, that they might be right to do what they do and we might be wrong.

In this sense, those who are subordinated or marginalized have, one might say, moral realism thrust upon them: that others might live differently is not just a matter for theoretical speculation. The mores of the dominant are everywhere around them, constantly being touted as the right way to live. In the light of those mores, the subordinated or marginalized see themselves stigmatized as culpably defective, their forms of life as inferior, either lacking in values or informed by the wrong ones. Whether we internalize these judgments of ourselves or reject them, we can hardly ignore them or see them as emanating from forms of life that are just different, neither better nor worse. Questions about right or wrong are not idle, nor can one say "this is what we do," as though that settles the matter, when the "we" one appeals to is stigmatized as perverse. Critical engagement, for some, is not a theoretical possibility; it is a necessity for survival.

From nonprivileged vantage points, moral realism is practical and concrete rather than metaphysical. It does some work because there is work that needs to be done. Moral questions are real questions, with real answers—moral judgments are true or false—because that is how they are treated, as matters literally of life and death, whether one is confronting gay-bashers or those who would deny food, shelter, and health care to children without two, married parents. Ultimate vindication in the light of principles that transcend any form of practice is beside the point: what makes moral judgments objective is the intelligibility of continuing dispute.[24]

The privileged, by contrast, might well come to a point where such intelligibility runs out, where it seems either that no-one really could, seriously, think or act differently, or that their doing so is of merely aesthetic interest: quaint or exotic or titillating. In either case, there's nothing to argue about, no real possibility that others might show me to be mistaken. One might subscribe nonetheless to metaphysical moral realism—holding on, as a matter of principle, to the intelligibility of dispute, without any idea of how in practice to carry it on, but the principle is an empty one. What it would take for one's spade *not* to be turned would be the actual chipping of the bedrock, a cracking open of the earth beneath one's feet, a real instability calling for a real effort to regain one's footing, to find a better ground for one's convictions, or, perhaps, a change in one's form of life.[25] Moral realism is a demand, from the less to the more privileged, that the latter take such a challenge seriously. To reply that the challenge can only truly be set, or met, by practice-transcendent values is to evade the demand. It is to counter, Let them eat pie-in-the-sky.

Here, however, once more the turn toward serious politics presumes a discursive space that in general does not exist: "Just say 'No'" works no better against metaphysics than it does against drugs. In both cases what is likely to be lacking is the justified belief in something to which to say, "Yes." One can admit that a serious moral conversation (or a well-paying, rewarding job) is what one really needs, but, if one thinks there is no chance of getting one, it can be hard to let go of one's surrogate satisfactions.

Privileged Access

Metaphysical and moral realism seem to offer protection from the abuses of power and privilege by positing a realm of truth that is beyond the grasp equally of prince and of pauper. The thesis of privileged access to our mental states offers such protection by putting those states equally within the grasp of each of us—and us alone. Each of us gets to be the ultimate insider, possessed of the insider's edge, when it comes to the crucial questions about what we believe or feel, desire or despise. Since it is those without sanctioned social power—for example, women, children, gays and lesbians, transsexuals, those declared insane—who are typically subjected to allegedly authoritative pronouncements by others as to what we really feel or mean or intend or want, it would seem that we would have particular reason to embrace a philosophical position that made us the only true ultimate authorities on such matters. It would seem helpful to be able to say, "You—whoever you are—are merely in the position of putting together pieces of evidence, trying to acquire reasons to believe what I, and I alone, already directly and infallibly know."

Certainly the problem of being subjected to others' socially sanctioned expertise over one's inner states is a real one. Children are told their anger is merely overtiredness (the word "cranky" exists largely for this purpose); women are told by men that our no's really mean yes; the meaning of homoerotic desire is claimed by those whose authority stems largely from their supposed immunity to it;[26] transsexuals have had to struggle with a range of expert discourses that claim to know better than they do what genders they are or can possibly be; and a declaration of insanity is tantamount to a loss of all epistemic authority over oneself. In these ways, it can be evident that what appears to be a metaphysical thesis, applying equally to everyone, functions instead like a property right: privileged access is just what it sounds like—a right to (epistemic) access that tracks privilege.[27] But why shouldn't we argue for granting in practice what the thesis offers in theory—privileged access for each of us to our own inner lives?

There are two reasons why such an offer is, like the offers of metaphysical and moral realism, more apparent than real, a distraction from the changes in our form of life that would address the real needs that privileged access appeals to. The first concerns what we don't get with privileged access; the second concerns what we too often do.

What we don't get is an acknowledgment of the roles that we play in each other's intelligibility, of the ways in which we "listen each other into speech," create the grounds of each other's possibility.[28] It is an illusion of privilege to believe that our inner lives have meaning and structure independently of the social worlds in which we are embedded. The illusion comes about from the closeness of fit the privileged are likely to experience, the ease with which they can make sense of themselves using the available language and explanatory frameworks—even when they are articulating their own supposed divergence from what they take to be the norm (there is, at least in the late twentieth-century United States, a ready vocabulary for disaffection, alienation, and eccentricity). It can seem that one just does directly encounter one's inner self, and that its meaning is clear.

As post-Freudian sophisticates, we naturally do not really believe in such simple self-transparency.[29] But, depending on our social locations, we have wildly diverse encounters with the various expert discourses that purport to have or to be able to uncover the truth about us, a truth of which we might be unaware or which we might actively resist. For the privileged, such encounters tend to be voluntary and to be aimed at providing explanations over which we exercise ultimate authority; and the terms of those explanations are likely to be familiar, even if their application in one's own case is initially disconcerting. The "designated others," by contrast, encounter experts implacable in their claims to ultimate authority, an authority that is quite independent of whether or not we ever come to accept their stories about us as the correct ones. Nor are the terms of those expert discourses likely to be useful to us in fashioning livable narratives of our own lives: it is certainly not a condition on their explanatory adequacy that they do so—as it is in practice for the explanatory stories about the privileged. In the face of such pervasive arrogance, it can be a matter of survival to be convinced that one has privileged access to one's own inner being.[30]

There is a burgeoning literature about and from the perspectives of those whose identities are, according to dominant constructions, "impossible." Marilyn Frye, for example, starts her essay "To Be and Be Seen" with a comment by Sarah Hoagland that lesbians are impossible beings, and that being so offers distinctive epistemic advantages.[31] María Lugones writes in "Hispaneando y Lesbiando" about the impossibility of being what she is: an Hispanic lesbian.[32] Jacob Hale, Kate Bornstein, Susan Stryker, and Sandy Stone write variously about the ways in which transsexual subjectivity is a struggle against a dichotomous sex/gender system that offers them intelligibility only at the cost of a continuous, truthful life story, and only if they agree to conform to stereotypical notions of gender.[33] In all these cases, the need is acute to be able to say: I exist as what I know myself to be, in the face of a normalizing discourse that says no one can possibly be such a thing—a lesbian (someone whose attention is drawn to women) or a Hispanic lesbian (rather than a pervert or an exotic caricature) or a person whose gender identity has shifted in varying relation to one's also shifting sexed body.

Though privileged access can seem especially appealing to those subject to routine epistemic predation, one striking feature of the writing of these theorists is that, though they may acknowledge temptations in that direction, they argue, explicitly or implicitly, against such access. For one, they are acutely aware that those who do not find usable representations of themselves, narratives in which to insert their own singularity, need more than mere permission to say how it is with them and a readiness on the part of others to accept what they say. They first need a language, and a set of stories, that make them intelligible, that let them string together descriptors that add up to something other than an "impossible being." Something needs to be there to make one's articulations of identity more than meaningless babble, even in one's own ears—a "something" that the privileged tend to take for granted.

Part of that "something" is provided by the discursive resources of our cultural surroundings. But we also need more focused uptake from those with whom we interact—we need acknowledgment and, beyond that, critical engagement with our ongoing projects of self-creation. Simply being left alone, as the ultimate authorities on ourselves, will too often leave us without the resources to figure out just what it is that we are supposed to know. We are neither as opaque to (all) others nor as transparent to ourselves as the thesis of privileged access would have it. To a great extent, we are what others take us to be, and, if we think that is not so, that is likely to be because the "others" are sufficiently culturally ubiquitous and sufficiently on our side for us to be oblivious to their contributions. When that is not the case, what we need is not to be left to our own devices, infallibly introspecting, supposedly protected by metaphysically guaranteed, universally privileged access. Locking others out serves equally to lock us in, deprived of sense-making resources.

We may, however, know that the culturally available discursive resources fail to make sense of our lives without ourselves knowing how better to tell the story. And an initial step toward constructing a usable narrative may well be the exposure of the contingency of those resources, an exposure that comes when the gaze of those who are rendered impossible is directed back at the structures of intelligibility. It is the invisibility of those structures to those for whom they work that fosters the illusion of direct self-knowledge, even as it allows for the idea that such self-knowledge may frequently fail and need to be supplemented by experts who can see the truth when we are ourselves unaware of it. Exposing structures of intelligibility as the contingent effects of normalizing practices is a first step in the concrete, political work of taking responsibility for our complicity in setting or refusing the conditions of each other's possibility.

If the notion of privileged access promises the discursively marginalized what it cannot deliver—unmediated access to an already existing coherent truth about themselves—it equally problematically imposes on them a form of self-knowledge from which they can have no distance and which is unusable in their hands. All they can do—what they are expected to do as "native informants"—is to hand over the infallible knowledge of themselves on which they will in all likelihood be impaled. Those designated "primitive" or "natives" are ironically taken to be in possession of (or to be possessed by) straightforward truths about their own lives, truths ready for consumption by those who take an interest in them.

These points have been made with greatest clarity by postcolonial theorists like Chandra Talpade Mohanty and Uma Narayan.[34] In a culture that privileges scientific knowledge—that is, knowledge gained by disciplined adherence to a prescribed method—the self-knowledge of the marginalized and subordinated is taken to inhere effortlessly in them and to exude naturally from them: a natural resource for more privileged knowers to gather up and refine in the production of "real" knowledge. Presumed incapable of real, disciplined understanding of their own situation, "natives" are no more empowered by their "privileged" relationship to the truths of their lives than indigenous peoples have been by their relation to the land on which they lived.

Elaine Scarry makes a similar point about pain, especially the pain of torture, on which the sufferer is impaled, disempowered by what she or he cannot but know but cannot say, the suffered pain made available for appropriation by the torturer. This pain comes to signify the torturer's power and control precisely because the torturer is the one who stands at the authoritative distance from it.[35] In arguing that the experience of pain is private, in the sense of being incommunicable, Scarry might seem to be at odds with Wittgenstein. But there is, I think, an insight they share. Both see knowledge as an achievement—a matter, as Wittgenstein would stress, of justification, reasoning, overcoming of challenges, establishment of grounds and of authority. That is why Wittgenstein says that we do not know our own pain. We do not stand in the right relation to it. We are not separate from it; it is not an object for us, hence not an object of knowledge.

Wittgenstein clearly does not mean to single out in particular the sort of pain Scarry writes about; he would include pain we can straightforwardly communicate, as when we tell the doctor where and how it hurts—or, for that matter, when we cry out or moan. Somewhat less clear is the question, Why pain? Isn't what Wittgenstein says true of all sensations, perceptions, and so on? My sense about that is that there *is* something special about pain, and that Scarry's discussion of the pain of torture strikingly brings it out. In general, my "inner states," including my pain, can be the objects of the knowledge of others; but, especially in the case of pain, what I may primarily need from others is not that they know how it is with me, but that they acknowledge it—and me.[36] When my pain is acknowledged, I am connected as a subject with others; and their knowledge, if grounded in that acknowledgment, is available to me: I am part of the community that comes to know how it is with me—even though my own relation to what I feel is not the same as that of the others. We are, reciprocally, subjects and objects for each other; and what I come to know about you inflects how I experience myself. In the absence of that reciprocity and trust—commonly, when my experiences put me beyond the range of what others are able to acknowledge, as can happen with extreme pain, or, horrifically, when the others are not to be trusted with my experience, as when, most extremely, they are my torturers—those experiences (and pain is at least the paradigm example here) are not known within a community of which I am an equal member. Instead, knowledge happens in the absence of acknowledgment. A chasm opens up between my having and others' knowing; each stands as a reproach to the other, contests the others' authority. My body becomes contested epistemic terrain—and the contest is one I cannot win, if the winner is the one who knows.

What is the "real need" of the marginalized and subordinated with respect to the truths of their/our own lives? The answer to that question starts from the recognition that, construed as a struggle for something that already exists, it is one we are doomed to lose. Insofar as such truths are seen as proper objects of knowledge, others are far better placed to possess them; and if such truths are seen as naturally inhering in us, they possess us rather than the other way around. If, however, the truths of our lives are to be created—not by making ourselves up, though we may need to do that, but by creating the explanatory and narrative frames within which we can make a sense we can live with—then what we need are contexts of trust and reciprocity, contexts in which, in Marilyn Frye's terms, we are "lovingly perceived."[37] It is the strength of perspectival realism, of the critique of diverse separatisms, to create such contexts. Moving beyond those confines has met with some, albeit limited, success, but to the extent that relationships with dominant discourses remain hostile, privileged access will retain its appeal to those who feel themselves wrongly stigmatized by those discourses.

What Philosophy Cannot Do, and Why

In suggesting that we rotate the axis of our examination, Wittgenstein presumably had in mind (not solely, but centrally) the examination he had undertaken in the *Tractatus* of language, the world, and the relationship between them. That examination had culminated—*philosophy*, he argued, therein culminated—in a proof by ostension (showing, not saying) that both language and the world were, necessarily, *mine*. The "real need" to which such a "proof" was meant to respond concerns one's belonging in, or to, the world—knowing and being known, understanding and being understood, mattering and having things matter. It makes no sense, in *Tractatus* terms, to think oneself marginal to or excluded from sense-making: wherever I am is the center of my world, the place from which sense is made.

Some interpreters of Wittgenstein have read especially the private language "argument" in the *Investigations* as continuing this line of thought, with the crucial shift from "I" to "we."[38] On this reading, Wittgenstein's later work provides the same sort of minimal metaphysical guarantee of intelligibility and deflection of the threat of radical skepticism as did the earlier work: by our use of language, we place ourselves within a form of life the living of which provides the ground for shared judgments. There is, I think, something right about this picture. To the extent that our judgments are grounded, this is what it comes to. But the air of bourgeois complacency many commentators attribute to Wittgenstein—we all go on the same, doing what we do, our spades turned—could not be more alien to his sensibility. The interlocutor's unwillingness to stop demanding something more absolute by way of bedrock can, I have argued elsewhere,[39] best be understood as an expression of anxiety on the part of someone whose attachment to "what we do" is by no means simple or to be taken for granted. It may well be that only if I take what we do for granted (which includes not worrying about just who "we" are) can I be fully intelligible, even to myself—but there is no guarantee that I *am* intelligible.

Intelligibility is not an all-or-nothing affair. As both subjects and objects of knowledge, each of us moves in the world as one medium-sized physical object among many, finding our way around with a degree of success—whoever we may be—sufficient to ground the objectivity of a plethora of judgments. We wouldn't (couldn't) argue as we do about, for example, preserving the environment, if we didn't agree about being mortal creatures inhabiting the same planet. But when it comes to more subtle and vexed ways of sense-making, our relationships to the practices that ground intelligibility differ widely. "What we do" is a matter of what Wittgenstein calls our natural history, including under that rubric "[c]ommanding, questioning, recounting, chatting" along with "walking, eating, drinking, playing" (PI §25). If one's commands are routinely ignored or mocked, one's questions consistently dismissed as silly, one's attempts to recount one's experiences rejected as fantasy, or one's chatting ignored as chattering; if one's ways of walking (or not) are unaccommodated or one's experiences around food and drink are the source of shame; or if, as a boy, one prefers playing with dolls over what is referred to as "rough and tumble play," one is likely to be regarded by those around one as not quite making sense.

It is understandable that one might try to argue that one *does* make sense—that there is a truth about who and what one is, as well as about the moral rightness of one's being, and that, no matter what anyone else says, there are things about oneself that one just directly knows. One might, that is, call on metaphysics as a shield against others who seem to get one wrong, gesturing toward something that is not a matter of shared practices in which to ground the truth and rightness of one's claims to intelligibility.

Such arguments—or gestures in the directions of arguments—are understandable, but they are not, I have argued, effective. Like the soaring arches of Gothic cathedrals, they draw our attention away from the practices that ground intelligibility and from the need for concrete political struggle to change those practices, to shift the ground. Wittgenstein had little or nothing to say about such struggle, as deeply disaffected as he was with the Europe of his day, except to express profound suspicion of the idea that philosophy could figure out what should be done. He clearly rejected the possibility of sitting down and deducing from first principles how and where to relocate the riverbed.

But a suspicion of theory-driven radical utopianism doesn't preclude recognizing the radical potential in the perspectives of those whose connections to "what we do" are neither simple nor unconflicted. As María Lugones has argued,[40] the tendency of privileged theorists to see all problems as matters to be dealt with by coming up with better theories expresses an unwillingness to engage with those who have been excluded or marginalized by dominant practices, including practices of theory-construction. What is avoided, Lugones points out, when we think what we need are better theories, is engagement, interaction, and submission by the privileged to the gaze of "others." By drawing our attention ("just look") to our practices, Wittgenstein can lead us to notice our complicity, our (diverse) investments and "real needs," and how what we do makes what others do—or try or want to do—difficult or impossible.

Needs and Demands

To successfully negotiate an indefinite sequence of emergent resistances
in the interplay of material, conceptual and social practices is a far more
impressive and admirable achievement than simply to conform to a list of
standards given in advance.

> Andrew Pickering, "Objectivity and the Mangle of Practice,"
> quoted in Heldke and Kellert, "Objectivity as Responsibility"

Need is also a political instrument, meticulously prepared, calculated, and
used.

> Michel Foucault, *Discipline and Punish*,
> quoted in Fraser, "Struggle over Needs"

We can get clearer about the nature of philosophical "demands" by looking at the paradox of analysis.[41] One way of putting the paradox is this: we are looking for the analysis of some concept, say knowledge. Now, either we know what it is—in which case, why do we have to look for it?—or we do not—in which case, how will we recognize it when we find it? For analytic philosophers, the usual resolution to the paradox is via some form of what Rawls calls "reflective equilibrium": we approach an analysis by tacking back and forth in response to the pressures on the one side from our considered judgments and on the other side from the demands of a theory meant to explain and justify those judgments; we have reached the analysis when we are, so to speak, becalmed.[42] "What we are inclined to say" is both a place to start and a pressure to which we need always to be responsive (otherwise we could not know that it was our concept we had analyzed), but it cannot be our only consideration, since there is no reason to believe that the concept itself will be perspicuously displayed in all our deployments of it. The concept "works" because of its underlying logic, which may or may not show up on the surface.

Philosophers' "demands" thus have at least two sources: on the one hand, an analysis must fit the form of whatever theoretical framework is being deployed; and, on the other, it must effectively account for our preanalytic judgments. There is, on the face of it, nothing to object to in this method; it seems laudably open to discovery and revision both from theoretical developments and from more careful examination of the data. Yet the problematic "a prioricity" to which Wittgenstein and Diamond draw our attention is smuggled in under cover of this apparent reasonableness, in what Wittgenstein refers to as "the initial move in the conjuring trick" (PI §308). We may be quite open as to the character of what fills the explanatory box; but the size, shape, and location of the box are set in advance: we are looking, for example, for a description of the state (event, process) that will play what we have determined is the necessary causal role in the explanatory scheme that seems to us to make sense of the phenomenon we are analyzing. Such a project may seem to leave everything open while actually—starting with the identification of "*the* phenomenon"—setting unargued-for constraints on what we are in a position even to notice, let alone adequately to describe.

But surely we have to start somewhere, and, if we have no idea of what it is we are explaining or of what an acceptable explanation looks like, how are we even to get started? Don't we have to place demands on what we do in order to do anything at all? What might Wittgenstein have in mind in urging us to attend not to the demands of philosophers but to our "real needs"? How do we determine what those needs are and what might count as meeting them? Aren't philosophers' demands meant precisely to meet our needs for clarity, understanding, and confidence in what we take to be our best-founded judgments?

What I want to suggest is that a serious attempt to meet our real needs involves us in an open-ended search to articulate what those needs might be. It involves us, that is, in what in the introduction to this essay I called serious politics—that circular, Aristotelian crafting of virtuous citizens and a virtuous polis as the conditions for each other's possibility. If for whatever reason one disdains or despairs

of such an attempt (and there are many reasons why one might: the understandable lack of trust on the part of the disenfranchised is the one that has most concerned me here, but equally worth noting is the cynicism of the overly comfortable),
then one will be drawn to ways of thinking it unnecessary, impossible, or both. One
way is to act as though real needs were discoverable without politics: thus, the
arrogance of the welfare state as Nancy Fraser describes it. Another is to replace
needs with demands: thus the understandable attractiveness of fighting for something one has specifically delineated (ideally by identifying it as a right, a legitimated
demand), the deeper meaning of which is nonnegotiable, when the circumstances
preclude the trust required for negotiating (discovering, creating) our real needs.

In this light, philosophers' demands are another evasion of serious politics,
though not because were we to turn from our books to the streets we would be
able to change the world (or even have a clue about what to do in order to change
the world) so as to "make all these words superfluous." It is not that philosophers
are fiddling while Rome burns when we should be helping to put out the fires.
That *may* be sometimes how to describe what we are and should be doing, but it
is hardly what Wittgenstein has in mind. Rather, we need to turn toward serious politics precisely because it is more, rather than less, open-ended than philosophy. It is, for example, more intellectually serious, more genuinely difficult
and challenging, more potentially revelatory of the deep structures of knowledge
and of reality, to take on the task of answering the doubts of those who are alienated from the practices of rationality than it is to attempt to answer the skeptic of
one's own imagination.[43]

Those of us who, for example, teach introductory logic classes may well be right
about the universal validity of, say, modus ponens; I can't imagine that we're not.
But my confidence that the impossibility stems from something deeper than the
limitations of my own imagination needs to be tested against my attempts to find
the grounds for mutual comprehension with those (who may be among my students) who claim not to recognize that validity. Modus ponens may seem to them
not to be implicated in the practices in which they are seriously engaged: it seems
to belong to an alien form of life confined to the classroom, to meet no needs deeper
or more pervasive than passing a required course. To take those students and their
skepticism seriously doesn't require that we think they might be right to deny the
validity of modus ponens. Rather, just as we need to teach them that modus
ponens is, in fact, woven into the fabric of their ordinary practices, they have to
teach us that also woven into that fabric are some very problematic practices of
domination. We may be convinced that, were we to reweave the fabric of our
practices in more equitable ways (in ways that more fully met real needs), modus
ponens would remain (as I said, I cannot imagine otherwise), but the proof that
that is so will come through those transformations in practice. And taking our
students, and the needs that would emerge from our engaging with them, seriously is one place to start.[44] Not only can we not know in advance what our
shared, real needs are (hence, we cannot satisfy them in the form of political demands), but there is no and cannot be an answer to that question outside of our
engaging with each other in creating one (hence, we cannot expect as philosophers meaningfully to articulate those demands).

Since most of us who are professional philosophers are among the relatively enfranchised, one thing we can do is work toward the conditions in which such engagement can occur, by doing what we can to make the trust required for serious politics neither an unnecessary expense for the privileged nor a fatally foolhardy gamble for the subordinated. One would "give philosophy peace" in part by shifting the perplexity that philosophers have taken on as our own back onto all of us, by stopping being the scapegoats for cultural anxieties. It would require the acknowledgment of the fact that there is nothing beyond or below human practice that obviates the need to create trust, nothing that either practically or conceptually sets the terms of truth or of right or determines our real needs— however unlikely it may seem that human practice is adequate to the task of doing so. In this light, arguments that undermine the allegedly practice-transcendent guarantors of truth are hardly nihilistic. To argue that there is nothing beyond or below "what we do" that grounds truth is to argue not for the superficiality of truth but for the depth of practice. There is no "merely" about our lives; it's "not as if we *chose* this game!" (OC §317).

NOTES

1. See Diamond's "Introduction II: Wittgenstein and Metaphysics," in her *The Realistic Spirit: Wittgenstein, Philosophy, and the Mind* (Cambridge, Mass.: MIT Press, 1991), pp. 13–38, and Fraser's "Struggle over Needs: Outline of a Socialist-Feminist Critical Theory of Late Capitalist Political Culture," in her *Unruly Practices: Power, Discourse, and Gender in Contemporary Social Theory* (Oxford: Polity Press, 1989).

2. Ludwig Wittgenstein, *Philosophical Investigations*, ed. G. E. M. Anscombe and R. Rhees, trans. G. E. M. Anscombe (Oxford: Basil Blackwell & Mott, 1958), §217. References hereafter will be to PI and will be made parenthetically in the text.

3. For particularly insightful discussions of these tensions, see the disputes between critical legal theorists and critical race theorists. The former argue against the discourse of rights as enshrining a problematically bourgeois conception of the individual; the latter historicize that discourse rather in terms of black antislavery and enfranchisement struggles and argue for its continuing relevance. See Patricia Williams, *Alchemy of Race and Rights: Diary of a Law Professor* (Cambridge, Mass.: Harvard University Press, 1991); and Richard Delgado, ed., *Critical Race Theory: The Cutting Edge* (Philadelphia: Temple University Press, 1995). Nancy Fraser's *Unruly Practices* also addresses these tensions in an especially illuminating way.

4. Wittgenstein, *Zettel*, ed. G. E. M. Anscombe and G. H. von Wright (Oxford: Blackwell, 1967), §314. References hereafter will be to Z and will be made parenthetically in the text.

5. Cornel West, *The American Evasion of Philosophy: A Genealogy of Pragmatism* (Madison: University of Wisconsin Press, 1989), p. 4.

6. Konstanty Gebert, the Polish journalist quoted in the epigraph to this section, goes on to say, "When we say [that something is history], it means just the opposite." I take this quote from an editorial in the the *New York Times*, August 28, 1997.

7. Carnap writes about the role of progressive politics in the discussions in the Vienna Circle in his "Intellectual Autobiography," in *The Philosophy of Rudolf Carnap*, ed. Paul Arthur Schilpp (La Salle, Ill.: Open Court, 1963), especially pp. 22–24. Whether or not political commitments ought explicitly to inform philosophizing was, according to Carnap's reminiscences, a frequent topic of conversation. His own view was that they should not; his main adversary in this regard was Otto Neurath.

8. My use of "we" (and, alternatively, "they") in this essay will be intentionally unstable and shifting, reflecting the unstable and shifting nature of my own identifi-

cations. In particular, I will sometimes say "we" and sometimes "they" when speaking either of those who are privileged or of those who are marginalized or subordinated. Not only do I and other radical academics occupy a variety of different subject positions, some privileged, some marginalized or subordinated, but we share a particular complex position I have elsewhere called "privileged marginality." See my "Forms of Life: Mapping the Rough Ground," in *The Cambridge Companion to Wittgenstein*, ed. Hans Sluga and David G. Stein (Cambridge: Cambridge University Press, 1996), pp. 389–390. Such complexity needs to be seen both as an epistemic tool and as a reminder of the importance of concrete forms of moral, political, and epistemic responsibility. For the first point, see Patricia Hill Collins, "Learning from the Outsider Within," *Social Problems* 33 (1986): 14–32.

9. Taking the problems of philosophy in this way seriously, as requiring us to ask why it is that they matter to us and matter in a way that brain-teasers or (mere) puzzles do not, in fact characterized much of my own philosophical education—explicitly from Stanley Cavell and, as importantly, implicitly from Burton Dreben. Whatever reservations either of them has about my current work attach, I am certain, not to my raising such questions but to my too quickly answering them.

10. See my *Engenderings: Constructions of Knowledge, Authority, and Privilege* (New York: Routledge, 1993).

11. I need to guard against a tendency to oversimplify the political and to believe I know more than I possibly can about what such changes can and should be like. What I want to argue here—as will, I hope, come clear below—is that what is at issue is not the actual achievement of specific political changes, but rather the commitment to what I am calling serious politics, which I see as connected to Wittgenstein's attempt to get us to acknowledge both the absence of anything underneath our practices and the depth of those practices.

12. The arguments have been around for quite some time but have recently taken a heated turn. See, for example, the fracas surrounding Alan Sokal's spoof of postmodern science studies: Alan Sokal, "Transgressing the Boundaries: Toward a Transformative Hermeneutics of Quantum Gravity," *Social Text* 46/47 (1996): 217–252 (the spoof); Sokal, "A Physicist Experiments with Cultural Studies," *Lingua Franca*, May/June 1996: 62–64. (Sokal's exposure of the spoof); and "Mystery Science Theater," *Lingua Franca*, July/August 1996: 54–64 (discussion by the editors of *Social Text*, Sokal, and others of the significance of the spoof). For a left-feminist attack on feminist and other approaches to science studies, see Barbara Ehrenreich and Janet McIntosh, "The New Creationism: Biology under Attack," *The Nation*, June 9, 1997: 11–16.

13. Scientific realists, such as Richard Boyd, want to emphasize that the independence emphatically does not go the other way around: we have good reason to conclude that those among our beliefs that are justified are so precisely because they are (approximately) true. See Boyd's "On the Current Status of Scientific Realism," in *The Philosophy of Science*, ed. Richard Boyd, Philip Gasper, and J. D. Trout (Cambridge, Mass.: MIT Press, 1991), pp. 195–222.

14. See Lorraine Code, *What Can She Know? Feminist Theory and the Construction of Knowledge* (Ithaca, N.Y.: Cornell University Press, 1991); Donna Haraway, "Situated Knowledge and the Privilege of Partial Perspective," *Feminist Studies* 14 (1988): 575–599; Sandra Harding, *The Science Question in Feminism* (Ithaca, New York: Cornell University Press, 1986); and Lisa M. Heldke and Stephen H. Kellert, "Objectivity as Responsibility," *Metaphilosophy* 26 (1995): 360–378.

15. To frame the issue this way may seem, on a metalevel, to beg the question against the metaphysical realist, who might either reject the question or answer it by saying that our real need is for the truth of the matter. The point supports my argument: metaphysical realism is attractive insofar as one does not historicize the question to which it is an answer.

16. See Helen Longino, *Science as Social Knowledge: Values and Objectivity in Scientific Inquiry* (Princeton: Princeton University Press, 1990).

17. Sandra Harding, *Whose Science? Whose Knowledge? Thinking from Women's Lives* (Ithaca, N.Y.: Cornell University Press, 1991), p. 161. The point is strikingly similar to Quine's call for a naturalized epistemology. However differently Harding and Quine might characterize the relevant explanatory sciences, they share the insistence that subjects of knowledge need equally to be objects and in the same terms as other objects. See Quine's "Epistemology Naturalized," in *Ontological Relativity and Other Essays* (New York: Columbia University Press, 1969).

18. Such antirealist, Archimedean-point conceptions of objectivity do not, it should be noted, follow from metaphysical realism: One can hold such a conception of realism alongside an equally robust realism about knowing subjects. But the placement of mind-independent conceptions of reality at the definitional heart of realism does in practice serve to deflect attention from subjects to objects of knowledge—so that, for example, the contamination of test tubes poses an obvious epistemic threat, while the sexual harassment of lab assistants does not.

19. For an explicit connection between scientific and moral realism, see Richard Boyd, "How To Be a Moral Realist," in *Essays on Moral Realism*, ed. Geoffrey Sayre-McCord (Ithaca, N.Y.: Cornell University Press, 1988), pp. 181–228.

20. Wittgenstein, *On Certainty*, ed. G. E. M. Anscombe and G. H. von Wright (Oxford: Blackwell, 1969), §110. References hereafter will be to OC and will be made parenthetically in the text.

21. See J. C. Nyri's "Wittgenstein's Later Work in Relation to Conservatism," in *Wittgenstein and His Times*, ed. Brian McGuinness (Oxford: Blackwell, 1982), pp. 44–68, and "Wittgenstein 1929–31: The Turning Back," in *Ludwig Wittgenstein: Critical Assessments*, ed. S. G. Shanker, vol. 4, *From Theology to Sociology: Wittgenstein's Impact on Contemporary Thought* (London: Croom Helm, 1986), pp. 29–59.

22. Sabina Lovibond, *Realism and Imagination in Ethics* (Minneapolis: University of Minnesota Press, 1983).

23. For approaches to extending this account, see my "Forms of Life" and Peg O'Connor's "Moving to New Boroughs: Transforming the World by Inventing Language Games," in *Feminist Readings of Wittgenstein*, ed. Naomi Scheman (University Park, Penn.: Penn State Press, forthcoming).

24. The issues here are similar to those raised by critical race theorists about, for example, talk of rights. Critical legal theorists argue against the appeal to rights, on the grounds that the concept lacks the sort of practice-transcendent ground that would give it standing independent of its use by those in power. Critical race theorists agree that the meaning of the concept is its use, but point to its use by, for example, blacks in the civil rights struggle. They argue that such use makes rights real in any meaningful sense of that term: real enough, that is, to use; too real to ignore.

25. One can evade the demand that one change one's life and attempt to regain one's footing on new, more democratic ground, by embracing the conditions of instability and mocking any call for grounding as theoretically suspect. Though my quarrel in this essay is with analytic philosophers, it is important to point out that many (not all) postmodern, anti-Enlightenment theorists are equally guilty of an evasion of politics. Rather than arguing, or assuming, that the structures of liberalism are adequate to liberatory politics, they argue against the notion that anything could be adequate, or even meaningfully responsive. Such theorists may be effective seismographs, in recognizing the instability of the ground that most analytic philosophers take to be quite stable, but their evasion of agency and responsibility is a refuge for privilege, as Elizabeth V. Spelman characterizes epistemic nihilism or relativism on the part of the privileged in her *Inessential Woman: Problems of Exclusion in Feminist Thought* (Boston: Beacon Press, 1988), pp. 183–185. For a discussion of the relationships between poststructuralist theory and (specifically feminist) politics, see Seyla Benhabib et al., *Feminist Contentions: A Philosophical Exchange* (New York: Routledge, 1995).

26. See David Halperin, "The Queer Politics of Michel Foucault," in *Foucault: Two Essays in Gay Hagiography* (New York: Oxford University Press, 1995).

27. For a fuller discussion of this point, see my "Anger and the Politics of Naming," in *Women and Language in Literature and Society*, ed. Sally McConnell-Ginet, Ruth Borker, and Nelly Furman (New York: Praeger, 1980), pp. 174–187. This essay is reprinted in my *Engenderings*.

28. See María Lugones, "Playfulness, 'World'-Travel, and Loving Perception," in *Hypatia* 2 (1987): 3–19. See also my "Feeling Our Way toward Moral Objectivity," in *Minds and Morals: Essays on Cognitive Science and Ethics*, ed. Larry May, Marilyn Friedman, and Andy Clark (Cambridge, Mass.: MIT Press, 1987), pp. 221–236.

29. Thanks to Mary Mothersill for reminding me of this.

30. And thanks to Peg O'Connor for reminding me of *this*.

31. Marilyn Frye, "To Be and To Be Seen: The Politics of Reality," in *The Politics of Reality* (Trumansburg, New York: The Crossing Press, 1983).

32. María Lugones, "Hispanenando y Lesbiando: On Sarah Hoagland's *Lesbian Ethics*," *Hypatia* 5 (1990): 138–146.

33. See Kate Bornstein, *Gender Outlaw: On Men, Women, and the Rest of Us* (New York: Routledge, 1994); Jacob Hale, "Transgendered Strategies for Refusing Gender," paper delivered at a meeting of the Pacific Division of the Society for Women in Philosophy in Los Angeles, May 20, 1995; Sandy Stone, "The Empire Strikes Back: A Posttranssexual Manifesto," in *Body Guards: The Cultural Politics of Gender*, ed. Julia Epstein and Kristina Straub (New York: Routledge, 1991), pp. 280–304; and Susan Stryker, "My Words to Victor Frankenstein above the Village of Chamonix," *GLQ: A Journal and Lesbian and Gay Studies* 1 (1994): 237–254.

34. See Chandra Talpade Mohanty, "Under Western Eyes: Feminist Scholarship and Colonial Discourses," in *Third World Women and the Politics of Feminism*, ed. Chandra Talpade Mohanty, Ann Russo, and Lourdes Torres (Bloomington: Indiana University Press, 1991), pp. 51–80; and Uma Narayan, *Dislocating Cultures: Identities, Traditions, and Third World Feminism* (New York: Routledge, 1997).

35. See Elaine Scarry, *The Body in Pain: The Making and Unmaking of the World* (Oxford: Oxford University Press, 1985), especially chapter 1, "The Structure of Torture: The Conversion of Real Pain into the Fiction of Power."

36. See Stanley Cavell, "Knowing and Acknowledging," in *Must We Say What We Mean?* (New York: Scribner's, 1969).

37. Marilyn Frye, "In and Out of Harm's Way: Arrogance and Love," in *Politics of Reality*.

38. See, for example, Jonathan Lear, "The Disappearing 'We,'" *Proceedings of the Aristotelian Society*, supplementary vol. 58 (1984): 219–242.

39. See my "Forms of Life."

40. María Lugones, "The Logic of Pluralist Feminism," in *Feminist Ethics*, ed. Claudia Card (Lawrence: University of Kansas Press), pp. 40–42.

41. The paradox of analysis is stated in semantic, rather than epistemic, terms (either the analysans has the same meaning as the analysandum, in which case the analysis is trivial, or it does not, in which case the analysis is false) by C. H. Langford, "The Notion of Analysis in Moore's Philosophy," in *The Philosophy of G. E. Moore*, ed. Paul Arthur Schilpp (New York: Tudor Publishing, 1952), pp. 319–342. Thanks to Ingvar Johansson for pointing out to me that the epistemic version of the paradox first appears in Plato's *Meno*.

42. John Rawls, *A Theory of Justice* (Cambridge, Mass.: Harvard University Press, 1971), p. 20.

43. Descartes may have believed that in constructing the evil genius he was posing to himself a challenge more stringent than any real-world interlocutor could devise, but, on my view, what he ended up doing was providing himself (and, more importantly, his heirs) with an all-purpose excuse for not attending to the voices of others, especially not to those others for whom the very structures of authoritative reasoning appear as part of the problem.

44. This discussion can be read as a reply to Martha Nussbaum's dismissive critique of Ruth Ginzberg's discussion of feminist logic pedagogy, which attempts just the sort of engagement I am urging here (and which I learned how to think about from Ginzberg). See Ruth Ginzberg, "Feminism, Rationality, and Logic" and "Teaching Feminist Logic," *APA Newsletter on Feminism and Philosophy* 88 (1989): 34–39 and 58–62; and Martha Nussbaum, "Feminists and Philosophy," a review of *A Mind of One's Own: Feminist Essays on Reason and Objectivity*, ed. Louise Antony and Charlotte Witt (Boulder, Colo: Westview Press, 1992), in the *New York Review of Books* 41 (October 20, 1994): 59–63. In a reply to a letter to the editor I wrote in response to her review, Nussbaum argued that "feminism needs to be able to avail itself of robust notions of reason and objectivity"; see Nussbaum, *New York Review* 42 (April 6, 1995): 48–49. I couldn't agree more. But the dispute concerns how to understand "robust." My argument has been that, seen as a real need, as I presume Nussbaum intends for us to see it, robustness requires precisely the sort of commitment to practical, politically aware engagement that feminist critics (and others: see the quote from Pickering that heads this section) urge. To be robust is to be willing and able to roll up one's sleeves, get to work, and get one's hands dirty. In this light, the philosopher's demands (for some practice-transcendent guarantor) are revealed as precisely not robust but effete, insisting that we disdain as not the "real thing" anything we actually do by way of resolving the disputes between us. Henry James's novella, *The Beast in the Jungle*, can be read as a parable of this sort of thinking. Henry Marcher spent his whole adult life waiting for and focused on the one big thing that was to happen to him, thereby failing to attend to his actual life, in particular to the love that (indeterminately) was or might have been between him and May Bartram, the woman friend who spent her life waiting with him. Focusing on what lies always just over the horizon assures that everything closer than optical infinity will be a blur and, consequently, that one will fail at just the sort of responsibility that, as Heldke and Kellert argue (in "Objectivity as Responsibility"), constitutes objectivity.

1950
Publication of Alan Turing's "Computing
Machinery and Intelligence" in *Mind*

15

Language as Social Software

ROHIT PARIKH

Computer science has generated much interest among philosophers in recent years, in part because of the existence of computer models of the mind, but also because of the relevance of Church's Thesis[1] to the discussion about the possibilities of artificial intelligence. Much of the sort of computer science invoked in these discussions, however, is fairly old, going back to the work of Church, Turing, and Gödel. Apart from connectionism, most recent work in computer science, especially the work on program correctness, compilers, and the semantics of programming languages has not influenced philosophical discussion. Perhaps philosophers see these topics as too technical, of interest only to computer scientists and having little or no bearing on philosophical issues. What I intend to show here is that, to the contrary, this work too, beginning with Floyd and Hoare, and developed by others like Pratt, Pnueli, Scott, Milner, and myself, can yield significant insights into philosophical issues.

In part I of this paper, I briefly describe some recent developments in computer science, especially in the areas of program correctness, dynamic logic, and temporal logic. In part II, I use analogies from computer science to approach contemporary philosophical puzzles such as Quine's indeterminacy thesis,[2] Searle's Chinese room puzzle,[3] and the Wittgenstein-Kripke plus-quus puzzle.[4] Part I is somewhat technical, but it can be followed with no more than high school algebra and elementary logic. Part II is intended to be fairly self-contained, so the reader who so desires may skim part I or even skip directly to part II.

The principal tool of part II is an analogy between two dichotomies: (1) the denotational semantics of a high-level programming language versus the operational semantics of the machine language and (2) a meaning theory for a natural language versus the actual linguistic and nonlinguistic behavior of the members of a speech community. I try to use this analogy to provide computer science counterparts for the various philosophical puzzles mentioned above. My hope is that these computer science counterparts will prove somewhat easier to understand, or at least to become clear about, and that this understanding can help to clarify the philosophical puzzles.

The view of language developed in part II is not primarily truth-theoretic but, as I see it, more Wittgensteinian. Language is thought of as part of the life of a community and its purpose is seen as enabling the community to function more effectively. Inasmuch as the conveying of information needs to be accurate (in some sense) to be useful, there is here an underlying notion of truth. But there are large parts of language which are not informational, for example, commands, exclamations, as well as performatives. Arthur Collins suggests that this applies also to propositional attitudes.[5] Moreover, though there is and must be a great deal of overlap in the way in which different members of a community use language, still different individuals in the same community, or even the same individual on different occasions, cannot, as I have argued elsewhere,[6] use language in literally the same way. An example of this are the uses of vague predicates. While attempts to specify truth-conditions and a logic for vague predicates have been notoriously unsuccessful, pragmatic approaches that do not assume uniformity in the use of language seem to work quite well.

Thus the reader will not go far wrong by thinking of the development in part II as a formal version of what Wittgenstein called "language games."[7]

I

Program Correctness

Computer programmers write programs for specific purposes and not just to pass the time. The question thus arises at once, for any given program, whether it has fulfilled its purpose. For example, a spell-checking program should take a document, say this very paper, and produce a list of misspelled words. The program then fulfills its purpose, or is *correct*, if it produces all and only words which are misspelled. If it produces words that are *not* misspelled, or fails to produce some that *are*, then it is not correct.

But how do we *know* that a given program is correct? The way in which most of us (including software companies like Microsoft) proceed in practice is to try the program and see if it works. If a program has worked satisfactorily for us a few times, we tend to feel secure and assume that it is correct. The difficulty with this procedure—called *testing*—is that a program may work correctly some of the time or even much of the time but not *all* of the time, in which case it may be risky to use it on a new input. As Dijkstra has remarked in this context, testing can only prove that an incorrect program is incorrect but not that a correct program is correct.[8] Those of us who regard programs as part of the natural world, and hence feel that falsifiability is all we can hope for, may think that this is all that one should want.

But not all have been satisfied by mere falsifiability. Since programs are human artifacts, one might think that there must be a better way, namely, to *prove* them to be correct. Mathematical techniques for this purpose were developed by Floyd and converted to formal logics by Hoare, Pratt, and others.[9] Let us see by means of a simple example how this works.

Let α_1 be the program $(x:=2);(y:= x \times z)$.

Here an instruction of the form "$x:=t$" means, set the variable x to the (current) value of the term t (here 2) and the symbol ";" stands for "and then." So α_1

is the program that first sets x to be the integer 2 and then sets y to be equal to x times z. How do we talk about the properties of α_1?

Hoare's notation for expressing properties of programs, which he uses in his logic, is $\{A\}\alpha\{B\}$ where A and B are ordinary first order formulas and α is some program. The meaning of the statement $\{A\}\alpha\{B\}$ is that, if the formula A is true when the program α starts, then the formula B will be true when it finishes.

We can now show that the formula $\{z=4\}\alpha_1\{y=8\}$ *must* hold, and we need not resort to any testing. For clearly, given that z is 4, after the step $x:=2$, z will still be 4 and x must now be 2 since it has just been set to that value. Now the next step sets y to $x \times z$. But since x is 2 and z is 4, $x \times z$ must be 8 and hence y is indeed set to 8. For any other values of z, it is clear that executing α_1 always results in $y = 2 \times z$ being true.

The above argument made implicit use of one of Hoare's rules: if some program α is the same as $\beta;\gamma$ and if the properties $\{A\}\beta\{B\}$ and $\{B\}\gamma\{C\}$ hold, then $\{A\}\alpha\{C\}$ must hold. In our example, β is ($x:=2$), and γ is ($y: = x \times z$). Also A is $z = 4$, B is $z = 4 \wedge x = 2$, and C is $y = 8$. It is evident that both $\{A\}\beta\{B\}$ and $\{B\}\gamma\{C\}$ hold.

A more sophisticated Hoare rule deals with the construct "*while—do.*" If β is a program we already have, then the program "*while A do β*" consists of repeatedly executing the program β as long as the condition A holds, and it terminates only when A is no longer true. The cooking instruction "stir until the sauce is thick" is of this form. It is (roughly) equivalent to, "*while* the sauce is not thick, *do* stir." Thus if β is the program "stir once," and A is "the sauce is not thick," then the instruction has the form "*while A do β.*" In general, "*while A do β*" means, "check if A is true and if it is, then do β once. Repeat until A is no longer true." Of course, if the sauce never gets thick, then you never stop stirring!

The Hoare rule (slightly simplified) for such a case is: If α is "*while A do β*" and $\{B\}\beta\{B\}$ holds, then derive $\{B\}\alpha\{B \wedge \neg A\}$. In other words, provided that β preserves the truth of B and if B holds when α begins, then B will still hold when α ends, and moreover, A will be false.

Suppose B is the formula "the baby needs changing," then provided that B is left invariant by one stirring, and provided that the baby needed to be changed at the beginning of the stirring, then, by Hoare's rule, at the end of all the stirrings the sauce will be thick (that is, not nonthick), but the baby will (still) need changing.

To take a somewhat more interesting example, consider the program α_g for computing the greatest common divisor (*gcd*) of two positive integers. It is given by

$$(x:=u);(y:=v);(while\ (x \neq y)\ do\ (if\ x < y\ then\ y:=y-x\ else\ x:=x-y))$$

The program sets x, y to u, v, respectively, and then repeatedly subtracts the smaller of x, y from the larger until the two numbers become equal. If u, v are positive integers, then this program terminates with $x = gcd(u,v)$, the greatest common divisor of u, v.[10] The reason is that after the initial $(x:=u);(y:=v)$ clearly $gcd(x,y) = gcd(u,v)$. Now both the instructions $x:= x-y$ and $y:= y-x$ leave the *gcd* of x,y unchanged. Thus if B is $gcd(x,y) = gcd(u,v)$, and β is ($if\ x < y\ then\ y:=y-x\ else\ x:= x-y$), then $\{B\}\beta\{B\}$ holds. Thus if the program α_g terminates, then by Hoare's rule for "*while,*" $x \neq y$ will be false, i.e. $x = y$ will hold, and moreover B will hold. Since $gcd(x,x) = x$, we will now have $gcd(u,v) = gcd(x,y) = gcd(x,x) = x$.

There is a feature of Hoare's logic which makes it logically incomplete. Suppose that α is $\beta;\gamma$, $\{A\}\alpha\{C\}$ holds, and we want to derive this fact from properties of β and γ. Then to use Hoare's rule, we need to find a B such that $\{A\}\beta\{B\}$ and $\{B\}\gamma\{C\}$ are both true. It turns out that, although such a B must always exist, it may not be expressible in first-order logic, even though both A and C are first-order formulae. That is to say, there may be no first-order description of the state of affairs that prevails when β has ended and γ has yet to begin.

Dynamic Logic

Pratt's solution to the inexpressibility problem is to extend the language of first-order logic by allowing program modalities $[\alpha]$. $[\alpha]B$ means that the situation *now* is such that if we do α, then B will hold if and when α terminates. Thus $\{A\}\alpha\{B\}$ holds if and only if A implies $[\alpha]B$. Also, to prove $\{A\}\beta;\gamma\{C\}$, the formula $[\gamma]C$ will work as the intermediate B whose absence was the problem for Hoare's rules described above. The argument for this last claim goes as follows.

First, suppose that $\{A\}\beta;\gamma\{C\}$ is true. Suppose also that A is true in some state s and we do β to reach a new state t. Clearly, if we *now* did γ, C would hold. So t satisfies $[\gamma]C$. But s was an arbitrary state satisfying A. Hence, $\{A\}\beta\{[\gamma]C\}$ holds. Second, $\{[\gamma]C\}\gamma\{C\}$ holds by the very meaning of $[\gamma]C$. For, if t satisfies $[\gamma]C$, then we know that if we did do γ we would reach a state in which we would have C. Hence if we do γ, we will evidently have C. Thus, if we take B to be $[\gamma]C$, then both $\{A\}\beta\{B\}$ and $\{B\}\gamma\{C\}$ hold. Since both $\{A\}\beta\{[\gamma]C\}$ and $\{[\gamma]C\}\gamma\{C\}$ hold, we can indeed derive $\{A\}\beta;\gamma\{C\}$.

Although first-order dynamic logic is highly undecidable, its propositional version, propositional dynamic logic (PDL) can be effectively axiomatized using the Segerberg axioms, a fact shown independently by Gabbay and by me. Dynamic logic also allows us to express dispositions. For example, an object is *fragile* if when thrown, it will break. So we can express $Fragile(x)$ by $[thrown]\ Broken(x)$. As Thorne McCarty has pointed out,[11] dynamic logic is appropriate for formalizing notions of permission and obligation, since the *permissible* and the *obligatory* characterize actions rather than propositions. Thus dynamic logic may well have a domain of applications even larger than foreseen.

An extension of dynamic logic is game logic, which can be used to show that many-person interactions can have certain desirable properties, for example, that there exists a fair algorithm for sharing something among n people.[12]

Suppose that n thieves have stolen a cake and, following the dictum of "honor among thieves," want to divide it fairly among themselves. One algorithm for this scenario goes as follows: thief number one cuts out a piece which she claims is her fair share. Then the other thieves look at it in turn, and any thief who thinks it is too big may reduce it. After all the thieves have looked at it, if no one has reduced it, then thief number one takes the piece. If it has been reduced, then the last one who did so takes the piece. In either case, we now have $n-1$ thieves to provide for, and we can repeat the algorithm.

Using game logic, one can show that this algorithm is fair in the sense that every thief has a strategy whereby she can get $1/n$ of the cake regardless of what the other thieves do. The strategy is: when asked to pick, pick exactly $1/n$. If asked to look at a piece that someone else has picked, then let it pass if it is at most $1/n$. If it is more than $1/n$, reduce it to $1/n$.

This case serves as an example of a program involving many different agents or computers, unlike the program α_g, which involves only one. Such multiagent programs or procedures occur constantly in social life, from traffic regulations to rules governing getting a building permit; and the study of their correctness and efficiency is therefore of the utmost importance.

Temporal Logic

Temporal logic, an alternative to dynamic logic followed by Pnueli and others, abandons modularity (or compositionality), the principle (implicit in Hoare's rules) that we should derive the properties of a program from those of its subparts. For instance, the Hoare rule for ";" derived the properties of $\beta;\gamma$ from the properties of β and γ. Temporal logic, by contrast, reasons about one program at a time, focusing on the passage of time as a program runs. Thus in temporal logic, we use operators such as "the property A will hold sometime in the future" or "A will hold until B does." The structure of time may be assumed to be linear or branching. The latter case arises if the course of the program is not determined but depends on random events like coin tosses or on external influence.[13]

II

Specification and Implementation

Clearly every program does *something* and therefore every program is correct if we are willing to accept whatever it does. Generally, however, the program was written for some purpose, and so we have some prior idea of what we want it to do. If this idea can be made precise, then it is called the *specification* of the program. A program is correct only relative to a specification, that is, it is correct if what it does is what the specification demands that it do. Our little α_1 of part I was correct with respect to the specification *make y equal to 2 times z* and incorrect with respect to the specification *make y equal to 4 times z*.

Compilers and Their Correctness

Computers come with their own mother tongue, what is usually called *machine language*. The commands in machine language tend to be rather primitive, like "store the contents of register x in register y," or "increment register y by 1." Programmers, however, rarely write their programs in machine language. Rather, they tend to write in what is called a high-level language. Such a language may contain complex commands like "sort the given list of numbers in increasing numerical order," or "change all occurrences of 'Dreben' to 'Burt' in the given document." Since the programmer writes his programs in one language and the machine understands another, some kind of translation mechanism is needed, and this mechanism—which is itself a program—is called the *compiler* for the particular high-level language. The compiler takes a high-level program α produced by the programmer and translates it into a machine language program $\beta = C(\alpha)$.

Whenever a high-level program α runs on a computer, it is first compiled. This process converts α into the machine language program $C(\alpha)$, the results of whose execution are then interpreted as outputs of α. There is an assumption that the operation of the compiled program *mimics* the mathematical properties of the source program α. We shall come back to this important assumption.

A high-level programming language L has a "denotational semantics" corresponding to the usual model-theoretic semantics for a formalized language; at the denotational level, α refers to an abstract mathematical object, perhaps a function. The machine language, by contrast, has an "operational semantics," which is essentially a description of what happens inside the computer when a compiled program is run.

Thus programs can be seen in two ways. There are also two ways in which we can see natural language. One way is to see it in terms of some meaning theory. The other is to see natural language purely (or at least in large part) behaviorally. There is thus a potential analogy between two dichotomies: (1) the denotational semantics of a high-level programming language versus the operational semantics of the machine language and (2) a meaning theory for a natural language versus the actual linguistic *and* nonlinguistic behavior of the members of the community of users of this language. In *Figure* 1 below, *DS* stands for denotational semantics, *OS* for operational semantics, *MT* for a meaning theory for a natural language, and *Beh* for linguistic and nonlinguistic behavior. The left side of the diagram is the computer science side, the right side is the natural language side.

$$DS \leftrightarrow MT$$
$$| \qquad |$$
$$OS \leftrightarrow Beh$$

Figure 1

In what follows, we will, as promised, try to use this analogy to sharpen some issues involving meaning, translation, and rule-following.

What does it now mean to say that a compiled program is correct with respect to some given specification? Clearly, if the compiler C is badly written, then, even if the program α is correct, the compiled program $C(\alpha)$ might not be. So we must ask that for a compiler to be correct it should transform correct high-level programs into correct machine language programs. This becomes a requirement we will impose before accepting the compiler. But to enforce this requirement, we need a precise criterion of what it amounts to for a compiled program to be correct.

We note now that the compiler is generally written by a person who will not know the specification which the programmer will have in mind in a particular case. A similar situation arises when someone writes a translation manual from English to German. To get to the station, I must formulate the right question in English—say, "Where is the station?" The translation manual yields a corresponding question in German, for example, "Wo ist der Bahnhof, bitte?" If we use the question that we got from the manual, there will, hopefully, then be some linguistic response, which, when converted from German back to English, will provide me with the directions to the station. I assume that the German speaker is knowledgeable and willing to help me get to the station. The process succeeds if I *do* get to the station. I know whether the German question, "Wo ist der Bahnhof, bitte?" is the correct question to ask for my purposes, *not by itself*, but only by the success of *the entire procedure*. That procedure is, formulating the question in English, translation to German, answer in German, translation back to English, following the translated answer with the hope of getting to the station.

Now the writer of the translation manual has no idea whether I will want to get to the station or to the bathroom or will need a beer. Rather, the translation manual must anticipate all possibilities and convert an arbitrary English question into one in German which "asks the same thing."

We know from Quine[14] that characterizing generally this notion of "asks the same thing" is problematic. But the compiler context allows us to be more specific about the difficulties. Suppose for simplicity that the program α implements some function f correctly, that is, given an input n, α produces an output $f(n)$. The compiled version of α is $C(\alpha)$. What does it mean to say that $C(\alpha)$ is correct, that is, that it also "computes" f?

What we need in order to use $C(\alpha)$ is a coding m of numbers into the kind of objects that machine language can manipulate. The number n will then be coded as the object $m(n)$. We ask that the compiled program work in such a way that, if its output on $m(n)$ is x, x should equal $m(f(n))$. That is, we should have

$$m(f(n)) = C(\alpha)(m(n)) \tag{1a}$$

or equivalently,

$$f(n) = m^{-1}[C(\alpha)(m(n))] \tag{1b}$$

We can compute f by coding the input, compiling the program α, applying the compiled program $C(\alpha)$ to $m(n)$ and then applying m^{-1}, the inverse or the decoding operation of m, to the output of $C(\alpha)$.

A correctness proof for a compiler C consists of showing that for each program α, its compiled version $C(\alpha)$, *together with* the coding operation m, produces a mathematical object which is the denotational-semantic "meaning" of α. In other words, conditions (1a) and (1b) hold.

Let us illustrate this apparently complex picture by means of an example.

Consider the (simplified) Pascal program $\alpha = (x:=2;y:=3;z:=x\times y)$, which means: make $x=2$, make $y=3$, and make $z=x\times y$. Suppose we represent the number n by the string a^n in the computer, where a^n stands for the symbol a repeated n times. Then $m(2) = aa$ and $m(3) = aaa$. Thus we will want the compiled version $\theta = C(\alpha)$ of the program α to store, first the string "aa" in the location marked x, then the string "aaa" in the location marked y, and finally the string "$aaaaaa$" in the location marked z. Thus we can think of both α and $C(\alpha)$ as performing the multiplication of 2 by 3.

But note that the operational semantics of $C(\alpha)$ does not actually fix the denotational semantics of α. For example, under our code the number 0 is represented by the empty string. But we might have preferred that the nonempty string a represent the number 0, and that a^{n+1} represents the number n. Our new coding m' has the property that $m'(0) = a$, $m'(1) = aa$ and $m'(2) = aaa$. So "aa" represents the number 1, "aaa" represents 2, and "$aaaaaa$" represents 5. The very same machine language program θ which produced "$aaaaaa$" from "aa" and "aaa" will now be seen as computing not 2×3, but $g(1,2)$ ($= 5$) where g is the function $g(m,n)=(m+1)\times(n+1)-1$. As for $g(2,3)$, it is not 6, but 11. Thus there is no unique answer to the question, "Which mathematical function is θ computing?" Rather it depends on the compiler C, the coding m, and the high-level program α, and cannot be recovered from θ alone. We *know* what the machine language program is *doing*, we just are not sure how to interpret its behavior.

Here we have a precise computer science analog to Quine's famed indeterminacy thesis. As Quine imagined it, an anthropologist landing on a remote island where a hitherto unknown language is spoken has a problem getting from the observed utterances of the natives to a translation manual for their language. This problem of "radical translation," of trying to learn the native language by *observation alone*, is exactly like the problem of determining the denotational semantics of a program α by watching the running of the compiled program $C(\alpha)$. We can figure out the denotational semantics of the original α only if α can be recovered, and this is possible only if the compiler C is known. But the anthropologist has no way of knowing the linguistic analog of the coding C. As Quine argues, when a native has responded to the appearance of a rabbit by saying "gavagai," we do not know whether he has referred to a rabbit, to a rabbit part, or perhaps to a rabbit seen while in the company of an anthropologist! We have a precise analogy here to the computer example for again we know *what* the natives are doing, we just don't know *how* to interpret it.

Moreover, a child born into such a community is also in the position of the anthropologist. This child has no data except his or her observation of what people do. The child too, then, initially takes in language at the observational level. To "understand" what other people are saying requires obtaining the denotational semantics of various procedures and going on no more data than the anthropologist practicing radical translation.

But what if we could actually look into the heads of people? Could we not then see what compiler is being used and recover both α and the intended meaning of whatever is being said? The answer to that is, No: such a procedure would still leave us at a syntactic level, albeit in a more detailed way. Moving to the computer part of the analogy, even if we were given the formal expressions for the original α, the program text for the compiler C, and the formula for the coding m, in our role as radical translators we still would not know *what* mathematical objects the program referred to. For instance, there is nothing in the structure of the original α to indicate whether the function denoted by $\times$ is multiplication or some other function. In fact, if α_1 is the program $(x:=2);(y:= x \times z)$, there is nothing in the notation even to indicate that the program is to read from the left to right rather than the other way round. It is our practice that we do read programs from left to right, but nothing in the notation itself forces us to do so, and nothing can.

This argument connects Quine's indeterminacy of translation thesis to a later argument offered by Kripke as an interpretation of Wittgenstein. In *Wittgenstein on Rules and Private Language*, Kripke presents arguments that seem to show that, even if there is a function *plus*, there is no way that we can unambiguously show that, when we use the symbol +, we are talking about the addition function and not some other function, for example *quus*, where $quus(x,y) = x+y$ if x and y are less than some very large number—for the sake of argument, 750—and $quus(x,y)$ = 5 otherwise. No matter how much I say about my understanding of the word "plus," it is always possible to find some other function *quus* that is not addition and fits all that I or indeed anybody else has said about *plus*. Of course, the function *quus* would need to be fitted to all that has been said about *plus* so far, so that the limit of 750 above might need to change, but there always *is* such a function. Parallel to this puzzle is this fact about denotational semantics: no matter how much we know about the operational semantics of a program, the ambiguity in the denotational semantics of the original high level program will remain.[15]

Should we allow ourselves to be moved to philosophical skepticism about meaning as a result of these sorts of arguments? Quine advocates only skepticism about observation-transcendent notions of meaning or propositions. Kripke, on behalf of Wittgenstein, suggests that the plus-quus puzzle leaves us without any notion of a *fact* of meaning for an individual speaker. He claims that Wittgenstein's answer is to bring in the behavior of a wider linguistic community to settle questions of meaning. But matters will not stand on any more solid a basis by appealing to community usage. For that too is only "correct" relative to an antecedent purpose or specification of what correctness consists in.

Am I suggesting that human mental life in general and language in particular is nothing but computation and behavior? Not exactly; I am only drawing a parallel. The most influential recent argument that the human mind is not a computer has been advanced by Searle. Searle wishes to make an ambitious point: that a computer (and even a robot) cannot know, say, Chinese. I shall leave aside the merits of Searle's stronger claim to argue instead that we should grant him a weaker point. And that is that, *given certain restrictions, neither* Searle *nor* a computer in his specific position can be said to know Chinese. In his thought experiment, Searle imagines himself locked in a room having been given some instructions (in English) for correlating certain questions posed in Chinese with certain other expressions (stories) in Chinese so as to produce certain other expressions (the answers) in Chinese. If the rules are sufficiently good, then presumably Searle's written answers, conveyed out of the room, will be indistinguishable from those given by a Chinese speaker based on the latter's actual understanding of the stories. But Searle says that these rules do not suffice to allow him to say that he *knows* Chinese. And he argues that, since a computer that has been programmed to follow these rules knows no more than he does, then it too cannot be said to know Chinese.

What we have here is in fact an example of a compiler. A question asked in Chinese notation is compiled into a question asked in English, and the answer in English is decompiled into an answer in Chinese notation. English plays here the role of machine language and Chinese of the high-level language. And Searle is quite right that a person who can carry out this process need not know the "semantics" of Chinese.

As we have seen, however, there is a strong sense of the word "semantics" in which even a Chinese speaker cannot know the semantics of Chinese. She was born into a Chinese community and only has the same sort of data at her disposal that a radical translator would have. We might think, with Chomsky, that perhaps the semantics might be hardwired in her brain and need not be learned. But since humans are capable of learning very many languages with different semantics, the "hardwiring," if it exists, cannot settle all uncertainties about which semantics is intended by certain utterances and certain behavior.

Is there then a sense in which a Chinese person *does* know Chinese but in which Searle, in his example, does not? A crucial difference is that the Chinese speaking person can also correlate her behavior to the real world. If she wants five potatoes, she can go to a grocer, ask her question in Chinese, and see to it that what she gets is five potatoes and not five tomatoes. But note that, at least in English, Searle's procedure cannot distinguish between potatoes and tomatoes.

To explain, suppose we have a procedure P for answering questions posed in English, correlated to situations described in English and yielding answers in English. And suppose that this procedure works properly. Now replace English by *Penglish*, in which the word "potato" means tomato and the word "tomato" means potato. The procedure P will also work perfectly for Penglish.

Consider the story, "Jane has no potatoes. John gives her five potatoes. Then he asks her to return three of the potatoes to him." And the question, "How many potatoes does Jane now have?" The answer is "two potatoes," which is clearly correct in English. But it is also correct in Penglish. In Penglish the story, the question, and the answer refer to tomatoes, using the Penglish word "potatoes," and the answer given by the procedure is still correct.

Knowing English implies knowing what potatoes are and that they are different from tomatoes. But someone who can answer questions like the above need not know the difference between English and Penglish and hence cannot necessarily be said to know English. Since a computer that has been programmed to follow the procedure also does not know the difference between a potato and a tomato, or between English and Penglish, we can say that it too does not know English. So Searle is quite right that merely knowing the rules for playing the question-answer game does not imply a knowledge of Chinese.

If Searle is able to memorize his rules so that he can use them in real life with facility, however, and, moreover, if he is able to ask in Chinese for potatoes and then not accept tomatoes, it would be hard to say just what it is that the average Chinese person knows (in such contexts) that Searle does not. A robot that knew how to answer questions and was also able to operate with the language in the real world would be in the same position as this (more retentive) Searle. If we still wanted to say that the robot did not know Chinese, it would have to be on some other basis than Searle's Chinese room puzzle.

Returning to the program context, suppose we are given a compiler and a high-level language together with a denotational semantics for the high-level language. Suppose now that there is a property P that high-level language programs may have or fail to have. Then we could say—with some abuse of language—that $C(\alpha)$ has property P if and only if α has property P. But if some machine language program θ is *not* of the form $C(\alpha)$ for some α, then—under that particular compiler—it would not have a mathematical meaning, though it would still do *something*, that is, still have operational semantics.[16] But we could not say either that it had or that it lacked the property P. Returning to the linguistic context, I offer the following parallel: there need not be a determinate answer to the question whether the word "slab" in the language of Wittgenstein's builders in §2 of the *Philosophical Investigations* is a noun or a single word sentence. To answer such a question requires a great deal more information about the builders than a mere description of what they do with the word.

In the linguistic context, what we are given is the linguistic behavior of individuals in a community, supplemented by nonlinguistic behavior. As we noted, the latter is missing in Searle's Chinese room, which is significant. We want to develop a meaning theory, that is, a high-level language L with a denotational semantics that will "compile" into actual utterances. Communication between two members of a community, something that takes place at the lower level, could be thought of as conveying these high-level meanings. But developing such a high-level language and its semantics may not always be possible. In addition, it will almost certainly not be unique. Thus, assigning a meaning theory to the behavior of a linguistic community will be problematic, as will be the question (the radical translation question) of correlating the (supposed) meanings associated with the linguistic behavior of one community with the meanings associated with the behavior of another. Indeed—as Quine has argued—we even have to give up the picture of a conversation between two members of the same community as conveying meanings, for the meanings of the speaker cannot really be conveyed to the listener.[17] Perhaps there is some way out of this "meaning solipsism," but finding such a way requires a deeper analysis.

Linguistic utterance is a social phenomenon that facilitates living in a community. It is undeniable that utterances *can* at times be interpreted in terms of a meaning theory—and such an interpretation, when it exists, yields significant benefits in terms of organizing our grasp of the workings of the language. (For example, first-order model theory, though not the only possible interpretation of first-order logic, makes it easier for us to understand the purely proof theoretic properties of first-order logic.) But such an interpretation may not always be available or be unique or be uniform over the different suburbs of the linguistic metropolis. The point of this observation is to suggest a shift in the way both computer scientists and philosophers should think about semantics.

NOTES

I thank Samir Chopra, Arthur Collins, Juliet Floyd, Konstantinos Georgatos, and Larry Moss for comments on previous versions of this paper. Research supported by a grant from the CUNY-FRAP program.

1. The philosophical thesis that every effectively computable function is recursive.

2. See W. V. Quine, *Word and Object* (Cambridge, Mass.: MIT Press, 1960), ch. 2.

3. See John Searle, "Minds, Brains and Programs," *Behavioral and Brain Sciences* 3 (1980): 417–457.

4. See Saul Kripke, *Wittgenstein on Rules and Private Language* (Cambridge, Mass.: Harvard University Press, 1982).

5. "Behaviorism and Belief," *Annals of Pure and Applied Logic* 96 (1999) 75–88.

6. "Vagueness and Utility: The Semantics of Common Nouns," *Linguistics and Philosophy* 17 (1994): 521–535.

7. In *Philosophical Investigations*, 3d ed., ed. G. E. M. Anscombe and R. Rhees, trans. G. E. M. Anscombe (Oxford: Basil Blackwell and Mott, 1958).

8. Edsger Dijkstra, *A Discipline of Programming* (New York: Prentice Hall, 1976), p. 20.

9. Some early references are: R. W. Floyd, "Assigning Meanings to Programs," *Proc. AMS Symp. on Applied Mathematics* 19, Amer. Math. Soc. (1967) 19–31; C. A. R. Hoare, "An Axiomatic Basis for Computer Programming," *Comm. Assoc. Comp. Mach.* 12 (1967) 516–580; V. R. Pratt, "Semantical Considerations on Floyd-Hoare Logic," *Proc. 17th Annual IEEE Symp. on Found. Comp. Sci.* (1976): 109–121; Dexter Kozen and Rohit Parikh, "An Elementary Completeness Proof for PDL," *Theoretical Computer Science* 14 (1981): 113–118; Amir Pnueli, "The Temporal Logic of Programs," *Proceedings of the 18th Annual IEEE Symposium on the Foundations of Computer Science* (1977): 46–57. My article on computation in the supplement to the MacMillan *Encyclopedia of Philosophy* (1996), pp. 86–87, contains a brief introduction to this area. More detailed surveys are given by Dexter Kozen and Jerzy Tiuryn, "Logics of Programs," in *Handbook of Theoretical Computer Science*, vol. B, ed. Jan van Leeuwen (Cambridge: Mass.: MIT Press/Elsevier, 1990), pp. 789–840, and Allan Emerson, "Temporal and Modal Logic," in *Handbook of Theoretical Computer Science*, vol. B, ed. Jan van Leeuwen (Cambridge, Mass.: MIT Press/Elsevier, 1990) pp. 995–1072.

10. For instance, if u, v are 10 and 8, respectively, then initially, x is set to 10 and y to 8. Subtracting y from x yields $x = 2$. Now x is repeatedly subtracted from y until both become 2. Thus the *gcd* of 10 and 8 is 2.

11. L. Thorne McCarty, "Permissions and Obligations," in *Proceedings of the Eighth International Joint Conference on Artificial Intelligence*, ed. Alan Bundy (Los Altos: William Kaufmann, 1983), pp. 287–294.

12. Rohit Parikh, "The Logic of Games," *Annals of Discrete Mathematics* 24 (1985): 111–140.

13. Jorge Luis Borges gives a nice example of branching time in "The Garden of Forking Paths," *Ficciones* (New York: Grove Press, 1962), pp. 89–101.

14. W. V. Quine, "Meaning and Translation," in *The Structure of Language*, ed. J. Fodor and J. Katz (New York: Prentice Hall, 1964), pp. 460–478.

15. Kripke himself suggests a connection with Quine's indeterminacy of translation thesis; see *Wittgenstein on Rules and Private Language*, pp. 14–15.

16. This is perhaps the point of Piero Sraffa's famous gesture to Wittgenstein. The gesture that Sraffa made—brushing his chin with his fingertips—had a meaning, at least to Italians (or at least to Neapolitans), but could not fit into the semantics provided by Wittgenstein in the *Tractatus*. See Ray Monk's *Ludwig Wittgenstein: The Duty of Genius* (New York: Penguin, 1990), pp. 260–261.

17. It is shown in my "Vagueness and Utility: The Semantics of Common Nouns," *Linguistics and Philosophy* 17 (1994): 521–535, and "Vague Predicates and Language Games," *Theoria* [Spain] 11, no. 27 (1996): 97–107, though, that the listener will usually be *helped* by what he hears.

1953
Publication of Wittgenstein's
Philosophical Investigations

16

Silences Noises Voices

STANLEY CAVELL

What could I have been thinking, those months ago when I was asked for a title for these remarks, in proposing the words "Silences Noises Voices"? Imagining the occasion on which I would see *The Claim of Reason* appear in French, I surely would have wanted to commemorate the painful elaboration of detail in that text marking the dangerous geography in which human urgency has to find its intelligibility. Moreover, my gratitude for having this occasion of remembering would have magnified my sense of danger, because the presence of my teacher J. L. Austin and of the later Wittgenstein in my text extends their desire, almost to obsessiveness, to depose philosophy's chronic efforts to neutralize the contexts of human utterance, as if neutralization would make our utterances pure. Extends their efforts, for are not nations, or do they not remain, contexts, and is not the occasion of translation one in which the difference of context is limitlessly at stake?—every passage to communication becoming a barrier to it. A text in translation has the chance of a new life. A speech of gratitude for that chance has only its present moment in which to give thanks for that new life. The odds of doing the moment justice are vanishing.

Considering those title words at this distance, as I set down my thoughts for this occasion, they seem to me to name the perceptual preoccupations of a child in a haunted house. Perhaps I wanted this resonance all along, since it is a fair way of describing a register of Thoreau's experience at Walden, not a fear of his surroundings but a sense of the strangeness and morbidity in the way his fellow townsmen inhabit their town; and also a way of capturing Emerson's experience of what he calls our "chagrin" in response to "every word they [his neighbors] say." Emerson claims indeed that in their fear of their own words they miss the discovery of their existence and hence can be said to haunt the world. (So, at any rate, I claimed for Emerson's words when he dawned on me as a philosopher; it was the year *The Claim of Reason* was published.)

No doubt, I was also recalling specific occurrences of noises in my book, as when it justifies the traditional epistemologist's fastidiousness (however much it seeks to avoid the animus of skepticism) by remarking, "There are not just noises in the air," in which I am commenting on the human being's responsibility for making sense of every particle or corpuscle of his or her experience. And I would have recalled the passage in Wittgenstein's *Philosophical Investigations*[1] in which he dramatizes this moral by inviting the image or memory of a noise we might produce:

> What reason have we for calling "S" the sign for a sensation? For "sensation" is a word of our common language, not of one intelligible to me alone. So the use of this word stands in need of a justification which everybody under-stands.—And it would not help either to say that it need not be a sensation; that when he writes "S," he has *something*—and that is all that can be said. "Has" and "something" also belong to our common language.—So in the end when one is philosophizing one gets to the point where one would like just to emit an inarticulate sound.—But such a sound is an expression only as it occurs in a particular language-game, which should now be described. (§261)

There could hardly be a stronger indication from Wittgenstein of his recognition of the dominance of the signifier. Even the expression of philosophical inarticu-lateness, my reduction to making a noise, is subject to its law.

And I know other noises that would have been on my mind—for example, the noises in the attic that the woman in Cukor's film *Gaslight* refuses to name, which are therefore cause and consequence of her maddening loss of all words and de-sires of her own; and the noises the wife in another of Cukor's films, *Adam's Rib*, hears her husband make in the night, whose interpretation she is willing to name and which leads her to take him to court.

But certainly I would have wanted my title words to evoke the earliest essay of mine in which I describe the experience of encountering Wittgenstein's *Philosophical Investigations* and characterize its all but incessant dialogues as occurring between two voices (at least) which I characterize as the voice of temptation and the voice of correctness and which I take to have two insistent implications: that since both voices are Wittgenstein's, neither is his (exclusively), and that there is a beyond of these voices, a before and an after, occupied in Wittgenstein's prose by parables, paradoxes, fantasies, aphorisms, and so on, which do not and did not strike me as expressing identifiable voices exactly but which I did not know then how to char-acterize further. That essay of mine formed the introduction to my doctoral thesis, large parts of which, sixteen years after it was submitted for my degree, were reconfigured, and much of the remainder of it hammered apart for certain irreplace-able elements, to become about half of what appears as *The Claim of Reason*.

The original introduction was dropped and was to be replaced by an account precisely of that beyond of the voices, the place, as it were, out of which they arise. In the lectures I had begun offering on Wittgenstein at the time I was writing my thesis, I characterized that sense of origin as expressed in a recognition that phi-losophy does not speak first, that it maintains silence, that its essential virtue is not assertiveness (since it has no information of its own to impart) but responsive-ness, awake after all the others have fallen asleep. The *Investigations*, for example, begins with the words of someone else, St. Augustine's description of, in effect, the silence of infancy, wandering among the elders whose powers of expression it is fated, and seeks blindly, to adopt. When a few years ago I got around to pub-

lishing my notes on those lectures,[2] mostly those concerning the beginning moments of the *Investigations*, I accounted for not having included them, as planned,
as a new introduction to *The Claim of Reason* on the ground that the book was
already too long. I might have said it was because I had not yet arrived at an understanding of the other silence (if it is other) at the other pole of the beyond of voice in
the *Investigations*, the silence not out of which philosophy arises but the silence in
which philosophical problems, according to Wittgenstein, end—he calls it peace.

Wittgenstein refers to this end of philosophy as the achievement, or construction, of perspicuous presentation, something that he claims captures the sense
of the form in which he casts his philosophizing. The arrival at perspicuous presentation is applied by Wittgenstein characteristically to the work of mathematical proof; only once does he apply it to the work of the investigations as a whole.
And it is only within the past year or two that I have been able to articulate to
my satisfaction how the concept of perspicuousness applies no more precisely to
Wittgenstein's interpretation of the mathematical than to his use of the aphoris-
tic—which is to say, to the most obviously literary passages of the *Investigations*—
as when its work describes itself as showing the fly the way out of the flybottle, or
speaks of the human body as the best picture of the human soul.

But my inability to relate satisfactorily the silences that surround philosophy
can hardly be what prevented my broaching the subject at the time I was trying
to let go of my *Claim of Reason*. A truer account seems to have awaited the context of my speaking in France. I wonder if I can say briefly how I see this.

The silence in which philosophy begins is the recognition of my lostness to
myself, something Wittgenstein's text figures as the emptiness of my words, my
craving or insistence upon their emptiness, upon wanting them to do what
human words cannot do. I read this disappointment with words as a function
of the human wish to deny responsibility for speech. The silence in which philosophy ends is the acceptance of the human life of words, that I am revealed
and concealed in every word I utter, that when I have found the word I had lost,
that is, displaced from myself, it is up to me to acknowledge my reorientation
(Wittgenstein describes the work of philosophy as having to turn our search
around, as if reality is behind us), that I have said what there is for me to say, that
this ground gained from discontent is all the ground I have, that I am exposed in
my finitude, without justification. ("Justifications come to an end" is a way
Wittgenstein says it.) That the end of philosophy here occurs as a punctuation
within philosophy, that it is dictated neither by the conclusion of a proof nor of a
system, that philosophy is brought so inconsequential a form of peace (to bring
which to philosophy Wittgenstein pronounces with pride) is the hardest news for
Wittgenstein's readers to accept. The news is expressed by his announcing that
philosophy has no place to advance theses.

What is hard in this news is that being at the end of my words strikes me as my
being at the end of my life, exposed to death.

It was just this past summer in Paris that I noted, in response to a request to
describe my interest in *Philosophical Investigations*, that taking as a rough measure the six-hundred ninety-three sections of the first and longest part of the *Investigations*, philosophy there comes to an end six-hundred ninety-three times. I had

noted that fact on other occasions, for various purposes. But this time I found myself going on to say that its endings are so many deaths to so many issues whose fervor has come to nothing, a nothing that Wittgenstein calls the ordinary; it is a field that we have never occupied. If—I went on then—one can say that this is Wittgenstein discovering philosophy as learning how to die, learning my separateness (I do not know if Wittgenstein read Montaigne), then one can say that arriving at the ordinary is its companion teaching of the commonness of our humanity. Putting these thoughts together, it seemed right to say that in ordinary language philosophy the ordinary is the scene of recognition of one's own death. Saying such a thing for the first time seems to be a condition for knowing it.

Why was it, as it seems, necessary for me to leave home in order to say and know that? What presents itself as unsayable at home, as if there what urges silence is not alone the fear of illogicality but of indecorousness? Have I, in finding the immeasurable relief of translation, found another or a truer home?

I learned from the review of *Les Voix de la raison* in *Le Monde* that I am spoken of by some of my American colleagues as a continental philosopher. Part of what I mean by the relief of translation is that in Europe I am taken as an American philosopher. The relief lies not in the correctness of either description but in the fact of their conflict, confirming my conviction of my role as insisting where I can on the split within the philosophical mind. It is something I have known about myself since at least the moment I recognized that Heidegger's characterization of the human task as one of dwelling, finding home, is intimately contradicted in Thoreau's dramatizing of its task as leaving home, the thing Emerson names abandonment, meaning both a yielding and a departure.

In a recent book of mine, *A Pitch of Philosophy*,[3] I characterize this split by claiming that for Wittgenstein—unlike the case of Heidegger and his aftermath, and for that matter unlike the case of John Dewey—there is no standing dispensation of philosophy that philosophy now, or what has replaced philosophy, is to overcome. It is as if Wittgenstein felt that, in the modern academization of philosophy, what in it is illusory will fall of its own weight. The issue for philosophy remains what it was from the beginning, the threat of human thinking to lead itself astray, to exempt itself from the need for human intelligibility, to torment itself with shadows of its language, to deny the world rather than to recognize its strangeness in the world, to deny its hand in its works, its interest in its concepts, to bore itself to distraction.

I suppose my favorite way of epitomizing the splitting of philosophy has been to invoke what I call the two myths of philosophical reading, that is, of the intellectual preparation for writing philosophy. In the one myth, the philosopher proceeds from having read, and knowing, everything; in the other, from having read, and knowing, nothing. Perhaps this duality is prefigured in the division between Plato's writing and Socrates' talking, but it is purely enough illustrated in this century by contrasting Heidegger's work, which assumes the march of the great names in the history of Western philosophy, with that of Wittgenstein, who may get around to mentioning half-a-dozen names, but then only to identify a remark he happens to have come across and which seems to get its philosophical importance solely from the fact that he is thinking about it then. Common to the two myths is an idea that philosophy begins only when there are no further texts to read, when the truth you seek has already been missed, escaped. In the myth of totality, philosophy has still not found itself—until at least it has found you; in the myth of blankness philosophy has lost itself in its first utterance.

Where does this leave us, who know the truth that we have read neither nothing nor everything? Or may we question this? We might consider how it looks to the Emerson of "Self-Reliance" and to the Thoreau of the chapter entitled "Reading" in *Walden*, who apparently judge that we have mostly not begun to read and that there is nothing in print necessary to read.

But I was saying, or asking why, in the dominant philosophical dispensation in the English-speaking world of philosophy, it would be indecorous to speak in unguarded terms, say untheoretical words, of the presence of death in speech. If philosophy must preoccupy itself with questions of what can and cannot be said, it must not shrink from utterances whose saying is merely indecorous.

It will help to articulate this matter if we distinguish the indecorous from the improper. The improper has on both sides of the Atlantic received its share of attention, in questioning and in asserting philosophy's quest for, its authorization by, the pure, say the self-possessed. The indecorous, we might say, speaks rather of the outside of that quest, of the communal requirement for rules, for the avoidance of the unseemly. (The improper risks nonsense, or emptiness, say estrangement; the indecorous courts excess, or outlandishness, say exile.) My writing has from its beginning been subject to both charges. That is, at all events, how I understand the most common charge brought against my writing by philosophers in my neighborhood of philosophy who disapprove of it, namely the charge that it is self-indulgent, some may have said instead self-absorbed. It would only have increased the sense of the indecorousness or impurity of my manner had I suggested a diagnosis of those charges. I have not in any case been moved to do so. But in the confidence that translation, in its overcoming of its impossibilities, brings to the sense of being understood, I register my sense of the philosophical stakes in this double charge.

The perception of impurity, or impropriety, I take as a displacement onto my writing of the sense that the appeal to the ordinariness of words—which is to say, the demonstration of our investment in words—is as such philosophically improper. Since this is a cause of the recurrent dismissals to which both Wittgenstein's late work and most of Austin's are open, I will add nothing here to what I have said elsewhere about this impropriety, nor any more about its bearing on philosophy's chronic flight from the ordinary. The twin perception of indecorousness remains to be located. That is what shows itself, I believe, in the repeated attention in negative reviews of *The Claim of Reason* to its opening sentence, where each time that sentence has been stated to run longer than two-hundred words. Imagine the reviewers in each case taking the trouble to count those words and verify the magnitude of their transgression. Why is so plain a thing the cause of distress? I can think of a number of reasons that I might have wanted to begin my book with a sentence about beginnings that fairly obviously dramatizes a problem about philosophical beginnings, hence about philosophical endings. And I can imagine that that itself is something which may strike a different philosophical sensibility as unnecessary or impertinent or ostentatious. But why as something bordering on the outrageous?

Consider that Wittgenstein's response to the passage from Augustine with which he opens the *Investigations* confesses, with a tentativeness and openness unusual for him, that "it seems to me" that "these words [of Augustine's] give us a picture of the essence of human language. It is this: the individual words in language name objects—sentences are combinations of such names." But that picture is given by the very first of Augustine's three cited sentences: "When they (my elders) named some object, and accordingly moved toward something, I saw this and I grasped that the thing was called by the sound they uttered when they meant to point it out." The last of Augustine's sentences goes on to give a companion picture, one equally under discussion throughout the *Investigations*: "Thus, as I heard words repeatedly used in their proper places in various sentences, I gradually learnt to understand what objects they signified; and after I had trained my mouth to form these signs, I used them to express my own desires." The companion picture I point to—concerning the expression of my own desires—is blurred, or rather ambiguous: it might suggest that to express my own desires is to indicate which objects I desire (which may or may not be the ones my elders desired); or it might suggest that my coming into possession of language means that my every proper utterance bespeaks my desire, as sign or as signal; that my language, like the mind and body from which it originates, or which originate in it, becomes as a whole a field of expression. As Freud says of us, "No mortal can keep a secret. If his lips are silent, he chatters with his fingertips; betrayal oozes out of him at every pore."[4] Emerson voices a comparable revelation by casting us as victims of expression. This avowal of radical subjection of the human to language is placed at odds in the text of the *Investigations* with philosophy's wish to escape what appears to it as the radical arbitrariness of our given language, as if it stands in need of logical repair.

Now I might say that my way of impressing upon myself, perhaps upon my reader, the human subjection to words as well as the human disappointment in words, is to get my writing to recognize, in every word if I can, that it does not know all that it knows. This may seem a terrible confession for a philosopher to make, and it is here that I understand the charge of the indecorous to fit what I do. But what it fits is not so much, I think, my own relatively mild tone of indecorousness as it does my sharp sense of, even my call for, an understanding with the indecorous. I suppose there can be no philosophical understanding in this field without philosophy's acknowledging the existence of psychoanalysis, not as posing something like a problem for the philosophy of science, but as an intellectual competitor in the placement of reason. In philosophy, I have to recognize the arrogance with which I arrogate the right to speak universally, for all other possessors of language; in psychoanalysis, I have to recognize the disgrace that I do not so much as speak for myself.

I conclude, accordingly, with a pair of passages, the first from a psychoanalyst, Lacan, the second from Wittgenstein's *Philosophical Investigations*.

In "The Freudian Thing"[5] from 1955—it was the year Austin came to Harvard to give as the William James Lectures *How to Do Things with Words*, along with two graduate and faculty seminars, the result of which was that I put aside plans for a Ph.D. thesis that I did not believe in, and other plans to leave the field of philosophy—Lacan devotes a section to a disquisition on the subject of speech that he attributes (the disquisition) to a speaking desk. I draw from the example at least the following moral: Even psychoanalysts (most egregiously perhaps the ego-psychologists among them) do not know what it means that certain things speak, that there are subjects; their treatment (and theory) of what is said to them fantasizes a source of speech that has about the consistency of a piece of furniture. Wittgenstein begins a section toward the middle of the *Investigations*, §361, with the fantasied claim: "The chair is thinking to itself," followed by indications of a long silence, and then the outburst, "WHERE? In one of its parts? Or outside its body? Or not anywhere at all? But then what is the difference between this chair's saying something to itself and another one's doing so, next to it?—But then how is it with man: where does he say things to himself? How does it come about that this question seems senseless . . . ?" I draw a companion moral: in our desperation for closure or order or sublimity in our concepts—in our disappointment with our criteria for their application—we ask criteria to do something or to go somewhere that they are not fit to do or to go, and so we repudiate, as it were, their intelligence. We can arrive at a philosophical position from which it seems that to ground the application of the concept of another's thinking to herself you have to be able to locate the place of that thinking. Then imagine applying the concept to a chair and you may transform disguised nonsense into patent nonsense.

There is evidently more than one form of human self-defeat, or temptation to emptiness in our aspirations, or distortions or neglect of our experience of things. Until it is shown that there is some general form that all human folly takes, it is not safe for us to do without any of the fields that have some perspective upon it.

In the course of writing these remarks, I asked myself why I had come to thoughts of the tragic character of human experience, of philosophy's requirement, hence I suppose that of any serious writing, to incorporate death (you might, more decorously, say finitude) into its reflections. I seem to have answered on this occasion, stirring memories that span the decades in which I have been writing publicly, that the appearance of *The Claim of Reason* as *Les voix de la raison* is a sign of life for my work so sharp as to perplex me with joy.

Postscript, December 2, 1997

The idea of submitting the preceding text in a volume marking the scholarly and pedagogical achievements to date of Burton Dreben occurred to me some time after it was composed for what is on the face of it a foreign occasion—not however before I knew of the plans for this volume. If I say that the idea of its appropriateness occurred to me without a concept, I mean to suggest that, as Kant implies (to my mind) about analogous judgments of aesthetic pleasure, reasons are bound to be drawn in, as it were to fill in the ground of concepts, after the fact of judgment. In the present case, the plain fact that my text presents a thought new to me about Wittgenstein's *Philosophical Investigations*—a work of undying interest for both Dreben and myself—is less important than the fact that the thought (about how philosophizing comes repeatedly to an end, or rather comes to an end repeatedly) is apt to seem to some readers outlandish (at least initially) and to others obvious (once it is articulated), no more nor less than the text asks to bear. This marks the importance as one, so I might put it, of challenging the obvious, a matter that goes back to conversations from the period in which Burt and I were graduate students.

I do not quite say graduate students together, since he was, though somewhat younger than I, a good two years ahead in graduate studies, and since he had, what is more, been an undergraduate at Harvard, he seemed to me virtually from a different generation. He was the first instance I recognized as satisfying a concept I acquired my entering year at Harvard, that of the famous graduate student. His fame rested—already—on the combination of an achievement of a result in logic together with a reputation for remarkable skills and standards of textual interpretation (including but not confined to texts in the history of analytic philosophy). Because, in addition, of his generosity as a teacher—he would, for example, hold concentrated logic scrimmages for those preparing for the annual death-defying twelve-hour games of the old Ph.D. written preliminary examinations—it was to him that I would sometimes submit the more questionable of my exercises in coming to terms with the dispensation of philosophy so formidably represented at Harvard. I remember particularly the long paper I had prepared for J. L. Austin on the occasion of his residence at Harvard for the spring semester of 1955 to offer the William James Lectures. The paper was entitled "The Theatricality of Everyday Life," itself indicating that, while full of Austin-inspired examples, it was not your ordinary analytic fare. Burt's timely response, after making it clear that he understood what I was after (accomplished, however else, by drawing the moral of certain of my purplish passages), was to say something like: "You're right to hold out for these effects of understanding. But there will be consequences. Not everyone is going to see that there is rigor here; it is not of an accustomed kind." The setting of those words, or ones close to them, I recall, was a walk through Harvard Yard, which has not changed much in the more than forty years since they were uttered. Neither has my gratitude for them.

I never assumed that later such occasions would uniformly prove to be so encouraging; Burt could also be harsh.

NOTES

A version of the present text was delivered in Paris in October 1996 on the occasion of the publication of the French translation of *The Claim of Reason* (Oxford: Oxford University Press, 1979), *Les voix de la raison*.

1. Ludwig Wittgenstein, *Philosophical Investigations*, 3d ed., ed. G. E. M. Anscombe and R. Rhees, trans. G. E. M. Anscombe (Oxford: Basil Blackwell and Mott, 1958; 1st edition 1953).
2. "Notes and Afterthoughts on the Opening of Wittgenstein's *Investigations*," in Cavell, *Philosophical Passages: Wittgenstein, Emerson, Austin* (Cambridge, Mass.: Blackwell, 1995), pp. 125–186.
3. *A Pitch of Philosophy* (Cambridge, Mass.: Harvard University Press, 1995).
4. "Fragment of an Analysis of a Case of Hysteria," in *The Standard Edition of the Complete Psychological Works of Sigmund Freud*, ed. and trans. James Strachey et al. (London: Hogarth Press, 1957–1966), vol. 7, pp. 77–78.
5. "The Freudian Thing," in *Écrits: A Selection*, trans. Alan Sheridan (New York: Norton, 1955).

1961
Abraham Robinson's lecture
on infinitesimals at the
Silver Anniversary Meeting of
the Association for Symbolic Logic

17

Long Decimals

W. D. HART

In the Fall semester of 1965, Burt Dreben taught a graduate seminar on Rudolf Carnap's book *The Logical Syntax of Language*.[1] Dreben used Carnap's book in part as a textbook from which to teach Gödel's proof of the incompleteness of number theory. It was somewhat as if one used Wittgenstein's *Tractatus* as a textbook for teaching truth-function theory; the truth tables are in there all right, but it is not so easy to winkle them out. The following Spring, Dreben inaugurated Philosophy 144, Gödel for all comers, in which he used Gödel's original 1931 paper (in an English translation) as his text.[2] That was not quite as extreme as teaching basic physics from Newton's *Principia*, but Dreben certainly stretched his classes. Many people who teach technical material like to present the cleanest, simplest versions possible. But Dreben is interested in history as well as mathematics; what impact did the result have when it was discovered? He wants to see the original presentation and its immediate descendants, warts and all, to understand how they were received, especially among philosophers.

Civilized people celebrate their differences. It is not as if we have to choose between the two approaches to exposition, the clean and the warty; each has its virtues. Consider, for example, infinitesimals. To calculate the slope or derivative of $y=x^2$ thus

$$\frac{dy}{dx} = \frac{(x+dx)^2 - x^2}{(x+dx)-x} \tag{1}$$

$$= \frac{x^2 + 2xdx + (dx)^2 - x^2}{dx}$$

$$= 2x + dx$$

$$= 2x$$

it would suffice to have an infinitesimal dx, a quantity so small that $2x+dx = 2x$, but nonetheless not zero, so that division by it is possible. (This is not to say that Newton or Leibniz did so calculate. That is a warty question.) Here a critic could well object that if $2x+dx = 2x$, then $dx=0$, so there are no such infinitesimals. (This is not to say that Berkeley did so object in *The Analyst*. That is another warty question.) In the nineteenth century, ε-δ methods supplanted infinitesimals. Then in the 1960s Abraham Robinson discovered non-standard analysis;[3] infinitesimals were, it seems, vindicated after all. Or were they?

Infinitesimals whet philosophical appetites, but in the thirty-odd years since Robinson vindicated infinitesimals, there has been precious little renewed philosophical attention paid to them. Why? The standard mathematical path to Robinson's infinitesimals is not easy for most philosophers, which may be one reason why so few make the trip. Let us review the high points along the way.

As always, ω is the set of natural numbers. A *filter* on ω is a collection F of subsets of ω such that $\omega \in F$, $A \cap B \in F$ whenever $A \in F$ and $B \in F$, and $B \in F$ whenever $A \subseteq B \subseteq \omega$ and $A \in F$. A filter is *proper* just in case it does not contain the empty set. A filter F' *properly extends* a filter F just in case F is a proper subset of F'. An *ultrafilter* is a proper filter that is maximal, that is, no proper filter properly extends it. Using the axiom of choice, it can be shown that every proper filter is included in an ultrafilter. The *cofinite* subsets of ω are those subsets whose complements in ω are finite. They form a filter, and, since the complement of the empty set in ω is ω, and so is not finite, these cofinite subsets form a proper filter. So there is an ultrafilter, which from now on we call F, including the cofinite subsets of ω.

Let M be a structure (in the model theoretic sense) for analysis and let $\mathcal{L}$ be a first-order language of the appropriate type for M. The domain D of M is the set of ordinary (standard) real numbers. The distinguished elements, subsets, and functions of the model are all those of the domain of M. $\mathcal{L}$ is the first-order language whose constants, predicates, and function signs are those needed to put the distinguished elements, subsets, and functions of M into words. We will be a bit more careful about M and $\mathcal{L}$ later on, but for now we can leave them comfortably hazy.

For functions f and g from ω to D, define

$$f \sim g$$

by

$$\{n \mid f(n)=g(n)\} \in F \tag{2}$$

The relation $\sim$ is an equivalence relation. Let $[f]$ be the equivalence class of f under $\sim$, and let D^* be the set of all these equivalence classes. We are going to describe a structure M^* of the same model theoretic type as M, but with domain D^*. This description will go a bit more briskly if we use Church's λ notation for functions. For example, (λx)(the father of x) is the fatherhood function, whose value at any person x is x's father, and $(\lambda n)(5)$ is the constant function whose value at any natural number n is 5. For any distinguished element c of M, let c^* be $[(\lambda n)(c)]$. For any distinguished function g of M, let

$$g^*([f_1], \ldots, [f_n]) = [(\lambda k)\,(g(f_1(k), \ldots, f_n(k)))] \tag{3}$$

For any distinguished relation R of M, let

$$R^*([f_1], \ldots, [f_n]) \text{ iff } \{k \mid R(f_1(k), \ldots, f_n(k))\} \in F \tag{4}$$

It can be shown that g^* and R^* are well-defined.

Note two special cases of (3) useful for a calculation to be carried out below:

$$[f] +^* [g] = [f + g] \tag{5}$$

since $\{k \mid f(k) + g(k) = (f+g)(k)\} = \omega \in F$, and,

$$[f] \cdot^* [g] = [f \cdot g] \tag{6}$$

since $\{k \mid f(k) \cdot g(k) = (f \cdot g)(k)\} = \omega \in F$.

Let M^* be the structure whose domain is D^*, whose distinguished elements are the c^*, whose distinguished functions are the g^*, and whose distinguished relations are the R^*.

M^* is called an *ultrapower* of M. Łoś' Theorem states that a structure is a model of a sentence of $\mathcal{L}$ just in case its ultrapower is also a model of that sentence. It follows that M and M^* agree on all sentences of $\mathcal{L}$. That is to say, M^* satisfies all the laws of real numbers stated in $\mathcal{L}$ and true in M.

There are very small positive members of D^*. Let $<$ be the ordinary less-than relation on D. For each r in D, let $\bar{r}$ be $(\lambda n)(r)$. Let i be (λn) $(\frac{1}{n+1})$. Then for all positive integers m

$$[i] <^* [\tfrac{\overline{1}}{m}] \text{ iff } \{k \mid \tfrac{1}{k} < \tfrac{1}{m}\} \in F \tag{7}$$

which holds since the set mentioned on the right hand side is cofinite. Also

$$[0] <^* [i] \text{ iff } \{k \mid 0 < \tfrac{1}{k+1}\} \in F \tag{8}$$

which holds since the set mentioned is ω. So, though M^* satisfies all the laws of real numbers stated in $\mathcal{L}$, it has a member i that is greater* than 0^* but less* than all positive* standard reals*.

A member x of D^* is *infinitesimal* if and only if $\mid x \mid^* <^* [\bar{r}]$ for all positive r in D. The i mentioned above is infinitesimal. A member x of D^* is *finite* if and only if $\mid x \mid^* <^* [\bar{r}]$ for some positive r in D. (The i mentioned above has a reciprocal*— that is, a member j of D^* such that $i \cdot^* j = [\bar{1}]$—that is not finite.) We can show that for each finite x in D^* there is a unique real r in D such that $\mid [\bar{r}]-x \mid^*$ is infinitesimal; this r is called $st(x)$, the standard part of x. (In fact $st(x)$ is the least upper bound in M of $\{r \in D \mid [\bar{r}] \leq^* x\}$.) We can also show that when g has a derivative g' then for finite x and non-zero infinitesimal h

$$g'\big(st(x)\big) = st\left(\frac{g^*(x +^* h) -^* g^*(x)}{h}\right) \tag{9}$$

Now let's recalculate the derivative of $y = x^2$. The function $g = (\lambda r)(r^2)$ of course has a derivative g'. So

$$g'(r) = st\left(\frac{g^*([\bar{r}] +^* h) -^* g^*([\bar{r}])}{h}\right) \tag{10}$$

because, given that r is a real number of D, $st([\bar{r}])=r$. Let's first calculate $g^*([\bar{r}])$:

$$g^*([\bar{r}])=[(\lambda k)(g(\bar{r}(k)))] \qquad (11)$$
$$=[(\lambda k)(g(r))]$$
$$=[(\lambda k)(r^2)]$$
$$=[\bar{r^2}]$$

And now, let's calculate $g^*([\bar{r}]+^* h)$ (note the use of (5) in moving to the last two lines):

$$g^*([\bar{r}]+^* h)=g^*([\overline{r+h'}]), \text{ where } h=[h'] \qquad (12)$$
$$=\left[(\lambda k)\left(g((\overline{r+h'})(k))\right)\right]$$
$$=\left[(\lambda k)\left(g(\bar{r}(k)+h'(k))\right)\right]$$
$$=\left[(\lambda k)\left(g(r+h'(k))\right)\right]$$
$$=\left[(\lambda k)\left(r^2+2r\cdot h'(k)+h'(k)^2\right)\right]$$
$$=\left[(\lambda k)(r^2)+(\lambda k)(2r\cdot h'(k))+(\lambda k)\left(h'(k)^2\right)\right]$$
$$=\left[(\lambda k)(r^2)\right]+^*\left[(\lambda k)(2r\cdot h'(k))\right]+^*\left[(\lambda k)\left(h'(k)^2\right)\right]$$
$$=[\bar{r^2}]+^*\left[(\lambda k)(2r\cdot h'(k))\right]+^*\left[(\lambda k)\left(h'(k)^2\right)\right]$$

Now we calculate their difference (note the use of (5) and (6)):

$$g^*([\bar{r}]+h)-g^*([\bar{r}])=\left[(\lambda k)(2r\cdot h'(k))\right]+^*\left[(\lambda k)\left(h'(k)^2\right)\right] \qquad (13)$$
$$=[(\lambda k)(2r)]\cdot^*[(\lambda k)(h'(k))]+^*$$
$$[(\lambda k)(h'(k))]\cdot^*[(\lambda k)(h'(k))]$$
$$=[(\lambda k)(2r)]\cdot^* h+^* h\cdot^* h$$

Finally, we calculate the derivative:

$$st\left(\frac{g^*([\bar{r}]+h)-g([\bar{r}])}{h}\right)=st([(\lambda k)(2r)]+h) \qquad (14)$$
$$=st([\overline{2r}]+h)$$
$$g'(r)=2r$$

So instead of $2x+dx = 2x$ for non-zero dx as in our original calculation, it is now st that wipes out the non-zero infinitesimal h when we move back to standard reals.

This construction is gorgeous. Moreover, we need only a somewhat more general version of this construction to prove the compactness of first-order logic (if every finite subset of a set of sentences has a model then the set itself has a model) directly from Łoś's Theorem. This proof does not proceed in the usual way via a syntactical detour through formal proofs, and so is conceptually important in showing that compactness is not just the finiteness of proofs writ large.

But even able and hard-working graduate students in philosophy with a taste for mathematics find the hike up ultrafilters to ultrapowers and Łoś' Theorem a strain on their powers of abstraction. Though that is not entirely a bad thing, it would be nice to have a low road to infinitesimals.

M^* is a *non-standard* model for analysis. Leon Henkin in his dissertation showed us a splendid shortcut to non-standard models for number theory.[4] To enjoy it again, suppose ω and identity on it are distinguished sets of M; 0 is a distinguished element; and successor, addition, and multiplication are distinguished functions. Then all the truths of first-order number theory under standard interpretation in M are sentences of $\mathcal{L}$. Let T be the set of these truths. Add to $\mathcal{L}$ a single new constant a. Add to T sentences saying that a is a natural number but different from 0, from 1, and so on. Call the expanded set T^+. For any *finite* subset A of T^+, let a denote the least (standard) natural number (in D) not mentioned in new difference claims from T^+ in A. Then, under this interpretation, A comes out true in M. It follows that every finite subset T^+ has a model. Hence, by compactness, T^+ itself has a model, call it M^+. M^+ has the same cardinality as M, but also contains a natural number different from all of 0, 1, 2, and so forth. M^+ is a non-standard model for number theory. Students find this argument from Henkin less of a strain on their powers of abstraction (even if it strains their powers of credulity).

All the sentences of T still hold in M^+, so no natural number of M^+ precedes its 0, and no natural number of M^+ comes between a natural number n of M^+ and its successor $n+1$. But of any two distinct natural numbers of M^+, one is greater than the other. So in M^+ a is greater than all the standard natural numbers of M^+. Nor is a alone out there. For any natural number has a successor, which has another, and so on; and any non-zero natural number has a predecessor, which has a predecessor, and so on. Since a is non-zero, it has infinitely many successors and predecessors. None of these predecessors is a standard natural number; for, if $a-k = n$, for example, and n is standard, then $a = k+n$ would be standard after all.

The upshot is that the non-standard a lies in a *clump* of non-standard natural numbers order-isomorphic to the standard integers (negative, zero, and positive) but all greater than all the standard natural numbers of M^+. Moreover, a, like any natural number, has a double, namely, $2a= a+a$. Now, $a+a > a+k$ for all standard k, since otherwise $a=n$ for some standard n. So for any clump, there is another wholly beyond the first.

Moreover, a is odd or even. If it is even, then $a=2b$ for some $b < a$ since $a \neq 0$. If a is odd, then $a+1 = 2b$ for some $b<a$. It follows that there is a clump around b wholly below that around a but wholly above the standard natural numbers of M^+. In other words, there is no clump farthest out, nor is there one lowest down but above the standard natural numbers.

Next, suppose b lies in one clump and c in another. Then $b+c$ is even or odd. If it is even, then it is $2d$ for some d strictly between b and c. If it is odd, then $b+c+1$ is twice some such d. In either case, there is a clump wholly between any two clumps.

The upshot is that, after its standard natural numbers, M^+ has clumps of non-standard natural numbers, any one clump order-isomorphic to the standard integers (negative, zero, and positive), and the clumps order-isomorphic to the standard rationals (a countable dense linear order without endpoints). Back when ω

was the order type of the (standard) natural numbers, ω^* was the reverse, that is, the order type of the (standard) negative integers, and η was the order type of the standard rationals. So one way to say what we have seen is that $\omega+(\omega^*+\omega)\eta$ is the order type of the natural numbers of M^+.

But these are just the natural numbers of M^+. They are preceded by a copy of them in reverse order, the negative integers of M^+. So the integers of M^+ (negative, zero, and positive) have the order type $(\omega^*+\omega)\eta$. Any of these integers is the numerator, and any non-zero one the denominator, of a ratio of M^+, and these ratios fix the rationals of M^+ according to the usual rule that $\frac{n}{p}=\frac{m}{q}$ if and only if $nq = mp$. The rationals of M^+ have order type η.

It is the reals of M^+ we have been after, and continuing our high-school style, we will think of reals in terms of decimals. A decimal like $3.14159\ldots$ is a sequence of digits. Such sequences may be represented by functions from the integers to the set of digits, that is, the set of natural numbers $\{0, 1, 2, 3, 4, 5, 6, 7, 8, 9\}$. The integers in their usual array,

$$\ldots, -2, -1, 0, 1, 2, \ldots \tag{15}$$

increase as we move to the right, but in decimal notation a step to the *left* is an increase in order of magnitude. This opposition produces irrelevant irritations. Let us picture the integers thus

$$\ldots, 2, 1, 0, -1, -2, \ldots \tag{16}$$

so as with decimals advancement is toward the left. (For all his interest in history, Dreben is not a reactionary.) It is required of any decimal d that there be an integer i such that for all $j > i$, $d(j) = 0$. Also, suppose d were a decimal such that for some i and all $j < i$, $d(j) = 9$. Let i' be the greatest such i. Then we exclude d in favor of the d' such that

$$d'(j)=d(j)\text{ for } j>i' \tag{17}$$
$$d'(i')=d(i')+1$$
$$d'(j)=0\text{ for } j<i'$$

Given these stipulations, for each non-negative (standard) real r there is a unique decimal d such that

$$r=\sum_i d(i)\cdot 10^i \tag{18}$$

the sum being taken over all integers. And, for each decimal d there is a unique non-negative (standard) real r obeying the same equation (18). For r negative, $-r$ is positive so we have a unique d such that

$$r=\sum_i -d(i)\cdot 10^i \tag{19}$$

and conversely. We may suppose that resources of $\mathcal{L}$ are sufficient to express these claims. So these claims are true in M, and thus members of T, which, recall, is the set of sentences of $\mathcal{L}$ true under the standard interpretation in M.

These claims are thus also true in M^+. But, in M^+, while the digits are as ever, the integers include the non-standard integers. We have reached the *long decimals*. For each real r of D^+ let d_r be its decimal. Then r is *finite* iff there is a standard integer i such that $d_r(j) = 0$ for all $j > i$, and r is *infinitesimal* iff $d_r(i) \neq 0$ at most for negative non-standard integers i. For each finite r, $st(r)$, the standard part of r, is the (standard) real in D fixed by restricting d_r to standard integers. Let us suppose that each standard real r in D was a distinguished member of M. It was then the denotation of a constant ρ of $\mathcal{L}$ under the standard interpretation of $\mathcal{L}$ in M. M^+ provides an interpretation of $\mathcal{L}$. Let r^+ be the denotation of ρ in D^+ under this interpretation. Then r^+ is always finite, and r and r^+ have the same standard digits. (Note that we do not, for example, pick $(\frac{1}{3})^+$ so that $d_{(\frac{1}{3})^+}(i) = 0$ for negative non-standard i because "To the right of the decimal point, every digit of $\frac{1}{3}$ is 3" should formalize in $\mathcal{L}$ as true in M and thus in M^+ also.) We treat functions and relations similarly. Where before we went by way of $(\lambda g)(g^*)$ to M^*, we now go by way of M^+ to $(\lambda g)(g^+)$; the order of exposition has been inverted. We now have (in st, g^+, r^+ and being finite and infinitesimal) all the pieces we need to reach the derivative in M of $(\lambda r)(r^2)$ via M^+ as we did *via M^**.

You can just hear Dreben: "OK, so there are infinitesimals, or at least a version of them, and maybe even a low road to them. But what can you *do* with them?"

Suppose first that suitable coordinate axes for space are the real line not of M but of M^+. Then space consists of a countable infinity of cubes each infinite in all three dimensions. (How do other geometries respond to non-standard reals?) Each cube on its own is rather as Euclid or Descartes or Newton pictured all of space, but they fit together seamlessly. "Is there room for a cube of gold whose edges are $\omega^* + \omega$ feet long but which does not fill up space?" (This question resonates with a remark made by Kripke about Robinson thirty years ago.)[5] The answer may turn on which real numbers serve best as spatial coordinates. Thus the philosophical presumption that mathematics has nothing interesting to say about physics may not survive the reciprocals of infinitesimals.[6] Even if mathematical natural science is a conservative extension[7] of a somehow de-mathematized natural science, *which* mathematics best extends natural science may still be a significant natural question, as Dreben's teacher Quine emphasizes. On another tack, if the laws of nature are uniform across space but there is a finite real maximum to the speed of any causal signal, then these aforementioned cubes will be utterly isolated from each other, and so perhaps might serve as a system of physically possible worlds within the metaphysically actual world.

Second, the infinitesimals we have described occur in *non*-standard models of *first*-order analysis. But *second*-order analysis is categorical, that is, any two structures satisfying its sentences are isomorphic. The isomorphism between models of second-order number theory that Dedekind described extends up the "construction" of integers, rationals, and reals from the natural numbers. Recently, increased attention has been paid to second-order systems, particularly by authors concerned to urge the virtues of such systems.[8] Suppose, however, we refuse to choose between standard and non-standard analysis, but prefer to enjoy the virtues of both. We might also refuse to choose between second- and first-order formalization, but prefer to enjoy the virtues of both these too. For while second-order systems sometimes get us categoricity (and so a sort of univocality),[9] first-order systems often do not, and that is how we got the pleasures of infinitesimals.

Third, an interesting problem appears to arise in this neighborhood. The categoricity of second-order number theory or of second-order analysis means, as we have seen, that all models of each share a single structure. But this does not by itself mean that this shared structure is that of the standard model. Exactly what could be said to explain why some non-standard countable model for first-order number theory is not the type of all models for second-order number theory? The mathematical basis for categoricity is this: given that there is a set S of exactly the standard natural numbers, second-order induction[10] implies that S exhausts the domain of a model for second-order number theory, and this excludes all non-standard models. If we are sure that "is a standard natural number" has an extension, S is it. But which are the standard natural numbers? One fairly obvious answer is that the standard natural numbers are those with only finitely many predecessors. This answer calls for a good story about the notion of finiteness that does not assume the standard natural numbers. Dedekind showed at least how to start such a story, but he was too early to appreciate the distinction between the standard and the non-standard.[11]

But maybe there is another issue here. We have been prising apart the concepts of finitude and of natural number, since our constructions show how it is possible to be a natural number, albeit a "non-standard" one, without having finitely many predecessors. But we have just urged that we don't have an independent account of standardness and non-standardness. So we don't, in fact, have a good way to show that each of the real natural numbers has only finitely many predecessors. For all we know, the real natural numbers have infinitely many predecessors. Similarly, for all we know, each real real number is surrounded by a haze of numbers that differ from it only infinitesimally. Of course, granted M, M^+ is *mathematically* inevitable. So, perhaps, the question of which of these structures is "*real*" may turn out to be a question about the structure of the space in which we live and move and have our being.[12]

NOTES

1. Trans. A. Smeaton (London: Kegan Paul, 1937).

2. Gödel's paper is, of course, "Über formal unentscheidbare Sätze der *Principia Mathematica* und verwandter Systeme, I," *Monatshefte für Mathematik und Physik* 38 (1931), 173–198. The translation Dreben used was the one Elliot Mendelson did especially for Martin Davis, ed., *The Undecidable* (Hewlitt, New York: Raven Press, 1965), pp. 4–38, entitled "On Formally Undecidable Propositions of *Principia Mathematica* and Similar Systems, I."

3. First presented in "Non-Standard Analysis," *Koninklijke Nederlandse Akademie van Wetenschappen* (Amsterdam), *Proceedings*, series A, vol. 64 (or *Indagationes mathematicae*, volume 23) (1961): 432–440.

4. *The Completeness of Formal Systems* (Ph.D. Dissertation, Princeton University, 1947), p. 70.

5. In conversation.

6. Recall that the reciprocal of an infinitesimal i is the nonstandard real number j such that $i \cdot * j = [\bar{1}]$.

7. A theory T' is a conservative extension over a theory T just in case any sentence in the vocabulary of T provable from T' is provable from T alone.

8. For example, Geoffrey Hellman, *Mathematics without Numbers* (Oxford: Oxford University Press, 1989); Stewart Shapiro, *Foundations without Foundationalism: A Case for Second-Order Logic* (Oxford: Oxford University Press, 1991); and George Boolos, *Logic, Logic, and Logic*, ed. Richard C. Jeffrey (Cambridge, Mass.: Harvard University Press, 1998), especially chapters 3–5.

9. A set of sentences is *categorical* just in case any two models of all the sentences (any two structures in which all the sentences are true) are isomorphic to one another.

10. $(\forall P)(P(0) \wedge (\forall n)(P(n) \rightarrow P(n+1)) \rightarrow (\forall n)P(n))$.

11. A set is finite in the Dedekind sense just in case there is no one-to-one mapping from it to one of its proper subsets. For more on the relationships among notions of finiteness and of natural number, see Charles Parsons, "Developing Arithmetic in Set Theory without Infinity: Some Historical Remarks," *History and Philosophy of Logic* 8 (1987): 201–213.

12. It is a blessing when one realizes one is not the culmination of history, but just a conduit between, for example, one's teacher, Burt Dreben, and one's student, Matt Moore. Without Moore, this essay would not exist.

In quite another way, it also owes its existence to Abraham Robinson, *Non-Standard Analysis*, rev. ed. (Princeton: Princeton University Press 1996); James M. Henle and Eugene M. Kleinberg, *Infinitesimal Calculus* (Cambridge, Mass.: MIT Press, 1979); and Albert E. Hurd and Peter A. Loeb, *An Introduction to Nonstandard Real Analysis* (New York: Academic Press 1985).

1970
Saul Kripke gives the lectures
of *Naming and Necessity*

18

Meaning, Rigidity, and Modality

SANFORD SHIEH

It is a platitude that Saul Kripke's *Naming and Necessity*[1] occupies a central position in contemporary analytic philosophy. Just about every philosopher educated in this tradition nowadays knows that in this book Kripke argued that proper names are rigid designators.[2] And nearly as many would know that Kripke's arguments put into question two doctrines central to the period of analytic philosophy dominated by linguistic analysis: the Fregean account of meaning in terms of the sense/reference distinction and the logical positivist alignment of the a priori/a posteriori distinction with the analytic/synthetic distinction.[3] Moreover, the notion of rigid designation, and the arguments that involve it, have been subjected to such thorough investigation that they are now thought of as a standard part of philosophy of language, routinely taught from systematic presentations such as that found in Nathan Salmon's *Reference and Essence*.[4] Thus, the fundamental concepts and arguments of *Naming and Necessity* appear to be such completely familiar ground that it is difficult to imagine how anything about them might not be fully understood.

An unsurprising consequence of this familiarity, to my mind, is that we have difficulty reading *Naming and Necessity* philosophically. Since we assume that we know everything there is to know about it, we do not raise certain elementary questions about this text, as we would if approaching a philosophical work from an unfamiliar tradition.

The principal aim of the present essay is twofold: to attempt to read *Naming and Necessity* afresh, by raising a simple question about some of its most familiar features, and then to reexamine one of its central arguments from the perspective that this question opens up.

The following are surely incontrovertible facts about *Naming and Necessity*:

- The principal target of the book is *the description theory of proper names*, according to which, as Kripke puts it, "really a proper name, properly used, simply [i]s a definite description abbreviated or disguised" (*NN*, p. 27).
- This theory has two variants, differing only in whether a single or a cluster of descriptions abbreviates a name. Both derive from a version of the sense/reference distinction: the definite description, or descriptions, express the sense of the name.

- The description theory can also be interpreted in two ways: either descriptions *give the meanings* of proper names, or they merely *fix the references* of names.
- One of the arguments Kripke employs against the description theory proceeds by trying to show, based on our understanding of sentences in which proper names interact with modal expressions, that proper names are rigid designators. This is the argument, in the first lecture of the book, now standardly called "the modal argument."[5]
- This argument is intended to be effective against *only* the *meaning-giving* interpretation of the description theory, *not* the *reference-fixing* interpretation (*NN*, pp. 32–33).

It follows from these facts that, in *Naming and Necessity* at least, Kripke's modal argument relies on a transition from

(R)   Proper names are rigid designators but definite descriptions are not.

to

(M)   Definite descriptions cannot give the meanings of proper names.

Now it is natural to ask: what justifies this inference? Clearly it is not simply the principles of first- (or higher-) order logic. Rather, the transition would seem to have to rely on nonlogical (although perhaps analytic) principles connecting the concept of rigid designation with that of meaning. But, so far as I know, there is no explicit statement of these principles, much less of their justification, in Kripke's writings, or in the secondary literature surrounding *Naming and Necessity*.

Of course the mere absence of an account of these principles is not in itself all that interesting. It becomes significant only in light of some further points. To begin with, once we raise the question of the last paragraph—which can be put more bluntly as, What does rigid designation have to do meaning?—we are in a position to see that the history of disputes over the modal argument is not wholly reducible to a set of fully resolved issues, as might appear in systematic presentations of the doctrines of *Naming and Necessity*. Specifically, as I will show in sections I and II below, there are certain lacunae in the familiar objections, replies, and clarifications surrounding this argument, all traceable to the fact that Kripke provides no account of what it is for an expression to "give the meaning" of another. Moreover, it is not obvious how the notion of "meaning giving" should be explained in order to fill in these gaps. Thus, our question about the relation between rigidity and meaning shows, at least, that Kripke's modal argument has yet to be *fully* understood. Accordingly, the task of the first half of the following essay is to establish the identity of, and the grounds for, the connection or connections between rigidity and meaning that underlie the modal argument.

My procedure here is to attempt to give an account of "meaning giving" that would preserve the cogency of the modal argument. This leads to a revised version of that argument, explicitly incorporating that account of "meaning giving."

But this revised modal argument, it is worth noting, contains little not found in the original version; its interest lies entirely in its making explicit the conception of meaning underlying the modal argument.

The significance of this conception, in turn, is twofold. First of all, it is clearly relevant to our understanding and evaluation of Kripke's achievement. Kripke's arguments in *Naming and Necessity*, as noted above, have led contemporary analytic philosophy by and large to abandon a Fregean picture of language. But surely we cannot be quite certain of why exactly we have rejected this picture, or what exactly we have committed ourselves to in its stead, if we don't know quite exactly what notion of meaning is involved in Kripke's arguments.[6]

Secondly, once it is clear how the modal argument turns on a conception of meaning, it becomes possible to reveal certain tacit presuppositions of Kripke's view of language. Specifically, in the second half of the following essay, sections III–V, I will develop some non-standard objections to the revised version of the modal argument. I show that, although none of these objections is decisive, it is not clear how any of them could be answered without undertaking a commitment to the notion of deep necessity formulated by Gareth Evans, Martin Davies, and Lloyd Humberstone.[7] My principal conclusion, therefore, is that a Kripkean view of language seems to *require* substantial commitments in the metaphysics of modality, rather than to furnish the basis of such commitments. Uncovering these commitments is the payoff of thinking about *Naming and Necessity* from the perspective of our initial question of the relation between rigidity and meaning.

In section VI, as something of a postscript, I briefly discuss the prospects of defending the Kripkean view on the basis of these metaphysical commitments.

I

The first wave of criticism directed at *Naming and Necessity* operated with a picture of the modal argument[8] suggested by passages such as the following:

The stronger version [of the description theory] would say that the name is simply *defined*, synonymously, as [a] cluster of descriptions. It will then be necessary—that [Aristotle]—had the disjunction of [properties in the cluster]—. I think it's clear that this is very implausible. . . . Most of the things commonly attributed to Aristotle are things that Aristotle might not have done at all. This is not a distinction of scope, as happens sometimes in the case of descriptions, where someone might say that the man who taught Alexander might not have taught Alexander; though it could not have been true that: the man who taught Alexander didn't teach Alexander. (*NN*, p. 61)

The facts that "the teacher of Alexander" is capable of scope distinctions in modal contexts and that it is not a rigid designator are both illustrated when one observes that the teacher of Alexander might not have . . . been the teacher of Alexander. . . . On the other hand, it is not true that Aristotle might not have been Aristotle. (*NN*, p. 62, n. 25)

These passages suggest that Kripke's argument rests on our linguistic intuitions about sentences such as:

(1) It might not have been true that the teacher of Alexander the Great was the teacher of Alexander the Great

(2) The teacher of Alexander the Great is such that he might not have been the teacher of Alexander the Great.

(3) It might not have been true that Aristotle was Aristotle

(4) Aristotle might not have been Aristotle

We intuitively take (1) to be false and (2) true; in contrast, we take both (3) and (4) to be false. So the scope of a proper name with respect to (expressions regimented as) modal operators in a sentence has no effect on its truth-value, whereas that of a definite description does.

These linguistic intuitions form the basis for an argument against the *synonymy* of coreferential proper names and descriptions such as "Aristotle" and "the teacher of Alexander the Great." If they are synonymous then surely (1) and (3) are also synonymous. But it is a rather plausible assumption that synonymous sentences have the identical truth conditions, and so must have the same truth-values when used in the same contexts. It follows that, contrary to our linguistic intuitions, (1) and (3) must have the same truth-values (when used in the same context). Let's call this argument "the simple modal argument." Note that, in ascribing this argument to Kripke, we implicitly interpret his notion of "meaning giving" as synonymy.

There is a well-known objection to the simple modal argument, given by, among others, Michael Dummett and Brian Loar.[9] This objection concedes that Kripke's argument establishes the non-synonymy of proper names and definite descriptions. But it claims that it is consistent with this argument to reformulate the description theory as claiming that the meaning of a proper name is given by a definite description and, in addition, by a convention that (every occurrence of) that description has wide scope with respect to all modal operators in sentences in which it occurs. In terms of the examples we have been using, this is the claim that both (3) and (4) are to be interpreted as:

(5) The teacher of Alexander is such that he might not be the same as himself.

Hence they are both false, as our intuitions demand.[10]

There are, of course, well-known replies to the wide scope theory, which I will discuss in a moment. But I want first to pose a question about this familiar theory, one which is perhaps a little hard to see *as* a question, precisely because of its familiarity. The wide scope theory, we have noted, concedes that coreferential definite descriptions and proper names are *not* synonymous. But, then, how could this theory pose *any* problems for the conclusion that definite descriptions *can't give the meanings* of proper names? Why, we might wonder, isn't the wide scope theory simply a nonstarter as an objection to the simple modal argument?

The only way in which the wide scope theory could have been accepted as an objection at all (albeit an unsuccessful one) is if "meaning giving" is a distinct notion from synonymy. And this by itself shows that a very natural interpretation of Kripke's notion of what it is for an expression to give the meaning of another—namely, that they are synonymous—cannot be sustained.

It is not difficult to make a little headway in explaining the notion of "meaning giving." Let's consider why the wide scope theory was taken to be a serious challenge to the simple modal argument. The basic motivation of the description theory is the Fregean idea that the reference of *any* singular term is to be analyzed in terms of the satisfaction of a condition by its referent. Let's call this idea *the conditionality of reference.* As far as respecting the motivation of this theory is concerned, it is more important to hold that proper names and definite descriptions *share this feature of the conditionality of reference* than to hold that they can be strictly synonymous. Now, the wide scope theory shows that it is possible to accept an argument showing that names and descriptions are not synonymous, *without* giving up the claim that the satisfaction of a descriptive condition is *part of* (the explanation of) the meaning of a proper name. So, on this view, the simple modal argument fails to show that there is anything wrong with the basic Fregean idea about the reference of names and establishes at most the need for a minor revision.

This should perhaps have been obvious to an attentive reader of *Naming and Necessity.* For, after giving the modal argument, Kripke claims that it shows that "*being the teacher of Alexander the Great* cannot be part of [the sense of] the name" (*NN*, p. 30). Now, if Kripke's argument merely showed that names and descriptions are not synonymous, this conclusion wouldn't be warranted. For there is a gap between saying that two expressions don't have the *same* meaning and saying that the meaning of one can't be *a part of* the meaning of the other.[11]

This discussion takes us to two preliminary points. First, we should distinguish between two kinds of semantic difference between proper names and definite descriptions. A weak kind is established by the simple modal argument, which shows no more than that these two sorts of singular terms cannot be synonymous. But, as I've just shown, Kripke is after a stronger kind of semantic difference. A plausible initial formulation of this stronger difference is:

It is *not* (*even*) part of the meanings of proper names that their referents satisfy descriptive conditions; in contrast, it *is* part of the meanings of definite descriptions that their referents satisfy descriptive conditions.

Let's call this claim the *Semantic Difference Thesis.* The claim is meant to imply that, at least with respect to referents, proper names and definite descriptions belong to different semantic kinds.

Of course, to invent terminology is not to clarify anything. This is especially true in the present case, where we have so far merely exchanged one unclarity—what it is for one expression to give the meaning of another—for a second—what it is for something to be, or fail to be, part of the meaning of an expression. But, I hold that this (yet to be clarified) thesis *is* what the claim that descriptions can't give the meanings of names really amounts to; that is, it is what (M) above really means, and it is the intended conclusion of Kripke's modal argument.

The second point is that, if Kripke's intended conclusion is the Semantic Difference Thesis, then the simple modal argument should not be attributed to him,
since it fails to establish that Thesis.

These conclusions set the agenda for the next section. I will try

  (i) to clarify the Semantic Difference Thesis, and
  (ii) to discover what argument(s) Kripke gives for it.

II

An argument for the Semantic Difference Thesis can be extracted from Kripke's
reply to the wide scope theory given in the Preface of *Naming and Necessity*.[12] The
reply is framed as a "restatement of the idea of rigid designation" (*NN*, p. 6):

> Consider:
>   (1) Aristotle was fond of dogs.
> A proper understanding of this statement involves an understanding both
> of the (extensionally correct) conditions under which it is in fact true, *and* of
> the conditions under which a counterfactual course of history, resembling
> the actual course in some respects but not in others, would be correctly (par-
> tially) described by (1). Presumably everyone agrees that there is a certain
> man—the philosopher we call "Aristotle"—such that, as a matter of fact, (1)
> is true if and only if *he* was fond of dogs. The thesis of rigid designation is sim-
> ply . . . that the same paradigm applies to the truth conditions of (1) as it
> describes *counterfactual* situations. That is, (1) truly describes a counter-
> factual situation if and only if the same aforementioned man would have
> been fond of dogs, had that situation obtained. . . . By contrast, Russell thinks
> that (1) should be analyzed as something like:
>   (2) The last great philosopher of antiquity was fond of dogs.
>   . . .
> The actual truth conditions of [(2)] agree extensionally with those mentioned
> above for (1), assuming that Aristotle was the last great philosopher of antiq-
> uity. But counterfactually, Russell's conditions can vary wildly from those
> supposed by the rigidity thesis. With respect to a counterfactual situation
> where someone other than Aristotle would have been the last great philoso-
> pher of antiquity, Russell's criterion would make *that other person's* fondness
> for dogs the relevant issue for the correctness of (1)! (*NN*, pp. 6–7)

In order to discuss this passage, I begin by fixing some terminology. Let's call
"the conditions under which a counterfactual situation would be correctly described by" a sentence its *counterfactual truth conditions*. The intuition Kripke presents in this passage is that there is a difference between the counterfactual truth
conditions of two sentences, neither of which contains (expressions regimentable
as) modal operators, and which differ only in that the one contains an occurrence
of a proper name wherever the other contains an occurrence of a coreferential

definite description. I will follow Kripke and call sentences that do not contain modal operators *simple* sentences. Let's call the simple sentence containing the name "Aristotle," *the name sentence*, and the simple sentence containing the description "the last great philosopher of antiquity," *the description sentence*. Let's call Kripke's account of this case *Kripke's Intuition*, and the actual and counterfactual truth conditions that it involves, *Kripke's Truth Conditions*.

One last piece of preliminary: the precise difference between Kripke's Truth Conditions of the name sentence and those of the description sentence requires some care to state. In particular, it is important to avoid the following account, naturally but erroneously suggested by the last quoted passage. In the case of the name sentence, *one and the same* person is relevant to its actual and counterfactual truth conditions; whereas, in the case of the description sentence, *distinct* persons are relevant to its actual and to its counterfactual truth conditions. Hence, the actual and counterfactual referents of the name are identical whereas those of the description are distinct.

The problem with this account is that it doesn't distinguish names from descriptions such as "the smallest prime number." Clearly, if a simple sentence contains *this* description, one and the same number is relevant to its truth in any possible world. That is to say, this account fails to respect two features of Kripke's views. First, it fails to respect the fact that Kripke distinguishes

> between "*de jure*" rigidity, where the reference of a designator is *stipulated* to be a single object, whether we are speaking of the actual world or of a counterfactual situation, and mere "*de facto*" rigidity, where a description "the x such that Fx" happens to use a predicate "F" that in each possible world is true of one and the same unique object. (*NN*, p. 21, n. 21)

Second, it fails to take into consideration the fact that for Kripke names are rigid *de jure*, not *de facto*. So the right account of the relevant difference in Kripke's Truth Conditions is this: in a counterfactual situation, the referent of the description is the unique satisfier of a condition, whereas the referent of the name is (stipulated to be) identical to the actual referent. One way to put the difference is that it consists in a difference in *the mechanism of reference determination* with respect to nonactual possible worlds.

With these preliminaries out of the way, I turn to the question whether, and if so how, Kripke's Intuition can be used to demonstrate the Semantic Difference Thesis.

To begin with, it is certainly possible to use the Intuition to give *an* argument, of a familiar type, against the description theory. Suppose the description theory is right. Then "Aristotle" and "the last great philosopher of antiquity" would be synonymous. So sentences (1) and (2) in Kripke's presentation of his Intuition would be synonymous. Now, if it is plausible that whenever two sentences are synonymous they have the same actual truth conditions, then it is no less plausible that they would have the same counterfactual truth conditions. But Kripke's Intuition shows that (1) and (2) don't have the same counterfactual truth conditions. Hence, these expressions are not synonymous.

Moreover, this argument is proof against the wide scope move. As Kripke puts it: "(1) and (2) are 'simple' sentences. Neither contains modal or other operators, so there is no room for any scope distinctions. No scope convention about more complex sentences affects the interpretation of *these* sentences" (*NN*, p. 11). Hence, Kripke's Intuition cannot be accounted for by the wide scope theory. This argument is more or less accepted in the secondary literature as Kripke's real modal argument against the description theory; let's call it "the standard modal argument."

The standard modal argument is certainly an improvement over the simple modal argument in its ability to handle the wide scope objection. A moment's reflection, however, indicates that it still fails to establish any more than a *weak* nonsynonymy claim. The crucial distinction in Kripke's Intuition is between the ways in which the references of two singular terms are determined *with respect to counterfactual situations*. But their references *with respect to the actual world* are determined in the *same* way. Hence, it is consistent with the standard modal argument to hold that *the satisfaction of a descriptive condition by its actual referent* is a part of the meaning of the proper name.

The problem can be formulated in a slightly different way. As Kripke presents his Intuition, there is something common to "Aristotle" and "the last great philosopher of antiquity," namely, the way in which their references are determined in the actual world. The divergence in their linguistic properties becomes apparent only when we consider how their references are determined with respect to counterfactual situations. Why not then say that this common factor, the way in which actual reference is determined, is a *shared* aspect of the *meanings* of these expressions? But if we say this, then surely we are committed to claiming that the satisfaction of a descriptive condition is a part of the meaning of "Aristotle." Hence, the standard modal argument still fails to establish the Semantic Difference Thesis.

As far as I know, there is no explicit explanation, either in *Naming and Necessity* or in the secondary literature, of how an argument from Kripke's Intuition to the Semantic Difference Thesis works. Nevertheless, I believe that a tacit line of reasoning underlies Kripke's overt claims. This reasoning I will now attempt to reconstruct.

The first step is an account of what it is for something to be *part of the meaning of* an expression. I will approach this question by looking at an account of the difference in meaning between proper names and definite descriptions given by A. D. Smith, based on Kripke's Intuition:

What is distinctive about *any* kind of definite description . . . is that [it] expresses, in virtue of its meaning, a descriptive condition to be met by a designatum. It is this relation between a definite descriptive expression and a descriptive condition that is genuinely semantic. The relation of designation between such an expression and an item in the world is, by contrast, *not* purely semantic. For definite descriptions of themselves do not determine the relation of designation to an item: it is also, in part, determined by the facts of the world. . . . *If things had gone differently that expression would have designated a different individual (or none) while its meaning would remain unchanged.*

Things are quite otherwise with proper names. It is a genuinely semantic fact about the name "Aristotle" that it designates, or, more precisely, *names* the particular individual Aristotle. Such a name *could not have a different reference without having changed in meaning.*[13]

I want to emphasize two features of Smith's account of Kripke's Intuition:

- The referent of a definite description *could be* different from its actual referent, without affecting its meaning.
- In contrast, the referent of a proper name *could not be* different from its actual referent, without affecting its meaning.

This difference suggests that, for a proper name, having a particular referent is *essential* or *necessary* to its meaning, whereas, for a definite description, the determination of reference by the satisfaction of a descriptive condition, rather than the possession of a particular referent, is what is essential to its meaning. Smith's account of Kripke's Intuition therefore suggests that the Intuition is governed by the following principle:

- For something to be a part of the meaning of an expression is for it to be an essential property of any expression having that meaning.

Thus, the difference in meaning involved in the Semantic Difference Thesis is precisely this difference in essential properties of meaning. The thesis can now finally be formulated thus:

(SDT) It is not an essential property of the meanings of proper names that their referents satisfy descriptive conditions; in contrast, it is an essential property of the meanings of definite descriptions that their referents satisfy descriptive conditions.

(SDT) is the interpretation of (M) I will henceforth employ.

Given this clarification of the Semantic Difference Thesis, the task of a reconstruction of the modal argument is to show how Kripke's Intuition implies a difference in essential semantic properties of names and descriptions. Within the framework of the analysis of modality in terms of counterfactual situations, the essential properties of an object are those that are true of it with respect to all counterfactual situations. Thus, the role of Kripke's Intuition is this: Kripke implicitly uses this Intuition to determine what holds true of singular terms occurring in simple sentences with respect to all counterfactual situations, and, thereby, the necessary properties of the meanings of these expressions.

Note that, in order for this determination to work, the counterfactual situations of Kripke's Intuition must be such that the meanings of the expressions at issue are constant over them. Kripke confirms this by the following remark:

When I say that a designator is rigid,—I mean that, as used in *our* language, it stands for [one and the same] thing, when *we* talk about counterfactual situations. . . . [W]hen we speak of a counterfactual situation, we speak of it in English, even if it is part of the description of that counterfactual situation that we were all speaking German. . . . [I]n describing that world, we use *English* with *our* meanings and *our* references. (*NN*, p. 77)

The reconstruction of the modal argument proceeds as follows.

To begin with, Kripke's Intuition shows that the use of the name sentence (with the same meanings as the name actually has) to describe counterfactual situations exhibits three features:

1. *The same person* is relevant to the truth-values of the sentence, whether we're describing the actual world or other possible worlds.
2. This person is determined as the referent of the name in the actual world because he is the object in this world that uniquely satisfies a descriptive condition.[14]
3. However, this person is determined as the referent of the name in a counterfactual situation *not* because he is the object in that situation that uniquely satisfies a descriptive condition, *but* because he is identical to the actual referent.

The use of the description sentence to describe counterfactual situations exhibits a corresponding set of three features:

1'. The person in the actual world relevant to the truth-value of the description sentence is *different from* the person(s) in other possible worlds relevant to the truth value of that sentence.
2'. The person in question is determined as the referent of the description in the actual world because he is the object in this world that uniquely satisfies a descriptive condition.
3'. However, the person in question is determined as the referent of the description in a counterfactual situation *because* he is the object in that situation that uniquely satisfies a descriptive condition, *and not* because he is identical to the actual referent.

The features of the use of the name sentence imply that what is constant across possible worlds for the use of a *name* is its *referent*, and *not* its *mechanism of reference determination*. Hence the referent, rather than the mechanism, is essential to the meaning of a proper name.

In contrast, what's constant across possible worlds for the use of a *description* is its *mechanism of reference determination*, and *not* its *referent*. So it is the mechanism, not the referent, that is essential to the meaning of a definite description.

These last two points, of course, imply the Semantic Different Thesis. Let's call this line of thought "the revised standard modal argument."

In light of this revision of Kripke's argument, we can state the principle that connects rigidity with meaning:

(RM) Whether a singular term is rigid determines whether having a
       particular referent is a necessary property of that expression when
       used with the meaning that it has.

The revised standard argument makes explicit the fact that this principle medi-
ates the inference from (M) to (SDT).

We have now arrived at the first main conclusion of this essay:

What Kripke intends to establish in Lecture I of *Naming and Necessity* is the
Semantic Difference Thesis, and his largely tacit argument for it proceeds by
inferring the contrasting necessary semantic properties of names and descriptions from his Intuition of the actual and counterfactual truth conditions of
simple sentences containing these expressions.

What I have been arguing so far can be summarized in the following way. The
standard modal argument establishes that proper names and definite descriptions
have different mechanisms of reference determination.[15] It is perfectly cogent; but
it does not establish the Semantic Difference Thesis and hence does not suffice to
overturn the description theory. The reason is that it fails to make explicit the relation between reference determination and meaning. The crux of the revised standard modal argument, accordingly, is to make this relation explicit and to use this
relation to effect the transition Kripke's Intuition to the Semantic Difference Thesis. This, then, is the explanation of how the inference from (R) to (M) is justified.

III

Since the revised standard modal argument hasn't been presented as such in the
literature, there are of course no extant discussions of it. But Dummett, in the final
Appendix to *The Interpretation of Frege's Philosophy*,[16] criticizes Kripke's Intuition,
which of course is the basis of this argument. From these criticisms it is possible
to extract an objection to the revised standard modal argument.[17] It is very difficult to be sure whether this objection is what Dummett had in mind, but I think
it is in any case worth considering independently.

The basis of the objection is a distinction between the "assertoric content" and
the "ingredient sense" of a sentence. The former may be equated with H. P. Grice's
notion of "what is said" in the assertoric utterance of a declarative sentence.[18] The
latter is the contribution that a sentence makes to the truth conditions of sentences
containing it as a subsentence. Kripke's Intuition may show that there is a difference between the ingredient senses of the two simple sentences, but we also have
an independent intuition that their assertoric contents *do not* differ. Hence, the
burden of proof is on Kripke to show that the rigidity of a singular term affects the
content of simple sentences containing it. But Kripke has given no noncircular argument for this claim. Call the foregoing "the simplified Dummett argument."

The difficulty in trying to evaluate this argument as an objection to the revised
standard modal argument lies in understanding how it pertains to Kripke's Intuition. This Intuition, as I have formulated it, is about the actual and counterfactual

truth conditions of simple sentences; so our question is how Kripke's Truth Conditions relate to the notions of assertoric content and ingredient sense. Since, according to the passage in which Kripke's Intuition is presented, the actual truth conditions of the name sentence and the description sentence are the same, whereas their
counterfactual truth conditions are different, a first guess is that assertoric content
corresponds to actual truth conditions, while ingredient sense corresponds to
counterfactual truth conditions. But if this is the right way to understand the simplified Dummett argument, it's hard to see how it could be effective against the revised
standard modal argument. For now the basis of the simplified Dummett argument
turns out to be nothing other than Kripke's Intuition, stated in a different terminology. In terms of this new terminology, the revised standard modal argument
may be described as attempting to demonstrate the Semantic Difference Thesis on
the basis of the Intuition that there is a difference between the ingredient senses of
the name sentence and the description sentence, *even though their assertoric contents
are the same*. Hence, it is a non sequitur to object to this argument by claiming that
the rigidity of a singular term does not make a difference to the assertoric contents
of simple sentences containing it.

Now perhaps this shows that we have to add a premise to the simplified Dummett
argument in order to arrive at an objection to the revised standard modal argument: assertoric content is alone relevant to the meaning of a sentence. But it is
unclear why we should accept this premise. After all, it is plausible that the meaning of an expression has *something* to do with the truth conditions of sentences
that contain it. The ingredient of a sentence is relevant to the truth conditions of
other sentences containing that sentence as a syntactic part. So, why doesn't the
ingredient sense of a sentence have anything to do with its meaning?

Even if this additional premise is granted, however, it remains unclear that the
expanded argument is an effective objection. The reason is that it contains no more
of an account of the notion of assertoric content than the claim that it is Grice's
notion of "what is said" in an assertoric utterance. Thus, it does not rule out a
Gricean account of assertoric content, consistent with Kripke's Intuition, along the
following lines.[19] The purpose of assertion, it might be held, is to distinguish possibilities. This view of assertion, in turn, suggests that to know what is said by an
assertion is to know which possibilities would make it true. That is, to know the
assertoric content of a sentence is to know which of the possibilities in the sentence
would be true. But now it appears to follow from this account that to know the
assertoric content of a simple sentence requires knowing its counterfactual truth
conditions. Given the suppressed premise, it follows that to know the meaning of a
simple sentence requires knowing its actual and counterfactual truth conditions.
So then it would be difficult to maintain that Kripke's Intuition is not relevant to
the meanings of the simple sentences in question.

IV

I now formulate another objection to the revised standard modal argument. Let's
begin by asking: do those features of names made explicit by Kripke's Intuition

belong *only* to names? Or, to put it differently, are names the only expressions whose actual reference is conditionally determined but whose counterfactual reference is determined by identity with the actual referent? If there are *descriptions* with these features, then, even if Kripke's Intuition is accepted, it does not establish the Semantic Difference Thesis.

It is fairly plausible that there are such definite descriptions. Indeed, their existence is suggested by Kripke himself, in his "intuitive test for rigidity":

> What's the difference between asking whether it's necessary that 9 is greater than 7 or whether it's necessary that the number of planets is greater than 7? . . . The answer to this might be intuitively "Well, look, the number of planets might have been different from what it in fact is. It doesn't make any sense, though, to say that nine might have been different from what it in fact is." (*NN*, p. 48).

I take the claim that "the number of planets might have been different from what it in fact is" to express the same claim as

(6) The number of planets might have been different from what it actually is.

That is,

(7) The number of planets might have been different from the actual number of planets.

Or,

(8) It is possible that the number of planets be different from the actual number of planets.

Surely what makes these statements true is a counterfactual situation, call it w_7, in which there are seven planets in the Solar System. So, when we talk about w_7, (the expression) "the number of planets" refers to something distinct from (the expression) "the actual number of planets." That is to say, in describing this world, w_7, (the expression) "the actual number of planets" refers not to the object in w_7 that satisfies the condition of being the number of planets, but to the object in the actual world that satisfies that condition.

For obvious reasons, I will call these definite descriptions *actualized descriptions*. They have, as advertised, just those properties that proper names have, according to Kripke's Intuition. What remains constant in their reference across counterfactual situations are their referents, *not* their mechanisms of reference determination. Their actual reference determination is conditional, whereas their counterfactual reference determination is by identity with their actual referents. All this is exactly like proper names. So it seems that we can say, about these descriptions, that they couldn't refer to something other than their actual referents without changing meaning. Which is to say that the essential properties of their meanings are just the same as those of proper names. Yet, it is clear enough, it seems, that they *are* definite descriptions; that is, the satisfaction of a condition is part of the meaning of each.[20]

These properties of actualized descriptions point to a reformulation of the description theory, using actualized descriptions, analogous to the wide scope theory. And this reformulation is the basis of an objection to the revised standard modal argument. This objection concedes to the revised standard modal argument that proper names and coreferential definite descriptions do not, in general, exhibit the same semantic features with respect to all possible worlds. But it is consistent with this concession to hold that the meanings of proper names are given by coreferential *actualized* definite descriptions, since, as we have just shown, these are of the *same* semantic type as proper names. And if we thus revise the description theory, it would follow

(a) that names and descriptions are *not semantically distinct types* of singular terms, and,

(b) that the references of names are conditionally determined.

Hence, the revised standard modal argument no more establishes the Semantic Difference Thesis than does the simple modal argument. Call the argument just presented *the objection from actualized descriptions*.

The cogency of this objection clearly depends on the account just given of how the reference of actualized descriptions is determined. So, this objection could be overturned by showing that there are problems with this account. I will consider one possible reply along these lines, based on David Bostock's account of the semantics of "actually" and "actual."[21] Bostock is concerned in particular to argue that "actually" should not be analyzed as a sentential modal operator distinct from "necessarily." For, "when we add an actuality-operator to our language," "the familiar criterion that a necessary truth is one that is true in all possible worlds . . . ceases to apply" (Bostock 1988, p. 357). Moreover, according to Bostock it is unclear whether there is an adequate replacement for this criterion since the alternative, developed by Davies and Humberstone,[22] that a necessary truth is "true in any possible world, *when* that world is taken to be the actual world" (Bostock 1988, p. 358) fails to capture all our intuitions about necessary truth. Bostock proposes avoiding these problems as follows:

> [T]he general idea is to treat "actually" not as a new modal operator but as a device for indicating relative scope, so that the word no longer occurs explicitly in our formal language, where scope is shown differently, by order and bracketing. On this approach, we suppose that "actually" has no logically significant role except when it is within the apparent scope of a modal operator, and that its role in that context is to remove what it modifies from the scope of that operator. (Bostock 1988, p. 360)

The proposal to treat "actually" as a scope shifter is not pertinent to the objection from actualized descriptions, since that concerns *simple sentences*, in which there are no scopes of modal operators. What is relevant is the suggestion that "actually" has "no logically significant role" except when it is within such a scope. If *this* proposal is adopted for "actual," then it seems to follow that there is "no logically significant role" for "actual" to play in simple sentences. At this point, it is not entirely clear what this suggestion amounts to, since Bostock has not explained what it is for an expression to have a logically significant role. But one interpretation is that simple sentences containing actualized descriptions have the same truth conditions as sentences in which these descriptions are replaced with their unactualized versions. This clearly constitutes a criticism of the objection from actualized descriptions.

But is this proposal plausible? Do the following claims

(9)   The actual number of planets is equal to the number of planets
(10) The number of planets is equal to the number of planets

have the same truth conditions, actual and counterfactual? Suppose we take these simple sentences as descriptions of w_7 in which there are seven planets; do they have the same truth value? My intuition is that they don't. Clearly (10) is true with respect to w_7; but (9) is false, since the actual number of planets is nine while the number of planets in w_7 is seven. Now I confess that I am not too confident of these intuitions. But consider the fact that (10) is plausibly true as a description of every possible world.[23] Hence, it follows from the proposal that so is (9). But then, surely, (9) is a necessary truth, and so its necessitation

(11) Necessarily, the actual number of planets is equal to the number of planets

is true. About my intuition of this sentence's falsehood I am much more confident.

It might be replied that these criticisms can be circumvented if we relied on a different analysis of the notion of counterfactual truth condition. Recall that the counterfactual truth conditions of a sentence are "the conditions under which a counterfactual situation would be correctly described by" it. Suppose we analyze the claim that w_7 is correctly described by (9) in terms of two conditions:

1. The sentence, "It is possible that the actual number of planets is equal to the number of planets" is true,

and,

2. w_7 is one of the worlds that make this sentence true.

So the falsity of either of these conditions implies that w_7 is not correctly described by (9). But now we can apply the scope shifter theory to the sentence in question, and we find that condition 2 fails, as required. More generally, the suggestion is that a simple sentence S involving actualized descriptions is true with respect to a counterfactual situation w just in case w is among the possible worlds that make ⌜It is possible that⌝S⌝ true.

Unfortunately, it is not clear that this proposal helps the revised standard modal argument. If it is adopted, then it should surely be taken to apply to the counterfactual truth conditions of the name sentence in Kripke's Intuition. That is, we would then be committed to holding that "Aristotle is fond of dogs" is true with respect to a counterfactual situation w just in case w is among the possible worlds that make "It is possible that Aristotle was fond of dogs" true. But then it is not clear that Kripke's Intuition represents an adequate response to the old wide scope theory.

Thus no genuine flaw has so far been found in the objection from actualized descriptions. In the absence of further criticisms of this objection, I provisionally advance the second main conclusion of this essay:

> Actualized descriptions make exactly the same contribution to the actual and counterfactual truth conditions of simple sentences in which they occur as do names. Hence, their necessary semantic features are no different from those of names, at least if differences in necessary semantic properties are determined in the same way as Kripke's Intuition determines the semantic differences between names and (unactualized) descriptions.

Before moving on, I'd like to make three points about the objection from actualized descriptions. First of all, I want to emphasize that since it is based on our intuitions about the actual and counterfactual truth conditions of certain simple sentences, it rests on *exactly the same sort* of grounds as does the revised standard modal argument. Secondly, I want to point out that the objection is not (obviously, at any rate) committed to a specific account of necessity. In particular, it does not presuppose the correctness of the Davies/Humberstone theory of two notions of necessity. Rather, since all it appeals to, to repeat yet again, are our intuitions about the truth conditions of certain sentences, its coherence stands or falls together with the coherence of Kripke's appeal to the idea of counterfactual truth conditions. Finally, it should be stressed that this objection does *not* establish the falsity of the Semantic Difference Thesis. At best it shows that the Thesis cannot be demonstrated on the basis of the revised standard modal argument, that is, on the basis of linguistic intuitions about differences in actual and counterfactual truth conditions.

V

The success of the objection from actualized descriptions depends on the claim that such expressions couldn't refer to something other than their actual referents without changing meaning. But we may well think that the sense in which they couldn't do so is, as it were, somewhat superficial. For, consider again the description, "the actual number of planets," and suppose that the world w_7 were the actual world. Now, if we were, in those circumstances, to use this expression in the same way that we do in fact use it, would it refer to the number nine? An intuitively attractive answer is: clearly not; the expression would refer to the number seven. So we might think that its reference *does depend on which world is the actual world.* Thus, we may grant that, *from the perspective of a given world, if it were actual,* the reference of this expression with respect to other possible worlds is identical to its actual referent. But, this doesn't show that the expression *couldn't* refer to anything else without changing its meaning. It could, *in the sense that,* if some other world were actual, it would refer to something other than what it refers to given that the actual world is actual.[24]

I want to stress that this reply to the objection from actualized descriptions *does not rescue* the revised standard modal argument. It does, however, enable us to say more precisely how the revised standard argument fails. To begin with, let me make explicit something that, so far, I have only suggested. I spoke earlier of the Fregean idea of the conditionality of reference of singular terms, that is, the idea that the referent of a singular term is determined as the object that satisfies some condition. It is natural to think that it must be possible for such terms to refer to something distinct from their actual referents without changing meaning, since it is surely in general possible for a condition to be satisfied by different objects. (Indeed, this is precisely what the quotation from Smith suggests.)

Now, what the objection to the revised standard modal argument shows is that the considerations it uses to determine the necessary properties of meaning fail to show that reference to a particular object is *not* a necessary property of actualized descriptions. And so this argument fails to discern the conditionality of reference of actualized descriptions. But the reply to this objection points the way to the right set of considerations for capturing this conditionality. Specifically, it shows that, in order to discover the essential properties of the meaning of an expression, it is not sufficient to consider the use of that expression to describe counterfactual situations, *considered merely as alternatives to the actual world.* Rather, we must consider the use of that expression to describe counterfactual situations, *if these were (part of) the actual world.* If actualized descriptions are considered in this way, the conditionality of their reference can be accounted for; in this way, we make more precise the superficiality of the objection from actualized descriptions.

We can thus envisage the possibility of a kind of rigid designation distinct from the one we've been discussing so far. For, on the basis of the new account of conditionality we have just outlined, we can now contemplate the possibility of a singular term whose reference is not conditional in this new sense. The referent of such a term is not merely constant across possible worlds, but is constant no matter which world is actual. Let's call such singular terms *deeply rigid* designators, in contrast to those we had been discussing, which we will call *superficially rigid* designators.[25]

What I have been arguing can now be summed up in the following claims.

- Actualized descriptions and proper names are both superficially rigid.
- But actualized descriptions are not deeply rigid.
- The reference of a term is conditional only if it is not deeply rigid.

From these claims it follows that, *if* it can be shown that proper names, unlike *any* descriptions, actualized or not, are deeply rigid, then the Semantic Difference Thesis can be demonstrated on the basis of a difference in the necessary semantic properties of names and descriptions.

Moreover, it seems that this conclusion has been embraced, unwittingly, by certain expositions of Kripke's arguments against the description theory. For example, Nathan Salmon's account of what he calls "the semantic arguments" against the description theory is in fact an attempt to argue for the deep rigidity of names:

> Consider the set of properties which might be associated with the name "Thales" as giving its sense according to the Fregean theory. . . . On the orthodox view, the name denotes whoever happens to satisfy this description. Suppose now that owing to some error or fraud the man . . . from whom our use of the name "Thales" derives, never genuinely believed that all is water. Suppose further that by a very strange coincidence there was indeed a Greek hermit-philosopher who did in fact hold this bizarre view, though he . . . bears no historical connection to us. To which of these two philosophers would our name "Thales" refer? This is a clear semantical question with a clear answer. The name would refer to Thales, the first of the two. Our use of the name would bear no significant connection to the second character whatsoever. It is only by way of a comical accident that he enters into the story at all.
>
> This example is not to be confused with the corresponding modal . . . arguments ("Thales might not have been the Greek philosopher who held that all is water"). In the modal . . . arguments, the main question is what the truth value of a sentence like "Thales is the Greek philosopher who held that all is water" . . . becomes when the sentence is evaluated with respect to certain [possible] circumstances. . . . The strategy in the semantical arguments is more direct. The issue here is not whom the name *actually* denotes *with respect to* the imagined circumstances; the issue is whom the name *would* denote if the circumstances described above *were to obtain*. (Salmon 1981, pp. 29–30)

The last sentence, on my reading, shows that Salmon is in this passage presenting a purported direct intuition of the *deep* rigidity of proper names.[26]

What this suggests is that an argument for the deep rigidity of names is the only clear way we have so far seen for a modal argument for the Semantic Difference Thesis to work. And clearly this fact is independent of whether there is a sound argument for the deep rigidity of names. Now it is quite controversial whether the notion of deep necessity underlying the concept of deep rigidity is even coherent. I clearly cannot, nor is it my intention to, resolve this controversy here. What I do want to emphasize here is that this notion of necessity arises in a natural way if we try to formulate the intuition that it is not a necessary feature of the meaning of an actualized description to have the reference it actually has. In addition, if we accept the objection from actualized descriptions, then the only clear way of spelling out the intuition that descriptions have essentially Fregean meanings, whereas names do not, requires the notion of deep necessity. That is to say, if the notion of deep necessity turns out to be incoherent, it is simply not clear how it would be possible to argue for the Semantic Difference Thesis based on modal semantic properties of expressions.[27] So the third and final conclusion of this paper is:

> To the extent that the conception of meaning underlying Kripke's modal argument requires that argument to rest on modal semantic properties, it is committed to the coherence of deep necessity.

One interesting consequence of this conclusion is that it appears to stand in some tension with certain aspects of Kripke's conception of his philosophical practice. A specific example is when Kripke argues for the coherence of certain identification of individuals across possible worlds thus: "it is *because* we can refer (rigidly) to Nixon, and stipulate that we are speaking of what might have happened to *him* . . . , that 'transworld identifications' are unproblematic in such cases" (*NN*, p. 49). So, in this case, a conclusion in the metaphysics of modality is based on linguistic intuitions. In contrast, if what I have been arguing is correct, Kripke's rejection of the Fregean account of language via the modal argument is based on a position in the metaphysics of modality.

VI

I am agnostic about the coherence of deep necessity. Still, it is interesting to speculate on the prospects of demonstrating the deep rigidity of proper names. And so in this final section, I provide a brief discussion of this topic, although one that is both tentative and inconclusive.

It could be argued that our intuitions of the deep rigidity of proper names are not in fact as clear or firm as Salmon's example in the last passage quoted from him suggests. This argument proceeds by reconsidering some aspects of Kripke's argument for the existence of contingent *a priori* statements.

Kripke's argument, let us recall, focuses on the by now rather notorious example of the standard meter stick. He begins with the "definition" of the expression "one meter" "by stipulating that one meter is to be the length of [a stick] S at a fixed time t_0" (*NN*, p. 54). He then argues that someone who gives this definition is not using it "to *give the meaning* of what he called the 'meter,' but to *fix the reference*" (*NN*, p. 54). Hence,

> Even if this is the *only* standard of length that he uses, there is an intuitive difference between the phrase "one meter" and the phrase "the length of S at t_0." The first phrase is meant to designate rigidly a certain length in all possible worlds, which in the actual world happens to be the length of the stick S at t_0. On the other hand "the length of stick S at t_0" does not designate anything rigidly. In some counterfactual situations the stick might have

been longer and in some shorter, if various stresses and strains had been applied to it. So we can say of this stick, . . . that if heat of a given quantity had been applied to it, it would have expanded to such and such a length. (*NN*, p. 55)

So, it is *not* "a necessary truth that stick *S* is one meter long at time t_0" (*NN*, p. 54). Kripke then concludes by arguing that this truth is, nevertheless, *a priori*.

But is the expression "one meter," as defined in Kripke's example, deeply rigid?

As we have seen, in order to determine whether a term is deeply rigid, we must investigate what semantic properties with respect to other possible worlds it would have, *if they were the actual world*. Let's consider one of the counterfactual situations Kripke specifies in this passage, the one in which *S* had been heated before t_0, so that, as a result, in this situation the length of *S* is greater than its actual length. Let's call this counterfactual situation w', the actual length of *S* at t_0, *l*, and the length of *S* in w', *l'*. Now let's suppose that w' were the actual world, and try to see what we would say about "one meter" in this situation. It seems, to begin with, intuitively plausible that, even if w' were actual, we could still make exactly the same stipulation to define "one meter" as we do in the actual world. That is, we could still decide that "one meter" refers to the length of stick *S* at t_0, that is, *l'*. Now, what about the use of this expression? It is surely indisputable that, in the actual world, to use "one meter" correctly requires, roughly and among other things, that one take the actual length of *S* at t_0 to be the standard for determining whether something is one meter long. It follows, we might think, that, to use "one meter," if w' were actual, in the same way as we actually do use it, is to take the length of *S* at t_0, in w', to be the standard for determining whether something is one meter long. Certainly, as things actually are, we wouldn't take the standard of correctness for applying "one meter" to be set by the length *S* has in counterfactual circumstances. So, by parity of reasoning, if circumstances were different, we wouldn't take the standard of correctness for applying "one meter" to be set by the length of *S* in what would then be nonactual circumstances.

Now it seems to follow from these intuitions that, if w' were actual, and if in those circumstances we continue to use "one meter" in the same way as we actually do, then the expression "one meter" would refer to a different length than it actually does. The upshot of this, of course, is that "one meter" is *not* deeply rigid.[28] Moreover, we might generalize from this upshot and conclude that, whenever a rigid designator is introduced by a reference fixing stipulation using a definite description, its rigidity is superficial and not deep. But, according to Kripke, at least one class of *proper names* is introduced by such stipulations. Since these names are thus not deeply rigid, they are not semantically of different type from definite descriptions. Hence, it follows that the Semantic Difference Thesis cannot, *in general*, be established by demonstrating the deep rigidity of proper names.

This argument clearly depends on the claim that "one meter" has the *same meaning* in w' as it does in the actual world, as a result of the reference-fixing stipulation. And this claim is in turn based on the thought that in both worlds the reference-fixing stipulations are the same, and the correct use of the terms is the same. Looking at the case in this way, my intuition is indeed that there is no reason to think that the expression has different meanings in these two worlds. From this perspective, the argument shifts the burden of proof to proponents of deeply rigid proper names. They would have to demonstrate either that

- the reference-fixing stipulation or the use of "one meter" is not in fact identical in the worlds of the example,

or, that

- the identity of the stipulation or the use of this expression *fails* to entail that it means the same in the two worlds.

I don't think any stronger conclusion can be sustained, because it seems to me that a plausible argument can be constructed to meet this burden of proof.

Consider, to begin with, Salmon's example in passage about "Thales." How might an opponent of deeply rigid names respond to it? It seems difficult to gainsay Salmon's intuition that, if the possible world he specifies—call it w''—were actual, "Thales" would no longer refer to the person it refers to, given the actuality of the actual world. But we might try to show that Salmon's example *merely seems* to support the deep rigidity of "Thales." Why do we think that, if w' were actual, the expression "one meter" would refer to l'? Surely it is because our use of the term, if w' were actual, is determined, through the reference-fixing stipulation, by l', rather than by l. But, in Salmon's counterfactual situation, our use of the name "Thales" is stipulated to "bear no significant connection to" the hermit-philosopher, presumably because this person "bears no historical connection to us." Moreover, it would seem that Salmon is at the same time tacitly stipulating that if w'' were actual our use of "Thales" *would* bear the appropriate historical connection to the person to whom "Thales" refers given the actuality of the actual world. So, in order to be genuinely parallel to the case of "one meter," Salmon's case would have to be altered to be about a counterfactual situation, now w''', in which our use of "Thales" is historically appropriately related to the hermit-philosopher, rather than to "our" Thales.

I think we would all grant that, if w''' were actual, we would be using the name "Thales" to refer to the hermit-philosopher. However, and this points the way to shouldering the burden of proof generated by the first argument, it is also not at all clear that if w''' were actual, we would take "Thales" to be still *the same name* as "Thales" is in the actual world. So now, since our uses of "Thales" in w''' no longer count as uses of the same name, its having a different referent fails to constitute grounds against its deep rigidity.

What underlies this intuition can be perhaps made somewhat clearer in the following way. Suppose that neither Salmon's story nor the one just sketched is completely right; suppose instead that both the hermit-philosopher and "our" Thales were named "Thales." Then we would have a familiar puzzle about this name. Although we might, as in actual cases we sometimes do, say that these people have the same name, we would be reluctant to say that it then follows that one and the same expression, "Thales," is ambiguous. The familiar response to this conundrum is to say that the expression type "Thales" when used to refer to one of these people counts as a different name than when used to refer to the other. And our intuition is that if an expression type were to be used, as a name, but bearing the appropriate historical connection to a different individual than it actually does, then, supposing those circumstances were actual, the expression would count as a different name than it does, given the actuality of the actual world.

I end with two relatively safe observations about the dialectical engagement staged in this postscript. First, the issue on which the deep rigidity of proper names depends emerges as that of the criteria for the transworld individuation of linguistic expressions. Second, it also emerges that our intuitions about this individuation seem to be determined by the way in which we deal with the phenomenon of apparently multiple bearers of what appears to be a single proper name.[29]

NOTES

1. (Cambridge, Mass.: Harvard University Press, 1980) (hereafter "*NN*").

2. Rigid designators are singular referring expressions that designate the same object in all possible worlds (in which it exists); see *NN*, p. 48.

3. Whether for Frege himself the sense/reference distinction played the same philosophical role as it did for analytic philosophy in the heyday of linguistic analysis seems to me to be an open question. And the same should be said for logical empiricism and the analytic/synthetic and *a priori/a posteriori* distinctions. For these reasons, I would like to emphasize that I use the term "Fregean" to refer, not to Frege's own views, but to the views attributed to him by Kripke and others.

4. (Princeton, N.J.: Princeton University Press, 1981) (hereafter Salmon 1981). For other systematic expositions, see Gregory McCulloch, *The Game of the Name: Introducing Logic, Language, and Mind* (Oxford: Clarendon Press, 1989) and Stephen Neale, *Descriptions* (Cambridge, Mass.: MIT Press 1990).

5. This terminology is used in Salmon (1981, section 2.1).

6. The modal argument is, of course, not the only one Kripke deploys against Fregeanism in *Naming and Necessity*. Another argument, or set of arguments, presented in Lecture II of that book, relies on cognitive, or epistemological, considerations.

7. Gareth Evans, "Reference and Contingency," in Evans, *Collected Papers* (Oxford: Clarendon Press, 1979), pp. 178–213 (hereafter Evans 1979); Martin Davies and Lloyd Humberstone, "Two Notions of Necessity," *Philosophical Studies* 38 (1980): 1–30 (hereafter Davies and Humberstone 1980). Note that Evans's concern is with deep and superficial *contingency*.

8. Two prominent examples of this interpretation of Kripke's modal argument are Leonard Linsky, *Names and Descriptions* (Chicago: University of Chicago Press, 1977) (hereafter Linsky 1977); and Michael Dummett, *Frege: Philosophy of Language*, 2d ed. (London: Duckworth, 1981), Appendix of chapter 5 (hereafter cited as Dummett 1981).

9. Brian Loar, "The Semantics of Singular Terms," *Philosophical Studies* 30(1976): 353–377, and again the Appendix of chapter 5 of Dummett (1981). There are, in fact, a rather large number of objections to Kripke given in Dummett's Appendix; moreover, even the one mentioned in the text is quite a bit more complex than my ensuing presentation suggests.

10. One point about this "wide scope" description theory is worth noting, for it is often misunderstood. Kripke, in the Preface to *Naming and Necessity*, seems to take it to consist in the claim "that the doctrine of rigidity simply *is* the doctrine that natural language has a convention that a name, in the context of any sentence, should

be read with a large scope including all modal operators," and adds that this claim contains a "technical mistake" (*NN*, p. 11). It seems to me that this account of the wide scope theory is itself simply a mistake, although not a technical one.

To begin with, what exactly is the technical mistake that Kripke is alluding to? I take it that it is the claim that for a designator to be rigid is *the same thing as* its having wide scope with respect to modal operators. This claim is, indeed, a mistake. Consider the truth conditions of a sentence in which a singular term occurs with wide scope, say, $[t]\Box F(t)$. This is true just in case $F(x)$ is true, with respect to some possible world, of the referent *of t* in the actual world. That is, $F(x)$ is true with respect to that possible world when x is assigned the actual referent of t. But now, in spelling out these truth conditions, no mention has been made of what t refers to in any world other than the actual world. So, clearly, it does not follow from this account of truth conditions that t has the same referent in all possible worlds. So, adoption of a wide scope convention for a singular term does not result in that term's being rigid (given Kripke's definition of rigidity).

But the wide scope theory, at least in the version proposed by Dummett, is *not* committed to this mistaken claim. What the wide scope theory claims is that all the intuitive linguistic phenomena that Kripke explains by the rigidity of proper names can be equally well explained by the existence of a tacit convention that the definite descriptions which proper names abbreviate take wide scope in modal contexts. Thus the wide scope theory is, at bottom, a theory that *dispenses* with rigid designation; it is not a theory that gives any particular account of rigidity, and certainly not the explanation Kripke attributes to it.

I should add, finally, that none of this note is meant to be a defense of Dummett's wide scope theory. It is no more than an account of what the theory really is.

11. Note that the distinction between reference fixing and meaning giving, by itself, is not evidence for the claim that Kripke is arguing for a stronger claim than nonsynonymy. This distinction might be interpreted as the claim that reference fixing does not give a complete account of meaning. But, equally, it could be interpreted as the claim that reference fixing gives *no* account of meaning *at all*.

12. There are a number of other replies along essentially the same lines: see J. Hudson and M. Tye, "Proper Names and Definite Descriptions with Widest Possible Scope," *Analysis* 40 (1980): 63–64; A. D. Smith, "Rigidity and Scope," *Mind* 93 (1984): 177–193 (hereafter Smith 1984); and Salmon (1981), p. 26, n. 28. One interestingly different reply is M. J. More, "Rigidity and Scope," *Logique et Analyse* 23 (1980): 327–330.

13. Smith (1984), pp. 189–190. Smith takes his characterization to be the right explanation of the passages that I've been calling "Kripke's Intuition." But he does not ascribe it to Kripke.

14. This must be accepted by Kripke in Lecture I since he there grants that the description theory gives the right account of *reference fixing* for names.

15. Linsky, for instance, writes that "Kripke's 'modal arguments' come down to the claim that[,] since names are always rigid designators and descriptions are not, names are not abbreviated . . . descriptions" (Linsky 1977), p. 59. And, Salmon takes what he calls "the modal arguments" to be intended to establish that proper names are *nondescriptional*, where an expression is nondescriptional just in case (roughly) its denotation is *not* determined (with respect to a possible world and a time) as the unique individual satisfying a set of properties (in that world at that time). See Salmon (1981), pp. 14–29.

16. *The Interpretation of Frege's Philosophy* (London: Duckworth, 1981b), pp. 557–603.

17. I'm indebted to Jason Stanley for suggesting this interpretation of Dummett's criticisms to me.

18. See, for example, H. P. Grice, *Studies in the Way of Words* (Cambridge, Mass.: Harvard University Press, 1989).

19. This account is described in Robert Stalnaker, "Assertion," in *Syntax and Semantics*, vol. 9, *Pragmatics*, ed. P. Cole (New York: Academic Press, 1978), pp. 315–322, on pp. 315–316.

20. The idea of using the notion of actuality to give a Fregean account of names has been discussed by A. Plantinga in "The Boethian Compromise," *American Philosophical Quarterly* 15 (1978): 129–138. Since Plantinga's overriding concern is not with the conception of meaning underlying Kripke's critique of Frege and Russell, his account differs in details and consequences from the one sketched in this essay. It is interesting to note that, as Plantinga points out, something like this view of names can be traced at least as far back as Boethius.

21. In "Necessary Truth and *A Priori* Truth," *Mind* 97 (1988): 343–379 (hereafter Bostock 1988).

22. Davies and Humberstone (1980), p. 30.

23. I am, of course, assuming that if there is no solar system then the number zero belongs to the concept expressed by the predicate "ξ is a planet of the Solar System."

24. This sense of "couldn't" expresses one of the two notions of necessity in Davies and Humberstone (1980), p. 30.

25. It is of course somewhat more than a happy coincidence that the present terminology dovetails with Gareth Evans's distinction between deep and superficial contingency. Another connection with Evans's views will be pointed out below, in section VI. I do want to emphasize, however, that, unlike Evans's distinction, the superficiality of rigid designation is based on its failure to capture the conditionality of reference of actualized descriptions.

For another development of the notion of rigidity on the basis of two dimensions of modality see H. Deutsch, "On Direct Reference," in *Themes from Kaplan*, ed. J. Almog, J. Perry, and H. Wettstein (Oxford: Oxford University Press, 1989), pp. 167–195.

26. Since Salmon presents his account of "the semantic arguments" as distinct from the modal argument, I doubt he would think of it, in the way that I do, as a modal argument for the Semantic Difference Thesis. So the claim that Salmon's example can be used in this way should not be attributed to him.

27. Note that it doesn't follow from this last conclusion that the Thesis cannot be established by means other than modal ones.

28. The argument just given is, in essence, a variation of Evans's argument that Kripke's contingent a priori statements are only superficially contingent, not deeply so. It tries to establish the corresponding claim that the designator "one meter" is only superficially rigid, not deeply so.

29. I am grateful to Stephen Angle, Emily Carson, Juliet Floyd, Michael Glanzberg, Michael Hallett, Steven Horst, Steven Menn, Joseph Rouse, Sahotra Sarkar, and Jason Stanley for questions about, and comments on, earlier versions of this paper.

Although I have never discussed the issues of this paper with Professor Burton Dreben, and although he would most likely have disapproved of just about every sentence of it (because of its dalliance with the metaphysics of modality); still, each of these very sentences, along with all other philosophical writing I do, bear the influence of his teaching. And for that, I am, necessarily, thankful.

1979
Publication of Richard Rorty's
Philosophy and the Mirror of Nature

19

Epistemology and Science in the Image of Modern Philosophy: Rorty on Descartes and Locke

GARY HATFIELD

As with most human activities, philosophy has been shaped by its past. More importantly, it is, like other intellectual pursuits, deeply conditioned by its conception of its own history. For this reason, the history of philosophy is never far from the center of philosophical consciousness. Indeed, history is a prominent mode of philosophizing because of the self-knowledge it provides.[1] The more we know about how our questions have been shaped by their original motivations, the better we will be able to see new possibilities in the problem-space to which they belong—new ways of posing old questions and new questions to pose.

In the past two decades, the most widely discussed attempt to use history for philosophical ends has been Richard Rorty's *Philosophy and the Mirror of Nature*.[2] Rorty draws on a popular account of the rise of modern philosophy in order to diagnose the ills of contemporary philosophy. He traces those ills to the epistemologies of Descartes and Locke and the attempt to frame a general picture of the relation between mind and world that could secure the foundations of knowledge. His prescribed cure is to give up the foundational quest—which, in his view, amounts to abandoning the characteristic aims of modern philosophy. Philosophers should instead engage in the sort of edifying and hermeneutic conversation found in literary criticism and cultural studies.

Although I share Rorty's reservations about some styles of contemporary philosophy, I accept neither his diagnosis nor his remedy. Rorty's critical evaluation of epistemology in Descartes and Locke is vitiated by his failure to give sufficient attention to—or by his outright misunderstanding of—the relation between philosophy and science in the early modern period. One recurrent theme in recent work in the history of modern philosophy has been the central importance of the rise of modern science as a motivation for and topical object of early modern epistemology and metaphysics.[3] If one adopts a contextual approach to modern philosophy from Descartes to Kant, the interplay between science and philosophy is apparent: the new science was at the center of Descartes' and Locke's philosophical projects, and Newton's new science powerfully conditioned the work of Berkeley, Hume, and Kant. To ignore modern science in discussing epistemology and metaphysics in these authors is to risk missing the point of their work entirely—which is what Rorty has done, to the detriment of his diagnostic efforts.

Rorty's Evaluation of Early
Modern Philosophy

Rorty intended his book to change the way philosophy is done. His argument that a change was both possible and desirable rested on his account of the aetiology of some philosophical problems—primarily epistemological—that were prominent in the mid twentieth century. His strategy was to use history to show that the "epistemological turn" of modern philosophy was based upon contingent (read, "dispensable") doctrines advanced by Descartes and Locke. His target was a particular image of philosophy, according to which philosophers stand apart from the intellectual concerns that engage scientists, historians, and critics, pose abstract questions about the nature and possibility of knowledge, and then promote their answers as binding on the cognitive practices of all. He believed that an evaluation of early modern epistemology would expose the illegitimacy of philosophy so conceived.

According to Rorty's diagnostic analysis (*PMN*, pp. 3–4 and chap. 1, 3), the direction of philosophy for the last three centuries was set by two mistakes made long ago: first, the interposition of ideas as third things between the knower and the world and, second, the attempt to do epistemology by doing psychology. The first mistake resulted in the creation of the "problem of knowledge" as a general problem admitting of a general solution (*PMN*, chap. 1, especially pp. 29–30, 45–61). As the story goes, this creation was made possible when Descartes "invented the mind" by conflating sensations and beliefs, thereby launching the "theory of ideas." According to this theory, we are immediately aware only of ideas; this doctrine allegedly locks us into a "thought world" by interposing a "veil of ideas" between us and the world we would know. The task of philosophy accordingly becomes that of ascertaining the representational accuracy of ideas, since ideas mediate knowledge. In using the theory of ideas to pose a skeptical challenge he could not meet, Descartes set the problematic for subsequent metaphysics and epistemology.

This first mistake made possible the second. According to Rorty, Descartes's "invention of the mind" enabled his successors to stake out the mental as a special domain of investigation, and thereby to secure their roles as epistemological gatekeepers for the rest of intellectual culture. As Rorty tells it, Descartes and Locke could claim such authority because they (or at least Locke) believed themselves to have provided something analogous to a scientific account of the mind (*PMN*, ch. 3, especially pp. 137–148). Because they had given an account of the instrument of knowledge, they could assert authority over all fields in which the instrument was used, that is, over all fields of human knowledge taken generally. Rorty contends that this claim of authority rested on a confusion between causal explanation of the interactions among mental states and the quite different task of analyzing the grounds of justification for knowledge. According to Rorty, from the time of Locke through Kant down to the present, philosophy's claim to intellectual authority has rested on a confusion between psychology and epistemology. It has rested, that is to say, on the fallacy of "psychologism."[4]

Response to Rorty has been mixed. On the one hand, his skills as philosophical pathologist have been criticized on the grounds that his diagnosis is mistaken about both disease and aetiology. In particular, it has been objected that his conception of epistemology as preeminently concerned with absolute foundations is out of touch with recent work and that his history is incorrect.[5] On the other hand, many philosophers have found his diagnosis to be on the mark and his outline of history acceptable.[6] Indeed, his history was largely based on received opinion.

My evaluation of Rorty's use of history examines the two central mistakes he attributes to Descartes and Locke. A brief review of recent contextually based scholarship will suffice to counter Rorty's lively rendition of the tired "veil of ideas" story. It remains unclear whether this scholarship demands a reassessment of Rorty's general historical critique, for it has been observed that, even if the details of Rorty's history were unsatisfactory, his central point about the ill effects of the "epistemological turn" and the consequent conception of philosophy's task could stand.[7] In assessing Rorty's diagnostic use of history, we must look not only at the accuracy of his analysis of the theory of ideas, but also at the broader question of whether he has understood the use to which that theory was put within early modern philosophy. Such an investigation must appeal to the history of science, inasmuch as Descartes' and Locke's queries about the representational accuracy or inaccuracy of ideas were motivated by their interest in discerning the proper categories of explanation in natural science. Their motivation for bringing "representational accuracy" into this endeavor becomes clearer against the background of scholastic Aristotelian theories of perception. Further, Rorty's charge of psychologism must also be rejected, despite its long acceptance (especially for Locke).[8] Descartes and Locke were not guilty of psychologism, and their discussions of the mind's activities in knowing are not best conceived as anticipations of naturalistic psychology.

The Theory of Ideas and the "Theory of Knowledge"

The theory of ideas has long been cast as an especially pernicious early modern doctrine, because it is alleged to have inevitably spawned the problematic of the "veil of ideas." In Rorty's account, the veil of ideas arose when a mistaken model of knowledge led to a mistaken ontology. The mistaken model of knowledge is expressed in the "visual metaphor": to know something is to see it clearly with the mind's eye. The "thing" known in this way is no ordinary object, but a special entity, an "idea" or "representation," interposed as a third thing between perceiver and external world.[9] The same model, applied to intellectual apprehension, spirited a special domain of intellectual objects into existence, which mediate all knowledge while placing a screen between knower and known.[10] Consequently, philosophy became fixated on the "representational accuracy" of ideas in relation to the (inaccessible) external world.

Rorty's reconstruction of the development of modern philosophy not only traces the origin of doctrines deemed "bad" because of their legacy in recent philosophy; it also suggests that acceptance of these doctrines allowed for, and perhaps was motivated by, a claim to intellectual authority on the part of philosophers. But in fact Rorty devotes little attention to determining what might actually have motivated Descartes and Locke, who serve as the main villains in his story. These authors are portrayed as if they blindly (or strategically) adopted the visual metaphor, or accepted an unreasoned demand for certainty, independent of questions of genuine intellectual interest. In evaluating this portrayal, we need to pay heed both to the "bad" doctrines attributed to them—in order to determine whether they in fact held them—and to the motivation for the doctrines they did in fact hold.

Rorty's story, despite its erstwhile popularity, does not withstand scrutiny. Descartes and Locke were not ontologically committed to ideas as third things. Attention to the formal constraints of Descartes's ontology has revealed that he treated ideas not as separate or "third" things, but as "modes" (or modifications) of minds.[11] Minds do not stand in a perceptual relation to ideas as separate existents; rather, minds *have* ideas. But what does this mean? An interpretation according to which minds "have" ideas of shape in the way bodies have shapes—by having the property of being shaped—will not do. Minds have ideas of shape and color without being shaped and colored. Descartes treated ideas as modes of minds; he did not hypostatize ideas as third things. But this doctrine by itself does not explain how ideas as objects of awareness are related to the minds that have them.

Descartes sought to explain the relations among minds, ideas, and the objects of ideas by appealing to a distinction between "formal" and "objective" reality.[12] When ideas are considered formally, they just are modifications of thinking substance: minds have ideas (formally) just as bodies have shape. But ideas may also be considered "objectively," or in terms of their "content"; ideas have the peculiar characteristic that objects are found "in" them objectively or by way of representation. Descartes treats the content of an idea as the object of that idea, where "object" is understood as intentional object or object of thought. To think of an absent friend, and to perceive that friend by sight, both involve having a mental state with a certain content or intentional object (that of the friend). The mental content presents the absent or present friend without being identical with the friend. There is a distinction between ideas and the external objects they purport to (and sometimes do) represent, but ideas are not something in addition to acts of perception and their contents. Ideas reduce to perceivings. Locke's talk of ideas has been given a similar reading, despite his use of reifying language.[13] Locke's interpreters have persuasively argued that his talk of "perceiving ideas" typically means simply that one has a perception of a certain kind, rather than that one stands in a perceptual relation to an idea considered as a thing.[14] Lockean ideas are then seen as acts of perception with intentional objects or contents.[15]

The suggestion that ideas be treated as perceivings in Descartes and Locke provides a handle on the notion that ideas are representations: they are representations just insofar as, qua perceptions, they have one or another "content" or intentional object. The expansion of "perceiving an idea" into the fulsome "having a modification of the mind with a certain intentional object" does not render talk of ideas and their contents any less problematic than talk of intentional objects. But it does remove the location of problem pertaining to the representative function of ideas from the "theory of ideas"; for even the "anti-idealist" Reid was committed to the notion that perceptions have objects, and that these objects may or may not coincide with external objects.[16] Moreover, although this interpretation does not remove the possibility of posing skepticism in conjunction with the theory of ideas, it makes it clear that skepticism is not the special heritage of that theory. The skeptic's wedge can find entry at the moment perceivers are distinguished from things perceived; skepticism about the senses only requires admission of the conceptual possibility that a state of the perceiver such as might be taken to constitute perception of an external object can occur in the absence of said object. This minimal requirement shows that the skeptical problematic does not depend on the theory of ideas. Indeed, the fact that skepticism toward the senses does not depend upon the "veil of ideas" is evident from its convertibility to "brain in the vat" skepticism. This latter skeptical challenge certainly does not presuppose the theory of ideas; it may require no more than a willingness to engage in science fiction.[17]

These considerations challenge the historical accuracy of Rorty's discussion of ideas, but they don't neutralize his description of the ills of modern philosophy. Rorty's plaint against the theory of ideas only begins with the theory's putative ontology. According to his analysis, its most pernicious effect was to promulgate the image of the mind as a "mirror of nature." The conception of the mind as a representational medium led philosophers to concentrate, without good reason, on assessing the representational accuracy of various groups of ideas. The claim that there was a general problem about accuracy that could be solved by a philosophical cum scientific theory abetted the development of a corps of professional philosophers who asserted their authority to adjudicate all cognitive claims.

Rorty is right that Descartes and Locke sought to assess the representational accuracy of ideas. An evaluation of his diagnostic polemic requires us to understand why they did so. Both authors formulated the question of "representational accuracy" in terms of the "resemblance" (or lack thereof) between the contents of ideas and external objects. Their much-maligned talk of resemblance is rendered understandable (and so less obviously objectionable) when put in context.[18] The notion of resemblance in perception was prominent in the seventeenth century as an interpretation of the Aristotelian notion of a "similitude" between perceptual contents and external objects.[19] According to the Aristotelian theory of the senses, the cause of our experience of color is the quality of color per se, considered as a primitive property of objects which is transmitted as a "form without matter" through the medium and into the brain; the cause of our experience of shape (at least as regards the two-dimensional spatial arrangement in vision) is an actually shaped pattern in the brain, which arises from the spatial arrangement of points in the visual field.[20]

Descartes and Locke denied that the sensory ideas of what (Locke called) secondary qualities are "resemblances" of material objects, but they allowed that ideas of "primary qualities" might be resemblances. In so doing, they were intent on denying that ideas of color and other secondary qualities accurately represent the basic properties of material objects. These denials did not arise out of a detached fixation on representational accuracy; they arose in the context of a project to determine the basic properties that should be admitted into physical explanations.[21] In this context, to say that color as experienced does not "resemble" anything in objects is to say that a proper scientific account of color perception will explain color as a property of objects by appeal to other, more basic properties—in particular, to size, shape, position, and motion. To say that ideas of shape are accurate representations is to say that the things perceived as having shape typically do possess that property in a way in which they don't have color. The reality of shape as a property makes it a viable candidate for inclusion among the fundamental properties of matter, in terms of which other properties of bodies are to be explained. The question of representational accuracy becomes the question of deciding which, among those properties of bodies that we perceive or mentally represent, should be made basic in physics. Descartes' and Locke's discussions of the "resemblance" or "accuracy" of sensory ideas do not reveal their idle (or seditious) concern with abstract "problems of epistemology"; these discussions arose from a central intellectual concern of the early modern period, the quest for an adequate science of nature.

In fact, Rorty does allow that a concern to further the "New Science" was present in Descartes. But he totally misperceives Descartes's relation to the new science. According to Rorty, Descartes understood his "cultural role" in terms of the warfare between science and religion: he was fighting "to make the intellectual world safe for Copernicus and Galileo" (*PMN*, p. 131). There is a grain of truth in this characterization, inasmuch as Descartes was, I would argue, sensitive to the need to free the metaphysics of natural science from an overly close connection with rational theology.[22] But Rorty misses Descartes's central mission, which was to discover the fundamental principles of physics. In Rorty's view, Descartes was committed to the distinction between primary and secondary qualities merely as a by-product of his project to provide a "philosophical foundation" for Galilean mechanics (*PMN*, p. 65). He thus presents Descartes's interest in the new physics as an instance of philosophy's claim to professional authority through its role as foundation-provider—a claim legitimized by the notion that philosophy must certify the cognitive tenets of other disciplines. As Rorty would have it, Galileo developed a general physics of nature which was seized upon as a possible object of foundation-providing by a parasitic Descartes.

This picture is doubly in error. First, Galileo didn't conceive of either a general mechanistic physics or a general mathematical science of nature: as far as his writings reveal, he was working within the framework of various mathematical *sciences* of nature, a framework that departed from the Aristotelian "mixed mathematical sciences" only by adding *Two New Sciences* to their number.[23] Second, it was Descartes, not Galileo, who first conceived of a general mechanistic physics and of a general science of nature founded upon a few simple laws of motion. Descartes's metaphysical investigations, far from constituting a mere pretext for professional authority, were instrumental in his arriving at this vision of a general physics, a vision that later was to inspire Newton.[24] Indeed, prior to his "metaphysical turn" of 1629, Descartes (together with Isaac Beeckman) had conceived only of the possibility of various physico-mathematical sciences; it was in connection with his search for a metaphysical justification for excluding substantial forms from matter that he came to develop his vision of a general physics of nature.[25]

Rorty's discussion of representational accuracy, which treats Descartes and Locke as the originators of a common problematic, masks an interesting difference between the arguments they provided for adopting their respective lists of primary qualities. Descartes claimed to provide a criterion for determining the basic properties of matter that is independent of the senses: this independent source is the intellect itself, conceived as a faculty capable of operating without sensory materials. His "clear and distinct perception" that extension is the essence of matter is provided by the intellect operating independently of the senses and imagination; in this use, the intellect finds that phenomenal color does not pertain to matter. With respect to matter, the objects of intellectual perception are the geometrical and kinematic properties: size, shape, position, and motion.[26] Sensory properties such as color, which are not found among those that are clearly and distinctly perceived by the intellect, are not basic properties of matter; they are at best secondary properties that depend on the basic properties.

Descartes's justification of the distinction between primary and secondary qualities was not open to Locke.[27] Despite the passages in the *Essay* that read like Descartes's appeal to conceivability (especially II.viii.9), Locke was not in a position to accept "pure conceivings" as a source of knowledge about the external world. He rejected the notion that the intellect can grasp essences independently of the senses; this rejection is one implication of the doctrine that all knowledge comes through the senses.[28] The passages on conceivability are best read as reflections on what is conceivable in accordance with the most plausible scientific account of the operation of the senses.[29] And indeed, immediately subsequent to these passages, Locke invokes a mechanistic account of sensory stimulation, according to which colors in objects are surface textures that cause light to be reflected so as to produce certain effects in the nervous system, which in turn produce various sensations or sensory ideas.[30]

I will return to the contrast between Locke's and Descartes's attitudes toward the relation between philosophy and natural science. For the moment, I should acknowledge that according to my reading, a fundamental difference in their arguments pertains to the power of a particular cognitive faculty, the intellect. This fact would seem to confirm the second part of Rorty's condemnation of Locke and Descartes, according to which Descartes's invention of the mind paved the way for Locke's proposal that philosophy has a special authority over other cognitive enterprises because it provides a scientific account of the mechanics of the mind. Let us then turn to Rorty's charge that Locke attempted to ground his account of human cognition in a natural science of the mind and so committed the "naturalistic fallacy."

Epistemology and Psychology

Rorty charges Locke with "confusedly thinking that an analogue of Newton's particle mechanics for 'inner space' would somehow 'be of great advantage in directing our Thoughts in the search of other Things' and would somehow let us 'see, what Objects our Understandings were, or were not fitted to deal with'."[31] Significantly, his support for this charge comes not from specific citations to Locke's *Essay*, but from extensive quotations of the works of T. H. Green, Wilfrid Sellars, and Thomas Reid; the upshot of these quotations is that Locke confused the "logical space of reasons" with that of causes, offering a causal analysis where he should have been concerned with reasons and grounds.[32] Rorty is surely correct that Locke thought he was engaged in an investigation that would determine the domain and limits of human understanding, an investigation that took as its object the faculties and powers of the human mind. But I deny that Locke was, for all his talk of probing the depths of our mental faculties, engaged in anything resembling a "mechanics of the mind" or a natural scientific theory of human mental processes. Rather, he was pursuing an epistemological inquiry of the sort that Rorty's quoted sources accuse him of confusing with psychology, an inquiry that yielded results Rorty would have found philosophically interesting, had he understood them.

That it was Locke's *intention* to engage in what we should call epistemology and not to entertain causal hypotheses about the operations of the mind is clear from the opening of sections of the *Essay*. Indeed, Locke explicitly sets his project apart from the sort of natural scientific "physiological" investigation with which Rorty would saddle him (*PMN*, pp. 141, 145, 146). Thus, he remarks that "my *Purpose* being to enquire into the Original, Certainty, and Extent of humane Knowledge; together with the Grounds and Degrees of Belief, Opinion, and Assent; I shall not at present meddle with the Physical Consideration of the Mind; or trouble myself to examine, wherein its Essence consists, or by what Motion of our Spirits, or Alterations of our Bodies, we come to have any Sensation by our Organs, or any *Ideas* in our Understandings." Setting aside any concern with the physiology or ontology of nervous system and mind, Locke firmly channels his investigation toward epistemological topics: the ways we acquire our "Notions of Things," the "Measures of the Certainty of our Knowledge," and the "Grounds of those Perswasions" which are found among human beings, and "the *Bounds* between Opinion and Knowledge" (*Essay*, I.i.2–3). True to his word, Locke leaves physiological speculation out of the *Essay*.[33]

Locke was investigating the grounds of belief, which fits into the "logical space of reasons" rather than that of causes. But he also claimed to be investigating the "original" of human knowledge, and the "ways" we attain our notions of things. This wording, taken together with his analysis of mental contents into simple and complex ideas, his discussion of innateness, and his avowal of the "plain, historical method," may make it look as if Locke were actually pursuing psychological questions, despite his other statements. His distinction between simple and complex ideas may seem like the first step in analyzing mental processes into their constituent elements, a hallmark of the old association psychology. Innateness, too, became a much disputed topic in psychology. In this light, Locke's talk of a "plain, historical method" may well seem like a statement of his intention to settle such questions through natural scientific observation.

The discrepancy between Locke's stated epistemological aims and the seemingly psychological character of his results reveals something about our retrospective application of the category "psychological." Our perspective of hindsight may cause us to perceive earlier authors as pursuing psychological projects because of surface similarities between their projects and later, benchmark instances of psychological or natural-scientific approaches to mind. David Hume, David Hartley, and legions of later associationists claimed to resolve complex ideas into simple constituent elements as a first step in a naturalistic account of the mind's operations (modeled on Newtonian lines). The question of whether various visual abilities are innate or learned was an object of controversy in the optical literature of the seventeenth and eighteenth centuries. Thomas Reid and others brought clinical evidence to bear on this controversy, and it became an organizing theme in Hermann Helmholtz's psychology of spatial vision.[34] Be that as it may, Locke's concern with similar topics should not be classified as psychological. Briefly put, the analysis into simple and complex ideas should be seen, not as an attempt to discover the psychological primitives from which to construct a mechanics of the mind, but as part of an empiricist analysis of mental contents. Some contents, Locke argues, are primitive, "given" atomic sensory ideas, while others are derived by composition from these atomic contents. This mental atomism is not driven by an interest in psychogenesis, but by a desire to investigate the epistemological standing of simple and complex notions. Notoriously, Locke contends that complex notions, such as that of substance, are epistemically inferior to those based in simple ideas.[35]

Locke's discussion of innateness also should not be assimilated directly to later discussions of innateness in psychology. When we ask today whether a concept or an ability is innate or acquired, we are simply asking whether it is inborn or results from learning, and such questions are typically considered to be distinct from the epistemological concern with the justification of knowledge claims. Hence, to link innateness with justification would appear to confuse causal origin with evidential basis, for mere innateness doesn't provide epistemic warrant. But as matters were understood in the seventeenth century, there was a clear basis for supposing that innateness could provide epistemic credentials. Locke was intent on showing that there are no ideas or principles "stamped upon the Mind of Man" by "Nature" or by a deity (*Essay*, I.ii.1, see also I.iv.12–17). Those, like Descartes, who posited innate principles bestowed by God argued that their divine origin gave them an epistemic warranty. The fact that philosophers today reject divine origins for innate ideas does not render the content of the earlier claims psychological, as if by default; even if rejected as false, the claims remain assertions about a cognitive guarantee. And so, though Locke did indeed ask whether certain ideas and principles are innate, his discussion should not be assimilated to later psychological discussions, for the stakes were different.

Finally, there is Locke's appeal to the plain, historical method. This phrase should be seen as asserting no more than Locke's commitment to reflecting on human cognitive practices in investigating the scope and limits of human knowledge. And unless one believes that philosophy can draw on a priori sources of knowledge, any conceptual investigation must rely upon experience as its source of instances and examples. If every appeal to human experience were to be counted as an appeal to empirical natural science, then every epistemologist and philosopher of mind who attended to examples drawn from actual practice could be charged with psychologism. Such a broad-scope charge loses its bite.

The considerations just canvassed could explain Rorty's misperception of Locke as engaged in a psychologistic project. Underlying this misperception is a deeper failure to distinguish adequately between early modern *mentalism* and nineteenth-century *psychologism*. Many philosophers in the seventeenth and eighteenth centuries undertook an investigation of the mind's powers and capacities as part of an investigation of the grounds of knowledge.[36] As we have seen in the case of Locke, such investigations may have been "empirical" in the sense that they appealed to experience, but they need not for that reason be seen as proto-natural-scientific investigations of mind. This point stands out especially clearly in the case of rationalistic philosophers such as Descartes and Spinoza, who believed that the mind possesses a truth-discerning power capable of recognizing substantive metaphysical truths and has access to ideas that reveal such truths independently of sensory experience. They each marked off a certain class of thoughts as privileged, which Descartes labeled "clear and distinct perception" and Spinoza called "the third kind of knowledge."[37] The privileged status of these thoughts was explained by divine warranty or by an appeal to the irreducible trustworthiness of the intellect. For these philosophers, investigation of the mind—the knowing power—was a reasonable means for evaluating the possibility and limits of knowledge.

The mentalism evident in the positions of Descartes, Spinoza, and Locke is in sharp contrast with the recognizably naturalistic and natural scientific approach to the mind that took root and grew in the eighteenth century. The natural scientific approach to the mind of authors such as David Hartley and Johann Lossius was characterized by a rejection of the framework of bare truth-perceiving powers, and the attempt to replace it with a description and explanation of mental phenomena that appealed only to a naturalistic vocabulary modeled after Newton's physics: a vocabulary of simple entities (ideas) characterized by a few dimensions of variation (say, quality and intensity) and governed by laws of interaction defined over those dimensions (typically, laws of association).[38] This sort of associationist psychology was one stream feeding the growth of self-described natural-scientific psychologies in the nineteenth century.[39] Perhaps because such genuine attempts at a natural science of the mind were ignored by Rorty, he failed to see how they differed from the projects of Descartes, Locke, and others.

Rorty's portrayal of Locke as simply a link in the chain from Descartes' "invention of the mind" to Kant's alleged assertion of philosophy's cultural hegemony caused him not only to miss the epistemological character of Locke's investigation; it also diverted him from some interesting results of Locke's *Essay* pertaining to the theory of knowledge itself. Locke granted what he termed "intuitive and demonstrative knowledge" the highest degree of certainty, and he explained this certainty in terms of the perception of agreement or disagreement between ideas;[40] to this extent, he embraced the model of the mind's eye examining the contents of ideas in order to determine their agreement or disagreement.[41] But Locke did not restrict his account of knowledge to this model. In addition to "intuitive" and "demonstrative" knowledge, he countenanced "knowledge of real existence"; and, at least in the case of ordinary objects, he did not think that this sort of knowledge could achieve the certainty of intuition. Locke denied that the intuitive certainty with which we perceive relations between ideas extends to the cognition of particular bodies.[42]

In point of fact, Rorty concedes that Locke did not retain—or as he puts it "could not hold on to"—Cartesian certainty, but he seems comfortable in assuming that Locke still supports his case. In treating this fact about Locke as a minor deviation from an alleged early modern fixation on foundational certainty, Rorty fails to appreciate one of the central thrusts of Locke's investigation of knowledge, which was to broaden the basis for rational assent beyond the model of intuitive and demonstrative certainty found in mathematics.[43] This aspect of Locke's epistemology, though relatively neglected, has been receiving attention of late.[44] A thorough reading of Book IV of the *Essay* reveals that Locke's admission of "sensitive knowledge" into the domain of knowledge, even though it lacks the certainty of intuition and demonstration, is not an embarrassing lapse in his program, but one step on the way to a second, more radical aim: that of legitimizing merely probable belief as worthy of rational assent.

Locke proposed that propositions possessing even less certainty than his "sensitive knowledge"—propositions which therefore do not meet the minimal standard for being called "knowledge"—nonetheless may be warranted for rational belief. In Chapters 14 through 17 of Book IV, he develops an account of propositions that may be affirmed through what he termed "judgment." Locke defines judgment as follows: "The Faculty, which God has given Man to supply the want of clear and certain Knowledge in Cases where that cannot be had, is *Judgment*: whereby the Mind takes its *Ideas* to agree, or disagree; or which is the same, any Proposition to be true, or false, without perceiving a demonstrative evidence in the Proofs" (*Essay*, IV.xiv.3). In surrounding passages, he distinguishes between a standard of certainty appropriate to knowledge and one that is appropriate for what he terms "probability." He goes on to give an account of probability, which is not to be understood as a mathematical calculus of chances but as a doctrine of judgmental approbation or epistemic probity. Probable propositions typically affirm what has been observed to be true always or "for the most part" (*Essay*, IV.xiv.1, IV.xvi.6–7). In Chapters 16 and 17, Locke works out the degrees of assent that may be accorded probable propositions, which range from assurance and confidence, through belief, conjecture, and guess, to doubt, wavering, distrust, disbelief, and others. Any doubt that Locke intends these to be gradations of *rational* assent is put to rest early in Chapter 17, where he includes within the purview of reason arguments whose discursive steps are each based on judgments of probability.[45]

If we now read the account of probable assent found in Book IV back into the discussions of real and nominal essences in Book III, and into the investigations of the idea of substance, and of adequate and inadequate ideas in Book II, a consistent picture begins to emerge. These earlier discussions do not simply reflect Locke's unfulfilled longing for rationalistic insight into real essences and necessary connections. Rather, they show Locke mounting his case that such longings will never be sated with respect to knowledge of substances or of the mechanical constitution of bodies. By contrast with Descartes, the privilege that Locke grants to the primary qualities in physical explanation will rest on weaker grounds than those found in mathematics. But that does not mean that the mechanical philosophy, as a systematic approach to nature, should be abandoned. Rather, it will rest on the Boylean grounds of what can be "probably said," or said with probity, in favor of the mechanical philosophy.[46] Locke concedes that a proper (demonstrative) *science* of body is beyond our means, and then proceeds to *replace* the ideal of a science of body with the conception of a system of probable doctrine. In brief, Locke denies metaphysics to make room for empirically grounded rational belief. Far from being trapped behind the mirrorlike surface of his glassy essence, Locke was prepared to explore conceptions of rational assent that break through the glassy surface of the intuitively evident to include a range of probable judgments regarding matters of fact.

According to this reading, Locke is a philosopher whose hermeneutic conversation Rorty might have enjoyed. In focusing so exclusively on his own diagnostic story, Rorty failed to appreciate Locke philosophically and so to use Locke's example to full advantage. But Rorty's own detached imperialism regarding Locke should come as no surprise. Examination of the full range of conceptions surrounding the theory of ideas and the relation of epistemology to psychology has demonstrated the extent to which the traditional story recounted by Rorty relies on a misconception of the history of modern philosophy. Much of this misconception arose from Rorty's failure to appreciate the relations between early modern philosophy and early modern science, including both the science of physics and the nascent science of psychology. Rorty failed to appreciate Descartes's genuine contribution to the vision of a unified science of nature. And he misconstrued Locke's epistemological project as psychological, thereby missing much of interest in Locke's analyses of knowledge and warranted belief.

Conclusion

Rorty's reliance on a distorted account of seventeenth- and eighteenth-century philosophy led him into serious error. Yet I doubt that he would be much distressed by this judgment. In fact, in his book he dismisses various revisionist readings of Descartes and Locke with the remark that if the traditional story is wrong, say, in singling out Descartes as the originator of the "Cartesian problematic," one must simply look elsewhere for its origin (*PMN*, pp. 49–50, note 19). For Rorty is certain that the problematic exists, and he is right.

Interestingly, Rorty was perfectly correct in his claim that he could ignore historical accuracy and still mount an effective attack on his quarry. But that is only because, despite promising a general diagnosis of all of modern philosophy, Rorty's effective target is an image of philosophy of recent vintage. According to this image, philosophy is detached and imperialistic, dictatorial and culturally alienated. I hope to have shown that this image could not have been drawn from a careful analysis of the historical relation between philosophy and other intellectual pursuits during the modern period. It is most likely a product of Rorty's personal acquaintance with a variant of the "professionalized philosophy" that arose after the wave of disciplinary specialization at the end of the nineteenth century. In any event, criticism of the alleged assumptions of Descartes, Locke, and others was a vehicle available to Rorty precisely because some contemporary epistemologists and philosophers of mind had assimilated or usurped the works of these authors for their own purposes. And so it was that during the middle decades of the twentieth century, a kind of legendary, even mythic image of various modern philosophers took hold. Descartes, for example, came to be known primarily through the use of the First Meditation as the standard introduction to veil-of-ideas skepticism and the problem of knowledge. Anyone who has taught the *Meditations* to graduate students schooled in the image of Descartes as an unmotivated skeptic knows the staying power of that image, notwithstanding the availability of historically and philosophically sophisticated treatments of the method of doubt.[47]

But is this objection to Rorty's version of history anything more than a quibble about historical accuracy? Rorty himself locates the "professional turn" of philosophy late in the nineteenth century. Perhaps he needn't care about history prior to this time. He knows that the "bad" philosophy he wants to attack has existed, and he knows that it has used the texts of Descartes and others to define its problematic. Indeed, Rorty's turn to history most likely was motivated by the admirable aim of stamping out the sort of philosopher who imperiously seeks to judge the ongoing intellectual projects of others without truly engaging those projects. I think his evidence for the existence of such boorish philosophers came not from his analysis of history, but from his acquaintance with colleagues who were rude at parties. Rorty no doubt has observed colleagues who *were* downright rude at parties—who listen to the conversation of nonphilosophers for a moment or two, and then jump in as know-it-alls when speaking on subjects in which their listeners are experts, but about which they are virtually unversed. Rorty probably believes such colleagues behave so badly because of their mistaken conception of the power of a priori analyses of the conditions for knowledge, or something of the like. He wants them to be more polite, perhaps so that he won't have to share the collective blame for their behavior. In Rorty's book of etiquette, philosophers should join into conversation not with the authority of judge or umpire, nor even with the voice of a full participant, but only as a kind of gossip. They should listen to the edifying words of others and then pass them on as opportunity arises. Philosophers should seek to facilitate the flow of ideas while at the same time acknowledging that they really have nothing to add; they should behave like caterer's assistants, who present the edifying morsels prepared by master chefs from other disciplines and are themselves allowed to contribute only to the arrangement of the items on their trays.

In offering this unappealing picture of philosophy and its future, Rorty has fallen prey, I contend, to his own distorted history. Indeed, his acontextual reading of the theory of ideas is an instance of the very trend that he laments. He has stood back from the philosophical tradition in an attempt to unmask errors latent in certain philosophical projects and positions. He effectively treats these projects and positions as timeless—as divorced from context or motive. Because he refused to engage his named quarries historically, he failed to benefit from history as he might have, and in two ways.

First, if he had really wanted to counter foundationalism in epistemology, he should have looked to the recent history of foundationalism. He would have found, I think, that twentieth-century foundationalism arose in the context of a particular philosophical program that took shape in the first two decades of the century. When the project of constructing the world out of incorrigibly-known sense-data failed, the continued philosophical fascination with sense-data came to appear futile and detached from questions of much interest. Rorty is thus right that a concern with representational accuracy is not of great interest in itself, any more than questions of historical accuracy are of interest in themselves. But he failed to diagnose the recent conditions leading to the fruitlessness of such questions.

The consequences of this first failure are compounded by a second. Rorty failed to appreciate a type of lesson that we philosophers can take from our history. He allows that we can gain self-understanding through history, by discovering how the problems we take seriously came to be regarded as problems (my criticism of him here is simply that he failed to make any interesting discoveries). But beyond self-knowledge, history can teach us about philosophy itself; it can stir us from musings on recent problematics by offering models of philosophical activity that was culturally engaged rather than imperiously detached. Attention to the great philosophers of the seventeenth and eighteenth centuries does not reveal Rorty's intellectual autocrats, but participants involved in producing and shaping the intellectual projects of their time. Attention to nineteenth-century discussions—especially by the neo-Kantians—of the relations among philosophy, other humanistic disciplines, and the natural sciences could offer additional models of the kind of outward-looking, humanistic stance Rorty might appreciate.[48] In these cases, genuine contact with the history of philosophy offers materials for redirecting philosophy now.

A theme of Rorty's book is that in the old days, beginning with Descartes, philosophers claimed a special authority for their craft. It is true that Descartes, as a metaphysician, claimed a certain authority over physics. But it was not the authority to bring a successful, ongoing research program before the independent tribunal of philosophy; rather, it was the "authority" to present an argument in favor of a new physics to replace the old. And although it is true that Descartes provided an account of the mind as knower in order to achieve a metaphysical perspective from which to argue for the new physics, not all philosophers adopted his strategy. Locke didn't. Like Descartes, he claimed no more authority than that which the reader can find in his arguments; but unlike Descartes, he attempted no "metaperspective" to undergird his foundational descriptions of the new science. We may reject Descartes's attempt at a "metaperspective," but not because he was detached and imperious. We will do so because we don't think his sort of metaphysical "metaperspective" is attainable; that is, we will do so because we have a substantive disagreement with his position.

When we examine the projects of authors such as Descartes and Locke in their contexts, they do not at all resemble Rorty's image of those philosophers as detached yet imperious, an image that does fit some epistemologists and philosophers of science of the twentieth century. Like more recent epistemologists, Descartes and Locke did claim to be investigating claims to knowledge and, more specifically, to be discerning the limits of human knowledge in general. But they did not attempt to investigate these limits in the abstract or with respect to mere "puzzle" problems, say, about tables and chairs, as epistemologists earlier in our century did, characteristically and regrettably. They undertook investigations of the scope and limits of human knowledge in the face of pressing and consequential questions about the existence and character of a deity, the nature of the soul, and the possibility and characteristics of a science of nature. These were live questions of great intellectual significance, and the work done by Descartes, Locke, and their successors in responding to them constitutes a permanent achievement of Western philosophy.

Rorty has suggested that philosophy should give up epistemology in favor of cultural criticism. But epistemologically oriented philosophy in the early modern period was already engaged in cultural criticism, both speculative and reactive. Philosophers in that period were onto the hot topics of their age; moreover, they proposed as well as disposed. Rorty's depressing image of contemporary philosophy notwithstanding, this kind of philosophy is alive and well. In reflections on social and political institutions and thought, in investigations of the concepts and methods of such sciences as physics, biology, psychology, and economics, in explorations of questions of interpretation in art and literature, and in analyses of the historical constitution of philosophy itself (and its relation to other dimensions of culture), philosophers continue a tradition of criticism and speculation at the horizons of thought.[49] Some of this reflection might be characterized as epistemology and even as the investigation of the foundations of knowledge. But here, an investigation of "foundations" is an inquiry into what is "basic" or "central," not into the "incorrigibly grounded." So we can hope that epistemology will continue to investigate foundations, in the spirit of Descartes's and Locke's engagement with live endeavors to know, even if we reject those authors' particular doctrines. More generally, we can admire the critically participatory philosophy that flourishes in our time.

My final assessment of the story told in *Philosophy and the Mirror of Nature* finds that the tarnished image of philosophy presented there is an optical artifact, a refraction from the local disputes of philosophers in the mid twentieth century. In presenting this image, Rorty hoped to act not merely as the pathologist, but also as the undertaker of philosophy in the modern tradition. I have sought to construct a counterimage to Rorty's unappealing portrait of this tradition by drawing on contextual readings of two modern philosophical projects. In doing so, I have endeavored to provide an historicist twist on the wise saying that philosophy buries its undertakers.

NOTES

An earlier version of this chapter was presented as an inaugural lecture in the Austin-Hempel Lecture Series at Dalhousie University, Nova Scotia, June 1991.

1. As Michael Ayers has argued, philosophers need to consider history because they need to understand the origin of the problems they continue to take seriously: see his "Analytical Philosophy and the History of Philosophy," in *Philosophy and Its*

Past, ed. Michael Ayers, Jonathan Reé, and Adam Westoby (Hassocks, U.K.: Harvester Press, 1978) (hereafter Ayers, Reé, and Westoby 1978), pp. 42–66, and his "The End of Metaphysics and the Historiography of Philosophy," in *Philosophy, Its History and Historiography*, ed. A. J. Holland (Dordrecht: Reidel, 1985), pp. 27–40 (hereafter Holland 1985). See also the editors' introduction and the chapters by Charles Taylor and Alasdair MacIntyre in *Philosophy in History*, ed. Richard Rorty, J. B. Schneewind, and Quentin Skinner (Cambridge: Cambridge University Press, 1984), (hereafter Rorty, Schneewind and Skinner 1984).

2. Richard Rorty, *Philosophy and the Mirror of Nature* (Princeton: Princeton University Press, 1979); hereafter *PMN*. Stephen Toulmin, *Cosmopolis: The Hidden Agenda of Modernity* (Chicago: University of Chicago Press, 1992) (hereafter Toulmin 1992), is a more recent attempt at diagnosing the modern mistake.

3. For example, Michael Friedman, *Kant and the Exact Sciences* (Cambridge, Mass.: Harvard University Press, 1992); Daniel Garber, *Descartes' Metaphysical Science* (Chicago: University of Chicago Press, 1992); and my "Metaphysics and the New Science" (hereafter Hatfield 1990a), in *Reappraisals of the Scientific Revolution*, ed. D. Lindberg and R. Westman (Cambridge: Cambridge University Press, 1990) (hereafter Lindberg and Westman 1990), pp. 93–166. In Toulmin's hands, the central role of science is equated with an obsession with formal validity in the case of Descartes, which is intended to explain much that is bad in subsequent philosophy (1992, pp. 20, 31, 72, 80, 177–178); on Descartes' lack of concern with formality, see Ian Hacking, "Proof and Eternal Truths: Descartes and Leibniz," in S. Gaukroger, ed., *Descartes: Philosophy, Mathematics and Physics* (Sussex: Harvester Press, 1980) pp. 169–180 (hereafter Hacking 1980).

4. Rorty does not use the term "psychologism" to name the fallacy he describes (rather, he compares it to the "naturalistic fallacy" in ethics, *PMN*, p. 141), but his charge fits the classical meaning of that term, according to which psychologism is the attempt to base epistemology on psychology. J. E. Erdmann apparently introduced the term with this meaning in his *Grundriss der Geschichte der Philosophie*, 2d ed., 2 vols. (Berlin, 1870), vol. 2, p. 636; see also J. Dewey, "Psychologism," in J. M. Baldwin, ed., *Dictionary of Philosophy and Psychology*, 3 vols. (New York: Macmillan, 1901–1905), vol. 2, p. 382.

5. Rorty's portrayal of contemporary epistemology is rejected by Alvin Goldman and Fred Dretske in their respective reviews of *PMN*: Goldman, "Review of *Philosophy and the Mirror of Nature*," *The Philosophical Review* 90 (1981): 424–429; and Dretske, "Review of *Philosophy and the Mirror of Nature*," *International Studies in Philosophy* 14 (1982): 96–98. S. Rosen in his "Review of *Philosophy and the Mirror of Nature*," *Review of Metaphysics* 33 (1980): 799–802, endorses Rorty's attack on contemporary philosophy and has only minor quibbles with the history; John W. Yolton argues that Rorty's account of the theory of ideas is seriously mistaken in his *Perceptual Acquaintance from Descartes to Reid* (Minneapolis: University of Minnesota Press, 1984) (hereafter Yolton 1984), pp. 5, 58–73, 222, and in his "Mirrors and Veils, Thoughts and Things: The Epistemological Problematic" (hereafter Yolton 1990), in *Reading Rorty*, ed. Alan R. Malachowski (Oxford: Basil Blackwell, 1990) (hereafter Malachowski 1990), pp. 58–73.

6. See Robert Bernstein, "Philosophy in the Conversation of Mankind," *Review of Metaphysics* 33 (1980): 743–775; Quentin Skinner, "Review of *Philosophy and the Mirror of Nature*," *New York Review of Books* 28 (19 March 1981): 46; Alasdair MacIntyre, "Review of *Philosophy and the Mirror of Nature*," *London Review of Books* 2 (5–18 June 1980): 15–16; Jennifer Hornsby, "Descartes, Rorty and the Mind-Body Fiction" (in Malachowski 1990, pp. 41–57) finds Rorty's conclusions "congenial" and accepts his "command of the history," but seeks to fill out the picture of Descartes so as to mitigate the grounds for Rorty's rejection of the philosophy of mind.

7. See the reviews of *PMN* by Robert Schwartz, "Review of *Philosophy and the Mirror of Nature*," *Journal of Philosophy* 80 (1983): 51–67, especially p. 64; and

Victoria Choy, "Review of *Philosophy and the Mirror of Nature*," *Synthese* 52 (1982): 515–541, especially p. 524.

8. Locke as pursuing psychology: Yolton (1984), pp. 16, 39, 105; Mary Hesse, "Epistemology without Foundations," in Holland (1985), pp. 49–68, p. 51. Rorty reviews earlier instances of the charge in T. H. Green and Wilfrid Sellars, *PMN*, pp. 140–143. Others see the naturalistic or psychological aspects of Locke's discussion of knowledge as a virtue: R. S. Woolhouse, *Locke* (Brighton, U.K.: Harvester Press, 1983), pp. 186–187; and E. J. Lowe, *Locke on Human Understanding* (London: Routledge, 1995), chapter 8. On Locke on knowledge, compare Michael Ayers, *Locke: Epistemology and Ontology*, 2 vols. (London: Routledge, 1991) (hereafter Ayers 1991), vol. 1, part 2.

9. The notion that the perceiver is placed at one remove from the external world did not need to rely on a mere analogy with vision in order to gain its plausibility, for it could also rely upon extant theories of vision as formulated in early modern optical writings. Typical seventeenth-century theories of sensory perception analyzed the perceptual process as a causal chain starting with external objects and ending with a mental sensation or idea. The earlier portions of the chain comprised the mechanical transmission of a sensory impression to the common sense or sensorium (a structure in the brain), where the impression caused its mental effect. But if the mind is locked away inside the brain, how could it be aware of objects at some distance from it? Yolton (1984) describes the contribution of theories of the senses to the doctrine of the veil of perception, while at the same time questioning the standard (and Rortyan) reading of Descartes and Locke, observing that this reading has been unduly influenced by Thomas Reid.

10. On the postulation of ideas as "entities modeled on retinal images," which are treated as "distinct particulars," see Rorty, *PMN*, pp. 30 and 45. Rorty doesn't keep straight whether ideas are distinct from the minds that have them, or are modes of mind (see p. 58), and doesn't seem to think it matters (*PMN*, pp. 49–50, n. 19).

11. Descartes' clearest statement of the ontology of ideas as modes of mind occurs in the *Principles*, part 1, articles 53, 56, 65 (in *The Philosophical Writings of Descartes*, trans. John Cottingham, Robert Stoothoff, and Dugald Murdoch, 3 vols. [Cambridge: Cambridge University Press, 1984–1985], volume 1).

12. See Brian E. O'Neil, *Epistemological Direct Realism in Descartes' Philosophy* (Albuquerque: University of New Mexico Press, 1974), p. 71 and chapter 4; Yolton (1984), pp. 34–38; and Yolton (1990), pp. 63–65; Steven Nadler, *Arnauld and the Cartesian Philosophy of Ideas* (Princeton: Princeton University Press, 1989), section 15. An extensive and rewarding discussion of objective reality and representational content in Descartes occurs in Wilfred Sellars, "Berkeley and Descartes: Reflections on the Theory of Ideas," in *Studies in Perception: Interrelations in the History and Philosophy of Science*, ed. Peter Machamer and Robert Turnbull (Columbus: Ohio State University Press, 1978), pp. 259–311.

13. See for example, Locke's *An Essay concerning Human Understanding*, ed. Peter H. Nidditch (Oxford: Oxford University Press, 1975) (hereafter cited as *Essay*), II.iii.1, where Locke speaks of ideas as things that "make their approaches to our minds," are conducted by the nerves "to their audience in the brain, the mind's presence room," and are perceived inasmuch as they "bring themselves into view." See also *Essay* II.vii.10 and II.x.14.

14. J. L. Mackie, *Problems from Locke* (Oxford: Clarendon Press, 1976), pp. 37–51, and Douglas Greenlee, "Locke's Ideas of 'Idea,'" in *Locke on Human Understanding*, ed. I. C. Tipton (Oxford: Oxford University Press, 1977), pp. 41–54 (including a discussion by Gunnar Aspelin, with Greenlee's reply).

15. Yolton (1984), chapters. 5–6; Vere Chappell, "Locke's Theory of Ideas," in *The Cambridge Companion to Locke*, ed. Vere Chappell (Cambridge: Cambridge University Press, 1994), pp. 26–55; Ayers (1991), vol. 1, part 1, discusses both "intentional object" and "blank effect" interpretations of Locke on ideas (according to the latter interpretation, ideas are mental effects having their own arbitrary character and are

used by the mind as signs). He favors treating ideas as images, having intentionality appropriate to imagistic representations.

16. Thomas Reid, *Works*, ed. W. Hamilton, 8th ed., 2 vols. (Edinburgh, 1895), vol. 1, pp. 135–137, 292b.

17. Even Berkeley's skepticism regarding material substance, while invoking veil-of-ideas arguments, is ultimately based on the comparative intelligibility of alternative causal chains for the production of sensory ideas; he argues that *matter* cannot coherently be ascribed the causal role, whereas God, an infinite active spirit, can; see *Treatise on the Principles of Philosophy* (Dublin, 1710) part 1, sections 25–30.

18. On resemblance theories in the history of philosophy, see Richard A. Watson, *Representational Ideas from Plato to Churchland* (Boston: Dordrecht, 1995).

19. On scholastic theories, see my "Cognitive Faculties," in *Cambridge History of Seventeenth Century Philosophy*, ed. Michael Ayers and Daniel Garber (Cambridge: Cambridge University Press, 1997), pp. 952–1001 (hereafter Hatfield 1997). Descartes, *Optics*, part 4, explicitly mentions the theory of the schools; in the *Essay*, II.viii.13, Locke introduces resemblance by denying it for the secondary qualities, without mentioning the Aristotelians, though their theory is in the background.

20. On Aristotelian theories as elaborated within the optical tradition, see Gary Hatfield and William Epstein, "The Sensory Core and the Medieval Foundations of Early Modern Perceptual Theory," *Isis* 70 (1979): 363–384; on Aristotelian theories more generally, see Alison Simmons, "Explaining Sense Perception: A Scholastic Challenge," *Philosophical Studies* 73 (1994): 257–275.

21. Peter Alexander, *Ideas, Qualities and Corpuscles: Locke and Boyle on the External World* (Cambridge: Cambridge University Press, 1985), chapters 4–6; Steven Nadler, *Malebranche and Ideas* (New York: Oxford University Press, 1992), pp. 15–18; and Hatfield (1990a), pp. 112–114.

22. Gary Hatfield, "Reason, Nature, and God in Descartes," in *Essays on the Philosophy and Science of René Descartes*, ed. Stephen Voss (New York: Oxford University Press, 1993), pp. 259–287, (hereafter Hatfield, 1993), pp. 259–287. By contrast, Toulmin (1992, p. 105) portrays Descartes as attempting to achieve theological dividends from natural philosophical work.

23. See my "Was the Scientific Revolution Really a Revolution in Science?" in *Tradition, Transmission, Transformation*, ed. Jamil Ragep and Sally Ragep (Leiden: Brill, 1996), pp. 489–525 (hereafter Hatfield 1996).

24. Newton made a close study of Descartes' *Principles* during the 1660s. It is true that the style of Newton's general mathematical physics of nature is closer to that of Galileo than to that of Descartes, for Descartes' mechanistic physics was not mathematical in the Newtonian manner: see Hatfield (1990a), pp. 114–115; and on Newton's relation to Galileo's style of mathematical science, I. Bernard Cohen, *The Newtonian Revolution: With Illustrations of the Transformation of Scientific Ideas* (Cambridge: Cambridge University Press, 1980), pp. 132–133. Nonetheless, Descartes was, as far as I know, the first to envision a general physics based on a few laws of motion.

25. On this account of Descartes' development, see Hatfield "Science, Certainty, and Descartes," in *PSA 1988*, vol. 2 (East Lansing, Mich.: Philosophy of Science Association, 1989) (hereafter Hatfield 1989), pp. 249–262; and Hatfield (1993).

26. See my "The Senses and the Fleshless Eye: The Meditations as Cognitive Exercises," in *Essays on Descartes' Meditations*, ed. Amélie Rorty (Berkeley: University of California Press, 1986), pp. 45–79 (hereafter Hatfield 1986), section IV.

27. Gary Hatfield, *The Natural and the Normative: Theories of Spatial Perception from Kant to Helmholtz* (Cambridge, Mass.: MIT Press, 1990) (hereafter Hatfield 1990b), pp. 56–57; the argument is summarized in the present paragraph together with the preceding one.

28. Locke says that the "materials of reason and knowledge" derive from sensation and reflection (*Essay*, II.i.2); since ideas of reflection have as their source the

operation of the mind in connection with sensory ideas, the latter are necessary if the mind is to have any "materials" whatsoever. Locke's denial of innate ideas and his discussion of the operation of the rational faculties (II.xi) are further evidence of his views that the mind's powers are always directed toward sense-derived ideas and that reason is unable to provide its own content.

29. In this connection, see *Essay*, IV.iii.16, which Peter Alexander discusses in his "Boyle and Locke on Primary and Secondary Qualities," *Ratio* 16 (1974): 51–67. On the role of the corpuscular hypothesis in Locke's distinction, see also E. M. Curley, "Locke, Boyle, and the Distinction between Primary and Secondary Qualities," *The Philosophical Review* 81 (1972): 438–464.

30. In the *Essay*, II.viii.11–14, Locke presents a mechanistic account of the operation of bodies upon the senses; in II.viii.15, he draws the resemblance thesis from this discussion.

31. *PMN*, p. 137; the second and third of the phrases placed in quotations by Rorty are from Locke's *Essay*, I.i.1 and the Epistle to the Reader.

32. *PMN*, pp. 140–147; Locke's *Essay* is quoted only once in these pages, to the effect that the mind must be aware of any "imprint" made upon it.

33. At II.viii.12, Locke conjectures about the manner in which insensible corpuscles act upon the senses; at II.xxi.73, he remarks that the details of the causal processes producing ideas are beyond the scope of his investigation, "my present purpose being only to enquire into the Knowledge the Mind has of Things, by those *Ideas*, and Appearances, which *God* has fitted it to receive from them, and how the Mind comes by that Knowledge; rather than into their Causes, or manner of Production."

34. On the associationist tradition, Reid, and Helmholtz, see Hatfield (1990b) chapters 2, 4, and 5. On Helmholtz and the innateness controversy, see R. Steven Turner, *In the Eye's Mind: Vision and the Helmholtz-Hering Controversy* (Princeton: Princeton University Press, 1994), chapters 5 and 9.

35. See Ayers (1991), vol. 1, part 1.

36. See Hatfield, "The Workings of the Intellect: Mind and Psychology," in *Logic and the Workings of the Mind*, ed. Patricia Easton (Atascadero, Calif.: North American Kant Society Publications, Ridgeview, 1997), pp. 21–45.

37. Benedict de Spinoza, *Ethics*, in Spinoza, *Collected Works*, ed. and trans. Edwin Curley (Princeton: Princeton University Press, 1985), vol. 1, pp. 477–478.

38. David Hartley, *Observations on Man, His Frame, His Duty, and His Expectations*, 2 vols. (London: 1749), part 1, proposition 12, corollary 10, and proposition 86 (vol. 1, pp. 79, 324–334), gives an associationist account of assent. So does Johann Lossius, *Physische Ursachen des Wahren* (Gotha, 1775), on which see Hatfield (1990b), pp. 71–72.

39. The old picture according to which natural-scientific psychology arose suddenly in the latter part of the nineteenth century is not viable. Work on a better understanding is underway: see Scheerer, "Psychologie," in Joachem Ritter, ed., *Historisches Wörterbuch der Philosophie* (Basel: Schwabe, 1971), vol. 7, columns 1599–1653; Fernando Vidal, "Psychology in the Eighteenth Century," *History of the Human Sciences* 6 (1993): 89–119; Gary Hatfield, "Remaking the Science of Mind: Psychology as a Natural Science," in Christopher Fox, Roy Porter, and Robert Wokler, eds., *Inventing Human Science* (Berkeley: University of California Press, 1995), pp. 184–231 (hereafter Hatfield 1995a).

40. Locke, *Essay*, IV.ii.1–2; Locke allowed that intuitive and demonstrative certainty could be extended beyond mathematics (IV.ii.9), even to "visible connections" among the primary qualities of things, for example, that figure presupposes extension (IV.iii.14). See also Hume's *A Treatise of Human Nature*, 2d ed., ed. P. H. Nidditch (New York: Oxford University Press, 1978), in which he argued that intuitive certainty extends to arithmetic and algebra, but not geometry (I.iii.1); in his *Enquiry Concerning Human Understanding* (in Hume, *Enquiries Concerning Human Understand-*

ing and Concerning the Principles of Morals, 3d ed., ed. P. H. Nidditch [New York: Oxford University Press, 1975]), he allowed that arithmetic, algebra, and geometry all admit of intuitive and demonstrative certainty (section IV, part 1).

41. Again, one might observe that, though Locke thereby fits Rorty's story inasmuch as he embraces a visual metaphor for knowledge, his doing so was not the product of an aimless pursuit of epistemological authority; instead, this model of knowledge was guided by the then-current best understanding of the basis for geometrical demonstration, at a time when geometry rightly served as the paradigm of certain knowledge, on which see Lisa Shabel, "Kant on the 'Symbolic Construction' of Mathematical Concepts," *Studies in History and Philosophy of Science* 29 (1998): 589–621.

42. Locke contrasts intuitive and demonstrative knowledge of relations among ideas with knowledge of "the particular existence of finite beings without us" (IV.ii.14); Locke's talk of relations is cast in terms of the perception of "agreement or disagreement" among ideas (IV.ii.1).

43. This broadening is illustrated in Locke's response to skepticism. He regarded the standards of certainty demanded by both Descartes and the skeptic as too high, and so he dismisses skepticism with regard to the senses, remarking that the certainty we have of things existing in nature, "when we have *the testimony of our Senses* for it, is not only *as great* as our frame can attain to, but *as our Condition needs*" (IV.xi.9; see also IV.ii.14; iv.4; xi.3).

44. Douglas Lane Patey, *Probability and Literary Form: Philosophic Theory and Literary Practice in the Augustan Age* (Cambridge: Cambridge University Press, 1984); Ernan McMullin, "Conceptions of Science in the Scientific Revolution," in Lindberg and Westman (1990), pp. 27–92, pp. 75–76; and Ayers (1991), vol. 1, part 2.

45. *Essay*, IV.17.2: "For as Reason perceives the necessary, and indubitable connexion of all the Proofs one to another, in each step of any Demonstration that produces Knowledge: so it likewise perceives the probable connexion of all the Proofs one to another, in every step of a Discourse, to which it will think Assent due. This is the lowest degree of that, which can be truly called Reason." The contrast found here and between "Demonstration that produces Knowledge" and "the probable connexion . . . to which [Reason] will think Assent due" may perhaps be understood by recalling that "knowledge" may have had the sense of the Latin *scientia*, which meant a systematic or demonstrative body of well-founded doctrine. Although Locke's probable judgments may be systematic, they lack the certainty of demonstration, and so fail to reach the level of knowledge or science. This reading squares with Locke's denial that humans can achieve a science of body, or a scientific physics, while affirming that the mechanical hypothesis should be adopted. Indeed, at IV.16.6, Locke accords the "highest degree of probability," but not the status of knowledge proper, to "all the stated Constitutions and Properties of Bodies, and the regular proceedings of Causes and Effects in the ordinary course of Nature."

46. Robert Boyle, "About the Excellency and Grounds of the Mechanical Philosophy," in Boyle, *Selected Philosophical Papers*, ed. M. A. Stewart (Manchester: Manchester University Press, 1979), pp. 138–154, p. 138. Locke was fully acquainted with Boyle and his corpuscularianism as he composed the *Essay* (over a period of some twenty years); by contrast, Newton's *Philosophiae naturalis principia mathematica* (London, 1687) appeared only three years before the *Essay* was published.

47. See, for instance, Margaret Wilson, *Descartes* (London: Routledge, 1978); E. M. Curley, *Descartes against the Skeptics* (Cambridge, Mass.: Harvard University Press, 1978); and Hatfield (1993).

48. Heinrich Rickert, *Limits of Concept Formation in the Natural Sciences: A Logical Introduction to the Historical Sciences,* abridged edition, ed. and trans. Guy Oakes (Cambridge: Cambridge University Press, 1986), introduction; Wilhelm Dilthey, *Pattern and Meaning in History: Thoughts on History and Society*, ed. and trans. H. P. Rickman (New York: Harper & Row, 1962), chapter 4. On Dilthey, see Rudolf A. Makkreel,

Dilthey: Philosopher of the Human Studies, 3d ed. (Princeton, New Jersey: Princeton University Press, 1992).

49. Examples include John Rawls, *A Theory of Justice* (Cambridge, Mass.: Harvard University Press, 1971); Michael Friedman, *Foundations of Space-Time Theories: Relativistic Physics and Philosophy of Science* (Princeton, New Jersey: Princeton University Press, 1983); Arthur Fine, *The Shaky Game: Einstein, the Quantum Theory* (Chicago: University of Chicago Press, 1986); Philip Kitcher, *Vaulting Ambition: Sociobiology and the Quest for Human Nature* (Cambridge, Mass.: MIT Press, 1985); Elliott Sober, *Reconstructing the Past: Parsimony, Evolution, and Inference* (Cambridge, Mass.: MIT Press, 1988); Dan Lloyd, *Simple Minds* (Cambridge, Mass.: MIT Press, 1989); Martin Carrier and Jurgen Mittelstrass, *Mind, Brain, Behavior: The Mind-Body Problem and the Philosophy of Psychology* (Berlin and New York: Walter de Gruyter, 1991); Daniel Hausman, *Essays on Philosophy and Economic Methodology* (Cambridge: Cambridge University Press, 1992); and Ayers, Reé, and Westoby (1978). See also Hatfield, "Philosophy of Psychology as Philosophy of Science," in *PSA 1994*, ed. David Hull, Mickey Forbes, and Richard Burian (East Lansing, Mich.: Philosophy of Science Association, 1995), vol. 2, pp. 19–23.

20

Formal Losses

GERALD E. SACKS

This short note touches on the losses incurred by formalization, but first a more pressing matter. Over the last thirty years, Burton Dreben has courteously but firmly refused to hear me out on any philosophical matter, so I am pleased to have this chance at long last to corner him at some length, brief though it be. Most likely he believes my interest in philosophy to be genuine but my attitude suspect or worse. The truth is: I am serious; and I mean what I say. Nonetheless, he has consistently refused to humor me on what I call the PH problem, a puzzle never far from my thoughts. The problem in short is, Is it possible to distinguish between a serious philosophical paper (P) and a humorous takeoff of the same (H)? Is there a test, effective or not, that detects the difference?

My position on the PH problem is definite and will be developed elsewhere.[1] For now I ask only that the reader reflect for a moment on whether or not the PH problem is serious. It should be clear that it is serious by virtue of the question it raises. With his fondness for self-reference, Dreben should be willing to accept this last point, or at least to take it seriously, which is all I ask.

There is all too soon an urge to formalize. Is there so much to fear from the indefinite? By the time we understand what it is we wish to formalize, the need to do so may well have passed. Formalize in haste, repent at leisure. Restraint can be helpful, even fruitful, if only in a negative sense. Must we be any clearer than we have to be? The more definite a mathematical notion becomes, the greater the likelihood of loss. Of course we want to be able to derive consequences of the notion, but we risk proving more about less. Why not move slowly toward the realm of the definite? Stalling may be the best tack even for a mathematician, even for a mathematical logician.

Proofs of a satisfactory sort can be given despite the absence of formal definitions. For example, conclusions about computable functions can be reached without a formal definition of computable function. An unsatisfactory example, however, is this: there exists a noncomputable function. For proof, recall Cantor's argument that the number of functions is uncountable. And yet, the number of computable functions, whatever they are, is countable.

Now a better proof relies on Gödel's diagonal argument. And for that some attempt has to be made at the definition of a computable function. So let us say, f is computable if and only if there exists a Pascal program P such that, for any natural number x, P with input x has output f(x). This last, formal as it sounds, is not formal at all. Yet it is enough for proofs in recursion theory.

Hartley Rogers greatly clarified computability theory by first presenting the fundamentals in an intuitive fashion and then proceeding to derive consequences in a more rigorous manner.[2] S. C. Kleene, the father of computability theory, objected, saying that Rogers did not prove anything; but Rogers' style of argument won out.

But computable functions are the last thing I want to talk about. I prefer to say something about the losses that attend first-order logic, the formal system presented in logic courses, thought by some to be the formalization of mathematical reasoning, by others of correct reasoning. No attack on first-order logic is intended. No one respects it more than I. First-order logic is an extraordinary artifact, a scientific achievement of the first water. Inside mathematics it has nontrivial applications *via* compactness and other model theoretic ideas, and outside it has the power to attack important questions. When is substitution of terms legal? Why is "$2 + 2 = 4$" true? What is meant by saying "'$2 + 2 = 4$' is true"?

But the more immersed I am in first-order logic, the more aware I am that something has been lost. I am not saying something is missing. First-order logic holds all it possibly can. There does not appear to be a way of adding anything to it without breaking it. And yet . . .

It is safer to allude to what is lost rather than to try to say precisely what is missing.

At the start many species of reasoning and argument are considered. But during the journey toward formalization some are thrown overboard. So the arrival at first-order logic is marred by a sense of loss. I feel it. And I see, of course, that I would stop feeling so if only I could forget what has been thrown away. Of course in the absence of memory, there is no experience of loss.

I will try to say more elsewhere about loss and sense of loss. The serious question here is whether my words are P or H.[3]

Postscript

For Burt on his seventieth birthday:

> Nothing begun
> Under the sun
> Reaches an end
> Lacking a friend.
> Glimpses of gold
> Not to be sold.

NOTES

1. Gerald Sacks, "The PH Problem with Applications, " in preparation.
2. Hartley Rogers, Jr., *The Theory of Recursive Functions and Effective Computability* (New York: McGraw-Hill, 1967).
3. The author is grateful for many helpful suggestions from two persons who insist on anonymity.

Afterword

A Reminiscence

JOHN RAWLS

Our Times at Harvard

Our times at Harvard and our lives before going there were quite different. Burton Dreben entered Harvard as a student in the summer term of 1945, as the war was ending, just after his graduation from the Boston Latin School. He came from a Jewish family in Chelsea, and his entering Harvard was an anxious moment for him. By contrast, I had been raised as an Episcopalian, graduating in 1939 from Kent School, a high-church school run by the Order of the Holy Cross. I entered Princeton that fall, the September Hitler invaded Poland. After I returned from the war, I went back to Princeton to get my Ph.D. degree. I taught first at Cornell and then at MIT. Burt, having been a Fulbright Fellow at Magdalen College, Oxford (1950–1951), a Junior Fellow in the Society of Fellows at Harvard (1952–1955), and an Instructor in the Graduate Faculty at the University of Chicago (1955–1956), became a member of the Harvard faculty in 1956 with only his undergraduate Summa B.A. degree and his Harvard M.A.—a distinction of which he was certainly not ashamed. We met at Harvard in the spring of 1957, where I gave the first draft of my paper "Justice as Fairness." Both of us received all of our formal education at the university we first entered and have remained rather proud of this: Burt is a "Harvard man" and I am a "Princeton man."

While I've often thought of myself as a displaced "Princeton man," and been amused by Harvard's self-congratulatory sense of importance, at the same time Harvard has been extremely good for me, and I don't regret a minute of my time here. But the administration of Harvard has never been the central focus for me, as it was for many years for Burt. Burt gave much energy during his best years to the service of Harvard, something I did not do except for the obligatory time I put in as department chair. He served from 1956–1960 on a central committee of the faculty, the Committee on Educational Policy (CEP), which was chaired by McGeorge Bundy, then Dean of the Faculty. Later, during the troubles over the student 2–S deferment, the student strike in April and May of 1969, and for several years afterward, Burt was heavily involved in university affairs, often as

Parliamentarian of the Faculty, a highly visible and important position demanding quick judgment and absolute confidence, both of which he had in abundance.
Burt was promoted to Dean of the Graduate School of Arts and Sciences, 1973–
1976, and then became Chair of the Society of Fellows, 1976–1989, and a Special Assistant to the Dean of the Faculty of Arts and Sciences, 1977–1989. The
latter position involved organizing approximately twenty *ad hoc* committees each
year, each composed of recognized, impartial, and wise experts, to assist the Presi-
dent of the University and the Dean in making tenure appointments. A man of
remarkable erudition and fairness, Burt was as well suited as anyone can be for
this difficult and controversial task.[1]

Lecturing Styles

There are a number of well-known kinds of lecturers. One was exemplified by the
great Cambridge physicist, P. A. M. Dirac, as illustrated in a biographical article
about the physicist Hans Bethe in *The New Yorker* some time ago. Bethe wanted
to leave Germany after Hitler came to power, and Sommerfeld, recognizing his
enormous gifts, gladly recommended him for a position at Cambridge. Bethe had
of course studied Dirac's great book on quantum mechanics, *The Principles of
Quantum Mechanics* (1930). While listening to Dirac's first lecture, he thought to
himself, "This sounds very familiar." Going up to the podium afterward, he saw
that Dirac had the page proofs and was reading from them. Bethe asked, "Don't
you think it would be better to amplify your text or to tackle other problems?"
Dirac replied, "I thought for a long time about the best way to express these matters and I think I put it right. I don't see the point of changing now."

A second kind of lecturer is exemplified by Joseph Schumpeter, the great econo-
mist. Coming into class, he would ask a student in the front row where he had
stopped last time. The student might say, "You were talking about Schmoller and
Roscher and the German Historical School, but for only a few minutes." Schumpeter
would pace up and down a moment or two and then start speaking. Pulling a pad
from his pocket, he took notes on his own lecture. He put these notes in his pocket
and later stuffed them in burlap bags in his office or study at home. Eventually,
they were sorted out and helped to form the basis of what he was writing.[2]

The philosopher of law Ronald Dworkin exemplifies yet a third kind. His lecturing style flows smoothly and effortlessly, and he never relies on notes. Once,
when he was about to deliver the Tanner lectures at Stanford, he suddenly found
himself without the written remarks he had prepared; someone had mistakenly
taken them away from the place near the podium where Dworkin had left them.
Remarkably, it seemed to make no difference. For three lectures, Dworkin proceeded calmly on. When his written remarks were returned to him at the end—
the person having realized the mistake—Dworkin said, "Thanks awfully, I had
wondered where they were. It's nice to have a record."[3]

Dreben offers a fourth lecturing style. He brings a suitcase full—it seems—of
xeroxes of numerous texts from Frege to Quine, with Russell, Wittgenstein, Carnap,
and Tarski, and many others in between. These xeroxes also include copies of

significant reviews, letters from autobiographies, and other records. He could answer invitations to lecture with: "Have xeroxes, will talk." And talk he does, often with a characteristic combination of fun and bravado. He will say, for example, that many misread Tarski's theory of truth, not understanding that Tarski is doing mathematics, proving a theorem in mathematical logic, and that Tarski's result on the theory of truth has nothing to do with philosophy. Tarski's result cannot be seen as a philosophical theory of truth, for there is no such thing. Philosophy doesn't contain such theories. Rather, it seeks understanding, and that is different.

Often in his lectures—or rather in his performances giving readings from and commentary on his own xeroxes—Dreben is extremely emphatic, sometimes even shouting as he refers to those he is attacking for their woefully misinformed and mistaken misreadings. When I was at Princeton as a student, there was a well-known mathematician in probability theory named William Feller whose proofs were frequently not very rigorous and sometimes even fallacious, though the theorem to be proved was almost always correct and often original. If he was questioned and the infelicities of the proof pointed out, his voice would rise to a loud volume in reply. Mark Kac, a fellow mathematician, referred to Feller's way of responding as "proof by intimidation."[4]

Likewise, Dreben may seem to want to intimidate, and it takes a lot of confidence for someone in the audience to challenge what he says. But if someone does, it becomes evident how wide and deep is Dreben's knowledge of the texts. What's more, he respects anyone who raises a challenge, welcoming questions. He is glad to be pressed. Actually, he would think his lecture a failure if no one were to question and challenge him.

I hesitate to mention my own lectures since I don't really have a lecturing style at all. My way was to write and rewrite my thoughts by hand; in recent years, it's been by typing at a computer. Until I started the physical movements of writing, I had only the vaguest idea of what I was going to say. My thoughts would grow and take shape only as I wrote them out and corrected them.[5] I also needed a written text to fall back on when I got confused in what I was saying, as I sometimes did. Voltaire is reputed to have said, "When he who hears doesn't know what he who speaks means, and when he who speaks doesn't know what he himself means—that is philosophy." I didn't want to give an exhibition of this claim, so I always had a complete prepared text and revised and added to it year by year. Eventually, my course lectures became longer than I could give in the allotted time, so I had them copied and made available to the class, and I would go over only the more important points. Yet, unlike Dirac, I never thought I got it right. Instead, I am reminded of a story about John Marin, the great American painter. He is well-known for his semi-abstract expressionist watercolor seascapes, many of which portray the islands around Stonington, Maine, where he went in the 1920s. A visitor to Stonington once asked one of the lobstermen there whether he had known Marin. The lobsterman replied: "Eeah, eeah, we all knew him. He went out painting in his little boat day after day, week after week, summer after summer. And you know, poor fellah, he tried so hard, but he never did get it right."[6]

The Sacks-Dreben Slugfest

On December 9, 1993, Burt had what was advertised as a no-holds barred debate at Boston University with Gerald Sacks, the well-known logician, about "The Fundamental Notions of Logic," as the announcement read. Close friends for many years, Sacks and Dreben had always differed over the nature of logic and philosophy, as Sacks noted in the prefaces of two of his books.[7] Hilary Putnam was to be the moderator. Beforehand, Sacks said to Dreben that he viewed Burt's influence on students about these matters as very bad. The debate, he predicted, could have one of three outcomes. Either Burt wouldn't speak to him for life; or he wouldn't speak to him for ten years; or he wouldn't speak to him for twenty years. After that it wouldn't matter anyway. Burt found this quite amusing and looked forward to the debate with relish. I asked him what he was going to say. He replied that he had no idea. Sacks would go first and Burt couldn't foresee what was coming. He would have to ad lib his performance.

Actually, the debate was quite friendly, with each cheerfully showing respect to the other. Sacks began by asking, How is it possible that Dreben—who knows so much about Frege, Wittgenstein, and Gödel, not to mention Carnap, Tarski, and Quine—can be so wrong about what is fundamental for logic? Sacks's answer was that Dreben lacks mathematical experience, which is the most satisfying thing in life.

Sacks then distinguished between syntax and structure, saying that what is important for logic is structure, not syntax. What we do in studying mathematics is learn about various structures. Sacks defined a structure as: (a) a universe (a nonempty set); and (b) relations among members of the set. Different kinds of groups are different kinds of structures; and so are algebras, vector spaces, topological spaces, and the rest. In learning mathematics, we become aware of and experience structures. That is what mathematical experience is. Finite sets are not enough, so axioms are used to define the structures. Axioms are used by Bourbaki, who regards mathematics as about structures. Hilbert and his followers used axioms, for example of geometry, to express structures. Gödel sometimes used syntactical language to prove a theorem about a structure. Sacks granted that syntax is simpler and that it therefore makes sense that we begin teaching logic with syntax. But, he argued, syntax is not what is fundamental. Sacks argued that Dreben thinks that syntax is fundamental because it is simple, and that this is simply wrong.

Dreben based his reply in part on his detailed studies of the history of modern logic.[8] He admitted that Sacks had greater mathematical experience than he, but countered that he had greater philosophical experience than Sacks. The fundamental problem of logic, as Dreben views it, is understanding. If one begins with model theory or mathematical structures as a way to understand logic, to gain clarity about it, then one has changed the subject of logic as Frege and Russell understood it. According to Dreben, we cannot use structures to get clear about language, to understand the basic logical notions. Sacks' view leads us to think there is something metaphysical about language and logic, that there is something deep about them to be discovered by uncovering structures. But this thought leads to mystification.

It came out in further discussion that Dreben's point was that no precise mathematical result can help us to understand any basic philosophical problem. This is because no mathematical argument can force us to accept a particular interpretation of a basic intuitive notion such as that of logical validity. This does *not* mean that, once we accept a mathematical argument, we can't go on to do various illuminating things with it. But we cannot begin with mathematical structures, relying on them to replace the basic logical notions. Whether we accept a mathematical structure as helping us to understand an intuitive logical notion like validity is up to us. It depends on our judgment upon critical reflection. It is one of Quine's great achievements, said Dreben, to have shown how little we can say about basic logical notions. I myself would interpret Dreben's view as similar to Kant's, who viewed reason as self-originating, self-authenticating, and alone competent to settle questions about its own authority.

On Logic and Philosophy

After his retirement from Harvard in 1990, Burt continued teaching, joining the faculty at Boston University in 1991. He told me that in one of his classes at Boston University the question once came up of what Wittgenstein was attacking in Frege. In response, Burt pointed to Frege's statement that it is a defect of natural languages that not every grammatically well-formed sentence is true or false. (Quine agrees with that statement.) Burt, like Wittgenstein, views this as a potentially misleading metaphysical statement. It is the basis of much metaphysics, of much of Quine, and certainly of Frege. It seems to suggest that we can attain an ideal language in which no grammatically well-formed sentence is meaningless, empty of content. Burt said that nothing that Wittgenstein says, or that he (Burt) says, is a decisive argument against this view. There is no way to present knock-down arguments against it, despite what much of philosophical practice suggests. Nevertheless, Wittgenstein and Burt try to show, by examining our practice and our use of logic and mathematics, that language need not be viewed in this way.

Burt often says that there are no theories in philosophy. This goes together with his calling metaphysics "nonsense," as he often does.[9] But what does Burt mean by saying this? One thing he means is that philosophical arguments rest on premises, or taking certain things as given—on "data," as he often says. One of Burt's favorite examples is the long dispute between Carnap and Quine about analyticity.[10] Carnap takes as his "data" that analytic statements are true in virtue of the meanings of their terms, and he presents a theory of meaning to support this claim. The statements Carnap takes to be paradigmatically analytic, however, Quine thinks are simply obvious. Anyone can see that they are true. For Quine, there is no particular kind of way in which they are true. They are simply true. Neither philosopher can convince the other of the premises, or the "data," of his argument.

Burt would not, of course, deny the plain fact that philosophers make many complicated arguments. But he thinks that at bottom there are no arguments one philosopher can use to convince another of a metaphysical point. At the basic level, philosophers simply rely on and appeal to different "data." It is a standoff with no resolution by *argument*. Burt has said that Quine is a metaphysician, a metaphysician of science. By that he means that Quine doesn't argue for physicalism, or scientific realism. He assumes it and works out his view from there.[11]

Another thing Burt means in saying that there are no theories in philosophy is that none of the so-called theories philosophers argue about is really a theory at all. There is no theory of truth, no theory of meaning, no theory of knowledge, no theory of perception, and the rest, despite centuries of philosophers discussing these things. Here the Sacks-Dreben slugfest is a typical example. As I have said, Burt agrees with Sacks that the theory of quantification is a theory, but he stresses that it is a theory in logic and mathematics. It is not philosophy, which has to do with understanding and should lead to that. For Burt, Tarski's so-called theory of truth is likewise not a philosophical theory, but rather belongs to logic and mathematics. Philosophy seeks to understand truth, but Tarski's theorem correctly seen as a theorem in logic can't help us to understand truth itself. The same, Burt thinks, can be seen in all other alleged theories. Recall here that great logicians and physicists have often worked much in philosophy and even theology. Newton and Gödel are familiar examples. Burt would not deny that their studies of these things may have inspired and motivated their scientific work. Nevertheless, he thinks their great achievements in mathematics are no help in achieving the very different aims of philosophy.

The crucial questions in understanding Burt's view are: What is philosophical understanding? What is it the understanding of? How does understanding differ from having a theory? How do we know understanding when we have it? And why is it worth having? I wonder how I can give answers to these questions in my work in moral and political philosophy, whose aims Burt encourages and supports.[12] Sometimes Burt indicates that my normative moral and political inquiries do not belong to philosophy proper. Yet this raises the question, Why not? And what counts as philosophy?

In February 1995, Burt spoke at a conference at Boston University in honor of Kurt Gödel.[13] Burt emphasized that Gödel was a great genius of logic. His great theorems mark an era in the subject and complement Frege's great achievements in modern logic beginning with his *Begriffsschrift* (1879). Yet, Burt claimed, Gödel was not a great philosopher. Indeed, his metaphysics and epistemology, his interest in Leibniz and Kant, all of it came to nothing. (I recall that all the volumes of Leibniz' collected works I looked at in the library while a student at Princeton had been signed out many times by Gödel.) This is not to deny, Burt said, that suggestions and modes of approach to his technical logical results may have been inspired by his intense interest in philosophy. Whether this is so or not can only be shown by careful examination of the texts. But even if Gödel's results were so inspired, this doesn't tend to support his philosophy.

Burt emphasized that Newton was much the same. He was perhaps the greatest mathematician and physicist who ever lived. It is amazing to think that, even as an old man, after his appointment at the Mint, and not having done mathematical work for years, Newton still felt challenged by scientific problems. He heard of the brachistochrone problem posed by Bernoulli. Eight months had been allowed to find the solution, but Newton wouldn't go to bed until he solved it that night![14] We must recognize, Burt thinks, that Newton was a much greater genius than Locke. But we must also recognize that Locke was a great philosopher and Newton was not. Locke was also a great man and Newton was not. Though Burt considers Wittgenstein one of the greatest philosophers, he thinks that he also was not a great or even a good man. Burt believes that his moral and religious ideas, his concern with his guilt and personal salvation, were indeed rather childish, and that Wittgenstein didn't know and didn't understand the religion of the prophets. What counted for them was the order of righteousness, justice, and humanity in the public world of the people and in their customs and practices of daily life. Sacrifices, prayers, and hymns cannot substitute for these.[15] Lincoln was not a philosopher, but Burt would say he was a great man. A truly great statesman in a position of enormous power, he seems to me (and Burt would agree), possibly the only person in such a position of whom even the first part of Acton's well-known aphorism fails to hold: "Power tends to corrupt and absolute power corrupts absolutely."[16] Lincoln understood the religion of the prophets, as the Second Inaugural makes clear, and Burt has said that a grove of oaks would have been a better memorial to Lincoln than the classical temple he was to have.

As Burt's Tutee

I can't think of any of my basic ideas that I got from Burt, yet I am convinced that replying to his criticisms always enormously improved the clarity and the organization of my thought—so much so that I often question whether my sense that I haven't gotten some basic ideas from him is delusionary on my part. I shouldn't be surprised if it is. I don't profess to understand our relationship, and I doubt that I ever shall. So how to be fair to him and to say how his work as tutor was really done?

Burt is six years younger than I, and he has never been my teacher in the normal sense of the word. Yet he often refers to me (in my presence) as his "tutee." I don't take offense at this; indeed, I am lucky to have him as a "tutor" when he has the time for it. Burt has given much of his time to other of his colleagues also. He has worked closely with Quine and Putnam (for years with Quine, much less often with Putnam), but I don't think he would refer to them in their presence as his "tutees." He has known Van Quine for over fifty years and has been thanked by Van in each of his books since *Word and Object* (1960).[17] *The Pursuit of Truth* (1990)[18] is dedicated thus: "To Burton Dreben—firm friend, constructive critic, down the decades." Van has also acknowledged Burt's advice and comments in nearly every one of his numerous articles written since the late 1950s. Burt has often had discussions with Hilary Putnam, and Hilary's *Representation and Reality* (1988)[19] is dedicated, "For Burton Dreben, who still won't be satisfied." Before Rogers Albritton left Harvard in the summer of 1972—a great loss to all of us—he and Burt talked often of philosophy; Stanley Cavell also expressed his gratitude for Burt's collegial and friendly offices in the foreword to *The Claim of Reason* (1979).[20] Earlier, as graduate students, Burt and Stanley assisted Morton White as teaching fellows in a course whose lectures eventually grew into White's *Toward Reunion in Philosophy* (1956);[21] and they are both thanked by Morty in his acknowledgments for their exceedingly generous care and mature insight. Three current members of the Harvard Philosophy Department, Charles Parsons, T. M. Scanlon, and Warren Goldfarb, as well as Harry Lewis, Professor of Computer Science and presently Dean of Harvard College, wrote their dissertations with Burt.

There are three periods in which Burt and I have worked closely together: the first 1962–1967, the second 1979–1987, and the third from 1994 to the present. What closed the first period was the political situation at Harvard in the late sixties and my preoccupation with certain political questions as they affected the university. This began with the faculty's discussion of the 2–S student deferment in December and January of 1966–1967. After the student strike in April of 1969 and the chaotic end of term in June, I left in August with my family for Stanford. It was there, at the Center for Advanced Study, that I wrote the first full draft of *A Theory of Justice* (1971).[22] I returned to Harvard to become department chair when the university opened in the fall.

Burt's work with me began again in the later seventies, especially in December of 1979 prior to the Dewey Lectures of April of 1980, and continued through the writing of several of the essays preparatory to my second book, *Political Liberalism* (1993, 1996),[23] a period ending in March of 1987. That month I went to Paris for a conference at the École Normale Supérieure, and I published the "Priority of the Right and Ideas of the Good"[24] in the summer of 1988.

Our third period of work began in the summer of 1994 when we discussed my "Reply to Habermas" and continues to the present day. It is noteworthy that, while I was actually writing my two books, I didn't work with Burt. Perhaps that is why, as he often says, the text reads as if it were translated from the original German. While my not working with him was partly the result of external circumstances, it was also by design: I knew that I could never complete a long text under the kind of intense scrutiny and penetrating criticism my writing receives from him. I decided that I would have to write the text alone and do it as best I could, mistakes and all. One day I explained this to him after he had remarked to me that he was sorry not to have seen *Political Liberalism* before it was published. He understood what I meant and accepted it.

A major change in our work took place after my stroke in late October of 1995. The stroke struck me in California, right after a meeting at Santa Clara in honor of the twenty-fifth anniversary of *A Theory of Justice*. I flew home and was immediately put in Mt. Auburn Hospital in Cambridge. I had a prior agreement with the Columbia University Press to write a second introduction to *Political Liberalism* (to be included following the first) for the paperback edition. Although most of this introduction had already been completed before Santa Clara, it still had to be finished and cleaned up. Burt insisted that we work on it, which we did, every day for the whole nine days I was in the hospital. As is his wont—those who know him won't be surprised—Burt was often late, arriving after visiting hours were over. Then our session would begin, continuing until the nurses asked him to leave. And we kept working after I came home. So although I had just suffered a serious stroke, the second introduction was completed on time and the paperback edition appeared in June of 1996. It is inconceivable that I could have carried on without Burt's enormous assistance and constant encouragement.

The same is true of the paper I published in the the *University of Chicago Law Review*, "The Idea of Public Reason Revisited,"[25] a revision of a lecture I gave at the University of Chicago Law School in November of 1993. In April of 1996, I suffered a nearly fatal attack of pancreatitis. I felt that this was perhaps the last paper I might ever be able to manage, so it had to show no falling off. Once I got going on this paper—I had a rough full draft by the end of the summer—Burt came out to our house in Lexington to discuss it with me twice and sometimes three times per week. We went over it line by line until gradually it fell into shape, and we started to think about sending it off in January. By this time, Burt himself was not feeling well; all fall he had been suffering from a worrisome cough. It turned out he had lymphoma. Yet none of this stopped him from continuing to help me on the paper. Indeed, the final checking of the *Review*'s edited "red-line" copy occurred while he was undergoing chemotherapy—we had to meet the deadline of the end of March. Burt and Juliet Floyd arrived at about 4 pm. Continuing after dinner, the four of us—Juliet and Mardy, my wife, took full part—finished around 9 pm. While I was flagging toward the end, Burt, not exactly to my surprise, was just getting warmed up.

At first Burt was coming to visit and comfort a sick friend; by the end, we were both among the sick, nevertheless endlessly working away at philosophy. Or so I view it, even if Burt might say it is not really philosophy. A significant aspect of Burt's character and of his attitude to such work is how much he cares both about philosophy and about how well his tutees do. He makes one feel that one's ideas are really important, as if much in the world depends on them. While this may seem odd for someone who holds his philosophical views—that there are no clinching arguments and no theories in philosophy—the fact is that he deeply loves the subject and intensely cares about it. The figures he most admires and studies—Frege and Russell, Wittgenstein and Moore, Carnap, Quine, and Austin (whom he met at Oxford during his year there)—he sees as exemplars, and he treasures their heroic efforts to write philosophy and to understand themselves in the world. This is evident in his intimate knowledge and study of their work, and his acquaintance with the biographical details of their personal lives and concerns.

Burt acts as his tutee's voice of conscience, and he does this in two ways. First, he keeps after one until he thinks one has gotten it right. There is to be no fudging or pretense. And it doesn't matter how long it takes or what effort is involved. The time and effort spent count for naught—about this he is relentless.[26] Sometimes he may seem to apologize for insisting that one's tenth or twentieth revision is still not right and needs to be done again. Yet it's not an apology, but all part of encouraging the tiring tutee to keep going. In fact, the more he expects of a tutee, the more relentless he is. It's a compliment, really.

Burt's criticisms are exacting, and sometimes minute. While I was working on "Basic Liberties and Their Priority,"[27] in which I was trying to reply to Hart's important objections to the account of liberty in *A Theory of Justice*, Burt called me in the morning to say that, in the passage on Brandeis we considered the previous day, the second comma should be taken out. I did so. Then in the afternoon, he called again saying he had thought further about it and the comma should go back in. It did.

Another kind of criticism Burt made was certainly not minute, but more Talmudic. He is an acute reader and is able to see the text as a whole—often better, I must say, than I see it myself. He works to articulate this whole. So his criticisms often take the form of rearranging the text. He will point out that some paragraphs are better put later, that others are not necessary and too repetitive. He will often say, "The argument is all there, we don't need to change or add to its basic parts, but it isn't organized correctly. Move this bit backward, bring that bit forward, and change the introductory lines to fit." In one draft of the *Chicago Law Review* paper, while every word and line was kept, the text was rearranged sentence by sentence. The same often happened in writing the "Reply to Habermas," particularly the second section, which seemed endlessly revised before it was done.

The second way Burt serves as a voice of conscience is that he insists on one's being fair to the persons one is criticizing. This means that one has to understand their view and how the problems looked to them. It means also that one has to understand how one's own view would look to them. While I was writing my "Reply to Habermas," I would occasionally make observations that could be taken amiss and were not quite accurate to Habermas's view, or had failed to express it correctly. These cases Burt noticed immediately and called to my attention. He insists on following Mill's maxim: no view is examined until it is examined in its best form.[28] I was glad Burt caught my lapses, since I wanted to be fair to Habermas; he is a great figure, the first major German philosopher since Kant and Hegel to play an honorable role in Germany's becoming a constitutional democratic state.

In all this work I sensed that Burt was doing what he could to make me be clear, to write forcefully and sharply, to be less guarded and muffled, a term he often used. He wanted me to find my own "voice," as we sometimes say. He would often comment by name on other people who were extraordinarily bright and knowledgeable but failed to express themselves clearly and with vigor. Their style was muffled and cramped, somehow they held back. He has always wanted to teach his tutees how to write, a seemingly small point, but it is not. Much of this surely comes from Burt's deep identification with his students, even his older tutees, and living through them when they do well. If they do good work, that's in part his effort also and belongs to his good as a teacher.

My Teaching

I don't know whether Burt influenced the development of my ideas about teaching, but I do know that here we agreed. We would often discuss historical texts, some of which I would be teaching at the time, and these conversations confirmed my ideas about how to proceed. Of course, I often taught the works of contemporary writers and presented my own views, yet Burt and I agreed that a knowledge of basic historical texts was essential.

Several maxims, with which I am confident Burt would agree, guided me in teaching. When lecturing, say, on Locke, Rousseau, Kant, or J. S. Mill, I always tried to do two things especially. One was to pose their problems as they themselves saw them, given what their understanding of these problems was in their own time. I often cited the remark of Collingwood that "the history of political theory is not the history of different answers to one and the same question, but the history of a problem more or less constantly changing, whose solution was changing with it."[29] (I would say "political philosophy" rather than "political theory.") Though this remark is an oversimplification, it is exactly right in telling us to look for a writer's view of the political world in order to see how political philosophy develops over time and why. I viewed each figure as contributing to the development of doctrines supporting constitutional democratic thought, and this included Marx, whom I always discussed.

The second thing I tried to do was to present each writer's thought in what I took to be its strongest form. I too took to heart Mill's remark in his review of Sedgwick: "A doctrine is not judged at all until it is judged in its best form."[30] I didn't say, not intentionally anyway, what I myself thought a writer should have said, but rather what that writer did say, supported by what I viewed as the most reasonable interpretation of the text. The text had to be known and respected, and its doctrine presented in its best form. Leaving aside the text seemed offensive, a kind of pretending. If I departed from it—no harm in that—I had to say so. Lecturing that way, I believed, made a writer's views stronger and more convincing, and a more worthy object of study.

I always took for granted that the writers we were studying were much smarter than I was. (Burt might say: as smart as he was.) If they were not, why was I wasting my time and the students' time by studying them? If I saw a mistake in their arguments, I supposed those writers saw it too and must have dealt with it. But where? I looked for their way out, not mine. Sometimes their way out was historical: in their day the question need not be raised, or wouldn't arise and so couldn't then be fruitfully discussed. Or there was a part of the text I had overlooked, or had not read. I assumed there were never plain mistakes, not ones that mattered anyway.

In doing this I followed what Kant says in the *Critique of Pure Reason* at B866, namely, that philosophy is a mere idea of a possible science and nowhere exists *in concreto*: "[W]e cannot learn philosophy; for where is it, who is in possession of it, and how shall we recognize it? We can only learn to philosophize, that is, to exercise the talent of reason, in accordance with its universal principles, on certain actually existing attempts at philosophy, always, however, reserving the right of reason to investigate, to confirm, or to reject these principles in their very sources."[31] Thus we learn moral and political philosophy—or indeed any part of philosophy— by studying the exemplars, those noted figures who have made cherished attempts at philosophy; and if we are lucky we find a way to go beyond them. My task was to explain Hobbes, Locke, and Rousseau, or Hume, Leibniz, and Kant as clearly and forcefully as I could, always attending carefully to what they actually said.

The result was that I was loath to raise objections to the exemplars; that's too easy and misses what is essential. However, it was important to point out difficulties that those coming later in the same tradition sought to overcome, or to point to views those in another tradition thought were mistaken. (I think here of the social contract view and utilitarianism as two traditions.) If this is not done, philosophical thought can't progress, and it becomes mysterious why later writers made the criticisms they did. In the case of Locke, for example, I remarked that his view allowed for a kind of political inequality we would not accept—inequality in basic rights of voting—and I discussed how Rousseau had tried to overcome this. Yet I would also emphasize that Locke was ahead of his time in his liberalism and opposed royal absolutism. During and after the Exclusion Crisis of 1679–1681, though a timid man, he didn't flinch from danger and remained loyal to his friend Lord Shaftesbury, even joining him, it seems, in the Rye House plot to assassinate Charles II in the summer of 1683. Locke fled for his life to Holland and barely escaped execution. He had the courage to put his head where his mouth was—perhaps the only one of the great modern figures to take such enormous risks.

With Kant I hardly made any criticisms at all.[32] My efforts were centered on trying to understand him so as to be able to describe his ideas to the students. Sometimes I would discuss well-known objections to his moral doctrine, such as those of Schiller and Hegel, Schopenhauer and Mill. Going over these is instructive and clarifies Kant's view. Yet I never felt satisfied with the understanding I achieved of Kant's doctrine as a whole. I never could grasp sufficiently his ideas on freedom of the will and reasonable religion, which must have been part of the core of his thought. All the great figures—Burt's as well as mine—lie to some degree beyond us, no matter how hard we try to master their thought. With Kant this distance often seems to me somehow much greater. Like great composers and great artists—Mozart and Beethoven, Poussin and Turner—they are beyond envy. It is vital in lecturing to try to exhibit to students in one's speech and conduct a sense of this, and why it is so. That can only be done by taking the thought of the text seriously, as worthy of honor and respect. This may at times be a kind of reverence, yet it is sharply distinct from adulation or uncritical acceptance of the text or author as authoritative. All true philosophy seeks fair criticism and depends on continuing and reflective public judgment.

If I have succeeded as a teacher, I owe it in part to many years of conversation with Burt, which strengthened my views and gave me the benefit of his remarkable knowledge and understanding.

Thanksgiving Day, 1997

NOTES

I should like to thank Juliet Floyd, Peter Hylton, Marcia Homiak, and Susan Neiman for many conversations about Burt and his work as a teacher.

1. See Henry Rosovsky's tribute to Burt in *The University: An Owner's Manual* (New York: Norton, 1990), pp. 200–202.

2. This story was told to me in 1953 by David Braybrooke, who attended Schumpeter's class in the late forties. (Schumpeter died in January of 1950.) It has,

I recognize, the ring of lore. For a more sober account, see Elizabeth Boody Schumpeter's editor's introduction to the *History of Economic Analysis* (New York: Oxford University Press, 1954), p. ix.

3. This story was passed around among many people. I don't recall who first told it to me but would guess it was Tom Nagel.

4. See Gian-Carlo Rota, *Indiscrete Thoughts*, ed. Fabrizio Palombi (Boston: Birkhauser, 1996), part 1, ch 1, "Fine Hall in its Golden Age," p. 8.

5. I had been a professor at Harvard for nearly ten years before I had written a book and twenty-two more years before I wrote another. All my writing has been done this way, slowly with almost endless revisions and additions. One needs time to shape one's thoughts, and I thank Harvard for giving it to me. None of my other colleagues tenured in the 1960s—Albritton, Cavell, Dreben, Nozick, and Putnam—had written a book before being appointed. This practice has not been uncommon in our department, and I hope it stays that way. In due course, we wrote our share.

6. I had thought that I read this story in Ruth E. Fine's splendid book, *John Marin* (Washington: National Gallery of Art, 1990), but I confess I have been unable to find it there.

7. See *Saturated Model Theory* (Reading, Mass.: W. A. Benjamin, 1972), pp. 1–2, and *Higher Recursion Theory* (Berlin and Heidelberg: Springer, 1990), p. xii.

8. See Burton Dreben and Warren Goldfarb, *The Decision Problem* (Reading, Mass.: Addison-Wesley, 1979); Jean van Heijenoort, ed., *From Frege to Gödel: A Sourcebook in Modern Logic, 1879–1931* (Cambridge: Harvard University Press, 1967) (in the latter volume, Dreben wrote ten notes for "Herbrand [*1930*]," pp. 525–581, and cowrote with van Heijenoort the introductory note to "Skolem [*1928*]," pp. 508–512); and Burton Dreben and Jean van Heijenoort, "Introductory note to *Gödel 1929, 1930, 1930a*," in *Kurt Gödel Collected Works*, ed. S. Feferman et al., vol. I. (Oxford: Oxford University Press, 1986), pp. 44–59.

9. Once I told Burt that someone had beaten him to the punch and recounted to him an aphorism that expresses an aspect of his view of philosophy. It goes: "Nonsense is nonsense, and the history of nonsense is scholarship." It is credited to Saul Lieberman, who was a great Talmud scholar, by Avishai Margalit in the *New York Review of Books*, Nov. 4, 1993, p. 68. When I told Burt of this aphorism, he was pleased, for he'd heard it before, as one might have expected. As he explained, Lieberman had been at the Jewish Theological Seminary of America in New York at the same time as Burt's late father-in-law, the great scholar Shalom Spiegel. Burt said that he saw Lieberman there occasionally and remembered him having said, "'Rubbish is rubbish, and the history of rubbish is scholarship.'"

10. See *The Philosophy of Rudolf Carnap*, ed. L. E. Hahn and P. A. Schilpp (La Salle, Ill.: Open Court, 1983), pp. 385–406, 915–921.

11. See Dreben's articles "Quine," in *Perspectives on Quine*, ed. Robert B. Barrett and Roger F. Gibson (Oxford: Basil Blackwell, 1990), pp. 81–95; "Putnam, Quine—and the Facts," in *Philosophical Topics* 20/1 (April 1991): 293–315; "*In Mediis Rebus*," in *Inquiry* 37/4 (December 1994): 441–447; and "Quine and Wittgenstein: The Odd Couple," in *Wittgenstein and Quine*, ed. Robert Arrington and Hans Glock (New York: Routledge, 1996), pp. 39–61.

12. See Dreben, "Cohen's Carnap, or Subjectivity is in the Eye of the Beholder," in *Science, Politics and Social Practice*, ed. Kostas Gavroglu, John Stachel, and Marx W. Wartofsky (Dordrecht: Kluwer Academic Publishers, 1995), pp. 27–42.

13. The conference was on Feb. 6, 1995. Hao Wang spoke, as did John Dawson, Warren Goldfarb, Jaakko Hintikka, Rohit Parikh, and Thomas Tymoczko. Burt spoke that evening. My remarks are based on conversation with Burt after the meeting.

14. See Richard S. Westfall's *Never at Rest* (Cambridge: Cambridge Univerity Press, 1980), pp. 581–583. The story of Newton's not going to bed until he had solved the problem was told by his niece.

15. See Isaiah 58.

16. See Lord Acton's correspondence with Bishop Creighton in Acton's *Collected Works*, vol. 11 (Indianapolis: Liberty Classics, 1985), p. 383.

17. W. V. Quine, *Word and Object* (Cambridge, Mass.: MIT Press, 1960).

18. W. V. Quine, *The Pursuit of Truth* (Cambridge, Mass.: Harvard University Press, 1990).

19. Hilary Putnam, *Representation and Reality* (Cambridge, Mass: MIT Press, 1988).

20. Stanley Cavell, *The Claim of Reason* (Oxford: Oxford University Press, 1979).

21. Morton White, *Toward Reunion in Philosophy* (Cambridge, Mass.: Harvard University Press, 1956).

22. *A Theory of Justice* (Cambridge, Mass.: Harvard University Press, 1971).

23. *Political Liberalism* (New York: Columbia University Press, 1993, 1996). The 1996, paperback edition includes a new, second introduction (pp. xxxvii–lxii) and my "Reply to Habermas" (pp. 372–434), which was originally published in the *Journal of Philosophy* 92 (1995): 132–180.

24. "The Priority of the Right and Ideas of the Good," *Philosophy and Public Affairs* 17 (1988).

25. "The Idea of Public Reason Revisited," *The University of Chicago Law Review* 64/3 (1997): 765–807.

26. Akihiro Kanamori, who is in the mathematics department at Boston University, has frequently worked with Burt—see, for example, "Hilbert and Set Theory," *Synthese* 110/1 (1997): 77–125—and addresses mail to him, "To the Dreaded Dreben." I know the feeling.

27. Tanner Lectures, 1982.

28. See Mills's review of the Cambridge geologist Alfred Sedgwick in Mill's *Collected Works*, vol. 10, *Essays on Ethics, Religion and Society*, ed. J. M. Robson (Toronto: University of Toronto Press, 1969), p. 52.

29. See R. G. Collingwood, *An Autobiography* (Oxford: Clarendon Press, 1939), p. 62.

30. As previously, Mill, *Collected Works*, vol. 10, p. 52.

31. Kant, *Critique of Pure Reason*, trans. Norman Kemp Smith (New York: St. Martin's Press, 1929), A838/B866.

32. See my lectures on Kant to be published by Harvard Univerity Press, ed. Barbara Herman and Christine Korsgaard. These are not serious works of scholarship but are aimed at helping the student and myself to understand and appreciate Kant's thought as expressed in the text.

Bibliography

Acton, John. 1985. *Collected Works*, vol. 11. Indianapolis: Liberty Classics.

Alexander, Peter. 1974. "Boyle and Locke on Primary and Secondary Qualities," *Ratio* 16: 51–67.

———. 1985. *Ideas, Qualities and Corpuscles: Locke and Boyle on the External World.* Cambridge: Cambridge University Press.

Alexandrov, P. S., ed. 1971. *Die Hilbertschen Probleme: Vortrag "Mathematische Probleme" von D. Hilbert.* Leipzig: Akademische Verlagsgesellschaft.

Améry, Jean. 1971. *Unmeisterliche Wanderjahre.* Stuttgart: E. Klett-Cotta.

Anderson, A. R. 1959. "Mathematics and the 'Language Game,' *Review of Metaphysics* 11: 446–458.

Anscombe, G. E. M. 1971 [1959]. *An Introduction to Wittgenstein's Tractatus.* Philadelphia: University of Pennsylvania Press.

Arendt, Hannah. 1971. *The Life of the Mind.* New York: Harcourt Brace Jovanovich.

———. 1982. *Lectures on Kant's Political Philosophy.* Chicago: University of Chicago Press.

Ayer, A. J. 1952. *Language, Truth and Logic.* New York: Dover.

———. 1959. "Editor's Introduction," in *Logical Postivism,* ed. A. J. Ayer. Glencoe, Ill.: Free Press, pp. 3–28.

Ayers, Michael. 1978. "Analytical Philosophy and the History of Philosophy," in *Philosophy and Its Past,* ed. Michael Ayers, Jonathan Reé, and Adam Westoby. Hassocks, U.K.: Harvester Press, pp. 42–66.

———. 1985. "The End of Metaphysics and the Historiography of Philosophy," in *Philosophy, Its History and Historiography,* ed. A. J. Holland. Dordrecht: Reidel, pp. 27–40.

———. 1991. *Locke: Epistemology and Ontology,* 2 vols. London: Routledge.

Ayers, Michael, Jonathan Reé, and Adam Westoby, eds. 1978. *Philosophy and Its Past.* Hassocks, U.K.: Harvester Press.

Baldwin, J. M., ed. 1901–1905. *Dictionary of Philosophy and Psychology,* 3 vols. New York: Macmillan.

Bar-Hillel, Yehoshua. 1950. "Bolzano's Definition of Analytic Propositions," *Theoria* 16: 91–117.

Beiser, Frederick. 1987. *The Fate of Reason: German Philosophy from Kant to Fichte.* Cambridge, Mass.: Harvard University Press.

431

————. 1992. *Enlightenment, Revolution, and Romanticism: The Genesis of Modern German Political Thought, 1790–1800*. Cambridge, Mass.: Harvard University Press.

Bell, David. 1994. "Reference, Experience, and Intentionality," in *Mind, Meaning and Mathematics: Essays on the Philosophical Views of Husserl and Frege*, ed. Leila Haaparanta. Dordrecht: Kluwer, pp. 185–209.

Bell, J. L., and William Demopoulos. 1996. "Elementary Propositions and Independence," *Notre Dame Journal of Formal Logic* 37: 112–124.

Benacerraf, Paul, and Hilary Putnam, eds. 1983. *Philosophy of Mathematics: Selected Readings*. Cambridge: Cambridge University Press.

Benhabib, Seyla, et al. 1995. *Feminist Contentions: A Philosophical Exchange*. New York: Routledge.

Bennett, Jonathan. 1966. *Kant's Analytic*. Cambridge: Cambridge University Press.

Berkeley, George. 1710. *Treatise on the Principles of Philosophy*. Dublin.

Bernays, Paul. 1959. "Comments on Ludwig Wittgenstein's *Remarks on the Foundations of Mathematics*," *Ratio* 2/1: 1–22.

Bernstein, Robert. 1980. "Philosophy in the Conversation of Mankind," *Review of Metaphysics* 33: 743–775.

Beth, Evert. 1963. "Carnap's Views on the Advantages of Constructed Systems over Natural Languages," in *The Philosophy of Rudolf Carnap*, ed. Paul Arthur Schilpp. La Salle, Ill.: Open Court, pp. 469–502.

Beyer, Christian. 1996. *Von Bolzano zu Husserl* (*Phenomenologica*). The Hague: Nijhoff.

Black, Max. 1964. *A Companion to Wittgenstein's* Tractatus. Ithaca, N.Y.: Cornell University Press.

Blackmore, John T. 1972. *Ernst Mach: His Work, Life, and Influence*. Berkeley: University of California Press.

Blackmore, John T., ed. 1992. *Ernst Mach—A Deeper Look: Documents and New Perspectives*. Dordrecht: Kluwer Academic.

————. 1995. *Ludwig Boltzmann: His Later Life and Philosophy, Book 1: A Documentary History*, Dordrecht: Kluwer Academic.

Boltzmann, Ludwig. 1974. *Theoretical Physics and Philosophical Problems*, ed. Brian McGuinness. Dordrecht: D. Reidel.

Bolzano, Bernard. 1889 [1851]. *Paradoxien des Unendlichen*, ed. F. Prihonsky. Berlin: Mayer and Müller.

————. 1972 [1837]. *Theory of Science*, abridged ed., trans. Rolf George. Berkeley: University of California Press.

Boolos, George. 1975. "On Second-Order Logic," *Journal of Philosophy* 72: 509–527.

————. 1998. *Logic, Logic, and Logic*, ed. Richard C. Jeffrey. Cambridge, Mass.: Harvard University Press.

Borges, Jorge Luis. 1962. "The Garden of Forking Paths," in Borges, *Ficciones*. New York, Grove Press, pp. 89–101.

Bornstein, Kate. 1994. *Gender Outlaw: On Men, Women, and the Rest of Us*. New York: Routledge.

Bostock, David. 1988. "Necessary Truth and *A Priori* Truth," *Mind* 97: 343–379.

Bouveresse, Jacques. 1988. *Le pays des possibles: Wittgenstein, les mathématiques, et le monde réel*. Paris: Les Éditions de Minuit.

Bouwsma, O. K. 1986. *Wittgenstein: Conversations 1949–1951*, ed. J. L. Cratz and Ronald E. Hustwit. Indianapolis: Hackett Publishing.

Boyd, Richard. 1988. "How to Be a Moral Realist," in *Essays on Moral Realism*, ed. Geoffrey Sayre-McCord. Ithaca, N.Y.: Cornell University Press, pp. 181–228.

————. 1991. "On the Current Status of Scientific Realism," in *The Philosophy of Science*, ed. Richard Boyd, Philip Gasper, and J. D. Trout. Cambridge, Mass.: MIT Press, pp. 195–222.

Boyle, Robert. 1979. "About the Excellency and Grounds of the Mechanical Philosophy," in Robert Boyle, *Selected Philosophical Papers*, ed. M. A. Stewart. Manchester: Manchester University Press, pp. 138–154.

Bradley, F. H. 1910. "On Appearance, Error, and Contradiction," *Mind* n.s. 19: 153–185.

Brandom, R. 1992. "Heidegger's Categories in *Being and Time*," in *Heidegger: A Critical Reader*, ed. H. Dreyfus and H. Hall. Cambridge, Mass.: Blackwell, pp. 45–64.

Bunge, Mario. 1992. "Mach's Critique of Newtonian Mechanics," in *Ernst Mach—A Deeper Look: Documents and New Perspectives*, ed. John T. Blackmore. Kluwer Academic, Dordrecht, pp. 243–261.

Bynum, Terrell W., ed. 1970. *Conceptual Notation and Related Articles*. Oxford: Oxford University Press.

Carnap, Rudolf. 1922. "Der Raum. Ein Beitrag zur Wissenschaftslehre," *Kant-Studien, Ergänzungshefte im Auftrag der Kant Gesellschaft*, 56.

———. 1928. *Der logische Aufbau der Welt*. Berlin: Weltkreis.

———. 1930. "Die Mathematik als Zweig der Logik," *Blätter für deutsche Philosophie* 4: 298–310.

———. 1930. "Die logizistische Grundlegung der Mathematik," *Erkenntnis* 2: 91–105.

———. 1934. *Die Aufgabe der Wissenschaftslogik*. Vienna: Gerold.

———. 1934. *Logische Syntax der Sprache*. Vienna: Springer.

———. 1934. "On the Character of Philosophical Problems," *Philosophy of Science* 1: 2–19.

———. 1935. "Formalwissenschaft und Realwissenschaft," *Erkenntnis* 5/1: 30–36.

———. 1935. *Philosophy and Logical Syntax*. London: Kegan Paul.

———. 1936. "Testability and Meaning," part I, *Philosophy of Science* 3: 420–471.

———. 1936. "Von der Erkenntnistheorie zur Wissenschaftslogik," in *Actes du Congrès international de philosophie scientifique*. Paris: Hermann et Compagnie.

———. 1937. "Testability and Meaning," part II, *Philosophy of Science* 4: 2–38.

———. 1937. *The Logical Syntax of Language*, trans. A. Smeaton. London: Kegan Paul.

———. 1939. "Foundations of Logic and Mathematics," *International Encyclopedia of Unified Science*, vol. I, no. 3. Chicago: University of Chicago Press.

———. 1942. *Introduction to Semantics*. Cambridge, Mass.: Harvard University Press.

———. 1950. "Empiricism, Semantics, and Ontology," *Revue Internationale de Philosophie* 11: 20–40.

———. 1950. *Logical Foundations of Probability*. Chicago: University of Chicago Press.

———. 1956. *Meaning and Necessity*, 2d ed. Chicago: University of Chicago Press.

———. 1953. "Formal and Factual Science," in *Readings in the Philosophy of Science*, ed. H. Feigl and M. Brodbeck. New York: Appleton-Century-Crofts.

———. 1963. "Intellectual Autobiography," in *The Philosophy of Rudolf Carnap*, ed. Paul Arthur Schilpp. La Salle, Ill.: Open Court, pp. 3–86.

———. 1963. "W. V. Quine on Logical Truth," in *The Philosophy of Rudolf Carnap*, ed. Paul Arthur Schilpp. La Salle, Ill.: Open Court, pp. 915–921.

———. 1963. "E. W. Beth on Constructed Language Systems," in *The Philosophy of Rudolf Carnap*, ed. Paul Arthur Schilpp. La Salle, Ill.: Open Court, pp. 927–932.

———. 1967. *The Logical Structure of the World*, trans. R. George. Berkeley: University of California Press.

———. 1987. "The Task of the Logic of Science," in *Unified Science*, ed. B. McGuinness. Dordrecht: Reidel, pp. 46–66.

Carnap, Rudolf, Arend Heyting, and Johan von Neumann. 1931. "Diskussion zur Grundlegung der Mathematik," *Erkenntnis* 2: 91–121.

Carrier, Martin and Jurgen Mittelstrass. 1991. *Mind, Brain, Behavior: The Mind-Body Problem and the Philosophy of Psychology*. Berlin and New York: Walter de Gruyter.

Carroll, Lewis. 1895. "What the Tortoise Said to Achilles," *Mind* n.s. 4: 278–280.

Cartwright, Richard. 1987. "A Neglected Theory of Truth," in Richard Cartwright, *Philosophical Essays*. Cambridge, Mass.: MIT Press, pp. 71–93.

Cavell, Stanley. 1969. *Must We Mean What We Say?* New York: Scribner's.
————. 1979. *The Claim of Reason.* Oxford: Oxford University Press.
————. 1995. *A Pitch of Philosophy.* Cambridge, Mass.: Harvard University Press.
————. 1995. "Notes and Afterthoughts on the Opening of Wittgenstein's *Investigations*," in *Philosophical Passages: Wittgenstein, Emerson, Austin.* Cambridge, Mass.: Blackwell, pp. 125–186.
————. 1996. *Les Voix de la raison,* trans. Nicole Balso and Sandra Laugier. Paris: Seuil.
Chappell, Vere. 1994. "Locke's Theory of Ideas," in *The Cambridge Companion to Locke,* ed. Vere Chappell. Cambridge: Cambridge University Press, pp. 26–55.
Chomsky, Noam. 1957. *Syntactic Structures.* The Hague: Mouton.
————. 1980 [1959]. Review of B. F. Skinner, *Verbal Behavior,*" *Language* 35/1: 26–58, reprinted in Ned Block, ed., *Readings in the Philosophy of Psychology,* vol. 1. Cambridge, Mass.: Harvard University Press, pp. 48–63.
————. 1965. *Aspects of the Theory of Syntax.* Cambridge, Mass.: MIT Press.
Choy, Victoria. 1982. "Review of *Philosophy and the Mirror of Nature,*" *Synthese* 52: 515–541.
Clark, P., and B. Hale, eds. 1994. *Reading Putnam.* Oxford: Blackwell.
Code, Lorraine. 1991. *What Can She Know? Feminist Theory and the Construction of Knowledge.* Ithaca, N.Y.: Cornell University Press.
Cohen, I. Bernard. 1980. *The Newtonian Revolution: With Illustrations of the Transformation of Scientific Ideas.* Cambridge: Cambridge University Press.
Collingwood, R. G. 1939. *An Autobiography.* Oxford: Clarendon Press.
Collins, Arthur. 1999. "Behaviorism and Belief," *Annals of Pure and Applied Logic* 96: 75–88.
Collins, Patricia Hill. 1986. "Learning from the Outsider Within," *Social Problems* 33: 14–32.
Conant, James. 1992. "The Search for Logically Alien Thought: Descartes, Kant, Frege and the *Tractatus,*" *Philosophical Topics* 20/1: 115–180.
Corry, Len. 1998. "Hilbert on Kinetic Theory and Radiation Theory (1912–14)," *The Mathematical Intelligencer* 20/3: 52–58.
Creath, R., ed. 1990. *Dear Carnap, Dear Van: The Quine-Carnap Correspondence and Related Work.* Berkeley: University of California Press.
Curley, E. M. 1972. "Locke, Boyle, and the Distinction between Primary and Secondary Qualities," *The Philosophical Review* 81: 438–464.
————. 1978. *Descartes against the Skeptics.* Cambridge, Mass.: Harvard University Press.
Davidson, Donald. 1985. "Reply to Quine on Events," in Ernest LePore and Brian McLaughlin, eds., *Actions and Events: Perspectives on the Philosophy of Donald Davidson.* New York: Basil Blackwell, pp. 172–176.
Davies, Martin, and Lloyd Humberstone. 1980. "Two Notions of Necessity," *Philosophical Studies* 38: 1–30.
Davis, Martin, ed. 1965. *The Undecidable.* Hewlett, N.Y.: Raven Press, 1965.
Dawson, John L., Jr. 1997. *Logical Dilemmas: The Life and Work of Kurt Gödel.* Wellesley, Mass.: A.K. Peters.
Delgado, Richard, ed. 1995. *Critical Race Theory: The Cutting Edge.* Philadelphia: Temple University Press.
Descartes, René. 1984–1985. *The Philosophical Writings of Descartes,* trans. John Cottingham, Robert Stoothoff, and Dugald Murdoch, 3 vols. Cambridge: Cambridge University Press.
Deutsch, H. 1989. "On Direct Reference," in *Themes from Kaplan,* ed. J. Almog, J. Perry and H. Wettstein. Oxford: Oxford University Press, pp. 167–195.
Diamond, Cora. 1988. "Throwing Away the Ladder," *Philosophy* 63: 5–27.
————. 1991. "Ethics, Imagination and the Method of Wittgenstein's *Tractatus,*" in *Bilder der Philosophie, Wiener Reihe V.* ed. R. Heinrich and H. Vetter. Vienna: R. Oldenbourg Verlag, pp. 55–90.

———. 1991. *The Realistic Spirit: Wittgenstein, Philosophy, and the Mind.* Cambridge, Mass.: MIT Press.

———. 1997. "Realism and Resolution," *Journal of Philosophical Research* 22: 75–86.

———. Forthcoming. "Truth before Tarski: After Sluga, after Ricketts, after Geach, after Goldfarb, Hylton, Floyd and van Heijenoort," *Perspectives on Early Analytic Philosophy: Frege, Russell, Wittgenstein.* ed. E. Reck. Oxford: Oxford University Press.

Dilthey, Wilhelm. 1962. *Pattern and Meaning in History: Thoughts on History and Society,* ed. and trans. H. P. Rickman. New York: Harper & Row.

Dijkstra, Edsger. 1976. *A Discipline of Programming.* New York: Prentice Hall.

Dirac, P. A. M. 1930. *The Principles of Quantum Mechanics.* Oxford: Clarendon Press.

Dreben, Burton. 1990. "Quine," in *Perspectives on Quine,* ed. Robert B. Barrett and Roger F. Gibson. Cambridge, Mass.: Basil Blackwell, pp. 81–95.

———. 1991. "Putnam, Quine—and the Facts," *Philosophical Topics* 20/1 (April): 293–315.

———. 1994. *"In Mediis Rebus,"* *Inquiry* 37/4 (December): 441–447.

———. 1995. "Cohen's Carnap, or Subjectivity Is in the Eye of the Beholder," in *Science, Politics and Social Practice,* ed. Kostas Gavroglu, John Stachel, and Marx W. Wartofsky. Dordrecht: Kluwer Academic Publishers, pp. 27–42.

———. 1996. "Quine and Wittgenstein: The Odd Couple," in *Wittgenstein and Quine,* ed. Robert Arrington and Hans-Johan Glock. London: Routledge, pp. 39–61.

Dreben, Burton, and Juliet Floyd. 1991. "Tautology: How Not to Use A Word," *Synthese* 87/1: 23–50.

Dreben, Burton, and Warren Goldfarb. 1979. *The Decision Problem.* Reading, Mass.: Addison-Wesley.

Dreben, Burton, and Jean van Heijenoort. 1986. "Introductory Note to Gödel 1929, 1930 and 1930a," in *Kurt Gödel: Collected Works,* vol. 1, ed. S. Feferman et al. New York: Oxford University Press, pp. 44–59.

Dreben, Burton, and Akihiro Kanamori. 1997. "Hilbert and Set Theory," *Synthese* 110/1 (January): 77–125.

Dretske, Fred. 1982. "Review of *Philosophy and the Mirror of Nature,*" *International Studies in Philosophy* 14: 96–98.

Dreyfus, Hubert. 1991. *Being-in-the-World.* Cambridge, Mass.: MIT Press.

Dreyfus, Hubert, ed. 1982. *Husserl, Intentionality and Cognitive Science.* Cambridge, Mass.: MIT Press

Dreyfus, Hubert, and H. Hall. 1992. *Heidegger: A Critical Reader.* Cambridge, Mass.: Blackwell.

Dummett, Michael. 1973. *Frege: Philosophy of Language.* London: Duckworth.

———. 1978. *Truth and Other Enigmas.* Cambridge, Mass: Harvard University Press.

———. 1981. *Frege: Philosophy of Language,* 2d ed. London: Duckworth.

———. 1981. *The Interpretation of Frege's Philosophy.* London and Cambridge: Duckworth and Harvard University Press.

———. 1991. *The Logical Basis of Metaphysics.* Cambridge, Mass.: Harvard University Press.

———. 1991. *Frege: Philosophy of Mathematics.* Cambridge, Mass.: Harvard University Press.

———. 1993. *Origins of Analytical Philosophy.* Cambridge, Mass.: Harvard University Press.

Easton, Patricia, ed. Forthcoming. *Logic and the Workings of the Mind.* North American Kant Society Publications, Atascadero, Calif.: Ridgeview.

Ehrenreich, Barbara, and Janet McIntosh. 1997. "The New Creationism: Biology under Attack," *The Nation,* June 9: 11–16.

Elliston, Frederick and Peter McCormick, eds. 1977. *Husserl: Expositions and Appraisals.* Notre Dame: University of Notre Dame Press.

————. 1981. *Husserl: Shorter Works*. Notre Dame: University of Notre Dame Press.

Embree, Lester, et al., eds. 1997. *Encyclopedia of Phenomenology*. Dordrecht: Kluwer Academic.

Emerson, Allan. 1990. "Temporal and Modal Logic," in *Handbook of Theoretical Computer Science*, vol. B, ed. Jan van Leeuwen. Cambridge, Mass.: MIT Press/Elsevier, pp. 995–1072.

Epstein, Williams, and Gary Hatfield. 1979. "The Sensory Core and the Medieval Foundations of Early Modern Perceptual Theory," *Isis* 70: 363–384.

Erdmann, J. E. 1870. *Grundriss der Geschichte der Philosophie*, 2d ed., 2 vols. Berlin.

Etchemendy, John. 1990. *The Concept of Logical Consequence*. Cambridge: Harvard University Press.

Evans, Gareth. 1979. "Reference and Contingency," in Gareth Evans, *Collected Papers*. Oxford: Clarendon Press, pp. 178–213.

————. 1982. *The Varieties of Reference*. Oxford: Clarendon Press.

Feigl, Herbert, and Wilfrid Sellars, eds. 1949. *Readings in Philosophical Analysis*. New York: Appleton-Century-Crofts.

Fine, Arthur. 1986. *The Shaky Game: Einstein, the Quantum Theory*. Chicago: University of Chicago Press.

Fine, Ruth E. 1990. *John Marin*. Washington: National Gallery of Art.

Floyd, Juliet. 1991. "Wittgenstein on 2,2,2 . . . : On the Opening of *Remarks on the Foundations of Mathematics*," *Synthese* 87/1: 143–180.

————. 1995. "On Saying What You Really Want to Say: Wittgenstein, Gödel and the Trisection of the Angle," in *From Dedekind to Gödel: Essays on the Development of the Foundations of Mathematics in the Twentieth Century*, ed. Jaakko Hintikka. Dordrecht: Kluwer, pp. 373–426.

————. 1998. "Frege, Semantics and the Double-Definition Stroke," in *The Story of Analytic Philosophy: Plot and Heroes*, ed. Anat Biletzki and Anat Matar. New York: Routledge, pp. 141–166.

————. 1998. "The Uncaptive Eye: Solipsism in Wittgenstein's *Tractatus*" in *Loneliness*, ed. Leroy S. Rouner. Notre Dame, Ind.: University of Notre Dame Press, pp. 79–108.

————. 2000. "Wittgenstein, Mathematics, Philosophy," in *The New Wittgenstein*, ed. A. Crary and R. Read. New York: Routledge.

Floyd, R. W. 1967. "Assigning Meanings to Programs," *Proceedings of the 19th AMS Symposium on Applied Mathematics*, pp. 19–31.

Fogelin, R. J. 1983. "Wittgenstein on Identity," *Synthese* 56: 141–154.

————. 1987. *Wittgenstein*. New York: Routledge and Kegan Paul.

Føllesdal, Dagfinn. 1969. "Husserl's Notion of Noema," *The Journal of Philosophy* 66: 680–687.

————. 1974. "Phenomenology," in *Handbook of Perception*, ed. Edward C. Carterette and Morton P. Friedman, vol. 1. New York: Academic Press, pp. 377–386.

————. 1978. "Brentano and Husserl on Intentional Objects and Perception," *Grazer philosophische Studien* 5: 83–94.

————. 1979. "Husserl and Heidegger on the Role of Actions in the Constitution of the World," in *Essays in Honour of Jaakko Hintikka*, ed. E. Saarinen et al. Dordrecht: Reidel, pp. 365–378.

————. 1986. "Quantified Modal Logic and Essentialism," in *Mérites et limites des méthodes logiques en philosophie*, ed. J. Vuillemin. Paris: Vrin, pp. 167–182.

————. 1988. "Husserl on Evidence and Justification," in *Edmund Husserl and the Phenomenological Tradition: Essays in Phenomenology*, ed. Robert Sokolowski. Washington, D.C.: Catholic University of America Press, pp. 107–129.

————. 1996. "Analytic Philosophy: What Is It and Why Should One Engage in It?" *Ratio* n.s. 9: 193–208.

Frascolla, P. 1994. *Wittgenstein's Philosophy of Mathematics*. New York: Routledge.

Fraser, Nancy. 1989. *Unruly Practices: Power, Discourse, and Gender in Contemporary Social Theory.* Oxford: Polity Press.

Frede, Dorothea. 1986. "Heidegger and the Scandal of Philosophy," in *Human Nature and Natural Knowledge,* ed. A. Donagan, A. N. Perovich Jr., and M.V. Wedin. Dordrecht: Reidel, pp. 129–151.

Frege, Gottlob. 1879. *Begriffsschrift, eine der arithmetischen nachgebildete Formelsprache des reinen Denkens.* Halle: L Nebert.

———. 1882. "Über den Zweck der Begriffsschrift," *Jenaische Zeitschrift für Naturwissenschaft,* supplementary, vol. 16: 1–10.

———. 1884. *Die Grundlagen der Arithmetik.* Breslau: W. Koebner.

———. 1891. *Funktion und Begriff.* Jena: Herman Pohle.

———. 1891. "Über das Trägheitsgesetz," *Zeitschrift für Philosophie und philosophische Kritik* 98: 145–161.

———. 1892. "Über Begriff und Gegenstand," *Vierteljahrsschrift für Philosophie und philosophische Kritik* 16: 192–205.

———. 1893. *Grundgesetze der Arithmetik, Begriffsschriftlich abgeleitet,* vol. 1. Jena: H. Pohle.

———. 1894. "Rezension von E. Husserl, *Philosophie der Arithmetik,*" Zeitschrift für Philosophie und philosophische Kritik 103: 313–332.

———. 1897. "Über die Begriffsschrift des Herrn Peano und meine eigene," *Berichte über die Verhandlungen der Königlich Sächsischen Gesellschaften der Wissenschaften zu Leipzig* (Mathematisch-physische Classe) 48: 362–378.

———. 1903. *Grundgesetze der Arithmetik, Begriffsschriftlich abgeleitet,* vol. 2. Jena: H. Pohle.

———. 1906. "Über die Grundlagen der Geometrie," *Jahresberichte der Deutschen Mathematiker-Vereinigung* 15: 293–309, 377–403, 423–430.

———. 1918. "Der Gedanke," *Beiträge zur Philosophie des deutschen Idealismus* 1: 58–77.

———. 1918. "Die Verneinung," *Beiträge zur Philosophie des deutschen Idealismus* 1: 143–157.

———. 1962. *Grundgesetze der Arithmetik.* Hildesheim: Georg Olms.

———. 1964. *The Basic Laws of Arithmetic: Exposition of the System,* ed. and trans. Montgomery Furth. Berkeley: University of California Press.

———. 1970. *Begriffsschrift, a Formula Language, Modeled upon that of Arithmetic, for Pure Thought,* in *Frege and Gödel: Two Fundamental Texts in Mathematical Logic,* ed. Jean van Heijenoort. Cambridge, Mass.: Harvard University Press.

———. 1976. *Wissenschaftlicher Briefwechsel.* Hamburg: Felix Meiner.

———. 1979 [1906]. "Introduction to Logic," in *Posthumous Writings,* ed. Hans Hermes, Friedrich Kambartel, and Friedrich Kaulbach, trans. Peter Long and Roger White. Chicago: University of Chicago Press, pp. 185–196.

———. 1979 [1897]. "Logic," in *Posthumous Writings,* ed. Hans Hermes, Friedrich Kambartel, and Friedrich Kaulbach, trans. Peter Long and Roger White. Chicago: University of Chicago Press, pp. 126–151.

———. 1979 [1914]. "Logic in Mathematics," in *Posthumous Writings,* ed. Hans Hermes, Friedrich Kambartel, and Friedrich Kaulbach, trans. Peter Long and Roger White. Chicago: University of Chicago Press, pp. 203–250.

———. 1979 [1915]. "My Basic Logical Insights," *Posthumous Writings,* ed. Hans Hermes, Friedrich Kambartel, and Friedrich Kaulbach, trans. Peter Long and Roger White. Chicago: University of Chicago Press, pp. 251–252.

———. 1979. *Posthumous Writings,* ed. Hans Hermes, Friedrich Kambartel, and Friedrich Kaulbach, trans. Peter Long and Roger White, Chicago: University of Chicago Press.

———. 1980. *Foundations of Arithmetic,* 2d. rev. ed., trans. J. L. Austin. Evanston, Ill.: Northwestern University Press.

————. 1980. *Translations from the Philosophical Writings of Gottlob Frege*, 3d ed., ed. Peter Geach and Max Black, index by E. D. Klemke. Totowa, N.J.: Rowman and Littlefield.

————. 1983. *Nachgelassene Schriften*. Hamburg: Felix Meiner.

————. 1984. *Collected Papers on Mathematics, Logic, and Philosophy*, ed. Brian McGuinness, trans. Max Black et al. Oxford: Blackwell.

————. 1984 [1892]. "On Sense and Meaning," in *Collected Papers*, pp. 157–177.

————. 1984 [1918]. "Thoughts," in *Collected Papers: On Mathematics, Logic, and Philosophy*, ed. Brian McGuinness, trans. Max Black et al. Oxford: Basil Blackwell, pp. 351–372.

Freud, Sigmund 1957–1966. *The Standard Edition of the Complete Psychological Works of Sigmund Freud*, ed. and trans. James Strachey et al. London: Hogarth Press.

Friedlander, Eli 1998. "Heidegger, Carnap, Wittgenstein: Much Ado About Nothing," in *The Story of Analytic Philosophy*, ed. Anat Biletsky and Anat Matar. London: Routledge.

Friedman, Michael. 1983. *Foundations of Space-Time Theories: Relativistic Physics and Philosophy of Science*. Princeton: Princeton University Press.

————. 1987. "Carnap's *Aufbau* Reconsidered," *Noûs* 21: 521–545.

————. 1988. "Logical Truth and Analyticity in Carnap's *Logical Syntax of Language*," in *History and Philosophy of Modern Mathematics*, ed. W. Aspray and P. Kitcher. Minneapolis: University of Minnesota Press.

————. 1992. *Kant and the Exact Sciences*. Cambridge, Mass.: Harvard University Press.

————. 1992. "Epistemology in the *Aufbau*," *Synthese* 93: 15–57.

————. 1995. "Carnap and Weyl on the Foundations of Geometry and Relativity Theory," *Erkenntnis* 42: 247–260.

————. 1997. "Carnap and Wittgenstein's *Tractatus*," in *Early Analytic Philosophy: Frege, Russell, Wittgenstein*, ed. W. Tait. La Salle: Open Court, pp. 19–36.

Frye, Marilyn. 1983. *The Politics of Reality*. Trumansburg, N.Y.: Crossing Press.

Garber, Daniel. 1992. *Descartes' Metaphysical Physics*. Chicago: University of Chicago Press.

Gauss, C. F. 1966 [1801]. *Disquisitiones Arithmeticae*, trans. A. A. Clarke. New Haven: Yale University Press.

Geach, Peter. 1972. *Logic Matters*. Oxford: Blackwell.

————. 1983. "Wittgenstein's Operator N," *Analysis* 41: 573–589.

Gerrard, S. 1991. "Wittgenstein's Philosophies of Mathematics," *Synthese* 87: 125–142.

Giere, Ronald N., and Alan W. Richardson, eds. 1996. *Origins of Logical Empiricism*. Minneapolis: University of Minnesota Press.

Ginzberg, Ruth. 1989. "Feminism, Rationality, and Logic," *APA Newsletter on Feminism and Philosophy* 88: 34–39.

————. 1989. "Teaching Feminist Logic," *APA Newsletter on Feminism and Philosophy* 88: 58–62.

Gödel, Kurt. 1931. "Über formal unentscheidbare Sätze der *Principia Mathematica* und verwandter Systeme, I," *Monatshefte für Mathematik und Physik* 38: 173–198.

————. 1965. "On Formally Undecidable Propositions of *Principia Mathematica* and Similar Systems, I," trans. Elliot Mendelson, in *The Undecidable*, ed. Martin Davis. Hewlitt, N.Y.: Raven Press, pp. 4–38.

————. 1986–. *Kurt Gödel: Collected Works*, ed. Solomon Feferman et al. New York: Oxford University Press.

Goldman, Alvin. 1981. "Review of *Philosophy and the Mirror of Nature*," *The Philosophical Review* 90: 424–429.

Goldfarb, Warren. 1979. "Logic in the Twenties: The Nature of the Quantifier," *Journal of Symbolic Logic* 44: 351–368.

————. 1995. "Introductory Note to Gödel *1953/1959," in *Kurt Gödel: Collected Works*, vol. 3, ed. Solomon Feferman et al. New York: Oxford University Press, pp. 324–333.

———. 1988. "Poincaré Against the Logicists," in *Minnesota Studies in the Philosopy of Science xi: History and Philosophy of Modern Mathematics*, ed. W. Aspray and P. Kitcher. Minneapolis: University of Minnesota Press, pp. 61–81.

———. 1997. "Metaphysics and Nonsense: On Cora Diamond's *The Realistic Spirit*," *Journal of Philosophical Research* 22, pp. 57–73.

Goldfarb, Warren, and Thomas Ricketts 1992. "Carnap and the Philosophy of Mathematics," in *Science and Subjectivity*, ed. D. Bell and W. Vossenkuhl. Berlin: Akademie.

Goodstein, R. L. 1957. "Critical Notice of *Remarks on the Foundations of Mathematics*," *Mind*: 549–553.

Greenlee, Douglas. 1977. "Locke's Ideas of 'Idea,'" in *Locke on Human Understanding*, ed. I. C. Tipton. Oxford: Oxford University Press.

Grice, H. P. 1989. *Studies in the Way of Words*. Cambridge, Mass.: Harvard University Press.

Griffin, Nicholas. 1985. "Russell's Multiple Relation Theory of Judgment," *Philosophical Studies* 47: 213–247.

Guignon, Charles. 1983. *Heidegger and the Problem of Knowledge*. Indianapolis: Hackett.

Haaparanta, L., and Jaakko Hintikka, eds. 1986. *Frege Synthesized*. Dordrecht: D. Reidel.

Hacker, P. M. S. 1986. *Insight and Illusion: Themes in the Philosophy of Wittgenstein*, rev. 2d ed., Oxford: Oxford University Press.

———. 1997. *Wittgenstein's Place in Twentieth-Century Analytic Philosophy*. Oxford: Basil Blackwell.

———. 1998. "Analytic Philosophy: What, Whence, and Whither?" in *The Story of Analytic Philosophy: Plots and Heroes*, ed. A. Biletzki and A. Matar. London: Routledge, pp. 3–34.

Hacking, Ian. 1980. "Proof and Eternal Truths: Descartes and Leibniz," in *Descartes: Philosophy, Mathematics and Physics*, ed. S. Gaukroger. Sussex:: Harvester Press, pp. 169–180.

Hahn, L. E., and Paul Arthur Schilpp, eds. 1986. *The Philosophy of W. V. Quine*. La Salle, Ill.: Open Court.

Hale, Jacob. 1995. "Transgendered Strategies for Refusing Gender," paper delivered at a meeting of the Pacific Division of the Society for Women in Philosophy, Los Angeles, May 20.

Haller, Rudolf. 1993. *Neopositivismus*. Darmstadt: Wissenschaftliche Buchgesellschaft.

Haller, Rudolf, and Friedrich Stadler, eds. 1988. *Ernst Mach: Werk und Wirkung*. Vienna: HoderPichler-Tempsky.

Halperin, David. 1995. *Foucault: Two Essays in Gay Hagiography*. New York: Oxford University Press.

Haraway, Donna. 1988. "Situated Knowledges and the Privilege of Partial Perspective," *Feminist Studies* 14: 575–599.

Harding, Sandra. 1986. *The Science Question in Feminism*. Ithaca, N.Y.: Cornell University Press. 1991. *Whose Science? Whose Knowledge? Thinking from Women's Lives*. Ithaca, N.Y.: Cornell University Press.

Hartley, David. 1749. *Observations on Man, His Frame, His Duty, and His Expectations*, 2 vols. London.

Hatfield, Gary. 1986. "The Senses and the Fleshless Eye: *The Meditations* as Cognitive Exercises," in *Essays on Descartes' Meditations*, ed. Amélie Rorty. Berkeley: University of California Press, pp. 45–79.

———. 1989. "Science, Certainty, and Descartes," in *PSA 1988*, vol. 2, ed. David Hull, Mickey Forbes, and Richard Burian. East Lansing, Mich.: Philosophy of Science Association, pp. 249–262.

———. 1990. "Metaphysics and the New Science," in *Reappraisals of the Scientific Revolution*, ed. D. Lindberg and R. Westman. Cambridge: Cambridge University Press, pp. 93–166.

———. 1990. *The Natural and the Normative: Theories of Spatial Perception from Kant to Helmholtz.* Cambridge, Mass.: MIT Press.

———. 1993. "Reason, Nature, and God in Descartes," in *Essays on the Philosophy and Science of René Descartes,* ed. Stephen Voss. New York: Oxford University Press, pp. 259–287.

———. 1995. "Philosophy of Psychology as Philosophy of Science," in *PSA 1994,* vol. 2., ed. David Hull, Mickey Forbes, and Richard Burian. East Lansing, Mich.: Philosophy of Science Association, pp. 19–23.

———. 1995. "Remaking the Science of Mind: Psychology as a Natural Science," in *Inventing Human Science,* ed. Christopher Fox, Roy Porter, and Robert Wokler. Berkeley: University of California Press, pp. 184–231.

———. 1996. "Was the Scientific Revolution Really a Revolution in Science?" in *Tradition, Transmission, Transformation,* ed. Jamil Ragep and Sally Ragep. Leiden: Brill, pp. 489–525.

———. 1997. "Cognitive Faculties," in *Cambridge History of Seventeenth Century Philosophy,* ed. Michael Ayers and Daniel Garber. Cambridge: Cambridge University Press, pp. 952–1001.

Hausman, Daniel. 1992. *Essays on Philosophy and Economic Methodology.* Cambridge: Cambridge University Press.

Heck, Richard. Forthcoming. "The Finite and the Infinite in Frege's *Grundgesetze der Arithmetik,*" in *Philosophy of Mathematics Today,* ed. M. Schirn. Oxford: Oxford University Press.

Heidegger, Martin. 1962. *Being and Time,* trans. J. Macquarrie and E. Robinson. New York: Harper & Row.

———. 1982. *The Basic Problems of Phenomenology,* trans. Albert Hofstadter. Bloomington: Indiana University Press.

———. 1984. *The Metaphysical Foundations of Logic,* trans. Michael Heim. Bloomington: Indiana University Press.

———. 1992. *History of the Concept of Time,* trans. Theodore Kisiel. Bloomington: Indiana University Press.

———. 1993 [1927]. *Sein und Zeit,* 7th. ed. Tübingen: Max Niemeyer.

———. 1996. *Being and Time,* trans. J. Stambaugh. Albany, N.Y.: State University of New York Press.

Heine, Heinrich. 1971. *Sämtliche Schriften,* Band 5, *Zur Geschichte der Religion und Philosophie in Deutschland.* München: Carl Hanser.

Heldke, Lisa M., and Stephen H. Kellert. 1995. "Objectivity as Responsibility," *Metaphilosophy* 26: 360–378.

Hellman, Geoffrey. 1989. *Mathematics without Numbers.* Oxford: Oxford University Press.

Henkin, Leon. 1947. *The Completeness of Formal Systems,* Ph.D. Dissertation, Princeton University.

Henle, James M., and Eugene M. Kleinberg. 1979. *Infinitesimal Calculus.* Cambridge, Mass.: MIT Press.

Henrich, Dieter. 1992. *Aesthetic Judgement and the Moral Image of the World.* Stanford: Stanford University Press.

Hersh, Reuben. 1997. *What Is Mathematics, Really?* New York: Oxford University Press.

Hesse, Mary. 1985. "Epistemology without Foundations," in *Philosophy, Its History and Historiography,* ed. A. J. Holland. Dordrecht: Reidel, pp. 49–68.

Hilbert, David, and Paul Bernays. 1934, 1939. *Grundlagen der Mathematik,* Berlin: Julius Springer, vols. 1 and 2.

Hintikka, Jaakko. 1956. "Identity, Variables and Impredicative Definitions," *Journal of Symbolic Logic* 21: 225–245.

———. 1962. *Knowledge and Belief.* Ithaca: Cornell University Press.

———. 1988. "On the Development of the Model-Theoretic Viewpoint in Logical Theory," *Synthese* 77: 1–36.

————. 1990. "G. H. von Wright on Logical Truth and Distributive Normal Forms," in *The Philosophy of G. H. von Wright*, ed. Paul Arthur Schilpp. La Salle, Ill.: Open Court, pp. 517–537.

————. 1991. "Towards a General Theory of Identifiability," in *Definitions and Definability*, ed. J. Fetzer, D. Shatz, and G. Schlesinger. Dordrecht: Kluwer Academic, pp. 161–183.

————. 1993. "Ludwig's Apple Tree," in *Scientific Philosophy: Origins and Developments*, ed. Friedrich Stadler. Dordrecht: Kluwer Academic, pp. 27–46.

————. 1993. "The Original *Sinn* of Wittgenstein's Philosophy of Mathematics," in *Wittgenstein's Philosophy of Mathematics*, ed. Klaus Puhl. Vienna: Hölder-Pichler-Tempsky, pp. 24–51.

————. 1994. "An Anatomy of Wittgenstein's Picture Theory," in *Artifacts, Representations and Social Practice*, ed. C. C. Gould and Robert S. Cohen. Dordrecht: Kluwer Academic, pp. 223–256.

————. 1996. "The Idea of Phenomenology in Wittgenstein and Husserl," in *Ludwig Wittgenstein: Half-Truths and One-and-a-Half-Truths*, ed. Jaakko Hintikka. Dordrecht: Kluwer Academic, pp. 55–77.

Hintikka, Jaakko, ed. 1995. *From Dedekind to Gödel: Essays on the Development of the Foundations of Mathematics in the Twentieth Century.* Dordrecht: Kluwer.

Hintikka, Jaakko, and Merrill B. Hintikka. 1986. *Investigating Wittgenstein.* New York: Blackwell.

Hoare, C. A. R. 1967. "An Axiomatic Basis for Computer Programming," *Communications of the Association of Computing Machines* 12: 516–580.

Hofman, V. 1998. "Ein Bostoner Streitgespräch über Wittgensteins *Tractatus*," *Frankfurter Allgemeine Zeitung* June 10, 1998.

Holland, A. J., ed. 1985. *Philosophy, Its History and Historiography.* Dordrecht: Reidel.

Holton, Gerald. 1992. "More on Mach and Einstein," in *Ernst Mach—A Deeper Look: Documents and New Perspectives*, ed. John T. Blackmore, Doredrecht: Kluwer Academic, pp. 263–276.

Hornsby, Jennifer. 1990. "Descartes, Rorty and the Mind-Body Fiction," in *Reading Rorty*, ed. Alan R. Malachowski, Oxford: Basil Blackwell, pp. 41–57.

Howard, Don. 1996. "Relativity, *Eindeutigkeit* and Monomorphism," in *Origins of Logical Empiricism*, ed. Ronald N. Giere and Alan W. Richardson. Minneapolis: University of Minnesota Press, pp. 115–164.

Hudson, J., and M. Tye. 1980. "Proper Names and Definite Descriptions with Widest Possible Scope," *Analysis* 40: 63–64.

Hume, David. 1975. *Enquiries concerning Human Understanding and concerning the Principles of Morals*, 3rd ed., ed. P. H. Nidditch. New York: Oxford University Press.

————. 1978. *A Treatise of Human Nature*, 2d ed., ed. P. H. Nidditch, New York: Oxford University Press.

Hurd, Albert E., and Peter A. Loeb. 1985. *An Introduction to Nonstandard Real Analysis.* New York: Academic Press.

Husserl, Edmund. 1897. "Review of E. Mach's 'Über das Prinzip der Vergleichung in der Physik,'" *Archiv für systematische Philosophie* n. f. 3: 241–244.

————. 1900. *Logische Untersuchungen*, vol. I. Halle: Niemeyer.

————. 1901. *Logische Untersuchungen*, vol. II. Halle: Niemeyer.

————. 1913a. *Logische Untersuchungen*, 2d. ed., vol. I and vol. II. part 1. Halle: Niemeyer.

————. 1913b. *Ideen zu einer reinen Phänomenologie und phänomenologischen Philosophie. Erstes Buch: Allgemeine Einführung in die reine Phänomenologie.* Halle: Niemeyer.

————. 1921. *Logische Untersuchungen*, 2d. ed., vol. II, part 2. Halle: Niemeyer.

————. 1930. "Nachwort zu meinen *Ideen zu einer reinen Phänomenologie und phänomenologischen Philosophie*," appendix to Edmund Husserl, *Ideen zu einer reinen Phänomenologie und phänomenologischen Philosophie, Drittes Buch* (*Husserliana* V), ed. Marly Biemel. The Hague: Nijhoff, 1952.

————. 1948. *Erfahrung und Urteil.* Hamburg: Claassen.

————. 1950 [1931]. *Cartesianische Meditationen: Einleitung in die transzendentale Phanomenologie* (posthumously published in *Husserliana* I), ed. Elisabeth Stroker. The Hague: Nijhoff.

————. 1950–. *Gesammelte Werke* (*Husserliana*, Band I-). The Hague: Nijhoff.

————. 1952. *Ideen zu einer reinen Phänomenologie und phänomenologischen Philosophie, Drittes Buch* (*Husserliana* V), ed. Marly Biemel. The Hague: Nijhoff.

————. 1960. *Cartesian Meditations: An Introduction to Phenomenology*, trans. Dorion Cairns. The Hague: Nijhoff.

————. 1970. *Logical Investigations*, trans. J. N. Findlay. London: Routledge and Kegan Paul.

————. 1970 [1891]. *Philosophie der Arithmetik* (*Husserliana* XII), ed. Lothar Eley. The Hague: Nijhoff.

————. 1970. *The Crisis of European Sciences and Transcendental Phenomenology*, trans. David Carr. Evanston, Ill.: Northwestern University Press.

————. 1973. *Ding und Raum* (*Husserliana* XVI), ed. Ulrich Claesges. The Hague: Nijhoff.

————. 1973. *Experience and Judgement*, trans. James S. Churchill and Karl Ameriks. Evanston, Ill.: Northwestern University Press.

————. 1980. *Ideas Pertaining to a Pure Phenomenology and to a Phenomenological Philosophy, Book 1: General introduction to a Pure Phenomenology*, trans. F. Kersten. The Hague: M. Nijhoff.

————. 1981. *Shorter Works*, ed. Peter McCormick and Frederick Elliston. Notre Dame: University of Notre Dame Press. 1984. *Logische Untersuchungen*, Zweiter Band, Erster Teil, *Husserliana*, vol. XIX/1. The Hague: Nijhoff.

Hylton, Peter. 1984. "The Nature of the Proposition and the Revolt against Idealism," in *Philosophy in History*, ed. R. Rorty, J. B. Schneewind, and Q. Skinner. Cambridge: Cambridge University Press, pp. 375–397.

————. 1990. "Logic in Russell's Logicism," in *The Analytic Tradition*, ed. David Bell and Neil Cooper. Oxford: Basil Blackwell, pp. 137–172.

————. 1990. *Russell, Idealism, and the Emergence of Analytic Philosophy*. Oxford: Oxford University Press.

————. 1994. "Functions and Propositional Functions in Principia Mathematica," in *Russell and Early Analytic Philosophy*, ed. A. Irvine and G. Wedeking. Toronto: University of Toronto Press, pp. 342–360.

————. 1995. "Review of *Origins of Analytical Philosophy*," *Journal of Philosophy* 92: 556–563.

————. 1997. "Functions, Operations and Sense in Wittgenstein's Tractatus," in *Early Analytic Philosophy*, ed. W. W. Tait. Chicago/Lasalle: Open Court, pp. 91–106.

James, William. 1950. *The Principles of Psychology*, vol. 2. New York: Dover.

Jammer, Max. 1961. *Concepts of Mass in Classical and Modern Physics*. Cambridge, Mass.: Harvard University Press.

Kaila, Eino. 1979. *Reality and Experience: Four Philosophical Essays*, ed. Robert S. Cohen. Dordrecht: D. Reidel.

————. 1926. *Die Prinzipien der Wahrscheinlichkeitslogik, Annales Universitatis Fennicae Aboensis* Series B, vol. IV, no. 1. Turku.

Kanger, Stig. 1957. *Provability in Logic*. Stockholm: Almqvist and Wiksell.

Kant, Immanuel. 1910–. *Kants gesammelte Schriften, Hrsg. von der königlich preussischen Akademie der Wissenschaften*. Vols. 1–8, Berlin: G. Reimer; vols. 8–28, Berlin: Walter de Gruyter.

————. 1929. *Critique of Pure Reason*, trans. Norman Kemp Smith. New York: St. Martin's Press.

————. 1958. *Critique of Pure Reason* abridged ed., ed. and trans. Norman Kemp Smith. New York: Random House.

Kemp Smith, Norman. 1979. *A Commentary to Kant's Critique of Pure Reason*, 2d rev. ed. London: Macmillan.

Kersey, Ethel M. 1983. "The Noema, Husserlian and Beyond: An Annotated Bibliography of English Language Sources," *Philosophy Research Archives* 9: 62–90.

Kitcher, Philip. 1985. *Vaulting Ambition: Sociobiology and the Quest for Human Nature.* Cambridge, Mass.: MIT Press.

Köhnke, Klaus Christian. 1986. *Enstehung und Aufstieg des Neukantianismus: Die deutsche Universität zwischen Idealismus und Positivismus.* Frankfurt am Main: Suhrkamp.

Koopmans, Tjalling C. 1949. "Identification Problems in Economic Model Construction," *Econometrica* 17: 125–144.

Kozen, Dexter and Rohit Parikh. 1981. "An Elementary Completeness Proof for PDL," *Theoretical Computer Science* 14: 113–118.

Kozen, Dexter, and Jerzy Tiuryn. 1990. "Logics of Programs," in *Handbook of Theoretical Computer Science*, vol. B, ed. Jan van Leeuwen. Cambridge: Mass.: MIT Press/Elsevier, pp. 789–840.

Kreisel, Georg. 1950. "Note on Arithmetic Models for Consistent Formulae of the Predicate Calculus," *Fundamenta Mathematicae* 37: 265–285.

———. 1958. "Review of Wittgenstein's *Remarks on the Foundations of Mathematics*," *British Journal for the Philosophy of Science* 9: 135–158.

———. 1959. "Wittgenstein's Theory and Practice of Philosophy," *British Journal for the Philosophy of Science* 11: 283–252.

———. 1978. "The Motto of 'Philosophical Investigations' and the Philosophy of Proofs and Rules," *Grazer philosophische Studien* 6: 13–38.

———. 1979. "Review of *Remarks on the Foundations of Mathematics*, second edition," *American Scientist* 67: 619.

———. 1982. "Einige Erläuterungen zu Wittgensteins Kummer mit Hilbert und Gödel," in *Epistemology and Philosophy of Science. Proceedings of the 7th International Wittgenstein Symposium*, ed. P. Weingartner and J. Czermak. Vienna: Hölder-Pichler-Tempsky, pp. 295–303.

———. 1989. "Zu Einigen Gesprächen mit Wittgenstein," in *Ludwig Wittgenstein Biographie-Philosophie-Praxis*. Vienna: Catalogue for the Exhibition at the Wiener Secession, 13 September–29 October.

Kreisel, Georg and G. Takeuti. 1974. "Formally Self-Referential Propositions for Cut Free Classical Analysis and Related Systems," in *Dissertationes Mathematicae*. Mathematical Institute of the Polish Academy/Polska Akademia Nauk, Instytut Matematyczny 118.

Kremer, Michael. 1992. "The Multiplicity of General Propositions," *Noûs* 26/4: 409–426.

Kripke, Saul. 1959. "A Completeness Theorem in Modal Logic," *Journal of Symbolic Logic* 24/1: 1–14.

———. 1963. "Semantical Considerations on Modal Logic," *Acta Philosophica Fennica* Fax. XVI: 83–94.

———. 1963. "Semantical Analysis of Modal Logic I: Normal Modal Propositional Calculi," *Zeitschrift für mathematische Logik und Grundlagen der Mathematik* 9: 63–96.

———. 1980. *Naming and Necessity*. Cambridge, Mass.: Harvard University Press.

———. 1982. *Wittgenstein on Rules and Private Language*. Cambridge, Mass.: Harvard University Press.

Küng, Guido. 1977. "The Phenomenological Reduction as 'Epoche' and Explanation," in *Husserl: Expositions and Appraisals*, ed. F. A. Elliston and P. McCormick. Notre Dame: University of Notre Dame Press, pp. 338–349.

Künne, Wolfgang. 1983. "Indexikalität, Sinn und propositionaler Gehalt," *Grazer philosophische Studien* 18: 41–74.

———. 1990. "The Nature of Acts—Moore on Husserl," in *The Analytic Tradition—Meaning, Thought and Knowledge*, ed. D. Bell and N. Cooper. Oxford: Blackwell, pp. 104–116.

———. 1992. "Hybrid Proper Names," *Mind* 101: 721–731.

Kusch, Martin. 1995. *Psychologism*. London: Routledge.

Lacan, Jacques. 1955. "The Freudian Thing," in *Écrits: A Selection*, trans. Alan Sheridan. New York: Norton.

Lambert, Karel. 1974. "Predication and Extensionality," *Journal of Philosophical Logic* 3: 255–264.

Lamberth, David C. 1997. *Metaphysics, Experience and Religion in William James' Thought*. Cambridge: Cambridge University Press.

Langford, C. H. 1952. "The Notion of Analysis in Moore's Philosophy," in *The Philosophy of G. E. Moore*, ed. Paul Arthur Schilpp. New York: Tudor Publishing, pp. 319–342.

Lear, Jonathan. 1984. "The Disappearing 'We,'" *Proceedings of the Aristotelian Society*, supplementary, vol. 58: 219–242.

Lehmann, Gerhard. 1987. "Kant im Spätidealismus," in *Materialien zur Neukantianismus Diskussion*, ed. Hans-Ludwig Ollig, Darmstadt: Wissenschaftliche Buchgesellschaft,

LePore, Ernest, and Brian McLaughlin, eds. 1985. *Truth and Interpretation: Perspectives on the Philosophy of Donald Davidson*. New York: Basil Blackwell.

Lewis, C. I. 1923. "A Pragmatic Conception of the *A Priori*," *Journal of Philosophy* 20: 169–177; reprinted in *Collected Papers of Clarence Irving Lewis*, ed. John D. Goheen and John L. Mothershead, Jr. Stanford, Calif.: Stanford University Press, 1970, pp. 231–239.

———. 1929. *Mind and the World Order*. New York: Scribner's; reprinted, New York: Dover Publishing, 1956.

———. 1918. *A Survey of Symbolic Logic*. Berkeley: University of California Press.

Lewy, C. 1967. "A Note on the Text of the *Tractatus*," *Mind* 76: 416–23.

Lindberg, D., and R. Westman, eds. 1990. *Reappraisals of the Scientific Revolution*. Cambridge: Cambridge University Press.

Linsky, Bernard. 1993. "Why Russell Abandoned Russellian Propositions," in *Russell and Analytic Philosophy*, ed. A. D. Irving and G. A. Wedeking. Toronto: University of Toronto Press, pp. 193–209.

Linsky, Leonard. 1977. *Names and Descriptions*. Chicago: University of Chicago Press.

———. 1988. "Terms and Propositions in Russell's Principles of Mathematics," *Journal of the History of Philosophy* 26: 621–642.

———. 1992. "The Unity of the Proposition," *Journal of the History of Philosophy* 30: 243–273.

Lloyd, Dan. 1989. *Simple Minds*. Cambridge, Mass.: MIT Press.

Locke, John. 1975. *An Essay Concerning Human Understanding*, ed. P. H. Nidditch. Oxford: Oxford University Press.

Loar, Brian. 1976. "The Semantics of Singular Terms," *Philosophical Studies* 30: 353–377.

Longino, Helen. 1990. *Science as Social Knowledge: Values and Objectivity in Scientific Inquiry*. Princeton: Princeton University Press.

Lossius, Johann. 1775. *Physische Ursachen des Wahren*. Gotha.

Lovibond, Sabina. 1983. *Realism and Imagination in Ethics*. Minneapolis: University of Minnesota Press.

Lowe, E. J. 1995. *Locke on Human Understanding*. London: Routledge.

Lugones, María. 1987. "Playfulness, 'World'-Travel, and Loving Perception," *Hypatia* 2: 3–19.

———. 1990. "Hispaneando y Lesbiando: On Sarah Hoagland's *Lesbian Ethics*," *Hypatia* 5: 138–146.

———. 1991. "The Logic of Pluralist Feminism," in *Feminist Ethics*, ed. Claudia Card. Lawrence, Kan.: University Press of Kansas, pp. 40–42.

Mach, Ernst. 1960 [1883]. *The Science of Mechanics*, trans. Thomas J. McCormack. La Salle, Ill.: Open Court.

———. 1959. *The Analysis of Sensations and the Relation of the Physical to the Psychical.* New York: Dover.

———. 1905. *Erkenntnis und Irrtum: Skizzen zur Psychologie der Forschung.* Leipzig: Johann Ambrosius Barth.

MacIntyre, Alasdair. 1980. "Review of *Philosophy and the Mirror of Nature*," *London Review of Books* 2 (5–18 June): 15–16.

Mackie, J. L. 1976. *Problems from Locke.* Oxford: Clarendon Press.

Makkreel, Rudolf A. 1992. *Dilthey: Philosopher of the Human Studies*, 3d ed. Princeton: Princeton University Press.

Malachowski, Alan R., ed. 1990. *Reading Rorty.* Oxford: Basil Blackwell.

Marcus, Ruth Barcan. 1946. "A Functional Calculus of First Order Based on Strict Implication," *Journal of Symbolic Logic* 11: 1–16.

———. 1947. "The Identity of Individuals in a Strict Functional Calculus of Second Order," *Journal of Symbolic Logic* 12: 12–15.

———. 1961. "Modalities and Intensional Languages," *Synthese* 13: 303–322.

Marion, Mathieu. 1998. *Wittgenstein, Finitism, and the Philosophy of Mathematics.* New York: Oxford University Press.

———. Forthcoming. "Operations and Numbers in the Tractatus," in *From the Tractatus to the Tractatus: Wittgenstein Studies*, ed. G. Oliveri. Dordrecht: Reidel.

Marion, Mathieu, and Alain Voizard. 1998. "Frege aujourd'hui," in *Frege: Logique et philosophie*, ed. Mathieu Marion and Alain Voizard. Montréal, Quebec, and Paris: l'Harmattan, pp. 10–11.

McCarty, L. Thorne. 1983. "Permissions and Obligations," in *Proceedings of the Eighth International Joint Conference on Artificial Intelligence*, ed. Alan Bundy. Los Altos: William Kaufmann, pp. 287–294.

McCulloch, Gregory. 1989. *The Game of the Name: Introducing Logic, Language, and Mind.* Oxford: Clarendon Press.

McDowell, John. 1994. *Mind and World.* Cambridge, Mass.: Harvard University Press.

McGinn, Marie. 1999. "Between Metaphysics and Nonsense: Elucidation in Wittgenstein's *Tractatus*," *The Philosophical Quarterly* 49: 491–513.

McGuinness, Brian. 1988. *Wittgenstein: A Life. Young Ludwig 1889–1921.* Berkeley: University of California Press.

McIntyre, Ronald. 1982. "Intending and Referring," in *Husserl, Intentionality and Cognitive Science*, ed. Hubert L. Dreyfus. Cambridge, Mass.: MIT Press, pp. 215–231.

McIntyre, Ronald, and David Woodruff Smith, eds. 1982. *Husserl and Intentionality.* Dordrecht: Reidel.

McKinsey, J. C. C., A.C. Sugar, and Patrick Suppes. 1953. "Axiomatic Foundations of Classical Particle Mechanics," *Journal of Rational Mechanics and Analysis* 2: 253–272.

McMullin, Ernan. 1990. "Conceptions of Science in the Scientific Revolution," in *Reappraisals of the Scientific Revolution*, ed. D. Lindberg and R. Westman. Cambridge: Cambridge University Press, pp. 27–92.

Menger, Karl. 1930. "Der Intuitionismus," *Blätter für deutsche Philosophie* 4: 311–325.

———. 1979. *Selected Papers in Logic and Foundations, Didactics, and Economics.* Dordrecht: Reidel.

———. 1994. *Reminiscences of the Vienna Circle and the Mathematical Colloquium*, ed. L. Golland, B. McGuinness, and A. Sklar. Dordrecht: Kluwer.

Mill, J. S. 1969 [1832–1874]. *Collected Works*, vol. 10, *Essays on Ethics, Religion and Society*, ed. J. M. Robson. Toronto: University of Toronto Press.

Mohanty, Chandra Talpade. 1991. "Under Western Eyes: Feminist Scholarship and Colonial Discourses," in *Third World Women and the Politics of Feminism*, ed. Chandra Talpade Mohanty, Ann Russo, and Lourdes Torres. Bloomington: Indiana University Press, pp. 51–80.

Monk, Ray. 1990. *Ludwig Witgenstein: The Duty of Genius*. New York: Penguin.

Moore, G. E. 1899. "The Nature of Judgment," *Mind* n.s. 8: 176–193.

———. 1901. "Truth and Falsity," in the *Dictionary of Philosophy and Psychology*, vol. 2, ed. John Mark Baldwin. New York: Macmillan, pp. 716–718.

———. 1903. *Principia Ethica*. Cambridge: Cambridge University Press.

———. 1959. *Philosophical Papers*. London: George Allen and Unwin.

———. 1959. "Proof of an External World," in Moore, *Philosophical Papers*. London: George Allen and Unwin, pp. 127–150.

More, M. J. 1980. "Rigidity and Scope," *Logique et Analyse* 23: 327–330.

Morton, Adam, and Stephen Stich, eds. 1996. *Benacerraf and His Critics*. Cambridge, Mass.: Blackwell.

Mulligan, Kevin. 1995. "Perception," in *The Cambridge Companion to Husserl*, ed. Barry Smith and David Woodruff Smith. Cambridge: Cambridge University Press, pp. 168–238.

Nadler, Steven. 1989. *Arnauld and the Cartesian Philosophy of Ideas*. Princeton: Princeton University Press.

———. 1992. *Malebranche and Ideas*. New York: Oxford University Press.

Nagel, Thomas. 1979. "What Is it Like to Be a Bat?" in *Mortal Questions*, ed. Nagel. Cambridge: Cambridge University Press.

Narayan, Uma. 1997. *Dislocating Cultures: Identities, Traditions, and Third World Feminism*. New York: Routledge.

Neale, Stephen. 1990. *Descriptions*. Cambridge, Mass.: MIT Press.

Nedo, Michael, and Michele Ranchetti, eds. 1983. *Wittgenstein: Sein Leben in Bildern und Texten*. Frankfurt am Main: Suhrkamp.

Neiman, Susan. 1994. *The Unity of Reason: Rereading Kant*. Oxford: Oxford University Press.

———. 1995. "Understanding the Unconditioned," *Proceedings of the 8th International Kant Congress*. Memphis, Tenn.: Marquette University Press, pp. 505–519.

———. 1997. "Metaphysics, Philosophy: Rousseau and the Problem of Evil," in *Reclaiming the History of Ethics: Essays in Honor of John Rawls*, ed. B. Herman, C. Korsgaard, and A. Reath. Cambridge: Cambridge University Press, pp. 140–169.

Newton, Isaac. 1687. *Philosophia naturalis principia mathematica*. London.

Nussbaum, Martha. 1994. "Feminists and Philosophy," review of *A Mind of One's Own: Feminist Essays on Reason and Objectivity*, ed. Louise Antony and Charlotte Witt. *New York Review of Books* 41 (October 20): 59–63.

———. 1995. "Reply," *New York Review of Books* 42 (April 6): 48–49.

Nyiri, J. C. 1982. "Wittgenstein's Later Work in Relation to Conservatism," in *Wittgenstein and His Times*, ed. Brian McGuinness. Oxford: Blackwell, pp. 44–68.

———. 1986. "Wittgenstein 1929–1931: The Turning Back," in *Ludwig Wittgenstein: Critical Assessments, vol. 4, From Theology to Sociology: Wittgenstein's Impact on Contemporary Thought*, ed. S.G. Shanker. London: Croom Helm, pp. 29–59.

O'Connor, Peg. Forthcoming. "Moving to New Boroughs: Transforming the World by Inventing Language Games," in *Feminist Readings of Wittgenstein*, ed. Naomi Scheman.

Okrent, M. 1988. *Heidegger's Pragmatism*. Ithaca, N.Y.: Cornell University Press.

Olafson, F. 1987. *Heidegger and the Philosophy of Mind*. New Haven: Yale University Press.

O'Neil, Brian E. 1974. *Epistemological Direct Realism in Descartes' Philosophy*. Albuquerque: University of New Mexico Press.

Ostrow, M. 1999. *Wittgenstein, Plato, and the Liberating Word*, Ph.D. Dissertation, Boston University.

Parikh, Rohit. 1978. "The Completeness of Propositional Dynamic Logic," *7th MFCS, Springer Lecture Notes in Computer Science* 64: 403–415.

———. 1985. "The Logic of Games," *Annals of Discrete Mathematics* 24: 111–140.

———. 1994. "Vagueness and Utility: The Semantics of Common Nouns," *Linguistics and Philosophy* 17: 521–35.

———. 1996. "Vague Predicates and Language Games," *Theoria* [Spain] XI/27: 97–107.

———. 1996. "Computation," in *Encyclopedia of Philosophy*, supplement. New York: MacMillan, pp 86–87.

Parsons, Charles. 1982 [1965]. "Frege's Theory of Number," in Charles Parsons, *Mathematics in Philosophy*. Ithaca, N.Y.: Cornell University Press, pp. 150–172.

———. 1982 [1974]. "The Liar Paradox," in *Mathematics in Philosophy*, ed. Charles Parsons. Ithaca, N.Y.: Cornell University Press, pp. 221–250.

———. 1982. "Objects and Logic," *Monist* 65: 491–516.

———. 1987. "Developing Arithmetic in Set Theory without Infinity: Some Historical Remarks," *History and Philosophy of Logic* 8: 201–213.

———. 1998. "Hao Wang as Philosopher and Interpreter of Gödel," *Philosophia Mathematica* 3/5: 3–24.

Patey, Douglas Lane. 1984. *Probability and Literary Form: Philosophic Theory and Literary Practice in the Augustan Age*. Cambridge: Cambridge University Press.

Peacocke, Christopher. 1992. *A Study of Concepts*. Cambridge, Mass.: MIT Press.

Pears, David. 1998. "Le Wittgenstein de Hintikka," in *Jaakko Hintikka, Questions de Logique et de Phénoménologie*, ed. Elisabeth Rigel. Paris: J. Vrin.

———. 1993. "Connections between Wittgenstein's Treatment of Solipsism and the Private Language Argument," in *A Wittgenstein Symposium*, ed. Josep-Maria Terricabras. Amsterdam: Rodopi, pp. 79–91.

———. 1993. "The Ego and the Eye: Wittgenstein's Use of an Analogy," *Grazer philosophische Studien* 44: 59–68.

Penrose, Roger. 1989. *The Emperor's New Mind: Concerning Computers, Minds, and the Laws of Physics*. New York: Oxford University Press.

Perry, John. 1993. *The Problem of the Essential Indexical and Other Essays*. Oxford: Oxford University Press.

Pessin, Andrew and Sanford Goldberg, eds. 1996. *The Twin Earth Chronicles: Twenty Years of Reflection on Hilary Putnam's "The Meaning of 'Meaning.'"* London and Armonk, N.Y.: M. E. Sharpe.

Philipse, Herman. 1994. "Husserl and the Origins of Analytical Philosophy," *European Journal of Philosophy* 2: 165–184.

Plantinga, Alvin. 1978. "The Boethian Compromise," *American Philosophical Quarterly* 15: 129–138.

Pnueli, Amir. 1977. "The Temporal Logic of Programs," *Proceedings of the 18th Annual IEEE Symposium on the Foundations of Computer Science*: 46–57.

Poincaré, Henri. 1904. *Science and Hypothesis*, trans. George Bruce Halsted. Walter Scott Publishing; reprinted, New York: Dover Publishing, 1952.

———. 1909. "La logique de l'infini," *Revue de Métaphysique et de Morale* 17: 461–482.

Post, Emil L. 1921. "Introduction to a General Theory of Elementary Propositions," *American Journal of Mathematics* 43: 163–85.

———. 1965. "Absolutely Unsolvable Problems and Relatively Undecidable Propositions—Account of an Anticipation," in *The Undecidable*, ed. Martin Davis. Hewlett, N.Y.: Raven Press.

Pratt, V. R. 1976. "Semantical Considerations on Floyd-Hoare Logic," *Proceedings of the 17th Annual IEEE Symposium on the Foundations of Computer Science*: 109–121.

Putnam, Hilary. 1962. "What Theories Are Not," in Hilary Putnam, *Philosophical Papers, vol. 1: Mathematics, Matter and Method*, 2d ed. Cambridge: Cambridge University Press, pp. 215–227.

———. 1978. *Meaning and the Moral Sciences*. London: Routledge and Kegan Paul.

———. 1979. *Philosophical Papers, vol. 1: Mathematics, Matter and Method*, 2d ed. Cambridge: Cambridge University Press.

———. 1988. *Representation and Reality*, Cambridge, Mass: MIT Press.

———. 1991. "Logical Positivism and Intentionality," in *Words and Life*, ed. Hilary Putnam. Cambridge, Mass.: Harvard University Press, pp. 85–98.

———. 1991. "Reichenbach and the Myth of the Given," in *Words and Life*, ed. Hilary Putnam, Cambridge, Mass.: Harvard University Press, pp. 115–130.

———. 1993. "Reichenbach and the Limits of Vindication," in *Words and Life*, ed. Hilary Putnam. Cambridge, Mass.: Harvard University Press, pp. 131–148.

———. 1994. "The Dewey Lectures 1994: Sense, Nonsense and the Senses; An Inquiry into the Powers of the Human Mind," *The Journal of Philosophy* 91: 445–517.

———. 1994. *Words and Life*. Cambridge, Mass.: Harvard University Press.

———. 1996. "On Wittgenstein's Philosophy of Mathematics," *Proceedings of the Aristotelian Society*, supplementary, vol. 70: 243–264.

———. 1997. "A Half Century of Philosophy Viewed from Within," *Daedelus* Winter 1997: 175–208.

———. Forthcoming. "Richard Rorty on Reality and Justification," in *Festschrift for Ben-Ami Scharfstein*, ed. Shlomo Biderman.

Quine, W. V. 1932. *The Logic of Sequences*, Ph.D. Dissertation, Harvard University; later published, New York: Garland Publishing, 1990.

———. 1936. "Truth by Convention," in *Philosophical Essays for A. N. Whitehead*, ed. O. H. Lee. New York: Longmans, pp. 90–124.

———. 1937. "Logic Based on Inclusion and Abstraction," *Journal of Symbolic Logic* 2: 145–152.

———. 1941. *Elementary Logic*. Boston: Ginn.

———. 1950. *Methods of Logic*. New York: Holt.

———. 1951. "Two Dogmas of Empiricism," *The Philosophical Review* 60: 20–43.

———. 1953. *From a Logical Point of View*. Cambridge, Mass.: Harvard University Press.

———. 1960. *Word and Object*. Cambridge, Mass.: MIT Press.

———. 1963. "Carnap and Logical Truth," in *The Philosophy of Rudolf Carnap*, ed. Paul Arthur Schilpp. La Salle, Ill.: Open Court, pp. 385–406.

———. 1964. "Implicit Definition Sustained," *The Journal of Philosophy* 61: 71–74.

———. 1964. "Meaning and Translation," in *The Structure of Language*, ed. J. Fodor and J. Katz. New York: Prentice Hall, pp. 460–478.

———. 1969. "Ontological Relativity," in *Ontological Relativity and Other Essays*. New York: Columbia University Press, pp. 69–90.

———. 1969. *Ontological Relativity and Other Essays*. New York: Columbia University Press.

———. 1971. "Homage to Rudolf Carnap," *Boston Studies in the Philosophy of Science* 8: xxii–xxv.

———. 1976. *Ways of Paradox*. Cambridge, Mass.: Harvard University Press.

———. 1981. *Theories and Things*. Cambridge, Mass.: Harvard University Press.

———. 1985. *Time of My Life*. Cambridge, Mass.: MIT Press.

———. 1986. "Autobiography," in *The Philosophy of W. V. Quine*, ed. Lewis Edwin Hahn and Paul Arthur Schilpp. LaSalle, Ill.: Open Court, pp. 3–46.

———. 1990. *The Pursuit of Truth*. Cambridge, Mass.: Harvard University Press.

———. 1991. "Two Dogmas in Retrospect," *Canadian Journal of Philosophy* 21: 265–274.

———. 1995. *From Stimulus to Science*. Cambridge, Mass.: Harvard University Press.

———. 1995. "Reactions," in *On Quine*, ed. Paolo Leonardi and Marco Santambrogio. Cambridge: Cambridge University Press, pp. 347–361.

———. 1995. *Selected Logic Papers*, enlarged ed. Cambridge, Mass.: Harvard University Press.

———. Unpublished. "From Stimulus to Science," lecture at Lehigh University, October 15, 1990.

Rajchman, John, and Cornel West, ed. 1985. *Post-Analytic Philosophy*, New York: Columbia University Press.

Ramsey, F. P. 1960. *The Foundations of Mathematics*, ed. R. B. Braithwaite. Paterson, N.J.: Littlefield, Adams.

Rawls, John. 1971. *A Theory of Justice*. Cambridge, Mass: Harvard University Press.

———. 1982. "Basic Liberties and Their Priority," *Tanner Lectures On Human Values* 3. Salt Lake City: University of Utah Press.

———. 1988. "The Priority of the Right and Ideas of the Good,"*Philosophy and Public Affairs* 17 (Fall): 251–276.

———. 1993. *Political Liberalism*. New York: Columbia University Press.

———. 1995. "Reply to Habermas," *Journal of Philosophy* 92 (March): 132–180, reprinted in John Rawls, *Political Liberalism*. New York: Columbia University Press, 1996.

———. 1996. *Political Liberalism*, paperback ed. New York: Columbia University Press.

———. 1997. "The Idea of Public Reason Revisited," *The University of Chicago Law Review* 64, no. 3 (Summer): 765–807.

Reichenbach, Hans. 1938. *Experience and Prediction*, Chicago: University of Chicago Press.

———. 1952. "Are Phenomenal Reports Absolutely Certain?" *Philosophical Review* 61: 147–159.

Reid, Thomas. 1895. *Works*, 8th ed., 2 vols., ed. W. Hamilton. Edinburgh.

Richardson, J. 1986. *Existential Epistemology*. Oxford: Clarendon Press.

Rickert, Heinrich. 1986. *Limits of Concept Formation in the Natural Sciences: A Logical Introduction to the Historical Sciences*, abridged ed., ed. and trans. Guy Oakes. Cambridge: Cambridge University Press.

Ricketts, Thomas. 1982. "Rationality, Translation, and Epistemology Naturalized," *The Journal of Philosophy* 79: 117–136.

———. 1985. "Frege, the *Tractatus*, and the Logocentric Predicament," *Noûs* 19: 3–14.

———. 1986. "Objectivity and Objecthood: Frege's Metaphysics of Judgment," in *Frege Synthesized*, ed. L. Haaparanta and J. Hintikka. Dordrecht: D. Reidel, pp. 65–95.

———. 1994. "Carnap's Principle of Tolerance, Empiricism, and Conventionalism," in *Reading Putnam*, ed. P. Clark and B. Hale. Oxford: Blackwell, pp. 176–200.

———. 1996. "Carnap: From Logical Syntax to Semantics," in *The Origins of Logical Empiricism*, ed. R. Giere and A. Richardson. Minneapolis: University of Minnesota Press, pp. 231–250.

———. 1996. "Logic and Truth in Frege," *The Aristotelian Society*, supplementary, vol. 70: 121–140.

———. 1996. "Pictures, Logic, and the Limits of Sense in Wittgenstein's *Tractatus*," in *The Cambridge Companion to Wittgenstein*, ed. H. Sluga and D. Stern. Cambridge: Cambridge University Press, pp. 59–99.

Ritter, Joachim, ed. 1971–. *Historisches Wörterbuch der Philosophie*. Basel: Schwabe.

Robinson, Abraham. 1961. "Non-standard Analysis," *Koninklijke Nederlandse Akademie van Wetenschappen* (Amsterdam), proceedings, series A, vol. 64 (or *Indagationes mathematicae*, vol. 23): 432–440

———. 1996. *Non-standard Analysis*, rev. ed. Princeton: Princeton University Press.

Rogers, Hartley. 1967. *Theory of Recursive Functions and Effective Computability*. New York: McGraw-Hill.

Rorty, Richard. 1979. *Philosophy and the Mirror of Nature*. Princeton: Princeton University Press.

———. 1982. *Consequence of Pragmatism: Essays 1972–1980*. Minneapolis, Minn.: University of Minnesota Press.

———. 1991. *Essays on Heidegger and Others*. Cambridge: Cambridge University Press.

———. 1991. "Heidegger, Contingency, and Pragmatism," in *Essays on Heidegger and Others*. Cambridge: Cambridge University Press, pp. 27–49.

Rorty, Richard, ed. 1967. *The Linguistic Turn*. Chicago: University of Chicago Press.

Rorty, Richard, J. B. Schneewind, and Quentin Skinner, eds. 1984. *Philosophy in History*. Cambridge: Cambridge University Press.

Rosen, Stanley. 1980. "Review of *Philosophy and the Mirror of Nature*," *Review of Metaphysics* 33: 799–802.

Rosovky, Henry. 1990. *The University: An Owner's Manual*. New York: Norton.

Rota, Gian-Carlo. 1996. "Fine Hall in its Golden Age," in *Indiscrete Thoughts*, ed. Fabrizio Palombi. Boston: Birkhauser.

Russell, Bertrand. 1903. *The Principles of Mathematics*. Cambridge: Cambridge University Press.

———. 1904. "Meinong's Theory of Complexes and Assumptions," *Mind* n.s. 13: 509–524.

———. 1905. "On Denoting," *Mind* n.s. 14: 479–493.

———. 1906. "On the Nature of Truth," *Proceedings of the Aristotelian Society* n.s. 7: 28–49.

———. 1908. "Mathematical Logic As Based on the Theory of Types," *American Journal of Mathematics* 30: 222–262.

———. 1910. "Some Explanations in Reply to Mr. Bradley," *Mind* n.s. 19: 372–378.

———. 1912. *The Problems of Philosophy*. London: William and Norgate.

———. 1919. *Introduction to Mathematical Philosophy*. London: Allen & Unwin.

———. 1926 [1914]. *Our Knowledge of the External World*. London: George Allen and Unwin.

———. 1936. "The Limits of Empiricism," *Proceedings of the Aristotelian Society* 36: 131–150.

———. 1945. *A History of Western Philosophy*. London: George Allen and Unwin.

———. 1948. "Whitehead and *Principia Mathematica*," *Mind* 57: 137–138.

———. 1956. "Logical Positivism," in Bertand Russell, *Logic and Knowledge*. New York: Macmillan, pp. 367–382.

———. 1959. *The Problems of Philosophy*. Oxford: Oxford University Press.

———. 1963. *Mysticism and Logic*. London: George Allen and Unwin.

———. 1963 [1901]. "Recent Work on the Principles of Mathematics," reprinted as "Mathematics and the Metaphysicians" in Bertrand Russell, *Mysticism and Logic*. London: George Allen and Unwin.

———. 1966. *Philosophical Essays*. London: George Allen and Unwin.

———. 1966 [1910]. "The Nature of Truth and Falsehood," in Bertrand Russell, *Philosophical Essays*. London: George Allen and Unwin, 1966, pp. 147–159.

———. 1967. *Autobiography I*. Boston: Little, Brown & Company.

———. 1983. *The Collected Papers of Bertrand Russell*, vol. 7, *Theory of Knowledge: The 1913 Manuscript*, ed. Elizabeth Eames. London: Routledge.

———. 1992. *The Collected Papers of Bertrand Russell*, vol. 6, *Logical and Philosophical Papers: 1909–1913*, ed. John G. Slater. London: Routledge.

———. 1994. *The Collected Papers of Bertrand Russell*, vol. 4, *Foundations of Logic: 1903–05*, ed. Alasdair Urquhart. London: Routledge.

———. 1994 [1905]. "Necessity and Possibility," in Bertrand Russell, *The Collected Papers of Bertrand Russell*, vol. 4, *Foundations of Logic: 1903–05*, ed. Alasdair Urquhart. London: Routledge, pp. 507–520.

———. 1994 [1905]. "The Nature of Truth," in Bertrand Russell, *The Collected Papers of Bertrand Russell*, vol. 4, *Foundations of Logic: 1903–05*, ed. Alasdair Urquhart. London: Routledge.

———. 1996. "Review of Ramsey's *Foundations of Mathematics*," in *The Collected Papers of Bertrand Russell*, vol. 10, *A Fresh Look at Empiricism 1927–1942*, J. G. Slater and P. Köllner, eds. New York: Routledge.

Sacks, Gerald. 1972. *Saturated Model Theory*. Reading, Mass.: W. A. Benjamin.

———. 1990. *Higher Recursion Theory*. Berlin, Heidelberg: Springer.

———. Forthcoming. "The PH Problem with Applications."

Salmon, Nathan U. 1981. *Reference and Essence*, Princeton: Princeton University Press.

Scarry, Elaine. 1985. *The Body in Pain: The Making and Unmaking of the World*. Oxford: Oxford University Press.

Scheman, Naomi. 1980. "Anger and the Politics of Naming," in *Women and Language in Literature and Society*, ed. Sally McConnell-Ginet, Ruth Borker, and Nelly Furman. New York: Praeger, pp. 174–187.

———. 1993. *Engenderings: Constructions of Knowledge, Authority, and Privilege*. New York: Routledge.

———. 1996. "Forms of Life: Mapping the Rough Ground," in *The Cambridge Companion to Wittgenstein*, ed. Hans Sluga and David G. Stein. Cambridge: Cambridge University Press, pp. 383–410.

———. 1996. "Feeling Our Way toward Moral Objectivity," in *Mind and Morals: Essays on Cognitive Science and Ethics*, ed. Larry May, Marilyn Friedman, and Andy Clark. Cambridge, Mass: MIT Press, pp. 221–236.

Scheman, Naomi, ed. Forthcoming. *Feminist Readings of Wittgenstein*. University Park, Penn.: Penn State Press.

Schilpp, Paul Arthur, ed. 1952. *The Philosophy of G. E. Moore*. New York: Tudor Publishing.

———. 1963. *The Philosophy of Rudolf Carnap*. LaSalle, Ill.: Open Court.

———. 1980. *The Philosophy of G. H. von Wright*. La Salle, Ill.: Open Court.

Schlick, Moritz. 1918. *Allgemeine Erkenntnislehre*. Julius Springer, Berlin.

———. 1938 [1930]. "Gibt es ein materiales Apriori?" in *Gesammelte Aufsätze, 1926–36*, ed. F. Waismann. Vienna: Gerold.

———. 1938. *Gesammelte Aufsätze, 1926–36*. Vienna: Gerold.

———. 1967. "The Future of Philosophy," in *The Linguistic Turn*, ed. Richard Rorty. Chicago: University of Chicago Press, pp. 43–53.

———. 1979. *Philosophical Papers*, vol. II (1925–1936), ed. Henk L. Mulder and Barbara F. B. van de Velde-Schlick. Dordrecht: Reidel.

Schopenhauer, Arthur. 1958. *The World As Will and Representation*, trans. E. F. J. Payne. New York: Dover.

Schuhmann, K. 1977. *Husserl-Chronik*. The Hague: Nijhoff.

———. 1993. "Husserl's Theory of Indexicals," in *Phenomenology—East and West*, ed. F. M. Kirkland and D. P. Chattopadhyaya. Dordrecht: Reidel, pp. 111–127.

Schumpeter, Joseph. 1990. *History of Economic Analysis*, ed. Elizabeth Boody Schumpeter. New York: Oxford University Press.

Schwartz, Robert. 1983. "Review of *Philosophy and the Mirror of Nature*," *The Journal of Philosophy* 80: 51–67.

Searle, John. 1980. "Minds, Brains and Programs," *Behavioral and Brain Sciences* 3: 417–457.

Sellars, Wilfrid. 1978. "Berkeley and Descartes: Reflections on the Theory of Ideas," in *Studies in Perception: Interrelations in the History and Philosophy of Science*, ed. Peter Machamer and Robert Turnbull. Columbus: Ohio State University Press, pp. 259–311.

Shabel, Lisa. Forthcoming. "Kant on the 'Symbolic Construction' of Mathematical Concepts," *Studies in History and Philosophy of Science*.

Shanker, S. G. 1988. "Wittgenstein's Remarks on the Significance of Gödel's Theorem," in *Gödel's Theorem in Focus*, ed. S. G. Shanker. London: Croom Helm, pp. 155–256.

Shanker, S. G., ed. 1986. *Ludwig Wittgenstein: Critical Assessments*, vol. 3. London: Croom Helm.

Shapiro, Stewart. 1991. *Foundations without Foundationalism: A Case for Second-Order Logic*. Oxford: Oxford University Press.

Simmons, Alison. 1994. "Explaining Sense Perception: A Scholastic Challenge," *Philosophical Studies* 73: 257–275.

Simon, Herbert A. 1977. *Models of Discovery: Topics in the Methods of Science*. Dordrecht: D. Reidel.

Simons, Peter. 1995. "Meaning and Language," in *The Cambridge Companion to Husserl*, ed. Barry Smith and David Woodruff Smith. Cambridge: Cambridge University Press, pp. 106–137.

Skinner, Quentin. 1981. "Review of *Philosophy and the Mirror of Nature*," *New York Review of Books* 28 (19 March): 46.

Sleigh, Robert. 1968. "On a Proposed System of Epistemic Logic," *Noûs* 2: 391–398.

Smith, A. D. 1984. "Rigidity and Scope," *Mind* 93: 177–193.

Smith, Barry and David Woodruff Smith, eds. 1995. *The Cambridge Companion to Husserl*. Cambridge: Cambridge University Press.

Smith, David. 1989. *The Circle of Acquaintance*. Dordrecht: Reidel.

Soames, Scott. 1983. "Generality, Truth Functions and Expressive Capacity," *Philosophical Review* 92: 573–589.

Sober, Elliott. 1988. *Reconstructing the Past: Parsimony, Evolution, and Inference*. Cambridge, Mass.: MIT Press.

Soffer, Gail. 1991. *Husserl and the Question of Relativism*. Dordrecht: Kluwer.

Sokal, Alan. 1996. "Transgressing the Boundaries: Toward a Transformative Hermeneutics of Quantum Gravity," *Social Text* 46/47: 217–252.

———. 1996. "A Physicist Experiments with Cultural Studies," *Lingua Franca* May/June: 62–64.

Sokal, Alan et al. 1996. "Mystery Science Theater," *Lingua Franca* July/August: 62–64.

Sommer, Manfred. 1988. "Denkökonomie und Empfindungstheorie bei Mach und Husserl: Zum Verhältnis von Positivismus und Phänomenologie," in *Ernst Mach: Werk und Wirkung*, ed. Rudolf Haller and Friedrich Stadler. Vienna: Hoder Pichler-Tempsky, pp. 309–328.

———. 1987. *Evidenz im Augenblick: Eine Phänomenologie der reinen Empfindung*. Frankfurt am Main: Suhrkamp.

———. 1985. *Husserl und der frühe Positivismus*. Frankfurt am Main: Vittorio Klostermann.

Spelman, Elizabeth V. 1988. *Inessential Woman: Problems of Exclusion in Feminist Thought*. Boston: Beacon Press.

Spiegelberg, Herbert. 1970. "Husserl in England: Facts and Lessons," *Journal of the British Society for Phenomenology*: 4–17.

Spiel, Hilde. 1987. *Vienna's Golden Autumn from the Watershed Year 1866 to Hitler's Anschluss 1938*. New York: Weidenfeld and Nicholson.

Spinoza, Benedict de. 1985. *Ethics*, in Benedict de Spinoza, *Collected Works*, vol. 1, ed. and trans. Edwin Curley. Princeton: Princeton University Press.

Stadler, Friedrich. 1992. "The 'Verein Ernst Mach'—What was it really?" in *Ernst Mach—A Deeper Look: Documents and New Perspectives*, ed. John T. Blackmore. Dordrecht: Kluwer Academic, pp. 363–377.

Stalnaker, Robert. 1978. "Assertion," in *Syntax and Semantics*, vol. 9, *Pragmatics*, ed. P. Cole. New York: Academic Press, pp. 315–322.

Steiner, Mark. 1975. *Mathematical Knowledge*. Ithaca, N.Y.: Cornell University Press.

———. 1996. "Wittgenstein: Mathematics, Regularities and Rules" in *Benacerraf and His Critics*, ed. Adam Morton and Stephen Stich. Cambridge, Mass.: Blackwell, pp. 190–212.

———. 1998. *The Applicability of Mathematics as a Philosophical Problem*. Cambridge, Mass., Harvard University Press.

———. 2001. "Wittgenstein As His Own Worst Enemy: The Case of Gödel's Theorem," *Philosophia Mathematica* 3 (9): 901–928.

Stone, Sandy. 1991. "The Empire Strikes Back: A Posttranssexual Manifesto," in *Body*

Guards: The Cultural Politics of Gender, ed. Julia Epstein and Kristina Straub. New York: Routledge, pp. 280–304.

Strawson, P. F. 1959. *Individuals: An Essay in Descriptive Metaphysics*. London: Methuen.

———. 1966. *The Bounds of Sense*. London: Methuen.

———. 1985. *Skepticism and Naturalism: Some Varieties*. New York: Columbia University Press.

Stroud, Barry. 1968. "Transcendental Arguments," *Journal of Philosophy* 65: 241–256.

———. 1984. *The Significance of Philosophical Scepticism*. Oxford: Clarendon Press.

———. 1989. "Understanding Human Knowledge in General," *Knowledge and Skepticism*, ed. M. Clay and K. Lehrer. Boulder, Colo: Westview Press, pp. 31–50.

Stryker, Susan. 1994. "My Words to Victor Frankenstein above the Village of Chamonix," *GLQ: A Journal of Lesbian and Gay Studies* 1: 237–254.

Sullivan, Peter. 1994. "Ramsey's Definition of Identity: A Tractarian Criticism," in *The British Tradition in 20th Century Philosophy*, ed. J. Hintikka and K. Puhl. Vienna: Austrian Ludwig Wittgenstein Society, pp. 501–507.

———. 1995. "Wittgenstein on the 'Foundations of Mathematics', June 1927," *Theoria* 61: 105–142.

Sundholm, Goran. 1992. "The General Form of the Operation in Wittgenstein's *Tractatus*," *Grazer Philosophische Studien* 42: 57–76.

Tarski, Alfred. 1983 [1935]. "On the Concept of Logical Consequence," in Alfred Tarski, *Logic, Semantics, Metamathematics: Papers From 1923 to 1938*, rev. ed., trans. J. H. Woodger, ed. John Corcoran. Indianapolis, Ind.: Hackett Publishing (1st ed., Oxford: Oxford University Press, 1956), pp. 409–420.

Tennant, Neil. 1994. "Carnap and Quine," in *Logic, Language, and the Structure of Scientific Theories*, ed. Wesley Salmon and Gereon Wolters. Pittsburgh: University of Pittsburgh Press, pp. 305–344.

Textor, Markus. 1996. *Bolzanos Propositionalismus*. Berlin: Walter de Gruyter.

Toulmin, Stephen. 1992. *Cosmopolis: The Hidden Agenda of Modernity*. Chicago: University of Chicago Press.

Turner, R. Steven. 1994. *In the Eye's Mind: Vision and the Helmholtz-Hering Controversy*. Princeton: Princeton University Press.

van Heijenoort, Jean ed. 1967. *From Frege to Gödel: A Sourcebook in Modern Logic, 1879–1931*. Cambridge, Mass.: Harvard University Press.

———. 1967. "Logic as Calculus and Logic as Language," *Synthese* 17: 324–330.

———. 1970. *Frege and Gödel: Two Fundamental Texts in Mathematical Logic*. Cambridge, Mass.: Harvard University Press.

Vidal, Fernando. 1993. "Psychology in the Eighteenth Century," *History of the Human Sciences* 6: 89–119.

Visser, Henk. 1992. "Mach, Utrecht, and Dutch Philosophy," in *Ernst Mach—A Deeper Look: Documents and New Perspectives*, ed. John T. Blackmore. Dordrecht: Kluwer Academic, pp. 703–730.

von Kries, Johannes. 1916. *Logik, Grundzüge einer kritischen und formalen Urteilslehre*. Tübingen: J. C. Mohr.

von Wright, G. H. 1979. "Introduction," in Eino Kaila, *Reality and Experience: Four Philosophical Essays*, ed. Robert S. Cohen. Dordrecht: D. Reidel, pp. ix–xliii.

Wang, Hao. 1986. *Beyond Analytic Philosophy: Doing Justice to What We Know*. Cambridge, Mass.: MIT Press.

———. 1987. *Reflections on Gödel*. Cambridge, Mass.: MIT Press.

———. 1991. "To and From Philosophy—Discussions with Gödel and Wittgenstein," *Synthese* 88/2: 229–277.

———. 1992. "Imagined Discussions with Gödel and Wittgenstein," *Jahrbuch 1992 der Kurt-Gödel-Gesellschaft*: 3–49.

Waismann, Friedrich. 1951. *Introduction to Mathematical Thinking: The Formulation of Concepts in Modern Mathematics*. New York: Harper Torchbooks.

————. 1982. *Lectures on the Philosophy of Mathematics*. Amsterdam: Rodopi.

Watson, Alister. 1930. "Mathematics and Its Foundations," *Mind* 47: 440–451.

Watson, Richard A. 1995. *Representational Ideas from Plato to Churchland*. Boston: Kluwer Academic Publishers.

Weiner, Joan. 1990. *Frege in Perspective*. Ithaca, N.Y.: Cornell University Press.

————. 1995. "Burge's Literal Interpretation," *Mind* 104: 585–597.

————. 1997. "Has Frege a Philosophy of Language?" in *Early Analytic Philosophy: Essays in Honor of Leonard Linsky*, ed. W.W. Tait. LaSalle, Ill.: Open Court, pp. 249–272.

————. Forthcoming. "Understanding Frege's Project," in *The Cambridge Companion to Frege*, ed. Thomas Ricketts. Cambridge: Cambridge University Press.

Weiss, Bernhard. 1995. "On the Demise of Russell's Multiple Relations Theory of Judgment," *Theoria* 61: 261–282.

West, Cornel. 1989. *The American Evasion of Philosophy: A Genealogy of Pragmatism*. Madison: University of Wisconsin Press.

Westfall, Richard S. 1980. *Never at Rest*. Cambridge: Cambridge Univerity Press.

Wharton, Edith. 1962 [1920]. *The Age of Innocence*. New York: New American Library.

White, Morton. 1956. *Toward Reunion in Philosophy*. Cambridge, Mass.: Harvard University Press.

White, R. 1979. "Wittgenstein on Identity," *Proceedings of the Aristotelian Society*, n.s. 78: 157–174.

Whitehead, Alfred North. 1898. *A Treatise on Universal Algebra with Applications*. Cambridge: Cambridge University Press.

————. 1911. *An Introduction to Mathematics*. London: Williams and Norgate.

Whitehead, Alfred North and Bertrand Russell. 1910. *Principia Mathematica*, vol. 1. Cambridge: Cambridge University Press.

————. 1912. *Principia Mathematica*, vol. 2. Cambridge: Cambridge University Press.

Wiener, Norbert. 1914. "A Simplification of the Logic of Relation," *Proceedings of the Cambridge Philosophical Society* 17: 387–390.

Williams, Bernard. 1978. *Descartes*. New York: Penguin.

Williams, Patricia. 1991. *Alchemy of Race and Rights: Diary of a Law Professor*. Cambridge, Mass.: Harvard University Press.

Wilson, Margaret. 1978. *Descartes*, London: Routledge.

Wittgenstein, Ludwig. 1913. "On Logic and How Not to Do It," *The Cambridge Review* 34: 351.

————. 1921. *Logische-Philosophische Abhandlung, Annalen der Naturphilosophie* 44: 185–262.

————. 1922. *Tractatus Logico-Philosophicus*, trans. C. K. Ogden. New York: Routledge and Kegan Paul.

————. 1929. "Some Remarks on Logical Form," *Proceedings of the Aristotelian Society*, supplementary vol. 9: 162–171.

————. 1958 [1953]. *Philosophical Investigations*, 3d ed., ed. G. E. M. Anscombe and R. Rhees, trans. G. E. M. Anscombe. Oxford: Basil Blackwell & Mott.

————. 1958. *The Blue and Brown Books*. Oxford: Blackwell.

————. 1961. *Tractatus Logico-Philosophicus*, trans. D. F. Pears and B. F. McGuinness. London: Routlege and Kegan Paul.

————. 1961. *Notebooks 1914–1916*, ed. G. H. von Wright and G. E. M. Anscombe, trans. G.E.M. Anscombe. Oxford: Blackwell.

————. 1967. *The Wittgenstein Papers*, microfilm. Cornell University.

————. 1967. *Zettel*, ed. G. E. M. Anscombe and G. H. von Wright, trans. G. E. M. Anscombe. Oxford: Blackwell.

————. 1969. *On Certainty*, ed. G. E. M. Anscombe and G. H. von Wright. Oxford: Blackwell.

————. 1973. *Ludwig Wittgenstein and the Vienna Circle*, shorthand notes recorded by F. Waismann, ed. B. McGuinness and J. Schulte, trans. B. McGuiness. Oxford: Blackwell.

———. 1974. *Philosophical Grammar*, ed. R. Rhees, trans. A. J. P. Kenny. Oxford: Blackwell.

———. 1975. *Philosophical Remarks*, ed. R. Rhees, R. Hargreaves, trans. R. White. Oxford: Blackwell.

———. 1977. *Vermischte Bemerkungen*. Frankfurt am Main: Suhrkamp.

———. 1976. *Remarks on the Foundations of Mathematics*, ed. G. H. von Wright, R. Rhees, G. E. M. Anscombe, trans. G. E. M. Anscombe, rev. ed. Cambridge, Mass.: MIT Press.

———. 1979. *Cambridge Lectures: 1932–1935*, from the Notes of Alice Ambrose and Margaret Macdonald, ed. Alice Ambrose. Chicago: University of Chicago Press.

———. 1979. *Notebooks, 1914–1916*, ed. G. H. von Wright and G. E. M. Anscombe. Chicago: University of Chicago Press.

———. 1980. *Culture and Value*, ed. G. H. von Wright, trans. Peter Winch. Chicago: University of Chicago Press.

———. 1980. *Wittgenstein's Lectures, Cambridge 1930–32, from the Notes of John King and Desmond Lee*, ed. Desmond Lee. Oxford: Blackwell.

———. 1989. *Wittgenstein's 1939 Lectures on the Foundations of Mathematics*, ed. C. Diamond. Chicago: University of Chicago Press.

———. 1992. *Geheime Tagebücher: 1914–1916*, 3d ed., ed. Wilhelm Baum. Vienna: Turia and Kant.

———. 1993. *Ludwig Wittgenstein: Philosophical Occasions 1912–1951*. Indianapolis: Hackett.

———. 1994. *Philosophische Bemerkungen*. New York: Springer Verlag.

———. 1997. *Ludwig Wittgenstein: Cambridge Letters: Conversations with Russell, Keynes, Moore, Ramsey and Sraffa*, ed. B. McGuinness and G. H. von Wright. Malden, Mass.: Blackwell.

———. Forthcoming. "Frühversion" or early version of the *Philosophical Investigations*, ed. G. H. von Wright and Heikki Nyman. Unpublished manuscript, Bergen Wittgenstein Archives.

Woolhouse, R. S. 1983. *Locke*. Brighton, U.K.: Harvester Press.

Yolton, John W. 1984. *Perceptual Acquaintance from Descartes to Reid*. Minneapolis: University of Minnesota Press.

———. 1990. "Mirrors and Veils, Thoughts and Things: The Epistemological Problematic," in *Reading Rorty*, ed. Alan R. Malachowski. Oxford: Basil Blackwell, pp. 58–73.

Wrigley, Michael. 1986. "Wittgenstein's Philosophy of Mathematics," in *Ludwig Wittgenstein: Critical Assessments*, vol. 3, ed. S. G. Shanker. London: Croom Helm, pp. 183–192.

———. 1987. *Wittgenstein's Early Philosophy of Mathematics*, Ph.D. Dissertation, University of California, Berkeley.

Index